Yale Language Series

BEGINNING
CHINESE

by John DeFrancis

with the assistance of
Yung Teng Chia-yee

SECOND REVISED EDITION

New Haven and London, Yale University Press

Published with assistance from the foundation
established in memory of Philip Hamilton McMillan
of the Class of 1894, Yale College.

Library of Congress catalog card number: 76–5099
ISBN: 0–300–02054–6 (cloth), 02058–9 (paper)

Printed in the United States of America by
The Murray Printing Company, Inc.,
Westford, Massachusetts.

14   13

TO KAY

ACKNOWLEDGMENTS

In the first edition of this book I was happy to acknowledge my indebtedness for the help and guidance of two men, Leonard Bloomfield and George A. Kennedy. Although both of these scholars are now no longer living, their influence persists, and I should like to record my continued indebtedness to them both in this revised edition.

The revision would not have been possible without the extensive support provided by Seton Hall University. I wish particularly to express my appreciation for the encouragement and help of Dr. John B. Tsu, Director of the Institute of Far Eastern Studies, who saw to it that I was provided with all the facilities and assistance I needed.

Dr. Tsu was also helpful in discussing many points regarding presentation of material. He deserves special credit for initiating the decision to base the Chinese work at Seton Hall University on the transcription used in this text.

Other Seton Hall personnel whose assistance I gratefully acknowledge are Dr. John C. H. Wu, Mr. C. S. Fu, Mrs. Teng Chia-yee, Mrs. Aileen Wei, and Mrs. Lucy Chao Ho. The assistance rendered by Mrs. Teng was particularly extensive. She was most active in the preparation of the dialogues, contributed largely to the various exercises, and helped me constantly at almost every step of the work.

Miss Diana Y. Ma is to be thanked for drawing the delightful illustrations.

I am grateful to my wife for taking on the appalling task of putting my scrawl into typewritten form.

I am indebted to David Horne of Yale University Press for seeing the book through the press, and to Elinor Horne for her expert and painstaking editorial revision.

J. De F.

Madison, Connecticut
March 1963

This revision has been made possible by the invaluable assistance provided by Mr. Patrick Destenay and Mr. Constantin Milsky, both of the Université de Provence in Aix-en-Provence, who kindly shared with me their unique knowledge of recent developments in the Chinese language obtained by their own long sojourns in the People's Republic of China and by their continuing contacts with exchange teachers, students, and other visitors to France from the PRC. I am also grateful to my long-standing associate, Mrs. Yung Teng Chia-yee, for assistance in compiling additional drill material along the lines worked out in the course of a summer's extensive consultations with my colleagues in France. Finally, I should like to thank the many users of the text, teachers and students alike, who have been kind enough to suggest corrections and revisions in the text.

John DeFrancis

Honolulu, Hawaii
January 1976

CONTENTS

Contents

PREFACE TO SECOND REVISED EDITION

The old saying "When in Rome do as the Romans do," which implies adjusting our behavior to whatever is appropriate to a given situation, if not taken too literally can be said to apply to the area of language as well as to other areas of human activity. It suggests that while we may not be able, or may not desire, to conform completely to the speech habits of people we may encounter, we should at the very least be aware that language usage varies. This is true within a single language as well as between different languages. There are different ways of saying (or writing) things—sometimes by different speakers in the same situation, sometimes by the same speaker in different situations.

As native speakers of a language, such as English, we are quite accustomed to attuning our ears and sometimes our tongues to variant forms of expression. Old friends may familiarly greet each other with "Hi!" but people who do not know each other well are likely to use a more formal greeting such as "How do you do?" An Eastern shopper requests a bag for his groceries, a mid-Westerner a sack. An American's "elevator" is an Englishman's "lift." "Sign here" and "Please put your signature here" are only partially identical since it is possible to think of situations where one would be more appropriate than the other. Yesterday's slang is today's oddity; today's will doubtless undergo the same transformation a few years hence. What some view as "America's generous financial contributions" may be denounced by others as "Yankee imperialism's silver bullets." As the last example especially makes clear, such different usages have a significance beyond the words themselves in that they suggest to us something about when and where and by whom a particular form might be used.

The Chinese language, spoken by over 800,000,000 people in the Chinese mainland, Taiwan, and overseas Chinese communities, is even more varied and unstable than English. In particular, the extensive changes that have taken place in Chinese society since the establishment of the Chinese People's Republic in 1949 have sparked changes in the Chinese language itself. While the basic features of the language have remained the same, so that Professor John McCoy is undoubtedly correct in saying that 98% of the language is identical everywhere,* some changes have taken place in the areas of pronunciation, vocabulary, syntax, and situational settings in which language usage occurs.

This new edition of Beginning Chinese has been prepared to take account of some of these changes. This has been done chiefly by the addition of twenty-four Supplementary Lessons paralleling those in the original text. In addition, some errors in the original text have been corrected and some improvements have been made in it without disturbing the basic content or approach, since these remain valid and continue to receive wide approval from students and teachers of Chinese.**

---

*Paper presented at annual meeting of Chinese Language Teachers Association on November 29, 1975.

**Among the improvements is the use of the enumerative comma. (See Beginning Chinese Reader, p. 13).

In the area of pronunciation, the attempt to promote Pǔtōnghuà 'Common Speech' in the People's Republic is leading toward lesser use of the r-ending typical of the Peking dialect. However, Common Speech is a hybrid norm, and Peking pronunciation remains quite acceptable as one variant of modern standard Chinese. Therefore in the original text I have retained the r-ending while showing its optional nature by enclosing it in parentheses in the vocabulary, as in the case of diànyǐng(r) 'movie,' but in the Supplementary Lessons I have emphasized non-r forms. This actually involves only four words out of 600-odd items in the text.

In the area of vocabulary, some ten items in the original text have been displaced by new usages in the People's Republic. A similar number are in competition with new usages and it is not yet clear which will eventually win out (or whether both will continue indefinitely to be used together). All of these changes are discussed in the Notes of the Supplementary Lessons and are drilled in the accompanying Exercises.

In the area of grammatical constructions, it so happens that none of the usages in the original text has been displaced by new structures.

In the area of situational changes, these also are noted and drilled in the Supplementary Lessons. They include such items as the new social relations and their effect on forms of address (Lesson 1), the merging of theory and practice as reflected in the new term for "to study" (Lesson 8), and the elimination of tipping (Lesson 21). In general there has been a decrease in stereotyped forms of politeness. In some cases, however, older forms have simply been replaced by other equivalents. In other cases the actual situation is confused by the tendency, especially marked in some PRC language-teaching materials, to reflect not actual usage but what the government aspires to have as ordinary usage. For example, the official attempts to broaden the use of the polite pronoun nín 'you' and to get people to call each other "Comrade" instead of using titles of rank or position are by no means universally accepted.

The new usages can be most clearly understood and most efficiently learned if they are contrasted with the older usages, especially since these "older" usages are still very much alive among Chinese outside the mainland of China and will be found in written materials that are still widely read. Students in the United States, and even in countries like France, which have had longer and closer contacts with the People's Republic, will have more occasion to speak to Chinese outside of China than in it. Most of these Chinese will be accustomed to the earlier uses of language. Hence students need to learn both the People's Republic and non-People's Republic forms and to use whichever is appropriate in the situations in which they find themselves. For example, students should not offer a tip to a waiter in the People's Republic of China, but they should not fail to do so to one in Taiwan or outside China. They may ask about someone's àirén 'lover' in the People's Republic but run the risk of getting their faces slapped if they use it in a conversation outside the mainland of China. Moreover, while students can limit what they say, they cannot limit what other speakers will say to them, or what they may encounter in reading, so they must acquire at least a passive command of variant forms of expression.

In order to cope with the present reality in which there are variant forms of Chinese all of which are valid and worth learning and yet are more or less distinctive, the new material has been placed in Supplementary Lessons so that teachers and students can choose whether to emphasize one or the other. Some things may be learned actively, others passively. As an aid to active mastery the new material in the Supplementary Lessons has for the most part been presented in the form of short dialogues or narratives that can be memorized.

A further reason for adopting the procedure noted here of leaving the original lessons basically intact and adding new material relevant to the People's Republic as Supplementary Lessons is in order to make the companion volume Character Text for Beginning Chinese even more useful as a reading text. Although not primarily designed for this purpose, the character version has been widely used as reading text by those who, with good pedagogical reasons, believe that it is useful to study in written form what one has already learned in spoken form. I believe strongly that foreign students must acquire a mastery of both regular and simplified characters, and that this is most efficiently accomplished by learning the regular first and the simplified second. Therefore in Character Text for Beginning Chinese the original content is presented, appropriately, in regular characters and the new material is presented, also appropriately, in simplified characters.*

One of the primary aims of these revisions is to impress on students that Chinese, like English and all other languages, uses different forms of expressions in different situations. Students must be prepared to encounter these varieties of linguistic usage, perhaps even among their own teachers, and must attempt to sharpen their command of the language by noting the sociolinguistic significance of these variations. Only thus can students progress from mechanical mastery of linguistic forms to a sensitive awareness of Chinese culture as embodied in its language.**

---

*This procedure has also been adopted in my Beginning Chinese Reader, a text specifically planned to accompany Beginning Chinese as a basic reading text. In the revision of this text the original division between regular and simplified characters has been preserved, but the material in simplified characters has been revised to bring the content more in line with usage in the People's Republic.

**For amplification of some of the remarks made in this Introduction see my "Sociolinguistic Aspects of Chinese Language Teaching Materials," Journal of Chinese Linguistics 3.2/3 (May−September 1975).

INTRODUCTION

TO THE READER

The study of a language generally requires the cooperative effort of at least three people: the textbook writer, the teacher, and the student. In my capacity as the first of these three I should like to address a few remarks to you, whether teacher or student, in the hope that they will help toward a more efficient utilization of this book.

My aim in writing this Chinese textbook has been to provide material that can be used at both the high-school and college levels. Its suitability will be apparent if we compare and contrast the needs of students at both levels.

One major point of similarity is that all students, of whatever age and whatever objective (whether a speaking or a reading knowledge), should start with spoken Chinese. Hence this book is primarily oriented toward helping you speak the language.

A second point of similarity is that high-school and college students have—in somewhat varying degrees, to be sure—the ability to absorb a systematic program of language study, as against the more informal approach of elementary grades with their emphasis on songs, stories, and limited subjects of conversation. In line with this, I have provided fairly extensive notes and explanations of the material. Nor have I hesitated to use a few technical terms. Actually these terms are minimal, amounting to far less than the technical terminology found in an introductory ninth-grade algebra text. In any case, technical expressions and explanations should not occupy too much of the teacher's and student's time. If a note or explanation is too hard to understand, ignore it. Don't waste time talking about Chinese when you should be talking Chinese. Much more important than the notes and explanations are the extensive drills concentrating on specific points of pronunciation or grammar. Provision of these drills reflects my confidence in the ability of high-school and college students alike to benefit from such structured material.

It may be true, however, that high-school students need more drill and review than older students. I have written the book with this requirement in mind. Units I–IV each consist of six lessons. The first five lessons of each unit introduce new material. Within each lesson, the new material should be studied first in the Sentence Build-Ups, various Pattern Drills, and Substitution Tables and then, in effect, reviewed at the end by means of the dialogues and various other exercises. The sixth and final lesson in each unit is a thoroughgoing review which introduces nothing new. Still further drill is provided in the tape recordings which accompany the text.

Extensive though this material is, it is not excessive. It is hard to conceive of too much drill material for students at any level. Extensive practice is the only road to fluency in a language; and after all, it is fluency—not agonizing translation à la Latin as traditionally taught—which should be the objective in studying a living language.

It is important to note that the relatively great size of this book is not due to any large amount of material. As a matter of fact, the vocabulary entries total less than 600, a comparatively small figure, and the structural patterns are by no means exhaustive. It is repetition and review which account for the bulk. With regard to the amount of material presented, it is a sobering thought that the Dialogues, which constitute the heart of the material and the basis for the extended drills in each lesson, represent less than one hour of actual speech, and that the entire Chinese contents of the book can be spoken by a native Chinese in just a few hours.

A major difference between college and high-school students is the fact that more is usually expected of the former than of the latter. Partly this is a matter of curricular programming which permits greater concentration on fewer subjects. Partly it is a matter of relative maturity. It is doubtful, however, whether there is any substantial difference in language ability on the part of the two groups, and if there is, it may well lie with those in the younger age bracket. Nevertheless, it is probably true that the two groups cannot proceed at the same pace. In view of this, I have attempted to make the book as flexible as possible so that it can be adapted to programs varying from two or three hours a week to intensive full-time courses. Some college programs may be able to complete all the material in a semester of intensive study, some semi-intensive high-school classes may be able to cover it all in one year, and others may be able to cover between eighteen and twenty-four lessons. The latter would probably be normal for high-school classes which have available no more than the usual four clock hours or less of classroom time per week. In any case, the emphasis, particularly at the beginning, should be on quality rather than quantity. Better to study a little well than a lot badly.

Another possible difference between high-school and college students is that the latter can more easily put up with material presented in a dull and humorless manner. Although there is much unavoidable drudgery in repetitive drills, a language text doesn't have to be dull, and I have attempted to enliven this one a bit by throwing in an occasional game, illustration, or other type of material that would be entertaining as well as instructive. College students who feel above this sort of thing can simply ignore it.

Partly as entertainment, partly with a serious end in view, I have provided two lessons introducing Chinese characters. These lessons can be studied either after completion of the rest of the material, or simultaneously with the first lesson. In the latter case, study of the characters should not distract us from the primary objective of mastering the speech sounds of Chinese. At this stage of our study, characters should be taken as a dessert, perhaps as an appetizer, but certainly not as the main course. At a later stage, the separate volume entitled Character Text for Beginning Chinese—though designed primarily as an aid for native Chinese teachers—can also be used for further character study.

The kind of spoken Chinese which we are studying here is the Peking dialect. This bears about the same relationship to other kinds of Chinese as Parisian French has to other varieties of French. It is understood by more people than any other language in the world. Apart from introducing you to the largest speech community, it also opens the gate to the largest continuous civilization the world has ever seen.

Chinese is thus an important as well as a fascinating language. But it is not an easy one for speakers of English. In this book, I have not glossed over the difficulties but have attempted to meet them head on. By so doing I hope to have done my part in easing the task of the teacher in presenting the Chinese language and that of the student in mastering it.

LANGUAGE AND WRITING

Man spoke long before he wrote.   Writing was invented only after hundreds of thousands of years in which the sole means of communication, other than gestures, was speech; only over the past few thousand years have various systems of writing, ranging from pictographic to alphabetic, been devised.   It is well to remember that even today only about half of the world's 4,000 or so languages have been reduced to writing.

The early creators of writing systems were, of course, not trained in the science of language.   We cannot therefore assume that the systems they created accurately represented the languages they spoke.   Furthermore, in the later evolution of these languages, what with shifts in pronunciation and other changes, the writing systems became even less reliable as indicators of the spoken word.

Changes have taken place in even so short a period as three hundred odd years in English, as is obvious to any reader of Shakespeare's plays.   That English writing does a poor job of representing the sounds of the language is also well known, and is caricatured by such jokes as the one about 'fish' being spelled <u>ghoti</u>: <u>gh</u> as in <u>tough</u>, <u>o</u> as in <u>women</u>, and <u>ti</u> as in <u>nation</u>.   It is plain that speech and writing cannot be mechanically equated.

The trouble is that the two things are commonly equated, especially when the term 'language' is loosely used in reference to both.   Instead, it is preferable to adopt the practice of reserving 'language' as a term synonymous with 'speech.'   This is the practice among linguists—that is, scholars engaged in the scientific study of language, not (as the term is often used) persons who speak a number of languages, more properly termed polyglots.

If we use 'language' to mean only 'speech,' then, we will avoid—or at least use with clearer understanding—such expressions as 'spoken language,' which is redundant, and 'written language,' which is a contradiction in terms.   We will also avoid the confusion which results from uncritically using 'language' in reference to both speech and writing.   This lack of discrimination leads to muddled ideas about the nature of language, which in turn leads to a confused approach to the teaching and learning of language.

The confusion in connection with Chinese is especially great because the term 'Chinese,' like the term 'language,' is used in more than one meaning. There is a widely held but quite erroneous idea that Chinese speak entirely in words of one syllable, that their language is ambiguous, and that they often have to resort to writing to make themselves understood.   The confusion can also be illustrated by the following dialogue:

A: I hear you've begun to study Chinese.

B: Yes.

A: It's a tough language, isn't it?

B: Sure is.

A: What's this Chinese character mean?

B: I don't know.

A: I thought you said you were studying Chinese.

B: I mean I'm learning how to speak Chinese.

Here A uses a catch-all expression 'Chinese' in the meaning of 'Chinese writing' and assumes that to study the Chinese language is to study Chinese writing.

Linguists are unanimously agreed, however, that since language is speech, to study a language is to study the speech of a given community.   Even if the ultimate and main objective is to read, this objective is most quickly and most efficiently reached by starting with speech. Such an approach is all the more necessary in the case of Chinese. The traditional Chinese system of writing has been from the beginning an exceedingly poor device for indicating the sounds of the language. Today the gap between writing and speech is greater in China than in any other country in the world.

In view of all this, it is not desirable to start the study of Chinese with the traditional script. We begin instead by representing Chinese speech with an alphabetic system, called p̄inyīn 'spelling,' which is widely used on the mainland of China. This orthography is the basis of education in the first few years of elementary school. It is also used in a variety of ways in dictionaries, journals, and other publications. Our use of the system provides not only a serviceable pedagogical tool but also an introduction to a great deal of material published in China.

It is likely that this orthography will have wider and wider application in the future in view of the current attempt to promote a single national language in China. In this connection it is worth noting that the catch-all term 'Chinese,' which we saw above was ambiguous because it failed to distinguish between speech and writing, also leads to confusion even when the term is applied only to speech. There are in fact many forms of speech in China, often called 'dialects'; and the situation is further confused by the fact that some so-called dialects of Chinese are as far apart as English is from Dutch, or Italian from Spanish.

Of the approximately two-thirds of a billion people who speak Chinese, some three-fourths of them speak Mandarin Chinese and the remainder speak mutually unintelligible forms of Chinese. The non-Mandarin 'dialects,' which include Cantonese, Wu (Shanghai), Hakka, Amoy-Swatow, and Foochow, are spoken by about 150,000,000 people. Mandarin Chinese, spoken by about half a billion people, is not intelligible to the rest of the population unless it has been learned as another language. Mandarin Chinese is subdivided into a number of genuine dialects—that is, mutually intelligible variants. Of these, the most important is the Peking dialect. An approximation of this dialect has for many years been the socially most acceptable form of speech.

The Peking dialect is the basis of what is being promoted in China as the standard national language. It is this dialect which is used here in beginning the study of Chinese.

THE SOUNDS OF CHINESE

1. Syllable Structure

The syllable in Chinese is made up of three parts: an initial, a final, and a tone. For example, in mă the m represents the initial, a the final, and ˘ the tone.

2. Tones

Although tones are a distinctive feature of Chinese, we have something akin to them in English. Thus the word 'yes' can convey many different shades of meaning according to just how it is uttered. Rudy Vallée once presented a radio skit in which he demonstrated a dozen or more ways of saying 'yes.' Varying his intonation, he expressed anger by 'Yes!,' inquiry by 'Yes?,' doubt by 'Y-e-s,' and so on, concluding the catalogue with the Sweet Young Thing's 'No.'

What makes Chinese tones unlike the expressive intonation of English is that they are an integral part of a syllable and help to distinguish quite. different words, in much the same way as the vowels a and u do in English hat and hut. Thus Chinese mā means 'mother,' while mǎ means 'horse.'

There are four basic tones in the Peking dialect. The accompanying Tone Chart demonstrates these, in relation to the range of a speaker's voice.

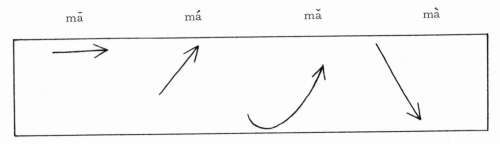

TONE CHART

The first tone starts near the top of a speaker's voice range and continues on that level until the end. The second tone starts at mid-range and rises rapidly to the top of the range. The third tone starts below mid-range, dips to the lowest pitch, and rises above mid-range. The fourth tone starts near the top of the range and falls very rapidly toward the bottom.

The four tones are represented by the following marks:

1. first tone, high level: mā 'mother'
2. second tone, high rising: má 'hemp'
3. third tone, low dipping: mǎ 'horse'
4. fourth tone, high falling: mà 'scold'

The tone mark is placed over a vowel letter. If there are three vowels in a syllable, it is written over the middle vowel. If there are two vowels, it is placed over the first, unless this is i or u:

āi, āo, ēi, ōu   iā, iē, iū   uā, uē, uī, uō

3. Simple Initials

The following are the simple initials:

b   like the p in spy (not like the b in buy; see description below)
p   as in pie, but with a much stronger aspiration, as described below
m   as in might
f   as in fight
d   like the t in sty (not like the d in die)
t   as in tie, but with a much stronger aspiration
n   as in night
l   as in light
g   like the k in sky (not like the g in guy)
k   as in kite, but with a much stronger aspiration
h   like the ch in German nach—that is, much rougher than English h

No two languages have the same speech sounds, and one of the first tasks of the language learner is to discover in what ways he must modify the pronunciation patterns of his native language in order to reproduce words in the new language—perfectly if possible, but in any event enough like the original to be understood. The new speech sounds do not "come naturally"; they must be learned and practiced.

Of the simple initials listed above, for example, six require special attention; they are like English sounds in some respects but different in others. These are the so-called STOP SOUNDS, represented by these pairs of letters:

b   p

d   t

g   k

The Chinese sounds represented by b, d, g differ from the corresponding English sounds (as in bay, day, gay) in this way: they are VOICELESS, which means they are not accompanied by voice sound, or vibration of the vocal cords. (You can hear this vibration as a loud buzzing if you pronounce "zzzzz" while pressing your hands over your ears. Now pronounce "sssss" and notice the absence of buzzing or "voicing"; s is a voiceless sound, while z is VOICED.)

Chinese b, d, g, then, are unlike English b, d, g in that they are voiceless. They are not, however, identical with English p, t, k. When English speakers say p, t, k (often spelled "c") at the beginning of words, our speech habits force us to pronounce them with a puff of breath (ASPIRATION) after them: you can feel this by holding the back of your hand to your lips while you pronounce pare, tear, care.

After "s" at the beginning of words, however, we pronounce p, t, k without aspiration: test this with your hand to your lips while you say spare, stare, scare. Now try out the contrast more strikingly by pronouncing pare, spare; tear, stare; care, scare. (The louder you speak, the more noticeable the difference.)

We say, then, that Chinese b is like the p sound of spy (unaspirated and voiceless) rather than like the b of buy (also unaspirated; but voiced). Similarly, Chinese d and g resemble the unaspirated, voiceless t and k sounds of sty and sky. Where English has three separate sounds in the b-p range, Chinese has only two, and similarly for d-t and g-k:

	Aspirated	Unaspirated	Voiced
English	p as in pie	p as in spy	b as in buy
Chinese	p as in pie	p as in spy	[no equivalent]
	(represented by p)	(represented by b)	
English	t as in tie	t as in sty	d as in die
Chinese	t as in tie	t as in sty	[no equivalent]
	(represented by t)	(represented by d)	
English	k as in kite	k as in sky	g as in guy
Chinese	k as in kite	k as in sky	[no equivalent]
	(represented by k)	(represented by g)	

The aspirated consonants of Chinese (represented by p, t, k) differ from their English counterparts (as in pie, tie, kite) mainly in that the aspiration is much stronger in Chinese. Hold a lighted match a few inches from your lips while saying pie. If you can make the flame go out, you are saying a good Chinese p sound.

4. Group-a Finals

a   as in father
an   between the an in can and the on in con
ang   a as in father and ng as in sing
ai   as in aisle
ao   like the au's in sauerkraut

5. Combinations of Simple Initials with Group-a Finals*

Initials	Finals				
	a	an	ang	ai	ao
∅ *	ā	ān	āng	ài	ǎo
b	bā	bān	bāng	bái	bào
p	pà	pān	páng	pái	pào
m	mā	màn	máng	mǎi	mào
f	fā	fān	fāng		
d	dá	dān	dāng	dài	dào
t	tā	tān	táng	tài	tào
n	ná	nán	náng	nài	nào
l	lā	lán	láng	lài	lǎo
g	gā	gān	gāng	gài	gào
k	kǎ	kàn	kàng	kāi	kào
h	hā	hán	háng	hài	hǎo

6. Group-o/e Finals

o   like the <u>wa</u> in <u>wall</u>

e   begins as the <u>e</u> of <u>error</u> and passes quickly into the <u>o</u> in <u>of</u>

en   like the <u>en</u> in <u>chicken</u>

eng   like the <u>ung</u> in <u>lung</u>

ei   as in <u>eight</u>

ou   as in <u>soul</u>

ong   like the <u>ung</u> in German <u>jung</u> or, roughly, <u>u</u> as in <u>put</u> plus <u>ng</u> as in <u>sing</u>

---

* It is convenient to speak of a syllable that consists only of a final as having a "zero initial," indicated in the table by the symbol ∅. Note that no combinations of <u>f</u> plus <u>ai</u> or <u>ao</u> occur.

7. Combinations of Simple Initials with Group-o/e Finals

Initials	Finals						
	o	e	en	eng	ei	ou	ong
∅		è	ēn	ēng		ǒu	
b	bō		bèn	bēng	bēi		
p	pō		pén	péng	péi	pōu	
m	mō		mén	mèng	méi	mǒu	
f	fó		fēn	féng	féi	fǒu	
d		dé		děng	děi	dōu	dōng
t		tè		téng		tōu	tóng
n			nèn	néng	nèi	nòu	nóng
l		lè	lèn	lěng	léi	lǒu	lóng
g		gē	gēn	gèng	gěi	gǒu	gōng
k		kè	kěn	kēng	kēi	kǒu	kōng
h		hē	hěn	héng	hēi	hòu	hóng

8. Group-u Finals

u   as in <u>rule</u>, but with more lip-rounding and with the tongue drawn
        farther back

ua   like the <u>wa</u> in <u>wander</u>

uo   like the <u>wa</u> in <u>waltz</u>

uai   like the <u>wi</u> in <u>wide</u>

ui   between <u>we</u> and <u>weigh</u> in the first and second tones, like <u>weigh</u> in
        the third and fourth tones.

uan   starts with a <u>w</u> ˖ sound and ends like the <u>an</u> in the group-a
        finals

un   somewhat like the <u>wen</u> in <u>Owen</u>

uang   starts with a <u>w</u>-sound and ends like the <u>ang</u> in the group-a
        finals

ueng   starts with a <u>w</u>-sound and ends like the <u>ung</u> in <u>lung</u>

9. Combinations of Simple Initials with Group-u Finals *

Initials	Finals								
	u	ua	uo	uai	ui	uan	un	uang	ueng
∅	wū	wá	wǒ	wài	wèi	wān	wèn	wáng	wēng
b	bù								
p	pù								
m	mù								
f	fū								
d	dù		duō		duì	duān	dūn		
t	tù		tuō		tuì	tuán	tún		
n	nú		nuó			nuǎn			
l	lù		luó			luàn	lún		
g	gǔ	guā	guó	guài	guì	guǎn	gǔn	guāng	
k	kū	kuā	kuò	kuài	kuì	kuǎn	kūn	kuāng	
h	hū	huà	huó	huài	huì	huān	hūn	huāng	

10. Retroflex and Sibilant Initials

Retroflex

zh   like the <u>ch</u> in <u>chew</u>, but unaspirated and with the tongue tip curled far back

ch   like the <u>zh</u> above, but aspirated, as the <u>ch-h</u> in <u>teach history</u>

sh   like the <u>sh</u> in <u>shoe</u>, but with the tongue tip curled far back

r   like the <u>r</u> in <u>crew</u>, but with the tongue tip curled far back

Sibilant

z   like the <u>t's</u> in <u>it's Al</u> (not the <u>dds</u> of <u>adds</u>), but with the tongue farther forward

c   like the <u>t's h</u> in <u>it's Hal</u>, but with much more breath and with the tongue farther forward

s   as in <u>soon</u>, but with the tongue farther forward

---

* The group-u finals can all occur by themselves (that is, with zero initial), but in this occurrence they are written with a <u>w</u> initial; note also the other spelling modifications in the ∅ row.

The four retroflex initials represent sounds made by curling the tongue far back, farther even than in pronouncing the r of English crew. The retroflex consonants are spoken by themselves with a sort of r-sound final, so that Chinese sh, for example, sounds somewhat like English shr in shrill. Similarly, the sibilant consonants are pronounced by themselves with a sort of buzzing sound like a prolonged z in buzz. These final sounds of both groups of consonants are written with the letter i. The sounds represented by this i are quite different from those of the group-i sounds discussed below. When referring to the former we shall write "i" in quotation marks to avoid confusion with the i-sounds as pronounced in other positions.

11. Combinations of Retroflex and Sibilant Initials with "i" and Group-a Finals

Initials	Finals					
	"i"	a	an	ang	ai	ao
zh	zhī	zhā	zhǎn	zhāng	zhái	zhāo
ch	chī	chà	chán	chāng	chái	chāo
sh	shī	shā	shān	shāng	shài	shāo
r	rì		rán	ràng		ráo
z	zì	zá	zān	zāng	zài	zǎo
c	cì	cā	cān	cāng	cāi	cǎo
s	sì	sà	sān	sāng	sài	sǎo

12. Combinations of Retroflex and Sibilant Initials with Group-o/e Finals

Initials	Finals					
	o	e	en	eng	ei	ou	ong
zh		zhě	zhēn	zhēng	zhèi	zhōu	zhōng
ch		chē	chén	chēng		chōu	chōng
sh		shé	shēn	shēng	shéi	shōu	
r		rè	rén	réng		róu	róng
z		zé	zěn	zēng	zéi	zǒu	zǒng
c		cè	cén	céng		còu	cóng
s		sè	sēn	sēng		sǒu	sòng

13. Combinations of Retroflex and Sibilant Initials
with Group-u Finals

Initials	Finals							
	u	ua	uo	uai	ui	uan	un	uang
zh	zhū	zhuā	zhuō	zhuāi	zhuī	zhuān	zhūn	zhuāng
ch	chū		chuò	chuǎi	chuī	chuān	chūn	chuáng
sh	shū	shuā	shuō	shuāi	shuǐ	shuàn	shùn	shuāng
r	rù		ruò		ruǐ	ruǎn	rùn	
z	zū		zuò		zuì	zuān	zūn	
c	cū		cuò		cuì	cuàn	cùn	
s	sú		suǒ		suì	suàn	sūn	

14. Group-i Finals

i   as in <u>machine</u>

ia   like the <u>ya</u> in <u>yacht</u>

iao   like the <u>yow</u> in <u>yowl</u>

ie   like the <u>ye</u> in <u>yet</u> (note that <u>e</u> after <u>i</u> is not the same as <u>e</u> in the group-o/e finals)

iu   in the first and second tones, close to <u>u</u> in <u>union</u>; in the third and fourth tones, close to <u>yo</u> in <u>yoke</u>

ian   like the <u>i</u> in <u>machine</u> plus a sound between the <u>an</u> of <u>man</u> and the <u>en</u> of <u>men</u> in English (note that <u>an</u> after <u>i</u> is not the same as the <u>an</u> in the group-a finals)

in   like the <u>ine</u> in <u>machine</u>

iang   like <u>i</u> in <u>machine</u> plus <u>ang</u> as in the group-a finals

ing   like <u>i</u> in <u>machine</u> plus <u>ng</u> as in <u>sing</u>

iong   like <u>i</u> in <u>machine</u> plus <u>ong</u> as in the group-o/e finals

15. Combinations of Simple Initials and Group-i Finals*

Initials	Finals									
	i	ia	iao	ie	iu	ian	in	iang	ing	iong
∅	yī	yá	yào	yě	yǒu	yán	yīn	yáng	yīng	yòng
b	bǐ		biǎo	bié		biān	bīn		bīng	
p	pí		piāo	piě		piān	pīn		píng	
m	mǐ		miào	miè	miú	mián	mín		mìng	
d	dì		diāo	diē	diū	diān			dīng	
t	tí		tiāo	tiē		tiān			tīng	
n	nǐ		niǎo	niè	niǔ	nián	nín	niáng	níng	
l	lǐ	liǎ	liáo	liè	liǔ	lián	lín	liáng	líng	

16. Palatal Initials

j   like the <u>tch</u> in <u>itching</u> (not voiced, like the <u>j</u> in <u>jeep</u>); made by pressing the flat part of the tongue against the palate or front roof of the mouth

q   like the <u>ch</u> in <u>cheap</u>, but with much more breath, as for the <u>ch-h</u> in <u>each house</u>; tongue position as for <u>j</u>

x   between the <u>s</u> in <u>see</u> and the <u>sh</u> in <u>she</u>; tongue position as for <u>j</u>

17. Combinations of Palatal Initials
with Group-i Finals

Initials	Finals									
	i	ia	iao	ie	iu	ian	in	iang	ing	iong
j	jī	jiā	jiāo	jiē	jiǔ	jiān	jīn	jiāng	jīng	jiǒng
q	qī	qià	qiāo	qiē	qiū	qiān	qīn	qiāng	qīng	qióng
x	xī	xiā	xiāo	xiè	xiū	xiān	xīn	xiāng	xīng	xiǒng

* The group-i finals can all occur by themselves—that is, with a zero initial—though they are written with a <u>y</u> initial in this occurrence, and with the spelling modifications shown. Note again that the <u>i</u> sound is altogether different from the "i" sound. Since they never occur after the same initials, it is unambiguous to use the same letter to represent both sounds; but learners must take special pains to differentiate their pronunciation. (See the Pronunciation Drills in Lesson 5.)

18. Group-ü Finals

ü   like the French u in rue or the German ü in über; made by pronouncing the i of machine with the lips rounded as for the oo of
ooze

üe   ü as above plus e as in ie in the group-i finals (not like the e of the
group-o/e finals)

üan   ü as above plus an as in ian in the group-i finals (not like the an of
the group-a finals)

ün   ü as above followed by a final n

19. Combinations of Palatal and Other Initials with Group-u Finals*

Initials	Finals			
	ü	üe	üan	ün
∅	yú	yuè	yuǎn	yún
j	jū	jué	juǎn	jūn
q	qù	què	quǎn	qún
x	xù	xué	xuān	xùn
n	nǚ	nüè		
l	lǚ	lüè		

20. Group-r Finals

Final r occurs as part of the syllable er and as a suffix attached to many of
the finals listed in the previous tables.

The syllable er is pronounced like the ur of fur in the first and second
tones, and between -ur and are in the third and fourth. This syllable is widely
used in other dialects as well as in that of Peking.

The suffix r modifies the spelling of a preceding final in various ways, as
follows:

---

* The group-ü finals can all occur by themselves. Although spoken with a
zero initial, they are written with a y initial and modified in spelling as indicated above. Note further that the two dots in ü are written only after n and l,
where they are needed to distinguish lu from lü and nu from nü. Be careful not
to confuse the sound of un in zhun with the un in jun, or the uan in chuan with
the uan in quan; the form un represents different sounds after different initials,
just as the letter i does (above, p. xxviii).

   I.   a, o, e, u, ng: add <u>r</u>. Examples: gē, gēr; fēng, fēngr.

  II.   ai, an, en: drop final letter and add <u>r</u>. Examples: hái, hár; wán, wár; fēn, fēr.

 III.   i, ü after consonants: add <u>er</u>. Examples: jī, jīer; yú, yuér.

 IV.   "i," in, un: drop final letter and add <u>er</u>. Examples: shì, shèr; xìn, xièr; zhǔn, zhuěr.

The suffix <u>r</u> is common to all speakers of the Peking dialect. Educated speakers, however, are aware that it is a substandard form in some other dialects, and so tend to limit their use of it, particularly in formal and public speech. For the same reason, the <u>r</u> suffix is generally minimized when the Peking dialect is being taught—whether as the National Language (to Chinese who speak other dialects natively) or to foreigners.

21. Juncture

Although the syllable is an important unit of sound in Chinese, it is by no means correct (as we pointed out above) to speak of the language as mono-syllabic. Some syllables can never stand alone but are always joined closely with others in speech. We say that these are in "close juncture" and write the syllables together as one word, as in <u>tàitai</u>. In the joining of syllables, unless there are special reasons for doing otherwise, we comply with the practices followed in other literature which uses the same writing system.

<u>N</u> before a vowel in the middle of a word is read as part of the following syllable. If <u>ng</u> occurs before a vowel in the middle of a word, <u>n</u> is read as part of the preceding syllable and <u>g</u> as part of the following. Exceptions to these rules are marked by an apostrophe.

yínán = yí + nán	yīn'àn = yīn + àn
míngē = mín + gē	míng'é = míng + é

We use hyphens to join two or more syllables which can under some conditions be separated by a pause or by the insertion of additional elements, but which in the specific case before us are spoken without a pause: <u>mǎi-shū</u>, <u>nǐ-tàitai</u>.

We use blank space to mark places where it is possible in slow speech to hesitate briefly or stop to catch one's breath: <u>Nèiběn-shū yě-kànwán-le</u>.

We use commas and periods to mark places where phrases or sentences are often separated by longer pauses: <u>Wǒmen-yǒu-shū, méi-yǒu-huàr</u>.

22. Stress

In a phrase or sentence, the last syllable with a tone mark on it usually receives the chief stress, that is, is spoken most loudly. If the chief stress is elsewhere, we mark it by a stress symbol or, more rarely, by a single underline (double if the sentence is already underlined):

<u>Wáng-Tàitai</u> (stress on <u>Tài</u>); '<u>Wáng-Tàitai</u> (stress on Wáng)

<u>Wǒ-shuō-jīntiān-qu</u> (stress on <u>tiān</u>)

In Chinese, as in English, a word which is strongly emphasized or strongly contrasted with something is spoken louder than the rest of the sentence. By shifting the stress from one word to another we can create differences in meaning within the same string of words. Note how this is done in the following English sentences:

He is leaving tomorrow.   He is <u>leaving</u> tomorrow.

He <u>is</u> leaving tomorrow.   He is leaving <u>tomorrow</u>.

23. Modification of Tones

A third tone (low dipping) has its full contour only when it is followed by a pause. Before any other tone, it is pronounced as a low tone without its final rise in pitch. We do not indicate this change of a full third tone to a 'half third tone,' as it is easily learned and quickly becomes automatic in connected speech.

If two third-tone syllables are spoken in uninterrupted succession, the first changes to a second tone. Thus hěn plus hǎo becomes hén-hǎo. We do indicate this change.

If three third tones occur in uninterrupted succession, the first two change to second tone. Thus yě plus hěn plus hǎo becomes yé-hén-hǎo. We mark these changes.

The above three changes in a third tone are illustrated in the accompanying chart, in which all syllables (except gāo) are original third tones.

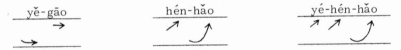

If four or more third-tone syllables occur together, various combinations of the changes noted above are possible.

Stressed syllables always have one of the four tones. The same syllables sometimes occur unstressed, in which case the tone often disappears. Some syllables never have stress. Such unstressed syllables are said to have neutral tone or to be toneless or neutral syllables and are written without tone marks.

If a neutral tone stands at the beginning of an utterance, as in bu-gāo, it is pronounced at about the mid-range of the speaker's voice. If a neutral tone comes at the end of an utterance, it is affected by the tone of the preceding syllable. The pitch of a neutral syllable after each of the four tones is indicated by the heavy dot in the accompanying chart.

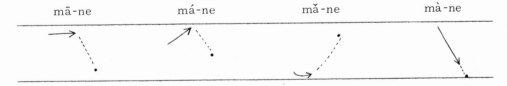

24. Intonation

In addition to the tones appearing on individual syllables, there are tone patterns (intonations) accompanying sentences: some statements, for example, have a different intonation from some types of questions. With certain questions—especially those asked out of genuine curiosity and interest and not merely from politeness—the whole pitch level is likely to be shifted slightly upward. This is illustrated by the following chart, in which the dotted figure represents the normal range for statements and the solid figure represents the range for questions.

Tā-hǎo-ma?

Questions

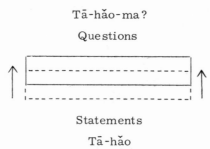

Statements

Tā-hǎo

It is essential to bear in mind that questions in Chinese do not have the same intonation patterns as questions in English. In English, questions which anticipate a "yes" or "no" answer normally end on a high pitch ("Is it raining? " "Are you happy? "), while questions asking for supplemental information are pronounced like statements, with dropping pitch at the end ("What time is it." "Where are you going."). In Chinese, on the contrary, it is the entire sentence which is uttered on a higher pitch—not merely the last word or some other part of it—regardless of the kind of answer expected.

25. Marking of Sounds

In the lessons which follow, we seek to provide all the information you need to pronounce the material correctly. We mark the required shift of a third tone to second before another third tone, together with a few other required tonal changes; we also indicate juncture and stress. Note that there are often several different ways of pronouncing the same sentence; different speakers may interpret the same sentence in different ways, for example in determining which part of the sentence should be stressed. Do not be disturbed if you hear native speakers pronounce a sentence differently from what we have indicated. It is always safe to imitate the native speaker.

SETTING THE STAGE

Cast of Characters

Bái Wénshān: Vincent White, an American college student spending his junior
                  year in China.

Gāo Měiyīng: A middle-school student, daughter of Mr. and Mrs. Gao.

Mr. Gao   : Manager of the Three Friends Bookstore.

Mrs. Gao   : Wife of Mr. Gao.

Mr. Mao   : A clerk in the Three Friends Bookstore.

Mr. Qian   : Friend and neighbor of the Gaos.

Mr. Wan   : Professor Wanamaker, a specialist in Chinese.

Ticket-seller on the No. 3 bus.

Waiter in the Ten Thousand Years Restaurant.

Place

A city in China

Time

September 7	Lesson 1	June 5	Lesson 20
September 10	Lesson 2	June 7	Lesson 21
September 14	Lesson 3	August 1	Lesson 22
September 16	Lesson 4	August 25	Lesson 23
January 22	Lessons 5−19		

UNIT I

Lesson 1 GREETING FRIENDS

" 'Gāo-Xiānsheng, nín-hǎo-a?"

Dialogue: Mr. White and Mr. Gao exchange greetings when they meet on the street. (Mr. White is younger than Mr. Gao and therefore uses more polite forms in addressing him.)

Bái:	'Gāo-Xiānsheng, nín-hǎo-a?		Mr. Gao, how are you?
Gāo:	Wó-hén-hǎo. Nǐ-ne?		I'm fine. And you?
Bái:	Hǎo, xièxie-nin. Gāo-Tàitai, Gāo-Xiáojie yé-hǎo-ma?		Fine, thank you. And how are Mrs. Gao and Miss Gao?
Gāo:	Tāmen-'dōu-hǎo, xièxie.	5	They're both well, thanks.
Bái:	Zàijiàn, 'Gāo-Xiānsheng.		Good-bye, Mr. Gao.
Gāo:	Zàijiàn, zàijiàn.		See you again.

VOCABULARY *

(For the abbreviations used below, see the list at the beginning of the Glossary and Index)

a	(question particle: Note 14)
bái	white (SV) (also, a surname)

---

* In all English translations of Chinese material, square brackets enclose more literal renderings of idiomatic equivalents; parentheses are used for English words with no equivalent in the Chinese but necessary for smoother English, as well as other explanatory material.

dōu   all, both, entirely (AD)

gāo   tall, high (SV) (also, a surname)

hǎo   good, well, fine, O.K. (SV)

hěn   very (AD)

ma   (question particle: Note 13)

men   (pluralizing suffix: Note 3)

ne   (question particle: Note 15)

nǐ   you (singular) (PR)

nín   you (polite form) (PR) (Note 3)

tā   he, him; she, her (PR)

tàitai   married lady (N); Mrs. (Note 7)

wǒ   I, me (PR)

xiānsheng   gentleman, husband (N); Mr. [lit. first born] (Note 7)

xiǎojie   young (unmarried) lady, daughter (N); Miss [lit. little sister] (Note 7)

xièxie   thank; thanks, thank you (TV)(Xiè is also a surname)

yě   also, too (AD)

zàijiàn   good-bye [lit. again see]

SENTENCE BUILD-UP

     nǐ   you (singular)
     hǎo   well
1.   Ní-hǎo?   How are you?

     nín   you (polite form)
2.   Nín-hǎo?   How are you?

     nǐ   you (singular)
     nǐmen   you (plural)
3.   Nǐmen-hǎo?   How are you?

     hǎo-a?   well (question form)
4.   Ní-hǎo-a?   How are you?

     hǎo-ma?   well (question form)
5.   Nín-hǎo-ma?   How are you?

     bái   white (also, a surname)
     Xiānsheng   gentleman; Mr.
     'Bái-Xiānsheng   Mr. White
6.   'Bái-Xiānsheng, ní-hǎo-ma?   How are you, Mr. White?

     gāo   tall, high (also, a surname)
     'Gāo-Xiānsheng   Mr. Gao
7.   'Gāo-Xiānsheng, nín-hǎo-ma?   How are you, Mr. Gao?

Xiáojie	young lady; Miss
'Gāo-Xiáojie	Miss Gao
8. 'Gāo-Xiáojie, ní-hǎo-ma?	Miss Gao, how are you?
Tàitai	married lady; Mrs.
'Gāo-Tàitai	Mrs. Gao
9. 'Gāo-Tàitai, nín-hǎo-ma?	How are you, Mrs. Gao?
xièxie	thank; thanks, thank you
10. Xièxie-ni.	Thank you.
wǒ	I
wǒmen	we
11. Wǒmen-xièxie-ni.	We thank you.
tā	he, him; she, her
tāmen	they
12. Tāmen-xièxie-ni.	They thank you.
hěn	very
hén-hǎo	very well
13. Wó-hén-hǎo.	I'm very well.
yě	also
yé-hén-hǎo	also very well
14. Tā-yé-hén-hǎo.	He's also very well.
dōu	all
dōu-gāo	all tall
15. Tāmen-dōu-gāo-ma?	Are all of them tall?
wó-hǎo	I'm fine
nǐ-ne?	how about you?
16. Wó-hǎo. Nǐ-ne?	I'm fine. And you?
zàijiàn	good-bye
17. Zàijiàn, 'Gāo-Tàitai.	Good-bye, Mrs. Gao.

PATTERN DRILLS *

Pattern 1.1. Statements with Stative Verbs
(Notes 8 and 11, below, p. 10)

S	AD	SV
Subject	Adverb	Stative Verb
Tā	hěn	hǎo.

'He's very well.'

---

* Each pattern is numbered by lesson and drill; Pattern 1.1, then, is the pattern demonstrated in Lesson 1, Drill 1.

1.	Hǎo.	Fine.
2.	Hén-hǎo.	Very well.
3.	Yé-hǎo.	(Someone) is also well.
4.	Wó-hǎo.	I'm fine.
5.	Wó-hén-hǎo.	I'm very well.
6.	Yé-hěn-gāo.	(Someone) is also very tall.
7.	Tāmen-dōu-hǎo.	They're all well.
8.	Tāmen-dōu-hěn-gāo.	They're all quite tall.
9.	'Gāo-Xiáojie yé-hǎo.	Miss Gao is also well.
10.	'Bái-Xiānsheng, 'Bái-Tàitai dōu-hěn-gāo.	Mr. and Mrs. Bai are both very tall.

Pattern 1.2. Statements with Transitive Verbs
(Notes 9 and 10, below, p. 10)

S	V	O
Subject	Verb	Object
Wǒ	xièxie	ni.

'I thank you.'

1.	Wǒ-xièxie-ta.	I thank him.
2.	Tā-xièxie-wo.	He thanks me.
3.	Tā-xièxie-ni.	He thanks you.
4.	Wó-yě-xièxie-ta.	I also thank him.
5.	Tāmen-dōu-xièxie-ni.	They all thank you.

Pattern 1.3. Questions Formed with the Particle ma
(Note 13, below, p. 11)

S	(AD)	SV	ma
Subject	(Adverb)	Stative Verb	Question Particle
Nǐ	yě	hǎo	ma?

'Are you also well?'

1.	Ní-hǎo-ma?	How are you?
2.	Tāmen-dōu-gāo-ma?	Are all of them tall?
3.	'Bái-Xiānsheng yé-hǎo-ma?	Is Mr. Bai also well?
4.	'Bái-Tàitai, 'Bái-Xiáojie dōu-háo-ma?	Are Mrs. Bai and Miss Bai both well?
5.	Nǐmen-dōu-hǎo-ma?	Are you (plural) all well?

SUBSTITUTION TABLES

Substitution tables are a device for rapid drill, as either individual study or classroom work. They enable the student to construct a number of different sentences on the same structural pattern, by substituting a variety of appropriate vocabulary items into a given sentence known to be grammatically correct. The number of sentences or phrases which can be formed from a table is indicated at the top of the table.

A break in a solid line above a substitution table indicates a place where it is possible to divide a table into two or more parts. Thus Table IV below can be divided into two parts and each part can be worked on separately, especially as a preliminary to forming the longer and more complicated sentences of the whole table.

A long dash in a column indicates you have the choice of selecting nothing from that column.

Taking Table IV, for example, you can get 48 sentences from the small vocabulary of Lesson 1 by varying only one item at a time. Half of these are statements formed by selecting nothing from the final column, and the other 24 are questions formed by adding ma to the sentences already created. One way to produce the first half of these sentences would be like this:

```
Bái Xiānsheng  yé hǎo        Bái Xiānsheng  hén hǎo
Gāo      "      "  "          Gāo       "     "   "
Bái Tàitai     "  "           Bái Tàitai       "   "
Gāo  "         "  "           Gāo       "      "   "
Bái Xiáojie    "  "           Bái Xiáojie      "   "
Gāo  "         "  "           Gāo       "      "   "
Bái Xiānsheng yě gāo          Bái Xiānsheng  hěn gāo
Gāo      "      "  "          Gāo       "     "   "
Bái Tàitai     "  "           Bái Tàitai       "   "
Gāo  "         "  "           Gāo       "      "   "
Bái Xiáojie    "  "           Bái Xiáojie      "   "
Gāo  "         "  "           Gāo       "      "   "
```

Substitution tables have varied uses. One of the simplest—the build-up drill or fluency drill—is performed by having the student repeat increasingly long sentences in direct imitation of the Chinese speaker, as follows:

Teacher	Student
Hǎo	Hǎo
Yé-hǎo	Yé-hǎo
Xiānsheng-yé-hǎo	Xiānsheng-yé-hǎo
Gāo-Xiānsheng-yé-hǎo	Gāo-Xiānsheng-yé-hǎo

Another useful exercise, the substitution drill, is performed by having the student substitute into a given sentence pattern, one by one, different vocabulary items called off by the teacher, as:

Teacher	Student
Gāo-Xiānsheng-yé-hǎo	Gāo-Xiānsheng-yé-hǎo
Tàitai	Gāo-Tàitai-yé-hǎo
Xiáojie	Gāo-Xiáojie-yé-hǎo

Each table should be used as the basis of as many drills as the teacher's ingenuity can invent.

I: 9 sentences (Notes 3, 14, 16)

nǐ	hǎo	—
nín		a
nǐmen		ma

II: 54 sentences (Notes 3, 4, 16)

Bái	Xiānsheng	–	hǎo	–
Gāo	Tàitai	nǐ		a
	Xiáojie	nín		ma

III: 36 sentences (Notes 7, 9, 10)

Bái	Xiānsheng	xièxie	wǒ	–
Gāo	Tàitai		nǐ	men
	Xiáojie		tā	

IV: 48 sentences (Notes 12–13)

Bái	Xiānsheng	yě	hǎo	–
Gāo	Tàitai	hěn	gāo	ma
	Xiáojie			

PRONUNCIATION DRILLS

I. The Unaspirated-Aspirated Contrast

(a) bà pà	(c) bái pái	(f) bǎo pǎo
(b) dā tā	(d) dài tài	(g) dào tào
	(e) gāi kāi	(h) gǎo kǎo

II. Contrasts in Tones

Read the following pairs first downward by columns, then across by rows, with pauses between syllables. (Digits indicate tone sequences.)

1,1 mā, mā	2,1 má, mā	3,1 mǎ, mā	4,1 mà, mā
1,2 mā, má	2,2 má, má	3,2 mǎ, má	4,2 mà, má
1,3 mā, mǎ	2,3 má, mǎ	3,3 mǎ, mǎ	4,3 mà, mǎ
1,4 mā, mà	2,4 má, mà	3,4 mǎ, mà	4,4 mà, mà

III. Combinations of Tones

Read the following phrases first down, then across. (The asterisked phrase involves a change of third tone to second tone.)

1,1 tā-bān	2,1 hái-gāo	3,1 mǎi-dāo	4,1 tài-gāo
1,2 tā-ná	2,2 hái-lái	3,2 mǎi-táng	4,2 tài-máng
1,3 tā-mǎi	2,3 hái-hǎo	3,3 mái-mǎ*	4,3 tài-hǎo
1,4 tā-pà	2,4 hái-kàn	3,4 mǎi-bào	4,4 tài-dà

IV. Changes in Third Tones
(See The Sounds of Chinese, 23)

A. Full Third Tone to Half Third Tone

wǒ gāo   >   wǒ-gāo

wǒ máng   >   wǒ-máng

wǒ dà   >   wǒ-dà

B. Third Tone to Second Tone

wǒ hǎo > wó-hǎo   wǒ hěn hǎo > wó-hén-hǎo

nǐ hǎo > ní-hǎo   nǐ hěn hǎo > ní-hén-hǎo

hěn hǎo > hén-hǎo   wǒ yě hǎo > wó-yé-hǎo

yě hǎo > yé-hǎo   nǐ yě hǎo > ní-yé-hǎo

V. Intonation Contrast
(See The Sounds of Chinese, 24)

Tā-yé-hǎo.   He's also well.

Tā-yé-hǎo-ma?   Is he also well?

Tāmen-hěn-gāo.   They're very tall.

Tāmen-hěn-gāo-ma?   Are they very tall?

BOY MEETS GIRL

State in English who says what to whom.

Bái: 'Gāo-Xiáojie, ní-hǎo?

Gāo: Hǎo. Nín-hǎo-ma?

Bái: Hén-hǎo. Gāo-Xiānsheng、 Gāo-Tàitai dōu-hǎo-ma?

Gāo: Dōu-hǎo, xièxie-nin.

Bái: Zàijiàn, zàijiàn.

Gāo: Zàijiàn, 'Bái-Xiānsheng.

NOTES

1. Chinese has parts of speech which we speak of as nouns, pronouns, verbs, adverbs. etc. These do not always have the same characteristics as the English parts of speech with the same names. In the English sentence 'All are well,' for example, 'all' is a noun or pronoun or perhaps an adjective, but in the corresponding Chinese sentence the word meaning 'all' is an adverb.

2. Chinese pronouns, unlike those of English, are not inflected for case or gender. Thus <u>tā</u> can mean 'he,' 'him,' 'she,' or 'her,' according to context.

3. Chinese personal pronouns are made plural by adding the suffix <u>men</u>:

wǒ	'I, me'	wǒmen	'we, us'
nǐ	'you' (singular)	nǐmen	'you' (plural)
tā	'he, him, she, her'	tāmen	'they, them'
nín	'you' (polite singular)	nínmen	'you' (polite plural)

<u>Nín</u> is also used without <u>men</u> as a polite plural form.

4. Chinese surnames generally consist of only one syllable. As in English, some of them are ordinary words, such as <u>bái</u> 'white.'

5. When foreigners take on Chinese names, they attempt to represent either the meaning or the sound of their original name. Thus someone with the surname 'White' would most likely call himself <u>Bái</u> in Chinese, translating the meaning; on the other hand, the name 'Gowan' would probably become <u>Gāo</u>, as a representation of the sound.

6. In the English translations of all Chinese material, we give the foreign equivalent of Chinese names which refer to non-Chinese; untranslated names will then be understood as referring to Chinese people.

7. A Chinese title follows the surname: <u>Bái-Xiānsheng</u> 'Mr. White.' Care should be taken to use appropriate titles. (See Supplementary Lesson 1, Note 1)

8. Chinese verbs, like English verbs, name actions (eat, come, are, etc.); unlike English verbs, they are not inflected for person, number, tense, or mood. Verbs may serve as grammatically complete sentences in Chinese: the subjects are often omitted if they can be inferred from the context. This is different from English; we say 'I'm fine' or 'Fine,' but not 'Am fine.'

9. Transitive verbs—those which take objects—are normally used (as in English) in the pattern Subject-Verb-Object: <u>Wǒ-xièxie-ni.</u> 'I thank you.'

10. Pronouns in object position often lose their tones, as with <u>ni</u> 'you' in the example in Note 9. However, if the sentence is spoken slowly, or if <u>nǐ</u> is stressed, the tone is retained.

11. Stative verbs are verbs which can be preceded by a word meaning 'very.' They describe a state of being and thus in meaning resemble adjectives in English: <u>hǎo</u> '(to be) good, (to be) well.' A statement containing a subject and a stative verb most often contains an adverb as well: <u>Wó-yé-hǎo.</u> 'I'm also well.'

12. Adverbs are words which can stand only before a verb or another adverb. The two adverbs appearing in Lesson 1 are <u>hěn</u> 'very,' as in <u>Hěn-gāo</u> '(Someone) is very tall' and <u>dōu</u> 'all,' as in <u>Dōu-hǎo</u> '(They) are all well.' Chinese adverbs are much more restricted than English adverbs, which can appear in various parts of a sentence. 'All' in the English sentence 'All of them are very well' is expressed in Chinese by the adverb <u>dōu</u>:

Tāmen-dōu-hén-hǎo. It is impossible to translate 'all of them' by placing dōu before tāmen, since Chinese adverbs occur only before verbs.

13. A statement is often turned into a yes-or-no question (a question that can be answered by 'yes' or 'no') without any change in word order, by the addition of a question particle at the end—the most common is ma. This form of question is nearly always used when the verb of the sentence is preceded by an adverb: Tā-hǎo-ma? 'Is he well?' Tā-yé-hǎo-ma? 'Is he also well?'

14. The particle a added to a statement changes it to a polite command, suggestion, or presumption. It often suggests that the speaker presumes his listener agrees with him; thus the Chinese sentence Ni-hǎo-a? is like English 'You are well, I suppose?' or 'How are you?' spoken as a greeting rather than as a real question.

15. The question particle ne makes questions from portions of speech which are less than a full sentence: Nǐ-ne? 'And you?' as a return greeting.

16. Conventional greetings are also expressed without a question particle. Three of the nine possible sentences from Substitution Table I, on page 7, for example, though they have the form of statements, would be understood in a conversational setting as questions:

    Ní-hǎo?   How are you? (singular)
    Nín-hǎo?   How are you? (polite form)
    Nǐmen-hǎo?   How are you? (plural)

17. The vast majority of Chinese words consist of one or more syllables each of which has meaning. Syllables have varying degrees of freedom. Some stand alone, like English 'Fine!' Others sometimes stand alone and sometimes combine with other syllables, like 'rail' and 'road' in 'railroad.' Still others, though they have meaning, never stand alone, like the suffix -er 'one who...' in 'teacher.' As it is sometimes helpful in memorizing words of more than one syllable to know how they are made up, we give meanings for individual syllables in the Vocabulary when it seems useful to do so. But be careful not to use the syllables in the meanings indicated unless you are sure the Chinese use them that way; some are combining forms rather than full words, and their use is restricted.

18. Coordinate items in succession are usually listed without intervening conjunctions and with or without pauses between them when spoken. In ordinary Chinese writing, that is in materials written in Chinese characters, they are generally separated by a special symbol which in Beginning Chinese Reader (p. 13) I have labelled the "enumerative comma." I have introduced this symbol into the present transcription text. Note that the use of the enumerative comma in contrast to the ordinary comma makes it possible to distinguish sentences which would otherwise be identical in writing but which are recognized in speech by quite different intonations, as in the following examples:

    'Máo-Xiānsheng, 'Gāo-Xiānsheng yé-hǎo-ma? 'Mr. Mao, is Mr. Gao also well?'
    'Máo-Xiānsheng、 'Gāo-Xiānsheng yé-hǎo-ma? 'Are Mr. Mao and Mr. Gao also well?'

Lesson 2   MEETING PEOPLE

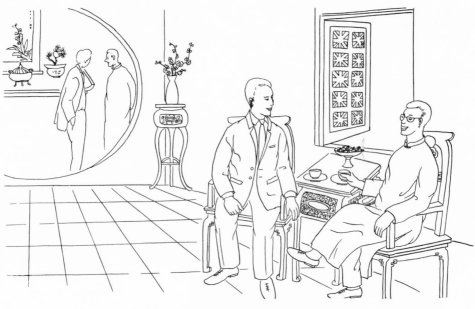

"'Nín-guìxìng?"

Dialogue: Mr. White, at a party, introduces himself to a Chinese gentleman.

Bái :	Qǐng-wèn-Xiānsheng, 'nín-guìxìng?		May I ask your name, Sir?
Qián:	Wǒ-xìng-Qián. Nín-shi 'Wáng-Xiānsheng-ba?		My name is Qian. I take it you're Mr. King?
Bái :	Bú-shi. Wǒ-xìng-Bái.	5	No, my name is White.
Qián:	Oh, nín-shi 'Bái-Xiānsheng. Nín-shi 'Yīngguo-rén-ma?		Oh, you're Mr. White. Are you English?
Bái :	Bú-shi. Wǒ-shi 'Měiguo-rén. Qǐng-wèn, nín-huì-shuō-'Yīngguo-huà-bu-huì?	10	No, I'm American. [May I ask,] do you speak English?
Qián:	Wǒ-'bú-huì. 'Jiù-huì-shuō 'Zhōngguo-huà.		No. I can only speak Chinese.

VOCABULARY

ba	(final particle) (Note 7)
bù, bú, bu	not; no (AD)
guìxìng?	What is your name? [lit. Honorable surname?—from guì, expensive, valuable, honorable' plus xìng 'surname']
guó	country, nation (N) (Note 1)
huà	speech, language (N)
huì	able to, can (V)
jiù	only, merely (AD)
Měiguo	America, United States (PW) [lit. beautiful country]
qián	money (N) (also, a surname)
qǐng	invite, request, ask; please (TV)
qǐng-wèn	May I ask?
rén	person, man, people (N)
shì, shi	be, am, is, are (EV) (Notes 3—6)
shuō	speak, talk, say (TV)
wáng	king (N) (also, a surname)
wèn	inquire, ask (TV)
xìng	have such-and-such surname, be called, named (EV)
Yīngguo	England (PW) [lit. brave country]
Zhōngguo	China (PW) [lit. middle country]

SENTENCE BUILD-UP

Wáng	King (a surname)
'Wáng-Xiānsheng	Mr. King
1. 'Wáng-Xiānsheng, 'nín-hǎo-ma?	Mr. King, how are you?
xìng	be called
xìng-Wáng	be called King
2. Wǒ-xìng-Wáng.	My name is King.
xìng-Bái	be called White
'bú-xìng-Bái	not be called White
3. Tā-'bú-xìng-Bái-ma?	His name isn't White?

shì   be, am, are, is
bú-shi   not be; am not, are not, is
                                         not
4. Tā-bú-shi 'Wáng-Xiānsheng.   He isn't Mr. King.

Zhōngguo   China
rén   person
'Zhōngguo-rén   Chinese person
5. Tā-shi-'Zhōngguo-rén.   He's Chinese.

Yīngguo   England
'Yīngguo-rén   Englishman
6. Wǒ-bú-shi 'Yīngguo-rén.   I'm not an Englishman.   or
                                         I'm not English.

Měiguo   America
'Měiguo-rén   American person
7. Wǒmen-dōu-shi 'Měiguo-rén.   We're all Americans.

shuō   say, speak
tā-shuō   he says, he speaks
8. Tā-shuō tā-xìng-Bái.   He says his name is White.

huà   language
'Zhōngguo-huà   Chinese language
9. Tāmen-shuō 'Zhōngguo-huà-   Are they speaking Chinese?
    ma?

shuō-'Zhōngguo-huà   speak Chinese
shuō-'Zhōngguo-huà-ba!   speak Chinese!
10. Wǒmen-shuō 'Zhōngguo-huà-   Let's speak Chinese! [lit. We,
    ba!   speak Chinese!]

huì   know how to, be able to
'huì-shuō 'Zhōngguo-huà   know how to speak Chinese,
                                         be able to speak Chinese
11. Wǒ-'bú-huì-shuō 'Zhōngguo-   I can't speak Chinese.
    huà.

'Yīngguo-huà   English language
'huì-shuō 'Yīngguo-   know how to or be able to
        huà   speak English
12. Nǐ-'huì-shuō 'Yīngguo-huà-   Can you speak English?
    ma?

jiù   only
'jiù-huì   only be able to, can only
13. Wǒ-'jiù-huì-shuō 'Zhōngguo-   I can only speak Chinese.
    huà.

Qián   Qian
'Qián-Xiānsheng   Mr. Qian
14. 'Qián-Xiānsheng shi-'Yīngguo-   Is Mr. Qian English?
    rén-ma?

shì	be, am, are, is
bú-shi	not be; am not, are not, is not
shì-bu-shi?	is or is not?
15. Tā-shì-bu-shi 'Yīngguo-rén?	Is he English?
shi-'Yīngguo-rén	be an Englishman, be English
bú-shi	is not
16. Tā-shì-'Yīngguo-rén-bu-shi?	Is he English?
huì	able to
'bú-huì	not be able to
'huì-bu-huì?	be able to or not be able to? can or can't?
17. Nǐ-'huì-bu-huì-shuō 'Zhōngguo-huà?	Can you speak Chinese?
huì-shuō 'Zhōngguo-huà	able to speak Chinese
'bú-huì	not able to
18. Nǐ-'huì-shuō 'Zhōngguo-huà-bu-huì?	Can you speak Chinese?
qǐng	request, ask
qǐng-ta	request him, ask him
19. Qǐng-ta-shuō 'Yīngguo-huà.	Ask him to speak English.
wèn	inquire, ask
tā-wèn-wo	he asked me
20. Tā-wèn-wo: "Nín-shi-'Yīngguo-rén-ma?"	He asked me: "Are you English?"
qǐng-wèn	may I ask
21. Qǐng-wèn, nín-shi-'Yīngguo-rén-ma?	May I ask, are you English?
guìxìng	honorable name
'nín-guìxìng?	(what is) your [honorable] name?
22. Qǐng-wèn, 'nín-guìxìng?	[May I ask,] what is your name?

PATTERN DRILLS

Pattern 2.1. Sentences with Equational Verbs (Note 3 below)

S	EV	C
Subject	Equational Verb	Complement
Tā	shì	'Yīngguo-rén.

'He is an Englishman.'

1. Wǒ-xìng-Wáng.   My name is King.

2. Tā-shi 'Qián-Xiáojie-ma?   Is she Miss Qian?

3. Tāmen 'dōu-xìng-Wáng-ma?   Are they all named King?

4. 'Wáng-Tàitai shi-'Yīngguo-rén.   Mrs. King is English.

5. Tā-'yě-xìng-Qián-ba?   I take it he's also called Qian?

6. Tā-shi-'Měiguo-rén, bú-shi-   He's American, not English.
    'Yīngguo-rén.

7. Tā-bú-xìng-Bái-ma?   Isn't his name White?

8. 'Wáng-Xiānsheng、'Wáng-Tàitai   Mr. and Mrs. King are both Eng-
    'dōu-shi-Yīngguo-rén.   lish.

9. 'Gāo-Tàitai 'yě-shi-Zhōngguo-   I suppose Mrs. Gao is also Chi-
    rén-ba?   nese?

10. Qǐng-wèn, nín-shi-'Yīngguo-   May I ask, are you English?
    rén-ma?

Pattern 2.2. Sentences with Auxiliary Verbs (Note 9 below)

S	AV	MV	O
Subject	Auxiliary Verb	Main Verb	Object
Tā	huì	shuō	'Yīngguo-huà.

'He can speak English.'

1. Tā-huì-shuō 'Zhōngguo-huà-   Can he speak Chinese?
    ma?

2. Tāmen-'bú-huì-shuō 'Yīngguo-   They can't speak English.
    huà.

3. 'Qián-Xiānsheng 'jiù-huì-shuō   Mr. Qian can only speak Chinese.
    'Zhōngguo-huà.

4. Wǒ-huì-shuō 'Yīngguo-huà, 'bú-   I can speak English but not Chi-
    huì-shuō 'Zhōngguo-huà.   nese.

5. Tāmen-'dōu-huì-shuō 'Zhōngguo-   They can all speak Chinese.
    huà.

Pattern 2.3. Choice-type Questions (Notes 4 and 6 below)

S	V	bu V	(O or.C)
Subject	Verb	Negative Verb	(Object or Complement)
Tā	shì	bu shi	'Yīngguo-rén?

'Is he an Englishman?'

1. Tā-'hǎo-bu-hǎo?   Is he well?
2. Nǐ-shì-bu-shi 'Qián-Tàitai?   Are you Mrs. Qian?
3. Nǐ-'huì-bu-huì-shuō 'Zhōngguo-   Can you speak Chinese?
   huà?
4. 'Wáng-Xiáojie shì-bu-shi-'Měigguo-   Is Miss King American?
   rén?
5. Tāmen-'huì-bu-huì-shuō 'Yīngguo-   Can they speak English?
   huà?

Pattern 2.4. Split Choice-type Questions (Notes 5 and 6 below)

S	V	O or C	bu V
Subject	Verb	Object or Complement	Negative Verb
Nǐ	shì	'Yīngguo-rén	bu shi?

'Are you English?'

1. Tā-shì-'Bái-Xiānsheng-bu-shi?   Is he Mr. White?
2. Tāmen-'huì-shuō-Zhōngguo-huà-   Can they speak Chinese?
   bu-huì?
3. Tāmen-shì-'Yīngguo-rén-bu-shi?   Are they English?
4. 'Gāo-Tàitai huì-shuō-'Yīngguo-   Can Mrs. Gao speak English?
   huà-bu-huì?
5. 'Wáng-Xiáojie shì-'Měiguo-rén-   Is Miss King American?
   bu-shi?

SUBSTITUTION TABLES

I: 36 sentences (Note 3)

wǒ	—	xìng	Bái	—
nǐ	bu		Gāo	ma
tā			Wáng	

II : 36 sentences (Note 3)

wǒ	–	–	shi	Měiguo	rén
nǐ	men	bú		Yīngguo	
tā				Zhōngguo	

III: 18 sentences (Notes 4 – 6)

wǒ	—	shì-bu-shi	Měiguo	rén?
nǐ	men		Yīngguo	
tā			Zhōngguo	

IV: 18 sentences (Notes 5 – 6)

wǒ	—	shì	Měiguo	rén	bu-shi?
nǐ	men		Yīngguo		
tā			Zhōngguo		

V: 12 sentences (Notes 5 – 6)

wǒ	—	huì	shuō	Yīngguo	huà	bu-huì?
nǐ	men			Zhōngguo		
tā						

PRONUNCIATION DRILLS

I. The e-en, e-eng Contrast
(See The Sounds of Chinese, 6)

(a) gē   gēn   (d) gè   gèng

(b) kě   kěn   (e) hé   héng

(c) hè   hèn   (f) lè   lèng

II. Lip-rounding versus No Lip-rounding
(See The Sounds of Chinese, 9)

(a) gù gè   (d) guò gè   (g) bō bā   (j) guǎn gǎn   (m) guāng gāng

(b) kù kè   (e) kuò kè   (h) pò pà   (k) kuǎn kǎn   (n) kuàng kàng

(c) hú hé   (f) huó hé   (i) mó má   (l) huàn hàn   (o) huáng háng

(p) guài gài   (r) gòng gèng   (t) kǔn kěn

(q) huài hài   (s) hóng héng

SNATCHES OF CONVERSATION

Imagine that you overhear the following bits of conversation. Translate the excerpts and invent some concrete situations in which they might be said.

1. Xiānsheng-guìxìng?
   Wǒ-xìng-Wáng.
   Oh! 'Wó-yě-xìng-Wáng.

2. Tā-shì-'Yīngguo-rén-bu-shì?
   Bú-shi. Tā-shì-'Měiguo-rén.

3. 'Gāo-Xiānsheng, zaìjiàn.
   Zaìjiàn, zaìjiàn.

4. Qǐng-wèn-Xiáojie, 'nín-guìxìng?
   Wǒ-xìng-Gāo. Nín-ne?

5. Nǐmen-hǎo-ma?
   Wǒmen-'dōu-hǎo, xièxie.

6. Ní-hǎo?
   Hǎo.
   Tàitai-'yé-hǎo-ma?
   Yé-hǎo, xièxie-ni.

7. Nǐ-'huì-shuō-Zhōngguo-huà-bu-huì?
   Bú-hui. 'Jiù-huì-shuō 'Yīngguo-huà.

8. Tā-bu-xìng-Bái-ma?
   Tā-'bú-xìng-Bái. Tā-xìng-Wáng.

9. Wǒ-wèn-ta: "Nǐ-shi-'Měiguo-rén-ma?"
   Tā-shuō: "Bú-shi. Wǒ-shi-'Yīngguo-rén."

10. Nǐ-shi-'Gāo-Tàitai-ma?
    Bú-shi. Wǒ-xìng-Qián.

11. 'Nǐ-huì-shuō 'Zhōngguo-huà-ma?
    'Wǒ-bú-huì. 'Wáng-Xiānsheng-huì.

12. Nǐ-shi-Wáng-Xiáojie-ba?
    Bú-shi. Wǒ-shi-Wáng-Tàitai.

13. Qǐng-ta-shuō-'Yīngguo-huà.
    Tā-shuō-tā-'bú-huì.

TO BE OR NOT TO BE?

Translate the following into Chinese. Be careful to translate 'is' with shì only when it is appropriate to do so.

1. He is very well.
2. He is Chinese.

3. He is able to speak Chinese.
4. He is named White.

PUTTING ON AN ACT

Act out the following conversation in Chinese, with each person taking turns in the roles of A and B. For individual practice, have one person take both parts.

A: May I ask, what is your name?
B: My name is King.
A: Mr. King, are you English?
B: No. I'm American.
A: Can you speak Chinese?
B: No.

NOTES

1. Chinese names of countries are formed most often, though not always, with the syllable guo or guó 'country.' Zhōngguo 'China' is made up of the two syllables zhōng 'middle' and guó 'country' or 'kingdom' (with the second syllable appearing in the neutral tone)—a reflection of the ancient notion that China was at the center of the universe. In Yīngguo 'England,' the syllable yīng is an approximation of the sound Eng., and the měi of Měiguo 'America' is also a representation of sound, probably of the syllable -mer-.*

2. Titles are used as polite forms in address as the equivalent of 'you.' Thus one might say Xiānsheng, nín-hǎo-ma? 'Sir, are you well?' or simply Xiānsheng-hǎo-ma? 'Is the gentleman well?'—that is, 'Are you well?' or 'How are you?'; Tàitai-hǎo-ma? 'How are you, madam?' Titles are also used in referring to persons who are not present: Tàitai-hǎo-ma? when addressing a husband would mean 'How is your wife?'

3. Equational verbs are verbs which connect or equate two nominal expressions on either side of the verb, like English 'is' in the sentence 'He is a man': here, 'is' equates 'he' with 'man.' The verb shì (often pronounced shi, with neutral tone) is the most common equational verb: Tā-shi-rén 'He is a man.' Remember that shì 'be' is used only to connect nominal expressions; it is not used in a sentence like Wó-hǎo 'I am well,' for hǎo is not a noun—it is a verb, meaning 'be well.'

4. Choice-type questions are formed by stating the affirmative and negative forms of a verb in rapid succession. For example, Tā-shì-bu-shì 'Yīngguo-ren? '[lit.] He is/is not an Englishman?' is answered by choosing either shì 'is' or bú-shi 'is not.' These forms can be used by themselves as an answer, or they can form part of fuller replies, such as:

---

* In addition to representing sounds, the syllables yīng and měi have complimentary connotations: yīng means 'brave' and měi means 'beautiful.'

Tā-'shì-'Yīngguo-rén. 'He is an Englishman.'
Tā-'bú-shi-Yīngguo-rén. 'He is not an Englishman.'

5. Split choice-type questions are formed by placing the negative form of the verb at the end: Tā-shì-'Yīngguo-rén-bu-shì? 'Is he an Englishman or not?' They are identical in meaning with the forms described in Note 4.

6. Stress in choice-type questions is on the first syllable: 'shì-bu-shi? Nǐ-'huì-bu-huì?

7. The final particle ba changes a statement to a request or suggestion, or adds a note of compliance or supposition:
     Tā-shi-'Měiguo-rén-ba. 'I suppose he's an American.'
     Wǒmen-shuō 'Zhōngguo-huà-ba. 'Let's talk Chinese.'
     Hǎo-ba. 'It's all right (with me).' 'Fine!'

8. English 'yes' and 'no' are used as answers to questions containing all sorts of verbs, such as:
     Are you well?   Yes.
     Can you speak English?   Yes.
     Are you an American?   Yes.
     Is your name King?   Yes.
     Do you have a notebook?   Yes.
     Do you want a pen?   Yes.
Chinese does not answer these questions with any single word meaning 'yes' or 'no.' Instead, it answers them with the affirmative or negative form of the verb used in the question, much as if we said in English:
     Can you speak English?   Can.
     Do you have a notebook?   Have.
Since the six questions listed above would all be expressed with different verbs in Chinese, there would be six different ways of saying 'yes.' Here are the Chinese questions and possible 'yes' answers for the first three questions:
     Nǐ-'hǎo-bu-hǎo?   Hǎo.
     Nǐ-'huì-shuō-Yīngguo-huà-
        bu-huì?   Huì.
     Nǐ-shì-'Měiguo-rén-bu-shì? Shì.
Be careful not to use shì and bú-shi for 'yes' and 'no' except when the question has shì or bú-shi as the main verb. (There is one situation, however, in which these forms do occur with any verb—when they are used as an initial affirmation or negation before the usual form. For example: Tā-huì-shuō-Yīngguo-huà-ma? . . . Shì, tā-huì-shuō-Yīngguo-huà. 'Can he speak English? . . . Yes, he can speak English.')

9. In Chinese, as in English, the auxiliary verb precedes the main verb:
     Tā-huì-shuō 'Yīngguo-huà. 'He can speak English.'

10. Note the differences in meaning conveyed by changes in word order in the following expressions:
     bù-dōu 'not all'   dōu-bù 'all not, none'
     bù-hěn 'not very'   hěn-bù 'very not'
     Wǒmen bù-dōu-shi-Měiguo-rén. 'Not all of us are Americans.'
     Wǒmen dōu-bú-shi-Měiguo-rén. 'None of us are Americans.'
     Tā-bù-hén-hǎo. 'He's not very good.'
     Tā-hěn-bù-hǎo. 'He's very bad.'

Lesson 3   SHOPPING AT A BOOKSTORE (1)

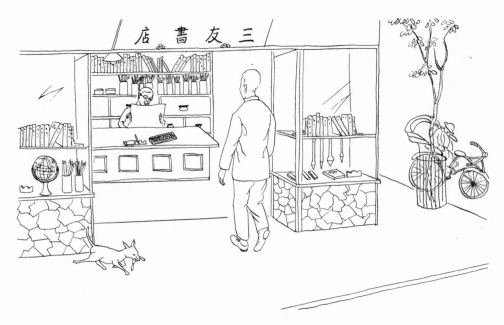

"Wǒ-yào-mǎi-shū."

Dialogue: A clerk, Mr. Mao, helps Mr. White make his purchases.

Máo :	Xiānsheng, nín-mǎi-shénmo?		What will you have, sir?
Bái :	Wǒ-yào-mǎi-shū. 'Nèibĕn-shū 'duōshao-qián?		I'd like to buy (some) books. (Points to a book.) How much is that book?
Máo :	'Néibĕn?	5	Which one?
Bái :	Nèibĕn-'Zhōngguo-shū.		That Chinese book.
Máo :	'Zhèibĕn-shū shi-liǎng-kuài-èrmáo-qián.		This book is two dollars and twenty cents.
Bái :	Hǎo, wó-mǎi-'liángbĕn.		Fine, I'll buy two copies.
Máo :	Nín-'hái-yào mǎi-shénmo-ne?	10	What else do you want to buy?
Bái :	Nǐmen-mài-'bǐ-bu-mài?		Do you sell pens?
Máo :	Mài. Wǒmen-mài 'Zhōng-guo-bǐ, yĕ-mài 'wàiguo-bǐ.	15	Yes. We sell Chinese pens, and also foreign pens.

Bái : Yìzhī-máobǐ 'duōshao-
qián?

How much for a Chinese writing
brush?

Máo: Yìzhī liǎngmáo-qián. Nín-
yào mái-'jǐzhī?

They're twenty cents each. How
many do you want to buy?

Bái : Sān-sìzhī. Bù. Wó-mái-
'wǔzhī.

20

Three or four. No. I'll buy five.

Máo: Wǔzhī yíkuài-qián.

Five—one dollar.

Bái : Yígòng 'duōshao-qián?

How much altogether?

Máo: Liángběn-shū, sìkuài-
sìmáo-qián. Wǔzhī-máobǐ,
yíkuài-qián. Yígòng wǔ-
kuài-sì.

25

Two books, four dollars and forty cents. Five Chinese writing
brushes, a dollar. Altogether,
five-forty.

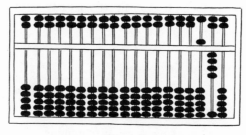

"wǔkuai-sì"

VOCABULARY

běn	volume, copy (M)
bǐ	pen, pencil (N)
duōshao	how many? how much? [lit. many few or much little]
èr	two (NU) (Note 10)
hái	additionally, in addition, still, more (AD)
jǐ	how many? (NU) (Note 9)
kuài	lump; dollar* (M)

---

* An earlier form of money in China consisted of silver chunks or lumps of
varying sizes. This use of kuài was extended to minted silver dollars and still
later to paper currency. (See also Supplementary Lesson 3, Note 1)

liǎng	two, a couple (NU) (Note 10)
mǎi	buy (TV)
mài	**sell, sell for (TV) (Note 18)**
máo	hair (N); feather (also, a surname)
máo	dime (M) (Note 12)
máobǐ	Chinese writing brush (N) [lit. hair pen]
nà, nèi	that (thing) (SP) (Note 19)
nǎ, něi	which (thing)? (SP) (Note 19)
sān	three (NU)
shénmo, shénme	what (thing)?
shū	book (N)
sì	four (NU)
wàiguo	foreign country (PW) [lit. outside country]
wǔ	five (NU)
yào	want (TV)
yī, yí, yì	one (NU) (Note 15)
yígòng	altogether, in all (MA) [lit. one together]
zhè, zhèi	this (thing) (SP) **(Note 19)**
zhī	(measure for long, slender objects)

SENTENCE BUILD-UP

	zhè	this (thing)
	shénmo?	what (thing)?
1.	Zhè-shi-shénmo?	What is this?
	zhèi	this (thing)
	shū	book
2.	Zhèi-shi-shū.	This is a book.
	nà	that (thing)
	shì-shénmo?	is what?
3.	Nà-shi-shénmo?	What is that?

	bǐ	pen
	Zhōngguo-bǐ	Chinese pen
4.	Nà-shi-'Zhōngguo-bǐ.	That's a Chinese pen.
	nèi	that (thing)
	nèi-yě-shi	that also is
5.	Nèi-'yě-shi-Zhōngguo-bǐ.	That's a Chinese pen, too.
	máo	hair
	máobǐ	Chinese writing brush
6.	Zhèi-shi-'máobǐ.	This is a writing brush.
	qián	money (also, a surname)
	'Qián-Tàitai	Mrs. Qian
7.	'Qián-Tàitai-hǎo-ma?	Is Mrs. Qian well?
	máo	hair (also, a surname)
	'Máo-Xiānsheng	Mr. Mao
8.	'Máo-Xiānsheng, 'nín-hǎo-ma?	How are you, Mr. Mao?
	máobǐ	Chinese writing brush
	shi-máobǐ	is a writing brush
9.	Zhèi-shi-'máobǐ-bu-shi?	Is this a writing brush?
	yào	want
	yào-shénmo?	want what?
10.	Tā-yào-'shénmo?	What does he want?
	běn	volume (also, measure for books)
	zhèiběn-shū	this book
11.	Wǒ-yào 'zhèiběn-shū.	I want this book.
	zhī	(measure for long objects)
	zhèizhī-bǐ	this pen
12.	Wǒ-yào 'zhèizhī-bǐ.	I want this pen.
	nèiběn-shū	that book
13.	Tā-yào 'nèiběn-shū.	He wants that book.
	yī	one
	máo	dime
	yìmáo-qián	one dime
14.	Zhèizhī-bǐ 'yìmáo-qián.	This pen (is) a dime.
	liǎng	two
	liǎngmáo-qián	twenty cents
15.	Nèizhī-bǐ yě-shi-liǎngmáo-qián.	That pen is also twenty cents.
	sān	three
	sānmáo-qián	thirty cents
16.	Tā-yào 'sānmáo-qián.	He wants thirty cents.

sì
sì máo-qián
17. Zhèizhī-máobǐ 'sìmáo-qián.

four
forty cents
This writing brush is forty cents.

wǔ
wǔmáo-qián
18. Zhèiběn-shū 'yě-shi-wǔmáo-
qián-ma?

five
fifty cents
Is this book also fifty cents?

kuài
yíkuài-qián
19. Zhèi-shi-'yíkuài-qián.

dollar
one dollar
This is one dollar.

liǎng
liǎngkuài-qián
20. 'Nèiběn-shū 'yě-shi-liǎngkuài-
qián.

two
two dollars
That book is also two dollars.

wúběn-shū
21. Tā-yě-yào wúběn-shū.

five books
He also wants five books.

jǐ?
jíběn-shū?
22. Nǐ-yào-'jíběn-shū?

how many?
how many books?
How many books do you want?

wǔkuài-qián
èrmáo-qián
23. 'Zhèizhī-bǐ wǔkuài-èrmáo-
qián.

five dollars
twenty cents
This pen is five dollars (and)
twenty cents.

wǔkuài-èr
24. Nèizhī-bǐ 'yě-shi-wǔkuài-èr.

five-twenty
That pen is also five-twenty.

něi?
něizhī bǐ?
25. Nǐ-yào 'něizhī-bǐ?

which (thing)?
which pen?
Which pen do you want?

liǎngzhī-bǐ
'néi-liǎngzhī-bǐ?
26. Tā-yào 'néi-liǎngzhī-bǐ?

two pens
which two pens?
Which two pens does he want?

duōshao?
duōshao-qián?
27. Zhèiběn-shū 'duōshǎo-qián?

how much?
how much money?
How much is this book?

yígòng
yígòng 'duōshao-qián?
28. Shū, bǐ 'yígòng-duōshao-qián?

altogether
how much altogether?
How much are the books and pens
altogether?

hái
hái-yào
29. Tā-'hái-yào-shénmo?

in addition
want in addition
What more does he want?

mǎi	buy
mǎi-shū	buy books
30. Nǐ-yào-mǎi-shū-ma?	Do you want to buy some books?

mài	sell
mài-shū	sell books
31. Tāmen-'mài-shū-ma?	Do they sell books?

wàiguo	foreign country
wàiguo-rén	foreign person
32. Tā-shi-'wàiguo-rén-ma?	Is he a foreigner?

wàiguo-huà	foreign language
shuō-wàiguo-huà	speak a foreign language
33. Wǒ-'bú-huì-shuō wàiguo-huà.	I can't speak a foreign language.

sì běn-shū	four books
wúběn-shū	five books
34. Tā-yào-mǎi 'sì-wúběn-shū.	He wants to buy four or five books.

zhèiběn-shū	this book
zhèiběn	this one
35. Zhèiběn 'yé-hén-hǎo.	This one is also very good.

PATTERN DRILLS

Pattern 3.1. Noun Phrases with Numbers and Measures
(Notes 2 — 6 below)

NU	M	N
Number	Measure	Noun
yì	běn	shū

'one book'

1. liǎngzhī-bǐ	two pens
2. liǎngmáo-qián	two dimes; twenty cents
3. sānkuài-qián	three dollars
4. wúběn-shū	five books
5. 'jǐzhī-bǐ?	how many pens?

6. 'jíběn-shū?   how many books?
7. liǎngzhī-máobǐ   two Chinese writing brushes
8. sìkuài-èrmáo-qián   four dollars and twenty cents
9. Zhèi-shi-sānkuài-qián.   This is three dollars.
10. Wǒ-yào-wǔzhī-bǐ.   I want five pens.
11. Tā-yào sìkuài-sānmáo-qián.   He wants four dollars and thirty
                                         cents.
12. Yìzhī-máobǐ liǎngmáo-qián.   One w r i t i n g brush is twenty
                                         cents.
13. Tāmen-yào-sānběn-shū.   They want three books.
14. Nǐ-yào-'jíběn-shū?   How many books do you want?
15. Bǐ 'yíkuài-èr, shū 'liǎngkuài-   The pen is a dollar twenty, the
    èr.   book two-twenty.

Pattern 3.2.   Noun Phrases with Specifiers and Measures (Note 7 below)

              SP   M   N
              Specifier   Measure   Noun
              zhèi   běn   shū

              'this book'

1. nèizhī-máobǐ   that Chinese writing brush
2. nèizhī-bǐ   that pen
3. zhèiběn-shū   this book
4. nèiběn-shū   that book
5. Tā-yào-'zhèiběn-shū-ma?   Does he want this book?
6. Zhèizhī-bǐ 'hǎo-bu-hǎo?   How's this pen?
7. Zhèizhī-bǐ 'jíkuài-qián?   How much [lit. how many dollars]
                                         is this pen?
8. Nèizhī-bǐ 'yě-shi-sānkuài-   That pen is also three dollars.
    qián.
9. Zhèizhī-máobǐ 'bù-hén-hǎo.   This writing brush isn't very
                                         good.
10. Nǐ-yào-'zhèiběn-shū-ma?   Do you want this book?

Pattern 3.3.   Noun Phrases with Specifiers, Numbers, and Measures
               (Note 7 below)

              SP   NU   M   N
              Specifier   Number   Measure   Noun
              zhèi   sān   běn   shū

              'these three books'

1. nèi-liǎngkuài-qián   those two dollars
2. 'nèi-sānzhī-bǐ?   which three pens?
3. zhèi-wǔmáo-qián   this fifty cents
4. 'nèi-sìběn-shū?   which four books?

5. zhèi-liǎngzhī-máobǐ   these two Chinese writing brush-
                                            es
6. Nǐ-yào 'néi-liángběn-shū?   Which two books do you want?
7. Zhèi-'sìzhī-bǐ 'yígòng-   How much altogether are these
    duōshao-qián?   four pens?
8. Nèi-sānzhī-máobǐ 'dōu-hén-   Those three writing brushes are
    hǎo.   all very good.
9. Zhèi-sānběn-shū 'yígòng-wǔ-   These three books are five dol-
    kuài-qián.   lars in all.
10. 'Wáng-Tàitai-shuō tā-yào-   Mrs. Wang says she wants these
    'zhèi-liǎngzhī-máobǐ.   two writing brushes.

SUBSTITUTION TABLES

I: 20 sentences

zhè	shi	shénmo?
zhèi		shū
nà		bǐ
nèi		máobǐ
		qián

II: 30 sentences

wǒ	—	yào	shénmo?
nǐ	men		shū
tā			bǐ
			máobǐ
			qián

III: 12 phrases (Note 7)

zhè	-zhī bǐ
zhèi	-běn shū
nà	-zhī máobǐ
nèi	

IV: 75 phrases (Notes 2–6, 10)

yí	-kuài	yī	—
liǎng		èr	máo
sān		sān	máo-qián
sì		sì	
wǔ		wǔ	

V: 72 Sentences (Notes 2–6)

zhèi shi	yì	-běn shū
wǒ yào	liǎng	-zhī bǐ
tā yào	sān	-kuài qián
	sì	-máo qián
	wǔ	
	jǐ	

<u>VI: 72 phrases</u>

zhèi	—	-běn shū
nèi	yī	-zhī bǐ
něi	liǎng	-máo qián
	sān	-kuài qián
	sì	
	wǔ	

PRONUNCIATION DRILLS

I. Non-Palatals versus Palatals

(a) bǎo	biǎo	(e) bàn	biàn
(b) pào	piào	(f) pān	piān
(c) máo	miáo	(g) màn	miàn
(d) dào	diào	(h) dàn	diàn

| (i) náng | niáng | (k) dé | dié |
| (j) láng | liáng | (l) tè | tiè |

II. The i-in, i-ing Contrast
(See The Sounds of Chinese, 14)

(a) lí	lín	(d) ní	nín	(g) dì	dìng
(b) bì	bìn	(e) mǐ	mǐn	(h) tí	tíng
(c) pǐ	pǐn	(f) lì	lìn	(i) mì	mìng

QUESTIONS AND ANSWERS

1. Zhèiběn-'Zhōngguo-shū 'duōshao-qián?
   'Nèiběn-shū wǔkuài-sì.

   How much is this Chinese book?

   That book is five-forty.

2. Zhèi-shi-shénmo?
   Nà-shi-máobǐ.

   What's this?

   That's a Chinese writing brush.

3. Nǐmen mài-'shū-bu-mài?
   Wǒmen-'jiù-mài 'Zhōngguo-shū.
   'Bú-mài 'wàiguo-shū.

   Do you sell books?
   We only sell Chinese books.
   We don't sell foreign books.

4. 'Wáng-Tàitai huì-shuō-'wàiguo-huà-ma?
   Tā-'bú-huì.

   Can Mrs. Wang speak a foreign language?
   No. [lit. She can't.]

5. Tā-yào 'duōshao-qián?
   Tā-yào 'sānkuài-qián.

   How much money does he want?
   He wants three dollars.

6. Nǐ-yào-mǎi jǐ zhī-bǐ?   How many pens do you want to buy?

   Qǐng-wèn, duōshao-qián-yìzhī?   (May I ask,) how much for one?

7. Zhè-'yígòng 'duōshao-qián?   How much is this altogether?
   'Yígòng sānkuài-yī.   Altogether (it's) three-ten.

8. Zhè-shi-'Měiguo-bǐ-bú-shi?   Is this an American pen?
   Bú-shi. Shi-'Yīngguo-bǐ.   No. It's an English pen.

9. Zhèizhī-bǐ 'duōshao-qián?   How much is this pen?
   Sìkuài-qián. Zhèizhī-bǐ hén-hǎo.   Four dollars. This pen is very fine.

10. Tàitai-yào-mǎi-shénmo?   What does the lady want to buy?
   Tā-yào-mǎi-shū.   She wants to buy some books.

11. Zhèizhī-bǐ wǔkuài-qián. Ní-mǎi-yìzhī-ma?   This pen is five dollars. Are you buying one?
   Xièxie, wǒ-bù-mǎi.   (No) thanks, I'm not [buying].

TRUE OR FALSE

Read each of the following statements aloud, then tell whether it is true or false.

1. Yìběn-shū sānkuài-qián. Yìzhī-máobǐ liǎngmáo-qián. 'Yígòng-wǔkuài-qián.

2. Wǒ-yào-mǎi liǎngzhī-'Zhōngguo-bǐ, yìzhī-'wàiguo-bǐ. Wǒ-'yígòng mǎi-'sānzhī-bǐ.

3. 'Bái-Xiānsheng-shuō tā-yào-mǎi sānběn-'Zhōngguo-shū.

4. 'Máo-Xiānsheng-shuō tāmen-mǎi 'wàiguo-bǐ.

5. 'Bái-Xiānsheng-shuō tā-yào-mǎi-shū, 'bú-yào-mái-bǐ.

6. Wó-mǎi-'yìběn-shū. Ní-mǎi-'liángběn-shū. Wǒmen-'yígòng mǎi-'sìběn-shū.

7. 'Bái-Xiānsheng xìng-Wáng.

WHAT WOULD YOU SAY?

Put yourself in the role of both customer and clerk and make up (either orally or in written form) a dialogue appropriate for the following situation:

A clerk in a store greets you by name as Mr. White and asks what you want to buy. You ask if they sell foreign books. The clerk answers that they don't, and adds that they only sell Chinese books. You ask if they sell foreign pens. He says they sell foreign pens, and also Chinese pens. You say you want to

buy a foreign pen, point to one, and ask how much it is. He mentions a price.
You tell him that that's fine and that you'll buy one. The clerk thanks you and
says good-bye.

NOTES

1. The first five Chinese numbers, plus the interrogation number, are:

    yī 'one'   sān 'three'   wǔ 'five'
    èr 'two'   sì 'four'   jǐ 'how many?'

2. A grammatical element that follows a number is a MEASURE: in yíkuài
    'one lump,' for example, kuài is a measure.

3. An element that can occur directly after a measure is a NOUN: the ex-
    pression yíkuài-qián 'one dollar' [lit. 'one lump (of) money'] consists of
    the number yī 'one' plus the measure kuài 'lump' plus the noun qián
    'money.'

4. Often, specific measures are used with certain nouns: zhī with the names
    of long slender objects, běn 'volume, copy' with shū 'books,' and so on.
    It is advisable to memorize the appropriate measure for each noun you
    learn.

5. The number or quantity of a Chinese noun is expressed not by a change in
    the noun itself but by the use of different expressions of amount before the
    noun: compare English 'three head of cattle,' 'four head of cattle.' Ex-
    amples:

    sānkuài-qián 'three dollars' [lit. 'three lumps money']
    sìkuài-qián 'four dollars' [lit. 'four lumps money']
    sānběn-shū 'three (volumes) books'
    sìběn-shū 'four (volumes) books'

    A measure must always intervene between a number and a noun (as,
    sānběn-shū); a number cannot precede a noun directly.

6. Different measures are often used with the same noun, just as with Eng-
    lish 'one grain of rice,' 'two bowls of rice,' 'three pounds of rice.' The
    measures kuài 'lump; dollar' and máo 'dime' are both used before qián
    'money':

    sānkuài-qián 'three dollars'
    sānmáo-qián 'three dimes'
    sānkuài-sānmáo-qián 'three dollars (and) thirty cents'

7. A SPECIFIER is a word which can precede or replace a number before a
    measure. Examples include zhèi 'this,' nèi 'that,' and the question word
    něi 'which?':

    zhèiběn-shū 'this book'
    nèiběn-shū 'that book'
    něiběn-shū 'which book?'
    zhèi-sānběn-shū 'these three books'

The alternate forms zhè for zhèi and nà for nèi are used as subjects in expressions not containing a number or measure:

Zhè-shi-shū. 'This is a book.'

8. Question words are used to form questions which cannot be answered by 'yes' or 'no.' In this, they resemble English 'how many?' 'who?' etc. Unlike these English expressions, however, they do not change the order of words in the sentence: Chinese question words occupy the same position in the sentence as the word which replaces them in the answer.

9. There are two differences between the question words duōshao 'how many? how much?' and jǐ 'how many?' First, duōshao is used as either a noun or a measure, whereas jǐ 'how many?' is used only before a measure. Second, duōshao suggests either an indefinite amount or a large number, whereas jǐ suggests less than ten:

duōshao-qián? 'how much money?' (an indefinite, or large, amount)
jǐkuài-qián? 'how many dollars?' (this question anticipates an answer of only a few dollars)

10. The number for 'two' before a measure is most often liǎng 'two, a couple.' The number èr is used in compound numbers (see next lesson), before máo 'dime,' and (optionally) when there is more than one measure:

liǎngkuài èrmáo-qián 'two dollars (and) twenty cents'

11. A noun may be omitted after a measure if it can be understood from the context:

Nǐ-yào jíběn-shū? 'How many books do you want?'
Wǒ-yào-sānběn. 'I want three.'
The measure, on the other hand, may NOT be omitted.

12. The measure máo 'dime' may be omitted from money expressions when they are compound: 'three dollars and forty cents,' for example, is either sānkuài-sìmáo-qián or sānkuài-sìmáo or simply sānkuài-sì. With 'two,' however, máo may be omitted only after èr, not after liǎng: for example, sānkuài-liǎngmáo-qián can only be abbreviated as sānkuài-èr.

13. English expressions like 'three or four' require no connecting form in Chinese: sān-sìběn-shū 'three (or) four books.'

14. The question words duōshao 'how many? how much?' and shénmo 'what?' are used either before a noun or independently:

Tā-yào shénmo-shū? 'What book does he want?' [lit. 'He wants what book?']
Tā-yào-shénmo? 'What does he want?'
Tā-yào-duōshao-qián? 'How much money does he want?'
Tā-yào-duōshao? 'How much does he want?'

15. The number 'one' is pronounced yī in isolation, yí before a fourth tone (yíkuài), and yì before other tones. When it is unstressed, it often becomes neutral in tone; if it is attached to an expression in object position, it may even disappear completely.

16.   Some Chinese sentences occur without verbs:

Zhèibĕn-shū wŭkuài-qián. 'This book (is) five dollars.'

17.   The particle <u>ne</u> often expresses the continuation of an action, especially
if the sentence also contains the adverb <u>hái</u> 'still':

Tā-hái-shuō-huà-ne. 'He's still talking.'

18.   Note the following uses of <u>mài</u> 'to sell, to sell for':

Tāmen-mài-shū-ma?   'Do they sell books?'
Zhèibĕn-shū mài-duōshao-qián? 'How much does this book sell for?'

19.   The Specifiers <u>nă</u>, <u>nà</u>, and <u>zhè</u> usually become <u>nĕi</u>, <u>nèi</u>, and <u>zhèi</u> before
Measure words:

Nà-shi-shénmo?   'What's that?'
Nèibĕn-shū duōshao-qián?   'How much is that book?'

Lesson 4   SHOPPING AT A BOOKSTORE (2)

" 'Yígòng-duōshao-qián? "

Dialogue: Mr. Mao helps Mr. White make some further purchases.

Máo :   Xiānsheng, nín-mǎi-shénmo?

Sir, what will you have?

Bái :   Wó-mǎi-yíge-běnzi. Zhèige-běnzi 'duōshao-qián-yìběn?

I'd like to buy a notebook. How much for one of these notebooks?

Máo :   'Nèige-běnzi liùmáo-wǔfēn-qián-yìběn.   5

That notebook is sixty-five cents.

Bái :   Wó-mǎi-'yìběn.

I'll buy one.

Máo :   Hǎo. Nín-'hái-mǎi-shénmo?

Fine. What else will you have?

Bái :   Yǒu-'mòshuǐ-ma?

Do you have any ink?

Máo :   Nín-mǎi 'shénmo-yánse-mòshuǐ?   10

What color ink do you want?

Bái :   Yǒu-'hóng-mòshuǐ-ma?

Do you have red ink?

Máo :   'Méi-yǒu. Yǒu-'hēi-mòshuǐ, 'lán-mòshuǐ.

No. We have black ink and blue ink.

Bái :   Yǒu-'qiānbǐ-méi-you?

Do you have pencils?

Máo :   Qiānbǐ, gāngbǐ, máobǐ—wǒ-men-'dōu-yǒu.   15

Pencils, fountain pens, writing brushes—we have them all.

Bái :   'Qiānbǐ duōshao-qián-yìzhī?

How much [each] are the pencils?

35

Máo: 'Jiǔfēn-qián-yìzhī.   Nine cents each.

Bái : Wó-mǎi-'liùzhī-qiānbǐ.   I'll buy six [pencils].

Máo: Liùzhī-qiānbǐ: 'liù-jiú-   20   Six pencils: six nines (are) fifty-
      wǔmáo-sì.   four cents.

Bái : Gāngbǐ duōshao-qián-yìzhī?   How much are the fountain pens?

Máo: Nín-mái-'něizhī?   Which are you buying?

Bái : 'Zhèizhī.   This one.

Máo: 'Zhèizhī liǎngkuài-bāmáo-   25   This one is two dollars (and)
      liù. Nín-mǎi-'máobǐ-ma?   eighty-six cents. Would you like
                                                       to buy some writing brushes?

Bái : Bù-mǎi, wó-yǒu. Nǐmen-   No, I have some. Do you have
      yǒu-dìtú-ma?   any maps?

Máo: Yǒu. 'Zhōngguo-dìtú,   Yes. We have both Chinese
      'Měiguo-dìtú, wǒmen-'dōu-   30   [maps] and American maps. What
      yǒu. Nín-mǎi 'něiguó-   country do you want a map of?
      dìtú?   [lit. What country map do you
                                                       buy?]

Bái : Wó-mǎi-'Zhōngguo-dìtú.   I'd like to buy a map of China.

Máo: 'Zhèige-dìtú-hén-hǎo. Nín-   This map is excellent. [I sug-
      'mǎi-yìzhāng-ba.   35   gest you buy one.]

Bái : 'Duōshao-qián-yìzhāng?   How much for one?

Máo: Liǎngkuài-jiǔmáo-qī-yì-   Two dollars (and) ninety-seven
      zhāng.   cents.

Bái : Oh, wǒ-'hái-yào-mǎi. Wǒ-   Oh, I want to buy something
      hái-mǎi 'wǔshízhāng-zhǐ.   40   more. I'd also like to buy fifty
      'Duōshao-qián?   sheets of paper. How much (are
                                                       they)?

Máo: Sìmáo-jiǔfēn-qián.   Forty-nine cents.

Bái : Yǒu-'zìdiǎn-ma?   Do you have any dictionaries?

Máo: Yǒu.   Yes.

Bái : Wǒ-yào-yìběn-'Zhōngwén-   45   I'd like a Chinese dictionary.
      zìdiǎn. 'Duōshao-qián?   How much is it?

Máo: Yíkuài-bāmáo-qián.   A dollar (and) eighty cents.

Bái : Yìběn-'Yīngwén-zìdiǎn   How much for an English dic-
      'duōshao-qián?   tionary?

Máo: Liǎngkuài-jiǔmáo-qián.   50   Two dollars and ninety cents.

Bái : Zhōng-Yīng-zìdiǎn-ne?   How about a Chinese-English
                                                       dictionary?

Máo: Zhōng-Yīng-zìdiǎn sìkuài-   A Chinese-English dictionary is
      qīmáo-qián.   four dollars and seventy cents.

Bái : 'Yígòng-duōshao-qián?   How much altogether?

Máo : Běnzi liùmáo-wǔ, 'qiānbǐ   55   Notebook 65 cents, pencils 54
wǔmáo-sì, 'gāngbǐ liǎng-   cents, fountain pen $2.86, map
kuài-bāmáo-liù, dìtú $2.97, paper 49 cents, Chinese
liǎngkuài-jiǔmáo-qī, zhǐ   dictionary $1.80, English dic-
sìmáo-jiǔ, 'Zhōngwén-   tionary $2.90, Chinese-English
zìdiǎn yíkuài-bā, 'Yīng-   60   dictionary $4.70. (Mao checks
wén-zìdiǎn liǎngkuài-jiǔ,   up each item on his abacus as he
'Zhōng-Yīng-zìdiǎn sìkuài-   speaks, so he is now ready to
qī. . . 'Yígòng shíliùkuài-   announce immediately:) Alto-
jiǔmáo-yìfēn-qián.   gether $16.91.

Bái : Hǎo.   65   O. K.

Máo : 'Xièxie-nin, 'zàijiàn.   Thank you, good-bye.

Bái : Zàijiàn, zàijiàn.   Good-bye.

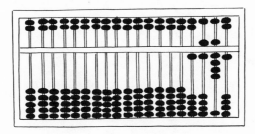

"Shíliùkuài-jiǔmáo-yìfēn-qián"

VOCABULARY

bā	eight (NU)
běnzi	notebook (N)
dìtú	map (N) [lit. land chart]
fēn	part; cent (M) (Note 7)
gāngbǐ	pen (fountain pen or pen with detachable point) (N) [lit. steel pen]
ge	(general measure: see Notes 3 and 4)
hēi	black (SV)
hóng	red (SV)
jiǔ	nine (NU)
lán	blue (SV); (also, a surname)
liù	six (NU)
méi	not (AD) (Note 8)

mòshuǐ	ink (N) [lit. ink water]
qī	seven (NU)
qiānbǐ	pencil (N) [lit. lead pencil]
shí	ten (NU) (Notes 5-6)
wén	language, literature (N) (Notes 1-2)
yánse	color (N) [lit. pigment color; yán is also a surname]
Yīngwén	English language and literature (N)
yǒu	have (V) (Note 8)
zhāng	(measure for flat objects; also, a surname)
zhǐ	paper (N)
Zhōngwén	Chinese language and literature (N)
zìdiǎn	dictionary (N) [lit. character book]

SENTENCE BUILD-UP

	yǒu	have
	yǒu-shū	have a book
1.	Ní-yǒu-shū-ma?	Do you have a book?
	méi-yǒu	not have
	méi-yóu-bǐ	not have a pen
2.	Wó-'yě-méi-yóu-bǐ.	I don't have a pen either [lit. I also don't have a pen].
	qiānbǐ	pencil
3.	Ní-yóu-'jǐ zhī-qiānbǐ?	How many pencils do you have?
	gāngbǐ	[steel] pen
4.	Zhèizhī-'gāngbǐ yíkuài-qián.	This pen is one dollar.
	liǎngge	two of something
	nèi-liǎngge-rén	those two people
5.	Nèi-liǎngge-rén 'dōu-shi-wàiguo-rén.	Both of those people are foreigners.
	běnzi	notebook
	sānge-běnzi	three notebooks
6.	Wó-yǒu-'sānge-běnzi.	I have three notebooks.
	wén	language and literature
	Zhōngwén	Chinese language
7.	Tāmen-'jiù-mài 'Zhōngwén-shū.	They sell only Chinese books.
	Yīngwén	English language

Yīngwén-shū
book in English

8. Zhèiběn-'Yīngwén-shū 'duōshao-qián?
How much is this English-language book?

zìdiǎn
dictionary

Zhōngwén-zìdiǎn
Chinese dictionary

9. Nǐmen-mài-'Zhōngwén-zìdiǎn-bu-mài?
Do you sell Chinese dictionaries?

Zhōng-Yīng
Chinese-English

Zhōng-Yīng-zìdiǎn
Chinese-English dictionary

10. Zhèiběn-Zhōng-Yīng-zìdiǎn 'duōshao-qián?
How much is this Chinese-English dictionary?

dìtú
map

Zhōngguo-dìtú
map of China

11. Zhè-shi-'Zhōngguo-dìtú.
This is a map of China.

zhāng
(measure for flat objects)

sānzhāng-dìtú
three maps

12. Sānzhāng-dìtú 'yíkuài-wǔ.
Three maps are a dollar fifty.

'Zhāng-Xiānsheng
Mr. Zhang

13. 'Zhāng-Xiānsheng, nín-hǎo-a?
How are you, Mr. Zhang?

zhǐ
paper

yìzhāng-zhǐ
one sheet of paper

14. Wǒ-'jiù-yǒu-yìzhāng-zhǐ.
I have only one sheet of paper.

mòshuǐ
ink

15. Zhèige-mòshuǐ-'hén-hǎo.
This ink is excellent.

hēi
black

hēi-mòshuǐ
black ink

16. Wǒ-'méi-yǒu hēi-mòshuǐ.
I don't have any black ink.

hóng
red

hóng-mòshuǐ
red ink

17. Ní-yǒu-'hóng-mòshuǐ-méi-yǒu?
Do you have any red ink?

lán
blue

lán-mòshuǐ
blue ink

18. Wǒmen-yé-yǒu-'lán-mòshuǐ.
We also have blue ink.

yánse
color

shénmo-yánse?
what color?

19. Zhèige-mòshuǐ shi-'shénmo-yánse?
What color is this ink?

fēn
cent

wǔfēn-qián
five cents

20. Yìzhī-qiānbǐ 'wǔfēn-qián.
One pencil is five cents.

liù	six
liùběn-shū	six books
21. Wó-yǒu-liùběn-'Zhōngwén-shū.	I have six Chinese books.
qī	seven
qīzhī-bǐ	seven pens
22. Qīzhī-bǐ 'sānmáo-qián.	Seven pens are thirty cents.
bā	eight
bākuài-qián	eight dollars
23. Wó-yǒu 'qī-bākuài-qián.	I have seven or eight dollars.
jiǔ	nine
sānmáo-jiǔ	thirty-nine cents
24. Sìzhāng 'sānmáo-jiǔ.	Four sheets are thirty-nine cents.
shí	ten
shíyī	eleven
25. Tā-'jiù-yǒu-shíyīkuài-qián.	He has only eleven dollars.
èrshí	twenty
èrshiyī	twenty-one
26. Shū-'yígòng-èrshiyīkuài-qián.	The books are twenty-one dollars in all.
'něiguó?	which country?
'něiguó-rén?	a native of which country?
27. 'Zhāng-Tàitai shi-'něiguó-rén?	What nationality is Mrs. Johnson?

SUBSTITUTION TABLES

I: 64 phrases

yī	-zhāng zhǐ
liǎng	-zhāng dìtú
sān	-ge běnzi
sì	-ge rén
zhèi	-ge Zhōngguo rén
nèi	-zhī gāngbǐ
něi	-zhī qiānbǐ
jǐ	-zhī máobǐ

II: 81 phrases

	-shi-	yī
——		yī
èr		èr
sān		sān
sì		sì
wǔ		wǔ
liù		liù
qī		qī
bā		bā
jiǔ		jiǔ

III: 60 phrases

yí	-kuài	liù	-máo	yī
liǎng		qī		èr
sān		bā		sān
sì		jiǔ		
wǔ				

PRONUNCIATION DRILLS

I. Contrast of Retroflexes and Sibilants

(a)	zhā	zā		(d)	zhé	zé		(g)	zhài	zài
(b)	chā	cā		(e)	chè	cè		(h)	chāi	cāi
(c)	shā	sā		(f)	shè	sè		(i)	shài	sài

(j)	zhōu	zōu		(m)	zhèng	zèng		(p)	zhōng	zōng
(k)	chòu	còu		(n)	chéng	céng		(q)	chóng	cóng
(l)	shōu	sōu		(o)	shēng	sēng				

II. Practice on Initial r

ráo	rè	ràng	ròu
rán	rén	rēng	róng

NUMBER PRACTICE

yī	1	shíyī	11	èrshí	20	èrshiyī	21
èr	2	shí'èr	12	sānshí	30	èrshi'èr	22
sān	3	shísān	13	sìshí	40	èrshijiǔ	29
sì	4	shísì	14	wǔshí	50	sānshiyī	31
wǔ	5	shíwǔ	15	liùshí	60	sìshisì	44
liù	6	shíliù	16	qīshí	70	wǔshiliù	56
qī	7	shíqī	17	bāshí	80	liùshiwǔ	65
bā	8	shíbā	18	jiǔshí	90	qīshibā	78
jiǔ	9	shíjiǔ	19			bāshisì	84
shí	10					jiǔshijiǔ	99

MULTIPLICATION TABLE

(See Note 6 below)

yī yī dé yī	èr yī dé èr	sān yī dé sān
yī èr dé èr	èr èr dé sì	sān èr dé liù
yī sān dé sān	èr sān dé liù	sān sān dé jiǔ
yī sì dé sì	èr sì dé bā	sān sì shí'èr
yī wǔ dé wǔ	èr wǔ yīshí	sān wǔ shíwǔ
yī liù dé liù	èr liù shí'èr	sān liù shíbā
yī qī dé qī	èr qī shísì	sān qī èrshiyī
yī bā dé bā	èr bā shíliù	sān bā èrshisì
yī jiǔ dé jiǔ	èr jiǔ shíbā	sān jiǔ èrshiqī

The rest of the tables can be made up on the model of the 3 table. Practice extending the table until you feel at ease with the numbers.

BOOM!

Practice numbers by playing 'Boom!' Count off in Chinese—one student says '1,' the next '2,' and so on—but the word 'Boom!' must be substituted for four and for every number containing or divisible by four. Play the game through the number 99. Those who survive the first round without forgetting to say an appropriate 'Boom!' can sit out the next round. Switch the taboo number from time to time.

NUMBERS AND MEASURES

A. Answer the following questions, using 'one' in the first sentence, 'two' in the second, and so on.

1. Ní-yóu-'jǐmáo-qián?

2. Tā-yóu-'jǐzhī-bǐ?

3. Ní-mái-'jǐzhāng-dìtú?

4. Nǐmen-'yígòng yóu-'jǐkuài-qián?

5. Nín-yóu-'jíběn-shū?

6. Tāmen-yào-mái-'jǐzhāng-dìtú?

7. Tā-yóu-'jǐfēn-qián?

8. Tāmen-'yígòng shi-'jǐge-rén?

9. 'Bái-Xiānsheng yào-'jǐzhī-qiānbǐ?

10. Wáng-Xiānsheng、Wáng-Tàitai 'yígòng-yóu-jǐge-běnzi?

B. Answer the following questions, using 'eleven' in the first sentence, 'twelve' in the second, and so on, taking care to use an appropriate measure in each case.

   1. Ní-yǒu-shū-ma?

   2. Tā-yào-dìtú-ma?

   3. Nǐmen-mài-bǐ-ma?

   4. Ní-yóu-zhǐ-ma?

   5. Tāmen-yào-mái-běnzi-ma?

   6. Nín-yǒu-'gāngbǐ-ma?

   7. Nǐmen-yǒu-qián-ma?

   8. 'Wáng-Xiānsheng mǎi-zìdiǎn-ma?

   9. 'Máo-Xiáojie yǒu-'máobǐ-ma?

  10. Tāmen-yào-qián-ma?

A CHARGE ACCOUNT

Suppose a Chinese bookstore which you patronize sends you the following bill at the end of the month. Translate the bill, state how much one of each item costs, add the figures, and tell how much change you would get back if you paid for the bill with a twenty-dollar check.

Zhōng-Yīng-zìdiǎn, liángběn	bákuài	qīmáo	liùfēn	qián
běnzi, sìběn	yíkuài	liùmáo		"
Zhōngguo-dìtú, yìzhāng		jiǔmáo	jiǔfēn	"
máobǐ, sānzhī	yíkuài	èrmáo		"
qiānbǐ, shí'èrzhī		bāmáo	sìfēn	"
gāngbǐ, yìzhī	liǎngkuài	liùmáo	bāfēn	"
zhǐ, qīshiwǔzhāng		qīmáo	wǔfēn	"

INFORMATION PLEASE!

(Answer in Chinese)

1. Nǐ-shi-'něiguó-rén?

2. Nǐ-shi-'Měiguo-rén-ma?

3. Ní-'yǒu-méi-yóu-běnzi?

4. Ní-yǒu-'duōshao-qián?

5. Nǐ-xìng-Wáng-ma?

6. Ní-yǒu-'Zhōngguo-dìtú-méi-yǒu?

7. Nǐ-yào-bu-yào-mǎi yìběn-'Zhōng-Yīng-zìdiǎn?

8. Ní-yǒu-'lán-mòshuǐ-ma?

9. Nǐ-huì-shuō 'Zhōngwén-bu huì?

10. Nǐ-quìxìng?

11. Ní-yóu-'jǐge-běnzi?

12. Nǐ-shi-'Bái-Xiānsheng-ma?

NOTES

1. Zhōngwén, although originally referring to Chinese writing, is also used more generally for 'Chinese language,' that is it includes Chinese speech. For 'to speak Chinese' some speakers prefer shuō-Zhōngwén over the more colloquial shuō-Zhōngguo-huà. Zhōngwén-shū refers specifically to a book in the Chinese language, as contrasted with Zhōngguo-shū, which might mean simply a book produced in China.

2. Many Chinese expressions occur sometimes in full form, sometimes in abbreviated form, the latter being especially common in combinations. Zhōngguo 'China' and Yīngguo 'England,' for example, are abbreviated in the combination Zhōng-Yīng 'Chinese-English, Sino-British.' Zhōngwén 'Chinese language' and Yīngwén 'English language' are also abbreviated in combination to Zhōng-Yīng, so that out of context this expression is ambiguous. In Zhōng-Yīng-zìdiǎn 'Chinese-English dictionary,' however, the combination is clearly an abbreviation of Zhōngwén and Yīngwén. Other similar abbreviations are Zhōng-Měi 'Sino-American' and Yīng-Měi 'British-American.'

3. The most widely used measure in Chinese is ge. If you do not know or cannot remember the appropriate measure for a noun, use ge.

4. Note the distinction in the Dialogue between the use of ge as a general measure for běnzi and of běn when referring specifically to one item or copy or volume:

> Wó-mǎi-yíge-běnzi. 'I'd like to buy a notebook.'
> Wó-mǎi-'yìběn. 'I'll buy one.'

5. A number following shí 'ten' is added to it; a number preceding shí multiplies it:

> shíyī 'eleven' ('ten and one')
> shí'èr 'twelve'
> shíjiǔ 'nineteen'
>
> èrshí 'twenty' ('two tens')
> sānshí 'thirty'
> jiǔshí 'ninety'
>
> èrshiyī 'twenty-one'
> jiǔshijiǔ 'ninety-nine'

6. The multiplication table is recited in various ways in Chinese. One of the simplest is the one given on page 42. Note the following points in connection with these:

(a) If the product contains only one syllable, the word dé 'get' is used,*
    as in yī-sān dé-sān 'one (times) three is three.'

(b) 'Two fives' and 'five twos' have the special form yìshí 'one ten' in
    order to retain the rhythm.

(c) The stress is on the first of the multipliers: 'qī-jiǔ liùshisān.

7. Qián 'money' and fēn 'cent' are often omitted at the end of an expression
   referring to dimes and cents or to dollars, dimes, and cents (cf. Note 12
   in Lesson 3, page 33):

   sānmáo-wǔ 'thirty-five cents'
   sānkuài-liǎngmáo-sì 'three dollars and twenty-four cents'

8. The special negative prefix méi is used with the verb yǒu 'have':

   Wǒ-'méi-yǒu-qián. 'I don't have any money.'

   'Ní-yǒu-méi-yǒu-qián?
             or   } 'Do you have any money?'
   'Ní-yǒu-qián-méi-yǒu?

9. In něizhī-bǐ? 'which pen?' the syllable zhī, of course, is a measure. In
   něiguó-dìtú? 'which country map?'—i.e. 'a map of what country?'—the
   syllable guó 'country' has the same function as zhī and is therefore also
   classified as a measure.   This flexibility of function is one of the special
   characteristics of the Chinese language.

10. The object of a verb is frequently transposed to the beginning of the sen-
    tence, especially for emphasis: Wǒ-jiù-mái-bǐ. Shū wǒ-bù-mǎi. 'I'm
    just buying a pen. (As for) books, I'm not buying (them).'

11. A number-plus-measure expression (like yìběn 'one volume') following a
    money expression means 'apiece' or 'per unit of that measure':

    sānkuài-qián-yìběn 'three dollars apiece'
    sānmáo-qián-yìzhī 'thirty cents each' (referring to pens or other
        long objects)

    When yíge is used in this way, the last syllable is pronounced with a fall-
    ing tone:

    sānmáo-qián-yígè 'thirty cents each' (referring to notebooks or other
        objects)

12. The syllables qī 'seven' and bā 'eight' change to qí and bá (i.e. second
    tone) before ge and (optionally) before a fourth tone:

    qī 'seven'   qíge rén 'seven people'
                      qīkuài qián or qíkuài qián 'seven dollars'

    bā 'eight'   báge rén 'eight people'
                      bākuài qián or bákuài qián 'eight dollars'

---

* Dé is introduced here just for the multiplication table. Other uses are
presented in Lesson 23, so do not attempt any further usage of it at this time.

Lesson 5 RECEIVING A PHONE CALL

"Shi-'Bái-Xiānsheng-jiā-ma?"

Dialogue: Mr. White receives a phone call from Mr. Gao.

Gāo: Wai! wai! Ní-năr? Shi-'Bái Xiānsheng-jiā-ma?	Hello, hello. Who's this? Is this Mr. White's home?
Bái: Shì. Nín-zháo-'něiwèi-shuō-huà?	Yes. Who are you calling?
Gāo: Qǐng-'Bái-Xiānsheng-shuō-huà. 5	I'd like to speak to Mr. White.
Bái: Wǒ-jiù-shì. Qǐng-wèn, 'nín-shi-shéi?	Speaking. Who's calling, please?
Gāo: Wǒ-xìng-Gāo.	This is Gao.
Bái: Oh, 'Gāo-Xiānsheng, 'háo-jiǔ-bú-jiàn. 'Nín-hǎo-ma? 10	Oh, Mr. Gao, (I) haven't seen you for a long time. How are you?
Gāo: 'Hén-hǎo. 'Ní-hǎo-ma?	Very well. How are you?
Bái: Wó-hén-hǎo. Gāo-Tàitai, Gāo-Xiáojie 'dōu-hǎo-ma?	I'm fine. Are Mrs. Gao and Miss Gao both well?
·Gāo: 'Dōu-hǎo, xièxie-ni. 'Jīn-tian-wǎnshang ní-yǒu-gōng-fu-ma? Wó-xiǎng qíng-ni-chī-fàn. 15	They're both well, thanks. Are you free this evening? I'd like to ask you to dinner.

46

Bái : Hǎo. Xièxie-nin. 'Jídiǎn-   (How) nice. Thank you. At what
zhōng?   20   time?

Gāo : 'Qīdiǎn-zhōng-kéyi-ma?   Can (you manage it) at seven
o'clock?

Bái : Qǐng-wèn, xiànzài-shi-   Could you tell me, please, what
'shénmo-shíhou?   time is it now?

Gāo : Xiànzài-'sìdiǎn-zhōng.   It's now four o'clock.

Bái : Kéyi.   25   I can (manage it).

Gāo : Wǒ-hái-qǐng yíwèi-'Yīng-   I'm also asking an English friend.
guo-péngyou. Yě-shi-wó-   He's a very good friend of mine
'hén-hǎode-péngyou.   too.

Bái : Hǎo, hǎo.   Very nice.

Gāo : Qīdiǎn-zhōng-jiàn.   30   See you at seven o'clock.

Bái : Qīdiǎn-zhōng-jiàn.   See you at seven.

"sìdiǎn-zhōng"

"qīdiǎn-zhōng"

VOCABULARY

chī	eat (TV)
de	(subordinating particle: Notes 2–4 below)
diǎn	dot, hour (of the clock) (M) (Note 5 below)
fàn	rice, food (N)
gōngfu	(leisure) time (N) (See Supplementary Lesson 5, Note 1)
'Háo-jiǔ-bú-jiàn	Haven't seen you for a long time
jiā	home, house (N)
jiàn	see, meet (people) (TV)
jīntian	today (TW) [lit. today day]
jiù	definitely, indeed, precisely (AD)
kéyi, kéyǐ	may, can (AV)
nǎr?	where? (PW)

péngyou   friend (N)

shéi   who?

shíhou(r)   time (by calendar or clock) (N)

wai   Hello! (on phone)

wǎnshang   evening (TW)

wèi   (polite measure for persons)

xiànzài   now (TW) [lit. present at]

xiǎng   think (of), think to, plan to (TV)

zhǎo   seek, look for, visit (TV)

zhōng   clock (N)

SENTENCE BUILD-UP

    chī   eat
    chī-shénmo?   eat what?
1. Nǐ-chī-shénmo?   What will you eat?

    fàn   food
    Zhōngguo-fàn   Chinese food
2. Wǒ-yào-chī 'Zhōngguo-fàn.   I want to eat Chinese food.

    gōngfu   leisure time
    yǒu-gōngfu   have the time (to do some-
                                          thing)
3. Nín-yǒu-'gōngfu-méi-you?   Do you have time?

    jīntian   today
4. Wǒ-jīntian 'méi-yǒu-gōngfu.   I don't have time today.

    wǎnshang   evening
    jīntian-wǎnshang   this evening
5. Nǐmen-jīntian-wǎnshang yǒu-   Do you have time this evening?
   gōngfu-ma?

    shíhou   time
    'shénmo-shíhou?   what time?
6. Wǒmen-'shénmo-shíhou-chī-   What time do we eat?
   fàn?

    zhōng   clock
    yǒu-zhōng   have clocks
7. Nǐmen-yǒu-zhōng-ma?   Do you have any clocks?

    yìdiǎn-zhōng   one o'clock
8. Wǒmen-'yìdiǎn-zhōng-chī-   We eat at one o'clock.
   fàn.

'jídiǎn-zhōng?

9. Wǒmen-'jídiǎn-zhōng-chī-fàn?

what o'clock?   what hour?

At what time do we eat?

wǎnshang-'jídiǎn-zhōng

10. Wǒmen-wǎnshang-'jídiǎn-zhōng chī-fàn?

what hour in the evening?

When are we having dinner this evening?

xiànzài

11. Xiànzài-'jídiǎn-zhōng?

now

What time is it now?

shéi?

12. Tā-shi-shéi?

who?

Who is he?

wǒde

wǒde-shū

13. Zhè-shi-'wǒde-shū.

my

my book

This is my book.

nǐde

14. Zhèibĕn-shū shi-nǐde.

your or yours

This book is yours.

péngyou

wǒmende-péngyou

15. Tāmen-shi-wǒmende-péngyou.

friend

our friend or our friends

They are our friends.

zhǎo

zhǎo-shénmo?

16. Ní-zhǎo-shénmo?

seek

seek what?

What are you looking for?

wèi

nèiwèi-tàitai

17. 'Nèiwèi-tàitai-shi-shéi?

(measure for people)

that lady

Who is that lady?

xiǎng

xiáng-mǎi-shū

18. Ní-xiáng-mǎi 'jíbĕn-shū?

think of, plan to

plan to buy books

How many books do you plan to buy?

jiā

Qián-jia

19. Nà-shi-Qián-jia-ma?

home

the Qian home

Is that the Qian home?

hǎo-péngyou

wǒde-hǎo-péngyou

20. Tā-shi-wǒde-hǎo-péngyou.

good friend

a good friend of mine

He's a good friend of mine.

hén-hǎode-péngyou

wó-hén-hǎode-péngyou

21. Tā-yĕ-shi wó-'hén-hǎode-péngyou.

very good friend

a very good friend of mine

He also is a very good friend of mine.

nǐde

hǎode

22. Hǎode-shi-nǐde.

your(s)

good one

The good one is yours.

	sānkuài-qián	three dollars
	sānkuài-qiánde-bǐ	a three-dollar pen
23.	Sānkuài-qiánde-bǐ 'yé-hén-hǎo.	A three-dollar pen is also very good.
	yíkuài-qiánde	a dollar one
	'bù-hén-hǎo	not very good
24.	'Yíkuài-qiánde 'bù-hén-hǎo.	A dollar one isn't very good.
	lánde	the blue one
	Bái-Xiānshengde	Mr. White's
25.	Lánde shi-'Bái-Xiānshengde.	The blue one is Mr. White's.
	hēide	the black one
	shéide?	whose?
26.	Hēide-shi-shéide?	Whose is the black one?
	kéyi	can or may
	kéyi-shuō-huà	may speak
27.	Wŏmen-kéyi-shuō-huà-ma?	May we speak?
	wai	hello!
	ní-năr?	who's this?
28.	Wai, ní-năr?	Hello, who's this?
	jiù	definitely
	jiù-shi	indeed is
29.	'Tā-jiù-shi 'Qián-Tàitai.	She is (indeed) Mrs. Qian.
	jiàn	see (people)
30.	Jīntian-wănshang-jiàn!	See you this evening!
	háo-jiŭ	a good while
	bú-jiàn	not see
31.	'Háo-jiŭ-bú-jiàn.	Haven't seen you for quite a while.
	něiwèi-Xiáojie	which young lady?
	'Zhāng-Xiáojie	Miss Johnson
32.	Něiwèi-Xiáojie shi-'Zhāng-Xiáojie?	Which young lady is Miss Johnson?

PATTERN DRILLS

Pattern 5.1. Subordination of Nouns and Pronouns with <u>de</u>
(Note 2 below)

N or P	-<u>de</u>	N
Noun or Pronoun	-de	Noun
Wáng-Xiānsheng	-de	shū

'Mr. King's book(s)'

1. tāmende-shū   their books

2. wǒde-běnzi   my notebook

3. wǒmende-máobǐ   our Chinese writing brushes

4. nǐde-zhǐ   your paper

5. 'shéide-jiā?   whose home?

6. 'sānkuài-qiánde-bǐ   a three-dollar pen

7. 'Wáng-Xiānshengde 'Zhōngguo-   Mr. King's Chinese friends
    péngyou

8. 'nèige-xiáojiede-zìdiǎn   that young lady's dictionary

9. Zhèi-shi-'shéide-shū?   Whose book is this?

10. 'Wǔmáo-qiánde-bǐ bù-hén-hǎo.   A fifty-cent pen isn't very good.

11. Tāde-běnzi shi-'bāmáo-qián.   His notebook is eighty cents.

12. Tāde-Yīngguo-péngyou xìng-   His English friend is called
    Wáng.   King.

13. Zhèi-shi-'tāde-qián, bú-shi-   This is his money, not yours.
    nǐde.

14. Wǒde-'yé-hén-hǎo.   Mine is also very good.

15. Zhè-shi-'nǐde-bu-shi?   Is this yours?

Pattern 5.2. Subordination of Stative Verbs with de
(Note 2 below)

AD	SV	-de	N
Adverb	Stative Verb	-de	Noun
hěn	hǎo	-de	shū

'a very good book'

1. 'bù-hǎode-zìdiǎn   a poor dictionary

2. hěn-'gāode-xiānsheng   a quite tall gentleman

3. hěn-'báide-zhǐ   very white paper

4. 'bù-hén-hǎode-bǐ   pens which aren't very good

5. hěn-'bù-hǎode-bǐ   pens which are very bad

6. Zhèi-shi-'hén-hǎode-zìdiǎn.   This is an excellent dictionary.

7. 'Hǎode-shi-wǒde, 'bù-hǎode 'yě-   The good one is mine, (and) the
    shi-wǒde.   bad one is also mine.

8. Tāmen-dōu-shi hěn-'gāode-rén.   They are all very tall people.

9. Báide shi-yíkuài-qián, lánde shi-   The white one is a dollar, (and)
    liǎngkuài-qián.   the blue one is two dollars.

10. Tāmende 'dōu-shi-hěn-hǎode-bǐ.   Theirs are all very good pens.

SUBSTITUTION TABLES

I: 16 phrases (Notes 6-7)

————	jǐ	diǎn zhōng
wǎnshang	liù	
	qī	
	bā	
	jiǔ	
	shí	
	shíyì	
	shí'èr	

II: 48 phrases (Notes 2-3)

Wáng	Xiānsheng	-de	————
Bái	Tàitai		shū
Qián	Xiáojie		péngyou
Gāo			zìdiǎn

III: 12 phrases (Notes 2-3)

bù	hǎo	-de	————
hěn	gāo		rén
			xiānsheng

PRONUNCIATION DRILLS

I. Contrast of Retroflexes and Palatals

(a)	zhā	jiā	(d)	zhào	jiào	(g)	zhàn	jiàn
(b)	chà	qià	(e)	chǎo	qiǎo	(h)	chán	qián
(c)	shā	xiā	(f)	shào	xiào	(i)	shān	xiān

(j)	zhāng	jiāng	(m)	zhǒng	jiǒng	(o)	zhǒu	jiǔ
(k)	cháng	qiáng	(n)	chóng	qióng	(p)	shòu	xiù
(l)	shāng	xiāng						

II. Some Sibilant-Retroflex-Palatal Contrasts

(a)	sā	shā	xiā	(d)	sāng	shāng	xiāng
(b)	sāo	shāo	xiāo	(e)	sǒu	shǒu	xiǔ
(c)	sān	shān	xiān				

CLOCK TIME

1. Xiànzài-'jídiǎn-zhōng?
   Xiànzài-'yìdiǎn-zhōng.

   What time is it now?
   It's now one o'clock.

2. Wǒmen-'jídiǎn-zhōng chī-fàn?
   Wǒmen-'liù-qīdiǎn-zhōng chī-fàn.

   At what time do we eat?
   We eat at 6:00 or 7:00.

3. Jīntian-wǎnshang 'bādiǎn-zhōng-hǎo-ma?
   Bādiǎn-zhōng 'hén-hǎo.

   Is this evening at 8:00 all right?
   Eight o'clock is fine.

4. 'Jiúdiǎn-zhōng-hǎo-ma?
   Jiúdiǎn-zhōng 'hén-hǎo.
   'Shídiǎn-ne?
   'Shídiǎn-zhōng 'yé-hǎo.

   Is nine o'clock all right?
   Nine o'clock is fine.
   How about ten o'clock?
   Ten o'clock is also fine.

5. Xiànzài-shi-'shénmo-shíhou?
   Xiànzài-shí-'yīdiǎn-zhōng.

   What time is it now?
   It's now one o'clock.

6. Wǒmen-'qīdiǎn-zhōng-chī-fàn 'hǎo-bu-hǎo?
   Chī-'shénmo-fàn?
   Wǒmen-chī-'wàiguo-fàn-ba.

   Is it all right to eat at 7:00?
   What (kind of) food shall we eat?
   Let's eat foreign food.

PIDGIN CHINESE

As you have probably noticed, a Chinese sentence that is translated into English word for word is likely to result in an intelligible but queer-sounding pattern—like Pidgin English. To express the meaning adequately, you must shape the Pidgin construction into a normal English pattern, which we might call the SITUATIONAL EQUIVALENT, as distinguished from the literal rendering.

The reverse translation process involves a similar problem. Literally translated English sentences make Pidgin Chinese. It is not enough to know the Chinese for each individual English word; you must then learn their proper groupings into Chinese patterns, so that your sentences are in fact Chinese and not Pidgin Chinese.

The examples below illustrate this dual process in proceeding from Chinese to English. Practice the opposite procedure by making up English sentences on the same patterns and putting them into smooth Chinese.

Chinese	Pidgin English	Situational Equivalent
Ní-nǎr?	You where?	Who's this?
Nín-zhǎo-'shéi-shuō-huà?	You looking for who talk?	Who are you calling?
Qǐng-'Wáng-Tàitai-shuō-huà.	Invite Mrs. King talk.	I'd like to speak to Mrs. King.

Chinese	Pidgin English	Situational Equivalent
Wǒ-jiù-shì.	I indeed am.	Speaking.
Wǒ-xìng-Gāo.	I name Gao.	This is Gao.
'Háo-jiǔ-bú-jiàn.	Good long-time no see.	Haven't seen you for a long time.
Ní-yǒu-'gōngfu-ma?	You have leisure time huh?	Are you free?
Nèige-rén-hěn-gāo.	That piece man very tall.	That man's very tall.
Ní-yóu-'bǐ-méi-yǒu?	You have pen not have?	Do you have a pen?

LISTENING IN

Imagine that you are a Chinese telephone operator eavesdropping on the following conversation between Mrs. Wang and Mrs. Qian. Relate what you heard.

Wáng : Wai, wai. Ní-nǎr? Shì-Qián-jia-ma?

Qián : Shì. Nín-zhǎo-'shéi-shuō-huà?

Wáng : Wó-qǐng 'Qián-Tàitai-shuō-huà.

Qián : Wǒ-jiù-shì.

Wáng : Oh, 'nín-jiù-shi-Qián-Tàitai. Wǒ. . .

Qián : Qǐng-wèn, 'nín-shi-něiwèi?

Wáng : Wǒ-xìng-Wáng.

Qián : Oh, 'Wáng-Tàitai, nín-hǎo-ma? Wáng-Xiānsheng 'yé-hǎo-ma?

Wáng : Wǒmen-'dōu-hǎo. Nín-ne?

Qián : Hǎo.

Wáng : Qián-'Xiānsheng-hǎo-ma?

Qián : Hǎo, xièxie-nin.

Wáng : Nǐmen-'jīntian-wǎnshang yǒu-'gōngfu-méi-you? Wǒmen-xiǎng 'qǐng nǐmen-chī-fàn.

Qián : Xièxie-nin. 'Shénmo-shíhou?

Wáng : 'Qī-bādiǎn-zhōng-kéyi-ma?

Qián : 'Bādiǎn-zhōng-kéyi.

Wáng : Wǒmen-hái-qíng-liǎngwèi 'Měiguo-péngyou. Yě-shi-wǒmende-'hǎo-péngyou.

Qián : Hén-hǎo.

Wáng : Bādiǎn-zhōng-jiàn.

Qián : Bādiǎn-zhōng-jiàn.

BRAIN-TWISTER

Find the answer to the question at the end.

Wó-yǒu liǎngzhī-'wàiguo-bǐ. Yìzhī shi-'Měiguo-bǐ, yìzhī shi-'Yīngguo-bǐ. Yīngguo-bǐ shi-hēide, Měiguo-bǐ shi-hóngde. Hēide shi-'bākuài-qiánde-bǐ, hóngde shi-'bāmáo-qiánde. 'Bākuài-qiánde-bǐ 'bù-hǎo. 'Bāmáo-qiánde hǎo. Nǐ-shuō, 'bù-hǎode-shi-'něiguó-bǐ?

NOTES

1. A general principle of word order in Chinese is that modifiers precede what they modify. We have seen this principle in compounds like Zhōng-guo-rén 'a Chinese (person)' [lit. 'China man']. The relationship of Zhōngguo to rén is here one of subordination: Zhōngguo, the modifier, is subordinate to rén, the main word of the construction.

2. Another construction of subordination is formed with the particle de. In a phrase A-de B, the A element modifies and is subordinate to the B element. The A element may be a pronoun, a noun, a time word, a stative verb, or (as we shall see later) a more complicated expression. The following are some examples of subordination with de:

wǒde-shū	'my book'
hǎode-shū	'good book'
jīntiande-fàn	'today's food'

3. The construction A-de (that is, the same construction as in Note 2 but without the modified element B) is often used when B can be understood from the context. Thus 'Zhèiběn-shū shi-wǒde 'This book is mine' is more common than 'Zhèiběn-shū shi-wǒde-shū 'This book is my book.'

4. It is important to distinguish between the constructions Noun-de Noun and Noun-Noun (both subordinate relationships), for they often have different meanings. For example, Zhōngguo-péngyou means 'Chinese friends,' but Zhōngguode-péngyou means 'friends of China.'

5. The particle de is often omitted under certain circumstances. One of these is when a pronoun is subordinated to a noun expressing personal relationship or itself closely followed by de, as:

nǐ-tàitai	'your wife'
wó-bǐde-yánse	'the color of my pen'

    Less often, de is omitted after a noun in certain fixed patterns:

Qián-jia	'the Qian home'

    It is regularly omitted after some frequently occurring combinations that contain certain unmodified stative verbs of one syllable, as in hǎo-rén 'a good person'—but not in an expression like hén-hǎode-rén 'a very good man,' where hǎo is itself preceded by a modifier, in this instance the adverb hěn 'very.'

6. The clock hours are expressed by the numbers one through twelve fol-
    lowed by the measure <u>diǎn</u> 'dot' and the noun <u>zhōng</u> 'clock':

    yì diǎn-zhōng   'one o'clock'
    liángdiǎn-zhōng   'two o'clock'
    shí'èrdiǎn-zhōng   'twelve o'clock'

    The word <u>zhōng</u> is often omitted in these expressions:

    Xiànzài jídiǎn-zhōng?   'What time is it now?'
    Shíyidiǎn.   'Eleven (o'clock)'

7. If more than one time expression is used in a phrase, the longer time
    precedes the shorter: <u>jīntian-wǎnshang shídiǎn-zhōng</u> 'ten o'clock this
    evening' — lit. 'today evening, ten o'clock.'

8. We saw in Lesson 2 (Note 7, page 21) that the final particle <u>ba</u> after
    a phrase can convey the idea of a suggestion or command, as in: <u>Wǒmen-</u>
    <u>shuō 'Zhōngguo-huà-ba</u> 'Let's talk Chinese.'   Similarly, the following
    forms are also used after a phrase:

    kéyi-ma 'is it possible to [do the foregoing]?'
    'kéyi-bu-kéyi 'is it possible to [do the foregoing]?'

    hǎo-ma 'is it all right to [do the foregoing]?'
    'hǎo-bu-hǎo 'is it all right to [do the foregoing]?'

    Examples:

    Wǒmen-'liùdiǎn-zhōng-chī-   Can we [or Will we be able to]
    fàn kéyi-ma?   eat at six?

    Wǒmen-'liùdiǎn-zhōng-chī-   Is it all right to eat at six?
    fàn hǎo-ma?

Lesson 6   REVIEW

PRONUNCIATION REVIEW

I.   Review of the Four Tones

This exercise includes only vocabulary introduced in Unit I, so that it also serves as a vocabulary review.

Read down by columns and across by rows.

1	2	3	4
dōu	bái	hǎo	huà
gāo	nín	hěn	huì
tā	qián	nǐ	jiù
shuō	rén	qǐng	shì
zhāng	Wáng	běn	wèn
Yīng	hái	bǐ	xìng
yī	máo	wǔ	èr
sān	guó	jiǔ	sì
qī	lán	jǐ	liù
bā	méi	liǎng	kuài
shū	shí	mǎi	mài
zhī	wén	něi	nà
fēn	shéi	yǒu	nèi
hēi	hóng	zhǐ	zhè
zhōng		diǎn	zhèi
chī		nǎr	fàn
jiā		xiǎng	jiàn
		zhǎo	wèi

II.   Review of the Neutral Tone

This exercise also includes only vocabulary introduced in Unit I.   Digits indicate tone sequences.

Read down by columns and across by rows.

10	20	30	40
xiānsheng	xiáojie	bĕnzi	tàitai
gōngfu	shénmo?	wŏmen	xièxie
tāmen	yánse	nĭmen	mài-ma?
sānge	yíge	liăngge	fàn-ne?
hēide	shíhou	wŏde	
tāde	péngyou	hăo-ma?	
shū-ne?	shéide?	nĭ-ne?	
chī-ma?	lánde	măi-ma?	

ANALOGY DRILL

The teacher asks each student a pair of questions. The student answers both questions on the model of the first, but adds the word y̆ĕ 'also' to his second answer. For example:

(1) Teacher asks: Tā-yŏu-shū-ma?
　　You answer　 : Tā-yŏu-shū.
　　Teacher asks: Nĭ-ne?
　　You answer　 : Wó-yé-yŏu-shū.

(2) Teacher asks: Nĭ-méi-yŏu-shū-ma?
　　You answer　 : Wŏ-méi-yŏu-shū.
　　Teacher asks: Bĭ-ne?
　　You answer　 : Wó-yĕ-méi-yóu-bĭ.

1. Tā-huì-shuō Zhōngguo-huà-ma? . . . Nĭ-ne? . . .

2. Tā-yŏu-gāngbĭ-ma? . . . Nĭ-ne? . . .

3. Ní-mái-bĕnzi-ma? . . . Tā-ne? . . .

4. Ní-măi-mòshuĭ-ma? . . . Tā-ne? . . .

5. Ní-măi-dìtú-ma? . . . Tā-ne? . . .

6. Nèige-xiānsheng xìng-Wáng-ma? . . . Xiáojie-ne? . . .

7. Ní-yŏu-qián-ma? . . . Tā-ne? . . .

8. Tā-shi-'Mĕiguo-rén-ma? . . . Nĭ-ne? . . .

9. Tā-yŏu-zìdiăn-ma? . . . Nĭ-ne? . . .

10. Ní-yŏu-'Zhōngguo-péngyou-ma? . . . Tā-ne? . . .

11. Ní-hăo-ma? . . . 'Wáng-Xiānsheng-ne? . . .

12. Nĭ-chī-'Zhōngguo-fàn-ma? . . . Tā-ne? . . .

13. Ní-yŏu-lán-mòshuĭ-ma? . . . Tā-ne? . . .

14. Tā-shi-'Zhōngguo-rén-ma? . . . Nĭ-ne? . . .

15. Tā-qǐng-Wáng-Xiānsheng chī-fàn-ma? . . . Wáng-Tàitai-ne? . . .

16. Ní-yǒu-máobǐ-ma? . . . Tā-ne? . . .

17. Nǐ-yào-zhǐ-ma? . . . Dìtú-ne? . . .

18. Ní-yóu-zhǐ-ma? . . . Tā-ne? . . .

19. Tāde-'gāngbǐ-shi 'sānkuài-qián-ma? . . . Nǐde-ne? . . .

20. Ní-mǎi-'hóng-yánse-mòshuǐ-ma? . . . Tā-ne? . . .

21. Ní-yóu-'Měiguo-dìtú-ma? . . . Tā-ne? . . .

22. Tā-yào-'Zhōngguo-dìtú-ma? . . . Nǐ-ne? . . .

23. Ní-yǒu-'Yīngguo-bǐ-ma? . . . Tā-ne? . . .

24. Jīntian ní-yǒu-gōngfu-ma? . . . Tā-ne? . . .

25. Tā-yǒu-'Zhōngguo-zhǐ-ma? . . . Nǐ-ne? . . .

26. Nèiwèi-xiáojie mǎi-shū-ma? . . . Nǐ-ne? . . .

27. Nèiwèi-xiānsheng xìng-Gāo-ma? . . . Nǐ-ne? . . .

28. Tā-yǒu-péngyou-ma? . . . Nǐ-ne? . . .

29. Tā-shuō-'Yīngguo-huà-ma? . . . Nín-ne? . . .

30. Tā-mǎi-qiānbǐ-ma? . . . Nǐ-ne? . . .

31. Ní-zhǎo 'Gāo-Xiānsheng-ma? . . . Tā-ne? . . .

32. Tā-zhǎo 'Wáng-Tàitai-ma? . . . Nǐ-ne? . . .

33. Ní-yǒu-tàitai-ma? . . . Tā-ne? . . .

34. Ní-yǒu-shū-ma? . . . Bǐ-ne? . . .

35. Ní-yǒu-mòshuǐ-ma? . . . Zhǐ-ne? . . .

36. Tā-yǒu-gāngbǐ-ma? . . . Máobǐ-ne? . . .

37. Tā-yǒu-gōngfu-ma? . . . Nǐ-ne? . . .

38. Tā-yóu-běnzi-ma? . . . Zìdiǎn-ne? . . .

39. Tā-yǒu-qián-ma? . . . Nǐ-ne? . . .

40. Tā-shi-'Zhōngguo-rén-ma? . . . Nǐ-ne? . . .

41. Ní-mǎi-dìtú-ma? . . . Tā-ne? . . .

42. Tāmen-chī-'Zhōngguo-fàn-ma? . . . Nǐ-ne? . . .

43. Tā-shi-'wàiguo-rén-ma? . . . Nǐ-ne? . . .

44. Tā-yǒu-'Yīngguo-péngyou-ma? . . . Nǐ-ne? . . .

45. Nǐ-shi-'Měiguo-rén-ma? . . . Tā-ne? . . .

46. Ní-yóu-běnzi-ma? . . . Tā-ne? . . .

47. Ní-yǒu-qián-ma? . . . Tā-ne? . . .

48. Wáng-'Tàitai-hǎo-ma? . . . Wáng-'Xiáojie-ne? . . .

49. Nǐ-méi-yǒu-qián-ma? . . . Tā-ne? . . .

50. Nǐ-méi-yǒu 'Zhōngguo-péngyou-ma? . . . Tā-ne? . . .

51. Tā-méi-yǒu-zìdiǎn-ma? . . . Nǐ-ne? . . .

52. Tā-méi-yǒu-tàitai-ma? . . . Nǐ-ne? . . .

53. Tāmen-mǎi-shū-ma? . . . Dìtú-ne? . . .

54. 'Wáng-Xiáojie méi-yóu-zhǐ-ma? . . . Qiānbǐ-ne? . . .

55. Nǐ-méi-yǒu 'Yīngguo-dìtú-ma? . . . Tā-ne? . . .

56. Tā-huì-shuō 'Yīngguo-huà-ma? . . . 'Zhōngguo-huà-ne? . . .

57. Nǐ-huì-shuō 'Yīngguo-huà-ma? . . . Tā-ne? . . .

58. Ní-xiǎng-chī-Zhōngguo-fàn-ma? . . . Tā-ne? . . .

59. Ní-zhǎo Wáng-Xiānsheng-ma? . . . Wáng-Tàitai-ne? . . .

60. Nǐ-jīntiān-mǎi-shū-ma? . . . Tā-ne? . . .

SINGLE REPLACEMENT DRILL

The teacher pronounces the sentence and the student repeats it. The teacher then pronounces an expression which can replace something in the original
sentence; the student pronounces the sentence again, making the replacement.
For example:

> Teacher says : Tā-shi-'Měiguo-rén.
> You say   : Tā-shi-'Měiguo-rén.
> Teacher says : Yīngguo
> You say   : Tā-shi-'Yīngguo-rén.

 1. Tā-yóu-wǔkuài-qián.   wǒ

 2. Ní-yǒu-máobǐ-ma?   tā

 3. Tāmen-yóu-běnzi-ma?   nǐmen

 4. Ní-yǒu-yìběn-zìdiǎn.   tā

 5. Wó-yǒu-gāngbǐ.   qiānbǐ

 6. Tā-yǒu-mòshuǐ.   yào

 7. Wó-yǒu-sānge 'Zhōngguo-péngyou.   sìge

 8. Tā-huì-shuō 'Zhōngguo-huà.   Yīngguo

 9. Wó-mǎi-shū.   zìdiǎn

10. Wǒ-yào-qiānbǐ.   gāngbǐ

11. Tā-yóu-zhǐ.   bǐ

12. Wǒ-yào-dìtú.   zìdiǎn

13. Nǐ-shi-'Yīngguo-rén-ma?   Měiguo

14. Wǒ-méi-yǒu 'Zhōngguo-péngyou.   wàiguo

15. Tāmen-dōu-shi-'Měiguo-rén.   Yīngguo

16. Zhèi-shi-'hóng-yánse.   lán

17. Wǒ-huì-shuō 'Zhōngguo-huà.   Yīngguo

18. Zhèige-shi-nǐde.   nèige

19. Hǎode-shi-tāde.   wǒde

20. Něige-shi-tāde?   nèige

DOUBLE REPLACEMENT DRILL

This exercise is to be conducted like the preceding one, except that the student must make whatever additional changes are required so that the replacement item can be used. For example:

        Teacher says : Wó-yǒu-sānběn-shū.
        You say   : Wó-yǒu-sānběn-shū.
        Teacher says : zhǐ
        You say   : Wó-yǒu-sānzhāng-zhǐ.

1. Wó-yě-bú-yào.   yǒu

2. Wó-yǒu-yìběn-shū.   zhǐ

3. Wǒ-yào-'yíge-běnzi.   bǐ

4. Wó-yǒu-yìzhāng-zhǐ.   shū

5. 'Wáng-Xiānsheng yóu-wǔkuài-qián.   shū

6. 'Wáng-Xiáojie yǒu-yìzhī-máobǐ.   běnzi

7. 'Gāo-Tàitai mǎi-yìběn-shū.   běnzi

8. 'Gāo-Xiáojie mǎi-liùzhī-qiānbǐ.   shū

9. 'Bái-Xiānsheng mǎi-yìzhāng-dìtú.   zìdiǎn

10. 'Gāo-Xiānsheng mái-wúběn-shū.   máobǐ

11. 'Gāo-Xiáojie mǎi-yìběn-zìdiǎn.   bǐ

12. 'Wáng-Xiānsheng jiù-yǒu-'yìběn-shū. qián

13. Tāmen-'yígòng yǒu-qīshizhāng-zhǐ.   shū

14. Tā-'jiù-yào-sānmáo-qián.   bǐ

15. Wǒ-méi-yǒu-qián.   yào

INSERTION DRILL

The teacher pronounces a sentence and then gives an expression which you are to insert in the sentence at some appropriate place. For example:

        Teacher says : Tā-yǒu-qián.
        You say   : Tā-yǒu-qián.
        Teacher says : duōshao
        You say   : Tā-yǒu 'duōshao-qián?

1.	Tā-shi-'Zhōngguo-rén.	yě
2.	Wǒ-jīntian-bù-chī-fàn.	wǎnshang
3.	Tā-shuō-'Yīngguo-huà.	huì
4.	Nǐ-shi-'Wáng-Xiānsheng-ma?	jiù
5.	Nǐ-chī-'shénmo-fàn?	xiǎng
6.	Zhèizhī-hén-hǎo.	máobǐ
7.	Tā-yào-qián.	hái
8.	Xiànzài-'shénmo-shíhou?	shì
9.	Zhèi-shi-shū.	wǒde
10.	Tāmen-huì-shuō 'Zhōngguo-huà.	dōu
11.	Nǐ-xièxie-ta-ma?	bú
12.	'Lánde-yé-hǎo.	mòshuǐ
13.	Zhèi-shi-'Bái-Xiānsheng.	jiā
14.	Sānkuài-qiánde yé-hén-hǎo.	bǐ
15.	Zhǐ, bǐ 'yígong-duōshao-qián?	shū
16.	Zhèibén-'duōshao-qián?	zìdiǎn
17.	Wó-yǒu-'bā-jiǔshikuài-qián.	jiù
18.	Wǒ-'jiù-yǒu 'qībén-shū.	liù
19.	Mòshuǐ-duōshao-qián?	hóng
20.	Wǒ-yào-mǎi-dìtú.	hái
21.	Wó-yóu-liǎngge-péngyou.	hǎo
22.	Tā-shuō-'Zhōngguo-huà.	huì
23.	Tāmen-'bù-mǎi-zìdiǎn.	yě
24.	Nín-mǎi-shénmo?	yào
25.	Tā-yě-shi-hǎo-péngyou.	wǒde

RAISE YOU ONE

Answer the following questions using the number next larger to the one mentioned in the immediately preceding sentence.

1. Wó-yóu-jiǔshikuài-qián. Nín-ne?

2. Wó-wǎnshang bādiǎn-zhōng-chī-fàn. Nín-ne?

3. Wǒ-yǒu liángbén-shū. Nín-ne?

4. Wó-yǒu liùkuài-qiánde-zhǐ. Nín-ne?

5. Wǒde-shū shi-sìkuài-qián. Nǐde-ne?

6. Wǒ-yào-mǎi wǔshiwǔzhāng-zhǐ. Nín-ne?

7. Wó-yǒu-sānge wàiguo-péngyou. Nín-ne?

8. Wǒde-bǐ-shi-wǔfēn-qián. Nǐde-ne?

9. Wǒ-'jiù-yǒu-yìzhāng-dìtú. Nín-ne?

10. Wǒ-péngyou yóu-'liǎngzhī-bǐ. Nǐ-ne?

11. Wó-qǐng-'bāge-péngyou-chī-fàn. Nín-ne?

12. Wó-yóu-jiǔshibākuài-qián. Nín-ne?

ANSWERING QUESTIONS

If the student has difficulty in answering, the two statements before the question may be repeated _after_ the question.

1. 'Wáng-Xiānsheng shi-'Zhōngguo-rén. 'Qián-Xiānsheng shi-'wàiguo-rén.
   'Zhōngguo-rén xìng-shénmo?

2. 'Bái-Xiáojie-huì-shuō 'Yīngguo-huà. 'Bái-Tàitai-huì-shuō 'Zhōngguo-huà. 'Shéi-huì-shuō 'Zhōngguo-huà?

3. 'Gāo-Xiānsheng shi-'Zhōngguo-rén. 'Máo-Xiānsheng shi-'Yīngguo-rén.
   Shéi-shi-'wàiguo-rén?

4. Gāo-Xiáojie yǒu-liùzhāng-zhǐ. Gāo-Tàitai yǒu-sìzhī-bǐ. 'Shéi-yóu-zhǐ?

5. 'Wáng-Xiānsheng shuō-'Zhōngguo-huà. 'Bái-Xiānsheng shuō-'Yīngguo-huà. Shéi-shuō-'Zhōngguo-huà?

6. 'Bái-Xiānsheng-mǎi-shū. 'Gāo-Xiānsheng-bù-mǎi-shū. Shéi-mǎi-shū?

7. 'Wáng-Xiáojie yóu-'Měiguo-dìtú. 'Gāo-Xiáojie yǒu-'Zhōngguo-dìtú.
   Shéi-yóu-Měiguo-dìtú?

8. 'Sānge-Zhōngguo-rén. 'Yíge-Yīngguo-rén. 'Jǐge-wàiguo-rén?

9. 'Bái-Xiáojie yóu-'Měiguo-bǐ. 'Máo-Xiáojie yǒu-'Yīngguo-bǐ. 'Bái-Xiáojie yóu-'něiguó-bǐ?

10. 'Wáng-Xiānsheng yǒu-'hóng-mòshuǐ. 'Bái-Xiānsheng yǒu-'lán-mòshuǐ.
    'Lán-mòshuǐ-shi-shéide?

11. 'Máo-Xiānsheng-yǒu-shū. 'Bái-Xiānsheng-yóu-bǐ. 'Máo-Xiānsheng-yǒu-shénmo?

12. 'Wáng-Tàitai-yóu-zhǐ. 'Bái-Tàitai-yǒu-shū. 'Shéi-yóu-zhǐ?

13. 'Gāo-Xiáojie-yǒu-zìdiǎn. !Wáng-Xiáojie-méi-yǒu-zìdiǎn. Shéi-yǒu-zìdiǎn?

14. Gāo-Tàitai yǒu-liùkuài-qián. Gāo-Xiānsheng yǒu-liùshikuài-qián. Gāo-Tàitai yǒu-'duōshao-qián?

15. 'Bái-Xiānsheng-yǒu-gāngbǐ. 'Máo-Xiānsheng-yǒu-qiānbǐ. 'Shéi-yǒu-
    gāngbǐ?

16. 'Yíge-Zhōngguo-rén. 'Liǎngge-Měiguo-rén. 'Yígòng-jǐge-rén?

17. 'Bái-Xiānsheng chī-'Měiguo-fàn. 'Gāo-Xiānsheng chī-'Zhōngguo-fàn.
    Shéi-chī-'Měiguo-fàn?

18. Zhèige-'Yīngguo-rén xìng-Máo. Zhèige-'Měiguo-rén xìng-Bái. Zhèige-
    'Yīngguo-rén xìng-shénmo?

19. Nèiwèi-'xiáojie xìng-Gāo. Nèiwèi-'tàitai xìng-Wáng. Nèiwèi-xiáojie
    xìng-shénmo?

20. Tā-yǒu-'máobǐ. Wó-yǒu-'gāngbǐ. 'Máobǐ-shi-shéide?

21. Gāo-'Tàitai-mǎi-dìtú. Gāo-'Xiáojie-mái-zhǐ. Gāo-'Tàitai-mǎi-shénmo?

22. 'Wáng-Xiānsheng mǎi-sìběn-shū. 'Bái-Xiānsheng mái-liángběn-shū.
    'Bái-Xiānsheng mái-'jíběn-shū?

23. Wó-yǒu-'Zhōngwén-shū. Tā-yǒu-'Yīngwén-shū. Shéi-yǒu-'Zhōngwén-
    shū?

24. 'Wáng-Xiānsheng-yóu-běnzi. 'Qián-Xiānsheng-yǒu-zìdiǎn. 'Shéi-yǒu-
    zìdiǎn?

25. 'Bái-Xiáojie-yǒu-zìdiǎn. 'Wáng-Xiáojie-yǒu-dìtú. 'Bái-Xiáojie-yǒu-
    shénmo?

QUESTIONING ANSWERS

This exercise is the opposite of the usual type: here, you are asked to supply the questions for which the given statements would be appropriate answers.
There may be several possibilities: a choice-type question, a split-choice-
type question, a question with the particle _ma_ or with a question word. Give
all the questions you can think of which might elicit the given statement. For
example:

Teacher says:	Tā-shi-Měiguo-rén.	'He is an American.'
You say	: Tā-shi-Měiguo-rén-ma?	'Is he an American?'
	Tā-shì-bu-shi-Měiguo-rén?	'Is he an American?'
	Tā-shì-'Měiguo-rén-bu-shi?	'Is he an American?'
	Tā-shi-'něiguó-rén?	'What nationality is he?'

After each question suggested by the student, the teacher should respond by
repeating the initial statement.

1. Bú-shi, wǒ-shi-'Měiguo-rén.

2. Wǒ-xìng-Bái. Nín-ne?

3. Wǒ-'bú-huì. 'Jiù-huì-shuō 'Yīngguo-huà.

4. Xiànzài-shi-'bādiǎn-zhōng.

5. Wǒ-jīntian-wǎnshang méi-yǒu-gōngfu.

6. Wǒmen-'bú-mài-wàiguo-shū. Jiù-mài-'Zhōngguo-shū.

7. Shū, bǐ 'yígòng-sānkuài-qián.

8. Tāmen-'dōu-hǎo, xièxie-ni.

9. Bù-dōu-shi-'Yīngguo-rén. Yíwèi-shi-'Měiguo-rén. Yíwèi-shi-'Yīng-guo-rén.

10. Wǒ-méi-yǒu-qián.

DIALOGUE I

Read aloud and translate into English.

M : Qǐng-wèn, nín-guìxìng?

W : Wǒ-xìng-Wáng.   Nín-ne?

M : Wǒ-xìng-Máo.

W : Nín-huì-shuō 'Zhōngguo-huà-ma?

M : Wǒ-huì-shuō 'Zhōngguo-huà.

W : Nín-shi-'Měiguo-rén-ma?

M : Shì, wǒ-'shì-Měiguo-rén.

W : Qǐng-wèn-nin, 'xiànzai-shi-shénmo-shíhou?   Wó-xiáng-zhǎo-yíge-péng-you.

M : Xiànzai-'sāndiǎn-zhōng.

W : Xièxie-nin.

DIALOGUE II

Read aloud and translate into English.

A : Qǐng-wèn-nin, 'nèige-rén shi-'Měiguo-rén-ma?

B : 'Něige-rén?

A : 'Nèige-rén.

B : Oh, 'nèige-rén. Tā-'bú-shi-Měiguo-rén. Tā-shi-'Yīngguo-rén.

A : Tā-xìng-shénmo?

B : Tā-xìng-Bái.

A : Oh! Tā-'bú-xìng-Wáng-a?

B : Tā-'bú-xìng-Wáng. Tā-xìng-Bái.

NARRATIVE

Read aloud and translate into English.

Jīntian wó-mǎi-shū. 'Wáng-Xiānsheng yé-mǎi-shū. Tā-hái-mǎi-qiānbǐ, máobǐ, zhǐ, běnzi. Wó-mǎi-yìběn-zìdiǎn, yìběn-Yīngwén-shū, yìzhāng-dìtú, yìzhī-gāngbǐ — yígòng-sìkuài-jiǔmáo-qián. Nèige-shíhou shi-liùdiǎn-zhōng. Wó-qǐng-Wáng-Xiānsheng-chī-fàn.

UNIT II

Lesson 7　INQUIRING ABOUT PLACES

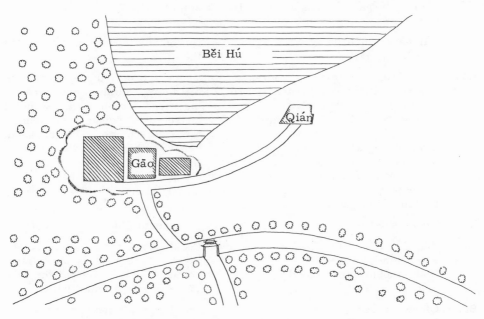

"Gāo-Xiānsheng-jiā zài-yíge-xiǎo-shānshang."

Dialogue: Mr. White is given a detailed answer to his inquiry about where Mr. Gao lives.

Máo : 'Bái-Xiānsheng, nín-hǎo-ma? Nín-yào-mǎi-shū-ma?

Mr. White, how are you? Do you want to buy some books?

Bái : Jīntian wǒ-bù-mǎi-shū. Wó-zhǎo-'Gāo-Xiānsheng. 'Gāo-Xiānsheng jīntian-wǎnshang 5 qíng-wǒ-chī-fàn. Nǐ-'zhīdao-bu-zhīdào shi-zài-zhèr-ne háishi-zài-ta-jiā-ne?*

I'm not buying books today. I'm looking for Mr. Gao. Mr. Gao asked me to dinner this evening. Do you know whether it's here or at his home?*

Máo : Zài-ta-'jiā-chī-fàn.

The dinner is at his home.

Bái : Ta-jiā-zài-nǎr? Shi-zài- 10 chéng-lǐtou háishi-zài-chéng-wàitou?

Where is his home? Is it inside the city or outside the city?

---

* It is a common practice among Chinese to entertain guests at their place of business (many business establishments have dining facilities) or at restaurants, as well as in their homes.

Máo : Gāo-Xiānsheng-jiā zài-chéng-   Mr. Gao's home is outside the
       wài, jiù-zài-zhèitiáo-lùde-   city, north of this road, on a
       běibiar, yíge-xiǎo-shān-   15   small hill.
       shang.

Bái : Zài-nèige-shānshang yóu-   How many houses are there on
       'jísuǒr-fángzi?   the hill?

Máo : Nèr-yígòng jiù-yǒu-'sānsuǒr-   There are only three houses [in
       fángzi. Xībiar yǒu-yìsuǒr-   20   all] there. To the west there's a
       'dà-fángzi. Dōngbiar yǒu-   big house. To the east is a small
       yìsuór-'xiǎo-fángzi. Zhōng-   house. The house in between is
       jiàrde-fángzi jiù-shi-Gāo-   Mr. Gao's home. To the south
       Xiānsheng-jiā. Nánbiar-   below the hill is Sun Yatsen Road.
       shānxià shi-Zhōngshān-Lù.   25   In front of Sun Yatsen Road is a
       Zhōngshān-Lù-qiánbiar yǒu-   big park. Behind the hill is a
       yíge-dà-gōngyuán. Shān-   small lake.
       hòutou yǒu-yíge-xiǎo-hú.

Bái : Nèige-shi-'Běi-Hú-ma?   Is it North Lake?

Máo : 'Shì-Běi-Hú. Húde-yòubiar   30   [Yes] it's North Lake. To the
       shi-'Qián-Xiānsheng-jiā.   right of the lake is Mr. Qian's
       Húde-zuǒbiar hái-yǒu-yíge-   home. To the left of the lake
       xiǎo-gōngyuán.   there is also a small park.

Bái : Oh, wǒ-zhīdao, wǒ-zhīdao.   Oh, I know, I know. Thank you.
       Xièxie-ni.   35

VOCABULARY

běi	north (PW)
biān, biār	side (PW) (See Supplementary Lesson 7, Note 1)
chéng	city (N)
dà	big (SV)
dōng	east (PW)
Dōngběi	Manchuria (PW) [lit. east north] (Note 11 below)
fángzi	house (N)
gōngyuán	park (N) [lit. public yard]
háishi	or [lit. still is] (Note 12 below)
hòu	rear (PW)
hú	lake (N)
Húběi	Hupeh province (PW) [lit. lake north] (Note 11 below)
Húnán	Hunan province (PW) [lit. lake south] (Note 11 below)
lǐ	inside (PW)
lù	road (N)

nán	south (PW)
nèr	there (PW)
qián	front (PW)
shān	hill, mountain (N)
Shāndong	Shantung province (PW) [lit. mountains east] (Note 11 below)
Shānxi	Shansi province (PW) [lit. mountains west] (Note 11 below)
shàng	top (PW)
suǒ, suǒr	(measure for buildings)
tiáo	(measure for roads)
tou	(substantive suffix) (See Supplementary Lesson 7, Note 1)
wài	outside (PW)
xī	west (PW)
xià	bottom, below (PW)
xiǎo	small (SV)
yòu	right [as opposed to left] (PW)
zài	occupy, be at (V) (Notes 1, 8, 9 below) at, in, on (CV) (Notes 3, 4, 7 below)
zhèr	here (PW)
zhīdào	know (that . . .) (V) (Note 13 below)
zhōngjiàr	middle (PW) [lit. middle interval]
Zhōngshān	Sun Yatsen [lit. middle mountain] (Note 10 below)
zuǒ	left [as opposed to right] (PW)

SENTENCE BUILD-UP

zài	at
zài-jiā	at home
1. Tā-zài-jiā-ma?	Is he at home?
zhèr	here
zài-zhèr	here, at this place
2. 'Gāo-Xiānsheng bú-zài-zhèr.	Mr. Gao isn't here.
nèr	there
zài-nèr	(at) there
3. Tāmen dōu-zài-nèr-ma?	Are they all there?
qiántou	front
zài-qiántou	be in front
4. Tāmen-zài-qiántou.	They're in front.

hòutou		rear, back
zài-hòutou		in the rear

5. 'Shéi-zài-hòutou?   Who's in back?

    qiánbian   front
    hòubian   rear

6. Wǒ-zài-qiánbian, tā-zài-   I'm in front, he's in back.
    hòubian.

    qiánbiar   front
    hòubiar   back

7. Tā-zài-qiánbiar, bú-zài-   He's in front, not in back.
    hòubiar.

    lǐtou   inside
    zài-lǐtou   be inside

8. Tāmen-dōu-zài-lǐtou.   They're all inside.

    wàibiar   outside
    zài-wàibiar   be outside

9. 'Gāo-Tàitai zài-wàibiar.   Mrs. Gao is outside.

    shàngtou   above
    xiàtou   below

10. 'Yíge-zài-shàngtou, 'yíge-   One is above, one is below.
    zài-xiàtou.

    fángzi   house
    'shéide-fángzi?   whose house?

11. Zhèi-shi-'shéide-fángzi?   Whose house is this?

    shān   hill
    'shénmo-shān?   what hill?

12. Nà-shi-'shénmo-shān?   What hill is that?

    dōng   east
    dōngbian   east (side)

13. Wǒ-jiā zài-dōngbian.   My house is to the east.

    xī   west
    xībiar   west (side)

14. Xī-Shān zài-xībiar.   The Western Hills are in the
                                          west.

    nán   south
    nánbiar   south (side)

15. Shénmo-zài-nánbiar?   What's in the south?

    běi   north
    běibiar   north (side)

16. Tā-jiā yě-zài-běibiar.   His home is also in the north.

gōngyuán	park
'shénmo-gōngyuán?	what park?
17. Zhèi-shi-'shénmo-gōngyuán?	What park is this?
hú	lake
Dōng-Hú	East Lake
18. Dōng-Hú-zài-nǎr?	Where is East Lake?
dà	big
'dà-bu-dà?	big or not?
19. Nèige-shān 'dà-bu-dà?	Is that mountain big?
xiǎo	small
xiǎo-fángzi	small house
20. Xiǎo-fángzi yě-shi-tāde-ma?	Is the small house also his?
zuǒ	left
zuǒbiar	left (side)
21. Dà-gōngyuán zài-zuǒbiar.	The big park is on the left.
yòu	right
yòubiar	right (side)
22. Xiǎo-gōngyuán zài-yòubiar.	The small park is on the right.
jiā	home
zài-jiāli	be in the house
23. Tāmen dōu-zài-jiāli.	They're all in the house.
chéng	city
chéng-lǐtou	inside the city
chéng-wàitou	outside the city
24. Wǒ-jiā-zài-chéng-lǐtou, bú-zài-chéng-wàitou.	My home is inside the city, not outside the city.
zài-shānshang	be on a hill
25. Tā-jiā zài-nèige-dà-shān-shang.	His home is on that big hill.
zài-shānxià	below the hill
26. Shéide-fángzi-zài-shānxià?	Whose house is below the hill?
Shāndong	Shantung (province)
Shānxi	Shansi (province)
27. Tāmen-zài-Shāndong, bú-zài-Shānxi.	They're in Shantung, not Shansi.
Húběi	Hupeh (province)
Húběi rén	a native of Hupeh
28. Tā-shi-Húběi-rén.	He's a native of Hupeh.

	Húnán	Hunan (province)
	Húnán-huà	Hunan dialect
29.	Tā-jiù-huì-shuō Húnán-huà.	He can only speak Hunan dialect.

	Dōngběi	the Northeast, Manchuria
	Dōngběi-rén	a native of Manchuria
30.	'Máo-Xiānsheng shi-Dōngběi-rén.	Mr. Mao is from Manchuria.

	zhīdao	know
	bu-zhīdào	not know
31.	Tā-zài-nǎr, nǐ-'zhīdao-bu-zhīdào?	Where is he, do you know?

	suǒr	(measure for houses)
	zhèisuǒr-fángzi	this house
32.	Zhèisuor-fángzi duōshao-qián?	How much is this house?

	zhōngjiàr	middle
	liángsuǒr-dà-fángzide-zhōngjiàr	between two big houses
33.	Xiǎo-fángzi zài-liángsuǒr-'dà-fángzide-zhōngjiàr.	The little house is between two big houses.

	tiáo	(measure for roads)
	lù	road
34.	Nèitiáo-lù 'hǎo-bu-hǎo?	How's that road?

	Zhōngshān	Sun Yatsen
	Zhōngshān-Lù	Sun Yatsen Avenue
35.	Qǐng-wèn, Zhōngshan-Lù zài-nǎr?	May I ask, where is Sun Yatsen Avenue?

	zài-lǐtou	be inside
	zài-lǐtou-chī-fàn	eat inside
36.	Tāmen-zài-lǐtou-chī-fàn.	They're eating inside.

	fángzide-dōngbiar	east of the house
37.	Xiǎo-hú zài-fángzide-dōngbiar.	The little lake is east of the house.

	dōngbiarde-fángzi	the house to the east
38.	Dōngbiarde-fángzi shi-'Wáng-Xiānshengde.	The house to the east is Mr. Wang's.

	zài-fángzi-wàitou	outside the house
	zài-fángzi-wàitoude-nèige-rén	that man outside the house
39.	Zài-fángzi-wàitoude-nèige-rén shi-shéi?	Who is that man outside the house?

	dà-gōngyuán	big park

zài-chéng-wàitou   outside the city
40. Dà-gōngyuán dōu-zài-chéng-   The big parks are all outside the
wàitou.   city.

zài-chéng-lǐtou   inside the city
yóu-xiǎo-gōngyuán   there are some small parks
41. Zài-chéng-lǐtou yóu-xiǎo-   There are some small parks in-
gōngyuán.   side the city.

jiāli   at home
méi-yǒu-rén   there isn't anybody
42. Jiāli-méi-yǒu-rén.   There isn't anyone at home.

zài-Húnán   in Hunan
háishi-zài-Húběi   or in Hupeh
43. Tāmen-zài-Húnán háishi-   Are they in Hunan or in Hupeh?
zài-Húběi?

PATTERN DRILLS

Pattern 7.1.   Location at a Place   (Note 1 below)

S   zài   P
Subject   is/are (at)   Place word
Rén   zài   lǐtou.

'The people are inside.'

1. Qiānbǐ-zài-nèr.   The pencil is there.

2. Máobǐ-zài-zhèr-ma?   Is the writing brush here?

3. Lán-mòshuǐ-zài-nǎr?   Where's the blue ink?

4. Tāmen-zài-lǐtou.   They're inside.

5. Tāmen-zài-fángzi-lǐtou.   They're inside the house.

6. Tāmen-zài-fángzili.   They're in the house.

7. 'Wáng-Xiānsheng zài-jiā-ma?   Is Mr. King at home?

8. Wǒ-péngyoude-jiā zài-chéng-   My friend's home is outside the
wài.   city.

9. Tāmen-bú-zài-jiā-ma?   Aren't they at home?

10. Tàitai-zài-jiā-ma?   Is the lady of the house at home?

11. Qíng-nǐ-wèn tā-jiā-zài-nǎr.   Please ask where his house is.

12. Tāde-jiā zài-Shāndong.   His home is in Shantung.

13. Tāde-fángzi zài-shānshang.   His house is on the hill.

14. Hóng-mòshuǐ-zài-nǎr, nǐ-   Where's the red ink, do you
zhīdao-ma?   know?

15. Dà-shān dōu-zài-dōngbiar.   The big mountains are all in the
                                            east.

                Pattern 7.2. The Coverb of Location (Notes 2-3 below)

         S   CV   P   MV   O

     Subject   Coverb   Place word   Main Verb   Object

     Rén   zài   lǐtou   chī   fàn.

     'The people are eating inside.'

1. Wǒ-jīntian bú-zài-jiā-chī-fàn.   I'm not eating at home today.

2. Wǒmen-'kéyi-bu-kéyi zài-zhèr-   Can we eat here?
    chī-fàn?

3. Wǒmen-zài-zhèr-chī-fàn kéyi-   Can we eat here?
    ma?

4. Wǒ-bù-xiǎng zài-nèr-mǎi-shū.   I'm not going to buy books there.

5. Nín-yào-zài-'nár-mǎi-zhōng?   Where do you want to buy a
                                            clock?

6. Tā-bú-zài-zhèr mǎi-mòshuǐ-   Isn't he buying the ink here?
    ma?

7. Nǐ-bú-zài-jiā chī-fàn-ma?   Aren't you eating at home?

8. Tāmen-zài-zhèr-mài-shénmo?   What do they sell here?

9. 'Wáng-Xiānsheng zài-'nǎr-   Where is Mr. King speaking?
    shuō-huà?

10. Tāmen dōu-zài-Gāo-Xiānsheng-   They're all eating at Mr. Gao's
    jiāli-chī-fàn.   home.

                Pattern 7.3. Existence at a Place (Note 8 below)

         (zài)   P   yǒu   N

         (at)   Place   there is/are   Noun

         (Zài)   lǐtou   yǒu   rén.

     'There are people inside.'

1. Jiāli-yǒu-rén-ma?   Is there anybody at home?

2. Zài-Húnán méi-yǒu-dà-   There are no big mountains in
    shān.   Hunan.

3. Chéng-wàitou méi-yǒu-fángzi.   There are no houses outside the
                                            city.

4. Zài-shānshang méi-yǒu-dà-   There are no big highways on
    lù.   the mountains.

5. Zài-Shāndong yǒu-dà-'hú-méi-
   yǒu?

   Are there any big lakes in Shantung?

6. Nèisuǒr-fángzishang yǒu-shén-
   mo?

   What's on top of that house?

7. Zài-Měiguo yé-yǒu-Zhōngguo-
   rén.

   There are also Chinese in America.

8. Fángzili yǒu-méi-yǒu-rén?

   Is there anyone in the house?

9. Zài-shānshang yǒu-fángzi-ma?

   Are there any houses on the
   mountain?

10. Zài-Wáng-Xiānsheng-jiā yǒu-
    dìtú-ma?

    Is there a map at Mr. King's
    house?

Pattern 7.4. Subordination of Place Words (Notes 6-7 below)

(zài)	P-_de_	N
(at)	Place-_de_	Noun
(zài)	lǐtoude	rén

'the people (who are) inside'

1. nèrde-rén

   the people there

2. wàitoude-rén

   the people outside

3. zài-wàitoude-rén

   the people who are outside

4. fángzi-wàitoude-rén

   the people outside the house

5. zài-fángzi-wàitoude-rén

   the people who are outside the
   house

6. zài-Dōngběide-dà-shān

   the big mountains in Manchuria

7. fángzi-qiántoude-nèiwèi-
   xiānsheng

   that gentleman in front of the
   house

8. zài-shānshangde-fángzi

   the houses on the hill

9. zài-lùshangde-rén

   the people on the road

10. zài-Měiguode-dà-hú

    the big lakes in America

11. Zài-dōngbiarde-fángzi yé-
    hén-hǎo.

    The houses in the east are also
    very nice.

12. Wáng-Xiānsheng-yòubiar-de-
    nèiwèi-xiáojie shi-shéi?

    Who is that young lady to the
    right of Mr. King?

13. Zài-nánbiarde-nèitiáo-lù shi-
    Zhōngshān-Lù-ma?

    Is the road on the south Sun Yat-
    sen Avenue?

14. Fángzi-hòutoude-shān bu-hěn-
    gāo.

    The hill behind the house isn't
    very high.

15. Fángzi-qiántoude-lù hěn-bu-
    hǎo.

    The road in front of the house is
    very bad.

16. Zìdiǎnshangde-nèiběn-shū   Is that book on the dictionary
     shi-nǐde-ma?   yours?

17. Běnzishangde-nèizhī-bǐ yě-   That pen on the notebook is also
     shi-wǒde.   mine.

18. Chéng-lǐtoude-shān dōu-hén-   The hills inside the city are all
     xiǎo.   very small.

19. Chéng-xībiande-nèitiáo-lù yě-   That road west of the city is also
     bu-hǎo.   no good.

20. Shānhòude-fángzi yě-shi-tāde-   Are the houses behind the hill
     ma?   also his?

Pattern 7.5.   Disjunctive Questions with Transitive Verbs
               (Note 12 below)

S	V₁ (ne)	háishi	V₂ (ne)
Subject	Verb 1 (ne)	háishi	Verb 2 (ne)
Nǐmen	'mǎi-shū	háishi	'mài-shū?

               'Do you buy books or sell books?'

1. Tāmen-chī-'Zhōngguo-fàn   Are they eating Chinese food or
    háishi-chī-'wàiguo-fàn?   foreign food?

2. Tāmen-shuō-'Zhōngguo-huà-ne   Are they speaking Chinese or
    háishi-shuō-'Yīngguo-huà-ne?   English?

3. Tāmen-'mǎi-shū háishi-'mài-   Do they buy books or sell books?
    shū?

4. 'Wáng-Xiānsheng zài-Zhōngguo-   Is Mr. King in China or abroad?
    ne háishi-zài-wàiguo-ne?

5. Tāmen-zài-lǐtou háishi-zài-   Are they inside or outside?
    wàitou?

6. Tā-shi-'Měiguo-rén shi-'Yīng-   Is he American or English, do
    guo-rén, nǐ-zhīdao-ma?   you know?

7. Nín-shi-zhǎo-Wáng-Tàitai-ne,   Are you looking for Mrs. King or
    háishi-zhǎo-Wáng-Xiáojie?   Miss King?

8. Wǒmen-zài-tā-jiā-chī-fàn hái-   Are we eating at his home or at
    shi-zài-tā-péngyoude-jiā-chī-   his friend's home?
    fàn-ne?

9. Wai, nǐ-shi-Wáng-Xiáojie hái-   Hello, is this Miss King or Mrs.
    shi-Wáng-Tàitai-ne?   King?

10. Nín-shi-zài-'jiā-chī-fàn háishi- Are you eating at home or out-
    zài-'wàitou-chī-fàn?   side?

11. Nínde-fángzi zài-shānshàng   Is your home on the mountain or
    háishi-zài-shānxià-ne?   at the foot of [lit. below] the
                                      mountain?

12. Nínde-jiā zài-chéng-lǐtou   Is your home inside the city or
     háishi-zài-chéng-wàitou-ne?   outside the city?

13. Wǒ-jīntiān-'mǎi-shū háishi-   Shall I or shall I not buy books
     'bù-mǎi-shū-ne?   today?

14. Tā-shi-tàitai háishi-xiáojie?   Is she [a] married [woman] or
                                        [an] unmarried [woman]?

15. Tā-mǎi-shū háishi-mái-bǐ?   Is he buying books or pens?

SUBSTITUTION TABLES

I: 54 sentences (Note 1)

wǒ	zài	qián	-tou
ní		hòu	-biar
tā		lǐ	-bian
		wài	
		shàng	
		xià	

II: 60 sentences (Note 1)

fángzi	zài	dōng	-biar
shān		xī	-bian
gōngyuán		nán	
dà-shān		běi	
xiǎo-hú		zuǒ	
		yòu	

III: 72 sentences (Note 1)

wǒ	—	—	zài	chéngwài
ní	jiā	bú		chéng-wàitou
tā				shānshang
				shānxià
				Shāndong
				Shānxi

IV: 64 sentences (Note 1)

wǒ	—	—	zài	dōng	-nán
ní	jiā	bú		xī	-běi
tā					

V: 64 sentences (Notes 2-3)

shéi	zài	qián	-tou	chī-fàn
tā		hòu	-biar	mǎi-shū
		lǐ		shuō-huà
		wài		mái-bǐ

VI: 72 phrases (Notes 1, 5)

——	fángzi	——	dōng	-biar
zài	gōngyuán	-de	xī	
	nèitiáo-lù		nán	
			běi	
			zuǒ	
			yòu	

VII: 72 phrases

dōng	-biar	-de	fángzi
xī	-bian		shān
nán			gōngyuán
běi			lù
zuǒ			xiǎo-hú
yòu			dà-shān

VIII: 64 phrases (Note 6)

——	wǒ-jiā	qián	-tou	-de	nèiwèi	xiānsheng
zài	fángzi	hòu	-biar			tàitai
		lǐ				
		wài				

IX: 60 sentences (Notes 8, 9)

——	fángzi-wàitou	——	yǒu	———	rén
zài	jiāli	méi		Zhōngguo	
	shānshang			wàiguo	
	gōngyuán-lǐtou				
	lùshang				

PRONUNCIATION DRILLS

I. The i - ü Contrast

(a) nǐ nǔ	(d) lǐ lǚ	(g) lì lǜ
(b) lí lǘ	(e) jí jú	(h) xī xū
(c) jī jū	(f) qī qū	(i) xǐ xǔ

II. The ie - üe Contrast

(a) liè lüè	(c) jié jué	(e) xiě xuě
(b) niè nüè	(d) qiē quē	(f) xié xué

III. The in - ün Contrast

(a) yín yún	(c) jīn jūn	(e) qín qún	(g) xìn xùn
(b) yìn yùn	(d) jìn jùn	(f) xīn xūn	

DEFINITE vs. INDEFINITE (Note 9)

1.	Shān-zài-nǎr?	Where are the mountains?
2.	'Nár-yǒu-shān?	Where are there (any) mountains?
3.	Rén-zài-fángzili.	The people are in the house.
4.	Fángzili-yǒu-rén.	There are (some) people in the house.
5.	Liángsuǒr-fángzi zài-shān-shang.	The two houses are on the hill.
6.	Zài-shānshang yóu-liángsuǒr-fángzi.	There are two houses on the hill.
7.	Sānge-rén-zài-lǐtou, wǔge-rén-zài-wàitou.	Three (of the) persons are inside, five persons are outside.
8.	Lǐtou-yǒu-sānge-rén, wàitou-yóu-wǔge-rén.	There are three people inside and five people outside.
9.	Rén-zài-nèr-ma?	Are the people there?
10.	Nèr-yǒu-rén-ma?	Are there any people there?
11.	Dà-fángzi zài-liǎngge-xiǎo-fángzide-zhōngjiàr.	The big house is between the two small houses.
12.	Zài-liǎngge-xiǎo-fángzide-zhōngjiàr yǒu-yíge-dà-fángzi.	Between the two small houses is a big house.

SAY WHERE

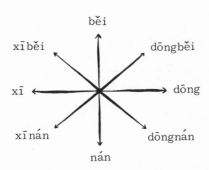

On a flat surface (such as the floor or a piece of cardboard on a desk) mark out the compass points as on the drawing on the left, but without writing down the Chinese names. Improvise a compass pointer and take turns spinning it and calling out the compass direction at which the pointer stops.

Copy the three figures at the top of page 82, omitting the Chinese, and practice identifying the locations without referring to the Chinese names.

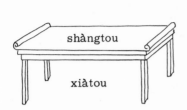

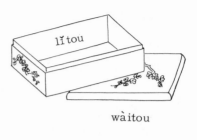

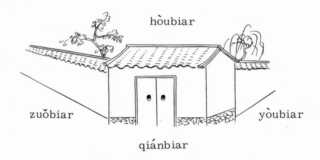

RELATIVITY PROBLEMS

The teacher makes a statement about a positional relationship and then asks you to comment on it from some other point of view. Here is an example:

Teacher says : Wǒ-zài-tā-qiántou. Tā-zài-nǎr?
'I am in front of him. Where is he?'

You answer   : Tā-zài-nǐ-hòutou.
'He is behind you.'

1. Tā-zài-nǐ-yòubiar. Nǐ-zài-nǎr?

2. Tā-jiā zài-nǐ-jiāde-běibiar. Nǐ-jiā-zài-nǎr?

3. Tāde-běnzi zài-ní-běnzide-shàngtou. Nǐde-běnzi-zài-nǎr?

4. Zhèitiáo-lù zài-nèitiáo-lùde-dōngbiar. Nèitiáo-lù-zài-nǎr?

5. Wǒde-zìdiǎn zài-nǐde-zìdiǎn-xiàbiar. Nǐde-zìdiǎn-zài-nǎr?

6. Húnán zài-Húběide-nánbiar. Húběi-zài-nǎr?

7. Shānxi zài-Shāndongde-xībiar. Shāndong-zài-nǎr?

8. Dà-chéng zài-xiǎo-chéngde-dōngbiar. Xiǎo-chéng-zài-nǎr?

9. Xiǎo-zhōng zài-dà-zhōngde-hòubiar. Dà-zhōng-zài-nǎr?

10. Zhōngshān-Lù zài-Běi-Húde-nánbiar. Běi-Hú-zài-nǎr?

11. 'Wáng-Xiānsheng zài-Bái-Xiānshengde-zuǒbiar. Bái-Xiānsheng-zài-nǎr?

12. Běnzi zài-zìdiǎnde-shàngtou. Zìdiǎn-zài-nǎr?

NOTES

1. Location at a place is expressed in Chinese by the construction <u>N zài P</u> 'N is at P':

   Shū-zài-zhèr. 'The book is here.'
   Tāmen-zài-lǐtou. 'They are inside.'

2. COVERBS are transitive verbs which precede the main verb of the sentence. Some coverbs, such as <u>zài</u> '(be) at,' are sometimes used as full verbs; a few are never anything but coverbs. All can be translated as prepositions in English.

3. The verb <u>zài</u> is used as a coverb indicating where the action of the main verb takes place:

   Tāmen-zài-lǐtou chī-fàn. 'They are eating inside.'

4. If a sentence contains a coverb, then the negative adverb <u>bu</u>, other adverbs, and auxiliary verbs usually appear directly before the coverb, rather than before the main verb:

   Tā-bú-zài-jiā chī-fàn. 'He is not eating at home.'
   Tā-yě-zài-jiā chī-fàn. 'He is also eating at home.'
   Tā-yào-zài-jiā chī-fàn. 'He wants to eat at home.'

5. Nouns usually precede place words without an intervening <u>de</u>, especially in frequently used phrases:

   fángzi-lǐtou 'inside (of) the house'

   In the same type of phrase, the place word often appears in the short form:

   fángzili 'in the house'
   shānshang 'on the hill'
   shānxià 'below the hill'

6. The verb <u>zài</u> is often omitted before place words which are subordinated to nouns:

   zài-shānshangde-nèige-rén 'that man who is on the hill'
   shānshangde-nèige-rén 'that man on the hill'

7. Place words are usually followed by <u>de</u> when subordinated to a following noun:

   lǐtoude-rén 'the people inside'

8. We have seen that the verb yǒu means 'have' when it is preceded by a subject:

   Wó-yǒu-qián. 'I have money.'

   When it is not preceded by a subject, and none is to be inferred from the context, yǒu means 'there is' or 'there are':

   Yǒu-qián. 'There is some money (at some understood place).'

   The location of the object of yǒu is indicated by a place word before the verb—sometimes with zài, but frequently without it:

   Zài-Shāndong méi-yǒu-dà-hú.   or
   Shāndong méi-yǒu-dà-hú.
   'There are no big lakes in Shantung.'

9. Chinese of course has no word corresponding to English 'the' for making nouns specific, but it has a grammatical device that serves a similar function—namely, the position the noun occupies in the sentence. A noun that occurs either in subject position or after a coverb usually refers to a definite person or thing (cf. English 'the'), as:

   Liǎngge-rén zài-jiāli. 'The two persons (whom we were talking about) are in the house.' or 'Two of the persons (we were talking about) are in the house.'

   In contrast, nouns in object position usually are indefinite, especially if a place word precedes the verb, as:

   Jiāli yóu-liǎngge-rén. 'There are two (unspecified) people in the house.'

10. Sun Yatsen, who founded the Chinese Republic in 1911, is also known as Sun Zhongshan. The latter part of his name—literally 'Middle Mountain'—is frequently used to name streets and so on, just as the name Washington is often used for this purpose in the United States.

11. Chinese place names, like those in other countries, are often based on geographical features: mountains, lakes, and so on. The provinces of Húnán 'Hunan' and Húběi 'Hupeh,' which mean ' South of the Lake' and 'North of the Lake' respectively, are named from their positions relative to Tungting Lake. Similarly, one of the names for Manchuria is Dōngběi, literally 'The Northeast.' The names of places as they appear on maps have long been standardized, unfortunately in a form which is different from the transcription used in this book.

12. The basic pattern for disjunctive questions—e.g. 'Are you eating Chinese food or (are you eating) foreign food?'—is simply to state the alternatives:

   Nǐ-chī-'Zhōngguo-fàn chī-'wàiguo-fàn?

   The pattern can be varied by the optional insertion of hái (lit. ' still') or háishi (lit.' still is') before the verbs and/or inserting ne at the end of one or both phrases. The most common form is the following:

   Subject   (shi)   Verb$_1$ háishi   Verb$_2$
   Tāmen   mài-shū   háishi   mǎi-shū?
   'Do they sell books or buy books?'

Note that if the verb is itself <u>shi</u>, the pattern usually has the following form:

Subject   <u>shi</u>   Noun₁   <u>háishi</u>   Noun₂
Tā   shi   'Yīngguo-rén   háishi   'Měiguo-rén?
'Is he an Englishman or an American?'

A useful way to drill this structure is for the teacher to present two expressions and ask the student to use them in a disjunctive question. For example:

Teacher: 'măi-shū . . . 'mài-shū
Student: Nĭmen-'măi-shū háishi-'mài-shū?

13. The verb <u>zhīdao</u>, which has a neutral second syllable in the affirmative form, is stressed on the second syllable in the negative: <u>bù-zhīdào</u>.

(See also Supplementary Lesson 7, Note 1)

14. The usual Chinese order of compass directions is <u>dōng</u> 'east,' <u>xī</u> 'west,' <u>nán</u> 'south,' <u>běi</u> 'north.' For compounds, the usual order is <u>xīnán</u> 'southwest,' <u>xīběi</u> 'northwest,' <u>dōngnán</u> 'southeast,' <u>dōngběi</u> 'northeast.'

15. Some speakers prefer to use the monosyllabic forms <u>lǐ</u> 'inside' and <u>wài</u> 'outside' after monosyllabic nouns:

Nĭ-jiā zài-chénglǐ háishi-zài-chéngwài? 'Is your home inside or outside the city?'
Wŏ-jiā-zài-chénglǐ. 'My home is in the city.'

Lesson 8   EXCHANGING INFORMATION

"Oh, 'Máo-Xiānsheng, wǒ-'hái-qǐng-wèn-ni."

Dialogue: Mr. White asks Mr. Mao about a library, and Mr. Mao asks
Mr. White about his studies.

Bái :	Oh, 'Máo-Xiānsheng, wǒ-'hái-qǐng-wèn-ni.	Oh, Mr. Mao, I have something more to ask you.
Máo :	Nín-hái-wèn-wǒ-shénmo?	What is it? [lit. What else are you asking me?]
Bái :	'Zhèr-yǒu-túshūguǎn-méi-yǒu? 5	Is there a library here?
Máo :	Yǒu. Zhèrde-túshūguǎn hěn-dà, shū-bù-shǎo. Měitiān yóu-hěn-duō-xuésheng zài-nèr-kàn-shū. Nín-yào-jiè-shū-ma? 10	Yes. The library here is pretty big and has quite a few books. Every day there are a lot of students reading there. Do you want to borrow some books?
Bái :	Wó-xiǎng-jiè-shū.	Yes. [lit. I'd like to borrow some books.]
Máo :	Nín-xiǎng-jiè-'shénmo-shū?	What books are you thinking of taking out [lit. borrowing]?
Bái :	Wó-xiǎng-jiè-'Zhōngwén-shū.	[I'm planning to take out] some Chinese books.
Máo :	Nín-zài-dàxué **xué-shénmo**? 15	What are you studying in college?

86

Bái :	Wǒ-niàn-wénxué.	[I'm studying] literature.
Máo:	**Nín-xué 'Zhōngguo-wénxué-ma?**	[Are you studying] Chinese literature?
Bái :	'Zhōngguo-wénxué, 'Yīngguo-wénxué, wǒ-dōu-niàn. 20	[I'm studying] both Chinese and English literature.
Máo:	Nín-xǐhuan 'Zhōngguo-wénxué-ma?	Do you like Chinese literature?
Bái :	Wó-hén-xǐhuan 'Zhōngguo-wén-xué.	I like Chinese literature very much.
Máo:	'Zhōngguo-wénxué-róngyi 25 háishi-'Yīngguo-wénxué-róngyi-ne?	Which is easier, Chinese or English literature?
Bái :	'Dōu-hěn-nán-xué.	Both are very difficult [to study].
Máo:	Yóu-hěn-duō-'wàiguo-rén néng-kàn-'Zhōngguo-shū, yě- 30 néng-xiě-'Zhōngguo-zì. Nín-ne?	Quite a few foreigners can read Chinese books and also write characters. What about you?
Bái :	Wǒ-néng-shuō-Zhōngguo-huà, néng-kàn-'jiǎndānde-Zhōngguo-shū, yě-huì-xiě-Zhōngguo-zì. 35	I can speak Chinese, read simple Chinese books, and also write characters.
Máo:	Zhōngguo-zì 'tài-nán-xiě.	Chinese characters are too hard to write.
Bái :	Hěn-duì. . . . Túshūguǎn-zài-nǎr? Lí-zhèr-yuǎn-ma?	Quite right. . . . Where is the library? Is it far from here?
Máo:	Túshūguǎn hén-yuǎn.	[The library is] quite far.
Bái :	Lí-zhèr-duó-yuǎn? 40	How far (is it) from here?
Máo:	Lí-zhèr-yǒu qīlǐ-duō-lù.	(It's) seven-odd (Chinese) miles [from here].
Bái :	Oh, qī-bālǐ-lù bú-'tài-yuǎn.	Oh, seven or eight (Chinese) miles isn't too far.
Máo:	Yě-bú-jìn.	It's not close either.
Bái :	Túshūguǎn lí-'Gāo-Xiānsheng-jiā 'yuǎn-bu-yuǎn? 45	Is the library far from Mr. Gao's home?
Máo:	'Hén-yuǎn.	Quite far.

VOCABULARY

dàxué	college, university (N) [lit. big study]
duì	correct (SV)
duō	numerous, many, much; -odd (SV) (Note 7 below)
duó(mo)	how? to what degree? (AD) (Notes 5, 7 below)
jiǎndān	simple, uncomplicated (SV) [lit. simple single]

jiè	borrow (TV)
jìn	near (SV)
kàn	look at, see, read (TV)
lí	(separated) from (CV)
lǐ	Chinese mile (= $\frac{1}{3}$ English mile) (M)
měi	each, every (M)
nán	difficult (SV)
néng	able to (AV) (Note 8 below)
niàn	study, read (aloud) (TV) (See Supplementary Lesson 8, Note 1)
róngyi	easy (SV)
shǎo	few, scarce, rare (SV) (Note 7a below)
tài	too, excessively (AD)
tiān	day (M)
túshūguǎn	library (N) [lit. chart book establishment]
wénxué	literature (N) [lit. writing study]
xiě	write (TV)
xǐhuan	like, like to (TV) [lit. joy rejoice]
xué	study (TV)
xuésheng	student (N)
yuǎn	far, a long way (off) (SV)
zì	character, word

SENTENCE BUILD-UP

yuǎn   far
'yuǎn-bu-yuǎn?   far or not?
1. Nǐ-jiā 'yuǎn-bu-yuǎn?   Is your home far away?

lí   from
lí-Měiguo   from America
2. Zhōngguo-lí-Měiguo hén-yuǎn.   China is quite far from America.

lǐ   (Chinese) mile
yìlǐ-lù   one (Chinese) mile
3. Wǒ-jiā lí-zhèr-yìlǐ-lù.   My home is one mile from here.

túshūguǎn`   library
lí-túshūguǎn   from the library
4. Tā-jiā-lí-túshūguǎn èrlǐ-lù.   His home is two miles from the
                                                     library.

dàxué   university

lí-dàxué   from the university
5. Túshūguǎn-lí-dàxué sānlǐ-lù.   The library is three miles from
                                            the university.

duō   many or much
hěn-duō   very much
6. Wǒde-qián bù-hěn-duō.   I don't have very much money.

duō   and a little more
sānlǐ-duō-lù   three miles and a little
                                            more
7. Wǒ-jiā-lí-zhèr sānlǐ-duō-lù.   My home is a little over three
                                            miles from here.

sānshilǐ-lù   thirty miles
sānshi-duō-lǐ-lù   thirty-odd miles
8. Běi-Hú-lí-Nán-Hú sānshi-   North Lake is thirty-odd miles
    duō-lǐ-lù.   from South Lake.

duó   how (much, of a quality)?
'duó-yuǎn?   how far?
lí-nèr-'duó-yuǎn?   how far from there?
9. Dàxué-lí-nèr 'duó-yuǎn?   How far is the university from
                                            there?

'duómo?   how (much, of a quality)?
'duómo-yuǎn?   how far?
10. Túshūguǎn-lí-zhèr 'duómo-   How far is the library from
    yuǎn?   here?

tài   excessively
tài-yuǎn   too far
11. Wǒ-jiā-lí-dàxué tài-yuǎn.   My home is too far from the uni-
                                            versity.

jìn   near
hěn-jìn   very near
12. Wǒ-jiā-lí-dàxué hěn-jìn.   My home is very near the uni-
                                            versity.

'jílǐ-lù?   how many miles?
lí-zhèr-'jílǐ-lù?   how many miles from here?
13. Xī-Shān-lí-zhèr 'jílǐ-lù?   How many miles from here are
                                            the Western Hills?

'duōshao-lǐ-lù?   how many miles?
lí-Měiguo 'duōshao-lǐ-lù?   how many miles from Amer-
                                            ica?
14. Zhōngguo-lí-Měiguo 'duōshao-   How many miles from America
    lǐ-lù?   is China?

lí-zhèr-'duó-yuǎn?   how far from here?
lí-zhèr yǒu-'duó-yuǎn?   how far from here?

15. Měiguo-lí-zhèr 'duó-yuǎn?   How far is America from here?
    or
    Měiguo-lí-zhèr yǒu-'duó-yuǎn?

        lí-zhèr-'jílǐ-lù?   how many miles from here?
        lí-zhèr-yóu-'jílǐ-lù?   how many miles from here?
16. Nǐ-jiā-lí-zhèr 'jílǐ-lù?   How far from here is your
    or   home?
    Nǐ-jiā-lí-zhèr yóu-'jílǐ-lù?

        lí-Yīngguo 'duōshao-lǐ-   how many miles from Eng-
            lù?   land?
        lí-Yīngguo yǒu-'duōshao-   how many miles from Eng-
            lǐ-lù?   land?
17. Zhōngguo-lí-Yīngguo 'duōshao-   How many miles is China from
    lǐ-lù?   England?
    or
    Zhōngguo-lí-Yīngguo yǒu-duō-
    shao-lǐ-lù?

        lí-nèr-bālǐ-lù   eight miles from there
        lí-nèr-yǒu-bālǐ-lù   eight miles from there
18. Wǒ-jiā-lí-nèr bālǐ-lù.   My home is eight miles from
    or   there.
    Wǒ-jiā-lí-nèr yǒu-bālǐ-lù.

        xuésheng   student
        nǐde-xuésheng   your students
19. Nǐde-xuésheng 'duō-bu-duō?   Do you have many students?

        xǐhuan   like
        hén-xǐhuan   like very much
20. Wó-hén-xǐhuan-ta.   I like him very much.

        kàn   look at, read
        kàn-shū   read books
21. Tā-bu-xǐhuan-kàn-shū.   He doesn't like to read.

        zì   character
        shénmo-zì?   what character?
22. Zhèi-shi-shénmo-zì?   What character is this?

        xiě   write
        xiě-zì   write characters
23. Nǐ-huì-xiě 'Zhōngguo-zì-   Do you know how to write Chi-
    ma?   nese characters?

        měi   each or every
        měige-rén   each person
24. Měige-rén yǒu-yìběn-shū.   Each person has one book.

        tiān   day
        měitiān   every day
25. Wó-měitiān chī-Zhōngguo-fàn.   I eat Chinese food every day.

ní-qǐng-shéi?   whom are you inviting?
'shéi-chī-fàn?   who is eating?
26. Ní-qǐng-'shéi-chī-fàn?   Whom have you invited to eat?

méi-you-xiáojie   there are no girls
xiáojie-xǐhuan-ta   girls like him
27. Méi-you-xiáojie xǐhuan-ta.   No girls like him.

hǎo   good
hǎo-kàn   good to look at, pretty
28. Nèige-xiáojie hén-hǎo-kàn.   That young lady is very pretty.

nán   difficult
nán-kàn   ugly
29. Nèisuǒr-fángzi hěn-nán-kàn.   That house is very ugly.

róngyi   easy
bu-róngyi-mǎi   not easy to buy
30. Xiànzài hǎo-fángzi bu-róngyi-   Nowadays it's not easy to buy
    mǎi.   good houses.

niàn   read, study
tài-nán-niàn   too hard to read
31. Zhèiběn-shū tài-nán-niàn.   This book is too hard to read.

niàn-shū   study
zài-dàxué-niàn-shū   study at a university
32. Tā-zài-'shénmo-dàxué-niàn-   At what university is he study-
    shū?   ing?

xué   study
xué-Zhōngguo-huà   study Chinese
33. Wó-hén-xǐhuan xué-Zhōngguo-   I enjoy studying Chinese very
    huà.   much.

shǎo   few
hén-shǎo   very few
34. 'Zhèrde-rén hén-shǎo.   There are very few people here.

jiè   borrow
jiè-zhèiběn-shū   borrow this book
35. Wó-xiǎng-jiè 'zhèiběn-shū.   I'd like to borrow this book.

néng   able to
'néng-xiě Zhōngguo-zì   able to write Chinese char-
                                      acters
36. Wǒ-bù-néng-xiě Zhōngguo-zì.   I can't write Chinese characters.

jiǎndān   simple
jiǎndānde-zì   simple characters
37. Wǒ-'jiù-néng-xiě jiǎndānde-   I can only write simple charac-
    zì.   ters.

wénxué   literature

	Yīngguo-wénxué	English literature
38.	Yīngguo-wénxué nán-niàn-ma?	Is English literature hard to study?

	duì	correct
	hěn-duì	quite correct
39.	Nǐde-huà hěn-duì.	Your statement is quite correct.

	xiě-Zhōngguo-zì	write Chinese characters
	hěn-nán	very hard
40.	Xiě-Zhōngguo-zì hěn-nán.	Writing Chinese characters is very hard.

	shi-zhèige-hǎo	is this good?
	háishi-nèige-hǎo	or is that good?
41.	Shi-'zhèige-hǎo háishi-'nèige hǎo-ne?	Which is better, this or that?

PATTERN DRILLS

Pattern 8.1. Distance between Places (Notes 3-5 below)

Pattern 8.1 a.

S	lí	P	yuǎn/jìn
Subject	'from'	Place	'far'/'close'
Túshūguǎn	lí	zhèr	yuǎn.

'The library is far from here.'

Pattern 8.1 b.

S	lí	P	(yǒu)	D
Subject	'from'	Place		Distance
Túshūguǎn	lí	zhèr	yǒu	sānlǐ lù.

'The library is three (Chinese) miles from here.'

1.	'Zhāng-Xiānsheng-jiā lí-zhèr-jìn.	Mr. Johnson's home is near here.
2.	Húběi-lí-zhèr 'hén-yuǎn.	Hupeh is far from here.
3.	Tā-jiā-lí-zhèr hěn-jìn.	His home is very near here.
4.	Gōngyuán-lí-wǒ-jiā 'tài-yuǎn.	The park is too far from my home.
5.	Dàxué-lí-zhèr hěn-jìn-ma?	Is the college very near here?
6.	Zhōngshān-Lù-lí-zhèr hén-yuǎn-ma?	Is Sun Yatsen Avenue very far from here?
7.	'Zuǒbiarde-fángzi lí -'yòubiarde-fángzi 'duómo-yuǎn?	How far is the house on the left from the house on the right?

8. Měiguo-lí-Yīngguo yǒu-'duó-yuǎn?

How far is America from England?

9. Wǒ-bu-zhīdào tā-jiā-lí-zhèr-'duó-yuǎn.

I don't know how far his home is from here.

10. Tā-jiā-lí-zhèr 'jílǐ-lù?

How many miles from here is his home?

11. 'Gāo-Xiānsheng-jiā lí-zhèr-yóu-'jílǐ-lù?

How many miles from here is Mr. Gao's home?

12. 'Bái-Xiānsheng-jiā lí-zhèr-'duōshao-lǐ-lù?

How many miles from here is Mr. White's home?

13. Túshūguǎn-lí-gōngyuán yǒu-qīlǐ-lù.

The library is seven miles from the park.

14. Shān-'qiántoude-fángzi lí-shān-'hòutoude-fángzi yǒu-èrlǐ-lù.

The house in front of the hill is two miles from the house behind the hill.

15. Gāo-Xiānsheng-jiā-lí-zhèr shí-liùlǐ-lù.

Mr. Gao's house is sixteen miles from here.

16. Xī-Shān-lí-zhèr bālǐ-duō-lù.

The Western Hills are eight or so miles from here.

17. Túshūguǎn-lí-gōngyuán bu-yuǎn-ma?

Isn't the library far from the park?

18. 'Wáng-Xiānsheng-jiā lí-túshū-guán-yuǎn-ma?

Is Mr. King's home far from the library?

19. 'Bái-Xiānsheng-jiā lí-'Máo-Xiānsheng-jiā jìn-ma?

Is Mr. White's home close to Mr. Mao's home?

20. 'Bái-Xiānsheng-jiā lí-nèr 'duōshao-lǐ-lù?

How far is Mr. White's home from there?

21. 'Dàxué-lí-túshūguǎn 'jílǐ-lù?

How many miles is the college from the library?

22. 'Máo-Xiānsheng-jiā lí-'Wáng-Xiānsheng-jiā hén-yuǎn-ma?

Is Mr. Mao's home very far from Mr. King's home?

23. Yīngguo-lí-Měiguo bù-hén-yuǎn-ma?

Isn't England a long way from America?

24. Nín-jiā-lí-túshūguǎn 'yuǎn-bu-yuǎn?

Is your home far from the library?

25. 'Nánbiarde-shān lí-'běibiarde-shān yóu-wǔshi-duō-lǐ-lù.

The mountains on the south are fifty-odd miles from the mountains on the north.

Pattern 8.2. Nouns Shared as Objects and Subjects (Note 2)

yǒu	N	V
there is/are	Noun	Verb
Yǒu	rén	kàn-shū.

'There are people reading.'

1. 'Bú-yào-shuō-huà. Yǒu-rén-
   kàn-shū.

   Don't talk. There are people
   reading.

2. Měitiān-yǒu-xuésheng zài-zhèr-
   kàn-shū.

   Every day there are students
   reading here.

3. Túshūguǎn jīntian-méi-yǒu-rén-
   kàn-shū.

   There isn't anyone reading in the
   library today.

4. Méi-yǒu-xiáojie-xǐhuan-ta.

   No girls like him.

5. Jīntian méi-yǒu-rén-mǎi-shū-
   ma?

   Isn't anyone buying books today?

6. Xiànzài yóu-hěn-duō-'wàiguo-rén
   yào-xué-'Zhōngguo-huà.

   Now there are a lot of foreigners
   who want to study Chinese.

7. Yóu-hěn-duō-xuésheng zài-nèr-
   kàn-shū.

   There are a lot of students reading there.

8. Yǒu-rén-zhǎo 'Wáng-Xiānsheng.

   There's someone looking for Mr.
   King.

9. Méi-yǒu-xiānsheng xǐhuan-nèige-
   xuésheng.

   There are no teachers who like
   that student.

10. Méi-yǒu-rén bù-xǐhuan-chī-
    Zhōngguo-fàn.

    Everyone likes to eat Chinese
    food.

11. Fángzili yǒu-rén-chī-fàn.

    There are some people eating in
    the house.

12. Yóu-hěn-duō-'Zhōngguo-rén huì-
    shuō-'Yīngguo-huà.

    There are lots of Chinese who
    can speak English.

13. Měitiān-yǒu-rén zài-zhèr-chī-
    fàn.

    Every day there are people eat-
    ing here.

14. Xiànzài méi-yǒu-'wàiguo-rén
    zài-nèige-dàxuéli-niàn-shū.

    There aren't any foreigners
    studying in that college now.

15. Méi-yǒu-rén bù-xǐhuan-'Gāo-
    Xiānsheng.

    There isn't anyone who doesn't
    like Mr. Gao.

16. Tā-kàn-wǒ-chī-fàn.

    He is watching me eat.

17. Nǐ-bu-qǐng 'Wáng-Xiānsheng-
    chī-fàn-ma? . . . Wǒ-bù-qǐng-
    Wáng-Xiānsheng. Wó-qǐng-
    Wáng-Xiáojie.

    Aren't you inviting Mr. Wang to
    dinner? . . . I'm not inviting Mr.
    Wang, I'm inviting Miss Wang.

18. Wó-hén-xǐhuan kàn-ta-xiě-
    Zhōngguo-zì.

    I like very much to watch him
    write Chinese.

19. Qíng-nǐ-kàn wó-xiě-'zhèige-
    zì.

Please watch me write this character.

20. Tā-zài-'nǎr-chī-fàn? Wó-qǐng-
    ta zài-'zhèr-chī-fàn.

Where is he eating? I've invited
him to eat here.

Pattern 8.3. Compound Descriptive Phrases (Note 1 below)

S	SV	TV
Subject	Stative Verb	Transitive Verb
Zhōngguo zì	nán	xiě.

'Chinese characters are hard to write.'

1. Zhōngguo-fàn-hǎo-chī.

Chinese food is delicious.

2. Zhōngguo-shū hěn-nán-niàn.

Chinese books are very hard to
read.

3. Zhōngguo-huà-nán-shuō.

Chinese is hard to speak.

4. Zhōngguo-zì tài-nán-xiě.

Chinese characters are too hard
to write.

5. Zhèiběn-shū róngyi-niàn.

This book is easy to read.

6. Zhōngguo-huà bù-róngyi-xué.

Chinese isn't easy to study.

7. Fángzi-shǎo róngyi-mài, fángzi-
   duō róngyi-mǎi.

(If) houses are scarce (they) are
easy to sell; (if) houses are plen-
tiful they're easy to buy.

8. Zhèiběn-shū hén-shǎo, bù-róng-
   yi-mǎi.

This book is quite rare; it's not
easy to buy.

9. Nèige-gōngyuán-hěn-dà, hěn-
   róngyi-zhǎo.

That park is very large; it's
very easy to find.

10. 'Gāo-Xiáojie hén-hǎo-kàn.

Miss Gao is very pretty.

11. Wó-yǒu 'hén-hǎo-kànde-bǐ.

I have a very pretty pen.

12. Zhèige-fàn bù-hǎo-chī.

This food is unpalatable.

13. Nèige-zì bù-róngyi-xiě.

That character isn't easy to
write.

14. Zhèiběn-shū bù-róngyi-niàn.

This book isn't easy to read.

15. Hǎo-kànde shi-wǒde, bù-hǎo-
    kànde shi-tāde.

The pretty one is mine, the ugly
one is his.

Pattern 8.4. Disjunctive Questions with Stative Verbs (Note 6 below)

shi	N₁	SV (ne)	háishi	N₂	SV (ne)
(is)	Noun₁	Stative Verb	or is	Noun₂	Stative Verb
Shi	gāngbǐ	hǎo	háishi	máobǐ	hǎo?

'Which is better, a fountain pen or a writing brush?'

shi	V₁	SV (ne)	háishi	V₂	SV (ne)
(is)	Verb₁	Stative Verb	or is	Verb₂	Stative Verb
Shi	shuō Zhōngguo huà	hǎo	háishi	shuō Yīngguo huà	hǎo?

'Is it better to speak Chinese or to speak English?'

1. 'Wáng-Xiáojie-gāo háishi-'Bái-Xiáojie-gāo?

Who is taller, Miss Wang or Miss Bai?

2. Shi-'zhèr-hǎo háishi-'nèr-hǎo?

Which is better, here or there?

3. 'Zhōngwén-nán shi-'Yīngwén-nán?

Which is harder, Chinese or English?

4. 'Zhōngwén-róngyi háishi-'Yīng-wén-róngyi? ... 'Yīngwén-róngyi.

Which is easier, Chinese or English? ... English is easier.

5. 'Dōngbiarde-shān-yuǎn háishi-'xībiarde-shān-yuǎn?

Which are farther away, the mountains to the east or those to the west?

6. Zhōngshān-Lù-jìn háishi-túshū-guǎn-jìn?

Which is closer, Sun Yatsen Avenue or the library?

7. 'Měiguo-rén-duō háishi-'Yīng-guo-rén-duō?

Which are more numerous, Americans or Englishmen?

8. Shānshàngde-fángzi-hǎo háishi-shānxiàde-fángzi-hǎo?

Which is better, a house on a hill or a house at the foot of [lit. below] a hill?

9. Zhèr-'xiānsheng-duō háishi-'tài-tai-duō?

Which are there more of here, gentlemen or ladies?

10. Shi-'zhèige-zìdián-hǎo-ne, shi-'nèige-zìdián-hǎo-ne?

Is this or that dictionary better?

11. Shi-'hóng-mòshuí-hǎo háishi-'lán-mòshuí-hǎo?

Which is better, red ink or blue ink?

12. 'Zhèige-túshūguán-hǎo háishi-'nèige-túshūguán-hǎo?

Which is better, this library or that library?

13. Chéng-'lǐtoude-rén-duō háishi-chéng-'wàitoude-rén-duō?

Are there more people inside the city or outside the city?

14. Shi-'zhèitiáo-lù-hǎo shi-'nèitiáo-lù-hǎo? ... Shi-'nèitiáo-lù-hǎo.

Which is better, this road or that road? ... That road is better.

15. Yǒu-péngyou-hǎo háishi-'méi-
    yǒu-péngyou-hǎo?

Which is better, to have friends or not to have friends?

16. Yǒu-qián-hǎo háishi-'méi-yǒu-
    qián-hǎo?

Which is better, to have money or not to have money?

17. Niàn-shū-hǎo háishi-'bú-niàn-
    shū-hǎo?

Which is better, to study or not to study?

18. Shi-'jiè-shū-hǎo-ne, háishi-'mǎi-
    shū-hǎo-ne?

Which is better, to borrow books or to buy books?

19. 'Qī diǎn-zhōng-chī-fàn-hǎo háishi-
    'bā diǎn-zhōng-chī-fàn-hǎo?

Is it better to eat at seven o'-clock or at eight o'clock?

20. Xiě-'Zhōngguo-zì-róngyi háishi-
    xiě-'Yīngguo-zì-róngyi?

Is it easier to write Chinese or English?

21. Shi-chī-'Zhōngguo-fàn-jiǎndān
    háishi-chī-'wàiguo-fàn-jiǎndān?

Is it simpler to eat Chinese food or to eat foreign food?

22. 'Zhèrde-fángzi-shǎo háishi-'nèr-
    de-fángzi-shǎo?

Are houses here scarcer than houses there?

23. Shi-'Yīngguo-rén-shǎo háishi-
    'Měiguo-rén-shǎo?

Which are there fewer of, Eng-lishmen or Americans?

24. Shi-kàn-'péngyou-hǎo háishi-niàn-
    'shū-hǎo? ... Wó-xiǎng háishi-
    niàn-shū-hǎo.

Which is better, to see friends or to study? ... I think it's bet-ter to study.

25. Wǒ-bù-zhīdào shi-zài-'jiā-niàn-
    shū-hǎo háishi-zài-'túshūguǎn-
    niàn-shū-hǎo-ne? ... Háishi-zài-
    'túshūguǎn-niàn-shū-hǎo.

I don't know whether it's better to study at home or at the libra-ry. .... It's better to study at the library.

SUBSTITUTION TABLES

I: 20 phrases (Notes 4, 7 b)

yì	-lǐ	——	lù
èr		duō	
sān			
.			
.			
.			
shí			

II: 18 phrases (Notes 4, 7 b)

——	shi	——	lǐ	lù
èr		duō		
sān				
.				
.				
.				
jiǔ				

III: 72 sentences (Notes 4, 7b)

dà-fángzi	lí	Zhōngshān-Lù	——	yì	-lǐ	——	lù
wǒ-jiā		gōngyuán	yǒu	èr		duō	
dàxué		túshūguǎn					

IV: 80 sentences (Notes 3, 5)

Húnán	lí	zhèr	duó	yuǎn
Húběi		nèr	duómo	jìn
Shāndong			hěn	
Shānxi			bu	
			tài	

V: 36 sentences (Note 2)

——	yǒu	xiānsheng	kàn-shū	——
méi		xuésheng	chī-fàn	ma
		rén	mǎi-shū	

VI: 72 sentences (Note 6)

		*			*
——	wǒ	hǎo	shi	xiānsheng	hǎo
shi	nǐ	gāo	háishi	tàitai	gāo
		dà		tā	dà

(The asterisk * indicates that the same word must be chosen from both columns.)

PRONUNCIATION DRILLS

I. The u - ü Contrast
(See The Sounds of Chinese, 19)

(a) wū yū	(e) nǔ nǚ	(i) zhū jū
(b) wú yú	(f) lú lǘ	(j) zhú jú
(c) wǔ yǔ	(g) lǔ lǚ	(k) zhǔ jǔ
(d) wù yù	(h) lù lǜ	(l) zhù jù

(m) chū qū	(q) shū xū
(n) chú qú	(r) shú xú
(o) chǔ qǔ	(s) shǔ xǔ
(p) chù qù	(t) shù xù

II. The un - ün Contrast
(See The Sounds of Chinese, 19)

(a) wén   yún   (d) zhūn   jūn

(b) wěn   yǔn   (e) chún   qún

(c) wèn   yùn   (f) shùn   xùn

III. The uan - üan Contrast
(See The Sounds of Chinese, 19)

(a) wán   yuán   (f) chuān   quān

(b) luǎn   lüǎn   (g) chuǎn   quǎn

(c) zhuān   juān   (h) chuàn   quàn

(d) zhuǎn   juǎn   (i) shuān   xuān

(e) zhuàn   juàn

CHECKERBOARD PROBLEM

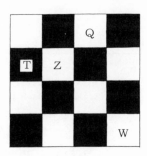

Suppose the accompanying figure represents a city laid out in a checkerboard pattern, in squares measuring one Chinese mile on each side. The white squares are residential blocks, while the black squares contain business establishments and public institutions, such as the library (T). In the blocks indicated by initials are residences occupied by Mr. Zhang, Mr. Wang, and Mr. Qian.

Answer the following questions based on straight-line distances (not diagonals) between the library and the residences, and between pairs of residences.

1. 'Zhāng-Xiānsheng-jiā lí-túshūguǎn 'jílǐ-lù?

2. 'Wáng-Xiānsheng-jiā lí-túshūguǎn 'duó-yuǎn?

3. Qián-jia-lí-Wáng-jia yǒu-'duó-yuǎn?

4. Túshūguǎn-lí-Qián-jia èrlǐ-lù. 'Duì-bu-duì?

5. 'Shéide-jiā lí-túshūguǎn yǒu-'sānlǐ-lù?

6. Qíng-nǐ-shuō, 'Wáng-Xiānsheng-jiā lí-'Qián-Xiānsheng-jiā 'duōshao-lǐ-lù?

7. Túshūguǎn lí-'Qián-Xiānsheng-jiā yǒu-'duó-yuǎn?

8. 'Zhāng-Xiānsheng-jiā lí-'Qián-Xiānsheng-jiā yǒu-'duó-yuǎn?

9. 'Wáng-Xiānsheng-jiā lí-'Zhāng-Xiānsheng-jiā yǒu-'duó-yuǎn?

10. Nǐ-shuō, túshūguǎn lí-'Zhāng-Xiánsheng-jiā 'jílǐ-lù?

11. 'Qián-Xiānsheng-jiā lí-'Zhāng-Xiānsheng-jiā yóu-'jílǐ-lù?

12. Túshūguǎn lí-'shéi-jiā-jìn, lí-'shéi-jiā-yuǎn?

13. 'Zhāng-Xiānsheng-jiā lí-'Qián-Xiānsheng-jiā-jìn-ne, háishi-lí-'Wáng-
     Xiānsheng-jiā-jìn?

14. 'Wáng-Xiānsheng-jiā lí-túshūguǎn-yuǎn háishi-lí-'Qián-Xiānsheng-jiā-
     yuǎn?

15. Túshūguǎn lí-'Wáng-Xiānsheng-jiā 'duōshao-lǐ-lù?

NOTES

1. Compound descriptive phrases are formed by using a stative verb before
    a transitive verb:

    > hǎo-chī 'good to eat, tasty'
    > róngyi-xiě 'easy to write'

2. Note the following types of sentences which we have already encoun-
    tered:

    (a) A full sentence used as the object of the verb shuō 'say,' as:

    > Tā-shuō 'Wáng-Xiānsheng-zài-jiā. 'He says (that) Mr. King is at
    > home.'

    Here shuō introduces the full sentence 'Wáng-Xiānsheng-zài-jiā 'Mr.
    Wang is at home.' Tā is the subject of shuō and 'Wáng-Xiānsheng is
    the subject of zài.

    (b) A sentence with a noun in the middle serving a double function, as:

    > Tā-qǐng-'Wáng-Xiānsheng-chī-fàn. 'He is inviting Mr. King to din-
    > ner.'

    This can be split into two sentences: Tā-qǐng-'Wáng-Xiānsheng 'He
    is inviting Mr. King' and 'Wáng-Xiānsheng-chī-fàn 'Mr. King eats.'
    The noun phrase 'Wáng-Xiānsheng serves double duty as the object of
    qǐng 'invite' and as the subject of chī-fàn 'eat.' A very frequent
    occurrence of this type of sharing is with the verb yǒu 'there is' or
    'there are': Yǒu-rén-zhǎo-ni 'There's someone looking for you'—with
    rén 'person' as the pivotal noun.

3. Separation of one place from another is expressed with the coverb lí
    '(separated) from' in sentences on this pattern: S lí P yuǎn 'S is sepa-
    rated from P far'—that is, 'S is far from P.' Qualifying adverbs, if any,
    are placed before the stative verb:

    > Wǒ-jiā lí-túshūguǎn hěn-jìn. 'My home is very close to the library.'

4. Expressing the distance separating one place from another involves the
    use of three elements: (1) the coverb lí 'from'; (2) a measure of distance
    (e.g. lǐ '[Chinese] mile'); and (3) the noun lù 'road':

    > Wǒ-jiā lí-túshūguǎn sānlǐ-lù. 'My home is three miles from the
    > library.'

The verb yǒu may be inserted before the expression for distance:

Wǒ-jiā lí-túshūguǎn yǒu-sānlǐ-lù.

5. Questions about distance are asked in the following ways:

S lí P yuǎn-ma? 'Is S far from P?'
S lí P 'yuǎn-bu-yuǎn? 'Is S far from P?'
S lí P (yǒu) 'duó-yuǎn? 'How far is S from P?'
S lí P (yǒu) 'duómo-yuǎn? 'How far is S from P?'
S lí P (yǒu) 'jílǐ-lù? 'How many miles is S from P?'
S lí P (yǒu) 'duōshao-lǐ-lù? 'How many miles is S from P?'

6. Disjunctive questions with stative verbs (e.g. 'Which is better, A or B?')
are usually expressed by stating the alternatives, often with shi before
the first alternative and shi or háishi before the second. A and B are
either noun expressions or verb expressions. Examples:

Shi-'zhèige-hǎo shi-'nèige-hǎo?   'Which is better, this or that?'
          or   [lit. Is this good (or) is that
Shi-'zhèige-hǎo háishi-'nèige-hǎo?   good?]

Shi-'qǐng-ta-hǎo háishi-'bù-qǐng-ta-hǎo?   'Is it better to invite him
or not to invite him?

In the answer, one alternative or the other is selected, with or without shi
or (for greater emphasis) háishi. For example:

'Zhèige-hǎo. 'This is better.'
Shi-'nèige-hǎo. 'That is better.'
Háishi-'zhèige-hǎo. 'This is better.'
Háishi-qǐng-ta-hǎo. 'It would be better to invite him.'

Note that Zhèige-hǎo out of context might be ambiguous. Context will
determine whether it is to be interpreted as 'This is good' or 'This is
better.'

7. Note the distinctions in tone and in usage between duō and duó:

(a) duō is a stative verb which is used as a predicate:

Wǒde-qián-bù-duō. 'My money isn't much'—that is, 'I don't have
very much money.'

This construction is much more common than the word-for-word
equivalent with the natural English corresponding to it (that is, 'I don't
have very much money'). Similarly with shǎo 'few, little':

Wǒde-qián hén-shǎo. 'I have very little money.'

(b) duō is used in the sense of '-odd' or 'and a little more.' With the
numbers from one to ten, it comes right after the measure:

yíkuài-duō-qián 'one dollar and a little more'
shíkuài-duō-qián 'ten-odd dollars'

With ten and multiples of ten (twenty, thirty, etc., to ninety), duō is
placed just before the measure:

shí-duō-kuài-qián 'ten-odd dollars'
èrshi-duō-kuài-qián 'twenty-odd dollars'
jiǔshi-duō-kuài-qián 'ninety-odd dollars'

With shí 'ten,' thus, there is a choice of two positions.

(c) duó (or duómo) is an adverb used before a stative verb to ask a question involving degree:

Nèige-běnzi-'duó-dà? 'How big is that notebook?'

8. The words néng, huì, and kéyi all mean 'can,' though sometimes in various senses, as follows:

(a) néng refers to a physical ability and might therefore be used in the sense of 'be able to' or 'strong enough to';

(b) huì refers to an acquired ability and might therefore be translated as 'know how to';

(c) kéyi asks for or grants permission, like 'may.'

These distinctions are by no means rigidly adhered to, however, just as 'can' and 'may' are often used interchangeably in English; néng and huì in particular are apt to fall together.

Lesson 9 ASKING DIRECTIONS

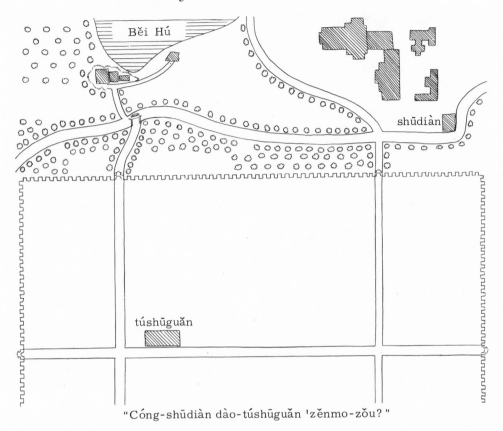

"Cóng-shūdiàn dào-túshūguǎn 'zěnmo-zǒu?"

Dialogue: Mr. White asks how to get to the library and to Mr. Gao's home.

'Bái-Xiānsheng-xiǎng 'xiān-dào-túshū- guǎn, 'hòu-dào-Gāo-Xiānsheng-jiā-qu. Tā-wèn-'Máo-Xiānsheng túshūguǎn-zài nǎr, 'zěnmo-zǒu, cóng-túshūguǎn dào- Gāo-Xiānsheng-jiā 'zěnmo-zǒu. 5

Mr. White plans to go to the library first and then to Mr. Gao's home. He asks Mr. Mao where the library is, how to get there, and how to go from the library to Mr. Gao's home.

Bái : Wǒ-hái-yào-wèn-ni, cóng-shū- diàn dào-túshūguǎn 'zěnmo- zǒu?

I'd also like to ask you, how do I get from the bookstore to the library?

Máo: Nín-cóng-zhèr wàng-nán-yì- zhíde-zǒu, wàng-xī-guǎi, 10 guò-báge-lù-kǒur, jiù-shi- túshūguǎn.

You go straight south from here, turn west, pass eight intersec- tions, and there's the library.

Bái :	Cóng-zhèr-dào-túshūguǎn-nèr yǒu-'shénmo-chē-kéyi-zuò-ne?	From here to the library what car can I take?
Máo :	Gōnggòng-qìchē diànchē 'dōu- 15 yǒu. Nín-xiǎng-zuò 'shénmo- chē-ne?	There are both busses and streetcars. What would you like to take?
Bái :	Wó-xiǎng-zuò gōnggòng-qì- chē-qu. Gōnggòng-qìchē-zhàn zài-nǎr? 20	I'd like to go by bus. Where's the bus stop?
Máo :	Lí-shūdiàn-bù-yuǎn. Nín- cóng-zhèr wàng-xī-zǒu, guò- yíge-lù-kǒur, jiù-shi-gōng- gòng-qìchē-zhàn.	Not far from the bookstore. You go west from here, pass one intersection, and you're at the bus stop.
Bái :	Zuò -'jǐhào-chē-ne? 25	What number bus do I take?
Máo :	Zuò-'sānhào-chē. Yìzhí- jiù-dào-túshūguǎn.	Take a No. 3 bus. It goes directly to the library.
Bái :	Cóng-túshūguǎn dào-'Gāo- Xiānsheng-jiā 'zěnmo-zǒu? Yǒu-gōnggòng-qìchē-ma? 30	How do I go from the library to Mr. Gao's home? Is there a bus?
Máo :	Yǒu. Nín-cóng-túshūguǎn wàng-xī-zǒu, guò-liǎngge- lù-kǒur, jiù-shi-gōnggòng- qìchē-zhàn. Nín-shàng-chē dào-Zhōngshān-Lù. Zài- 35 gōngyuán-mén-kǒur-xià-chē, zài-shàng-xiǎo-shān, jiù-shi- 'Gāo-Xiānsheng-jiā.	There is. You go west from the library, pass two intersections, and there's the bus stop. You get on the bus and go to Sun Yatsen Avenue. Get off the bus at the park gate, go up the little hill, and you come to Mr. Gao's home.
Bái :	Zuò-'jǐhào-chē-ne?	What number bus do I take?
Máo :	Nín-zuò-'jiǔhào-chē, 'liù- 40 hào-chē 'dōu-kéyi.	You can take either a No. 9 or a No. 6 bus.
Bái :	Xièxie-ni.	Thanks.
Máo :	Nín-míngtian 'lái-bu-lái?	Are you coming tomorrow?
Bái :	Huòzhě wǒ-míngtian 'hái- lái-mǎi-shū. 45	Perhaps I'll come again tomorrow to buy some books.
Máo :	Míngtian-jiàn.	See you tomorrow.

VOCABULARY

chē	vehicle (N)
cóng	from (CV)
dào	go to (TV) arrive (at) (IV) to (CV)
diànchē	streetcar (N)

guò	pass (TV)
guǎi	turn (IV)
gōnggòng	public
hào	number (M)
hòu	afterwards (AD)
huòzhě	perhaps (MA)
kǒu, kǒur	mouth, opening (N)
lái	come (IV)
mén	door, gate (N)
míngtian	tomorrow (TW)
qìchē	motor vehicle (N)
qù	go (IV)
shàng	ascend; go to (TV) to (CV)
shūdiàn	bookstore (N)
wàng, wǎng	toward (CV)
xià	descend (TV)
xiān	first (AD)
yìzhí(de)	straight (AD)
zài	again (AD)
zěnmo, zěnme	how? how come (that . . .)? (AD)
zhàn	stop, station (N)
zǒu	walk, travel, depart, go (V)
zuò	ride (on a vehicle) (TV) by means of (a vehicle) (CV)

SENTENCE BUILD-UP

lái	come
'lái-bu-lái?	come or not?
1. Tā-jīntian 'lái-bu-lái?	Is he coming today?

qù	go
'shídiǎn-zhōng-qù	go at ten o'clock
2. Wó-xiǎng 'shídiǎn-zhōng-qù.	I plan to go at ten o'clock.

dào	arrive (at a place)
'shénmo-shíhou-dào?	arrive at what time?
3. 'Bái-Xiānsheng 'shénmo-shíhou-dào?	When will Mr. White arrive?

dào
dào-túshūguǎn
4. Nǐ-'shénmo-shíhou dào-
túshūguǎn?

go to a place
go to the library
When are you going to the library?

shūdiàn
dào-shūdiàn
5. Nǐ-'shénmo-shíhou dào-shūdiàn?

bookstore
go to the bookstore
When are you going to the bookstore?

dào
dào-shūdiàn-lái
6. Qǐng-nín 'sìdiàn-zhōng-dào-
shūdiàn-lái.

to (a place)
come to the bookstore
Please come to the bookstore at
four o'clock.

dào
dào-shūdiàn-qu
7. Nǐ-'shénmo-shíhou dào-
shūdiàn-qu?

to (a place)
go to the bookstore
When are you going to the bookstore?

míngtian
míngtian-wǎnshang
8. Tā-míngtian-wǎnshang dào-
nèr-qu.

tomorrow
tomorrow evening
He will go there tomorrow.

wǒ-míngtian-lái
mǎi-shū
9. Wǒ-míngtian-lái-mǎi-shū.

I'll come tomorrow
buy books
I'll come tomorrow to buy some
books.

wǒ-míngtian-mǎi-shū
10. Wǒ-míngtian-mǎi-shū-lai.

I'll buy some books tomorrow
I'll come tomorrow to buy some
books.

dào-shūdiàn-qu
mǎi-shū
11. Wǒ-dào-shūdiàn-qu mǎi-
shū.

go to the bookstore
buy books
I'm going to the bookstore to buy
some books.

cóng-Yīngguo-lái
12. Tā-míngtian cóng-Yīngguo-
lái.

come from England
He will come from England tomorrow.

cóng-Yīngguo
dào-Zhōngguo
13. Cóng-Yīngguo-dào-Zhōngguo
'duó-yuǎn?

from England
to China
How far is it from England to
China?

zěnmo?
'zěnmo-shuō?
14. Zhèige 'Zhōngguo-huà-zěnmo-
shuō?

how?
say how?
How does one say this in Chinese?

	zǒu	walk, travel, depart
	'zěnmo-zǒu	how does one go?
15.	Dào-shūdiàn 'zěnmo-zǒu?	How do you get to the bookstore?
	zǒu	travel
	zǒu-lù	walk (along a road)
16.	Wó-hén-xǐhuan-zǒu-lù.	I like walking very much.
	sānlǐ-lù	three miles
	zǒu-sānlǐ-lù	walk three miles
17.	Wó-měitiān zǒu-sānlǐ-lù.	I walk three miles every day.
	wàng	toward
	wàng-xī	toward the west
18.	Wàng-xī-zǒu-ba!	Go west!
	wàng-dōng-zǒu	go east
	bālǐ-lù	eight miles
19.	Wàng-dōng-zǒu bālǐ-lù.	Go east for eight miles.
	guǎi	turn
	wàng-nán-guǎi	turn toward the south
20.	Bú-yào-wàng-nán-guǎi.	Don't turn south.
	chē	vehicle
	'shénmo-chē	what vehicle?
21.	Zhèi-shi-'shénmo-chē?	What vehicle is this?
	chē	vehicle
	qìchē	motor vehicle
22.	Zhèi-bú-shi-'Zhōngguo-qì-chē.	This is not a Chinese car.
	diànchē	streetcar
23.	Zhèr-yǒu-diànchē-ma?	Are there streetcars here?
	gōnggòng	public
	gōnggòng-qìchē	bus
24.	Zhèr-'méi-yǒu-gōnggòng-qìchē.	There are no busses here.
	zuò	ride (on a vehicle)
	zuò-diànchē	ride a streetcar
25.	Wǒ-'bù-xǐhuan zuò-diànchē.	I don't like to ride streetcars.
	zuò-diànchē	ride a streetcar
	zuò-'diànchē-lái	come by streetcar
26.	Qǐng-nín-zuò-'diànchē-lái.	Please come by streetcar.
	shàng	ascend, get on
	shàng-chē	board a car
27.	Wǒ-zài-'nǎr-shàng-chē?	Where do I board the car?

xià   descend, get off
xià-shān ·   descend the mountain

28. Tāmen-jīntian xià-shān-   Are they descending the moun-
     ma?   tain today?

xiān   first
'xiān-niàn-shū   first study

29. Wó-xiǎng 'xiān-niàn-shū.   I plan to study first.

hòu   afterwards
hòu-kàn-péngyou   afterwards see friends

30. Wǒ-'xiān-niàn-shū, 'hòu-   I'll study first, and see friends
     kàn-péngyou.   afterwards.

zài   again
'zài-shuō   say again

31. Qǐng-nín-'zài-shuō.   Please repeat.

mén   door, gate
chéng-mén   city gate

32. Wǒ-jiā lí-chéng-mén-hěn-   My home is very close to the
     jìn.   city gate.

kǒur   opening
mén-kǒur   doorway, gateway

33. Mén-kǒur bù-róngyi-zhǎo.   The doorway isn't easy to find.

lù-kǒur   street intersection
lí-lù-kǒur-bù-yuǎn   not far from the intersection

34. Shūdiàn lí-lù-kǒur-bù-yuǎn.   The bookstore is not far from
                                       the intersection.

guò   pass
guò-lù-kǒur   pass an intersection

35. Nǐ-xiān-guò sānge-lù-   First you pass three intersec-
     kǒur.   tions.

zhàn   stop, station
diànchē-zhàn   streetcar stop

36. Qǐng-wèn, diànchē-'zhàn-   May I ask, where is the street-
     zài-nǎr?   car stop?

yìzhí   straight
yìzhí-wàng-běi   straight toward the north

37. Nǐ-yìzhí wàng-béi-zǒu.   Go straight north.

hào   number
bāhào-chē   Number Eight car

38. Xiān-zuò-'bāhào-chē.   First take car No. 8.

huòzhě   perhaps
huòzhě-'bù-néng-qù   perhaps can't go

39. Tā-míngtian huòzhě-'bù-   Perhaps he can't go tomorrow.
     néng-qù.

yǒu-'shénmo-xuésheng?   what students are there?
kéyi-zài-zhèr-niàn-shū   can study here
40. Yǒu-'shénmo-xuésheng kéyi-   What students [are there who]
zài-'zhèr-niàn-shū?   can study here?

yǒu-'shénmo-fàn?   what food is there?
kéyi-chī   can eat
41. Yǒu-'shénmo-fàn kéyi-chī?   What food is there to eat?

yǒu-'shénmo-chē?   what car is there?
kéyi-zuò   it is possible to ride
42. Yǒu-'shénmo-chē kéyi-zuò?   What car can you take?

PATTERN DRILLS

Pattern 9.1.   Motion to a Place (Note 1 below)

S	dào	P	lái/qu
Subject	to	Place	come/go
Wǒ	dào	shūdiàn	qu.

'I'm going to the bookstore.'

1. Tā-dào-'Měiguo-lái.   He is coming to America.

2. Tā-dào-'Měiguo-qu.   He is going to America.

3. Tā-dào-nǎr-qu?   Where is he going?

4. 'Qián-Xiānsheng 'bú-dào-   Mr. Qian isn't coming to Amer-
Měiguo-lái.   ica.

5. 'Wáng-Xiānsheng dào-shū-   Is Mr. King going to the book-
diàn-qu-ma?   store?

6. Jīntian-wǎnshang 'Máo-Xiān-   This evening Mr. Mao is going to
sheng dào-túshūguǎn-qu.   the library.

7. Tā-dào-wǒ-jiā-lái.   He's coming to my home.

8. 'Gāo-Xiáojie dào-Wáng-jia-   Miss Gao is going to the King
qu.   home.

9. Wǒ-míngtian bú-dào-'Bái-   I'm not going to Mr. White's
Xiānsheng-jiā-qu.   home tomorrow.

10. Wǒ-dào-'wàitou-qu, tā-dào-   I'm going outside, he's coming
'lǐtou-lái.   inside.

11. Tā-xǐhuan dào-'shūdiàn-lái-   Does he like to come to the
ma?   bookstore?

12. 'Qián-Xiānsheng dào-Húběi-   Mr. Qian is going to Hupeh, Mr.
qu, 'Gāo-Xiānsheng dào-   Gao is coming to Hunan.
Húnán-lái.

13. Jīntian-wǎnshang nǐ-dào-   Are you going to Mr. Gao's home
    'Gāo-Xiānsheng-jiā-qu-ma?   this evening?

14. 'Gāo-Xiānsheng 'hén-xǐhuan-   Mr. Gao likes coming here very
    dào-zhèr-lái.   much.

15. Wǒ-míngtian dào-chéng-lǐtou-   I'm going into town tomorrow.
    qu.

Pattern 9.2.   Purpose with <u>lái</u> and <u>qù</u>   (Note 6 below)

Pattern 9.2 a.

	S	qù	V	O
	Subject	go	Verb	Object
	Wǒ	qù	kàn	péngyou.

'I'm going (in order) to see some friends.'

Pattern 9.2 b.

	S	V	O	qu
	Subject	Verb	Object	go
	Wǒ	kàn	péngyou	qu.

'I'm going (in order) to see some friends.'

 1. Wǒ-lái-zhǎo-'Wáng-Xiānsheng.   I've come to find Mr. King.

 2. Wǒ-jīntian 'bú-qù-mǎi-shū.   I'm not going (to some place or
                                       other) to buy books today.

 3. Tā-qù-niàn-shū.   He's going (somewhere) to study.

 4. Wǒ-'bú-qù-mǎi-qiānbǐ.   I'm not going (there) to buy pen-
                                       cils.

 5. Tā-lái-mǎi-shénmo?   What's he come to buy?

 6. Tā-jīntian 'bú-kàn-shū-qu.   He's not going (there) today to
                                       read.

 7. Wǒ-míngtian jiè-shū-lái.   I'll come tomorrow to take out
                                       some books.

 8. Wó-xiǎng-mǎi-shū-qu.   I plan to go and buy some books.

 9. Tā-jīntian lái-jiè-shū-ma?   Is he coming today to borrow the
                                       books?

10. Wó-xǐhuan dào-túshūguǎn   I like going to the library to
    kàn-shū-qu.   read.

11. Wǒ-míngtian 'hái-lái-mǎi-   I'll come again tomorrow to buy
    shū.   some books.

12. Tā-'bù-dào-shūdiàn mǎi-   He's not going to the bookstore
    zìdiǎn-qu.   to buy a dictionary.

13. Ní-'yé-xǐhuan dào-túshūguǎn-
    qu kàn-shū-ma?

Do you also like going to the library to read?

14. 'Gāo-Xiáojie méi-yǒu-'lán-
    mòshuǐ.

Miss Gao doesn't have any blue
ink.

15. 'Wáng-Xiānsheng méi-yóu-
    běnzi. Tā-jīntian-bú-qu-
    mǎi-ma?

Mr. King doesn't have a notebook. Isn't he going to buy one
today?

16. 'Bái-Xiānsheng méi-yǒu-
    Zhōngwén-shū. Tā-jīntian-
    lái-jiè.

Mr. White doesn't have any Chinese books. He's coming today
to borrow (some).

17. Wǒ-qù-chéng-wàitou kàn-
    péngyou.

I'm going outside the city to see
some friends.

18. Tā-bú-dào-Yīngguo-qu niàn-
    shū.

He's not going to England to
study.

19. Tā-dào-'Měiguo-lái niàn-shū-
    ma?

Is he coming to America to
study?

20. Xiànzài 'jídiǎn-zhōng? Wǒ-
    qu-kàn-péngyou.

What time is it now? I'm going
to see some friends.

Pattern 9.3.   Motion To and From Places   (Notes 2–3 below)

Pattern 9.3 a.

S	cóng	P	lái
Subject	from	Place	come
Tā	cóng	Měiguo	lái.

'He is coming from America.'

Pattern 9.3 b.

S	cóng	P_1	dào	P_2	lái
Subject	from	P_1	to	P_2	come
Tā	cóng	Měiguo	dào	Zhōngguo	lái.

'He is coming to China from America.'

1. Nǐ-cóng-'nǎr-lái?

Where are you coming from?

2. Nǐ-cóng-'Gāo-Xiānsheng-jiā-
   lái-ma?

Are you coming from Mr. Gao's
house?

3. Tā-cóng-'Yīngguo-lái-ma?

Is he coming from England?

4. Wǒ-cóng-'dàxué-lái.

I'm coming from the university.

5. 'Qián-Xiānsheng míngtian-'wú-
   diǎn-zhōng cóng-'Měiguo-lái.

Mr. Qian will come from America tomorrow at 5:00.

6. Wǒ-cóng-nèr dào-túshūguǎn-qu.

I'm going to the library from there.

7. 'Máo-Tàitai cóng-túshūguǎn dào-gōngyuán-qu.

Mrs. Mao is going from the library to the park.

8. 'Máo-Xiānsheng jīntian-sìdiǎn-zhōng cóng-túshūguǎn dào-'zhèr-lái.

Mr. Mao will come here from the library today at 4:00.

9. 'Zhāng-Xiānsheng cóng-Měiguo-dào-Yīngguo-qu.

Mr. Johnson is going from America to England.

10. 'Gāo-Xiānsheng cóng-'Máo-Xiānsheng-jiā dào-túshūguǎn-qu.

Mr. Gao is going from Mr. Mao's home to the library.

11. 'Qián-Xiānsheng cóng-'nǎr-lái? Dào-'nǎr-qù?

Where is Mr. Qian coming from? Where is he going?

12. Cóng-zhèr-dào-'Gāo-Xiānsheng-jiā 'zěnmo-qù?

How does one go from here to Mr. Gao's home?

13. Nǐ-cóng-zhèr-dào-tā-jiā 'zěn-mo-qù?

How are you going from here to his home?

14. Tāmen-bù-cóng-tā-ner dào-'zhèr-lái-ma?

Aren't they coming here from his place there?

15. 'Gāo-Tàitai-yǒu-péngyou cóng-Měiguo-dào-'Zhōngguo-lái?

Does Mrs. Gao have friends coming from America to China?

16. 'Máo-Xiānsheng-bù-cóng-shū-diàn dào-túshūguǎn-qu.

Mr. Mao isn't going to the library from the bookstore.

17. Cóng-zhèr-dào-'Gāo-Xiānsheng-jiā 'zěnmo-zǒu?

How do you get from here to Mr. Gao's home?

18. Cóng-nǐ-nèr dào-túshūguǎn 'zěnmo-zǒu?

How does one get from your place there to the library?

19. Tāmen-dōu-cóng-zhèr dào-gōngyuán-qu-ma?

Are they all going from here to the park?

20. Cóng-chéng-lǐtou dào-chéng-wàitou 'zěnmo-qù?

How do you get from inside the city to outside the city?

Pattern 9.4. Motion Toward a Place (Note 4 below)

wàng	P	zǒu
toward	Place	go
Wàng	nán	zǒu.

'Go south!'

1. Cóng-shūdiàn wàng-zuó-guǎi.

From the bookstore turn left.

2. Cóng-túshūguǎn wàng-yòu-guǎi.

Turn right at the library.

3. Cóng-Zhōngshān-Lù wàng-xī- | From Sun Yatsen Avenue turn
   guǎi. | west.

4. Cóng-zhèr wàng-xī-zǒu. | Go west from here.

5. Cóng-'Máo-Xiānsheng-jiā | Go north from Mr. Mao's home.
   wàng-béi-zǒu. |

6. Wàng-'dōng-guǎi háishi-wàng- | Does one turn east or west?
   'xī-guǎi? |

7. Cóng-nǎr wàng-dōng-zǒu? | From where do you go east?

8. Cóng-zhèr wàng-dōng-zǒu. | Go east from here.

9. Cóng-zhèr-dào-shūdiàn wàng- | Go north from here to the book-
   béi-zǒu. | store.

10. Cóng-zhèr-dào-túshūguǎn-qu, | To go from here to the library,
    wàng-béi-guǎi. | turn north.

Pattern 9.5. Coverb of Conveyance (Note 5 below)

(S)	zuò	N	qù
(Subject)	by	Noun	go
Wǒ	zuò	chē	qù.

'I go by car.'

1. Zuò-'diànchē-lái. | Come by streetcar.

2. Tā-jīntian zuò-'gōnggòng- | He's coming by bus today.
   qìchē-lái. |

3. Nǐ-míngtian zuò-'shénmo- | What sort of vehicle are you tak-
   chē-qù? | ing tomorrow?

4. 'Bái-Xiáojie bú-zuò-'qìchē- | Isn't Miss Bai coming by auto-
   lái-ma? | mobile?

5. Nǐmen dōu-zuò-'gōnggòng-qì- | All of you go by bus.
   chē-qù. |

6. Wǒ-cóng-gōngyuán zuò-qìchē- | I'm taking a car from the park.
   qu. |

7. 'Gāo-Xiānsheng zuò-gōnggòng- | Mr. Gao is coming to the library
   qìchē dào-túshūguǎn-lái. | by bus.

8. Wó-xiǎng-cóng-zhèr zuò- | **I plan to go by streetcar to the**
   diànchē dào-Gāo-jia-qu. | **Gao home from here.**

9. Nǐmen-cóng-zhèr dōu-zuò- | Are you all going from here to
   qìchē dào-gōngyuán-qu-ma? | the park by car?

10. Wǒ-cóng-Gāo-jia zuò-diànchē | I'm going from the Gao home to
    dào-túshūguǎn-qu. | the library by streetcar.

SUBSTITUTION TABLES

I: 72 sentences (Note 1)

wǒ	dào	túshūguǎn	lái
nǐ		gōngyuán	qù
tā		dàxué	
shéi		shūdiàn	

II: 64 sentences (Note 1)

tā	shénmo-shíhou	dào	túshūguǎn	lai
tāmen	míngtian		gōngyuán	qu
	wǎnshang		dàxué	
	sāndiǎn-zhōng		shūdiàn	

III: 72 sentences (Note 6)

(The asterisk * indicates positions in either of which lái or qù may be used.)

		*			*
wǒ	———	lái	kàn-'Gāo-Xiānsheng	lái
nǐ	men	qù	zhǎo-péngyou	qù
tā			mǎi-dìtú	

IV: 72 sentences (Note 6)

(The asterisk * indicates that only words on the same line may be selected from these two columns.)

		*			*
wǒ	dào	túshūguǎn	lái	jiè-shū
nǐ		shūdiàn	qù	mǎi-dìtú
tā		Gāo-jia		kàn-'Gāo-Xiānsheng
wǒmen		gōngyuán		zhǎo-péngyou
nǐmen		dàxué		niàn-shū
tāmen		túshūguǎn		kàn-shū

V: 72 sentences (Note 2)

wǒ	cóng	túshūguǎn	lái	———
nǐ		gōngyuán	zǒu	ma?
tā		dàxué		
		shūdiàn		
		nèr		
		Dōngběi		

VI: 64 sentences (Note 3)

cóng	zhèr	dào	túshūguǎn	'zěnmo-zǒu?
	nèr		gōngyuán	yǒu-sānlǐ-lù
	tā-jiā		dàxué	'duó-yuǎn?
	Wáng-jia		shūdiàn	yóu-'jílǐ-lù?

VII: 70 sentences (Note. 4)

cóng	túshūguǎn	wàng	dōng	zǒu
	gōngyuán		xī	guǎi
	dàxué		nán	
	shūdiàn		béi	
	Wáng-jia		yòu	
			zuó	
			nár	

VIII: 72 sentences (Note 5)

wǒ	zuò	chē	_____
nǐ		qìchē	lái
tā		diànchē	qù
		gōnggòng-qìchē	dào-shūdiàn
		shénmo-chē	
		tāde-chē	

PRONUNCIATION DRILLS

I. Contrast of "i" after Retroflexes and "i" after Sibilants

(a) zhī   zī   (d) zhì   zì

(b) chí   cí   (e) chì   cì

(c) shǐ   sǐ   (f) shì   sì

II. Contrast of "i" and <u>i</u>

(a) zhī   jī   (d) zī   jī

(b) chí   qí   (e) cí   qí

(c) shī   xī   (f) sī   xī

JUST THE OPPOSITE

Change each of the following sentences to a sentence of opposite meaning by substituting one new word. For example, change <u>Wàng-zuǒbiar-zǒu</u> 'Go toward the left' to <u>Wàng-yòubiar-zǒu</u> 'Go toward the right.'

1. Cóng-zhèr wàng-běibiar-guǎi.

2. Tā-míngtian dào-shūdiàn-lái.

3. Wǒ-zài-'nǎr-shàng-chē?

4. Wó-xiǎng-'xiān-kàn-shū.

5. Wǒmen-túshūguǎnde-shū hěn-duō.

6. Dàxué-lí-zhèr hén-yuǎn.

7. Tāmen-dōu-zài-lǐtou chī-fàn.

8. Zhèige-běnzi bú-tài-xiǎo-ma?

9. 'Yīngguo-huà hěn-róngyi-xué.

10. Fángzi-qiántou méi-yǒu-rén.

TAKE YOUR PICK

Answer each of the following questions by choosing one of the two alternatives.
For example: <u>Tā-zài-zhèr-'shàng-chē</u> háishi-'xià-chē?   ' Does he get on or
off the car here?' can be answered by either <u>Tā-zài-zhèr-'shàng-chē</u> 'He gets
on the car here' or <u>Tā-zài-zhèr-'xià-chē</u> 'He gets off the car here.'

1. Gōngyuán-mén-kǒur zài-běibiar háishi-zài-nánbiar?

2. Guò-'liǎngge-lù-kǒur háishi-guò-'sānge-lù-kǒur?

3. Tā-'jīntian-lái háishi-'míngtian-lái?

4. Nǐ-zuò-'qìchē-qù háishi-zuò-'diànchē-qù?

5. Wàng-'dōng-guǎi háishi-wàng-'xī-guǎi?

6. Zuò-'sānhao-chē háishi-zuò-'sìhao-chē-ne?

7. Shi-zuò-'diànchē-hǎo háishi-zuò-'gōnggòng-qìchē-hǎo?

8. Shi-'zhèrde-rén-duō háishi-'nèrde-rén-duō?

9. Shi-zǒu-'lù-hǎo háishi-zuò-'chē-hǎo?

10. Tāmen-'yìzhí-zǒu háishi-xiān-wàng-'béi-guǎi?

CHECKING UP

Answer the following questions based on the Dialogue.

1. 'Bái-Xiānsheng xiān-dào-nǎr-qu?

2. 'Bái-Xiānsheng xiǎng-cóng-shūdiàn dào-nǎr-qu?

3. Gōnggòng-qìchē-zhàn lí-shūdiàn-yuǎn-ma?

4. Cóng-shūdiàn dào-túshūguǎn yǒu-méi-yǒu-diànchē-kéyi-zuò?

5. Cóng-shūdiàn dào-túshūguǎn-qu dōu-yǒu-'shénmo-chē?

6. Cóng-shūdiàn guò-'jǐge-lù-kǒur jiù-shi-gōnggòng-qìchē-zhàn-ne?

7. Cóng-shūdian dào-túshūguǎn shi-wàng-béi-zǒu háishi-wàng-nán-zǒu?

8. Zuò-'jǐhào-chē 'yìzhí-jiù-dào-túshūguǎn-ne?

9. Cóng-shūdiàn-dào-túshūguǎn yào-zuò-'jǐhào-chē?

10. 'Bái-Xiānsheng zài-'nǎr-xià-chē?

11. Dào-'Gāo-Xiānsheng-jiā 'shàng-shān háishi-'xià-shān?
12. 'Bái-Xiānsheng-shuō tā-míngtian 'zài-dào-shūdiàn-lái-ma?

NOTES

1. Motion to an intended destination is expressed by the coverb dào 'to' with the verbs lái 'come' and qù 'go':

  Tā-dào-zhèr-lai. 'He is coming here.'
  Tā-dào-nèr-qu. 'He is going there.'

  Note that lái and qù are here written without a tone, as they often become neutral when used after other verbs.

2. Motion from a place is expressed by the coverb cóng 'from' with the verbs lái 'come' and zǒu 'walk, travel, depart':

  Tā-cóng-nèr-lai. 'He is coming from there.'
  Tā-cóng-nèr-zǒu. 'He is leaving from there.'

3. Motion from one place to another is expressed by the coverbs cóng 'from' and dào 'to' —always in this order—followed by a verbal phrase.

  Cóng-zhèr-dào-nèr 'zěnmo-zǒu? 'How does one go from here to there?'

4. Motion in the direction of a place which is not one's final destination is expressed by the coverb wàng 'toward' with the verbs zǒu 'travel' and guǎi 'turn':

  Wàng-dōng-zǒu. 'Go east.'
  Wàng-yòu-guǎi. 'Turn right.' or 'Make a right turn.'

  To indicate the place where (or from where) this direction is to take effect, use a cóng ('from') phrase followed by a wàng ('toward') phrase:

  Cóng-shūdiàn wàng-yòu-guǎi. 'Turn right from the bookstore.' or 'Turn right at the bookstore.'

5. The verb zuò 'sit' as a main verb also means 'ride in a conveyance':

  Wǒ-bu-xǐhuan zuò-diànchē. 'I don't like to ride streetcars.'

  As coverb it introduces the means of conveyance:

  Tā-zuò-diànchē-qu. 'He's going by streetcar.'

  Occasionally zuò is used between the coverbs cóng 'from' and dào 'to':

  Wǒ-cóng-zhèr zuò-chē-dào-tā-jiā-qu. 'I'm going from here to his home by car.'

6. Lái and qù express purpose when followed immediately by another verb:

  Wǒ-lái-jiè-shū. 'I've come to borrow some books.'
  Wǒ-qù-jiè-shū. 'I'm going (in order) to borrow some books.'

Less commonly they are used in this meaning at the end of a sentence:

Wŏ-jiè-shū-lai. 'I've come to borrow some books.'

7. The noun-sharing construction shown in Pattern 8.2 (above, p. 94) demonstrated the use of a noun as the object of the preceding verb and the subject of the following one:

Wŏ-qĭng-ta chī-fàn. 'I'm inviting him to dinner.'

Another type of noun-sharing is illustrated in this sentence:

Wŏ-méi-yŏu-shū kéyi-kàn. ' I don't have any books (which I) can read.'

Here, the noun shū 'book' is simultaneously the object of the two verbs kàn 'read' and yŏu 'have.'

8. The particle ne is often used at the end of a sentence containing a question word, particularly when the question is emphatic:

Nĭ-bú-dào-nèr-qu-ma? Dào-năr-qu-ne? ' You're not going there? Where are you going?'

9. Movable adverbs, like other adverbs, must come before the verb. Unlike other adverbs, which must be placed immediately before the verb, movable adverbs can occur before or after the subject:

Wŏ huòzhĕ míngtian qu. or Huòzhĕ wŏ míngtian qu. 'Perhaps I'll go tomorrow.'

10. The expression huòzhĕ is used singly in the meaning 'or.' It occurs singly or doubly in the meaning 'either . . . or':

Tā-(huòzhĕ)-jīntian huòzhĕ-míngtian-qù. 'He'll go (either) today or tomorrow.'

It is also used singly in the meaning 'perhaps':

Tā-huòzhĕ-míngtian-lái. 'Perhaps he'll come tomorrow.'

(See also Supplementary Lesson 9, Note 1)

Lesson 10 CONVERSING WITH A TICKET SELLER

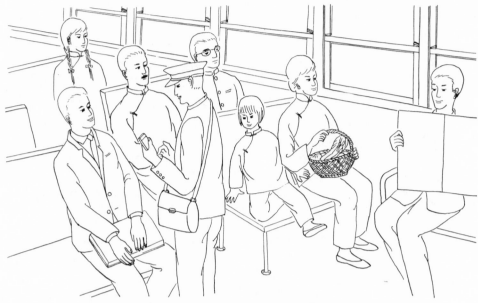

"Xiānsheng, qíng-mǎi-piào."

Dialogue: Mr. White boards a bus and gets to talking with the ticket seller.

'Bái-Xiānsheng, màipiàoyuán liǎngge-rén zài-gōnggòng-qìchēshang tán-huà.	Mr. White and the ticket seller converse on the bus.
MPY: Xiānsheng, qíng-mǎi-piào.	Sir, get your ticket here. [lit. Please buy a ticket.]
Bái : 'Duōshao-qián?	How much?
MPY: Nín-dào-nǎr-qu? 5	Where are you going?
Bái : Wǒ-dào-túshūguǎn-qu.	To the library.
MPY: Dào-túshūguǎn 'liǎngmáo-qián. Nín-Zhōngwén shuōde-'zhēn-hǎo.	To the library (is) twenty cents. You speak Chinese very well.
Bái : Wǒ-shuōde-'bù-hǎo. Shuōde- 10 tài-màn. Yóu-hěn-duō-wài-guo-rén shuōde-bí-wó-hǎo-de-duō.	I don't speak (it) well. I speak too slowly. There are lots of foreigners who speak much better than I do.
MPY: Nín-shi-'něiguó-rén-ne?	What country are you from?
Bái : Wǒ-shi-'Měiguo-rén. 15	I'm an American.

MPY: Nín-zài-zhèr niàn-shū   Are you studying or working
      háishi-zuò-shì-ne?   here?

Bái : Wǒ-niàn-shū-ne.   I'm studying.

MPY: Nín-zài-Yuǎndōng-Dàxué   Are you studying at Far Eastern
      niàn-shū-ma?   20   University?

Bái : Shì. Wǒ-zài-Yuǎn-Dà-   Yes. I'm studying at Far East-
      niàn-shū.   ern.

MPY: Yuǎndōng-Dàxué wàiguo-   Are there many foreign students
      xuésheng-duō-ma?   at Far Eastern University?

Bái : Hěn-duō.   25   Quite a few.

MPY: Zài-Měiguode-dàxué yé-   Are there also foreign students
      yǒu-'wàiguo-xuésheng-ma?   at American universities?

Bái : Měiguo-dàxué-lǐtou wàiguo-   There are even more foreign
      xuésheng-'gèng-duō. . . .   students in American universi-
      Zhèr-dào-túshūguǎn yào- 30   ties . . . . How long does it take
      'duōshao-shíhou?   from here to the library?

MPY: Gōnggòng-qìchē bǐ-diànchē   The bus is a little faster than
      zǒude-'kuài-yìdiǎr. Chàbu-   the streetcar. We can get there
      duō-'èrshifēn-zhōng jiù-   in about twenty minutes.
      kéyi-dào.   35

Bái : Xiànzai-'jídiǎn-zhōng?   What time is it now?

MPY: Chà-yíkè-wúdiǎn. Bù.   A quarter of five. No, it's ten
      Chà-shífēn-wúdiǎn. Nín-   of five. Are you going to the li-
      dào-túshūguǎn qu-kàn-shū-   brary to read?
      ma?   40

Bái : Wǒ-qù-'jiè-shū.   I'm going to check out some
                                     books.

MPY: Nín-jiā-zài-zhèr-ma?   Is your home here?

Bái : Bú-zài-zhèr. Wǒ-jiā-zài-   No. My home is in America.
      Měiguo.

MPY: Nín-jiāli dōu-yǒu-'shénmo- 45   What family do you have?
      rén?

Bái : Wǒ-jiāli-yǒu-fùqin-mǔqin,   In my family there's my father
      hái-yǒu-yíge-dìdi、 yíge-   and mother, and also a younger
      mèimei.   brother and a younger sister.

MPY: Dìdi-dà háishi-mèimei-dà- 50   Which is older, (your) younger
      ne?   brother or (your) younger sis-
                                     ter?

Bái : Dìdi-bǐ-mèimei-dà.   My [younger] brother is older
                                     than my [younger] sister.

MPY: Tāmen-dōu-niàn-shū-ma?   Are they both studying?

Bái : Tāmen-dōu-niàn-shū. Dìdi-   They both are. My brother is
      zài-'zhōngxué-niàn-shū. 55   studying in high school, and my
      Mèimei-zài-'xiǎoxué-niàn-   sister is studying in elementary
      shū.   school.

MPY : Nín-fùqin-zuò-'shénmo-   What does your father do?
shì ?

Bái : Wǒ-fùqin shi-'zhōngxué-   60   My father's a high-school teach-
jiàoyuán. Mǔqin shi-   er. (My) mother is a grade-
'xiǎoxué-jiàoyuán. 'Nǐ-   school teacher. Who's in your
jiāli dōu-yǒu-'shénmo-   family?
rén?

MPY : Wó-yǒu-tàitai, hái-yóu-   65   I have a wife and two children.
liǎngge-háizi.

Bái : Nán-háizi háishi-nǚ-hái-   Boys or girls?
zi-ne?

MPY : Yíge-'nán-háizi, yíge-   One boy, one girl.
'nǚ-háizi.   70

Bái : Tāmen-duó-dà?   How old are they?

MPY : Nán-háizi-qīsuì, nǚ-háizi-   The boy is seven, the girl two.
liǎngsuì. Zhēn-qíguài.   It's really amazing. This girl
Zhèige-nǚ-háizi 'yìsuì-   could walk at one year of age.
jiù-huì-zǒu-lù. Tā-xiàn-   75   Now she can run, and runs very
zài-huì-pǎo, yé-pǎode-hěn-   fast, too.
kuài.

Bái : Tāmen-míngzi dōu-jiào-   What are their names?
shénmo?

MPY : Nán-háizi-jiào-Láohu.   80   The boy is called Tiger. The
Nǚ-háizi-jiào-Xiǎomèi.   girl is called Little Sister.

Bái : Nán-háizi-niàn-shū-ma?   **Does the boy go to school?**

MPY : Niàn-shū. Zài-xiǎoxué-   Yes. He goes to grade school.
niàn-shū.

Bái : Nǐ-tàitai-yě-zuò-shì-ma?   85   Does your wife work too?

MPY : Tā-bú-zuò-shì . . . .   No, she doesn't . . . . Sir, see,
Xiānsheng, nín-kàn, qián-   up ahead is the library.
tou jiù-shi-túshūguǎn.

Bái : Hǎo, wǒ-xià-chē. Zàijiàn.   Fine. I'll get off. Good-bye.

MPY : Zàijiàn, zàijiàn.   90   Good-bye.

VOCABULARY

bǐ	compared to (CV)
chà	differ, fall short, lack (V)
chàbuduō	almost [lit. differ not much]
dìdi	younger brother (N)
fēn	(measure for minutes)
fùqin	father (N) [lit. father relative]

gèng	(still) more (AD)
háizi	child (N)
jiào	be called (EV) name, call; call, summon (TV)
jiàoyuán	teacher (N) [lit. teach person]
jiù	immediately, then (AD)
kè	quarter (of an hour) (M)
kuài	fast (SV)
láohu	tiger (N) [lit. old tiger]
màipiàoyuán	ticket seller (N) [lit. sell-ticket person](See Supplementary Lesson 10, Note 1)
màn	slow (SV)
mèimei	younger sister (N)
míngzi	name (N)
mǔqin	mother (N) [lit. mother relative]
nán	male
nǔ	female
pǎo	run (IV)
piào	ticket (N)
qíguài	amazing; amazed (SV) [lit. strange queer]
shì	affair, matter, work (N) (See Supplementary Lesson 10, Note 2)
suì	year (of age) (M)
tán	converse, talk (IV)
xiǎoxué	elementary school (N) [lit. small school]
yìdiǎr	a little [lit. one dot]
Yuǎndōng	Far East (PW)
zhēn	really (AD)
zhōngxué	middle school (in China), high school (in U.S.) (N)
zuò	do, make (TV)

SENTENCE BUILD-UP

bǐ	compared to
bǐ-hóngde	compared to a red one
1. Lánde-bǐ-hóngde-hǎo.	A blue one is better than a red one.
bǐ-nèige-hǎo	better than that
bǐ-nèige-hǎo-yìdiǎr	a little better than that

2. Zhèige-bǐ-nèige hǎo-yìdiǎr.   This is a little better than that.

    bǐ-diànchē-hǎo   better than streetcars
    bǐ-diànchē-háo-diar   somewhat better than street-
                                                            cars
3. Qìchē-bǐ-diànchē háo-diar.   Autos are somewhat better than
                                                     streetcars.

    bǐ-nèige-hǎo   better than that
    bǐ-nèige-hǎode-duō   a lot better than that
4. Zhèige-bǐ-nèige hǎode-duō.   This is a lot better than that.

    bǐ-nèige-hǎo   better than that
    bǐ-nèige-'gèng-hǎo   even better than that
5. Zhèige-bǐ-nèige 'gèng-hǎo.   This is even better than that.

    jiàoyuán   teacher
    bǐ-jiàoyuán-duō   more numerous than teach-
                                                            ers
6. Xuésheng-bǐ-jiàoyuán-duō.   There are more students than
                                                     teachers.

    láohu   tiger
    bǐ-nèige-láohu-dà   bigger than that tiger
7. 'Zhèige-láohu bǐ-'nèige-dà.   This tiger is bigger than that
                                                     one.

    bǐ-Máo-Tàitai-dà   older than Mrs. Mao
    bǐ-Máo-Tàitai-dà-yìdiǎr   a little older than Mrs. Mao
8. 'Gāo-Tàitai bǐ-'Máo-Tàitai-   Mrs. Gao is a little older than
    dà-yìdiǎr.   Mrs. Mao.

    bǐ-xiě-zì   compared to writing
    bǐ-xiě-zì-róngyi   easier than writing
9. Shuō-huà bǐ-xiě-zì-róngyi.   Speaking is easier than writing.

    kuài   fast
    zǒude-kuài   walk fast
10. Tā-yé-zǒude-kuài.   He also walks fast.

    zǒude-kuài   walk fast
    zǒude-'kuài-bu-kuài?   walk fast or not?
11. Tāmen-dōu-zǒude 'kuài-bu-   Are they all walking fast?
    kuài?

    chīde-duō   eat a lot
    chīde-tài-duō   eat too much
12. Nèige-xuésheng chīde-tài-   That student eats too much.
    duō.

    chīde-shǎo   eat little
    chīde-tài-shǎo   eat too little
13. Nèiwèi-xiáojie chīde-tài-   That young lady eats too little.
    shǎo.

       pǎo   run

       pǎode-kuài   run fast

14. Láohu yé-pǎode-hěn-kuài.   Tigers also run fast.

       màn   slow

       zǒude-hěn-màn   travel very slowly

15. Diànchē-zǒude-hěn-màn.   Streetcars go very slowly.

       fùqin   father

       bí-wǒ-fùqin   compared to my father

16. Wó-bí-wǒ-fùqin gāo-yìdiǎr.   I'm a little taller than my father.

       mǔqin   mother

       Zhāng-Xiānshengde-mǔqin   Mr. Johnson's mother

17. Zhāng-Xiānshengde-mǔqin shi-   Mr. Johnson's mother is Chi-
     Zhōngguo-rén.   nese.

       bǐ-tā   compared to him

       shuōde-hǎo   speak well

18. Ní-bǐ-tā-shuōde-hǎo.   You speak better than he does.

       bǐ-tā-hǎo   better than he

19. Nǐ-shuōde-bǐ-tā-hǎo.   You speak better than he does.

       bǐ-tā-hǎo   better than he

       bǐ-tā-hǎode-duō   a lot better than he

20. Nǐ-shuōde bǐ-tā-hǎode-duō.   You speak a lot better than he
                                     does.

       mài-Zhōngwén-shū   sell Chinese books

       màide-hěn-duō   sell a lot

21. Tāmen-mài-Zhōngwén-shū   They sell a lot of Chinese books.
     màide-hěn-duō.

       zuò   do

       zuò-shénmo?   do what?

22. Tā-zuò-shénmo?   What's he doing?

       shì   task <u>or</u> job

       zuò-shì   work <u>at</u> something

23. 'Wáng-Xiānsheng zuò-'shén-   What sort of work does Mr. King
     mo-shì?   do?

       nán   male

       nán-de   man <u>or</u> men

24. Nǐmende-jiàoyuán dōu-shi-   Are all your teachers men?
     nán-de-ma?

       nǚ   female

       nǚ-péngyou   girl friend

25. Tāde-nǚ-péngyou-bù-shǎo.   He has quite a few girl friends.

       háizi   child

       xuéde-tài-màn   learn too slowly

26. Nèige-háizi xué-Yīngguo-huà   That child is learning English
     xuéde-tài-màn.   too slowly.

         xiě-Zhōngguo-zì   write Chinese characters
         xiěde-bí-wó-hǎo   write better than I do
27. Tā-xiě-Zhōngguo-zì xiěde-bí-   He writes Chinese characters
     wó-hǎo.   better than I do.

         xiěde-bí-wó-hǎo   write better than I do
         bí-wó-xiěde-hǎo   write better than I do
28. Tā-xiě-Zhōngguo-zì bí-wó-   He writes Chinese characters
     xiěde-hǎo.   better than I do.

         zhēn   real or really
         xiěde-zhēn-hǎo   write really well
29. Nǐde-háizi-xiě-Zhōngguo-zì   Your child writes Chinese char-
     xiěde-zhēn-hǎo.   acters really well.

         dìdi   younger brother
         chīde-duō   eat a lot
30. Dìdi-chīde-bí-wǒ-duō.   (My) younger brother eats more
                                             than I do.

         mèimei   younger sister
         mèimei-xuéde-hǎo   younger sister learns well
31. Shi-'dìdi-xuéde-hǎo háishi-   Who learns better,   younger
     'mèimei-xuéde-hǎo?   brother or younger sister?

         jiào   call or summon
32. Jiào-tā-lái.   Tell him to come.

         jiào   be called
         jiào-shénmo?   called what?
33. Zhèige-jiào-shénmo?   What's this called?

         míngzi   name
         jiào-'shénmo-míngzi?   called by what name?
34. Zhèige-jiào-'shénmo-míngzi?   What's the name of this?

         míngzi   name
         míngzi-jiào-shénmo?   called by what name?
35. Mèimei míngzi-jiào-shénmo?   What's (your) younger sister's
                                             name?

         fēn   (measure for minutes)
         shísānfēn   thirteen minutes
36. Liùdiǎn-shísānfēn.   Six thirteen.

         chà   lack, be short
         chà-sānkuài-qián   be short three dollars
37. Bù-néng-mǎi, wǒ-chà-sānkuài-   I can't buy it; I'm short three
     qián.   dollars.

         chà-sānfēn   lacking three minutes
38. Xiànzài bādiǎn-chà-sānfēn.   It's now three of eight.

         chà-sānfēn   lacking three minutes
39. Xiànzài chà-sānfēn-bādiǎn.   It's now three of eight.

guò   pass
guò-sānfēn   three minutes after
40. Xiànzài bādiǎn-guò-sānfēn.   It's now three after eight.

kè   quarter hour
yíkè   one quarter hour
41. Tā-qīdiǎn-yíkè-lái.   He's coming at quarter after
                                            seven.

chàbuduō   almost
42. ·Xiànzài-chàbuduō liùdiǎn-   It's now almost 6:45.
    sānkè.

suì   year of age
shíliùsuì   sixteen years of age
43. Nèige-nǚ-xuésheng shíliùsuì.   That girl student is sixteen
                                            years old.

Yuǎndōng   Far East
44. Zhōngguo-zài-Yuǎndōng.   China is in the Far East.

piào   ticket
mǎi-piào   buy a ticket
45. Wǒ-zài-'nǎr-mǎi-piào?   Where do I buy a ticket?

mài-piào   sell tickets
màipiàoyuán   ticket seller
46. Màipiàoyuán shi-'sānshi-duō-   The ticket seller is a little over
    suìde-rén.   thirty years old.

xiǎoxué   elementary school
zài-xiǎoxué-niàn-shū   study in elementary school
47. Wǒ-dìdi zài-xiǎoxué-niàn-   My younger brother goes to ele-
    shū.   mentary school.

zhōngxué   middle school
'zhōngxuéde-xuésheng   middle-school student
48. Wǒmen-dōu-shi 'zhōngxuéde-   We are all middle-school stu-
    xuésheng.   dents.

tán   converse
tán-huà   converse
49. Tāmen-zài-jiāli-tán-huà.   They're having a chat in the
                                            house.

qíguài   amazing, strange
qíguàide-shì   amazing matter
50. Zhèi-shi-hěn-qíguàide-shì.   This is quite a strange affair.

qíguài   amazed
wó-hěn-qíguài   I'm amazed
51. Wó-hěn-qíguài. Sānsuìde-   I'm amazed! A three-year-old
    háizi néng-kàn-shū!   child can read!

      jiù   immediately
52. Wǒ-'jiù-zǒu.   I'm leaving immediately.

      shì   task, job
      yǒu-shì   have something to do
53. Nǐ-xiànzài-yǒu-shì-ma?   Are you busy now?

      duì   correct, true, right
      shuōde-duì   speak correctly
54. Nǐ-shuōde-hěn-duì.   You're quite right in what you
                                                  say.

                        PATTERN DRILLS

              Pattern 10.1. Comparison (Note 1 below)

      A   bǐ   B   SV

      A   compared to   B   is/are more SV

   Zhèige   bǐ   nèige   hǎo.

   'This is better than that.'

1. 'Nǐ-bǐ-wǒ-gāo.   You are taller than I.

2. Nǐ-bǐ-wǒ-gāo-diar.   You are a bit taller than I.

3. Nǐ-bǐ-wǒ-'gāo-yìdiǎr.   You're a little taller than I.

4. Nǐ-bǐ-wǒ-gāode-duō.   You're a lot taller than I.

5. Nèige-xuésheng bǐ-xiānsheng   That student is a little taller
    'gāo-yìdiǎr.   than the teacher.

6. Nèige-fángzi bǐ-zhèige-fángzi   That house is a little bigger than
    'dà-yìdiǎr.   this house.

7. Tā-bǐ-wǒ-dàde-duō.   He is a lot older than I.

8. Nèige-láohu bǐ-zhèige 'dà-   That tiger is a little bigger than
    yìdiǎr.   this one.

9. Gōngyuán bǐ-túshūguán-yuǎn.   The park is farther away than
                                                  the library.

10. Wǒ-jiā bǐ-nǐ-jiā-jìn.   My home is closer than your
                                                  home.

11. Gāngbǐ bǐ-qiānbǐ-hǎo.   A pen is better than a pencil.

12. Tāde-dìtú bǐ-wǒde-hǎo. Nǐde-   His map is better than mine.
    bǐ-tāde 'gèng-hǎo.   Yours is still better than his.

13. 'Qián-Xiǎojie bǐ-'Máo-Xiáojie   Miss Qian is a little older than
    'dà-yìdiǎr.   Miss Mao.

14. 'Gāo-Xiáojie bǐ-'Máo-Xiáojie   Miss Gao is a little younger than
    'xiǎo-yìdiǎr.   Miss Mao.

15. Nǐde-qián bǐ-wǒde-qián 'duō-   You have a little more money
     yìdiǎr. Tāde-qián bǐ-nǐde-   than I. He has a little more even
     qián 'gèng-duō-yìdiǎr.   than you.

16. 'Wàitoude-rén bǐ-'lǐtoude-   There are a few more people
     rén duō-yìdiǎr.   outside than inside.

17. Zhèige-jiàoyuán bǐ-nèige-   This teacher is better than that
     hǎo.   one.

18. Niàn-shū bǐ-xiě-zì-róngyi.   Reading is easier than writing.

19. Shuō-huà bǐ-niàn-shū-nán.   Speaking is harder than reading.

20. Mǎi-shū bǐ-jiè-shū-hǎo.   It's better to buy books than to
                                          borrow books.

Pattern 10.2.   Adverbs of Manner   (Note 2 below)

       S   V   -de   SV

    Subject   Verb   -de   Stative Verb
      Tā   chī   -de   kuài.

    'He eats fast.'

1. Tā-shuōde-kuài-ma?   Does he talk fast?

2. Tā-chīde-tài-màn.   He eats too slowly.

3. Tā-xuéde-bú-kuài.   He learns slowly.

4. Láohu pǎode-'kuài-bu-kuài?   Do tigers run fast?

5. Tā-mǔqin xiěde-hǎo. Tā-fùqin   His mother writes well. His fa-
    xiěde-'gèng-hǎo.   ther writes even better.

6. 'Wáng-Xiānsheng-zǒude-màn.   Mr. Wang walks slowly. Mr. Bai
    'Bái-Xiānsheng-zǒude-hěn-kuài.   walks very fast.

7. Nèige-xuésheng niànde-hén-hǎo.   **That student reads aloud very**
    'Wáng-Xiáojie niànde-bù-hǎo.   **well. Miss Wang reads badly.**

8. Tāmen-màide-hěn-duō.   They sell a lot.

9. Tāmen dōu-chīde-tài-shǎo.   They all eat too little.

10. 'Wáng-Xiánsheng shuōde-'hǎo-   Does Mr. Wang speak well?
    bu-hǎo?

Pattern 10.3.   Comparison with Adverbs of Manner   (Note 3 below)
Pattern 10.3a.

       S   bǐ   O   V   -de   SV

    Subject   compared to   Object   Verb   -de   Stative Verb
      Tā   bǐ   wǒ   shuō   -de   hǎo.

    'He speaks better than I do.'

Pattern 10.3 b.

S	V	-de	bǐ	O	SV
Subject	Verb	-de	compared to	Object	Stative Verb
Tā	shuō	-de	bí	wó	hǎo.

'He speaks better than I do.'

1. Tā-bí-wó-xiěde-hǎo.

He writes better than I do.

2. Nǐ-fùqin bí-wǒ-fùqin shuōde-hǎo.

Your father speaks better than my father does.

3. 'Xiáo-láohu bǐ-'dà-láohu-chī-de-gèng-duō.

Young tigers eat even more than old tigers.

4. Ní-bǐ-tā niànde-'gèng-hǎo.

You read aloud even better than he does.

5. Zhèiwèi-jiàoyuán bǐ-nèiwèi-jiàoyuán xiěde-hǎo.

This teacher writes better than that teacher.

6. Tā-bí-wó-zǒude-màn.

He walks more slowly than I do.

7. 'Gāo-Xiānsheng xiěde-bí-wó-hǎode-duō.

Mr. Gao writes a lot better than I do.

8. Tā-bí-wǒ-chīde-duō.

He eats more than I do.

9. 'Zhāng-Xiānsheng shuōde-bí-wǒ-'kuài-yìdiǎr.

Mr. Johnson talks a little faster than I do.

10. Dìdi-bǐ-mèimei zǒude-kuài-diar.

My (younger) brother walks a little faster than my (younger) sister.

Pattern 10.4. Objects with Adverbs of Manner (Note 4 below)

S	(V)	O	V	-de	SV
Subject	(Verb)	Object	Verb	-de	Stative Verb
Tā	(shuō)	**Zhōngwén**	shuō	-de	hǎo.

'He speaks Chinese well.'

1. **Nǐ-Zhōngwén shuōde-hén-hǎo.**

You speak Chinese very well.

2. Ní-xiě-Zhōngguo-zì xiěde-hén-hǎo.

You write Chinese characters very well.

3. Tā-chī-fàn chīde-'duō-bu-duō?

Does he eat a lot?

4. Tā-niàn-shū niànde-tài-shǎo.

He studies too little.

5. Bái-Xiānsheng-kàn-shū kànde-duō.

Mr. Bai reads a lot.

6. Tā-kàn-shū kànde-tài-duō.	He reads too much.
7. 'Gāo-Xiáojie-mǎi-shū mǎide-hěn-duō.	Miss Gao buys a lot of books.
8. 'Bái-Xiānsheng-chī-fàn chīde-tài-kuài.	Mr. White eats too fast.
9. 'Qián-Xiānsheng-shuō-Yīngwén shuōde-bú-kuài.	Mr. Qian speaks English slowly.
10. 'Zhèige-shūdiàn 'Zhōngwén-shū màide-duō.	This bookstore sells lots of Chinese books.
11. Shūdiàn gāngbǐ-màide-shǎo.	The bookstore sells few fountain pens.
12. Xuésheng-mái-běnzi mǎide-tài-duō.	Students buy too many notebooks.
13. Tāmen-qǐng-péngyou qǐngde-hěn-duō.	They invite lots of friends.
14. 'Wáng-Xiānsheng Zhōngwén-shū kànde-hěn-duō.	Mr. King reads lots of Chinese books.
15. Wǒ-fùqin-zǒu-lù zǒude-hěn-duō.	My father walks quite a bit.

Pattern 10.5.   Objects with Comparisons and Stative Verbs   (Note 4 below)

Pattern 10.5 a.

S	(V_1)	O_1	bǐ	O_2	V_1	-de	SV
Subject	(Verb)	Object	compared to	Object	Verb	-de	Stative Verb
Tā	mǎi	shū	bǐ	wó	mǎi	-de	duō.

'He buys more books than I do.'

Pattern 10.5 b.

S	(V_1)	O_1	V_1	-de	bǐ	O_2	SV
Subject	(Verb)	Object	Verb	-de	compared to	Object	Stative Verb
Tā	mǎi	shū	mǎi	-de	bǐ	wǒ	duō.

'He buys more books than I do.'

1. Ní-mǎi-shū bí-wó-mǎide-duō.	You buy more books than I do.
2. Ní-mǎi-shū mǎide-bí-wǒ-duō.	You buy more books than I do.
3. Tā-zuò-chē zuòde-bí-wǒ-duō.	He rides more than I do.
4. Tā-zuò-chē bí-wǒ-zuòde-duō.	He rides more than I do.
5. 'Gāo-Xiānsheng-kàn-shū bí-wǒ-kànde-duō.	Mr. Gao reads more than I do.

6. 'Wáng-Xiānsheng-kàn-shū kànde-   Mr. King reads more than I do.
    bǐ-wǒ-duō.

7. 'Bái-Xiáojie-shuō-huà bǐ-'Gāo-   Miss Bai speaks less than Miss
    Xiáojie-shuōde-shǎo.   Gao does.

8. 'Wáng-Xiānsheng-shuō-huà   Mr. King talks more than Mr.
    shuōde-bǐ-'Bái-Xiānsheng-duō.   White does.

9. Nǐ-Zhōngwén shuōde-bǐ-tā-   You speak Chinese better than
    hǎo.   he does.

10. Tā-Zhōngguo-huà bǐ-wǒ-shuō-   He speaks Chinese better than I
    de-hǎo.   do.

11. Gāo-'Xiānsheng-chī-fàn bǐ-Gāo-   Mr. Gao eats faster than Mrs.
    'Tàitai-chīde-kuài.   Gao does.

12. 'Máo-Xiānsheng-xiě-zì xiěde-   Mr. Mao writes better than Mr.
    bǐ-'Bái-Xiānsheng-hǎo.   Bai does.

13. Tā-kàn-shū kànde-bǐ-wǒ-duō.   He reads more than I do.

14. Tā-zǒu-lù bǐ-wó-zǒude-duō.   He walks more than I do.

15. 'Zhèige-shūdiàn Zhōngwén-shū   This bookstore sells more Chi-
    màide-bǐ-'nèige-shūdiàn-duō.   nese books than that bookstore
                                        does.

SUBSTITUTION TABLES

I: 96 sentences (Note 1)

nèiwèi-xiānsheng	bǐ	wǒ	hǎo	——
wǒde-péngyou		tā	gāo	diar
nèige-xuésheng			dà	yìdiǎr
nèiwèi-jiàoyuán				-de-duō

II: 80 sentences (Note 2)

wǒ	shuō	-de	——	kuài
nǐ	zǒu		hěn	màn
	xué		bú	
	pǎo		tài	
			gèng	

III: 96 sentences (Note 3)

(The asterisk * indicates columns either one of which may be chosen.)

	*			*		
wó	bǐ-nǐ	shuō	-de	bǐ-nǐ	kuài	——
	bǐ-tā	chī		bǐ-tā	màn	yìdiǎr
		zǒu				-de-duō
		xué				

IV: 80 sentences (Notes 2, 4)

In columns A, B, and C, only items in the same row may
be taken together. Column A may be omitted altogether.

	A	B	C			
tā	shuō	Yīngguo-huà	shuō	-de	———	kuài
	chī	Zhōngguo-fàn	chī		hěn	màn
	zuò	shì	zuò		bú	
	xiě	Zhōngguo-zì	xiě		tài	
					gèng	

V: 96 sentences (Notes 2–4)

In columns A, B, and C, only items in the same row may
be taken together. Column A may be omitted altogether.
Either (but not both) of the asterisked columns may be
used.

	A	B	*	C		*	
tā	shuō	Yīngguo-huà	bí-wǒ	shuō	-de	bí-wǒ	kuài
tāmen	xiě	Zhōngguo-zì	bí-nǐ	xiě		bí-nǐ	màn
	chī	Zhōngguo-fàn		chī			

VI: 54 sentences (Note 5)

yì	-diǎn	———	shíyīfēn
liǎng		chà	èrshijiǔfēn
sān		guò	yíkè
sì			
shí			
shí'èr			

PRONUNCIATION DRILLS

I. Contrast of "i" and e after Retroflexes

(a) zhī   zhē   (d) zhǐ   zhě   (h) zhì   zhè

(b) chī   chē   (e) chǐ   chě   (i) chì   chè

(c) shí   shé   (f) shǐ   shě   (j) shì   shè

                     (g) rì   rè

II. Contrast of "i" and e after Sibilants

(a) zì   zè   (b) cì   cè   (c) sì   sè

WHAT'S IN A NAME?

1. Nín-guìxìng?
   Wǒ-xìng-Wáng.
   Nín-míngzi-jiào-shénmo?
   Wǒ-míngzi-jiào-Dōngshēng.

   What is your [sur-]name?
   My [sur-]name is Wang.
   What is your given name?
   My given name is Dongsheng.

2. Tā-xìng-shénmo?
   Tā-xìng-Wáng.
   Míngzi-jiào-shénmo?
   Míngzi-jiào-Dōngshēng.

   What is his surname?
   His surname is Wang.
   What is his given name?
   His given name is Dongsheng.

3. 'Wáng-Xiānsheng, qǐng-wèn,
   nínde-míngzi-jiào-shénmo?

   Mr. Wang, may I ask, what is
   your given name?

4. Wó-xiǎng-zhīdao tāmen-jiào-
   shénmo.
   Wǒ-bù-zhīdào tāmen-jiào-
   shénmo.

   I'd like to know what their names
   are.
   I don't know what their names
   are.

5. Nín-yǒu-'Zhōngguo-míngzi-
   méi-yǒu?
   Yǒu. Wǒde-'Zhōngguo-míngzi
   jiào-Wáng-Dōngshēng.

   Do you have a Chinese name?

   Yes. My Chinese name is Wang
   Dongsheng.

6. Zhèige-jiào-shénmo?
   Zhèige-jiào-máobǐ.

   What's this called?
   This is called a writing brush.

7. Zhèige-jiào-shénmo-míngzi?
   Zhèige-jiào-máobǐ.

   What's the name of this?
   This is called a writing brush.

8. Nèige-jiào-shénmo?
   Nèige-méi-yǒu-míngzi.

   What's that called?
   That doesn't have a name.

9. Zhèiběn-shū jiào-shénmo-
   míngzi?
   Nèiběn-shū jiào-Zhōngguo-
   Wénxué.

   What's the title of this book?

   That book is entitled Chinese
   Literature.

10. Zhèige Zhōngguo-huà-jiào-
    shénmo?

    What's this called in Chinese?

11. Láohu Yīngguo-huà-jiào-
    shénmo-míngzi?

    What's the English word for
    láohu?

12. 'Tiger' Zhōngguo-huà-zěn-
    mo-shuō?

    How do you say 'tiger' in Chi-
    nese?

13. 'Tiger' Zhōngguo-huà-shi-
    láohu-ma?

    Is 'tiger' láohu in Chinese?

FRÈRE TIGER

This round can be sung to the tune of Frère Jacques.

Sānge-láohu,
Sānge-láohu,
Pǎode-kuài,
Pǎode-kuài.

Yíge-méi-you-wěiba,*
Yíge-méi-you-wěiba,
Zhēn-qíguài,
Zhēn-qíguài.

"Yíge-méi-you-wěiba"

MATCH AND FINISH

Below are ten Chinese sentences. For each, an incomplete English translation appears, but not opposite the corresponding Chinese sentence. First,
match the Chinese and the English by inserting the letters of the appropriate
Chinese sentence after the numbers of the English sentences; then complete
the translations.

a. Xiànzài-chàbuduō shíyīdiǎn-

    sānkè.

b. Xiǎomèi zài-xiǎoxué-niàn-

    shū-ma?

c. Zhōngxuéde-xuésheng bǐ-

    dàxuéde-duō. Xiǎoxuéde-

    xuésheng bǐ-zhōngxuéde

    'hái-duō.

1._____ Is his father in the Far East

    or _____

2._____ Who learns faster,_____

    _____

3._____ It's now almost _____

    _____

    _____

    _____

* Wěiba 'tail.'

d. Piào-'duōshao-qián-yìzhāng,
   nǐ-zhīdao-ma?

e. Xiànzài-chà-shífēn-yì-
   diǎn.

f. Shi-nán-háizi-xuéde-kuài
   háishi-nǚ-háizi-xuéde-
   kuài?

g. Diànchē, gōnggòng-qìchē
   dōu-yǒu-màipiàoyuán-
   ma?

h. Tāmen-zài-nèr-tán-huà
   háishi-niàn-shū?

i. Tā-fùqin zài-Yuǎndōng-ne
   háishi-zài-Měiguo-ne?

j. Láohu Yīngwén-jiào-shén-
   mo-míngzi?

4._____ What's the English word for
   _____

5._____ Does Little Sister study ____
   _____

6._____ Are they carrying on a conversation or _____
   _____

7._____ There are more middle-
   school students than _____
   _____

8._____ How much is one _____
   _____

9._____ Do both streetcars and ____
   _____

10._____ It's now ten _____
   _____

NOTES

1. The coverb **bǐ** 'compared to' is used in comparing two things:

   Nǐ-bǐ-wǒ-gāo.   'You're taller than I am.'

   Often **yìdiǎr** 'a bit' (or its shortened form **diǎr**) is added after the verb; if **yìdiǎr** is stressed, it means 'just a little." The verb is sometimes preceded by **hái** 'still,' **yào** lit. 'want,' or **hái yào** lit. 'still want.'

   Nǐ-bǐ-wǒ-'gāo-yìdiǎr.   'You're somewhat taller than I am.'
   Nǐ-bǐ-wǒ gāo-'yìdiǎr.   'You're just a little taller than I am.'
   Nǐ-bǐ-wǒ hái-yào-gāo.   'You're taller than I am.'

   The idea 'much' or 'much more' is expressed by adding **de-duō** to the verb:

   Nǐ-bǐ-wǒ-gāode-duō.   'You're much taller than I am.'

   If three things are compared, **hái**, **hái yào**, or—for even greater emphasis—**gèng** 'still more' are used before the verb:

   Nǐ-bǐ-wǒ-gāo, tā-bǐ-nǐ-'gèng-gāo.   'You're taller than I, and he is even taller than you.'

2. To express the manner in which the action of a verb takes place, Chinese
    attaches the particle de to the action verb:

  chīde-màn 'eat slowly'
  Tā-zŏude-kuài. 'He walks fast.'

Adverbs may be placed before either the action verb or the stative verb,
according to which one they modify:

  Tāmen-dōu-chīde-duō. 'They all eat a lot.'
  Tāmen-chīde-bu-shǎo. 'They eat not a little.' (Euphemism for
  'They eat quite a lot.')

3. Comparison of the manner in which two actors perform an action com-
    bines the patterns of the preceding notes, as follows:

  Tā-bǐ-wǒ-chīde-màn. 'He eats more slowly than I do.' [lit. 'He,
  compared to me, eats slowly.']

The phrase expressing comparison (here bǐ-wǒ) may follow rather than
precede the action verb:

  Tā-chīde-bǐ-wǒ-màn. 'He eats more slowly than I do.' [lit. 'He
  eats, compared to me, slowly.']

4. When an action verb followed by an expression of manner has an object,
    the object is mentioned before the verb:

  Nǐ-Yīngwén shuōde-hén-hǎo. 'You speak English very well.' [lit.
  'You English speak very well.'

Alternatively, the verb is said twice, first with its object and then
with de:

  Nǐ-shuō-Yīngwén shuōde-hén-hǎo. 'You speak English very well.'
  [lit. 'You speak English speak very well.'

The object cannot intervene between the verb and the particle de.

5. Time before and after the even hours is expressed with the verbs chà
    'lack' and guò 'pass':

  yìdiǎn-chà-wǔfēn 'five minutes of one' [lit. 'one o'clock lacking five
  minutes']
  yìdiǎn-guò-wǔfēn 'five minutes after one'
  yìdiǎn-guò-yíkè '1:15'
  yìdiǎn-chà-yíkè '12:45'
  yìdiǎn-guò-sānkè '1:45'

Guò may be omitted before the quarter hours and before minute expressions of more than two syllables:

  yìdiǎn-yíkè '1:15'
  yìdiǎn-èrshifēn '1:20'

Minute expressions with chà may be placed before the hour expressions
rather than after them:

  yìdiǎn-chà-wǔfēn
   or   } 'five minutes of one'
  chà-wǔfēn-yìdiǎn

6. In comparisons involving people, the stative verbs <u>dà</u> 'big' and <u>xiǎo</u> 'little' most often have the meanings 'older' and 'younger' respectively:

> Tā-bǐ-wǒ-dà. 'He is older than I am.'

7. A series of nouns is often followed by a summarizing expression like <u>tāmen</u> 'they' and/or some appropriate numerical expression:

> Xiānsheng, tàitai, xiáojie tāmen-dōu-zài-zhèr.   <u>or</u>
> Xiānsheng, tàitai, xiáojie sānge-rén-dōu-zài-zhèr.   <u>or</u>
> Xiānsheng, tàitai, xiáojie tāmen-sānge-rén dōu-zài-zhèr.
> 'The gentleman, the lady, and the girl are all here.'

Note that <u>dōu</u> 'all' is also frequently used to summarize a series or to express totality.

8. The Chinese educational system consists of six years of elementary school (<u>xiǎoxué</u>), six years of middle school (<u>zhōngxué</u>), and four years of college (<u>dàxué</u>). Elementary and secondary schools are divided into lower and higher schools, each three years in length.

9. Chinese expressions composed of two or more two-syllable words are often abbreviated, usually by selecting key syllables and dropping the rest:

> Yuǎndōng-Dàxué 'Far Eastern University' is abbreviated to Yuǎn-Dà

> Běijīng-Dàxué 'Peking University' is abbreviated to Běi-Dà

(The name <u>Yuǎndōng-Dàxué</u> was intended as fictitious. Since this book was written I find that a university with this name has indeed come into existence on Taiwan.)

10. There are two words for 'name.' <u>Xìng</u> means 'surname' and <u>míngzi</u> means either 'whole name' or 'given name,' depending on the context. Chinese often have more than one given name, one used during infancy, another used while they are growing up, and perhaps still others assumed while they are attending school or engaging in more advanced scholarly pursuits. In the Dialogue, the names 'Little Sister' and 'Tiger' are of course childhood names. A given name like <u>Dōngshēng</u> 'East Born,' which might be given to a child born in the eastern part of the country, could be either a childhood name or a permanent one. Parents with scholarly aspirations for their children are particularly fond of selecting names with literary connotations, such as <u>Wénshān</u> 'Literature Mountain.' <u>Wénshān</u> is a typical name for a man, suggesting two desirable qualities, learning and strength. A foreigner with the name Vincent might well be called <u>Wénshān</u> in Chinese, first because of its meaning connotation, and second as an approximation of the sound.

11. In asking for the name of a person, a commonly used pattern is:

> N(de) míngzi-jiào-shénmo? 'What is N's name?'

For the names of things, the most usual pattern is:

> N jiào-shénmo(-míngzi)? 'What is the name of N?'

Lesson 11 DISCUSSING TRAVEL

"Oh, 'Qián-Xiānsheng, 'háo-jiǔ-bú-jiàn."

Dialogue: Mr. White encounters Mr. Qian and is asked about his travels.

Qián: 'Háo-jiǔ-bú-jiàn. Hǎo-ma?

Haven't seen you for a long time. How are you?

Bái : Oh, 'Qián-Xiānsheng, 'háo-jiǔ-bú-jiàn. Nín-hǎo-ma?

Oh, Mr. Qian, I haven't seen you for a long time. How are you?

Qián: Hén-hǎo. Nín-shi-lái-kàn-shū-ma?　　5

Very well. Have you come (here) to read?

Bái : Wǒ-bú-shi-lái-'kàn-shū. Wǒ-lái-'jiè-shū.

No, not to read. I've come to take out some books.

Qián: Nín-shi-cóng-'nǎr-lái-de?

Where have you come from?

Bái : Wǒ-cóng-Sān-Yǒu-Shūdiàn*-lái-de.　　10

[I've come] from the Three Friends Bookstore.

---

* In Sān-Yǒu-Shūdiàn 'Three Friends Bookstore,' the syllable yǒu is short for péngyou 'friend.' The expression Sān Yǒu 'Three Friends' appears in a number of literary works which have come into existence in the past 2,500 years. In one of these works—the Chinese historical novel Romance of the Three Kingdoms—the Sān Yǒu are three heroes.

Qián: Nín-shi-zuò-'chē-lái-de-   Did you come by car?
ma?

Bái : Shì. Wǒ-shi-zuò-'chē-lái-   Yes. [I came by car.]·
de.

Qián: Nín-zuò-'shénmo-chē-lái-   15   What (sort of) car did you take?
de? Zuò-gōnggòng-'qìchē-   Did you come by bus or by
lái-de háishi-zuò-'diànchē-   streetcar?
lái-de-ne?

Bái : Wǒ-zuò-gōnggòng-'qìchē-   I came by bus.
lái-de.   20

Qián: Nín-cháng-dào-túshūguǎn-   Do you come to the library of-
lái-ma?   ten?

Bái : Bù. Wǒ-jīntian shi-dì-   No. Today is the first time [I've
yícì-lái. Nín-ne?   come]. How about you?

Qián: 'Wó-yě-bù-cháng-lái. . . . 25 I don't come often either. . . .
Oh, 'Bái-Xiānsheng, nín-   Oh, Mr. White, when was it that
shi-'shénmo-shíhou dào-   you came to China? Did you
Zhōngguo-lái-de? Nín-shi-   come last year?
'qùnian-lái-de-ma?

Bái : Shì. Wǒ-shi-qùnian-báyue-   30 Yes. I came on August seventh
qīhào-lái-de.   of last year.

Qián: Nín-yīzhí jiù-dào-Zhōng-   Did you come straight to China?
guo-lái-de-ma?

Bái : Bú-shi. Wǒ-shi-qùnian líkai-   No. I left the United States last
Měiguo, xiān-dào-Rìběn, hòu- 35   year, went first to Japan, and
cóng-Rìběn dào-Zhōngguo-   then came to China from Japan.
lái-de.

Qián: Nín-zuò-'chuán-lái-de hái-   Did you come by boat or by
shi-zuò-'fēijī-lái-de?   plane?

Bái : Wǒ-dào-Rìběn shi-zuò-   40 I came by boat to Japan, and by
chuán, cóng-Rìběn-dào-   plane from Japan to China.
Zhōngguo shi-zuò-'fēijī-
lái-de.

Qián: 'Chuán-zǒude-hěn-màn-   I suppose the boat traveled very
ba.   45 slowly.

Bái : Suírán-hěn-màn, kěshi-   [Although] it was very slow, but
zuò-chuán hén-yǒu-yìsi.   traveling by boat is quite inter-
Kéyi-rènshi hěn-duō-péng-   esting. One can make a lot of
you.   friends.

Qián: Wó-yé-hén-xǐhuan zuò-   50 I also like to travel by boat. I
chuán. Wó-xiǎng jīnnian-   plan to take a boat trip to Japan
zuò-chuán dào-Rìběn-qu.   this year.

Bái : Rìběn hén-yǒu-yìsi. . . .   Japan is very interesting. . . .
Nín-shénmo-shíhou líkai-   When are you leaving the libra-
túshūguǎn?   55 ry?

Qián: Xiànzài-'shénmo-shíhou?   What time is it now?

Bái : Xiànzài-wúdiǎn-bàn.   It's [now] 5:30.

Qián: Wó-yǒu-yìdiǎr-shì. Zuó-   I have a little matter (to attend
tian yǒu-yíge-péngyou-shuō   to). Yesterday a friend told me
jīntian-wǎnshang-liùdiǎn-   60   he was coming to my home this
zhōng tā-dào-wǒ-jiā-lǐtou-   evening at six. I think I'll leave
lái. Wó-xiǎng xiànzài-jiù-   right now.
zǒu.

Bái : Wǒmen-zài-jiàn.   We'll be seeing each other again.

Qián: Oh, wǒ-zài-lùshang-yùjian-   65   Oh, I ran into Mr. Gao on the
'Gāo-Xiānsheng. Tā-gàosù-   way here. He mentioned to me
wǒ jīntian-wǎnshang tā-   that he had invited you to their
qǐng-nín-dào-tāmen-jiā   home for dinner tonight.
chī-wǎnfàn.

Bái : Shì.   70   Yes.

Qián: Wǒ-nèr lí-'Gāo-Xiānsheng-   My place is very close to Mr.
jiā-hěn-jìn. Rúguǒ-nín-jīn-   Gao's home. If you have time
tian-wǎnshang yǒu-gōngfu,   this evening I'd like to invite you
yé-qǐng-dào-wǒ-jiā-lái   to drop in at my home too [to sit
zuòyizuò-tántan.   75   a while and chat].

Bái : Hǎo. Xièxie-nín. Rúguó-   How nice. Thank you. If I have
wǎnshang-yǒu-gōngfu, wǒ-   time [this evening] I'll [certain-
'yídìng-dào-fǔshang-bài-   ly] stop in [at your home to vis-
fang.   it].

Qián: Xīwang-nín-wǎnshang 'yí-   80   I hope you really will [come this
dìng-néng-lái.   evening].

Bái : Hǎo, 'xièxie-nín. Yǒu-   Fine, thanks. (If) there's time
gōngfu wǒ-'yídìng-lái.   I'll certainly come.

Qián: Wǒmen-zài-tán.   Good-bye. [lit. We'll talk fur-
                                           ther.]

Bái : Zài-tán, zài-tán.*   85   Good-bye.*

VOCABULARY

bàn   half (M)

bàifang   make a formal call on (someone) (TV) [lit. salute
                           visit

cháng   often (AD)

chuán   boat, ship (N)

---

* The final exchange between Mr. Qian and Mr. White (lines 71–84) illustrates an aspect of Chinese etiquette. Since Mr. Qian lives close to Mr. Gao,
social convention requires that he should invite Mr. White to drop in, and that
Mr. White should express eagerness to do so, even though it is unlikely that he
will.

cì	time, occasion (M)
dì	(ordinalizing prefix)
fēijī	airplane (N) [lit. flying machine]
fŭshang	(your) residence (N) (See Supplementary Lesson 11, Note 1)
gàosu	inform (TV) [lit. tell inform]
hào	day of the month (M)
jīnnian	this year (TW) [lit. now year]
kànjian	see (TV) [lit. look see
kĕshi	however, but (MA) [lit. may be]
líkai	leave, depart from (TV) [lit. leave open]
nián	year (M)
qùnian	last year (TW) [lit. go year]
rènshi	recognize, be acquainted with (TV) [lit. recognize know]
Rìbĕn	Japan (PW) [lit. sun source]
rúguŏ	if (MA) [lit. if result]
suírán	although (MA) [lit. even is]
wănfàn	dinner (N) [lit. late food]
xīwang	hope (TV) [lit. hope expect] hope (N)
yídìng	be certain (SV) [lit. one settled]
yìsi	meaning (N) [lit. thought think]
-yue	month of the year (M)
yùjian	encounter, meet (TV) [lit. meet see]
zuótian	yesterday (TW) [lit. yesterday day]

SENTENCE BUILD-UP

hào	day of the month
yíhào	first day of the month
1. Jīntian-yíhào.	Today is the first of the month.
yíyue	first month of the year, January
yíyue-yíhào	January first
2. Jīntian-shi-yíyue-yíhào.	Today is January first.
jĭyue	which month of the year?
3. Xiànzài-shi-jĭyue?	What month is it now?

	zuótian	yesterday
	jǐhào?	what day of the month?
4.	Zuótian-shi-jǐhào?	What day of the month was yesterday?

	nián	year
	yī-jiǔ-liù-yī-nián	1961
5.	Yī-jiǔ-liù-yī-nián nǐ-zài-nǎr?	Where were you in 1961?

	nián	year
	jīnnian	this year
6.	Jīnnian tā-xiǎng dào-Měiguo-lái.	This year he plans to come to America.

	qùnian	last year
	něinián?	what year?
7.	Qùnian-shi-něinián?	What year was last year?

	jīnnian	this year
	shíyue	October
	èrshiwǔhào	25th day of the month
8.	Wǒ-jīnnian shíyue-èrshiwǔhào-zǒu.	I'm leaving this year on the 25th of October.

	Rìběn	Japan
	dào-Rìběn-qu	go to Japan
9.	Tā-xiǎng jīnnian-qīyue dào-Rìběn-qu.	He plans to go to Japan in July of this year.

	kànjian	see, visit
	kànjian-'Gāo-Xiānsheng	see Mr. Gao
10.	Wǒ-huòzhě-èryue kànjian-'Gāo-Xiānsheng.	Perhaps I'll see Mr. Gao in February.

	yùjian	encounter
	yùjian-nèiwèi-xiānsheng	encounter that gentleman
11.	Wǒ-chàbuduō-měitiān yùjian-'nèiwèi-xiānsheng.	I meet that gentleman almost every day.

	wǎnfàn	dinner
	qíng-wǒ-chī-wǎnfàn	ask me to dinner
12.	Tā-jiǔyue-qīhào qíng-wǒ-chī-wǎnfàn.	He asked me to dinner on the 7th of September.

	zuótian	yesterday
	shi-'zuótian-lái-de	came yesterday
13.	Tā-shi-'zuótian-lái-de.	He came yesterday.

	shi-'zuótian-lái-de	came yesterday
	'zuótian-lái-de	came yesterday
14.	Tā-'zuótian-lái-de.	He came yesterday.

	fēijī	airplane
	zuò-fēijī	ride in an airplane

15. Tā-shi-zuò-'fēijī-lái-de.   He came by plane.

       chuán   boat
       zuò-chuán   take a boat
16. Tā-shi-zuò-'chuán-qù-de.   He went by boat.

       cháng   often, frequently
       cháng-lái   come frequently
17. Tā-shi-'cháng-lái-de.   He came frequently.

       yídìng   be certain
       bù-yídìng   not be certain
18. Wǒ-'bù-yídìng-qù.   I'm not sure of going.

       yìsi   meaning
       'shénmo-yìsi?   what meaning?
19. Zhèige-zì shi-'shénmo-yìsi?   What does this word mean?

       qián   money
       hén-yǒu-qián   be very wealthy
20. Nèige-rén 'hén-yǒu-qián.   That man is very wealthy.

       yìsi   meaning
       yǒu-yìsi   be interesting
21. Zhèibén-shū 'hén-yǒu-yìsi.   This book is very interesting.

       xīwang   hope
       wó-hěn-xīwang   I hope very much
22. Wó-hěn-xīwang nín-néng-lái.   I hope very much that you can come.

       xīwang   hope
       méi-yǒu-xīwang   have no hope
23. Wǒ-méi-yǒu-xīwang dào-nèr-qù.   I have no hope of going there.

       gàosu   inform
       gàosu-ta   inform him
24. Gàosu-ta wǒ-bù-néng-qù.   Tell him I can't go.

       líkai   depart from, leave
       líkai-Yīngguo   leave England
25. Tā-shénmo-shíhou líkai-Yīngguo?   When will he leave England?

       dì   (ordinalizing prefix)
       dì-yī   the first
       dì-yītian   the first day
26. **Dì-yītiān wó-xiǎng-bú-zuò-shì.**   I plan to do nothing the first day.

       cì   occasion, time
       dì-yícì   the first time
       zhèi-shi-dì-yícì   this is the first time

27. Zhèi-shi-dì-yícì wǒ-chī-   This is the first time I've had
     Zhōngguo-fàn.   Chinese food.

        rúguǒ   if
        rúguó-wó-yǒu-qián   if I had money
        wǒ-'yídìng-mǎi-zhèibén-   I'll surely buy this book
           shū
28. Rúguó-wó-yǒu-qián wǒ-'yídìng-   If I had money I would certainly
     mǎi-zhèibén-shū.   buy this book.

        kěshi   however
        kěshi-wǒ-méi-yǒu-qián   but I don't have any money
29. Wó-xiáng-mǎi, kěshi-wǒ-méi-   I'd like to buy (it), but I don't
     yǒu-qián.   have any money.

        suírán   although
        suírán-tā-shi-wàiguo-   although he's a foreigner
           rén
30. Suírán-tā-shi-wàiguo-rén,   Although he's a foreigner, (he)
     kěshi-Zhōngwén shuōde-hén-   speaks Chinese very well.
     hǎo.

        rènshi   recognize, know
        rènshi-zhèige-zì   know this character
31. Nǐ-rènshi-zhèige-zì-ma?   Do you know this character?

        fǔshang   (your) home
32. Qǐng-wèn, fǔshang-zài-nǎr?   May I ask, where is your home?

        bàifang   make a call on
        bàifang-péngyou   call on a friend
33. Wó-xiǎng míngtian-qu-bàifang-   I plan to call on a friend tomor-
     péngyou.   row.

        bàn   half
        sìdiǎn-bàn   four-thirty
34. Wó-xiǎng 'sìdiǎn-bàn-jiù   I plan to leave immediately at
     zǒu.   four-thirty.

        yíbàn   one half
        yíbàn-shi-nǐde   half is yours
35. Yíbàn-shi-wǒde, yíbàn-shi-   Half is mine, half is yours.
     nǐde.

PATTERN DRILLS

Pattern 11.1. Time Expressions with Year, Month, Day (Note 1 below)

     (Year)   (Month)   (Day)
     jīnnian   shíyue   bāhào

     'October 8 of this year'

1. Tā-'qīhào-lái.   He will come on the seventh.

2. Tā-qīyue-'sìhào-lái.   He will come on July 4th.

3. Tā-jīnnian-qīyue-'sìhào-lái.   He will come on July 4th of this
                                          year.

4. 'Máo-Xiānsheng báyue-jiǔhào-   Mr. Mao is coming on August
   lái.   9th.

5. 'Gāo-Xiānsheng jīnnian-wǔyue-   Mr. Gao is leaving on May 8th of
   bāhào-zǒu.   this year.

6. Yī-jiǔ-sì-jiǔ-nián nǐ-hái-zài-   Were you still in China in 1949?
   Zhōngguo-ma?

7. Jīnnian-qīyue wó-xiǎng-dào-   In July of this year I plan to go
   Yīngguo-qu.   to England.

8. **Wó-mǔqin jīnnian-shíyīyue**   My mother is coming by boat
   zuò-chuán-lái.   this November.

9. Wǒ-dìdi jīnnian-jiǔyue-niàn-   My younger brother will (start
   shū.   to) study this September.

10. Wǒ-fùqin jīnnian-báyue-sān-   My father is coming by plane on
    hào zuò-fēijī-lái.   August 3 of this year.

11. Huòzhě-wǒ-jīnnian néng-dào-   Perhaps I can go to China this
    'Zhōngguo-qù.   year.

12. Tā-tàitai-jīnnian-liùyue xiǎng-   His wife is planning to come
    dào-zhèr-lái.   here this June.

13. Tā-xiǎng-jīnnian-qīyue-'èrshi-   He plans to come to China on Ju-
    hào dào-Zhōngguo-lái.   ly 20th of this year.

14. Tāmen-liùyue-'sānshihào dào-   They are going to Hunan on June
    Húnán-qu.   30th.

15. 'Máo-Xiānsheng yī-jiú-wǔ-qī-   Mr. Mao was studying at the uni-
    nián-wǔyue zài-dàxué-niàn-shū.   versity in May of 1957.

Pattern 11.2.   The (shi)...Vde Construction   (Note 2 below)

S	(shi)	A	V	-de
Subject	(shi)	A	Verb	-de
Wǒ	(shi)	zuótian	lái	-de.

'I came yesterday.'

1. 'Wáng-Xiānsheng shi-'zuótiān-   It was yesterday that Mr. King
   dào-de.   arrived.

2. 'Bái-Xiānsheng 'shénmo-shíhou-   When was it that Mr. White
   lái-de?   came?

3. 'Qián-Xiānsheng jīnnian-èryue   Mr. Qian left from here in Feb-
   cóng-zhèr-zǒu-de.   ruary of this year.

4. Wǒ-qùnian-shí'èryue-bāhào zuò-fēijī-lái-de.	I came by plane on December 8th of last year.
5. Wǒ-fùqin shi-jīnnian-èryue èrshiwǔhào-zǒu-de.	My father left on February 25th of this year.
6. 'Gāo-Xiānsheng-shuō zuótian-wǎnshang tā-cóng-Rìběn-lái-de.	Mr. Gao says he came from Japan yesterday evening.
7. Tā-shi-'xiān-dào-gōngyuán 'hòu-dào-túshūguǎn-qù-de.	He went first to the park and then to the library.
8. Tā-jīntian-'jiúdiǎn-zhōng dào-túshūguǎn-lái-de.	He came to the library at nine today.
9. 'Wáng-Xiáojie bú-shi-zuótian zuò-'fēijī-lái-de-ma?	Didn't Miss King come by plane yesterday?
10. 'Gāo-Tàitai yī-jiǔ-sì-wǔ-nián jiǔyue-bāhào-lái-de.	Mrs. Gao arrived on September 8, 1945.
11. Nǐ-dìdi qùnian-cóng-zhèr-zǒu-de-ma?	Did your younger brother leave from here last year?
12. Nǐ-shi-'jīntian-mǎi-de hái-shi-'zuótian-mǎi-de?	Did you buy it today or yesterday?
13. 'Bái-Xiansheng shi-'sānhào-zǒu-de háishi-'sìhào-zǒu-de?	Did Mr. White leave on the 3d or the 4th?
14. Tā-shi-'yìzhíde-lái-de-ma?	Did he come directly?
15. Tā-bú-shi-'yìdiǎn-bàn-lái-de. Tā-shi-'liángdiǎn-bàn-lái-de.	It wasn't at 1:30 that he came. It was at 2:30.

Pattern 11.3.   The (shi)...V de Construction with Object (Note 3 below)

Pattern 11.3 a.

S	(shi)	A	V	O	de
Subject	(shi)	A	Verb	Object	de
Wǒ	shi	jīnnian	líkai	Měiguo	de.

'I left America this year.' (i.e. 'It was this year that I left America.')

Pattern 11.3 b.

S	(shi)	A	V	de	O
Subject	(shi)	A	Verb	de	Object
Wǒ	shi	jīnnian	líkai	de	Měiguo.

'I left America this year.' (i.e. 'It was this year that I left America.')

1. Wǒ-shi-zuótian dào-Měiguo-de.	I arrived in America yesterday.

2. Tā-'jīntian-mǎi-de-shū.   He bought the books <u>today</u>.

3. 'Gāo-Xiáojie-gàosu-wǒ, tā-   Miss Gao informed me that she
    'jīntian-qù-mǎi-de-shū.   went to buy the books <u>today</u>.

4. 'Gāo-Xiānsheng-shuō tā-shi-   Mr. Gao says it was last year
    qùnian mǎi-de-nèisuǒr-fángzi.   that he bought that house.

5. Nǐ-shi-dì-yícì líkai-Měiguo-   Is this the first time you've left
    de-ma?   America?

6. Wǒ-shi-dì-yícì-líkai-Měiguo-   This is the first time I've left
    de.   America.

7. Tā-zài-Sān-Yǒu-Shūdiàn mǎi-   He bought the books at the Three
    de-shū.   Friends Bookstore.

8. Gāo-Xiáojie-zài-nǎr xià-fēijī-   Where did Miss Gao get off the
    de?   plane?

9. 'Wáng-Xiáojie cóng-Yīngguo-   Miss King came to China from
    dào-de-Zhōngguo.   England.

10. 'Wáng-Xiānsheng shi-zuótian-   Mr. King sold the house yester-
    mài-de-fángzi.   day.

11. Nǐ-péngyou shi-shénmo-shíhou-   When did your friend meet him?
    yùjian-ta-de?

12. Tā-shi-'shénmo-shíhou-gàosu-   When was it that he told you?
    nǐ-de?

13. Nǐ-shi-'jídiǎn-zhōng chī-de   When did you eat dinner?
    wǎnfàn?

14. Nǐ-shi-'shénmo-shíhou kànjian-   When did you see Mr. King?
    'Wáng-Xiānsheng-de?

15. Tāmen-shi-zuótian xià-de-shān.   They went down the mountain
                                              yesterday.

16. Wǒmen-shi-zuótian guò-de-hú.   We crossed the lake yesterday.

17. Wǒ-shi-qùnian mǎi-de-zhèiběn-   I bought this dictionary last year.
    zìdiǎn.

18. Tā-mèimei-shi-sānyue-'èrhào   His younger sister boarded the
    shàng-de-chuán.   boat on March 2d.

19. Wǒ-dìdi-èryue-sānhào shàng-   My younger brother boarded the
    chuán-de.   boat on February 3d.

20. Tā-shi-zài-diànchēshang mǎi-   He bought the ticket on the
    de-piào.   streetcar.

SUBSTITUTION TABLES

I: 64 phrases (Note 1)

———	yí	-yue	yí	-hào
jīnnian	wǔ		èr	
qùnian	shí		èrshiwǔ	
1962 nián	shí'èr		sānshiyī	

II: 96 sentences (Note 2)

tā	—	qùnian	èr	-yue	wǔ	-hào	lái	de
	shi	1962 nián	sān		liù		qù	
			sì		qī			

III: 48 sentences (Note 2)

wǒ	—		zuò	diànchē	lái	de
nǐ	shi			chuán	qù	
tā				fēijī		
				shénmo		

IV: 72 sentences (Note 2)

wǒ	—	yìzhí(de)	lái	de
nǐ	shi	shénmo-shíhou	qù	
tā		cóng-nèr		

V: 64 sentences (Note 3)

(The asterisks * indicate positions either of which may be occupied by
<u>de</u>. From columns A and B, only items in the same row may be taken
together.)

tā	—		A	*	B	*
	shi	zuótian	shàng	-de	chuán	-de
		qùnian	líkai		Měiguo	
		sānyue	dào		Zhōngguo	
		jīntian	xià		shān	

PRONUNCIATION DRILLS

I. The Tone-Toneless Contrast

The following pairs of syllables are distinguished in meaning
by the presence or absence of tones on the second syllable.

(a) dōng-xī, dōngxi   (e) tā-dà, tāde

(b) xíng-lǐ, xíngli   (f) mái-mǎ, mái-ma

(c) lǎo-mā, lǎo-ma   (g) mǎi-má, mǎi-ma

(d) kuàilè, kuàile   (h) dàodé, dàode

II. Tonal Shifts in Stressed bù and yī

(a) 'bù-dā   (e) 'bù-gāo   (i) 'yìzhī

(b) 'bù-dá   (f) 'bù-máng   (j) 'yìmáo

(c) 'bù-dǎ   (g) 'bù-hǎo   (k) 'yìběn

(d) 'bú-dà   (h) 'bú-lèi   (l) 'yíkuài

                                          (m) 'yíge

QUESTIONS AND ANSWERS

1. Nǐ-rúguó-yǒu-qián nǐ-zuò-
   shénmo?
   Rúguó-wó-yǒu-qián wǒ-jiu-
   mǎi-fángzi.

   What would you do if you had
   money?
   If I had money, I'd buy a house.

2. Nǐ-shi-něinián líkai-Měiguo-
   de?
   Wǒ-shi-qùnian líkai-Měiguo-
   de.

   What year did you leave America?
   I left America last year.

3. Wǒmen-zài-zhèr-'zuòyizuò,
   'hǎo-bù-hǎo?
   Kéyi, kéyi.

   Let's sit here a while, O.K.?

   All right.

4. Nǐ-dì-yícì-kànjian-ta shi-
   'shénmo-shíhou?
   Wǒ-dì-yícì-kànjian-ta shi-jiǔ-
   yue-wǔhào.

   When was the first time you saw
   him?
   The first time I saw him was
   September 5th.

5. Suírán-nèitiáo-lù bù-háo-zǒu,
   kěshi-nǐ-'yídìng-yào-qù-ma?

   Shì, wǒ-'yídìng-yào-qù.

   Although that road is not good to
   travel on, do you insist on going?
   Yes, I insist on going.

6. Xiànzài-wǒmen kéyi-'tányitán-'
   ma?
   Wǎnshang 'liùdiǎn-yíkè-kéyi-
   ma?

   May we chat a while now?

   Will this evening at 6:15 be all
   right?

7. Nín-zhè-shi-dì-yícì dào-
   Zhōngguo-lái-ma?
   Bú-shi, wǒ-shi-dì-'èrcì
   dào-Zhōngguo-lái.

   Is this the first time you've
   come to China?
   No, this is my second trip to
   China.

8. Nín-'cháng-dào-'wàiguo-qù-
   ma?
   Shì. Wó-hén-xǐhuan dào-
   wàiguo-qu. Hén-yǒu-yìsi.

   Do you often go abroad?

   Yes, I like going abroad very
   much. It's very interesting.

9. Nǐ-shi-zài-'fēijīshang-yùjian-   Did you run into him on the plane
   ta-de háishi-zài-'chuánshang-yù-   or on the boat?
   jian-ta-de?
   Wǒ-shi-zài-'chuánshang-yù-   I met him on the boat.
   jian-ta-de.

10. Nǐ-'shénmo-shíhou rènshi-ta-de?   When did you get to know him?
    Wǒ-'qùnian-jiu-rènshi-ta-de.   I became acquainted with him
                                        just last year.

11. Nǐ-'shénmo-shíhou qù-zhǎo-   When are you going to look him
    ta?   up?
    Wó-xiǎng-míngtian bàifang-   I'm thinking of calling on him
    ta.   tomorrow.

12. Nín-jiā-zài-nǎr?   Where is your home?
    Wǒ-jiā-zài-chéngwài, lí-   My home is outside the city, not
    Zhōngshān-Lù-bù-yuǎn.   far from Sun Yatsen Avenue.

13. Nǐ-huì-shuō 'Zhóngwén-ma?   Can you speak Chinese?
    ma?
    Wǒ-huì-shuō, kěshi-shuōde-   I can, but I don't speak very
    bú-tài-hǎo.   well.

14. Tā-shi-sìdiǎn-'yíkè-láide-ma?   Did he come at 4:15?
    Bú-shi. Tā-shi-sìdiǎn-'sānkè-   No. He came at 4:45.
    láide.

15. Tā-shi-cóng-'Zhōngguo-lái-de   Did he come from China or Ja-
    háishi-cóng-'Rìběn-lái-de?   pan?
    Tā-shi-cóng-'Zhōngguo-lái-   He came from China.
    de.

16. Fēijī shi-shénmo-yìsi?   What does fēijī mean?
    Fēijī-shi-'airplane'-de-yìsi.   Fēijī means 'airplane.'

17. Nǐ-cháng-dào-tā-jiā-qù-ma?   Do you go to his home   fre-
                                        quently?
    Wǒ-chàbuduō měitiān-dōu-qù.   I go almost every day.

18. Nín-jīntian-wǎnshang qīdiǎn-   Would it be possible for you to
    bàn dào-wǒmen-zhèr-lái   come to our (place) here this
    tányitán-kéyi-ma?   evening at 7:30 [to chat a while]?
    Jīntian-wǎnshang wó-yǒu-   This evening I have a little mat-
    yìdiǎr-shì.   ter to attend to.

19. Wǒ-zhèige-zì xiěde-'duì-bu-   Have I written this character
    duì?   correctly?
    Nǐ-nèige-zì xiěde-bú-duì.   You've written that character in-
                                        correctly.

20. Tā-'zěnmo-bù-lái?   How is it that he's not coming?
    Tā-shuō tā-méi-yǒu-gōngfu.   He says he doesn't have time.

LET'S BE REASONABLE

Each of the following sentences contains an expression which makes the meaning absurd or unlikely.   Make whatever changes are necessary to turn the sentence into a reasonable statement.   For example, <u>Wó-wǎnshang-yìdiǎn-zhōng chī-wǎnfàn</u> 'I eat dinner at 1:00 in the evening' might be changed to <u>Wó-wǎnshang-liùdiǎn-zhōng chī-wǎnfàn</u> 'I eat dinner at 6:00 in the evening.'

1. Tā-gàosu-wo zhèi-liǎngge-běnzi yígòng-'yìfēn-qián.

2. Tā-shi-qùnian èryuè-sānshiyíhào dào-Zhōngguo-láide.

3. Wǒ-dìdi-bāsuì; tā-jīnnian-zài-'zhōngxué-niàn-shū.

4. Tā-shi-zuò-gōnggòng-qìchē cóng-Měiguo dào-Zhōngguo-lái-de.

5. Tāmen-zài-fángzishang chī-fàn.

6. Láohu yídìng-pǎode-hěn-màn.

7. 'Bái-Xiānsheng zài-chēshang mǎi-qiānbǐ.

8. Nèige-xuésheng cháng-dào-Sān-Yǒu-Shūdiàn-qù-mài-shū.

9. Shāndong-zài-Rìběn.

10. Tā-shuō ta-zuótian dào-gōngyuán-qu-jiè-shū.

DOUBLE JEOPARDY

Use the word on the right to replace something in the sentence to the left; doing this will require you to make one or more additional changes. Watch out! Your chances of making a mistake are doubled.

1. Ní-fúshang lí-zhèr-hěn-jìn.   wǒ

2. Dìdi-shi-nán-háizi.   mèimei

3. Rìběn-lí-Zhōngguo-bù-yuǎn.   Měiguo

4. 'Zhōngguo-rén dōu-shuō-'Zhōngguo-huà.   Měiguo-rén

5. Wǒ-zài-chēshang-mǎi-piào.   màipiàoyuán

6. Tā-zài-xiǎoxué-niàn-shū.   wénxué

7. Xià-shān hěn-róngyi.   shàng

8. Zhōngguo-huà hěn-nán-shuō.   xiě

9. Fùqin shi-nán-rén.   mǔqin

10. Zhèiběn-shū 'jǐkuài-qián?   fángzi

NOTES

1. In time expressions, larger units precede smaller units: <u>jīnnian-yíyue-sānhào wǎnshang-bādiǎn-èrshifēn</u> 'this year, January third, evening, eight-twenty.'

2. When a sentence emphasizes the time, place, purpose or some other aspect of a past occurrence, rather than the occurrence itself, the following
   pattern is used:

   S (shi) A V de. 'S did V under A time or place conditions.' or 'It
   was under A time or place conditions that S did V.'

   For example:

   Tā-shi-'zuótian-lái-de. 'He came yesterday.' or 'It was yesterday
   that he came.'
   Tā-shi-zuò-'chē-lái-de. 'He came by car (i.e. not on foot).'

   In this pattern, shi may be omitted if it is not modified by bu or some
   other adverb:

   Tā-'jīntian-lái-de. 'He came yesterday.'

       but:

   Tā-bú-shi-'jīntian-lái-de. 'It wasn't today that he came.' or 'He
   didn't come today.'

   Note that this is not a general past tense. Other ways of expressing the
   Chinese equivalent of English past tense are presented in lessons 13 and
   14.

3. If the verb of the construction described in Note 2 has a pronoun object,
   this must come directly after the verb:

   Wǒ-shi-'jīntian-kànjian-ta-de. 'It was today that I saw him.'

   With the verbs mǎi 'buy,' mài 'sell,' and chī 'eat,' the preferred position
   for the object is at the end:

   Wǒ-shi-'jīntian-mǎi-de-shū. 'I bought the book today.'

   In other cases, the object is either placed right after the verb or is separated from the verb by the particle de:

   Wǒ-shi-yíyue-dào-Měiguo-de. or Wǒ-shi-yíyue-dào-de-Měiguo. 'I
   arrived in America in January.'

   See Substitution Table V, p. 148, for further examples.

4. Note the following sentences stating the ordinal occurrence of an action:

   Jīntian-shi-dì-yícì kànjian-ta. '[lit.] Today is the first time seeing
   him.'

   Zhè-shi-dì-èrcì chī-Zhōngguo-fàn. '[lit.] This is the second time
   eating Chinese food.'

   When a sentence on this pattern has a subject, it is normally placed at the
   very beginning of the sentence:

   Wǒ-jīntian-shi-dì-yícì kànjian-tā. 'Today is the first time I've seen
   him.' [lit. '(As for) me, today is the first time seeing him.']

   Wǒ-zhè-shi-dì-èrcì chī-Zhōngguo-fàn. 'This is the second time I've
   eaten Chinese food.'

5. It is a common device to pair introductory words of similar or comple-
    mentary meanings in consecutive clauses in a sentence:

    suírán 'although' . . . . kěshi 'nevertheless'
    rúguǒ 'if' . . . . jiù   'then'

    For example:

    Suírán-tā-shi-'Zhōngguo-rén kěshi-tā-bu-huì shuō-Zhōngwén. 'Al-
    though he's Chinese, he can't speak Chinese.'

    Rúguó-wó-yǒu-gōngfu, wǒ-jiù-qu-kàn-'Wáng-Xiānsheng. 'If I had
    the time, (then) I'd go see Mr. King.'

    Jiù 'then' is a fixed adverb and hence comes directly before the verb; the
    other words in the list are movable adverbs, and can be placed either
    before or after the subject.

6. The doubling of a verb, with or without yi between the two forms, gives a
    touch of informality to the verb and suggests the idea 'for a while':

    Nǐ-kankàn. or Nǐ-'kànyikàn. 'Take a look.'

    Wǒmen-tántan. or Wǒmen-'tányitán. 'Let's talk for a while.'

7. Calendar years are expressed by putting numbers in telephone style (that
    is, simply listing them) in front of nián 'year':

    yī-jiǔ-sì-yī-nián '1941'

Lesson 12 REVIEW

PRONUNCIATION REVIEW

I. Review of Two-Syllable Tonal Combinations

The lists in this and the following exercise use vocabulary from Units I and II. Digits indicate tone sequences: e.g. '10' means first tone followed by neutral tone. Asterisks indicate expressions in which the first syllable changes from third tone to second tone.

1 0	1 1	1 2	1 3	1 4
sānyue	shān-dōng	sānmáo	dōu-hǎo	sānkuài
shānshang	Zhōngshān	Zhōngwén	sānběn	shuō-huà
zhīdao	sānfēn	gōngyuán	qiānbǐ	shūdiàn
jīntian	tā-shuō	zhōngxué	tā-yǒu	gōnggòng
jiāli	gāo-shān	dōu-lái	Dōngběi	chī-fàn
gōngfu	fēijī	sāntiáo	gāngbǐ	sāncì

2 0	2 1	2 2	2 3	2 4
xuésheng	shéi-shuō	wénxué	nín-hǎo	duó-dà
háizi	nín-chī	suīrán	máobǐ	yídìng
zuótian	shíyī	néng-xué	bái-zhǐ	shíhào
chuánshang	nín-shuō	shéi-lái	Húběi	lí-zhèr
yánse	néng-chī	nán-xué	hái-yǒu	chéngwài
míngzi	nán-shuō	Húnán	shéi-mǎi	shéi-mài

3 0	3 1	3 2	3 3	3 4
mǔqin	hěn-gāo	liǎngmáo	wúlǐ *	wǒ-qù
něige	wǔfēn	zhǎo-shéi	hén-shǎo *	hěn-dà
kěshi	mǎi-shū	wǒ-lái	jiúsuǒr *	wǎnfàn
wǔyue	hěn-duō	něiguó	wó-zǒu *	xiě-zì
fǔshang	něizhī	yǒu-qián	yé-xiǎo *	zǒu-lù
zǒude	Yuǎndōng	xiǎoxué	hén-yuǎn *	wǔhào

4 0	4 1	4 2	4 3	4 4
dìdi	xìng-Gāo	dìtú	mòshuǐ	liùkuài
mèimei	diànchē	jiàoyuán	tài-shǎo	sìhào
fùqin	kàn-shū	xìng-Bái	zìdiǎn	guìxìng
gàosu	xià-shān	yìzhí	Rìběn	jiù-huì
rènshi	tài-duō	dàxué	mài-bǐ	zài-zhèr
yìsi	qìchē	zài-lái	wàng-nǎr	dào-nèr

154

II. Review of i and "i"

sì cì	dìdi	jǐ zhī	yí cì	shí yī
yì si	sì shí	yì lǐ	shí sì	sì zhī
dì-yī	yì zhí	nǐ-chī	dì-shí	dì-qī
qī zhī	dì-sì	shí zhī	shí cì	yì shí

ANALOGY DRILL

Answer both questions affirmatively. Add yě 'also' in the answer to the second question.

1. 'Gāo-Xiānsheng-jiā zài-chéngwài-ma? 'Qián-Xiānsheng-jiā-ne?

2. Shānshang yǒu-yì suǒ-dà-fángzi-ma? 'Xiǎo-fángzi-ne?

3. Ní-qǐng-péngyou chī-wǎnfàn-ma? Tā-ne?

4. Nǐ-jiā zài-shānshang-ma? 'Tā-jiā-ne?

5. Nǐ-jīntian mái-běnzi-ma? Tā-ne?

6. Nǐ-jiā-zài-Húběi-ma? 'Tā-jiā-ne?

7. 'Qiánbiar-shi-dà-shān-ma? Hòubiar-ne?

8. Nǐ-dào-túshūguǎn-ma? Tā-ne?

9. Nǐ-jiā zài-chéng-lǐtou-ma? Nǐ-'péngyou-jiā-ne?

10. Nǐ-jiā zài-Zhōngshān-Lù-zuǒbiar-ma? 'Tā-jiā-ne?

11. Wáng-Xiānsheng shi-'Shāndong-rén-ma? Wáng-Tàitai-ne?

12. Nǐ-jiā-hòutou yóu-xiǎo-hú-ma? 'Tā-jiā-ne?

13. Nǐde-fángzi shi-'lán-yánse-de-ma? 'Tāde-fángzi-ne?

14. Nǐ-yào-jiè-shū-ma? Nǐ-péngyou-ne?

15. Ní-xǐhuan-kàn-shū-ma? Nǐ-péngyou-ne?

16. Nǐ-huì-xiě 'Zhōngguo-zì-ma? Nǐ-péngyou-ne?

17. Nǐ-jiā-lí-zhèr hén-yuǎn-ma? 'Tā-jiā-ne?

18. Tāmen-dōu-shi-xuésheng-ma? Nǐmen-ne?

19. Gōngyuán-lí-zhèr yuǎn-ma? Túshūguǎn-ne?

20. Nǐ-xué 'Zhōngguo-wénxué-ma? Tā-ne?

21. 'Zhōngguo-wénxué-róngyi-ma? 'Yīngguo-wénxué-ne?

22. Nǐ-néng-shuō Zhōngwén-ma? Tāmen-ne?

23. Túshūguǎn lí-'Gāo-Xiānsheng-jiā yuǎn-ma? Gōngyuán-ne?

24. Nǐ-néng-kàn jiǎndānde-Zhōngguo-shū-ma? Tāmen-ne?

25. Nǐ-zài-dàxué niàn-shū-ma? 'Bái-Xiānsheng-ne?

26. Nǐ-zuò-gōnggòng-qìchē-qù-ma? Tāmen-ne?

27. Cóng-zhèr-yìzhíde jiù-dào-nǐ-jiā-ma? 'Tā-jiā-ne?

28. Gōnggòng-qìchē-zhàn zài-nǐ-jiā-mén-kǒur-ma? 'Tā-jiā-ne?

29. Cóng-zhèr-yìzhíde-wàng-xī shi-nǐ-jiā-ma? 'Tā-jiā-ne?

30. Cóng-zhèr-dào-nǐ-jiā wàng-'dōngbiar-guǎi-ma? Nǐ-'péngyou-jiā-ne?

31. Nǐ-jiā-lí-zhèr yǒu-'bālǐ-lù-ma? Tā-jiā-ne?

32. Nǐ-jīntian dào-shūdiàn-qu-ma? 'Bái-Xiānsheng-ne?

33. Tā-mǔqin-shi-jiàoyuán-ma? Tā-'fùqin-ne?

34. Tā-dìdi zài-'xiǎoxué-niàn-shū-ma? 'Nǐ-dìdi-ne?

35. Tā-shuō-huà shuōde-hěn-kuài-ma? Nǐ-ne?

36. 'Zhèige-màipiàoyuán hén-hǎo-ma? Nèige-ne?

37. Nǐ-zài-chēshang mǎi-piào-ma? Tāmen-ne?

38. Nǐ-mèimei-shí sānsuì-ma? 'Tā-mèimei-ne?

39. Ní-yǒu-piào-ma? Tā-ne?

40. Tā-yǒu-háizi-ma? Nǐ-ne?

41. Tā-shi-'Měiguo-rén-ma? Nǐ-ne?

42. Nǐ-fùqin-zuò-shì-ma? 'Tā-fùqin-ne?

43. Tā-dìdi-zuò-shì-ma? 'Nǐ-dìdi-ne?

44. Tā-shi-zuò-'chē-láide-ma? Nǐ-ne?

45. Nǐ-míngtian bàifang-péngyou-ma? Tā-ne?

46. Nǐ-shi-zuò-'fēijī-lái-de-ma? Tā-ne?

47. Nǐ-shi-'qùnian-lái-de-ma? Tā-ne?

48. Zhèibén-shū yǒu-yìsi-ma? 'Nèibén-ne?

49. Nǐ-rènshi 'Bái-Xiānsheng-ma? Tā-ne?

50. 'Bái-Xiānsheng xiǎng-dào-Rìběn-qu-ma? Nǐ-ne?

51. Nǐ-shi-zuò-'chuán-lái-de-ma? Tā-ne?

52. Tā-shi-'zuótian-lái-de-ma? Nǐ-ne?

53. Nǐ-shi-cóng-'Zhōngguo-lái-de-ma? Tāmen-ne?

54. Nǐ-rènshi-nèige-rén-ma? Tā-ne?

55. Tā-shi-sānyue-'wǔhào-lái-de-ma? Nǐ-ne?

56. Nǐ-shi-jīntian yùjian-'Gāo-Xiānsheng-de-ma? 'Bái-Xiānsheng-ne?

57. Tā-shi-zuò gōnggòng-qìchē-lái-de-ma? Nǐmen-ne?

58. Nǐ-shi-xiān-dào-Rìběn hòu-dào-'Zhōngguo-qù-de-ma? Tā-ne?

59. Tā-jiā zài-Měiguo-ma? 'Nǐ-jiā-ne?

60. Tā-shi-'qùnian-lái-de-ma? Nǐ-ne?

61. Nǐ-xīwang dào-'Zhōngguo-qù-ma? Tā-ne?

62. 'Qiānbǐ-zài-zhèr-ma?   'Gāngbǐ-ne?

63. Tāmen-zài-diànchēshang mǎi-piào-ma?   Chuánshang-ne?

64. Zhèige-dàxué yǒu-'Yīngguo-xuésheng-ma?   'Měiguo-xuésheng-ne?

65. 'Chuánshangde-rén dōu-shi-'Zhōngguo-rén-ma?   Fēijīshang-ne?

66. Túshūguǎn lí-zhèr-yuǎn-ma?   Shūdiàn-ne?

67. 'Zhōngguo-wénxué nán-xué-ma?   'Yīngguo-wénxué-ne?

68. Běi-Hú-lí-nèr yǒu-'bālǐ-lù-ma?   Xī-Shān-ne?

69. Ní-xǐhuan-zuò-chuán-ma?   Fēijī-ne?

70. Zài-'nèige-túshūguǎn yóu-hěn-duō-'Zhōngguo-rén-kàn-shū-ma?   'Wài-guo-rén-ne?

71. Tā-shi-qùnian-'bāyue-lái-de-ma?   Nín-ne?

72. Tā-shi-zuótian mǎi-de-shū-ma?   Nǐ-ne?

73. Ní-xiǎng qīyue-sìhào-qù-ma?   Tā-ne?

74. Tā-bǐ-'Bái-Xiānsheng-gāo-ma?   Nǐ-ne?

75. Tā-shi-qùnian líkai-jiā-de-ma?   Nǐ-ne?

76. Tā-niànde-hǎo-ma?   Nǐ-ne?

77. Nǐ-lái-jiè-shū-ma?   Tā-ne?

78. Tā-bǐ-'Bái-Xiānsheng xuéde-hǎo-ma?   Nǐ-ne?

79. Nǐ-shi-cóng-Měiguo dào-'Zhōngguo-lái-de-ma?   Tā-ne?

80. Tā-'Zhōngguo-huà shuōde-hǎo-ma?   Rìběn-huà-ne?

REPLACEMENT DRILL

Replace some element in the sentence to the left with the word to the right.

1.	Tā-shi-'Rìběn-rén.	Zhōngguo
2.	Tā-xǐhuan-niàn-shū.	xiě-zì
3.	Tā-yǒu-mèimei.	dìdi
4.	Tā-'Zhōngguo-huà shuōde-hěn-kuài.	màn
5.	Tā-fùqin shi-jiàoyuán.	mǔqin
6.	Tā-míngzi jiào-Láohu.	Xiǎomèi
7.	Tā-bu-mǎi-zìdiǎn.	běnzi
8.	Tā-jiā-zài-shānshang.	shānxià
9.	Dōngbian-shi-túshūguǎn.	shūdiàn
10.	Wǒ-jiā-zài-Húnán.	Shāndong
11.	Fángzi-'lǐtou-yǒu-rén.	wàitou
12.	Wǒde-fángzi zài-zhōngjiàr.	zuǒbiar

13. Wǒ-zài-zhōngxué niàn-shū.   dàxué

14. 'Zhōngguo-zì róngyi-xiě.   nán

15. Wǒ-jiā lí-túshūguǎn-tài-yuǎn.   jìn

16. Wǒ-néng-shuō Zhōngguo-huà.   huì

17. Wǒ-qu-'jiè-shū.   mǎi

18. Wǒ-dào-túshūguǎn.   gōngyuán

19. Wǒ-huì-xiě 'Zhōngguo-zì.   néng

20. Dào-tā-jiā cóng-zhèr-wàng-dōng-guǎi.   xī

21. Tā-shi-zuò-'diànchē-lái-de.   qìchē

22. Zhōngshān-Lù-hòutou yǒu-gōngyuán.   qiántou

23. Nèige-hú shi-Běi-Hú.   Nán-Hú

24. Húde-yòubiar shi-'Qián-Xiānsheng-jiā.   hòubiar

25. Shānshang yǒu-yìsuǒr-fángzi.   sānsuǒr

26. Rén-zài-fángzi-lǐtou.   wàitou

27. Túshūguǎn yǒu-rén-kàn-shū.   jiè

28. Mèimei-bǐ-dìdi-dà.   xiǎo

29. Cóng-zhèr wàng-'béi-guǎi shi-wǒ-jiā.   dōng

30. Zhèiběn-shū-bù-hǎo.   zhēn

31. Tā-dìdi-mǎi-shū.   zuò-shì

32. Xiànzài chàbuduō-yìdiǎn-zhōng.   sān

33. Xiànzài chà-yíkè-sāndiǎn.   wǔfēn

34. Fēijī-bǐ-qìchē-kuài.   chuán

35. Tāde-míngzi hěn-qíguài.   bù

36. Tā-cháng-qu bàifang-péngyou.   lái

37. Tā-rènshi 'Wáng-Xiānsheng.   yùjian

38. Nèiběn-shū méi-yǒu-yìsi.   hén

39. Tā-yídìng-lái.   xǐhuan

40. Tā-xīwang-kànjian 'Gāo-Xiānsheng.   yídìng

41. Wǒ-zhèi-shi-dì-yícì lái-Měiguo.   sān

42. Shi-zuò-'chuán-hǎo háishi-zuò-'fēijī-hǎo? kuài

43. Tāmen-cóng-zhèr wàng-nán-zǒu.   běi

44. Tāmen-dōu-xuéde-hěn-kuài.   zhēn

45. Nǐ-shi-jiè-'shū-lái-de-ma?   dìtú

INSERTION DRILL

At an appropriate place in each of the following sentences, insert the word to
the right of the sentence.

1.	Wó-'měitiān dào-túshūguǎn-qu.	dōu
2.	Wǒ-yìdiǎn-bàn-zhōng-lái.	zài
3.	Wǒ-shi-dì-yícì lái-Zhōngguo.	yě
4.	Wó-zǒu-lù bǐ-tā-kuài.	gèng
5.	Tā-dìdi zài-zhōngxué-niàn-shū.	bú
6.	Jīntian wǒ-dào-túshūguǎn-qu.	wǎnshang
7.	Gōngyuán-qiántou yǒu-yìtiáo-lù.	dà
8.	Zhōngjiàrde-fángzi-shi-shéide?	zài
9.	Rúguǒ-bú-dào-gōngyuán, dào-túshūguǎn-qu.	jiù
10.	Zhèizhī-bǐ-hǎo.	zhēn
11.	Zhèige-zì-jiǎndān.	bù
12.	'Wáng-Xiáojie-shuōde-kuài.	yìdiǎr
13.	Xiànzài-'sìdiǎn-yíkè.	chà
14.	Wǒ-jīnnian-shíbāsuì.	chàbuduō
15.	Nǐmen-rènshi nèiwèi-xiānsheng-ma?	dōu
16.	Míngtian-wǒ-lái.	zài
17.	Nèiběn-shū hén-yǒu-yìsi.	méi
18.	Tā-bù-chī-fàn.	zěnmo
19.	Nèige-rén bù-chī-fàn.	xǐhuan
20.	'Shísuìde-háizi yě-jiè-shū-ma?	néng
21.	Wǒ-sānyue-yíhào líkai-zhèr.	xiǎng
22.	Tā-rúguǒ-sìdiǎn-bù-lái, wǒ-jiù-zǒu.	bàn
23.	Nèige-háizi-jiào-shénmo?	míngzi
24.	Wǒ-zhèige-zì xiěde-'duì-bú-duì?	qǐng-wèn
25.	Cóng-zhèr wàng-dōng-zǒu.	yìzhí(de)

ANSWERING QUESTIONS

Read aloud and answer in Chinese.

1. Gāo-Tàitai-qu-'mǎi-shū. Gāo-Xiānsheng-qu-'jiè-shū. 'Shéi-qu-mǎi-
   shū?

2. 'Wáng-Xiānshengde-jiā zài-chénglǐ. 'Gāo-Xiānshengde-jiā zài-
   chéngwài. 'Shéide-jiā zài-chénglǐ?

3. 'Qiántou-yǒu-gōngyuán. 'Hòutou-yǒu-hú. 'Qiántou-yǒu-shénmo?

4. Húde-zuǒbiar shi-xiǎo-gōngyuán. Yòubiar shi-'Qián-Xiānsheng-jiā.
    'Qián-Xiānsheng-jiā zài-nǎr?

5. Zhōngshan-Lù-zuǒbiar yǒu-dà-gōngyuán. Yòubiar yóu-xiǎo-hú. Dà-
    gōngyuán-zài-nǎr?

6. 'Máo-Xiānsheng mài-shū. 'Bái-Xiānsheng zài-dàxué-niàn-shū. 'Shéi-
    niàn-shū?

7. 'Bái-Xiānsheng dào-túshūguǎn-qu-jiè-shū. 'Máo-Xiānsheng qu-kàn-shū.
    'Shéi-qu-jiè-shū?

8. 'Bái-Xiānsheng néng-kàn-Zhōngguo-shū. 'Máo-Xiānsheng néng-xiě-
    Zhōngguo-zì. Shéi-néng-kàn-Zhōngguo-shū?

9. Wáng-Xiānsheng-jiā lí-túshūguán-hěn-jìn. 'Qián-Xiáojie-jiā lí-túshū-
    guán-hén-yuǎn. Shéi-jiā lí-túshūguán-hěn-jìn?

10. 'Gāo-Xiānsheng-shuō Zhōngguo-zì-róngyi-xiě. 'Bái-Xiānsheng-shuō
    'bù-róngyi-xiě. Shéi-shuō-Zhōngguo-zì 'bù-róngyi-xiě?

11. Túshūguǎn-lí-zhèr 'sānlǐ-lù. Gōngyuán-lí-zhèr 'bālǐ-lù. Túshūguǎn-
    lí-zhèr 'jílǐ-lù?

12. 'Bái-Xiānsheng shi-xuésheng. 'Qián-Xiānsheng shi-jiàoyuán. Shéi-
    niàn-shū?

13. 'Bái-Xiānsheng xiān-dào-túshūguǎn 'hòu-dào-Gāo-jia-qu. Tā-'xiān-dào-
    nǎr?

14. 'Bái-Xiānsheng zài-Yuǎndōng-Dàxué niàn-shū. 'Wáng-Xiānsheng zài-
    Měiguo-dàxué niàn-shū. 'Shéi-zài-Yuǎndōng-Dàxué niàn-shū?

15. 'Wáng-Tàitai yǒu-ge-'nǚ-háizi. 'Gāo-Tàitai yǒu-ge-'nán-háizi. 'Shéi-
    yóu-nǚ-háizi?

16. 'Gāo-Xiānsheng cóng-shūdiàn-lái. Máo-Xiānsheng cóng-gōngyuán-lái.
    Shéi-cóng-gōngyuán-lái?

17. 'Qián-Xiānsheng zuò-'qìchē. 'Gāo-Xiānsheng zuò-'diànchē. 'Qián-
    Xiānsheng zuò-'shénmo-chē?

18. 'Gāo-Xiáojie dì-'yícì-lái. 'Qián-Xiáojie dì-'sāncì-lái. 'Gāo-Xiáojie
    dì-'jǐcì-lái?

19. 'Bái-Xiānsheng zuò-'chuán-lái-de. 'Máo-Xiānsheng zuò-'fēijī-lái-de.
    'Bái-Xiānsheng shi-zuò-'shénmo-lái-de?

20. Fēijī-kuài. Chē-màn. 'Shénmo-kuài?

21. 'Gāo-Xiānsheng 'qùnian-líkai-Měiguo. 'Máo-Xiānsheng 'jīnnian-líkai-
    Měiguo. 'Shéi-qùnian-líkai-Měiguo?

22. 'Qián-Xiānsheng yùjian-'Gāo-Xiānsheng. 'Máo-Xiáojie yùjian-'Bái-
    Xiānsheng. 'Shéi-yùjian-Qián-Xiānsheng?

23. 'Bái-Xiānsheng jiè-'Yīngwén-shū. 'Máo-Xiānsheng jiè-'Zhōngwén-shū.
    'Shéi-jiè-Yīngwén-shū?

24. Dìdi zài-'zhōngxué-niàn-shū. Mèimei zài-'xiǎoxué-niàn-shū. Dìdi-
    zài-'nǎr-niàn-shū?

25. 'Wáng-Xiáojie xǐhuan-niàn-'Yīngwén. 'Máo-Xiáojie xǐhuan-niàn-'Zhōng-wén. 'Shéi-xǐhuan-niàn-Yīngwén?

26. 'Wáng-Xiáojie cháng-dào-túshūguǎn. 'Máo-Xiáojie bù-cháng-dào-túshū-guǎn. 'Shéi-cháng-dào-túshūguǎn?

27. Gāo-Xiānsheng-yǒu-tàitai. 'Wáng-Xiānsheng méi-yǒu-tàitai. 'Shéi-yǒu-tàitai?

28. Màipiàoyuán rènshi-'Bái-Xiānsheng. Wǒ-'bú-rènshi-Bái-Xiānsheng. 'Shéi-rènshi-Bái-Xiānsheng?

29. 'Qián-Xiáojie dào-shūdiàn-lái. 'Wáng-Xiáojie 'bú-dào-shūdiàn-lái. 'Shéi-dào-shūdiàn-lái?

30. Wǒ-qu-bàifang 'Gāo-Xiānsheng. Tā-qu-bàifang 'Wáng-Xiānsheng. 'Shéi-qu-bàifang 'Wáng-Xiānsheng?

31. 'Bái-Xiānsheng dào-Rìběn. 'Gāo-Xiānsheng dào-Yīngguo. 'Shéi-dào-Rìběn?

32. 'Wáng-Xiānsheng niàn-shū. 'Máo-Xiānsheng zuò-shi. 'Wáng-Xiānsheng zuò-shénmo?

33. Wó-xǐhuan-zuò-chuán. Tā-xǐhuan-zuò-fēijī. Tā-xǐhuan-zuò-chuán-hái-shi-xǐhuan-zuò-fēijī?

34. Nǐ-shuōde bí-wó-hǎo. Tā-shuōde-bí-nǐ-'gèng-hǎo. 'Shéi-shuōde-hǎo?

35. Dào-túshūguǎn wàng-'dōng-guǎi. Dào-shūdiàn wàng-'xī-guǎi. Dào-tú-shūguǎn wàng-'nár-guǎi?

NARRATIVE

Read aloud and translate into English.

Wǒ-fùqin-mǔqin zuótian-cóng-Yīngguo dào-'Zhōngguo-lái. Tāmen-shi-'xiān-dào-Rìběn 'hòu-dào-Zhōngguo-lái-de. Tāmen-hén-xǐhuan dào-'wài-guo-qu. Tāmen-'gèng-xǐhuan dào-'Zhōngguo lái. Zuótian-wǎnshang wó-qǐng-tāmen-qu-chī-'Zhōngguo-fàn. Tāmen-suírán-shi dì-yícì-chī-'Zhōng-guo-fàn, kěshi 'hén-xǐhuan-chī. Wǒ-fùqin chīde-hěn-duō. Tā-gàosu-wǒ tā-zài-Rìběn kànjiàn-hěn-duō tāde-péngyou. Tā-hái-gàosu-wǒ xiànzài-wǒ-dìdi-mèimei dōu-hěn-gāo. Wǒmen-zài-gōnggòng-qìchēshang yùjian-'Wáng-Tàitai. Tā-kànjian-wǒde-fùqin-mǔqin tā-qǐng-tāmen-míngtian dào-tā-jiā-qu-chī-fàn. Tā-wèn: "'Míngtian-wǎnshang yǒu-gōngfu-ma?" Wó-mǔqin-shuō: "Xièxie, yǒu-gōngfu." Wǒ-fùqin-shuō: "Wó-hěn-xǐwang dào-yíge-'Zhōngguo-péngyou-jiā-qù."

DIALOGUE

Read aloud, preferably with two students acting out the roles, and translate into English.

'Zhāng-Xiānsheng 'Wáng-Xiānsheng liǎngge-rén zài-gōnggòng-qìchē-shang yùjian-tán-huà.

Zhāng: Wáng-Xiānsheng, 'háo-jiǔ-bú-jiàn. Hǎo-ma?

Wáng : 'Zhāng-Xiānsheng, nín-hǎo-ma?

Zhāng: Fǔshang-dōu-hǎo-ma?

Wáng : 'Dōu-hǎo, xièxie-nín.

Zhāng: Nín-dào-nǎr-qu?

Wáng : Wǒ-qu-bàifang yíge-péngyou. Nín-ne?

Zhāng: Wǒ-dào-túshūguǎn-qu-kàn-shū.

Wáng : Zhèr-'túshūguǎn wǒ-hái-bù-zhīdào zài-nǎr-ne. Wó-yé-hén-xǐhuan dào-'túshūguǎn-qù-kàn-shū.

Zhāng: Nín-bù-zhīdào túshūguǎn-zài-nǎr-ma?

Wáng : Wǒ-bù-zhīdào-ne.

Zhāng: Lí-Zhōngshān-Gōngyuán bù-yuǎn. Hěn-róngyi-zhǎo. Zuótian-wǎn-shang wǒ-yùjian-'Qián-Xiānsheng. Tā-shuō sānyue-èrshiwǔhào tā-dào-'Rìběn-qu.

Wáng : Shì. Zuótian tā-dào-wǒ-jiā-qu. Tā-yě-gàosu-wǒ sānyue-dào-Rìběn.

Zhāng: Wó-xiǎng qǐng-ta-chī-fàn. Yé-qǐng-nín, qǐng-nín-'tàitai liǎngge-háizi dōu-lái.

Wáng : Xièxie-nín.

Zhāng: Nín-shíjiǔhào yǒu-gōngfu-ma? Wó-xiǎng-shíjiǔhào-wǎnshang-qǐng.

Wáng : Yǒu-gōngfu. Xièxie-nín.

Zhāng: Qǐng-nín-tàitai-háizi yídìng-lái.

Wáng : Wǒmen-yídìng-lái.

Zhāng: Nín-zài-nǎr-xià-chē?

Wáng : Qiántou-bù-yuǎn jiù-shi-wǒ-péngyou-jiā. Wǒ-jiù-zài-zhèige-chē-zhàn xià-chē.

Zhāng: Zài-guò-liǎngge-lù-kǒur, wàng-xī-guǎi, jiù-dào-túshūguǎn. Wǒ-zài túshūguǎn-mén-kǒur xià-chē. Zàijian. Shíjiǔhào yídìng-lái.

Wáng : Yídìng-lái, yídìng-lái.

QUESTIONNAIRE

Assume both roles in the following oral questionnaire, to practice getting information about another person as well as providing it about yourself.

Q: May I ask, what is your [sur]name?

A: My [sur]name is King.

Q: What is your Chinese given name?

A: I don't have a Chinese given name.

Q: When did you come to China?

A: I came on February 1.

Q: You speak Chinese very well. Did you study it in America?

A: I studied in America. I speak badly.

Q: You speak really well. Who is in your family?

A: I have a father, mother, and younger brother.

Q: How old is your younger brother? Does he study?

A: My younger brother is ten. He studies in elementary school.

Q: How old [lit. ten and how many years] are you this year?

A: I'm eighteen.

Q: What does your father do?

A: He works at a university.

Q: How about your mother?

A: My mother doesn't work.

Q: Did you come by boat or by plane from America to China?

A: I came first from America to England, then from England to China. I came from America to England by boat, and from England to China by plane.

Q: Are you coming to China to study or to work?

A: I'm coming to study.

Q: At what university are you studying?

A: I'm studying at Far Eastern University.

Q: What are you studying?

A: I'm studying literature.

Q: Are you studying Chinese literature or foreign literature?

A: I'm studying English literature, and also studying Chinese literature.

Q : My home is east of Sun Yatsen Road, number 15.   If you have time, I hope
     you will come often to my home.   We'll talk a while.

A : Thank you.   If I have time I will certainly go to your home to call on
     you.

UNIT III

Lesson 13 GETTING ACQUAINTED

" 'Gāo-Xiáojie, ní-hǎo-ma?"

Dialogue: Mr. White and Miss Gao meet on the bus and get further
acquainted.

Bái : 'Gāo-Xiáojie, ní-hǎo-ma?
      Shàng-nǎr-qu-le?

Miss Gao, how are you? Where
have you been?

Gāo : 'Bái-Xiānsheng, nín-hǎo-
      ma? Wǒ-shàng-xuéxiào-
      qu-le. Xiànzài-huí-jiā.   5

Hello, Mr. White. I've been at
school. I'm on my way home
now.

Bái : Nǐ-cóng-xuéxiào huí-jiā-
      hén-wǎn-ne.

You're returning home very late,
(aren't you?)

Gāo : Yīnwei-xià-kè-yǐhòu
      wǒmen-xuéxiào-yǒu-yì-
      diǎr-shì, suóyi-'wǎn-le-   10
      yìdiǎr. Nín-dào-nǎr-qu?
      Shi-dào-wǒmen-jiā-qu-
      ma?

After class we had something to
do at school, so I'm a little late.
Where are you going? [Are you
going] to our home?

Bái : Shì.

Yes.

Gāo : Jīntian-wǎnshang wǒ-fù-   15
      qin-qǐng-nín-chī-fàn,
      'duì-bu-duì?

My father invited you to dinner
this evening, isn't that so?

165

Bái : Duì-le. Tài-'máfan-nǐmen-   Yes. It puts you to too much
le.   trouble.

Gāo : 'Bù-máfan. Huānyíng-nín-   20   It's no trouble.   We're glad
lái.   you're coming.

Bái : Wǒ-hái-bu-zhīdào nǐ-zài-   [I still don't know] at what school
'něige-xuéxiào niàn-shū-ne.   are you studying?

Gāo : Wǒ-zài-Dì-'yī-Zhōngxué-   [I'm studying] at No. 1 Middle
niàn-shū.   25   School.

Bái : 'Jǐniánjí?   What year?

Gāo : Gāozhōng-'sānniánjí. Jīn-   Third year higher middle.   I'll
nián wǒ-jiù-bìyè-le.   be graduating this year.

Bái : Wó-xiǎng nǐ-'yídìng-hěn-   [I think] you must be very bright.
cōngming.   30

Gāo : 'Bù-cōngming. Bènjíle.   I'm not [bright. I'm awfully stu-
pid].

Bái : Nǐ-kèqi-ne.   You're being polite.

Gāo : Nín-zài-Yuǎn-Dà 'jǐniánjí?   What year are you in at Far
Eastern?

Bái : Wǒ-zài-sānniánjí.   [I'm in] the junior year.

Gāo : Wǒ-fùqin-shuō nín-'yòu-   35   My father says you're clever
cōngming 'yòu-yònggōng.   and hard-working.

Bái : Wǒ-bènjíle. Yě-'bú-yòng-   I'm not. [lit. I'm awfully stupid.
gōng.   Also, I don't work hard.]

Gāo : Wǒ-xiànzài-mángjíle, yīn-   I'm terribly busy now, as we're
wei-xuéxiào kuài-kǎoshì-le.   40   [lit. our school is] about to have
Nín-ne?   exams. What about you?

Bái : Wǒmen-'yě-méi-kǎo-ne.   We haven't had our exams yet
'Kuài-yào-kǎo-le. . . . Ní-   either. We'll be having them
xǐhuan kàn-diànyǐngr-ma?   soon. . . . Do you like [to see]
movies?

Gāo : Wǒ-'hén-xǐhuan. Chàbuduō- 45   [I like to] very much.   Almost
liǎngge-xīngqī jiù-qù-kàn-   every other week I go to one.
yícì.

Bái : Ní-kǎoshì-yǐhòu, wó-qíng-   After your exams may I invite
ni-kàn-diànyǐngr, hǎo-ma?   you to see a movie?

Gāo : 'Nín-yé-xǐhuan kàn-diàn-   50   Do you like movies too?
yǐngr-ma?

Bái : Wó-'yé-xǐhuan kàn-diàn-   Yes. [lit. I like movies too.]
yǐngr. Yǐqián zài-Měiguo-   [Previously,] when I was in
de-shíhou, wó-'měige-xīng-   America, I went to the movies
qī 'dōu-qù-kàn-diànyǐngr.   55   every week. Let's take one in
Kǎoshì-yǐhòu wǒmen-qù-   after exams. Be my guest.
kàn. Wó-qíng-ni.

Gāo : Xièxie-nin. Jīntian-   Thank you.   This evening we

wǎnshang wǒmen-hái-qǐng-
le yíwèi-'Yīngguo-péngyou-   60
ne. Nín-rènshi-ma?

have also invited an English
friend. (I take it) you're acquainted?

Bái : Wǒ-'bú-rènshi. Shi-xiānsheng, shi-tàitai, háishi-
xiáojie-ne?

No, I'm not. Who is it? [lit. Is
it a gentleman, a married lady,
or a girl?]

Gāo: Shi-xiānsheng. Wǒ-fùqin   65
méi-gàosu-nín-ma?

It's a gentleman. Didn't my
father tell you?

Bái : Tā-'méi-shuō. 'Jiù-shuō
shi-yíwèi-'Yīngguo-péng-
you.

He didn't say. He said only that
it was an English friend.

Gāo: Jīntian-wǎnshang nǐmen-   70
jiù-rènshi-le.

You'll get acquainted this evening.

Bái : Lí-fǔshang hái-yǒu-'duō-
yuǎn?

How much farther is it to your
home?

Gāo: Yǐjing-kuài-dàole. Zài-
guò-'sìge-lù-kǒur jiù-dào-   75
le.

We'll soon be there. It's just
four more blocks [lit. After
passing four more intersections
then we'll arrive.]

Bái : Wǒ-dì-'yícì-lái. Rúguǒ-
méi-yùjiàn-ni, hěn-nán-zhǎo-
le.

(This is) the first time I've come
(to your home). If I hadn't met
you, it would have been hard to
find.

Gāo: 'Bái-Xiānsheng, qǐng-wèn,   80
xiànzài-'jídiǎn-zhōng-le?
Wó-zǎochen-hěn-máng.
Chīle-zǎofàn-jiù-zǒule,
wàngle-dài-biǎo-le.

Mr. White, [may I ask,] what
time is it [lit. has it become]? I
was very busy this morning. I
left right after breakfast [lit. after eating breakfast I left imme-
diately], and forgot to wear my
watch.

Bái : Xiànzài chà-yíkè-qīdiǎn.   85

It's now quarter of seven.

Gāo: Dào-jiā jiù-chàbuduō-qī-
diǎnle.

By the time we get home it will
be just about seven.

VOCABULARY

bèn   stupid (SV)

biǎo   watch, timepiece (N)

bìyè   graduate (IV) [lit. finish job] (Bì is also a surname)

cōngming   intelligent, clever, bright (SV) [lit. clever bright]

dài   wear (on the hands or head) (TV); (also, a surname)

diànyǐng(r)   motion picture, movie (N) [lit. electric shadow]

gāozhōng   higher middle school (N) [lit. high middle]

'huānyíng	welcome (TV) [lit. pleased receive]
huí	return (to) (TV)
jíle	in the extreme, extremely [lit. extremely finished] (Note 15)
kǎo	take or give an examination (in a subject, or for school) (TV)
kǎoshì	take or give an examination (IV) [lit. test try]
kè	class (N) lesson (M)
kèqi	polite, ceremonious, formal (SV) [lit. guest air]
le	(suffix indicating perfective aspect: Notes 1-8, 17)
máng	busy (SV)
máfan	cause trouble to, disturb (TV) troublesome (SV)
niánjí	year of school (M) [lit. year rank]
suóyi	therefore (MA)
wǎn	late (SV)
wàng	forget (V)
xīngqī	week (N) [lit. star period] (Notes 13-14 below)
xuéxiào	school (N) [lit. study school]
yǐhòu	after, afterwards (TW) [lit. take rear] (Note 11 below)
yǐjing	already (AD) [lit. already pass]
yǐqián	before, previously (TW) [lit. take front] (Note 11 below)
yīnwei	because, since (MA) [lit. because be]
yònggōng	work hard, be studious (V) [lit. use service]
yòu	again (AD)
zǎochen	morning, forenoon (TW) [lit. early morning]
zǎofàn	breakfast (N) [lit. early food]

SENTENCE BUILD-UP

lái	come
lái-le	came
1. Tāmen-'dōu-lái-le.	They've all come.

bìyè	graduate
bìyè-le	graduated
2. Tā-dìdi qùnian-jiù-bìyè-le.	His younger brother graduated last year.

zǎochen   morning
zuótian-zǎochen   yesterday morning
3. Nǐ-zuótian-zǎochen dào-nǎr-   Where did you go yesterday
qù-le?   morning?

mǎi-shū-qu   go to buy books
mǎi-shū-qu-le   gone to buy books
4. Tā-bú-zài-jiā, mǎi-shū-qu-   He's not at home, (he's) gone to
le.   buy some books.

'chī-fàn   eat food
chī-fàn-le   have eaten
5. Nǐ-chī-fàn-le-ma?   Have you eaten?

chī-fàn-le   have eaten
chī-le-fàn-le   have eaten
6. Nǐ-chī-le-fàn-le-ma?   Have you eaten?

dàole-túshūguǎn   arrived at the library
jiù-jiè-shū   then take out books
7. Tā-dàole-túshūguǎn jiù-jiè-   When he gets to the library,
shū.   he'll take out some books.

jiù-jiè-shū   then take out books
jiù-jiè-shū-le   then took out books
8. Tā-dàole-túshūguǎn jiù-jiè-   After he got to the library, he
shū-le.   took out some books.

huí   return (to a place)
huí-jiā   return home
9. Nǐ-'shénmo-shíhou-huí-jiā?   When are you returning home?

huí-jiā   return home
huí-jiā-le   returned home
10. Tā-'mǎile-zìdiǎn jiù-huí-jiā-   He returned home after buying
le.   the dictionary.

zǎofàn   breakfast
chīle-zǎofàn   having eaten breakfast
11. Wǒ-chīle-zǎofàn jiù-zǒu.   I'll leave after [eating] break-
        fast.

biǎo   watch
mǎile-biǎo   bought the watch
12. Wó-mǎile-biǎo jiù-huí-jiā.   I'll return home after I've bought
        the watch.

dài   wear
dài-biǎo   wear a watch
13. Wó-měitiān dōu-dài-biǎo.   I wear a watch every day.

wǎn   late
wǎnle   become late
14. Xiànzài-wǎnle, wǒ-yào-zǒu.   It's [gotten to be] late. I must go.

cōngming | clever, bright
cōngmingde-xuésheng | bright student

15. 'Gāo-Xiáojie shi-yíge-cōng-
mingde-xuésheng. | Miss Gao is a bright student.

bèn | stupid
bènde-duō | much more stupid

16. Wó-bǐ-tāmen-'bènde-duō. | I'm a lot more stupid than they
are.

máng | busy
'máng-bu-máng? | busy or not?

17. Nǐ-xiànzài máng-bu-máng? | Are you busy now?

kèqi | polite
zhēn-kèqi | really polite

18. 'Zhōngguo-rén 'zhēn-kèqi. | Chinese are really polite.

jiè-yìběn-shū | borrow a book
jièle-yìběn-shū | borrowed a book

19. Wǒ-zuótian jièle-yìběn-shū. | I borrowed one book yesterday.

jièle-yìběn-shū | borrowed one book
jièle-yìběn-shū-le | have borrowed one book
'hái-yào-jiè-yìběn | want to borrow another one

20. Wǒ-jīntian jièle-yìběn-shū-
le, 'hái-yào-jiè-yìběn. | I've borrowed one book today
and want to borrow another.

yǐjing | already
yǐjing-qǐngle | already invited

21. Wó-yǐjing-qǐngle 'sānge-
péngyou-le. | I've already invited three
friends.

xīngqī | week
yíge-xīngqī | one week

22. 'Yíge-xīngqī yǒu-'qītiān. | A week has seven days.

xīngqītiān | Sunday
xīngqīyī | Monday

23. Tā-xīngqī'tiān-lái-de, xīng-
qī'yī-zǒu-de. | He arrived on Sunday and left on
Monday.

diànyǐngr | movie
kàn-diànyǐngr | see a movie

24. Wó-měi-xīngqīliù kàn-diàn-
yǐngr. | I go to the movies every Satur-
day.

yícì | one time
yícì-diànyǐngr | one movie

25. Wó-měi-xīngqī kàn-yícì-
diànyǐngr. | I see one movie a week.

xuéxiào | school
zài-'něige-xuéxiào? | at what school?

26. Nǐ-zài-'něige-xuéxiào-niàn-   At what school are you study-
     shū?   ing?

          zǒule   have left
          kuài-zǒule   will soon have left
27. 'Bái-Xiānsheng kuài-zǒule.   Mr. White will leave very soon.

          kǎo   take an examination
          kǎo-shū   have examinations
28. Wǒmen-'míngtian-kǎo-shū.   We have examinations tomorrow.

          kǎo   take an examination
          kǎo-dàxué   take an examination for col-
                                               lege
29. Wǒmen-bìyè jiù-kǎo-dàxué.   After graduating we take the
                                          exams for college.

          kǎoshì   examine or be examined
          'jiù-kǎoshìle   will soon have examinations
30. Wǒmen-xuéxiào jiù-yào-kǎo-   Our school is about to have ex-
     shìle.   ams.

          kè   class
          shàng-kè   go to class
          yào-shàng-kè-le   will go to class
31. Wǒ-xiànzài yào-shàng-kè-le.   I'm going to class now.

          kè   lesson
          dì-sānkè   third lesson
32. Wǒmen-jīntian yào-niàn-dì-   We're going to **read** Lesson
     'sānkè-le.   Three today.

          yòu   again
          'yòu-láile   came again
33. Tā-'zuótian-láile. Jīntian tā-   He came yesterday. He came
     'yòu-láile.   again today.

          Zhōngguo-zì   Chinese characters
          nán-xiě   hard to write
          nán-niàn   hard to read
34. 'Zhōngguo-zì 'yòu-nán-xiě   Chinese characters are [both]
     'yòu-nán-niàn.   hard to write and hard to read.

          máfan   cause trouble to
35. Nǐ-bú-yào-máfan-ta.   Don't disturb him.

          máfan   troublesome
36. Zuò-zhèige-shì hěn-máfan.   It's a lot of trouble to do this
                                          job.

          yǐqián   before
          shàng-chē-yǐqián   before getting on the street-
                                               car
37. Shàng-chē-yǐqián yào-mǎi-   Before you get on the car you
     piào.   have to buy a ticket.

yǐhòu   after
shàng-chē-yǐhòu   after getting on the car
38. Shàng-chē-yǐhòu yào-mǎi-   After you get on the car you have
piào.   to buy a ticket.

shíhou   time
shàng-chē-de-shíhou   when getting on the car
39. Shàng-chē-de-shíhou yào-   When you get on the car you have
mǎi-piào.   to buy a ticket.

wǒ-méi-yǒu-qián   I don't have any money
suóyi   therefore, so
bù-néng-mǎi-shū   can't buy books
40. Wǒ-méi-yǒu-qián, suóyi-bù-   I don't have any money, so I
néng-mǎi-shū.   can't buy any books.

yīnwei   because, since
yīnwei-wǒ-méi-yǒu-   since I don't have any money
qián
41. Yīnwei-wǒ-méi-yǒu-qián,   Since I don't have any money, I
suóyi-bù-néng-mǎi-shū.   can't buy any books.

yònggōng   studious, hard-working
hěn-yònggōng   very diligent
42. Nèige-xuésheng hěn-yòng-   That student works very hard.
gōng.

bù-chī   not eat
bù-chī-le   not eat any more
43. Xièxie, wǒ-bù-chīle.   Thanks, I won't have any more.

niánjí   year of school
èrniánjí   second year of school
44. Tā-bú-zài-èrniánjí-le.   He's no longer in the second
year.

gāozhōng   higher middle school
niàn-gāozhōng   study in h i g h e r m i d d l e
school
45. Tā-xiānzài bú-niàn-gāo-   He's no longer in higher middle
zhōng-le.   school [now].

'huānyíng   welcome
dào-wǒ-jiā-lái   come to my home
46. Wǒ-huānyíng-nín-míngtian   I look forward to your coming to
dào-wǒ-jiā-lái.   my home tomorrow.

jíle   awfully
hǎojíle   awfully good
47. Tāde-Zhōngguo-huà hǎojíle.   His Chinese is awfully good.

láile   came
'méi-yǒu-lái   did not come
48. Tāmen-'méi-yǒu-lái.   They didn't come.

láile	came
'méi-lái	did not come
49. Tā-'hái-méi-lái-ne.	He <u>still</u> hasn't come.
láile	came
méi-you	not have
50. Tā-'láile-méi-you?	Did he come?
bù-chī-le	not eat any more
51. Nǐ-bù-chī-le-ma?	Aren't you eating any more?
méi-yóu-bǐ	not have a pen
méi-bǐ	not have a pen
52. Nǐ-méi-bǐ-ma?	Don't you have a pen?
shàng-xué	attend school
xīngqīliù	Saturday
53. Wǒmen-xīngqīliù bú-shàng-xué.	We don't go to school on Saturday.
shàng-zhōngxué	attend middle school
shàng-dàxué	attend college
54. Nǐ-shàng-'zhōngxué háishi-shàng-'dàxué?	Do you go to middle school or college?
shàng-Yīngguo	go to England
55. Tā-kuài-shàng-Yīngguo-le.	He's going to England soon.
shàng-xīngqī	last week
zuò-shénmo?	do what?
56. Nǐ-shàng-xīngqī zuò-shén-mo-le?	What did you do last week?
xià-xīngqī	next week
xià-xīngqīsān	next Wednesday
57. Wǒ-xià-xīngqīsān qu-'kàn-diànyǐngr.	I'm going to see a movie next Wednesday.
niàn-xiǎoxué	study in grade school
niàn-zhōngxué	study in middle school
58. Nǐ-dìdi-niàn-'xiǎoxué háishi-niàn-'zhōngxué?	Is your younger brother going to grade school or middle school?
gāozhōng-'jǐniánjí?	what year of higher middle school?
niàn-'jǐniánjí?	be in what year of school?
59. Nǐ-niàn-gāozhōng-jǐniánjí?	What year of higher middle school are you in?
wàng	forget
wàngle-míngzi-le	forgot a name
60. Wǒ-wàngle-tāde-míngzi-le.	I've forgotten his name.

PATTERN DRILLS

Pattern 13.1. Le Indicating Completed Action or New Situation
(Notes 1 – 2 below)

Pattern 13.1 a.

S	V	le
Subject	Verb	le
Tā	zǒu	le.

'He has left.'

Pattern 13.1 b.

S	V(-le)	O	le
Subject	Verb(-le)	Object	le
Tā	chīle	fàn	le.

'He has eaten.'

1. 'Gāo-Xiáojie zǎochen-lái-le.

Miss Gao came in the morning.

2. Wó-mǔqin zuótian-zǎochen-zǒu-le.

My mother left yesterday morning.

3. 'Qián-Tàitai chīle-fàn-le-ma?

Has Mrs. Qian eaten?

4. Wó-dìdi jīntian-zǎochen-lái-le.

My brother came this morning.

5. 'Máo-Xiānsheng mǎile-'zì-diǎn-le-ma?

Did Mr. Mao buy a dictionary?

6. Nǐ-chīle-fàn-le-ma?

Have you eaten?

7. Tā-bìyè-le-ma?

Has he graduated?

8. 'Gāo-Xiáojie zhǎo-shéi-qu-le?

Whom has Miss Gao gone to visit?

9. 'Bái-Xiānsheng zhǎo-'Gāo-Xiānsheng-qu-le-ma?

Did Mr. White go to visit Mr. Gao?

10. 'Zhāng-Xiānsheng dào-shū-diàn-qu-le.

Mr. Zhang has gone to the bookstore.

11. Wǒ-gàosu-ni-le. Nǐ-wàng-le-ma?

I told you. Did you forget?

12. Míngtian-wǎnshang tā-qǐng-ni-chī-fàn. Nǐ-zhīdao-le-ma?

He's inviting you to dinner tomorrow. Did you know?

13. Jīntian-zǎochen wǒ-zuòle-diànchē-le.

I took a streetcar this morning.

14. Wǒ-zuótian-yùjian-ta-le.

I met him yesterday.

15. Tā-jīntian-zǎochen shàng-
    fēijī-le.

He took the plane this morning.

16. 'Wáng-Xiānsheng jīntian-
    shàng-shān-le-ma?

Did Mr. King go up the mountain
today?

17. Wǒ-zài-túshūguǎn jièle-
    liángběn-shū-le.

I've borrowed two books at the
library.

18. Wó-mǎile-gāngbǐ-le.

I've bought a pen.

19. Bái-Xiānsheng-lái-le-ma?

Did Mr. White come?

20. Wǒ-zuótian kànle-hěn-duō-
    shū-le.

I read a lot yesterday.

Pattern 13.2.   Completed Action with le in Dependent Clauses
                (Note 3 below)

Pattern 13.2 a.

S	V₁-le	O	jiù	V₂
Subject	Verb₁-le	Object	'then'	Verb₂
Wǒ	chīle	fàn	jiù	zǒu.

'After eating I will leave.'

Pattern 13.2 b.

S	V₁-le	O	jiù	V₂	le
Subject	Verb₁-le	Object	'then'	Verb₂	le
Wǒ	chīle	fàn	jiù	zǒu	le.

'After eating, I left.'

1. Tā-mǎile-shū jiù-huí-jiā-le.

He returned home after buying
the books.

2. Tā-xiàle-chē jiù-dào-gōngyuán-
   qu-le.

After he got off the car he went
to the park.

3. Qián-Xiānsheng-chīle-fàn jiù-
   zǒu-le-ma?

Did Mr. Qian leave after he ate?

4. Gāo-Xiānsheng-chīle-fàn jiù-
   dào-xuéxiào-qu-le.

After eating, Mr. Gao went to
school.

5. 'Bái-Xiānsheng láile-jiù-zǒu-
   le.

Mr. White came and then left
immediately.

6. Tā-mǎile-běnzi jiù-zǒu.

He will leave after buying the
notebook.

7. Nǐ-shàngle-chē jiù-mǎi-
   piào.

You buy the ticket right after
you get on the car.

8. Tā-mǎile-shū jiù-zǒu.

He will leave right after buying
the books.

9. Tāmen-mǎile-máobǐ jiù-xiě-   They will write some Chinese
    Zhōngguo-zì.   characters after buying writing
                                        brushes.

10. 'Bái-Xiānsheng chīle-zǎofàn-   Mr. White will leave right after
    jiù-zǒu.   (eating) breakfast.

11. Tā-chīle-zǎofàn jiù-dào-gōng-   He will go to the park after (eat-
    yuán.   ing) breakfast.

12. Tā-dàole-gōngyuán jiù-dào-   After going to the park he will
    túshūguǎn-qu.   go to the library.

13. Tā-mǎile-shū jiù-huí-jiā.   He will return home after buying
                                        the books.

14. Tā-shuōle-jiù-zǒu-le.   He mentioned it and left.

15. 'Bái-Xiānsheng jièle-shū-jiù-   Mr. White returned home after
    huí-jiā-le.   borrowing the books.

Pattern 13.3.   Le with Stative Verbs and Time Expressions
                (Note 4 below)

Pattern 13.3 a.

(S)	(AD)	SV	le
(Subject)	(Adverb)	Stative verb	le
Wǒ	xiànzài	hǎo	le.

'I'm well now.'

Pattern 13.3 b.

(AD)	TW	le
(Adverb)	Time word	le
Xiànzài	sāndiǎn	le.

'It's become 3:00.'

1. Wǒde-fángzi 'tài-xiǎo-le.   My home has become too small.

2. Xiànzài chà-yíkè-sìdiǎn-le.   It's [gotten to be] 3:45.

3. Nèige-háizi 'tài-gāo-le.   That child is too tall.

4. Tā-jiā-lí-zhèr 'tài-yuǎn-le.   His home is too far from here.

5. Nèige-xuéxiàode-xuésheng   There are too many students in
    'tài-duō-le.   that school.

6. Dào-Gāo-jia-qu 'tài-yuǎn-le.   It is too far to go to the Gao
                                        home.

7. Zhèibǎn-zìdiǎn tài-dà-le.   This dictionary is too big.

8. Ní-mǔqin-hǎo-le-ma?   Has your mother recovered?

9. Nèige-háizi xiànzài pǎode-hěn-   That child runs very fast now.
    kuài-le.

10. Xiànzài-'hén-wǎn-le. 'Yìdiǎn-   It's late now. It's one o'clock.
    le.

11. 'Gāo-Tàitai tài-kèqi-le.   Mrs. Gao is too polite.

12. Wǒ-tài-máng-le. Bù-néng-dào-   I'm too busy. I can't go to the
    gōngyuán-qu.   park.

13. Qián-tài-shǎo-le.   I have too little money.

14. Xiànzài-'jídiǎn-zhōng-le?   What time is it now?

15. 'Máo-Xiānsheng shū-tài-duō-le.   Mr. Mao has too many books.

Pattern 13.4. Single and Double le with Quantified Objects
               (Note 5 below)

Pattern 13.4a.

    S   (TW)   V-le   NU-M   O

    Subject   (Time word)   Verb-le   Number-Measure   Object
    Wǒ   jīntian   kànle   liángběn   shū.

    'I read two books today (and that's all I'm reading).'

Pattern 13.4b.

    S   (TW)   V-le   NU-M   O   le

    Subject   (Time word)   Verb-le   Number-Measure   Object   le
    Wǒ   jīntian   kànle   liángběn   shū   le.

    'I've read two books today (and I'm not done yet).'

1. Wǒ-zuótian mǎile-liángběn-   I bought two books yesterday.
    shū.

2. 'Gāo-Xiānsheng kànle-yícì-   Mr. Gao has been to a movie
    diànyǐngr.   once.

3. Wǒ-jīntian yǐjing-kànle   Today I've already read three
    'sānběn-shū-le.   books.

4. 'Bái-Xiáojie mǎile-wǔzhī-bǐ.   Miss Bai bought five pens. All
    'Dōu-hén-hǎo.   of them are very good.

5. 'Qián-Xiānsheng yǐjing-mǎile-   Mr. Qian has already bought one
    yìzhāng-dìtú-le. Hái-yào-'zài-   map. He still wants to buy an-
    mǎi-yìzhāng.   other.

6. 'Qián-Xiānsheng zài-Gāo-   Mr. Qian bought a house to the
    Xiānsheng-yòubiar mǎile-yì-   right of Mr. Gao('s house).
    suǒr-fángzi.

7. Tāmen-kànle 'wǔcì-diànyǐngr.   They saw five movies.

8. Bái-Xiānsheng-dào-túshūguǎn   Mr. White went to the library
    jièle-liángběn-zìdiǎn.   and took out two dictionaries.

9. Ní-yǐjing-qǐngle-'báge-péng-   You've already ·invited eight
    you-le. 'Hái-yào-qǐng-duō-   friends. How many more are
    shao?   you going to invite?

10. Wó-hěn-máng. Zhèige-xīngqī   I'm very busy. I've seen only
    jiù-kànle-'yícì-diànyǐngr.   one movie this week.

11. Tā-shuō tā-yào-mǎi-'sānběn-   He says he wants to buy three
    shū. Yǐjing-mǎile-'liángběn-   books. He's already bought two.
    le.

12. Wǒmen-yǐjing-zǒule chàbuduō-   We've already walked almost ten
    'shílǐ-lu-le. 'Hái-yào-zǒu-   miles. How far do we still have
    duó-yuǎn?   to go?

13. Wǒ-qùnian-zài-**chéngwài**   I bought a house outside the city
    mǎile-yìsuǒr-fángzi.   last year.

14. Wó-mǎile-yìzhāng-dà-dìtú.   I bought a large map.

15. Tā-xiěle-wǔge-zì. 'Dōu-bù-   He wrote five characters. They
    hǎo.   were all no good.

Pattern 13.5. Imminent Action with <u>le</u>   (Note 6 below)

	(kuài)	V	le
Subject	('soon')	Verb	le
Tā	kuài	zǒu	le.

'He is leaving soon.'

1. Wǒ-dìdi jiù-yào-cóng-Měiguo-   My younger brother will come
    lái-le.   from America soon.

2. Wǒmen-xuéxiào xiànzài-kuài-   Our school is about to have ex-
    yào-kǎoshì-le.   ams now.

3. Wúdiǎn-sānkè tā-jiù-lái-le.   He'll come at 5:45.

4. Wǒ-kuài-zǒu-le. Wǒmen-jiù-   I'm leaving. We're about to go
    yào-shàng-kè-le.   to class.

5. 'Gāo-Xiáojie 'sāndian-zhōng-   Miss Gao came at three o'clock
    láide, 'sìdian-zhōng-jiù-yào-   and will leave at four.
    zǒu-le.

6. Xiànzai kuài-dào-qīdiǎn-   It will ·soon be seven o'clock
    zhōng-le.   [now].

7. Wǒ-'jiù-yào-chī-fàn-le.   I'm about to eat.

8. Hái-yǒu-yíkè-zhōng jiù-dào-   In another quarter of an hour it
    wúdiǎn-le.   will be five o'clock.

9. **Wǒ-'jiù-yào-kàn-shū-le.**   **I'm about to read.**

10. Yǐjing-'bādiǎn-zhōng-le.   It's already eight o'clock. I'm
     Wǒ-'jiù-yào-zhǎo-Gāo-Xiān-   about to go visit Mr. Gao.
     sheng-qù-le.

Pattern 13.6. Clauses Expressing Relative Time (Note 11 below)

Pattern 13.6 a.

S	V	yǐqián/yǐhòu
Subject	Verb	'before'/'after'
nǐ	lái	yǐqián

'before you come'

Pattern 13.6 b.

S	V	de-shíhou
Subject	Verb	'when'
nǐ	lái	de-shíhou

'when you come'

1. Nǐ-lái-de-shíhou xiān-dào-   When you come, will you first go
    'Gāo-Xiānsheng-jiā-qu-ma?   to Mr. Gao's home?

2. Nǐ-láile-yǐhòu, wǒmen-kàn-   After you come, let's read —
    shū 'hǎo-bu-hǎo?   O.K.?

3. Nǐ-qù-de-shíhou qíng-ni-mǎi   When you go (to the bookstore),
    yìběn-zìdiǎn.   please buy a dictionary.

4. Wǒmen-kǎole-yǐhou qu-kàn-   How about going to a movie after
    diànyǐngr 'hǎo-bu-hǎo?   we've had our exams?

5. Wó-zǒu-de-shíhou wàngle-dài-   When I left, I forgot tó wear my
    biǎo-le.   watch:

6. Wó-mǎi-shū-de-shíhou xiān-   Whenever I buy books, I [first]
    zhǎo-'Máo-Xiānsheng.   look up Mr. Mao.

7. 'Bái-Xiānsheng dào-xuéxiào-   When Mr. White comes to school
    lái-de-shíhou, xiān-zháo-wo-   he will visit me first for a chat.
    tántan.

8. Wǒ-dào-xuéxiào-yǐqián xiān-   Before I go to school I [first] eat
    chī-zǎofàn.   breakfast.

9. 'Bái-Xiānsheng dào-Měiguo-   When Mr. White goes to America,
    qù-de-shíhou, xiān-lái-bài-   he will first come and visit you.
    fang-ni.

10. Wó-mǔqin-dào-zhèr-yǐhòu,   After my mother arrived here a
    hěn-duō-péngyou qǐng-ta-chī-   lot of friends invited her to din-
    fàn.   ner.

11. Wǒ-kàn-shū-de-shíhou bù-   When I read I don't like people
    xǐhuan-rén-zháo-wo.   to visit me.

12. Wǒ-xià-chuán-yǐhòu 'xiān-dào-   After getting off the boat, I go
     Gāo-jia-qu.   first to the Gaos'.

13. Wǒ-huí-jiā-yǐqián 'xiān-dào-   Before returning home, I'm
     túshūguǎn-qu.   [first] going to the library.

14. Wǒ-shàng-chuán-yǐhòu rènshi-   After boarding the boat I made
     le-hěn-duō-péngyou.   [the acquaintance of] numerous
                                          friends.

15. Wǒ-chī-fàn-de-shíhou bù-xǐ-   When I eat I don't like to talk.
     huan-shuō-huà.

Pattern 13.7. Le with Negative Verbs (Note 7)

         S   bu   V   le

      Subject   bu   Verb   le

         Wǒ   bù   chī   le.

      'I'm not eating any more.'

1. 'Gāo-Xiānsheng bú-zài-shūdiàn-   Mr. Gao is no longer at the book-
     le. Tā-huí-jiā-le.   store. He's gone home.

2. 'Bái-Xiānsheng jīntian-tài-   Mr. White is too busy today. He
     máng-le. Tā-bú-dào-túshū-   isn't going to the library.
     guǎn-qu-le.

3. Jīntian wǒ-kànle-sānběn-shū-   I've read three books today, so
     le, suóyi-wǒ-bú-kàn-le.   I'm not reading any more.

4. Jīntian wǒmen-huānyíng-yí-   Today we're meeting [lit. wel-
     wèi-péngyou. Wǒ-bú-dào-'nǐ-   coming] a friend. I'm not going
     nèr-qu-le.   to your place (after all).

5. 'Qián-Xiānsheng jīntiān-yǒu-   Mr. Qian has something to do to-
     shì, suóyi-tā-bù-lái-le.   day, so he's not coming (after
                                         all).

6. Tā-méi-yǒu-qián. Bù-néng-   He doesn't have any money. He
     'zài-niàn-shū-le.   can't study any more.

7. Tā-jīntian-méi-yǒu-qián-le,   He has no more money today, so
     suóyi-tā-'bù-mǎi-shū-le.   he's not buying any more books.

8. Zhèige-fàn bù-hǎo-chī. Wǒ-   This food is unappetizing. I'm
     bù-chī-le.   not eating any more.

9. 'Gāo-Xiáojie méi-yǒu-mòshuǐ-   Miss Gao doesn't have any more
     le. Tā-xiǎng-qù-mǎi.   ink. She's going to go buy some.

10. Tā-suíran-hén-xiǎo, kěshi   [Although] he's very young, but
     méi-yǒu-fùqin-le.   he's already lost his father [lit.
                                         nevertheless he no longer has a
                                         father].

SUBSTITUTION TABLES

I : 50 Sentences (Note 2)

tā	—	lái	le	—
	jīntian	,qù		ma
	zuótian	zǒu		
	jīnnian	dào		
	qùnian	bìyè		

II: 60 Sentences (Note 2)

(The asterisks here and in Tables III and V below indicate
that only items in the same row may be taken together.)

	*		*		
nǐ	chī	—	fàn	le	—
tā	mǎi	-le	bǐ		ma
tāmen	xiě		zì		
	shàng		shān		
	jiè		shū		

III: 96 Sentences (Note 3)

(See note at head of Table II)

	*		*			
wǒ	chī	-le	fàn	jiù	zǒu	—
wǒmen	mǎi		bǐ		lái	le
tā	xiě		zì		qù	
tāmen	jiè		shū			

IV: 15 Sentences (Note 4)

—	duō	—
tài	shǎo	le
	hǎo	
	wǎn	
	gāo	

V: 96 Sentences (Note 5)

(See note at head of Table II)

	*			*	
wǒ	kàn	-le	yì	-běn shū	—
tā	mǎi		liǎng	-zhī bǐ	le
	kàn		sān	-cì diànyǐngr	
	zǒu		sì	-lǐ lù	
	mǎi			-ge biǎo	
	jiè			-běn zìdiǎn	

VI: 48 Sentences (Note 6)

wǒ	----	lái	le
nǐ	yào	zǒu	
tā	kuài	qù	
	jiù	mǎi	

VII: 48 Sentences (Note 7)

wǒ	chī-fàn	yǐqián
nǐ	kàn-shū	de-shíhou
tā	xiě-zì	yǐhou
	dào-nèr-qu	
	mǎi-piào	
	gàosu-ta	

VIII: 24 Sentences (Note 8)

wǒ	----	bu	chī	le
nǐ	men		mǎi	
tā			zǒu	
			qù	

PRONUNCIATION DRILLS

I. The in - ian - an Contrast

(a)	yīn	yān	ān
(b)	bīn	biān	bān
(c)	pīn	piān	pān
(d)	mín	mián	mán
(e)	lín	lián	lán

II. The ou - uo Contrast

(a) gōu guō	(f) dōu duō	(k) zhōu zhuō
(b) gǒu guǒ	(g) lóu luó	(l) shōu shuō
(c) gòu guò	(h) kòu kuò	(m) zǒu zuǒ
(d) tóu tuó	(i) hòu huò	(n) còu cuò
(e) chōu chuō	(j) ròu ruò	(o) sōu suō

III. Contrast between h and Zero Initial

(a) wā   huā   (e) wàn   huàn

(b) wǒ   huǒ   (f) wáng   huáng

(c) wài   huài   (g) wú   hú

(d) wèi   huì   (h) wèn   hùn

EXPANSION DRILLS

The following exercise provides an opportunity to build up long sentences step
by step. Practice them until you are fluent at every step. Observe the changes
in meaning through the successive steps of the expansion.

I
qù

qù-le

dào-nèr-qu-le

dào-'tā-nèr-qu-le

wǒ-dào-'tā-nèr-qu-le

wǒ-zuótian-dào-'tā-nèr-qu-le

Wǒmen-zuótian-dào-'tā-nèr-qu-le.

II
shū

mǎi-shū

mǎi-yìběn-shū

mǎile-yìběn-shū

mǎile-yìběn-shū-le

jīntian-mǎile-yìběn-shū-le

wǒ-jīntian-mǎile-yìběn-shū-le

Wǒ-jīntian-yǐjing-mǎile-yìběn-shū-le.

III
chī

chī-fàn

chīle-fàn

chīle-fàn-jiù-zǒu

chīle-fàn-jiù-zǒu-le

xiānsheng-chīle-fàn-jiù-zǒu-le

Bǎi-Xiānsheng-chīle-fàn-jiù-zǒu-le.

<u>I V</u>

mǎi

mǎi-le

dōu-mǎi-le

tā-dōu-mǎi-le

shū, bǐ tā-'dōu-mǎi-le

Shū, bǐ tā-dōu-'mǎi-le-méi-you?

QUESTIONS AND ANSWERS

Practice the following questions and answers. The questions all contain <u>le</u>, and the negative answers require the use of <u>méi</u> or <u>méi-you</u>.

1. 'Bái-Xiānsheng 'shénmo-
   shíhou-huí-jiā-le?

   'Bái-Xiānsheng hái-'méi-huí-
   jiā-ne.

2. Ní-mǎi-'shū-le-méi-you?

   Wó-'méi-you-mǎi-ne.

3. Ní-mǔqin-zuótian-dào-le-
   ma?

   Wó-mǔqin-zuótian-'méi-dào.
   Jīntian-jiù-dào.

4. Nǐ-zuótian dào-túshūguǎn-le-
   ma?

   Wǒ-zuótian-'méi-dào-túshūguǎn.

5. 'Gāo-Xiānsheng zuótian-'lái-
   le-méi-you?

   Tā-zuótian-'méi-lái. Tā-shuō-
   'jīntian-lái.

6. Míngtian wǒmen-dōu-dào-'Bái-
   Xiānsheng-nèr-qu. Tā-gàosu-
   ni-le-ma?

   Wǒ-bù-zhīdào. Tā-'méi-gàosu-
   wo.

7. Ní-yǐjing-niàn-'dàxué-le-méi-
   you?

   Méi-you. Wǒ-xiànzài-niàn-
   'zhōngxué.

8. Nǐde-shū mǎile-'jíběn-le?

   Wó-mǎile-'liángběn-le. Hái-
   yǒu-'sānběn-méi-mǎi-ne.

9. Nǐ-chī-'fàn-le-méi-you?

   Wǒ-'méi-chī-fàn-ne.

10. 'Gāo-Xiáojie-kǎoshì-le-ma?

    Hái-méi-you-ne.

11. Jīntian-zǎochen nǐ-zuò-diàn-
    chē-le-ma?

    Méi-you. Wǒ-'méi-zuò-diànchē.

12. 'Qián-Xiānsheng 'shénmo-shí-
    hou dàole-Měiguo-le?

    Tā-hái-'méi-dào-Měiguo-ne.

13. Gāngbǐ, mòshuǐ nǐ-'dōu-yǒu-
    le-ma?

    Méi-you. Gāngbǐ, mòshuǐ wǒ-
    'dōu-méi-mǎi.

14. 'Máo-Xiānsheng dào-shūdiàn-
    le-ma?

    Méi-you. Tā-'jiù-qù-le.

15. 'Gāo-Xiáojie 'lái-le-méi-you?

    Gāo-Xiáojie-'méi-lái.

16. Zuótian nǐ-dào-Gāo-Xiānsheng-
    jiā-qu-le-ma?

    Zuótian wǒ-'méi-dào-Gāo-Xiān-
    sheng-jiā-qu.

17. Nǐ-shàng-'Húnán-qù-le-méi-
    you?

    Wǒ-'méi-qù.

18. Nǐ-dào-túshūguǎn qu-jiè-shū-
    le-ma?

    Méi-you. Wǒ-'méi-dào-túshū-
    guǎn-qù-jiè-shū.

19. Zìdiǎn, dìtú nǐ-'dōu-mǎi-le-
    méi-you?

    Zìdiǎn, dìtú wǒ-'dōu-méi-mǎi-
    ne.

20. Zuótian nǐ-kàn-diànyǐngr-le-
    ma?

    Zuótian-wǒ-'tài-máng. 'Méi-
    kàn-diànyǐngr.

MONOLOGUE

Wǒ-yīnwei-xǐhuan-'Zhōngguo-wénxué, xiǎng-dào-'Zhōngguo-qu-niàn-shū, suóyi zài-yī-jiǔ-liù-èr-nián-èryue wǒ-cóng-Měiguo-dào-Zhōngguo-de. Wǒ-bú-shi-yìzhíde dào-Zhōngguo-lái-de. Wǒ-shi-cóng-Měiguo-zuò-chuán, xiān-dào-Rìběn, wǒ-zài-Rìběn-'yíge-xīngqī, yòu-zuò-fēijī-dào-Zhōngguo-lái-de. Rìběn yé-hén-yǒu-yìsi. Wǒ-zuò-chuán-de-shíhou, rènshile-bù-shǎode-péng-you. Dào-Zhōngguo-yǐhòu, wǒ-yòu-rènshile-hěn-duō-'Zhōngguo-péngyou: Gāo-Xiānsheng, Gāo-Tàitai, Gāo-Xiáojie, 'Máo-Xiānsheng, 'Qián-Xiānsheng, tāmen-'dōu-shi-wó-hén-hǎode-péngyou. Wǒ-zài-Yuǎndōng-Dàxué-niàn-shū. Wǒ-niàn-wénxué. Yuǎndōng-Dàxué yóu-hěn-duō-'wàiguo-xuésheng. Wǒ-'Zhōngguo-wénxué, 'Yīngguo-wénxué 'dōu-niàn-le. Zhōngguo-wénxué 'hěn-nán. Zhōngwén bù-róngyi-xué. Zhōngguo-zì 'yòu-nán-xiě. Suírán-nán, kěshi-wó-hén-xǐhuan. Yǒu-yìsi-jíle. Yīnwei-wǒ-zài-Měiguo-dàxué yǐjing-niàn-'èrniánjí-le, suóyi-wǒ-dào-Yuǎndōng-Dàxué jiù-niàn-'sānniánjí-le. Wǒ-shuōde-Zhōngguo-huà suírán-bú-tài-hǎo, kěshi wǒ-chàbuduō-'dōu-huì-shuō-le. Wó-xiǎng wǒ-bìyè-de-shíhou, yídìng-bǐ-xiànzài 'hǎo-yìdiǎr. Wǒ-xī-wang-wǒ-bìyè-de-shíhou néng-kàn-shū, néng-xiě-zì, yě-néng-shuō 'gèng-hǎode-Zhōngguo-huà.

SETTING THINGS RIGHT

The following sentences based on the Dialogue contain false statements. Make
whatever changes are necessary to turn them into true statements.

1. 'Gāo-Xiáojie cóng-túshūguǎn-huí-jiā.

2. 'Bái-Xiānsheng zhīdao-'Gāo-Xiáojie zài-něige-xuéxiào-niàn-shū.

3. Gāo-Xiānshengde-Yīngguo-péngyou shi-yíwèi-tàitai.

4. 'Bái-Xiānsheng wàngle-dài-biǎo-le.

5. Yuǎn-Dà yǐjing-kǎoshì-le.

6. Gāo-Xiáojiede-mǔqin-shuō 'Bái-Xiānsheng 'yòu-cōngming yòu-yònggōng.

7. 'Gāo-Xiáojie 'bù-xǐhuan-kàn-diànyǐngr.

8. 'Gāo-Xiáojie shàng-kè-yǐqián yǒu-yìdiǎr-shì.

9. 'Bái-Xiānsheng zài-Yuǎn-Dà-'sìniánjí-niàn-shū.

10. 'Gāo-Xiáojie chàbuduō-'měige-xīngqī dōu-qù-kàn-diànyǐngr.

WHAT WOULD YOU SAY?

Improvise a Chinese conversation along the following lines between an American student and a Chinese acquaintance.

You ask the acquaintance where he is studying. He says he is studying at the
No. 3 Middle School. You ask what year. He answers that he's in the third
year of higher middle school, and that he's graduating this year. Then he asks
what you are studying. You reply that you're studying literature. He asks
whether it's English literature or Chinese literature, and you mention the
latter in reply. He tells you that you speak Chinese very well. You remark
that he's too polite, and that you don't speak Chinese well. He insists that you
are certainly very intelligent and very hard-working. You reply that you're
really awfully dumb and don't work very hard. He asks what time it is. You
say you forgot to bring your watch, but that you think it will soon be six-thirty.
You ask him if he has something to do. He says he has and suggests further
conversation later. You exchange farewells.

NOTES

1. The suffix -le is attached either to verbs or to entire sentences.* It has no precise English equivalent, though in many of its uses it corresponds roughly to the 'have (has, had)' of perfect-tense constructions, which denote past-flavored actions (had done, have been eating, have seen, have been writing, will have gone, will have been studying, having bought). Some specific uses of -le are described in Notes 2–9 below.

2. At the end of a sentence, -le indicates that the foregoing actions are completed or past, or that there has been a change to a new situation:

    Tāmen-dōu-lái-le. Wǒmen-jiù-'tányitán-le. 'They all came, and then we had a chat.'

    If the verb has a simple direct object, the verb may have a second -le attached to it, reinforcing the -le at the end:

    Tāmen-dōu-chīle-fàn-le. 'They have all eaten.'

    See pp. 174–75 for more examples.

3. The suffix -le attached to a verb in a dependent clause indicates that the action of the clause is completed with respect to the action of the main clause ('after having . . . -ed'). In a sentence of this structure, the main clause is commonly introduced by jiù 'then, and then, after that':

    Wǒ-jièle-shū jiù-yào-dào-ta-jiā-qu. 'After having borrowed the book I will go to his home.'

    Wǒ-jièle-shū jiù-dào-ta-jiā-qu-le. 'After borrowing the book I went to his home.'

    Note that a phrase like Wǒ-chīle-fàn, with a single le attached to the verb, is not complete; it does not mean 'I ate' but rather 'after I ate,' and one expects something to follow.

    See pp. 175–76 for more examples.

4. When -le is attached to a stative verb (e.g. hǎo 'is good') or to a time expression (e.g. shídiǎn-zhōng 'ten o'clock'), it means 'is (am, are)' in the special sense 'has (now) become,' as:

    Wó-hǎo-le. 'I'm fine, now [as contrasted to my previous ill state].' (Cf. Wó-hǎo. 'I'm fine,' in answer to a queried greeting.)

    Xiànzài-shídiǎn-zhōng-le. 'It's ten o'clock (already).' 'It's (now become) ten o'clock [and time to get on with a scheduled activity].' (Cf. Xiànzài-shídiǎn-zhōng. 'It's ten o'clock,' with no special emphasis.)

    Tā-jiā-lǐ-zhèr 'tài-yuǎn-le. 'His home is too far from here.' (Spoken in a situation where the house is now farther from the speaker than in some other envisaged situation.)

    See pp. 176–77 for more examples.

    * In our transcription, we attach -le to sentences by a hyphen (Tā-hǎo-le.) and to non-terminal verbs directly (chīle-fàn).

5. In sentences containing an object preceded by a number, -le may indicate a simple past action (corresponding to English simple past tense):

  Wǒ-jièle-sānběn-shū. 'I borrowed three books [and that is the end of my borrowing].'

  Addition of a second -le at the end alters the connotation of the past action: it implies that the (completed) action bears a relation to another present or future action (cf. the English present perfect tense):

  Wǒ-jièle-sānběn-shū-le. 'I've borrowed three books [in preparation for some other activity—borrowing more books, doing something with the books already borrowed, etc.].'

  See pp. 177–78 for more examples.

6. A verb plus -le can mean 'be about to [do]' or 'be on the point of [do]ing':

  Lái-le. 'I'm (on the point of) coming!' ['In another second, I'll have arrived.']

  Wó-zǒu-le. 'I'm about to go.' ['I will have left in no time.']

  The verb in this usage is often accompanied by a word which reinforces the sense of imminence—yào 'will,' jiù 'immediately,' kuài 'soon' (also 'fast') or the like:

  Wǒ-jiù-zǒu-le. 'I'm just about to leave.'

  Wǒ-kuài-yào-zǒu-le. 'I'm leaving soon.'

  See pp. 178–79 for more examples.

7. A méi or bu negative verb suffixed with -le means either 'doesn't [do] any more' or 'no longer intends to [do],' depending on the context:

  Wǒ-bu-chī-le. 'I'm not eating any more (because I'm full).' or 'I no longer intend to eat it.'

  Zuótian-qián-hěn-duō. Jīntian-'méi-yǒu-le. 'Yesterday (I) had a lot of money. Today there isn't any more (left).'

  See pp. 184–85 for more examples.

8. Except for the usage described in the preceding note, le appears only in affirmative sentences. Corresponding negative sentences have méi-yǒu, or méi, before the verb (or coverb, if there is one):

  Tā-méi-yóu-zǒu. or Tā-méi-zǒu. 'He hasn't gone.'

  See p. 180 for more examples.

9. One way of making -le sentences interrogative is to add ma at the end:

  Tā-lái-le-ma? 'Has he come?'

  Alternatively, affirmative (not negative!) -le sentences can be made into questions by adding méi-you at the end:

  Tā-'lái-le-méi-you? 'Has he come?'

  See pp. 184–85 for more examples.

10. Méi-yǒu may be abbreviated to méi before nouns as well as before verbs:

Wǒ-méi-yǒu-qián.   or Wǒ-méi-qián.   'I don't have any money.'

11. The relative-time words yǐqián 'before,' yǐhòu 'after,' and shíhou 'when, while' appear at the END of the clause, rather than at the beginning as in English:

nǐ-niàn-shū-YǏQIÁN   'BEFORE you study'

nǐ-niàn-shū-YǏHÒU 'AFTER you study'

nǐ-niàn-shū-de-SHÍHOU 'WHEN you study'

These subordinate time clauses must come BEFORE the main clause in Chinese sentences:

Nǐ-niàn-shū-de-shíhou yào-yònggōng.   'When you study, you have to work hard.'

Yǐhòu 'after' is optional in the type of changes mentioned above in Note 3:

Tā-chīle-fàn jiù-zǒu-le.
  or   } 'After he ate, he left.'
Tā-chīle-fàn-yǐhòu jiù-zǒu-le.

12. Xīngqī 'week' is compounded with tiān 'day' to form xīngqītiān 'Sunday,' and with the numbers from one to six to name the remaining days of the week:

xīngqīyī 'Monday'   xīngqīsì   'Thursday'

xīngqī'èr 'Tuesday'   xīngqīwǔ 'Friday'

xīngqīsān 'Wednesday'   xīngqīliù 'Saturday'

13. The verb shàng 'ascend, go up; get on [a vehicle],' which we have encountered in the phrases shàng-shān 'ascend a mountain' and shàng-chē 'board a car,' also means 'go to (a place), attend,' as:

shàng-kè   'go to a class'

shàng-xué   'go to school' [lit. 'go to study']

shàng-xuéxiào   'go to (one's) school'

shàng-xiǎoxué   'go to elementary school'

shàng-Yīngguo   'go to England'

shàng-dàxué-èrniánjí   'attend second year of college'

Shàng and xià are also used before xīngqī 'week' and its compounds in the meanings 'last' and 'next' respectively:

shàng-xīngqī   'last week'

xià-xīngqīsān   'next Wednesday'

14. The verb niàn 'study' is used in various senses: (a) with a general meaning, as in niàn-shū; (b) with a specific object, as in niàn-wénxué 'study literature'; and (c) to refer to studying at a particular school or in a particular year of school:

Wǒ-niàn-zhōngxué. 'I'm studying in middle school.'

Wǒ-niàn-Yuǎndōng-Dàxué. 'I'm studying at Far Eastern University.'

Wǒ-niàn-dàxué-èrniánjí. 'I'm a sophomore in college.'

(See also Supplementary Lesson 8, Note 1)

15. The expression jíle is added to a stative verb as an intensifier:

    hǎo   'good'

    hǎojíle   'excellent'

16. The exchange in the Dialogue between Miss Gao and Mr. White regarding their diligence and intelligence (lines 29–38) sounds stilted and unnatural to native speakers of English, but it is characteristic of traditional China. Traditional social custom requires that a Chinese speak very deprecatingly about himself and with exaggerated praise for the person he is speaking to:

    nín-fǔshang 'your residence'   but
    wǒ-jiā 'my home'

    Nín-guìxìng? 'What is your [honorable] surname?'
    Bìxìng   'My [miserable] surname is . . .'
    (These polite forms, the last especially, are now considered out of date by some Chinese.)

After you, a foreigner, say a few words of Chinese to a native speaker, you will probably be told—however halting your delivery—that you speak Chinese very well. Remember on the one hand to take such remarks with a grain of salt, and on the other hand to participate in this Oriental practice as much as possible, by exalting the other person and humbling yourself. (These remarks apply especially to more traditionally minded Chinese such as are likely to be encountered in Taiwan or as long-time residents abroad. In the People's Republic some of the older polite expressions have been replaced by newer polite expressions or have been eliminated altogether. Care must be taken to use the appropriate form, depending on the given social situation.)

17. The particle le forms part of a number of frequently occurring fixed phrases that are very useful and therefore worth memorizing. The following examples occur in this lesson:

    Hǎojíle.   'Fine! Excellent!'
    Duìle.   'Right!'
    Wàngle.   '(I've) forgotten'

Lesson 14 DISCUSSING SCHOOL WORK

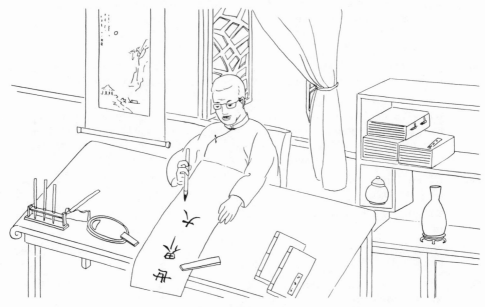

"Tā-chàbuduō-měitiān 'yé-xiě-zì."

Dialogue: Mr. White and Miss Gao continue their conversation.

Bái :	'Gāo-Xiáojie, nǐmen-xué- xiào yígòng-yǒu-'duōshao- xuésheng?		Miss Gao, how many students does your school have altogeth- er?
Gāo :	Wǒmen-xuéxiào yǒu-'yì- qiān-duō-rén.	5	[Our school has] over a thou- sand.
Bái :	'Nán-xuésheng-duō háishi- nǚ-xuésheng-duō-ne?		Which are (there) more (of), boys or girls?
Gāo :	'Nán-xuésheng-duō. 'Bái- Xiānsheng, nǐmen-Yuǎn-Dà yǒu-'duōshao-xuésheng?	10	There are more boys. [Mr. White,] how many students do you have at Far Eastern?
Bái :	Yǒu-'sānqiān-wúbǎi-duō- rén.		[There are] over 3,500.
Gāo :	Wó-xiǎng nǐmen-zài-'dà- xué-niàn-shū-de-xuésheng yídìng-'dōu-shi-hěn-cōng- ming-de.	15	I guess you college students must all be pretty bright.
Bái :	Yé-yǒu-cōngmingde, yé-yǒu- bènde. Yǒu-rén-niànde-hén- hǎo, yǒu-rén-niànde-hěn-bù- hǎo.	20	Some are bright, some are stu- pid. Some [people] study very well, some [people] study very badly.

191

Gāo: Qùnian-dào-Yuǎn-Dà-kǎo-
shì-de-xuésheng yígòng-
yǒu-yíwàn-duō-rén. Kǎo-
shangde zhí-yǒu-yìqiān-
rén. Suóyi-wǒ-shuō 'dà-   25
xuéde-xuésheng 'dōu-hěn-
cōngming.

Last year over ten thousand students took the exams for Far
Eastern. Only a thousand passed
the exams. So I say university
students are all very bright.

Bái: 'Gāo-Xiáojie, nǐ-zhōngxué-
bìyè-yǐhòu xiǎng-xué-shénmo-ne?   30

[Miss Gao,] what do you plan to
study after graduating from middle school?

Gāo: Wó-xiǎng-xué-wénxué, kěshi
wǒ-yòu-bú-yònggōng yòu-bù-
cōngming. Wó-xiǎng wǒ-
yídìng-kǎobushàng-dàxué.

I'd like to study literature, but
I don't work hard and I'm not
bright. I'm sure I can't pass the
college exams.

Bái: Nǐ-kèqi-ne. 'Yídìng-   35
kǎodeshàng.

You're being polite. You certainly can pass.

Gāo: Nǐ-shuō-wó-kǎodeshàng-
ma?

Do you think [lit. say] I can
[pass]?

Bái: Wǒ-shuō nǐ-'yídìng-
kǎodeshàng.   40

I think you certainly can [pass].

Gāo: Ní-xiáng-wǒ-xué-wénxué
xuédeliǎo-ma?

Do you think I will be able to
study literature?

Bái: Ní-'zěnmo-xuébuliǎo-ne?
Wó-yé-hěn-xīwang nǐ-xué-
wénxué.   45

Why shouldn't you be able to?
And I hope very much that you
will [study literature].

Gāo: Rúguó-wó-kǎobushàng-
dàxué wǒ-jiù-xué-huà-
huàr.

If I can't pass the exams for college, then I'll study painting.

Bái: Wó-xiáng-nǐ-'yídìng-huì-
huà, nǐ-huàde-huàr 'yídìng-   50
yé-hén-hǎo.

I'm sure you can paint and that
what you do is very good.

Gāo: Huà-huàr wǒ-shi-xuéguo-de,
kěshi-wǒ-huàde-bu-hǎo.

It's true I've studied painting
[lit. drawing pictures I have
studied], but I paint badly.

Bái: Yìhuěr wǒ-jiu-kéyi-kànjian
nǐ-huàde-huàr-le.   55

In a little while I'll be able to
see the paintings you've done.

Gāo: Huàde-'bù-hǎo. Zuì-hǎo-
nín-bú-kàn. 'Bái-Xiān-
sheng, 'nín-shi-xué-shén-
mo-de?

They're badly done. It would be
best if you didn't see them.
What are you studying, Mr.
White?

Bái: Wǒ-yuánlái shi-xiǎng-xué-   60
'kēxué-de, kěshi-wǒ-duì-
'wàiguo-huà hén-yǒu-xìng-
qu, 'gèng-xǐhuan-Zhōngguo-
huà, suóyi-wǒ-zài-Měiguo
jiù-xué-Zhōngguo-huà, niàn-   65
Zhōngguo-shū. Xiànzài-wǒ-

I originally planned to study science, but I'm very much interested in foreign languages,
especially Chinese, so in America I studied (spoken) Chinese
and read Chinese books. Now
I've come to China to study

dào-Zhōngguo-lái xué-
Zhōngguo-wénxué, yě-xué-
yǔyánxué.

Chinese literature, and also to
study linguistics.

Gāo: Xué-yǔyánxué 'zěnmo-xué-   70
ne? Jiù-shi-xué-shuō-wài-
guo-huà-ma?

How does one study linguistics?
Is it simply studying (how) to
speak a foreign language?

Bái: Bú-shi. Xué-yǔyánxué shi-
yòng 'kēxuéde-fāngfǎ yán-
jiu-yǔyán. Yǒu-rén-néng-   75
shuō hén-hǎode-wàiguo-huà,
dōu-tīngdedǒng, yě-shuōde-
shífēn-hǎo, kěshi-bù-dǒng
yòng-'kēxué-fāngfǎ yánjiu-
yǔyán.   80

No. [Studying] linguistics is
analyzing languages by scientific
means. Some people are quite
proficient in foreign languages—
they can understand everything
and speak very well—but they
don't understand (how) to use
scientific means to analyze foreign languages.

Gāo: Nín-xǐhuan-xiě-Zhōngguo-
zì-ma? Nín-yòng-Zhōng-
wén-xiě-xìn xiědeliǎo-xiěbuliǎo?

Do you like to write Chinese
characters? Can you use Chinese in writing letters?

Bái: Suírán-xiědeliǎo, kěshi-xiě-   85
de-bu-hǎo. Wó-gěi-Zhōng-
guo-péngyou-xiě-xìn xǐhuan-
yòng-Zhōngwén-xiě.

I can [do so], but I write badly.
(When) I write letters to Chinese
friends, I like to write in Chinese.

Gāo: Nín-néng-yòng-'máobí-xiě-
zì-ma?   90

Can you write characters with a
brush?

Bái: Néng-yòng, kěshi-xiěde-bu-
hǎo.

I can, but I don't write well.

Gāo: Rúguǒ-nín-néng-yòng-máobí
nín-xiěde-zì yídìng-hén-hǎo.
Xiànzài-hěn-duō-Zhōngguo-   95
rén dōu-bù-néng yòng-máobi-
xiě-zì-le. Chàbuduō dōu-
yòng-gāngbǐ-xiě-zì.

If you can use a writing brush,
the characters you write are
sure to be good. Nowadays many
Chinese no longer can write
characters with a brush. Almost
all of them write with (fountain)
pens.

Bái: Nǐ-fùqin-duì-wǒ-shuō nǐde-
zì xiěde-hén-hǎo.   100

Your father told me that your
calligraphy is excellent.

Gāo: Bù-hǎo-bù-hǎo. Suírán-wǒ-
fùqin měitiān-chīguo-le-
wǎnfàn-yǐhòu jiào-wǒ-yòng-
máobí-xiě-zì, kěshi-wǒ-
hái-xiěde-bu-hǎo.   105

No, no. [Although] my father
has me write with a brush every
day after dinner, but I still write
badly.

Bái: Zuì-nánde shi-xiě-Zhōng-
guo-zì-le. Nǐ-fùqin-zì
xiěde-hén-hǎo. Wó-xiǎng-
nǐ-yídìng xiěde-yé-hén-
hǎo.   110

The most difficult thing is writing Chinese characters. Your
father writes [characters] very
well. I'm sure you write well
too.

Gāo: Yīnwei-wǒ-fùqin-xiěde-hǎo
suóyi-tā-měitiān-jiào-wó-

Since my father writes well, he
has me write every day. He

	xiě-zì-ne. Tā-chàbuduō- měitiān yé-xiě-zì.	practices calligraphy almost ev- ery day too.
Bái :	Nǐ-méi-tīngshuō-ma: Huó-dào-lǎo, Xué-dào-lǎo, Hái-yóu-sānfēn Xuébudào.	115	Haven't you heard it said: Live to old age, Study to old age, There's still three-tenths That one can't learn.
Gāo :	Bù-zhí-yǒu-'sānfēn-ba!	120	It's not just three-tenths !

VOCABULARY

bǎi	hundred (NU) (Note 7 below)
dǒng	understand (TV)
duì	(facing) toward, to, regarding (CV)
'fāngfǎ	method, technique (N) [lit. means method]
gěi	give (TV) for, to (CV) (Note 1 below)
guo	(verb suffix: Note 5 below)
huà	paint, draw (TV)
huàr	painting, drawing (N)
huó	live (IV)
kēxué	(study of) science (N)
lǎo	old (chiefly animate things) (SV)
liǎo	(resultative verb ending: Note 6 below)
qiān	thousand (NU)
shífēn	very (AD) [lit. ten part]

tīng	listen (to) (TV)
tīngshuō	hear (it said) that (TV) [lit. hear say]
wàn	ten thousand, myriad (also, a surname) (NU)
xìn	letter (N)
xìngqu	interest (in) (N) [lit. feelings interest] (Note 15)
yánjiu	study, make a study of, investigate (TV) [lit. research investigate] study, research (N)
yìhuěr	a moment (TW) [lit. one moment]
yòng	use (TV) using, with (CV) (Note 1 below)
yǔyán	language (N) [lit. language word]
yǔyánxué	linguistics, linguistic science (N) [lit. language word study]
yuánlái	**originally, actually (MA)** [lit. origin come]
zhǐ	only (AD)
zuì	most (AD)

SENTENCE BUILD-UP

	yòng	use
	yòng-máobǐ	use a writing brush
1.	Wǒ-bú-huì-yòng-máobǐ.	I don't know how to use a writing brush.
	yòng-máobǐ	use a writing brush
	xiě-zì	write characters
2.	Wǒ-huì-yòng-máobí-xiě-zì.	I can write characters with a brush.
	duì	toward, to
	duì-shéi?	to whom?
3.	Tā-duì-shéi-shuō-huà?	Who is he talking to?
	xìngqu	interest
	hén-yǒu-xìngqu	be greatly interested
4.	Tā-duì-wénxué hén-yǒu-xìngqu.	He's greatly interested in literature.
	gěi	give
	gěi-ta-qián	give him money
5.	Ní-gěi-ta-qián-ma?	Are you giving him any money?
	gěi-ta	give him
	gěi-ta-mǎi	buy for him
6.	Ní-gěi-ta-mǎi-shū-ma?	Are you buying him a book?

xìn   letter
xiě-xìn   write a letter
7. Ní-gěi-ta-xiě-xìn-ma?   Are you writing him a letter?

zuì   most
zuì-hǎo   best
zuì-hǎode   the best one
8. Zuì-hǎode shi-'duōshao-qián?   How   much   is   the   best   one?

huàr   painting
zhèizhāng-huàr   this painting
9. Zhèizhāng-huàr hén-yǒu-yìsi.   This painting is very interesting.

huà   paint
huà-huàr   paint paintings
10. Tā-měitiān huà-yìzhāng-huàr.   He does one painting a day.

dǒng   understand
'dōu-dǒng   understand everything
11. Nǐ-'dōu-dǒng-ma?   Do you understand everything?

bù-dǒng-Zhōngguo-huà   not understand Chinese
bù-dǒng-Zhōngguo-huà-de-   people who don't under-
rén   stand Chinese
12. Bù-dǒng-Zhōngwén-de-rén   Can people who don't understand
yě-néng-zài-zhèr-niàn-shū-ma?   Chinese also study here?

tā-xiě-zì   he writes characters
tā-xiěde-zì   the characters which he
                                             writes
13. Tā-xiě-de-zì dōu-bú-duì.   The characters that he wrote
                                             are all incorrect.

zài-zhèr-niàn-shū   study here
zài-zhèr-niàn-shū-de   those who study here
14. Zài-zhèr-niàn-shū-de dōu-shi-   Is everyone studying here a for-
'wàiguo-rén-ma?   eigner?

tā-shuō   he says
tā-shuō-de   that which he says
15. Tā-shuō-de nǐ-dōu-dǒng-ma?   Do you understand all of what he
                                             says?

kēxué   science
xué-kēxué-de.   those who study science
16. Nürén yé-yǒu-xué-kēxué-de.   There are also some women who
                                             study science.

yánjiu   do research in
yánjiu-kēxué   do research in science
17. Yánjiu-kēxuéde-rén xiànzài-   There are even more people do-
'gèng-duō-le.   ing research in science now.

yǔyán   language

yánjiu-yǔyán
18. Yánjiu-yǔyán-de-rén yǒu-
    duōshao?

    do research in language
How many people are doing research in language?

yǔyánxué
  xué-yǔyánxué
19. Xué-yǔyánxué-de-xuésheng
    'duō-bu-duō?

    linguistics
    study linguistics
Are many students studying linguistics?

'fāngfǎ
  tā-yòng-de-'fāngfǎ
20. Tā-yòng-de-'fāngfǎ hén-
    jiǎndān.

    method
    the method he uses
The method he uses is very simple.

chī-'Rìběn-fàn
  chīguo-'Rìběn-fàn
21. Nǐ-chīguo-'Rìběn-fàn-ma?

    eat Japanese food
    have eaten Japanese food
Have you ever eaten Japanese
food?

chīguo-'wàiguo-fàn
  méi-chīguo-'wàiguo-fàn

22. Nǐ-méi-chīguo-'wàiguo-fàn-
    ma?

    have eaten foreign food
    have never eaten foreign
      food
Have you never eaten foreign
food?

chīguo-'Zhōngguo-fàn
  méi-you-chīguo-'Zhōng-
    guo-fàn
23. Nǐ-chīguo-'Zhōngguo-fàn-méi-
    you?

    have eaten Chinese food
    have never eaten Chinese
      food
Have you ever eaten Chinese
food?

tīng
  'tīngyitīng
24. Bú-yào-shuō-huà. Nǐ-'tīng-
    yitīng.

    listen
    listen (for a while)
Don't talk. Listen!

tīngshuō
25. Wǒ-tīngshuō-ta-hǎo-le.

    hear it said
I hear he's recovered.

lǎo
  lǎo-le
26. Tā-lǎo-le, bù-néng-zǒu-lù-
    le.

    old
    become old
He's old and can't walk any
more.

kànjian
  kànbujiàn
27. Kànbujiàn-Xī-Shān, yīnwei-
    tài-yuǎn-le.

    see
    unable to see
It's impossible to see the Western Hills because they're too far
away.

kàndejiàn
  kànbujiàn
28. Nǐ-kàndejiàn-kànbujiàn?

    able to see
    unable to see
Can you see it or not?

liǎo — (resultative suffix)
chīdeliǎo — able to eat
chībuliǎo — unable to eat

29. Zhèige-fàn nǐ-chīdeliǎo-chībuliǎo? — Can you eat this food?

huó — live
huóbuliǎo — unable to live

30. Tā-yídìng-huóbuliǎo. — He certainly can't survive.

kǎoshang — pass an entrance exam
kǎobushàng-zhōngxué — unable to pass an entrance exam for middle school

31. Tā-bènjíle, kǎobushàng-zhōngxué. — He's awfully stupid. He couldn't pass an entrance exam for middle school.

mǎidào-le — have succeeded in buying
méi-mǎidào — did not succeed in buying

32. Zhèiběn-shū 'wǒ-méi-mǎi-dào, kěshi-'tā-mǎidào-le. — I didn't succeed in buying this book, but he did.

zhǐ — only
zhǐ-yǒu-yíge-rén — there is only one person

33. Wǒmen-zhǐ-yǒu-yíge-rén méi-xuéguo-Zhōngwén. — There is only one person among us who has never studied Chinese.

bǎi — hundred
sìbǎikuài-qián — four hundred dollars

34. Wǒmen-yígòng-yǒu-'sìbǎi-kuài-qián. — We have four hundred dollars in all.

qiān — thousand
liǎngqiān-duō-běn-shū — over two thousand books

35. Zhèige-shūdiàn yíge-xīngqī mài-liǎngqiān-duō-běn-shū. — This bookstore sells over two thousand books every week.

wàn — ten thousand
yíwàn-duō-lǐ-lù — over ten thousand miles

36. Zhōngguo-lí-Měiguo yíwàn-duō-lǐ-lù. — China is over ten thousand miles from America.

yìqiān-sānbǎi èrshibáge-xuésheng — one thousand three hundred twenty-eight students

37. Dì-sì-Xiǎoxué yǒu-yìqiān-sānbǎi-èrshibáge-xuésheng. — No. 4 Elementary School has 1,328 students.

yíwàn-qīqiān — seventeen thousand

38. Wǒmen-xuéxiào yǒu-yíwàn-qīqiānge-xuésheng. — Our school has seventeen thousand students.

wànwàn — one hundred million
bāwànwàn-duō — over eight hundred million

39. Zhōngguo yǒu-bāwànwàn-duō-
    rén.

    China has over eight hundred
    million people.

        yuánlái   originally
        mǎibuliǎo-fángzi   unable to buy a house
40. Yuánlái-zài-chénglǐ   Originally it was not possible to
    mǎibuliǎo-fángzi.   buy a house in the city.

        bāfēn   eight parts (of ten)
        bāfēnde-xīwang   eight parts hope
41. Tā-kǎoshang-dàxué yǒu-bāfēn-   There is an eight-tenths chance
    de-xīwang.   that he will pass the college en-
                                                 trance test.

        shífēn   very
        shífēn-hǎo   very good or very well
42. Tā-Rìběn-huà shuōde-shífēn-   He speaks Japanese very well.
    hǎo.

        yìhuěr   a little while
43. Wǒ-yìhuěr-jiù-lái-le.   I'll come in a moment.

        zuì-hǎo   best
44. Wǒmen-zuì-hǎo-'bú-qù.   It would be best if we didn't go.

        yě-mài-shū   also sell books
        yě-mài-bǐ   also sell pens
        yě-mài-zhǐ   also sell paper
45. Tāmen-yě-mài-shū, yě-mài-   They sell books and pens and
    bǐ, yě-mài-zhǐ.   also paper.

        tā-dàile   he wore
        tā-méi-yǒu-dài   he did not wear
46. Tā-'dàile-méi-you?   Did he wear it?

        biǎo-dàile   the watch was worn
        biǎo-méi-dài   the watch wasn't worn
47. Biǎo-'dàile-méi-you?   Was the watch worn?

        nèige-xuésheng   that student
        hěn-cōngming   very bright
48. Nèige-xuésheng-hěn-cōngming.   That student is very bright.

        hěn-cōngming   very bright
        shi-hěn-cōngmingde   is a very bright one
49. Nèige-xuésheng shi-hěn-cōng-   That student is very bright.
    mingde.

PATTERN DRILLS

Pattern 14.1. The Coverbs <u>yòng</u>, <u>gěi</u>, <u>duì</u> (Note 1 below)

S	CV	O₁	V	O₂
Subject	Coverb	Object₁	Verb	Object₂
Tā	yòng	bǐ	xiě	zì.

'He writes with a pen.'

Tā	gěi	ni	mǎi	shū.

'He is buying the books for you.'

Tā	duì	ni	shuō	shénmo?

'What is he saying to you?'

1. 'Bái-Xiānsheng néng-yòng-'máobí-xiě-zì.

Mr. White can write with a Chinese writing brush.

2. 'Zhāng-Xiānsheng bù-néng-yòng-máobí-xiě-zì.

Mr. Johnson cannot write with a brush.

3. 'Bái-Xiānsheng néng-yòng-'máobí-xiě-zì-ma?

Can Mr. White write with a brush?

4. 'Wáng-Xiānsheng yòng-'Zhōng-wén-xiě-xìn.

Mr. King writes letters in Chinese.

5. 'Zhāng-Xiáojie néng-yòng-'Yīng-wén-xiě-xìn.

Miss Zhang can write letters in English.

6. 'Gāo-Xiáojie xǐhuan-yòng-'lán-mòshuí-xiě-zì.

Miss Gao likes to write characters with blue ink.

7. 'Bái-Xiānsheng kéyi-yòng-máo-bǐ xié-hén-hǎode-Zhōngguo-zì.

Mr. White can write very nice Chinese characters with a brush.

8. Zuótian-'Máo-Xiānsheng-lái duì-ni-shuō-shénmo?

What did Mr. Mao come to tell you yesterday?

9. Jīntian-Gāo-Tàitai duì-Gāo-Xiáojie shuōle-hěn-duō-huà.

Today Mrs. Gao talked a lot with Miss Gao.

10. 'Gāo-Xiáojie géi-ni-xiě-xìn-le-ma?

Did Miss Gao write you a letter?

11. 'Bái-Xiānsheng duì-Gāo-Xiáo-jie-shuō tāmen-yào-kǎoshì-le.

Mr. White told Miss Gao that they were about to have exams.

12. 'Bái-Xiānsheng duì-'Gāo-Xiáo-jie-shuō tā-bènjíle.

Mr. White told Miss Gao that he was awfully stupid.

13. 'Qián-Xiānsheng duì-Gāo-Xiānsheng-shuō tā-kàn-diàn-yǐngr-le.

Mr. Qian told Mr. Gao that he had seen a movie.

14. 'Zhāng-Xiānsheng-shuō tā-duì-'wénxué méi-yǒu-xìngqu.

Mr. Zhang says he is not interested in literature.

15. 'Qián-Xiānsheng-shuō tā-duì-
    'wénxué-yǒu-xìngqu-ma?

    Did Mr. Qian say he was inter-
    ested in literature?

16. Qián-Tàitai duì-Qián-'Xiān-
    sheng-shuō tā-qu-bàifang-
    péngyou.

    Mrs. Qian told Mr. Qian that she
    was going to visit a friend.

17. 'Gāo-Xiáojie duì-tā-mǔqin-
    shuō tā-dào-túshūguǎn-qu.

    Miss Gao told her mother she
    was going to the library.

18. 'Máo-Xiānsheng gěi-'Bái-
    Xiānsheng jièle-hěn-duō-shū.

    Mr. Mao borrowed a lot of books
    for Mr. White.

19. 'Qián-Xiānsheng duì-ta-péng-
    you-shuō tā-duì-wénxué-méi-
    xìngqu.

    Mr. Qian told his friend he was-
    n't interested in literature.

20. 'Qián-Xiānsheng duì-ta-tài-
    tai-shuō jīntian-wǎnshàng
    tā-'bù-huí-jiā chī-wǎnfàn.

    Mr. Qian told his wife that he
    wasn't going home for dinner to-
    night.

21. 'Qián-Xiáojie duì-'Zhāng-
    Xiānsheng-shuō tā-'bù-xǐhuan-
    kàn-diànyǐngr.

    Miss Qian told Mr. Zhang that
    she didn't like to see movies.

22. 'Gāo-Xiáojie duì-kàn-diànyǐngr
    hén-yǒu-xìngqu-ma?

    Is Miss Gao very much interest-
    ed in seeing movies?

23. 'Qián-Xiānsheng duì-kàn-shū
    méi-yǒu-xìngqu.

    Mr. Qian isn't interested in
    reading.

24. 'Zhāng-Xiānsheng géi-ni-mǎi-
    le hěn-duō-shū-ma?

    Did Mr. Zhang buy a lot of books
    for you?

25. 'Bái-Xiānsheng duì-shuō-wài-
    guo-huà yǒu-xìngqu-ma?

    Is Mr. White interested in speak-
    ing foreign languages?

Pattern 14.2. Subordination of Transitive and Intransitive Verbs to Nouns
(Notes 2—4 below)

Pattern 14.2 a.

S	V	de	(N)
Subject	Verb	de	(Noun)
xuésheng	jiè	de	shū

'books which students borrow'

Pattern 14.2 b.

V	O	de	(N)
Verb	Object	de	(Noun)
jiè	shū	de	xuésheng

'students who borrow books'

1. Tā-xiě-de-zì-hén-hǎo.

The characters he writes are very nice.

2. Nǐ-shuō-de-huà wǒ-'dōu-dǒng.

I understand everything you say.

3. Zuótian 'Gāo-Xiáojie-jiède-nèibén-shū 'zhēn-yǒu-yìsi.

The book that Miss Gao borrowed yesterday is really interesting.

4. Tā-shuō-de 'dōu-shi-zhēn-huà.

What he says is always the truth.

5. Tā-zuótian-kàn-de-shū jīn-tian-jiù-wàng-le.

The book he read yesterday he's forgotten today.

6. Nèiwèi-Měiguo-xuésheng wǒ-men-shuō-de-huà tā-'dōu-dǒng.

That American student understands all of what we say.

7. Wǒ-zuótian-jiè-de-nèibén-shū hěn-nán-niàn.

The book I borrowed yesterday is very hard to read.

8. Bái-Xiānsheng-jiè-de-nèibén-shū zuì-yǒu-yìsi.

The book that Mr. White borrowed is most interesting.

9. Zhāng-Xiānsheng-mǎi-de-nèizhāng-huàr hén-hǎo-kàn.

The painting that Mr. Zhang bought is very pretty.

10. Zuótian-lái-de-nèige-xuésheng shi-yánjiu-yǔyánxué-de.

The student who came yesterday is studying linguistics.

11. Nèiwèi-cóng-Yīngguo-lái-de-xuésheng shi-yánjiu-kēxué-de.

That student who has come from England is studying science.

12. Nèige-xué-huà-huàr-de-'nǔ-xuésheng bù-dǒng-Zhōngwén.

That girl student who is studying painting does not understand Chinese.

13. 'Gāo-Xiáojie zuótian-mǎi-de-nèibén-shū shi-'yánjiu-huà-huàr-fāngfǎ-de.

The book that Miss Gao bought yesterday is [one] for studying techniques of painting.

14. Zuótian-'Máo-Xiānsheng zài-túshūguǎn-jiè-de-shū 'dōu-méi-you-yìsi.

The books that Mr. Mao borrowed at the library yesterday are all uninteresting.

15. Shàng-xīngqī wǒ-zài-Sān-Yǒu-Shūdiàn-mǎi-de-shū wǒ-kàn-le-'dōu-bù-dǒng.

The books I bought last week at the Three Friends Bookstore I've read but don't understand.

16. Nèiwèi-néng-yòng-máobí-xiě-zì-de-wàiguo-xuésheng cōng-ming-jíle.

That foreign student who can write with a brush is tremendously bright.

17. Zài-nèige-xuéxiào-niàn-shū-de chàbuduō-dōu-shi-'wàiguo-xuésheng.

The ones who are studying at that school are almost all foreign students.

18. Jīntian-wǎnshang dào-Gāo-jia-chī-fàn-de dōu-shi-Gāo-Xiānshengde-hǎo-péngyou.

The people [lit. the ones] who are going to the Gaos' home for dinner this evening are all good friends of Mr. Gao.

19. Dào-Zhōngguo-lái-niàn-shū-de-wàiguo-xuésheng chàbuduō-dōu-shi-yánjiu-yǔyán huòzhě-wénxué-de.

Almost all foreign students who come to China to study take up either language or literature.

20. Zài-nèige-dàxué-niàn-shū-de-xuésheng chàbuduō-yǒu-èrshi-ge-Měiguo-xuésheng.

Among the students studying at that university, there are almost twenty American students.

21. Nèige-háizi-tài-bèn-le. Xiān-sheng-shuō-de-huà tā-dōu-wàng-le.

That child is too stupid. He has forgotten everything that the teacher said.

22. Qián-Xiānsheng-zuótian-mǎide-bǐ 'dōu-bu-néng-yòng.

The pens that Mr. Qian bought yesterday are all useless.

23. Zài-nèige-dàxué-niàn-shū-de-xuésheng nán-xuésheng-shǎo nǚ-xuésheng-duō.

Of the students studying at that university, there are few men [students] and many girls [lit. girl students].

24. Zhèi-shi-wǒ-zài-túshūguǎn 'jiè-de-shū.

This is the book I borrowed at the library.

25. Qián-Xiānsheng-jīntian-mǎi-de shi-Měiguo-bǐ.

What Mr. Qian bought today is an American pen.

26. Nèiwèi-mǎi-shū-de-wàiguo-xué-sheng jiù-shi-'Bái-Xiānsheng-ma?

Is that foreign student who is buying books Mr. White?

27. Gāo-Xiáojie-cōngming-jíle. Xiě-de-zì, huà-de-huàr 'dōu-hǎo.

Miss Gao is very intelligent. The characters she writes (and) the paintings she does are all fine.

28. Nèiwèi-kàn-shū-de-xiānsheng shi-Gāo-Xiānshengde-péngyou.

That gentleman who is reading is Mr. Gao's friend.

29. Mài-shū-de-'Máo-Xiānsheng shi-'Yīngguo-rén-ma?

Is the Mr. Mao who sells books an Englishman?

30. Gāo-Xiānsheng-mǎi-de-fángzi zài-shānshang-ma?

Is the house that Mr. Gao bought located on a hill?

Pattern 14.3.   Completed Action with <u>guo</u> (Note 5 below)

Pattern 14.3a.   (Sentences 1–10 below)

S	(AD)	V	-<u>guo</u>	(O)
Subject	(Adverb)	Verb	-guo	(Object)
Wǒ	méi	chī	-guo	Zhōngguo-fàn.

'I have never eaten Chinese food.'

Pattern 14.3 b.   (Sentences 11—20 below)

S	(TW)	V	-guo	le
Subject	(Time word)	Verb	-guo	le
Tā	zuótian	shuō	-guo	le.

'He mentioned it yesterday.'

1. Wǒ-dàoguo-Rìběn.

I've been to Japan.

2. Nǐ-chīguo-'Měiguo-fàn-méi-you?

Have you ever eaten American food?

3. Nèige-lǎo-rén méi-kànguo-diànyǐngr.

That old man has never seen a movie.

4. Wǒ-xuéguo-yǔyánxué.

I've studied linguistics.

5. Wǒ-méi-xuéguo-kēxué.

I've never studied science.

6. Wǒ-zài-zhōngxué-niàn-shū-de-shíhou méi-yòngguo-gāngbǐ.

When I was studying in middle school, I never used a fountain pen.

7. Wó-mǔqin-méi-zuòguo-fēijī.

My mother has never ridden on a plane.

8. 'Máo-Xiānsheng méi-kànguo-Zhōngwén-shu.

Mr. Mao has never read any Chinese books.

9. Nǐ-dàoguo-Shāndong-ma?

Have you ever been to Shantung?

10. Nǐ-kànjianguo tā-huà-de-huàr-ma?

Have you ever seen the painting he's done?

11. 'Qián-Xiānsheng 'zuótian-lái-guo-le.

Mr. Qian came yesterday.

12. Tā-zuótian-shuōguo-le tā jīntian-'bù-lái-le.

He mentioned yesterday that he wouldn't come today.

13. Tā-yǐjing chīguo-wǎnfàn-le.

He's already eaten dinner.

14. 'Gāo-Xiáojie zuótian-dàoguo-'Qián-Xiáojie-jiā.

Miss Gao went to Miss Qian's home yesterday.

15. Wǒ-jīntian-dàoguo-túshūguǎn-le.

I've been to the library today.

16. Zhèige-zì wǒ-zuótian-xuéguo, kěshi-jīntian-yòu-wàng-le.

I studied this character yesterday, but today I've forgotten it.

17. 'Bái-Xiānsheng jīntian-dào-shūdiàn-qùguo-le.

Mr. White went to the bookstore today.

18. Nǐ-zuótian dàoguo-'Gāo-Xiānsheng-jiā-ma?

Did you go to Mr. Gao's home yesterday?

19. Nǐ-'shàng-xīngqī kànguo-'Wáng-Xiānsheng-le-ma? Wǒ-qùguo-le, kěshi-tā-méi-zài-jiā.

Did you see Mr. Wang last week? I went (to see him), but he wasn't at home.

20. Nǐ-zuótian zhǎoguo-'Máo-   Did you visit Mr. Mao yester-
     Xiānsheng-le-ma? Wǒ-   day? I didn't visit him.
     méi-zhǎoguo-ta.

Pattern 14.4. Resultative Verbs (Note 6 below)

S	V₁	(bu/de)	V₂	(O)
Subject	Verb₁	(bu/de)	Verb₂	(Object)
Wǒmen	kàn	-bu	jiàn	hú.

'We can't see the lake.'

Wǒmen	kàn	-de	jiàn	hú.

'We can see the lake.'

A. Resultative-verb Phrases Composed from Vocabulary of Lessons 1–14
    (Note 6 below)

1. kànjian   see

2. kàndejiàn   be able to see

3. kànbujiàn   be unable to see

4. tīngjian   hear

5. tīngdejiàn   be able to hear

6. tīngbujiàn   be unable to hear

7. yùjian   encounter

8. yùdejiàn   be able to encounter

9. yùbujiàn   be unable to encounter

10. kàndedǒng   be able to understand by reading

11. kànbudǒng   be unable to understand by reading

12. tīngdedǒng   be able to understand by hearing

13. tīngbudǒng   be unable to understand by hearing

14. hǎodeliǎo   be able to get well

15. hǎobuliǎo   be unable to get well

16. mǎideliǎo   be able to buy (because funds are adequate)

17. mǎibuliǎo   be unable to buy (because funds are inadequate)

18. chīdeliǎo   be able to eat (because there is not too much)

19. chībuliǎo   be unable to eat (because there is too much)

20. niàndeliǎo   be able to read or study

21. niànbuliǎo   be unable to read or study

22.	tīngdeliǎo	be able to understand (aurally)
23.	tīngbuliǎo	be unable to understand (aurally)
24.	xiědeliǎo	be able to write
25.	xiěbuliǎo	be unable to write
26.	zǒudeliǎo	be able to go
27.	zǒubuliǎo	be unable to go
28.	zuòdeliǎo	be able to do
29.	zuòbuliǎo	be unable to do
30.	zuòdeliǎo	be able to ride <u>or</u> sit
31.	zuòbuliǎo	be unable to ride <u>or</u> sit
32.	dǒngdeliǎo	be able to understand
33.	dǒngbuliǎo	be unable to understand
34.	huódeliǎo	be able to live
35.	huóbuliǎo	be unable to live
36.	yòngdeliǎo	be able to use
37.	yòngbuliǎo	be unable to use
38.	màideliǎo	be able to sell
39.	màibuliǎo	be unable to sell
40.	mǎidào	succeed in buying
41.	mǎidedào	be able to buy (because the item is available)
42.	mǎibudào	be unable to buy (because the item is not available)
43.	zhǎodào	succeed in finding
44.	zhǎodedào	be able to find
45.	zhǎobudào	be unable to find
46.	jièdào	succeed in borrowing
47.	jièdedào	be able to borrow
48.	jièbudào	be unable to borrow
49.	kàndào	succeed in seeing
50.	kàndedào	be able to see
51.	kànbudào	be unable to see
52.	xuédào	study up to (i.e. study as far as)
53.	xuédedào	be able to study up to
54.	xuébudào	be unable to study up to
55.	zǒudedào	be able to arrive at
56.	zǒubudào	be unable to arrive at
57.	kǎoshang	pass entrance examinations

58.	kǎodeshàng	be able to pass examinations
59.	kǎobushàng	be unable to pass examinations
60.	niàndeshàng	be able to study (because funds are adequate)
61.	niànbushàng	be unable to study (because funds are inadequate)
62.	gěideshàng	be able to give (i.e. make payments)
63.	gěibushàng	be unable to give (i.e. make payments)
64.	chīdexià	be able to eat (because there is not too much)
65.	chībuxià	be unable to eat (because there is too much)
66.	zuòdexià	be able to sit down (because there is enough room)
67.	zuòbuxià	be unable to sit down (because there is not enough room)
68.	xiědexià	be able to write down (because there is enough room)
69.	xiěbuxià	be unable to write down (because there is not enough room)
70.	niàndeguò	be able to surpass in studies (i.e. do better than someone else)
71.	niànbuguò	be unable to surpass in studies

B. Sentences Illustrating Use of Resultative Verbs

1.	Nèiwèi-lǎo-tàitai bù-néng-chī-fàn-le. Hǎobuliǎo-le.	That old lady can no longer eat. It's no longer possible for her to get well.
2.	Nèiběn-shū-'tài-hǎo-le, kěshi-wǒ-méi-qián. Mǎibuliǎo.	That book is excellent, but I don't have any money. I can't buy it.
3.	Zhèiběn-shū zài-shūdiànli-mǎibudào. Nǐ-'yídìng-mài-deliǎo.	This book can't be bought in a bookstore. You certainly will be able to sell it.
4.	Zhèiběn-shū hěn-duō-shūdiàn 'dōu-mǎibudào-le.	This book can't be bought any more in lots of bookstores.
5.	Fàn-tài-duō-le. Wǒ-chībuliǎo.	There's too much food. I can't eat it all.
6.	Xièxie-nin. Wǒ-chīde-tài-duō-le. Chībuxià-le.	Thank you. I've eaten too much. I can't eat any more.
7.	Wǒ-zuótian-mǎide-yìběn-shū 'jīntian-jiù-zhǎobudào-le.	Today I can't find a book that I bought yesterday.
8.	Qǐng-wèn-nin, Gāo-Xiānsheng-	May I ask, on what hill is Mr.

jiā zài-'něige-shānshang?   Gao's home?   How is it that I
Wó-zěnmo zhǎobudào-ne?   can't find it?

9. Nǐ-kànjian-'Zhāng-Xiānsheng-   Did you see Mr. Zhang?   No.
    le-ma? Méi-you. Tā-jiā-lí-   His home is too far from my
    wǒ-jiā tài-yuǎn. Wǒ-kànbu-   home. I can't (go) see him.
    jiàn-ta.

10. Zhèitiáo-lù-xībiar yǒu-yíge-   West of this road is a little red
    xiǎo-hóng-fángzi. Nǐ-kànde-   house. Can you see it? It's too
    jiàn-ma? Tài-yuǎn-le. Wǒ-   far. I can't see it.
    kànbujiàn.

11. Jīntian-mǎile-yìběn-shū. Róng-   I bought a book today. It's aw-
    yi-jíle. Wǒ-dōu-kàndedǒng.   fully easy. I can understand it
                                         all.

12. Tā-shuō-huà shuōde-tài-kuài-   He talks too fast. I can't under-
    le. Wǒ-tīngbudǒng.   stand him.

13. Wǒ-shuōde-huà nǐ-tīngjian-   Did you hear what I said? I did-
    le-ma? Nǐ-shuōde-huà wǒ-   n't hear what you said.
    méi-tīngjian.

14. Wǒ-tài-bèn-le. Wǒ-yídìng-   I'm too stupid. I certainly can't
    niànbuliǎo-dàxué.   do college work.

15. Wǒ-méi-qián. Wó-xiáng-wǒ-   I don't have any money. I guess
    niànbushàng-dàxué.   I can't attend college.

16. Yòng-Zhōngwén-xiě-xìn ní-   Can you write letters in Chi-
    xiědeliǎo-ma? Wó-xiěbuliǎo.   nese? I can't. It's too hard.
    Tài-nán-le.

17. Nǐ-míngtian-dào-gōngyuán-   Are you going to the park tomor-
    qù-ma? Yīnwei-wó-yóu-hěn-   row? I have a lot to do, so I
    duō-shì, 'míngtian-wó-qù-   can't go tomorrow.
    buliǎo.

18. Tā-zǒude-tài-màn-le. Yìtiān-   He walks too slowly. He can't
    zǒubuliǎo-èrlǐ-lù.   walk two miles a day.

19. Tāde-shì-tài-máfan-le. Wǒ-   His work is too difficult [lit.
    zuòbuliǎo.   troublesome]. I can't do it (for
                                         him).

20. Tā-bu-néng-shuō-huà-le.   He's no longer able to speak.
    Yídìng-huóbuliǎo-le.   He certainly can't live any long-
                                         er.

21. Tāde-fángzi-tài-xiǎo-le. Yǒu-   His house is too small. (If he)
    péngyou jiù-zuòbuxià-le.   has friends he can't seat them.

22. Yìzhī-gāngbǐ-liǎngkuài-qián.   A fountain pen is two dollars. It

Yòngbuliáo-'wŭkuai-qián.   couldn't be five dollars.

23. Wǒ-zài-túshūguǎn yùjian-   I met Miss Johnson in the li-
     'Zhāng-Xiáojie-le.   brary.

24. Zhèibĕn-shū qíng-ni-gĕi-   May I ask you to give this book
     Wáng-Xiáojie kéyi-ma? Wǒ-   to Miss Wang? I'm not likely to
     jīntian yùbujiàn-ta.   run into her today.

25. Zhèibĕn-shū zài-túshūguǎn-   Is it possible to borrow this
     jièdedào-ma?   book at the library?

26. Nǐ-dào-túshūguǎn-qu zŏude-   (On the way) to the library can
     dào-Sān-Yŏu-Shūdiàn-ma?   you get to the Three Friends
     Rúguó-zŏudedào qíng-ni-géi-   Bookstore? If you can [get to it]
     wo-mǎi-yìbĕn-shū.   please buy a book for me.

27. Nèizhāng-zhǐ-'tài-xiǎo-le.   That sheet of paper is too small.
     Xiĕbuxià-hĕn-duō-zì. Nǐ-   You can't write many characters
     zì-xiĕde-'xiǎo-yìdiǎr jiù-   on it. Write the characters a
     xiĕdexià-le.   little smaller and you'll be able
                                       to get them on.

28. Tā-shuō-huà shuōde-'tài-kuài-   He talks too fast. I can't under-
     le. Wǒ-'dōu-tīngbudŏng.   stand anything (he says).

29. 'Wáng-Xiānsheng Zhōngwén-   Mr. King speaks Chinese awfully
     shuōde-hǎojíle. Wǒ-'dōu-   well. I can understand every-
     tīngdedŏng.   thing (he says).

30. Wó-xiǎng-xià-xīngqī wǒmen-   I don't think we'll be able to get
     xuébudào-dì-'shíqīkè.   to Lesson 17 by next week.

31. 'Zhāng-Xiáojie kǎoshang-dà-   Miss Zhang has passed the ex-
     xué-le.   ams for college.

32. Tā-yòu-cōngming yòu-yòng-   He's bright and he works hard.
     gōng. Yídìng-kǎodeshàng-   He can certainly pass the exams
     dàxué.   for college.

33. 'Nèige-xuésheng yòu-bèn-yòu-   That student is stupid as well as
     bú-yònggōng. Kǎobushàng-dà-   lazy. He can't pass the college
     xué.   entrance exams.

34. Wáng-Xiānsheng-'tài-cōng-   Mr. King is too brilliant. Al-
     ming-le. Wǒ-suírán-hĕn-   though I work very hard I [still]
     yònggōng kĕshi-'hái-niànbu-   can't beat him [in studying].
     guò-ta.

35. Nèige-xuésheng-'tài-cōngming-   That student is extremely in-
     le. Tā-'yídìng-niàndeguò-   telligent. He can certainly do
     Zhāng-Xiānsheng.   better than Mr. Johnson [in
                                       studying].

Pattern 14.5. Large Numbers (Note 7)

Pattern 14.5a. Numbers into the Tens of Thousands

(Each of the unit-numbers may be preceded by a digit from one to nine)

wàn	qiān	bǎi	shí
10,000's	1,000's	100's	10's
sānwàn	sìqiān	wúbǎi	liùshí

'thirty-four thousand five hundred sixty'

Pattern 14.5b. Numbers into the Hundreds of Millions

(As above, followed by <u>wàn</u> '10,000')

wàn	qiān	bǎi	shí	wàn
10,000's	1,000's	100's	10's	10,000's
sānwàn	sìqiān	wúbǎi	liùshí	wàn

'34,560 ten-thousands = 345,600,000'

1. Tīngshuō-Měiguo xiànzài-chà-buduō yóu-liǎngwànwàn-rén.

   I hear that the United States now has almost 200,000,000 people.

2. Zhōngguo-rén-zuì-duō. Chà-buduō-yǒu-jiǔwànwàn-rén.

   Chinese are the most numerous. There are almost 900,000,000 of them.

3. Měiguo-lí-Zhōngguo-hén-yuǎn— 'yíwàn-duō-lǐ-lù.

   America is a long way from China—over 10,000 miles.

4. Qián-Xiānsheng-'hén-xǐhuan-niàn-shū. Tā-jīnnian-yǐjing-mǎile yìbái-jiǔshíběn-shū-le.

   Mr. Qian is very fond of reading. He's already bought 190 books this year.

5. Tāde-qián-tài-duō-le. Chàbu-duō-yǒu-qībái-wǔshiwànkuài-qián.

   He has too much money—(he has) almost $7,500,000.

6. 'Zhāng-Xiānsheng yǒu-qián-jiù-mǎi-shū. Tā-yígòng-yǒu yí-wàn-wǔqiān-duō-běn-shū-le. Tāde-jiā jiù-shi-yíge-xiǎo-tú-shūguǎn.

   If Mr. Johnson has money he buys books. He has acquired a total of over 15,000 books. His home is a miniature (public) library.

7. Rúguǒ wó-yóu-liǎng-saṅ-qiān-kuài-qián wǒ-jiù-dào-wàiguo-qu.

   If I had two or three thousand dollars I'd go abroad.

8. 'Wáng-Xiānsheng mǎile-yìsuǒr-dà-fángzi. Yòngle-jiǔwàn-wǔ-qiān-duō-kuài-qián.

   Mr. Wang bought a big house. He spent over $95,000 (for it).

9. Nèige-xuéxiào yígòng-yǒu-

   That school has 3,000 students

sānqiān-xuésheng : 'nán-xué-
sheng yìqiān-jiúbǎi-rén, nǔ-
xuésheng yìqiān-yìbǎi-rén.

in all: 1,900 boys [lit. male stu-
dents], 1,100 girls [lit. female
students].

10. Zhèige-chéng-hěn-dà. Chàbuduō yǒu-shíqīwàn-wǔqiān-
rén.

This city is quite large. It has
almost 175,000 people.

SUBSTITUTION TABLES

I: 36 sentences (Note 1)

wǒ	yòng	máobǐ	xiě	xìn	—
nǐ		qiānbǐ		zì	ma
tā		gāngbǐ			

II: 54 sentences (Note 1)

wǒ	gěi	xiānsheng	mǎi-piào	—
nǐ		tàitai	xiě-xìn	ma
tā		xiáojie	jiè-shū	

III: 54 sentences (Note 1)

wǒ	duì	Wáng	Xiānsheng	shuō	huà
nǐ		Qián	Tàitai		shénmo
tā		Gāo	Xiáojie		

IV: 27 phrases (Note 2)

wǒ	jiè	de	zìdiǎn
nǐ	mǎi		shū
tā	yào		běnzi

V: 72 phrases (Notes 2–3)

(Asterisks indicate columns either of which may be used)

*				*	
———	jiè	zìdiǎn	de	———	xiānsheng
zhèige	mǎi	shū		zhèige	rén
nèige	yào			nèiwèi	

VI: 72 sentences (Note 5)

nǐ	—	yòng	-guo	máobǐ	—
tā	méi	jiè		gāngbǐ	ma
		jiàn		qiānbǐ	

<u>VII a:</u> 8 phrases (Note 6)

kàn	-de-	jiàn
tīng	-bu-	dǒng

<u>VII b:</u> 12 phrases (Note 6)

jiè	-de-	dào
xué	-bu-	liǎo
mǎi		

<u>VIII:</u> 64 phrases (Note 7)

yí	-wàn	yì	-qiān	yì	-bǎi
èr		èr		èr	
sān		sì		wǔ	
liù		qī		bā	

PRONUNCIATION DRILLS

I. Contrasts in <u>ui</u>: tones 1–2 versus tones 3–4

(The Sounds of Chinese, 8)

(Not all Chinese speakers make these contrasts; some pronounce all of these finals like those of tones 3–4.)

(a) guī guǐ	(e) huī huǐ	(i) tuí tuì
(b) guī guì	(f) huí huì	(j) suí suì
(c) kuī kuì	(g) duī duì	(k) zhuī zhuì
(d) kuí kuǐ	(h) tuī tuǐ	(l) cuī cuì

II. Contrasts in <u>iu</u> and <u>you</u>: tones 1–2 versus tones 3–4

(The Sounds of Chinese, 13)

(Not all Chinese speakers make these contrasts; some pronounce all of these finals like those of tones 3–4.)

(a) niú niǔ	(c) jiū jiǔ	(e) xiū xiǔ
(b) liú liù	(d) jiū jiù	(f) xiū xiù

(g) yōu yǒu	(i) yōu yòu
(h) yóu yǒu	(j) yóu yòu

III.   Contrasts in Stress (The Sounds of Chinese, 22)

1. Shi-Wáng-'Xiānsheng-láide shi-   Is it Mr. King or Mrs. King who
    Wáng-'Tàitai-láide?   has come?

2. Shi-'Wáng-Xiānsheng-láide shi-   Is it Mr. King or Mr. White who
    'Bái-Xiānsheng-láide?   has come?

3. Tā-shi-jīntian-'mǎi-de-chē   Did he buy or sell a car today?
    háishi-'mài-de-chē?

4. Tā-shi-jīntian-mǎi-chē háishi-   Is he buying a car or a house to-
    mǎi-fángzi?   day?

5. Tā-'jīntian-lái háishi-'míng-   Is it today or tomorrow that he's
    tian-lái?   coming?

6. Tā-jīntian-lái háishi-jīntian-   Is he coming or going today?
    zǒu?

7. Wǒ-shuō-jīntian, méi-shuō-   I said today, not yesterday.
    zuótian.

8. Wǒ-shuō-jīnnián, méi-shuō-   I said this year, not this day.
    jīntiān.

IV.   Contrasts in Juncture (The Sounds of Chinese, 21)

(a) yínán   yīn'àn

(b) míngē   míng'é

(c) fāngài   fáng'ài

THE TOPIC-COMMENT CONSTRUCTION (Note 8 below)

1. Ní-mǎile-piào-le-ma?   Piào-   Did you buy the tickets? The
    mǎi-le.   tickets have been bought.

2. Nǐ-kéyi-shuō-'Zhōngguo-huà-   Can you speak Chinese? (I) can
    ma? Zhōngguo-huà-kéyi-shuō.   speak Chinese.

3. 'Bái-Xiānsheng mǎile-'bǐ-   Did Mr. White buy the pens? He
    méi-you? Tā-bí-mǎi-le.   bought the pens.

4. 'Qián-Xiānsheng dào-túshū-   Did Mr. Qian go to the library?
    guǎn-le-ma? 'Qián-Xiān-   Mr. Qian has been to the library.
    sheng túshūguǎn-dàoguo-le.

5. 'Zhāng-Xiáojie zuótian-   Did Miss Zhang see a movie
    'kànguo-diànyǐngr-le-ma?   yesterday? Miss Zhang saw a
    'Zhāng-Xiáojie zuótian   movie yesterday.
    diànyǐngr-kànguo-le.

6. Nèige-xuésheng niànguo-   Has that student attended col-
    'dàxué-le-ma? Ta-'zhōng-   lege? He's been to middle

xué-niànguo-le, 'dàxué-hái-
méi-niàn-ne.

school, but has not yet been to
college.

7. Nǐ-niàn-shū-le-ma?   Shū-
niàn-le.

Did you do (your) studying?   The
studying's done.

8. Ní-mǎi-shū-gěi-'qián-méi-
you?   Qián-gěi-le.

Did you pay the money when you
bought the books?   The money
has been paid.

9. Nǐ-chīle-fàn-le-ma?   Fàn-
chīguo-le.

Have you eaten?   I've already
eaten.

10. Nǐ-néng-xiě-'Zhōngguo-zì-
ma?   'Zhōngguo-zì néng-
xiě.

Can you write Chinese characters?   (I) can write Chinese
characters.

11. Ní-géi-ni-mǔqin xiě-xìn-le-
ma?   Géi-wó-mǔqin-de-xìn
xiě-le.

Did you write a letter to your
mother?   The letter to my mother has been written.

12. Ní-mǎi-'mòshuǐ-le-méi-you?
Mòshuí-mǎi-le.

Did you buy the ink?   The ink
has been bought.

13. Nǐ-zuótian-shuō-mǎi-zìdiǎn,
mǎi-dìtú.   Dōu-'mǎi-le-méi-
you?   Zìdián-mǎi-le, dìtú-
hái-méi-mǎi-ne.

Yesterday you said (you were
going) to buy a dictionary and a
map. Did you buy both? I bought
the dictionary, but have not yet
bought the map.

14. Ní-xiě-zì-le-ma?   Zì-xiě-
le.

Did you write the characters?
The characters have been written.

15. 'Gāo-Xiānsheng-mǎile nèi-
suǒr-dà-fángzi-ma? Nèi-
suǒr-dà-fángzi tā-mǎi-le.

Did Mr. Gao buy that big house?
He bought that big house.

MONOLOGUE

Wǒ-shi-yíge-Měiguo-xuésheng.   Wǒ-dào-Zhōngguo lái-niàn-shū.   Xiàn-
zài-'Zhōngguo-shū wǒ-néng-kàndedǒng-le. 'Zhōngguo-huà yě-dōu-néng-shuō-
le. Wǒ-duì-xiě-zì zuì-yǒu-xìngqu.   Wó-měitiān dōu-yòng-máobí-xiě-zì.
'Gāo-Xiānsheng, 'Qián-Xiānsheng tāmen-kànjian-wó-xiě-de-zì, dōu-shuō-
xiěde-hǎojíle. Bù-zhīdào tāmen-shi-kèqi-ne háishi-zhēn-huà-ne. Yòng-máo-
bí-xiě-zì hěn-nán. Zhōngguo-rén chàbuduō-yě-dōu-yòng-gāngbǐ huòzhě-
qiānbǐ xiě-zì-le. 'Gāo-Xiānsheng-duì-xiě-zì hén-yǒu-yánjiu.   Wó-xiě-de-
zì cháng-qǐng-ta-kàn. Tā-yě-gàosu-wo xiě-zì-de-'fāngfǎ,   suóyi-wó-hěn-
xièxie-ta.

CHECKING UP

The questions below are based on material in the Dialogue at the beginning of this lesson.

1. 'Gāo-Xiáojie-xuéxiào yígòng-yǒu-'duōshao-xuésheng?

2. Dào-Yuǎndōng-Dàxué-kǎoshì-de-xuésheng yígòng-yǒu-'duōshao-rén?

3. 'Gāo-Xiáojie-shuō ta-'zěnmo-kǎobushàng-dàxué?

4. 'Bái-Xiānsheng-shuō 'Gāo-Xiáojie kǎodeshàng-dàxué-ma?

5. 'Gāo-Xiáojie-shuō ta-rúguó-kǎobushàng-dàxué ta-jiù-xué-shénmo?

6. 'Bái-Xiānsheng xīwang-'Gāo-Xiáojie-xué-shénmo?

7. 'Gāo-Xiáojie xuéguo-huà-huàr-ma?

8. 'Bái-Xiānsheng yuánlái-xiǎng-xué-shénmo-ne?

9. Yuǎndōng-Dàxué yǒu-'duōshao-xuésheng?

10. 'Duōshao-rén kǎoshang-Yuǎndōng-Dàxué-le?

11. Xué-yǔyánxué 'zěnmo-xué-ne?

12. 'Bái-Xiānsheng gěi-'Zhōngguo-péngyou-xiě-xìn, yòng-'Zhōngwén háishi-yòng-'Yīngwén?

13. 'Gāo-Xiáojiede-fùqin 'zì-xiěde-hǎo-bu-hǎo?

14. 'Gāo-Xiáojie-shuō xiànzài-Zhōngguo-rén dōu-yòng-'shénmo-bí-xiě-zì?

15. 'Shéi-duì-Bái-Xiānsheng-shuō Gāo-Xiáojiede-zì xiěde-hén-hǎo?

NOTES

1. The verb yòng 'use' also functions as a coverb meaning 'by, with, by means of':

> 'Zhōngguo-rén yòng-máobí-xiě-zì. 'Chinese write characters with a writing brush.'

The verb gěi 'give,' which is similar to its English equivalent in that it takes both direct and and indirect objects (Tā-gěi-wó-bǐ. 'He gave me a pen.'), is also used as a coverb meaning 'to' or 'for':

> Wǒ-jīntian-gěi-ta-xiě-xìn. 'I'm writing him a letter today.' 'I'm writing a letter for him (i.e. to someone else) today.'

> Wǒ-jīntian-gěi-ta-mǎi-shū. 'I'm buying him a book today.' 'I'm buying a book for him today.' *

---

* Note that the second of these English sentences is ambiguous: it could mean either 'I bought a book to give him as a present' or 'I bought a book to save him the effort of doing so himself.' The Chinese, however, is not ambiguous; it can only have the first English meaning. However, in a few cases, such as gěi-ta-xiě-xìn, the sentence is ambiguous out of context.

The verb <u>duì</u> 'face toward' is used as a coverb. Most often it corresponds to English 'toward' or 'to':

> Tā-duì-wǒ-shuō tā-bù-lái-le.   'He told me [lit. said to me that] he isn't coming any more.'

Occasionally it corresponds more closely to 'with respect to':

> Wǒ-duì-wénxué hén-yǒu-xìngqu.   'With respect to literature, I'm very interested.' Or, more freely, 'I'm very much interested in literature.'

2. Subordination of transitive and intransitive verbs to nouns is an extension of subordination of nouns and stative verbs (Lesson 5, Note 2, p. 55):

> wǒ-péngyoude-shū 'my friend's book'
> hén-xiǎode-shū 'a very small book'

With other verbs as well, <u>de</u> occurs between the verb phrase and the following noun:

> dào-túshūguǎn-qù-de-xuésheng 'students who go to the library'
> xué-wénxué-de-xuésheng 'students who study literature'
> xuésheng-kàn-de-shū 'books which students read'

The verb phrases often correspond to English relative clauses; but in Chinese the clauses always come <u>before</u> the modified noun—not after it, as in English.

3. Specifiers (e.g. <u>zhèi</u> 'this,' <u>nèi</u> 'that') used with subordinate clauses can come either before the clause or before the noun:

> nèige-mǎi-shū-de-rén ⎫
>   or   ⎬   'the person who is buying books'
> mǎi-shū-de-nèige-rén ⎭

If the clause is a long one, the specifier is more likely to occur before the noun.   In this usage the specifier more often has the force of the definite article 'the' in English rather than its basic meaning 'this' or 'that.'

4. The noun to which a clause is subordinated can be omitted:

> Zài-nèr-kàn-shū-de-rén bu-dōu-shi-'Zhōngguo-rén.
>   or
> Zài-nèr-kàn-shū-de bu-dōu-shi-'Zhōngguo-rén.
>
> 'Not all those reading there are Chinese.'

5. The verb suffix -<u>guo</u> has two meanings:

(a) In a context where no specific time is mentioned, it suggests that an action has (or has not) been experienced at some indefinite time in the past:

> Wǒ-chīguo-'Rìběn-fàn.   'I've eaten Japanese food (at some time or other).'
> Wǒ-méi-chīguo-'Rìběn-fàn.   'I have never [= not ever] eaten Japanese food.'
> Nǐ-chīguo-'Rìběn-fàn-méi-you?   'Have you ever eaten Japanese food?'

(b) In a context where a specific time is mentioned or understood, -guo places emphasis on the fact that an action has already been completed. Thus in answer to a question about whether you accomplished the task of borrowing a certain book from the library today, you might answer:

Jièguo-le. 'I've borrowed it (already).'

6. Resultative verbs (RV) are compound transitive verbs. Some of the compounds have a clear action-result relationship:

tīng 'listen' + jiàn 'see, perceive' = tīngjian 'perceive by listening' — i.e. 'hear'

Often, however, these compounds have meanings which are not predictable from the separate meanings of the parts (cf. English 'understand'), so that you cannot form your own resultative compounds by combining two likely-sounding verbs; you must learn each one individually as you encounter it.

Resultative verbs, as distinguished from other verbs, have special forms for adding the meanings 'be able' and 'be unable.' For 'be able,' de is inserted between the two parts:

tīngjian 'hear' > tīngdejiàn 'able to hear, can hear'

For 'be unable,' bu is inserted:

tīngjian 'hear' > tīngbujiàn 'unable to hear, can't hear'

Resultative compounds whose second member is liǎo (which here has no meaning in itself but only the grammatical function of forming compounds) have no simple verb + liǎo forms; they occur only in de and bu combinations:

chīdeliǎo 'can eat'
chībuliǎo 'can't eat'

The latter forms are interchangeable with the auxiliary-plus-verb pattern:

néng-chī or chīdeliǎo 'able to eat, can eat'

The two patterns may even be combined, so that there is a double expression for 'can':

néng-chīdeliǎo 'able to eat, can eat'

Resultative verb compounds are made negative by méi or méi-you:

Wǒ-méi-kànjian-ta. 'I didn't see him.'

Rarely, however, are they preceded by bu; instead, the verb-bu-verb form is used, expressing a 'cannot' rather than a 'does not' negative:

Nǐ-tīngjian-ma? 'Do you hear?'
Wǒ-tīngbujiàn. 'I can't hear.'

7. Numbers over 99 are expressed with combinations using bǎi 'hundred,' qiān 'thousand,' wàn 'ten thousand'; the larger units precede the smaller:

sānbǎi-sìshiwǔ '345'
yíwàn-èrqiān-sānbǎi-sìshiwǔ '12,345'

Numbers above 10,000 are expressed in multiples of ten thousand (not, as in English, in multiples of one thousand or one million):

    shíwàn   '100,000'
    bǎiwàn   '1,000,000'
    qiānwàn   '10,000,000'
    wànwàn   '100,000,000'

The numbers <u>bǎi</u>, <u>qiān</u>, and <u>wàn</u>, when combined with '2,' take <u>liǎng</u> or <u>èr</u>:

    liángbǎi <u>or</u> èrbǎi '200'

The measure <u>ge</u> is often omitted after <u>bǎi</u>, <u>qiān</u>, and <u>wàn</u>, and also after <u>duō</u> when the following word refers to people:

    yìbǎi-rén '100 people'
    sānqiān-duō-rén 'over 3,000 people'

8. Chinese subject-verb (SV) constructions may have two different interpretations, according to the context. For example, this sentence may have the following separate meanings:

    Wáng-Xiānsheng yě-kàn-le.

> (a) Mr. King also read (the book which has been under discussion).

> (b) I also saw Mr. King (among other of my acquaintances).

In meaning (a), the subject (S) performed the action of the verb (V); this can be called an Actor-Action relationship and considered a special subtype of the S-V construction.

In meaning (b), the relationship between the parts is different: the subject (S) is commented on by—but did not perform the action of—the verb (V). Meanings of the (b) type might be referred to as T-C, or Topic-Comment, constructions, and considered another subtype of the S-V construction.

In constructions of the T-C type, the word order of the Chinese sentence often corresponds loosely with the word order of English passive sentences:

    Fàn-chī-le. '(About) the food—eat(ing) has (been done to it).' (Cf.:
    'The food has been eaten.')

It is misleading, however, to translate the T-C construction with an English passive sentence, since the English passive construction has quite different connotations from the Chinese T-C pattern. The T-C pattern names something, then says something about it; the effect is often to emphasize the V, or Comment, part of the sentence.

Here are more examples:

    A-A: Nǐ-dōu-mǎi-le-méi-you? 'Did you buy everything?'

    T-C: Shū-dōu-mǎi-le-méi-you? 'The books . . . . did buy them
          all?'

    T-C: Zhèibǎn-shū xiànzài-shūdiàn-mǎibudào. '(About) this book....
          now [in] bookstores it can't be bought'—or, more freely, 'You
          can't buy this book in bookstores nowadays.'

The Topic-Comment construction is used more often in speech than in writing. It would be preferable not to use it in writing isolated sentences and to limit its use where appropriate in connected speech.

9. An alternative, and slightly less blunt, way of saying N-V is the construction N shi V de:

Wǒ-chīguo. 'I've eaten (it).'
Wǒ-shi-chīguo-de. 'I've eaten (it).'   [lit. ' I am the one who ate it.']
Zhèibén-shū hěn-dà. 'This book is very large.'
Zhèibén-shū shi-hěn-dà-de. 'This book is a very large one.'

Context will determine whether the form with shi . . . de has the same connotation as the simpler form, or whether a more literal translation is a closer representation of what the Chinese expresses.

10. The word zuì is used in two meanings: '-est' and 'very, extremely':

Zhèi-sìge-rén-lǐtou, tā-shi-zuì-gāo-de. 'Among these four men, he is the tallest.'
Tā-shuōde zuì-hǎo. Wǒ-dōu-tīngdedǒng. 'He speaks extremely well. I can understand everything (he says).'

The word tài is also used in two meanings, 'excessively, too' and 'very, extremely':

Rén-tài-duō. 'There are too many people.'
Tā-Zhōngguo-huà shuōde-tài-hǎo-le. 'He speaks Chinese extremely well.'

11. Other ways of expressing extreme or excessive degrees of an attribute, in addition to those described in Note 10, are:

(a) Giving special stress to a word. Observe the effect of stress in the following pairs of sentences:

Tā-hén-hǎo. 'He's O. K.'
Tā-'hén-hǎo. 'He's very good.'

(b) Suffixing jíle 'extremely' to the stative verb:

Tā-bènjíle. 'He's extremely stupid.'

(c) Repeating the phrase containing the stative verb:

Tā-shuō-Zhōngguo-huà shuōde hén-hǎo hén-hǎo. 'He speaks Chinese very well.'

12. The expression zuì-hǎo 'best' is used either before or after the subject to mean 'had better [do so-and-so]':

Wǒ-jīntian-méi-qián. Wǒ-zuì-hǎo míngtian-mǎi-shū. 'I don't have any money today. It would be best if I bought the books tomorrow.'
Zuì-hǎo-wǒmen-bu-qù. 'We'd better not go.'

13. The measure fēn 'part,' which we have encountered in expressions of time and money (yìfēn-zhōng 'one minute,' yìfēn-qián ' one cent'), is occasionally used in the meaning ' one-tenth,' usually in a figurative sense:

Tā-huó-de-xī̄wang zhí-yǒu-sānfēn.   'There is only a three-tenths hope of his living.'

The expression shífēn 'ten-tenths' is used as an intensifying adverb in the meaning 'very,' comparable to the English expression 'one hundred per cent' (a hundred per cent acceptable, etc.):

Zhèizhī-bǐ shífēn-hǎo. 'This pen is very good.'

14. The adverb yě 'also' is repeated in two or more consecutive parallel verbal expressions to mean 'both. . . and . . .,' or, if more than two, 'X and Y and Z . . . all three,' and so on:

Jīntian shū-yě-niàn-le, zì-yé-xiě-le.   'Today I have done both the studying and the writing.'

15. Note carefully that expressions with xìngqu 'interest (in)' require human subjects and do not permit inanimate subjects, which require the form yǒu-yìsi 'be interesting':

Wǒ-duì-yǔyanxué hén-yǒu-xìngqu.   'I'm very much interested in linguistics.'

Yúyanxué hén-yǒu-yìsi.   'Linguistics is very interesting.'

(See also Supplementary Lesson 14, Note 1)

Lesson 15 STUDYING AND TRAVELING

"Tīng-lùyīn shi-xué-yǔyán-'zuì-hǎode-fāngfǎ-le."

Dialogue: Mr. White and Miss Gao speak of their studies and travels.

Gāo: 'Bái-Xiānsheng, nín-xuéle 'jǐniánde-Zhōngwén-le?

Mr. White, how many years have you been studying Chinese?

Bái : Wǒ-zài-zhōngxué jiu-kāishǐ-niàn-'Zhōngwén. Gāozhōng-'èrniánjí wǒ-jiù-niàn-Zhōng-   5
wén-le.

I began (to study Chinese) in high school. [It was] in my second year in senior high [that I studied Chinese].

Gāo: Nín-Zhōngwén xuéde-'zhēn-bù-shǎo-le.

You've been studying it for quite a while.

Bái : Wǒ-niàn-'Zhōngwén chàbù-duō-yǐjing-yóu-'wǔnián-le.   10

[I've been studying it] for almost five years.

Gāo: Suóyi-nínde-Zhōngwén nènmo-hǎo-ne.   Nín-zài-Měiguo-xué-Zhōngwén 'zěn-mo-xué-ne?

That's why your Chinese is so good. How did you study Chinese in America?

Bái : Wǒmen-kāishǐ-'xué-de-shí-   15
hou měitiān-shàng-'yíge-zhōngtóude-kè. Jiàoyuán-jiāo-wǒmen-shuō. Xià-kè-yǐhòu wǒmen-jiu-tīng-lùyīnjīde-lùyīn.   20

At the beginning [lit. when we began to study], we went to class one hour a day. The teacher taught us to speak. After [leaving] class we listened to recordings on a tape recorder.

Gāo: Tīng-lùyīn shi-xué-yǔyán-   Listening to recordings is the
      'zuì-hǎode-fāngfǎ-le.   best way to study languages.

Bái: Duì-le.   That's right.

Gāo: Nín-měitian-tīng-lùyīn   How much time did you listen to
      yào-tīng-'duōshao-shíhou-   25   recordings each day?
      ne?

Bái: Zài-'zhōngxué-de-shíhou   We listened less in high school—
      tīngde-shǎo-yìdiǎr. Měi-   [we listened] thirty or forty
      tiān-tīng 'sān-sìshífēn-   minutes a day.   When I was in
      zhōngde-lùyīn. Zài-'dà-   30   college we had [to listen for] one
      xué-de-shíhou měitian-yào-   or two hours a day.
      tīng 'yì-liǎngge-zhōngtóu.

Gāo: Nín-zhēn-yònggōng.   You really work hard.

Bái: Xué-yǔyán bìděi-yònggōng.   You have to work hard to study a
      Xué-yǔyán hén-yǒu-yì si.   35   foreign language.   Language
      Kāishǐ-de-shíhou hěn-nán   study is very interesting. At the
      xué. Yǐhòu jiù-róngyi-le,   beginning it was hard going.
      gèng-yǒu-xìngqu-le. Wǒ-   Later it got easier and I became
      nèige-shíhou-jiù-xiǎng   even more interested.   It was
      jiānglái-yídìng-dào-Zhōng-   40   then that I got the idea of [surely
      guo-qu-niàn-shū.   in the future] going to China to
                                         study.

Gāo: Nín-xiànzài 'zhēn-dào-   Now you've really come to China
      Zhōngguo-lái-niàn-shū-le...   to study. . . . Did you come by
      Nín-dào-Zhōngguo zuò-'fēijī   plane or by boat?
      háishi-zuò-'chuán-lái-de-ne? 45

Bái: Wǒ-xiān-cóng-Niǔyue zuò-   First I went by car from New
      qìchē dào-Sānfánshì. Wǒ-   York to San Francisco, arriving
      zuòle-'liùtiān-de-qìchē cái-   there after a six-day drive.
      dào-ner.

Gāo: Tīngshuō-Sānfánshì 'Zhōng-   50   I hear there are a lot of Chinese
      guo-rén-hěn-duō. Shi-'zhēn-   in San Francisco. Is that right?
      de-ma?

Bái: Nèr-'Zhōngguo-rén-bù-shǎo.   There are quite a few [Chinese
      Zài-Sānfánshì zhùle-bātiān.   there]. I stayed in San Francis-
      Wǒ-yòu-zuòle-shítiānde-   55   co for eight days.   Then I
      chuán dào-Rìběn. Zài-Rì-   traveled for ten days by boat to
      běn zhùle-yíge-xīngqī, jiù-   Japan. I stayed in Japan for a
      zuò-fēijī dào-'Zhōngguo-lái-   week, and then came to China by
      le.   plane.

Gāo: Cóng-Rìběn-zuò-fēijī-dào-   60   How much time does it take by
      Zhōngguo yào-'duōshao-   plane from Japan to China?
      shíhou-ne? 'Yào-bu-yào   [Does it take] seven or eight
      qī-bāge-zhōngtóu-ne?   hours?

Bái: Yòngbudào-qī-bāge-zhōng-   It doesn't take that long [lit. It
      tóu. Sān-sìge-zhōngtóu jiù- 65   can't take seven or eight hours].
      dào-le.   You can make it in three or four
                                         [hours].

Gāo: Nín-zuòguo-'jǐcì-fēijī-le?

How many times have you been on a plane?

Bái: Wó-yǐjing-zuòguo-'hěn-duō-cì-le.

[I've been] quite a few times [already].

Gāo: Wǒ-hái-méi-zuòguo-fēijī-ne. 70
Yǒu-jīhui wó-děi-'zuò-yícì.

I haven't even been on a plane yet. If I have a chance I must go up in one [lit. sit once].

Bái: Jiānglái nǐ-bìyè-yǐhòu
yīnggāi-zuò-fēijī dào-biéde-dìfang-qu-wárwar.

[In the future] after you graduate you should take a plane somewhere and go have fun.

Gāo: Wó-xiǎng bìyè-yǐhòu gēn- 75
wǒ-fùqin-mǔqin-tāmen yí-kuàr-dào-Rìběn-wárwar.
Hěn-duō-rén-shuō Rìběn-hén-yǒu-yìsi. Wǒ-xīwang-dào-Rìběn-yǐhòu zài-nèr- 80
zhù-yì-liǎngge-yuè.

I think that after I graduate I'll go to Japan with my father and mother for a vacation [lit. to have fun]. Many people say Japan is quite interesting. I hope [after getting to Japan] to stay there for a month or two.

Bái: Rìběn-'shì-hén-yǒu-yìsi.
Yīnggāi-qu-wárwar.

Japan is very interesting. You should go there and have fun.

Gāo: Wǒ-fùqin-mǔqin dōu-qùguo- 85
Rìběn. Tāmen-'hén-xǐhuan-Rìběn. Tāmen-zài-nèr
zhùle-liǎngge-duō-yuè-ne,
hái-mǎile-hěn-duō Rìběn-dōngxi.

My father and mother have both been to Japan. They liked it very much. They stayed there for more than two months, and bought a lot of Japanese things.

Bái: Ní-'zěnmo-méi-gēn-tāmen 90
yíkuàr-qù-ne?

How come you didn't go along with them?

Gāo: Yīnwei-wǒmen-xuéxiào-kǎoshì, wǒ-méi-gōngfu-qù.
Wǒ-yuánlái-xiǎng kǎowán-yǐhòu gēn-liǎng-sānge- 95
'péngyou-yíkuàr-qù, kěshi-wǒ-bìng-le, suóyi-jiù-méi-qu.

Because our school was having exams, I didn't have time. I had planned originally to go with two or three friends after exams were over, but I got sick, so I didn't go.

Bái: Nǐ-bìyè-yǐhòu xīwang-nǐ-zhēn-néng-qù-yícì. 100

After you graduate I hope you really can go [once].

Gāo: 'Dāngrán-néng-qù-le. Yīn-wei-wo-fùqin-mǔqin tāmen-'dōu-xǐhuan-qù, bìyè-yǐhòu
huòzhě-gēn-tāmen-'yíkuàr-qù. 105

Of course I'll be able to [go]. Since my father and mother would both like to go, perhaps I'll go with them after I graduate.

Bái: Nǐ-fùqin-mǔqin tāmen-qù-Rìběn zhùzai-nǎr-ne?

When your father and mother go to Japan, where do they stay?

Gāo: Wǒ-fùqin-zai-Rìběn yǒu-yíwèi-Rìbén-lǎo-péngyou.
Tāmen-qùdao-Rìběn jiu- 110
zhùzai-tā-jiā.

[In Japan] my father has an old Japanese friend. When they go to Japan they stay at his home.

Bái : Nǐ-huì-huà-huàr 'gèng-   Your knowing how to paint is
       yīnggāi dào-biéde-dìfang-   even more reason why you
       qu-kànkan.   should go have a look at other
                                         places.

Gāo: Nǐ-zhènmo-shuō wǒ-yí-   115   The way you talk I certainly
      dìng-děi-dào-Rìběn-qù-   must take a trip to Japan.
      yícì.

VOCABULARY

bì	must, have to (AV) (Note 14)
bìděi	must, have to (AV) (Note 14)
bié(de)	other
bìng	sick (SV) sickness (N)
cái	(only) then, not until then (AD) (Note 13)
dāngrán	naturally, of course (MA) [lit. ought be]
děi	must, have to (AV) (Note 13)
dìfang	place, space (N) [lit. earth region]
dōngxi	(concrete) thing, object (N)
gāi	should, ought to (AV) (Note 15)
gēn	(together) with (CV)
jiānglái	in the future, hereafter (TW) [lit. about to come]
jiāo	teach (TV) (See Supplementary Lesson 15, Note 3)
jīhui	opportunity (N)
kāishǐ	begin (to do) (AV) [lit. open beginning]
lù-yīn	record (sound) (VO)
lùyīn	recording (N)
lùyīnjī	(tape) recorder (N) [lit. record sound machine]
nènmo, nàme	in that case (MA) so, that (AD) (Note 18)
Niǔyue	New York (PW)
Sānfánshì	San Francisco (PW) (See Supplementary Lesson 15, Note 4)
wán	finished, completed, done (IV)
wár	amuse oneself (with), play (with), have fun (IV)
yíkuàr	together (AD) [lit. one lump]
yīngdāng	should, ought to (AV) [lit. should ought] (Note 15)

yīnggāi	should, ought to (AV) [lit. should must] (Note 15)
yuè	month (N) (Note 1)
zènmo, zhènmo zènme, zhènme	so, this (AD) (Note 18)
zhōngtóu	hour (N)
zhù	live (at) (TV); stop, cease (IV)

SENTENCE BUILD-UP

yuè   month
shí'èrge-yuè   twelve months

1. Yìnián yǒu-shí'èrge-yuè.   One year has twelve months.

zhōngtóu   hour
èrshisìge-zhōngtóu   twenty-four hours

2. Yìtiān yǒu-èrshisìge-zhōng-
tóu.   One day has twenty-four hours.

lù   record, make a recording
yīn   sound

3. Wǒmen-xiànzài-lù-yīn kéyi-
ma?   Can we record now?

lùyīn   a recording
lùde-bù-hǎo   record badly

4. Zhèige-lùyīn lùde-bù-hǎo.   This recording is badly done.

lùyīnjī   recording machine
yòng-lùyīnjī   use a recorder

5. Wǒmen-yòng-lùyīnjī xué-
yǔyán.   We use recorders in studying
languages.

kāishǐ   begin
kāishǐ-xué-Zhōngwén   begin to study Chinese

6. Wǒmen-shi-jiǔyue kāishǐ-
xué-'Zhōngwén-de.   We began to study Chinese in
September.

zhù   live (in or at a place)
zhù-Měiguo   live in America

7. Tāmen-dōu-zhù-Měiguo.   They all live in America.

zài-Měiguo   in America
zài-Měiguo-zhù   live in America

8. Tāmen-dōu-zài-Měiguo-zhù.   They all live in America.

Niǔyue   New York
zhù-Niǔyue   live in New York

9. Ní-xǐhuan-zhù-Niǔyue-ma?   Do you like to live in New York?

         Sānfánshì   San Francisco
         zài-Sānfánshì-zhù   live in San Francisco

10.   Tīngshuō-zài-Sānfánshì-zhù   I hear it's very interesting to
      hén-yǒu-yìsi.   live in San Francisco.

         jiāo   teach
         jiāo-tāmen   teach them

11.   Wǒ-jiāo-tāmen-Zhōngwén.   I teach them Chinese.

         jiāo   teach
         jiāo-shū   teach

12.   Tā-zài-Niǔyue-jiāo-shū.   He teaches in New York.

         jiāo-shū   teach
         jiāo-yíge-zhōngtóu-shū   teach for one hour

13.   Wǒ-xiànzài yào-jiāo-yíge-   I'm going to teach for one hour
      zhōngtóu-shū.   now.

         jiāo-shū   teach
         jiāo-liǎngge-zhōngtóude-   teach for two hours
             shū

14.   Wó-měitiān jiāo-liǎngge-zhōng-   I teach two hours every day.
      tóude-shū.

         zài-Niǔyue-zhù   live in New York
         sānge-yuè   three months

15.   Wó-xiǎng-zài-Niǔyue zhù-   I plan to live in New York for
      sānge-yuè.   three months.

         bìng   sickness
         yǒu-bìng   have a sickness

16.   Tā-yǒu-'shénmo-bìng?   What illness does he have?

         bìng   sick
         bìng-le   become sick

17.   Tā-qùnian-bìngle-bātiān.   He was sick for eight days last
                                year.

         wár   have a good time
         wárwar   have a good time

18.   Wǒmen-dào-nèr-qu-wárwar-   How about going there and hav-
      hǎo-ma?   ing a good time?

         wár   have fun
         wárle   had fun
         wárle-yíge-xīngqī   had fun for a week

19.   Tāmen-èryue wárle-yíge-   They had fun for a week in Feb-
      xīngqī.   ruary.

         jiāo-sìge-zhōngtóu-   teach for four hours
            shū
         jiāole-sìge-zhōngtóu-   taught for four hours
            shū

20.   Wǒ-zuótian jiāole-sìge-zhōng-   I taught for four hours yester-
      tóu-shū.   day.

cái · just, then and only then
cái-zǒu · just left
21. Tā-bú-zài-jiā. Cái-zǒu. · He isn't at home. He just left.

wán · finish
wán-le · finished
22. Dōu-wán-le-ma? · Is everything finished?

chīwán · finish eating
chīwánle-fàn · finished eating
23. Wǒmen-chīwánle-fàn cái-zǒu. · We'll go after we've finished eating.

chīdewán · able to finish eating
chībuwán · unable to finish eating
24. Nǐ-shífēn-zhōng chīde-wán-chībuwán? · Can you eat [lit. finish eating] in ten minutes?

dāngrán · naturally
dāngrán-xiěbuwán · naturally unable to finish writing
25. Wǒ-yíkè-zhōng dāngrán-xiěbuwán. · Of course I can't finish writing in a quarter of an hour.

biéde · other
méi-yǒu-biéde · not have any other
26. Ní-yǒu-'biéde-méi-you? · Do you have any other?

biéde · other
biéde-shì · other tasks
27. Wǒ-méi-yǒu-biéde-shì. · I have no other tasks.

dìfang · place
nèige-dìfang · that place
28. Nèige-dìfang méi-yǒu-'wài-guo-rén. · There are no foreigners in that place.

dōngxi · thing
zhèige-dōngxi · this thing
29. Zhèige-dōngxi-jiào-shénmo? · What's this thing called?

jiānglái · some time in the future
bǐ-xiànzài · compared to now
shuōde-hǎo · speak well
30. Nǐ-jiānglái-shuōde bǐ-xiàn-zài-hǎo. · You will speak better in the future than (you do) now.

děi · must
31. Wó-déi-zǒu-le. · I must go.

bìděi · must
bìděi-kànwán · must finish reading
32. Wǒ-jīntian bìděi-kànwán-zhèiběn-shū. · I must finish reading this book today.

bú-bì	don't have to
bú-bì-xiě	don't have to write
33. Zhǐ-niàn, bú-bì-xiě.	Just read, (you) don't have to write.
gāi	ought to
34. Wǒ-xiànzài-gāi-zǒu-le.	I ought to go now.
yīnggāi	ought to
35. Wǒ-yīnggāi-'míngtian-qù.	I should go tomorrow.
yīngdāng	ought to
36. Wǒ-yīngdāng-qù-kàn-ta.	I should go see him.
gēn	with
gēn-shéi?	with whom?
37. Tā-gēn-'shéi-shuō-huà?	Who is he talking with?
nènmo	so
nènmo-dà	so big, that big
38. Nènmo-dàde wǒ-bú-yào.	I don't want such a big one.
zènmo	so
zènmo-bèn	so stupid, this stupid
39. Ní-zěnmo-'zènmo-bèn?	How come you're so stupid?
zhènmo	so
zhènmo-kèqi	so polite, this polite
40. Ní-zěnmo-zhènmo-kèqi?	Why are you so polite?
jīhui	opportunity
yǒu-jīhui	have an opportunity
41. Tā-méi-yǒu-jīhui-kàn-shū.	He doesn't have a chance to read.
yíkuàr	together
yíkuàr-qù	go together
42. Wǒmen-yíkuàr-qù-hǎo-ma?	Shall we go together?
cì	time, occasion
shuō-yícì	say once
43. Qǐng-nín-'zài-shuō-yícì.	Please say it one more time.
chī-sāncì	eat three times
chī-sāncì-Zhōngguo-fàn	eat Chinese food three times

44. Wó-zhǐ-chīguo 'sāncì-
Zhōngguo-fàn.

I've eaten Chinese food only
three times.

nǐ-qù

you are going

45. Shì-'nǐ-qù-ma?

Are you going?

tā-míngtian-qù

he is going tomorrow

46. Tā-shi-'míngtian-qù-ma?

Is he going tomorrow?

yòng
yǒu-yòng

use, make use of
be useful

47. Zhèige-zìdiǎn-méi-yǒu-yòng.

This dictionary is useless.

zài-jiāli
xiě-zì

in the house
write characters

48. Tā-zài-jiāli-xiě-zì.

He is writing characters in the
house.

xiězai

write on

49. Tā-xiězai-zhǐshang.

He is writing on paper.

zhùzai

live at or in a place

50. Tā-zhùzai-Niǔyue.

He lives in New York.

PATTERN DRILLS

Pattern 15.1. Duration of an Action in the Future (Note 4 below)

S	(yào)	V	T	(-de)	(O)
Subject	(yào)	Verb	Time	(-de)	(Object)
Wǒ	yào	kàn	yíge zhōngtóu	-de	shū.

'I will read a book for one hour.'

1. 'Qián-Xiānsheng yào-dào-
Rìběn-qù-bànnián.

Mr. Qian will go to Japan for
half a year.

2. Yīnwei-yào-kǎoshì-le, 'Bái-
Xiānsheng yào-niàn-liǎngge-
xīngqī-shū.

Because he's about to have exams, Mr. White is going to study
for two weeks.

3. 'Gāo-Xiáojie-shuō tā-kǎoshì-
yǐhòu yào-huà-liǎngge-yuède-
huàr.

Miss Gao says that after she has
her exams she will paint for a
couple of months.

4. Wó-xiǎng-xià-xīngqī qu-mǎi-
yíge-lùyīnjī, xià-kè-yǐhòu
měitiān-tīng-yíge-zhōngtóu-
de-lùyīn.

I plan to buy a recorder next
week and listen to recordings an
hour a day after class.

5. 'Zhāng-Xiānsheng hén-xǐhuan-
Sānfánshì. Tā-xiǎng-yíge-

Mr. Zhang is delighted with San
Francisco. A week from now he

xīngqī-yǐhòu dào-Sānfánshì
zhù-liǎng-sānge-xīngqī.

intends to go to San Francisco
and stay two or three weeks.

6. 'Máo-Xiānsheng xiáng-qǐng-
yíwèi-xiānsheng jiāo-ta-yì-
niánde-Yīngwén.

Mr. Mao plans to ask a teacher
to teach him English for a year.

7. 'Gāo-Tàitai xiǎng-dào-Niǔyue
qù-liǎngge-yuè.

Mrs. Gao intends to go to New
York for two months.

8. 'Zhāng-Xiáojie xiáng-měitiān
xué-liǎngge-zhōngtóude-Yīng-
wén.

Miss Zhang plans to study English two hours a day.

9. Tā-xiǎng-dào-Húnán qù-
liǎngge-xīngqī.

He intends to go to Hunan for
two weeks.

10. Tā-xiǎng-cóng-míngtian-
kāishǐ tā-yào-xué 'sānge-
yuède-Zhōngwén.

He plans to study Chinese for
three months beginning tomorrow.

11. Máo-Tàitai-shuō tā-yào-dào-
Shāndong-qu-bànnián.

Mrs. Mao says she will go to
Shantung for half a year.

12. Zhāng-Xiānsheng-shuō tā-
xiǎng-dào-Yīngguo-qu-yì-
nián, zài-dào-Měiguo-qu-
sānge-yuè.

Mr. Zhang says he plans to go
to England for a year, and then
to America for three months.

13. Wó-xiǎng-bànnián-yǐhòu dào-
'Zhōngguo-qu-zhù-yìnián.

Half a year from now I plan to
go to China for a year.

14. Wǒ-duì-xiě-Zhōngguo-zì hén-
yǒu-xìngqu.   Wó-xiǎng yǐ-
hou-měitiān xiě-yíge-zhōng-
tóude-zì.

I'm very much interested in
writing Chinese characters. I
plan to write characters for an
hour a day hereafter.

15. Máo-Xiānsheng-xiǎng dào-
Zhōngguo-qù-yíge-yuè.

Mr. Mao intends to go to China
for a month.

Pattern 15.2.   Duration of an Action in the Past   (Note 5 below)

S	V	-le	T	(-de)	(O)
Subject	Verb	-le	Time	(-de)	(Object)
Wǒ	kàn	-le	yíge zhōngtóu	-de	shū.

'I read for one hour.'

1. 'Gāo-Xiáojie xuéle-'sānnián-
de-huàr.

Miss Gao studied painting for
three years.

2. 'Qián-Xiānsheng bìngle-bàn-
nián-cái-hǎo.

Mr. Qian was sick for half a
year before he recovered.

3. Qùnian-wǒ-dào-Rìběn wárle-
liǎngge-yuè.

I went to Japan last year for a
pleasure trip for a couple of
months.

4. Zhèibĕn-Yīngwén-shū wŏ-xué-le-yìnián.

I studied this English book for one year.

5. Tā-duì-'Zhōngwén méi-xìngqu. Jiù-xuéle-bànnián.

He was not interested in Chinese. He studied it for only half a year.

6. Wŏ-xuéle-'liùniánde-Zhōngwén, kĕshi-shuōde-'hái-bu-hăo.

I studied Chinese for six years, but I still speak it badly.

7. 'Wáng-Xiānsheng xuéle-wŭnián-de-Rìbĕn-huà.

Mr. King studied Japanese for five years.

8. Tā-niànle-'liăngge-xīngqīde-shū jiù-bu-niàn-le.

He studied for two weeks and then didn't study any more.

9. 'Zhāng-Xiānsheng zài-Zhōngguo jiāole-wŭnián-bànde-shū.

Mr. Johnson taught in China for five and a half years.

10. Wó-hén-xǐhuan chī-Zhōngguo-fàn. Zài-Zhōngguo-de-shíhou chīle-yìniánde-Zhōngguo-fàn.

I'm very fond of Chinese food. I ate it [lit. Chinese food] for a year when I was in China.

Pattern 15.3.   Duration of an Action into the Present (a)
                (Note 6 below)

S	V	-le	T	(-de)	(O)	le
Subject	Verb	-le	Time	(-de)	(Object)	le
Wŏ	kàn	-le	yíge zhōngtóu	-de	shū	le.

'I have been reading for an hour.'

1. Bái-Xiānsheng-xué-Zhōngwén xuéle-wŭnián-le.

Mr. White has been studying Chinese for five years.

2. Qián-Xiānsheng-zài-Rìbĕn yǐ-jing-zhùle-bànnián-le.

Mr. Qian has been living in Japan for half a year [already].

3. Wŏ-jīntian-niànle-'wŭge-zhōng-tóude-shū-le.

I've been studying for five hours so far today.

4. Máo-Xiáojie-xuéle liăngnián-bànde-Yīngwén-le.

Miss Mao has been studying English for two and a half years.

5. Gāo-Xiānsheng-shuō tā-dào-'Mĕiguo-láile yóu-wŭnián-duō-le.

Mr. Gao says he has been in America for over five years.

6. 'Wáng-Xiānsheng jiāole-chàbu-duō-sānshiwŭnián-shū-le.

Mr. King has been teaching for almost thirty-five years.

7. Wŏ-jīntian-zài-túshūguăn kàn-le-'sìge-zhōngtóude-shū-le.

I've been reading in the library for four hours so far today.

8. Wŏ-jīntian tīngle-yíge-bàn-zhōngtóude-lùyīn-le.

I've been listening to recordings for an hour and a half so far today.

9. Wǒ-jīntian xiěle-yíge-zhōng-
    tóu-zì-le.

I have been writing characters
for an hour so far today.

10. Tāmen-yǐjing tánle-wǔshifēn-
     zhōngde-huà-le.

They've been conversing for fifty minutes [already].

11. Nèige-háizi yǐjing-zuòle-'liǎng-
     ge-zhōngtóude-diànchē-le, 'hái-
     bù-xiǎng-xià-chē.

That youngster has been riding
the streetcar for two hours already and still has no thought of
getting off.

12. Tāmen-zǒule-'yíge-zhōngtóude-
     lù-le.

They have been walking for an
hour.

13. 'Máo-Xiānsheng zuòle-'yíge-
     zhōngtóu-shì-le.

Mr. Mao has been working for an
hour.

14. 'Zhāng-Xiānsheng jiāole-liǎng-
     ge-zhōngtóude-shū-le.

Mr. Johnson has been teaching
for two hours.

15. Wǒ-jīntian jiù-xuéle-bànge-
     zhōngtóude-Zhōngwén.

I've studied Chinese for just half
an hour today.

Pattern 15.4. Duration of an Action into the Present (b)
(Note 7 below)

S	V	O	(yǐjing)	(yǒu)	T	le
Subject	Verb	Object	('already')	('there is')	Time	le
Wǒ	kàn	shū	yǐjing	yǒu	yíge-zhōngtóu	le.

'I've already been reading for an hour.'

1. Tā-zuò-shì yǐjing-yíge-zhōng-
    tóu-le.

He's already been working for
an hour.

2. 'Qián-Xiānsheng zhùzai-Rìběn
    yóu-liǎngnián-le.

Mr. Qian has been living in Japan for two years.

3. Wǒ-jiāo-shū yǐjing-'sānshí-duō-
    nián-le.

I've already been teaching for
thirty-odd years.

4. Wǒ-xué-Zhōngwén yǐjing-yóu-
    wǔnián-le.

I've [already] been studying Chinese for five years.

5. Bái-Xiáojie-xué-huà-huàr yǐjing-
    wǔnián-le.

Miss Bai has [already] been
studying painting for five years.

6. Qián-Xiānsheng-xué-wénxué yǐ-
    jing-sānnián-le.

Mr. Qian has [already] been
studying literature for three
years.

7. Máo-Xiānsheng-lái-Yīngguo yóu-
    liǎngge-xīngqī-le.

It's been two weeks since Mr.
Mao came to England.

8. Wǒ-dào-Měiguo yǐjing-'yíge-
    yuè-le.

It's been a month [already] since
I arrived in America.

9. Wáng-Xiānsheng-xué-Zhōng-
    wén yŏu-yì nián-le.

    Mr. King has been studying Chi-
    nese for a year.

10. Wŏ-rènshi-ta yĭjing-yóu-wŭ-
    niánle.

    I've known him for five years.

.

Pattern 15.5. Number of Occurrences (Note 8 below)

S	V	(le)	NU	-ci	(O)
Subject	Verb	(le)	Number	-ci	(Object)
Wŏ	zuò	le	sān	-cì	fēijī.

'I've ridden on a plane three times.'

1. Nèige-diànyĭngr 'tài-yŏu-
    yì si. Wŏ-kànle-liăngcì.

    That movie is extremely inter-
    esting. I saw it twice.

2. Shàng-xīngqī wŏ-kànle-
    liăngcì-diànyĭngr.

    I saw two movies last week.

3. Qùnian wŏ-qùle-yícì-Rìbĕn.

    I went to Japan once last year.

4. Nèige-zì wó-xiĕle-'wŭcì.
    'Hái-bu-huì-xiĕ.

    I wrote that character five
    times. I still can't write it.

5. Wŏ-bù-dŏng. Qĭng-nín-'zǎi-
    shuō-yícì.

    I don't understand. Please say
    it once more.

6. Nèige-'Zhōngguo-zì bù-róng-
    yì-xiĕ. Jiāoyuán-jiāole-wŏ-
    sìcì wŏ-hái-bu-huì-xiĕ.

    That Chinese character is not
    easy to write. The teacher
    taught it to me four times and I
    still can't write it.

7. Wŏ-dào-'Zhōngguo-lái yĭjing-
    chī guo-'jiŭcì-Zhōngguo-fàn.

    (Since) coming to China I've al-
    ready eaten Chinese food nine
    times.

8. Kăoshì-yĭhòu wó-dĕi-qù-kàn-
    yícì-diànyĭngr.

    After exams I must go see a
    movie.

9. Gāo-Xiānsheng-bìngle. Wŏ-
    yīngdāng qù-'kàn-ta-yícì.

    Mr. Gao is [lit. has become] ill.
    I certainly must go see him
    [once].

10. Zhōngshān-Gōngyuán wŏ-hái-
    bu-zhīdào-zài-năr-ne. Míng-
    tian wó-dĕi-gēn-ta-qù-yícì.

    I still don't know where Sun
    Yatsen Park is. I must go
    (there) with him [once] tomor-
    row.

SUBSTITUTION TABLES

I: 24 phrases (Notes 1–2)

bàn	-nián
yī	-ge yuè
liǎng	-tiān
sān	-ge zhōngtóu
sì	
wǔ	

II: 48 phrases (Notes 1–2)

yì	-nián	——
liǎng	-tiān	bàn
sān		duō
liù		
qī		
bā		

III: 54 phrases (Notes 1–2)

yí	-ge	——	yuè
liǎng		bàn	xīngqī
sān		duō	zhōngtóu
jiǔ			
shí			
shíyī			

IV: 96 sentences (Notes 3 c and 4)

(Here and in the following Tables, where columns are marked with asterisks, items must be taken from the same horizontal row.)

tā	*					*
	yào	jiāo	jǐ	-ge-zhōngtóu	—	shū
	xiǎng	lù	yī	-tiān	de	yīn
		tīng		-ge-xīngqī		lùyīn
		niàn				shū

V: 80 sentences (Note 5)

(See note at head of Table IV)

tā	*					*
	zuò	-le	jǐ	-ge-zhōngtóu	—	shì
	jiāo		liǎng	-tiān	de	shū
	tīng			-ge-xīngqī		lùyīn
	niàn					shū

VI: 80 sentences (Note 6)

		*					*	
tā	zuò	-le	jǐ	-ge-zhōngtóu	—	shì	le
	jiāo		sān	-tiān	de	shū	
	tīng			-ge-xīngqī		lùyīn	
	niàn			-ge-yuè		shū	
				-nián			

VII: 96 sentences (Note 7)

tā	niàn	-le	———	——	yī	-ge-zhōngtóu	le
	zhù		yǐjing	yǒu	liǎng	-tiān	
	jiāo				sì		
	xué						

VIII: 96 sentences (Note 8)

		*				*
tā	kàn	—	jǐ	-cì	diànyǐngr
	qù	-le	yí		Rìběn
	chī	-guo	sì		Zhōngguo-fàn
	bàifang		wǔ		Gāo-Xiānsheng
	zuò				fēijī
	lái				Zhōngguo

IX: 54 sentences (Note 3 d)

tā	jǐ	-nián	méi	chī Zhōngguo fàn	—
	yī	-ge-yuè		niàn Zhōngwén	le
	liǎng	-tiān		kànjian ta	

PRONUNCIATION DRILLS

(See The Sounds of Chinese, 20)

I. Suffixed r with final a, o, e, u, ng: add r

(a) bǎ	bǎr	(g) fǎ	fǎr
(b) gē	gēr	(h) zhè	zhèr
(c) suǒ	suǒr	(i) duǒ	duǒr
(d) tù	tùr	(j) shù	shùr
(e) dèng	dèngr	(k) gǒu	gǒur
(f) māo	māor	(l) fēng	fēngr

II. Suffixed r with ai, an, en: drop final letter and add r

    (a) wán   wár   (d) bàn   bàr

    (b) fēn   fēr   (e) mén   mér

    (c) hái   hár   (f) miàn   miàr

III. Suffixed r with final i, u after consonants: add er

    (a) jī   jiēr   (d) yú   yuér

    (b) yí   yiér   (e) yǔ   yuěr

    (c) qì   qièr   (f) xù   xuèr

IV. Suffixed r with final "i," in, un: drop final letter and add er

    (a) shì   shèr   (d) xìn   xièr

    (b) zǐ   zěr   (e) jīn   jiēr

    (c) cì   cèr   (f) zhǔn   zhuěr

EXPANSION DRILLS

I

kàn

kànwán

kàndewán

shū-kàndewán

zhèiběn-shū-kàndewán

zhèiběn-shū tā-kàndewán

zhèiběn-shū ta-jīntian-kàndewán

zhèiběn-shū ta-jīntian-kéyi-kàndewán

zhèiben-shū ta-jīntian-yídìng-kéyi-kàndewán

zhèiben-shū ta-shì-bu-shi-jīntian-yídìng-kéyi-kàndewán?

Nǐ-shuō-zhèiben-shū ta-shì-bu-shi-jīntian-yídìng-kéyi-kàndewán?

II

shū

kàn-shū

kàn-Zhōngwén-shū

wǒ-kàn-Zhōngwén-shū

wǒ-kàn-sānge-zhōngtóu-Zhōngwén-shū

wǒ-kàn-sānge-zhōngtóude-Zhōngwén-shū

wǒ-kànle-sānge-zhōngtóude-Zhōngwén-shū

wǒ-kànle-sānge-zhōngtóude-Zhōngwén-shū-le

wǒ-kànle-chàbuduō-sānge-zhōngtóude-Zhōngwén-shū-le

wǒ-yǐjing-kànle-chàbuduō-sānge-zhōngtóude-Zhōngwén-shū-le

Wǒ-xiànzai-yǐjing-kànle-chàbuduō-sānge-zhōngtóude-Zhōngwén-shū-le.

A LITTLE VARIETY

This exercise shows how to give variety to your speech by saying the same thing (or virtually the same thing) in two different ways.

1. Zhāng-Xiānsheng-shi-jiàoyuán.
   'Zhāng-Xiānsheng zài-xuéxiào-jiāo-shū.

2. Tā-yǐqián shi-xué-kēxué-de.
   Yuánlái tā-shi-xué-kēxué-de.

3. Zhèige-zì bù-róngyi-xiě.
   Zhèige-zì hěn-nán-xiě.

4. 'Wáng-Xiānsheng hén-yǒu-qián.
   'Wáng-Xiānsheng qián-hěn-duō.

5. Tā-jiā-lí-zhèr bù-hén-yuǎn.
   Tā-jiā-lí-zhèr hěn-jìn.

6. Nèige-háizi-hěn-qíguài, 'yísuì-bàn jiù-huì-pǎo.
   Nèige-háizi 'yísuì-bàn jiù-huì-pǎo. 'Zhēn-qíguài.

7. Tā-zài-túshūguǎn-zuò-shì.
   Tā-zuò-shì shi-zài-túshūguǎn.

8. Wǒmen-dōu-'huānyíng nín-dào-'zhèr-lái.
   Nín-dào-'zhèr-lái wǒmen-dōu-'huānyíng.

9. Ní-zóu-yǐqián bú-yào-wàngle-dài-biǎo.
   Ní-zóu-yǐqián xiān-dài-biǎo.

10. Nèibĕn-shū bĭ-zhèibĕn-shū-jiăndān.
     Nèibĕn-shū bĭ-zhèibĕn-shū róngyi-niàn.

11. Xiànzài chà-wŭfēn-zhōng shídiăn-le.
     Xiànzài jiúdián-wŭshiwŭfēn-le.

12. Zhèr-lí-Zhōngshān-Lù bù-yuăn.
     Cóng-zhèr-dào-Zhōngshān-Lù hĕn-jìn.

13. Yīnwei-wŏ-méi-qián, suóyĭ-bù-măi-fángzi.
     Wŏ-bù-măi-fángzi shi-yīnwei-wŏ-'méi-yŏu-qián.

14. Zhí-yŏu-yíkuài-qián bù-néng-măi-nèibĕn-shū.
     Yíkuài-qián măibuliăo-nèibĕn-shū.

15. Tā-zài-'dàxué-niàn-shū shi-xué-wénxué-de.
     Tā-zài-dàxué-niàn-wénxué.

16. 'Qián-Xiānsheng xīwang-dào-'Yīngguo-qù-yícì.
     'Qián-Xiānsheng xīwang-qù-Yīngguo-yícì.

17. Dào-'gōngyuán-qù tài-yuăn-le, suóyĭ wŏ-bù-xiăng-qù.
     Gōngyuán-'nènmo-yuăn wŏ-'bù-xiăng-qù.

18. 'Zhènmo-shuō nĭ-jīntian-'bù-yídìng-lái-le.
     Tīng-nĭ-zènmo-shuō nĭ-jīntian-huòzhĕ-'bù-lái-le.

19. Tā-huóbuliăo-le, bù-néng-shuō-huà-le.
     Tā-huà-yĭjing-bù-néng-shuō-le, 'yídìng-huóbuliăo-le.

20. Wŏ-'cháng-dào-chéng-lĭtou-qu.
     Chéng-lĭtou wŏ-'cháng-qù.

ANSWERING QUESTIONS

Each of the following items consists of one or more statements followed by a
question. Read each aloud, and answer the question orally in Chinese.

1. 'Bái-Xiānsheng hén-xĭhuan-xué-yŭyánxué.   Tā-duì-shénmo-hén-yŏu-
    xìngqu?

2. Tā-mĕitiān-zăochen bādiăn-zhōng-chī-fàn. Tā-nèige-shíhou-chī-de shi-
    'zăofan háishi-'wănfàn?

3. Qùnian shi-yī-jiŭ-liù-yī-nián. 'Jīnnian-shi-jĭnián?

4. Tā-zuótian-tīngle èrshiwŭfēn-zhōngde-lùyīn. Wŏ-tīngle-'èrshifēn-zhōng.
    'Shéi-tīngde-duō?

5. Jīntian-shi-shíyīyue-shíliùhào. Wŏ-shi-jīnnian-jiŭyue-shíliùhào kāishĭ-
    niàn-Zhōngwén-de. Wó-yĭjing-niànle 'jĭge-yuède-Zhōngwén?

6. Wǒ-péngyou-niàn-gāozhōng-'èrniánjí.   Tā-niàn-'zhōngxué háishi-niàn-'dàxué?

7. Nèige-rén-bènjíle. Tā-niànle-'liùniánde-gāozhōng 'hái-méi-bìyè-ne. Nǐ-shuō ta-kǎodeshàng-dàxué kǎobushàng-dàxué?

8. Zhèige-zìdiǎn zì-'tài-shǎo-le. Zhèige-zìdiǎn 'yǒu-yòng-méi-yǒu-yòng?

9. Wǒ-huì-shuō-Zhōngguo-huà, bú-huì-xiě-Zhōngguo-zì.   Wǒ-'huì-bú-huì yòng-Zhōngguo-zì-xiě-xìn?

10. 'Shíge-rén xiǎng-zuò-'yíge-xiǎo-qìchē. Nǐ-shuō tāmen-'zuòdexià-zuò-bu-xià?

NOTES

1. The neutral syllable yue, as you know, is used to form names of the months: wǔyue 'May.' Here it functions as a measure, since it can be preceded directly by a number. When yuè has a fourth tone, it is a noun meaning 'month.' It is used to count months, rather than name them, and is preceded not by a number but by a measure: wǔge-yuè 'five months.'

2. Chinese time words as a group are a good example of the differences in classification of Chinese and English words. The English words 'year,' 'month,' 'week,' 'day,' and 'hour' are all nouns—that is, they are grammatically the same kind of word. The corresponding Chinese words, however, are of two different types:

Nouns	Measures
yuè 'month'	nián 'year'
xīngqī 'week'	tiān 'day'
zhōngtóu 'hour'	

The measures nián and tiān can be preceded directly by a number:

wǔnián 'five years'
wǔtiān 'five days'

The nouns cannot be preceded directly by a number but must have an intervening measure:

wǔge-yuè 'five months'
wǔge-xīngqī 'five weeks'
wǔge-zhōngtóu 'five hours'

3. Observe the differences among the following kinds of time expressions and their positions within the sentence:

(a) Time expressions indicating the WHEN of an occurrence (or non-occurrence) come BEFORE the verb:

Wǒ-míngtian-qù. 'I'm going tomorrow.'
Wǒ-míngtian-bú-qù. 'I'm not going tomorrow.'

(b) Time expressions indicating the PERIOD WITHIN WHICH of an occurrence (or non-occurrence) come BEFORE the verb:

Wó-(měi-)sānge-xīngqī kàn-yíběn-shū. 'I read one book every three
weeks.'
Wǒ-zhèi-sāntiān kànle-sìběn-shū-le. 'I've read four books within
the past [lit. these] three days.'

(c) Time expressions indicating the DURATION of an occurrence come
AFTER the verb:

Tā-yào-zài-Zhōngguo zhù-sānnián. 'He will live in China for three
years.'

(d) Time expressions indicating the DURATION of a NON-occurrence
come BEFORE the verb:

Wǒ-sānnián méi-xué-Zhōngwén. 'I didn't study Chinese for three
years.'
Wǒ-sānnián bú-xué-Zhōngwén. 'I'm not going to study Chinese for
three years.'

4. A direct object in the construction described in Note 3 c can come at the
end:

Tā-yào-xué sānnián-Zhōngwén.
        or   } 'He will study Chinese for three
Tā-yào-xué sānniánde-Zhōngwén.   years.'

Or, the verb may be said twice, followed first by the object and then by
the time expression:

Tā-xué-Zhōngwén yào-xué-sānnián. 'He will study Chinese for
three years.'

5. The pattern described in Notes 3 c and 4 is made past by suffixing -le to
the verb:

Tā-zài-Zhōngguo zhùle-sānnián. 'He lived in China for three years
(but is doing so no longer).'
Tā-xuéle-sānnián-Zhōngwén.   ⎫
        or   ⎪
Tā-xuéle-sānniánde-Zhōngwén.   ⎬ 'He studied Chinese for three years
        or   ⎪   (but is doing so no longer).'
Tā-xué-Zhōngwén xuéle-sānnián.   ⎭

6. If the pattern described in Notes 3 c and 4 has two occurrences of le—one
attached to the verb, the other at the end of the sentence—the construction
means 'has been doing V (and still is)':

Tā-zài-Zhōngguo zhùle-sānnián-le. 'He has been living in China for
three years (and still is).'
Tā-xuéle-sānnián-Zhōngwén-le.   ⎫
        or   ⎪
Tā-xuéle-sānniánde-Zhōngwén-le.   ⎬ 'He has been studying Chinese
        or   ⎪   for three years.'
Tā-xué-Zhōngwén xuéle-sānnián-le. ⎭

7. In the construction just described ('has been—and still is—doing'), the

words yǐjing [lit. 'already'] or yǒu [lit. 'there is'] or both may be added, as follows:

(a) If the verb with le is not followed by an object, yǐjing may be inserted BEFORE this verb, or yǐjing or yǒu or both may be inserted AFTER the verb:

'He's been studying Chinese for three years.'

Tā-xué-Zhōngwén yǐjing-xuéle-sānnián-le.
or
Tā-xué-Zhōngwén xuéle-yǐjing-sānnián-le.
or
Tā-xué-Zhōngwén xuéle-yǒu-sānnián-le.
or
Tā-xué-Zhōngwén xuéle-yǐjing-yǒu-sānnián-le.

(b) If the verb is followed by an object (in which case there is no verb suffix le), yǐjing or yǒu or both may be inserted after the object:

'He's been studying Chinese for three years.'

Tā-xué-Zhōngwén yǐjing-sānnián-le.
or
Tā-xué-Zhōngwén yǒu-sānnián-le.
or
Tā-xué-Zhōngwén yǐjing-yǒu-sānnián-le.

8. The measure cì 'occasion,' which we encountered in Lesson 11 as a measure for movies (yícì-diànyǐngr ' one movie'), is used also as a measure meaning 'number of times':

Wó-xiǎng-xià-xīngqī qù-kàn-liǎngcì-diànyǐngr.   'I plan to go see two movies next week.'   or   'I plan to go to the movies twice next week.'

Also:

Tā-láile-sāncì, kěshi-nǐ-'dōu-bú-zài-jiā. 'He came three times, but you were never at home.'
Nǐ-chīle-'jǐcì-Zhōngguo-fàn? 'How many times have you eaten Chinese food?'

In this pattern, an object referring to a person comes BEFORE, not after, the expression for number of times:

Wǒ-kànle-tā-sāncì. 'I saw him three times.'

9. An ordinal expression of time of occurrence or non-occurrence ('the first time,' 'the third time,' etc.) comes BEFORE the verb:

Dì-yícì tā-méi-zài-jiā. 'The first time he wasn't at home.'
Zhèi-shi-wǒ dì-yícì-lái. 'This is the first time I've come.'

10. Zài 'in' or 'at' has two separate grammatical functions:

(a) It is used as a coverb if its subject and that of the main verb are identical:

Tā-zài-jiāli xiě-xìn. 'He's writing letters in the house.' [lit. 'He is in the house (and is) writing letters.']

(b) It is used as a postverb (that is, suffixed to a preceding verb) if the subjects of the two verbs are different:

Tā-xiězai-shūshang. 'He wrote (it) on the book'—that is, 'He wrote (it and it is) on the book.'

In some cases the two functions of zài are interchangeable:

Tā-zài-Niǔyue-zhù.
      or   } 'He lives in New York.'
Tā-zhùzai-Niǔyue.

When the main verb is zhù 'live,' zài may be omitted altogether:

Tā-zhùzai-Niǔyue.
      or   } 'He lives in New York.'
Tā-zhù-Niǔyue.

11. The verbs lái 'come' and qù 'go' may take a direct object, without the co-verb meaning 'to':

Nǐ-shi-shénmo-shíhou lái-Zhōngguo-de? 'When was it that you came to China?'
Wǒ-lái-Měiguo yǒu-sānnián-duō-le. 'It's been over three years since I've come to America.'

12. The adverbs zài, yòu, hái, and yě all have similar meanings but distinctly different usages. Zài means 'again, more, also, (and) then' with respect to future action:

Wǒ-míngtian-'zài-lái. 'I'm coming again tomorrow.'

Chī-fàn-yǐhòu wǒmen-zài-qù-kàn-diànyǐng, 'hǎo-bu-hǎo? 'After eating let's go see a movie, O.K.?'

Yòu means 'again, more, also' referring to past action:

Tā-zuótian-láile-yícì, jīntian-ta-'yòu-láile-yícì. 'He came once yesterday and he came once more today.'

Hái means ' still, in addition, more' and refers to conditions now in existence:

Tā-hái-zài-zhèr. 'He is still here.'
Wǒ-hái-yào. 'I want some more.' [lit. 'I still want some.']
Wó-mǎile-sānběn-shū, wǒ-hái-yào-mǎi-yìběn. 'I bought three books and want to buy one more.' [lit. 'I bought three books and still want to buy one.']

Yě means 'also, too, besides' and refers generally to the subject or topic of the sentence:

Máo-Xiānsheng-zài-zhèr, Wáng-Xiānsheng-yě-zài-zhèr. ' Mr. Mao is here, and Mr. Wang is also here.'

13. The adverb cái 'then; then and only then' is used before the second of two verbs to indicate that the action of the second verb occurred only after that of the first verb was completed. The verb modified by cái is never followed by le:

Wǒ-shuōle-sāncì, tā-cái-tīngjian. 'I said it three times, and only then did he hear me.'

14. Notice that English 'have to' and 'must' mean the same thing when they are affirmative, but that when made negative their meanings diverge:

(a) 'don't have to' means 'need not';

(b) 'must not' means 'permission is denied'

Chinese děi (bìděi) corresponds to both affirmative 'have to' and 'must'; but in the negative, which has the special form bú bì, it matches only the (a) negative above: 'don't have to, need not.'

15. The auxiliary verbs gāi, yīnggāi, and yīngdāng 'ought to, should' are used interchangeably. The affirmative forms often have a stronger meaning, corresponding to English 'must,' while the negative forms have the force of 'must not':

Wǒ-gāi-zǒule. 'I must go.'
Nǐ-'bù-yīngdāng-nènmo-shuō. 'You shouldn't speak so.' or 'You mustn't talk that way.'

These words, then, are nearly identical with those described in the preceding note.

16. Gēn ' (together) with' is used as a coverb to join coordinate nouns:

Wǒ-gēn-ni-qù. 'I'm going with you.'
Shū-gēn-bǐ dōu-shi-wǒde. 'The books and the pens are all mine.'

17.

Shì 'be' with heavy stress emphasizes what the sentence is asserting:

Zhèiběn-shū 'shì-hén-yǒu-yìsi. ' This book is very interesting.'

Unstressed shi, bu-shi, and shi-bu-shi occur in sentences stating a contrast of some kind; their use indicates that it is some other word in the sentence to which attention is directed:

Shi-'Wáng-Xiānsheng-yào-lái-ma? . . . Bu-shi-'Wáng-Xiānsheng-yào-lái, shi-'Bái-Xiānsheng-yào-lái. 'Is it Mr. King who's coming?... It isn't Mr. King who's coming, it's Mr. White.'

Similarly:

Shi-Wáng-'Tàitai-yào-lái-ma? 'Is it Mrs. King who's coming?'
Tā-shi-'míngtian-qù. 'He's going tomorrow.'
Tā-míngtian shi-dào-'Zhōngguo-qù. 'He's going to China tomorrow.'

Compare the shi . . . háishi pattern in Lesson 7, Note 12, pp. 84–85.

18. The adverbs zhènmo or zènmo 'this sort' and nènmo 'that sort' are used in the sense 'so, as, to such-and-such an extent.' Zhènmo or zènmo refers to something close by and nènmo to something farther away or at no specified place or distance:

Nǐ-zěnmo-zènmo-wǎn-ne? 'How come you're so late?'
Tā-jiā-nènmo-yuǎn wǒ-bù-xiǎng-qù. 'His home is so far away that I don't think I'll go (there).'

Lesson 16 VISITING FRIENDS

" 'Xià-yǒu-Sū-Háng."

Dialogue: Mr. White, accompanied by Miss Gao, arrives at the Gao home and visits with the Gaos and another guest.

Gāo: Yǐjing-dào-le. 'Qiántou-gōngyuán-mén-kǒur jiù-shi-chē-zhàn. Wǒmen-jiù-xià-chē. 'Xiàle-chē shàng-shàn-jiu-dào-le. 5

Here we are. The park gate ahead is the bus stop. [We get off now.] After we get off and climb the hill we'll be there.

Bái: Fǔshang-zhèige-dìfang hén-hǎo-a. 'Yòu-yǒu-shān 'yòu-yóu-shuǐ. 'Zhènmo-piào-liang!

This area around your home is very nice. You have hills and you have water. So beautiful!

Gāo: Suóyi-wǒ-fùqin 'měitiān- 10
dōu-yào-chūqu-zóuzou.
Lián-xīngqītiān tā-méi-shì dōu-yào-chūqu. Chū-qu-huílai dōu-shi-zǒu-lù.

That's why my father likes to go out for a walk every day. Even on Sundays when he doesn't have to work, he always goes out for a walk [lit. going out and returning is always (a matter of) walking].

Bái: Nǐ-fùqin 'yé-xǐhuan-lǚxíng- 15
ma?

Does your father also like to travel?

Gāo: Tā-'zuì-xǐhuan-lǚxíng-le.

He likes nothing better than

244

Tā-měinián dōu-lǚxíng-
jǐcì.

traveling. Every year he takes
a few trips.

Bái : Tā-dōu-dàoguo 'shénmo-
dìfang?

20

Where has he been?

Gāo: Zhōngguo-chàbuduō 'suó-
yǒude-dìfang tā-dōu-dào-
guo-le.

He's been almost everywhere in
China.

Bái : Tā-zuì-xǐhuan 'shénmo-
dìfang?

25

What place does he like best?

Gāo: Yīnwei-tā-shi-'Hángzhou-
rén, suóyi-tā-shuō tā-zuì-
xǐhuan-Sūzhou-Hángzhou.

Since he comes from Hangchow,
he says he likes Soochow and
Hangchow best of all.

Bái : Lǚxíng 'shì-hén-yǒu-yìsi.
'Ní-xǐhuan-lǚxíng-ma?

30

Travel is interesting. Do you
like to travel?

Gāo: Wó-xǐhuan, kěshi-méi-
jīhui. Wǒ-'shénmo-dìfang-
dōu-méi-qùguo. . . . Dào-
le. Wǒmen-xià-chē-ba.

35

I do, but I don't have any oppor-
tunities (to do so). I haven't
been anywhere. . . . Here we
are. Let's get off.

Bái : Wàng-'něibiar-zǒu?

Which way do we go?

Gāo: **Wàng-' zuó-guǎi-jiu-shàng-
shān.**

We turn left and go up the hill.

Bái : Zhèige-dìfang-'zhēn-hǎo.
Ní-měitiān-dào-xuéxiào
zuò-chē háishi-zǒu-lù-ne?

40

This place is really nice. [Ev-
ery day] do you take the bus to
school, or do you walk?

Gāo: Wǒ-chàbuduō-dōu-zuò-chē.

I nearly always take a bus.

Bái : Zuò-chē yào-'duōshao-shí-
hou-ne?

How long does it take to go by
bus?

Gāo: 'Èrshifēn-zhōng jiu-dào-le.

45

It takes twenty minutes.

Bái : Fǔshang-lí-xuéxiào yě-bu-
hěn-jìn.

Your home isn't very close to
the school.

Gāo: Bú-tài-yuǎn. . . . Dào-le.*

It's not too far. . . . Here we
are.* (She knocks.)

Gāo-Tàitai: Shéi-a?

Who (is it)?

Gāo-Xiáojie: Wǒ. Mā! Kāi-mén!
'Kèren-lái-le.

50

Me. Mom! Open the door! The
guest has come.

---

* The layout of the Gao home is as follows. The main door or gate leads
into a courtyard. On the left are utility rooms, the kitchen, and a store-
room; on the right is a study; and straight ahead, facing south, is a combined
living room and dining room, flanked on both sides by bedrooms. The gate is
barred on the inside, not locked. When Miss Gao knocks, Mrs. Gao comes out
of the kitchen to let her in, and Mr. Gao comes out of the living room to receive his guest.

(Gāo-Tàitai-chūlai duì-Bái-
Xiānsheng-shuō:)

(Mrs. Gao comes out and says to
Mr. White:)

Gāo-Tàitai: Oh, 'Bái-Xiānsheng-
lái-le. 'Háo-jiǔ-bu-jiàn.   55
Ní-hǎo-ma? 'Máng-bu-
máng?

Oh, Mr. White, you're here! I
haven't seen you for a long time.
How are you? Have you been
busy?

Bái : Gāo-Tàitai, 'háo-jiǔ-bú-
jiàn. Nín-hǎo? Gāo-
'Xiānsheng-hǎo-ma?   60

Mrs. Gao, I haven't seen you for
a long time (either). How are
you? How is Mr. Gao?

Gāo-Tàitai: Hǎo, xièxie-ni.

Fine, thanks.

(Gāo-Xiānsheng tīngjian-'Bái-
Xiānsheng-lái-le yě-chūlai-
le.)

(Mr. Gao, on hearing that Mr.
White has arrived, also comes
out.)

Gāo-Xiānsheng: 'Bái-Xiānsheng,   65
hǎo-ma? Lái-lái. Wó-
géi-nǐmen-liǎngwèi-'jiè-
shao-jièshao. Zhèiwèi-shi-
'Wàn-Jiàoshòu. Zhèiwèi-
shi-'Bái-Xiānsheng.   70

Mr. White, how are you? Come
(in), come (in). I'll introduce
the two of you. This is Professor Wanamaker. This is Mr.
White.

Bái : Jiúyǎng.

Pleased to meet you.

Wàn: Ní-hǎo.

Pleased to meet you.

Wàn: Wǒ-'cháng-tīng-Lǎo-Gāo*
tán-dào-ni.

I've often heard [Old] Gao* speak
of you.

Gāo: Jīntiān-hǎojíle. Nǐmen-   75
liǎngwèi dōu-shuō-'Zhōng-
wén. Rúguǒ nǐmen-
shuō-'Yīngwén wǒ-nèirén-
lián-'yíge-zì yě-tīngbu-
dǒng. Tā-jiu-méi-fázi gēn-   80
kèren-shuō-huà-le. Nǐmen-
liǎngwèi búdàn-néng-shuō,
érqiě-shuōde-'shífēn-hǎo.

This is wonderful. You can both
speak Chinese. If you spoke
English my wife wouldn't understand even one word, and she
wouldn't have any way of talking
to you [lit. to the guests]. Not
only can you both speak (Chinese), but you both speak very
well.

Bái : Gāo-Xiānsheng-kèqi.

Mr. Gao is being polite.

Wàn: 'Bái-Xiānsheng, nǐ-'shén-   85
mo-shíhou dào-'Zhōngguo-
lái-de?

Mr. White, when did you come to
China?

Bái : Wǒ-shi-qùnian-'báyue-láide.
Nín-ne?

I came last August. And you?

Wàn: Wó-yǐjing-láile-'liǎngnián- 90
le. Nǐ-zài-'něige-dàxué?

I've been here two years now.
At what university are you?

---

* Friends of about the same age address each other either by their given
names or by their surnames preceded by the word lǎo 'old': Lǎo-Qián 'Old
Qian.'

Bái : Wǒ-zài-'Yuǎndōng-Dàxué-
nìan-shū.

I'm studying at Far Eastern University.

Wàn: Yuǎn-Dà wǒ-hái-yóu-jǐge-
péngyou. Nǐ-shi-xué-shén-   95
mo-de?

I have a few other friends at Far Eastern. What are you studying?

Bái : Wǒ-xué-yǔyán-gēn-wénxué.

(I'm studying) language and literature.

Wàn: Hǎojíle. Wǒmen-'dōu-shi
yánjiu-yǔyán-gēn-wénxué-
de.   100

Wonderful. We're both students of language and literature.

Bái : Wǒ-kànguo-nín-zuò-de-
nèibén 'Zhōngguo-Wénxué-
Yánjiu. Nín-xiě-de-zhēn-
hǎo. Duì-wǒmen-xué-wén-
xué-de-rén hén-yǒu-yòng.   105

I've read your Studies in Chinese Literature. You've done a really fine job of writing. It's a great help for those of us studying literature.

Wàn: Wǒ-xiànzài-'yòu-xiěle-
yìbén yánjiu-wénxué-de-
shū.

I've just finished (writing) another book of literary research.

Gāo : 'Bái-Xiānsheng, Lǎo-Wàn-
de-xuéwen 'zhēn-bú-cuò.   110
Nǐmen-liǎngge-rén kéyi-
cháng-zài-yíkuàr 'yánjiu-
yánjiu.

Mr. White, [Old] Wan's scholarship is really good. You two should get together often to carry on your studies.

Wàn: Lǎo-Gāo, nǐ-bié-zhènmo-
kèqi 'hǎo-bù-hǎo?   115

[Old] Gao, don't flatter so, [all right?]

(Wàn-Jiàoshòu duì-Gāo-'Xiáojie-
shuō:)

(Professor Wanamaker says to Miss Gao:)

Měiyīng, lái, zuòxia. Wǒ-
men-yíkuàr-tántan. Gāo-
Xiáojie cōngming-piàoliang. 120
Shū-niànde-hǎo, huàr-huà-
de-hǎo.

Meiying, come sit down. Let's talk together. (To the others:) Miss Gao is intelligent and attractive. She studies well, she paints well.

Bái : Duì-le. 'Gāo-Xiáojie,
wǒmen-déi-'kànkan-nǐde-
huàr-le.   125

That's right. Miss Gao, we must look at your paintings.

Gāo Xiáojie: Bié-kàn-le. Wǒ-huà-
de-bù-hǎo.

Don't look (at them). I paint badly.

Bái : Bié-kèqi-le. Qíng-ní-bǎ-
huàr-náchulai wǒmen-kàn-
kan.   130

Don't be polite. Please bring out the paintings for us to look at.

Gāo-Xiānsheng: Měiyīng, bá-nǐ-
'suóyǒu-de-huàr dōu-náchu-
lai. Qíng-tāmen-liǎngwèi-
kànkan.

Meiying, bring all your paintings out. Let [both of] them have a look.

Gāo-Xiáojie: Wǒ-zhèr zhí-yóu-   135
jǐzhāng-huàr.

I have only a few paintings here.

(Gāo-Xiáojie náchu-sì-wǔzhāng-
huàr-lai.)

(Miss Gao brings out four or five
paintings.)

Bái : Huàde-hǎojíle. Nǐ-xuéguo-
jǐnián-le?   140

They're wonderfully well done.
How many years have you studied?

Gāo-Xiānsheng: Zhèige-háizi tā-
'hén-xǐhuan-huà-huàr. Xué-
le-'méi-yǒu-jǐnián.

This child loves to paint. She
hasn't studied many years.

Gāo-Xiáojie: Wǒ-xuéle-'sānnián.

I've studied three years.

Wàn : 'Zhēn-cōngming. Xuéle-   145
'sānnián jiu-huàde-'zhèn-
mo-hǎo. Dōu-shi-xiànzài-
huà-de-ma?

Really talented. Three years of
study and you paint so well. Did
you paint them all just recently
[lit. now]?

Gāo-Xiáojie: Bú-shi. Yǒude-shi
kāishǐ-'xué-de-shíhou-   150
huà-de. Yǒude-shi 'xiàn-
zài-huà-de.

No. I painted some when I began
to study and some just recently.

Bái : Zhèizhāng-shānshuǐ-huàr
'zhēn-hǎo. Huà-de-shi-
nǎr-a?   155

This landscape painting is really
nice. What place is it [that's
shown]?

Gāo-Xiáojie: Zhèi-jiu-shi-Hángzhou-a.

Why, this is Hangchow.

Bái : Oh, zhè-jiu-shi-Hángzhou-
a. 'Zhēn-piàoliang.

Oh, so this is Hangchow. It's
really attractive.

Wàn : Zhōngguo yǒu-yíjù-huà-
shuō: 160

China has a saying:

'Shàng-yǒu-tiāntáng,
'Xià-yǒu-Sū-Háng.

Above is heaven,
Below are Soochow and Hangchow.

Shuōde-yì 'diár-yě-bú-cuò.

The saying is not at all an exaggeration.

VOCABULARY

bǎ	take (CV)
bié	don't (AV)
búdàn	not only (MA) [lit. not merely]
chū	exit from (TV)
cuò	wrong, mistaken (CV)
érqiě	but also (MA) [lit. and moreover]
fázi	method, plan (N)
Hángzhou	Hangchow (PW)
jiàoshòu	professor (N) (also, a title)

jièshao	introduce (TV)
jìn	enter (TV)
jiúyǎng	Pleased to meet you. [lit. long look up to] (See Supplementary Lesson 16, Note 1)
jù	(measure for sentences)
kāi	open (door, etc.); drive (car) (TV)
kèren	guest (N) [lit. guest person]
lián	even, even including (CV); (also, a surname)
lǔxíng	travel (IV) [lit. travel go]
mā	(one's own) mother (N) (Note 15)
ná	hold, grasp, carry, take (TV)
nèiren	(one's own) wife (N) (Note 16)
piàoliang	attractive, elegant, beautiful (SV) [lit. bleach bright]
shānshuǐ	scenery, landscape (N) [lit. mountain water]
shuǐ	water (N)
'suóyǒude	all (before nouns)
Sūzhou	Soochow (PW) (Sū is also a surname)
tiāntáng	heaven (N) [lit. sky hall]
xuéwen	learning, scholarship (N) [lit. study ask]
yǒude	some (before nouns)

SENTENCE BUILD-UP

bié   don't!
bié-tīng   don't listen!
1. Nǐ-bié-tīng-tāde-huà.   Don't you listen to him.

ná   take
bié-ná   don't take!
2. Bié-ná-wǒde-dōngxi.   Don't take my things.

jìn   enter
jìn-chéng   enter the city
3. Qìchē-bù-kéyi-jìn-chéng.   Cars cannot enter the city.

chū   exit from, leave
chū-chéng   leave the city
4. Wǒmen-yíkuàr-chū-chéng   Can we leave the city together?
   kéyi-ma?

jìn   enter
jìnlai   come in
5. Qǐng-jìnlai!   Please come in!

jìnqu

go in

kéyi-jìnqu

can go in

6. Wǒmen-kéyi-jìnqu-ma?

May we go in?

chū

leave

chūlai

come out

7. Qǐng-nín-chūlai-kànkan.

Please come out and take a look.

chūqu

go out

8. Tāmen-dōu-chūqu-le.

They've all gone out.

ná

carry

náqu

take away

9. Dōu-'náqu-le-méi-you?

Have they all been taken out?

nálai

bring

10. Nǐ-nálai-ba!

Bring it!

nèiren

wife

wǒ-nèiren

my wife

11. Wǒ-nèiren bú-zài-jiā.

My wife isn't home. She's gone

Tā-chūqu-le.

out.

kèren

guest

qǐng-kèren

invite guests

12. Qǐng-kèren-jìnlai.

Invite the guests to come in.

jiàoshòu

professor

'Máo-Jiàoshōu

Professor Mao

13. 'Máo-Jiàoshòu xià-'kè-le-

Has Professor Mao left class?

méi-you?

zǒulái

walk toward

zǒuqù

walk away from

zǒulái-zǒuqù

pace back and forth

14. Háizi-zài-lùshang zǒulái-

The child is walking back and

zǒuqù.

forth on the road.

xiǎnglái-xiǎngqù

think over and over

yīnggāi-'zěnmo-zuò

how it should be done

15. Wó-xiǎnglái-xiǎngqù bù-zhī-

I thought and thought (but still)

dào-yīnggāi-'zěnmo-zuò.

don't know how it should be done.

huí-jiā

return home

huí-jiā-qu

go back home

16. Nǐ-'shēnmo-shíhou huí-

When do you go back home?

jiā-qu?

huí-jiā

return home

huí-jiā-lai

come back home

17. Tā-jīntian 'bù-huí-jiā-lai.

He isn't coming [back] home to-

day.

mā	mother
18. Mā! Wǒmen-'shénmo-shí-hou-chī-fàn?	Mom! When do we eat?
lǚxíng	travel
lǚxíng-liǎngcì	make two trips
19. Wó-měinián-lǚxíng-liǎngcì.	I make two trips a year.
Hángzhou	Hangchow
dà-chéng	big city
20. Hángzhou shi-'dà-chéng-ma?	Is Hangchow a big city?
Sūzhou	Soochow
lí-Sūzhou	from Soochow
21. Hángzhou-lí-Sūzhou 'bù-yuǎn.	Hangchow is not far from Soochow.
yǒude	some
yǒude-hǎo	some are good
22. Yǒude-hǎo, yǒude-'bù-hǎo.	Some are good, some are bad.
'suóyǒude	all
'suóyǒude-rén	all the people
23. Qíng-'suóyǒude-rén-dōu-lái.	Invite everyone to come.
jìnqu	go in
nájinqu	take in
24. Dōu-'nájinqu-le-méi-you?	Have they all been taken in?
nádejìnqù	able to carry in
nábujìnqù	unable to carry in
25. Yǒude-'nádejìnqù, yǒude-'nábujìnqù.	Some can be carried in, some can't [be carried in].
shuǐ	water
méi-yóu-shuǐ	there's no water
26. Húli-méi-yóu-shuǐ.	There's no water in the lake.
fázi	method, way, means
zhèige-fázi	this method
27. Zhèige-fázi bú-tài-hǎo.	This method isn't very good.
méi-yǒu-fázi	have no means (of doing something)
méi-fázi-niàn-shū	have no way to study
28. Yīnwei-wǒ-'méi-qián, suóyi-'méi-fázi-niàn-shū.	Since I have no money I have no way of studying.
kāi	open
kāi-mén	open the door
29. Qíng-nǐ-qu-kāi-mén.	Please go open the door.

      kāi   drive

      kāi-qìchē   drive a car

30. Nǐ-huì-bu-huì-kāi-qìchē?   Do you know how to drive a car?

      'náhuíqu   take back

      'náhuí-jiā-qu   take back home

31. Nǐ-'dōu-náhuí-jiā-qu-le-ma?   Did you take them all back home?

      jù   (measure for sentences)

      liǎngjù-huà   two sentences

32. Zhèi-liǎngjù-huà shi-'shén-mo-yìsi? What is the meaning of these two sentences?

      xuéwen   learning

      tāde-xuéwen   his scholarship

33. Tāde-xuéwen-hǎojíle.   He is extremely learned. [lit. His scholarship is extremely good.]

      xuéwen   learning

      yǒu-xuéwen   be learned

34. 'Wàn-Jiàoshòu hén-yǒu-xué-wen.   Professor Wanamaker is very learned.

      piàoliang   attractive

35. 'Nèige-nǚ-xuésheng 'hěn-piàoliang. That girl student is very attractive.

      shānshuǐ   scenery

      zhèrde-shānshuǐ   the scenery here

36. Zhèrde-shānshuǐ hěn-piào-liang.   The scenery here is very attractive.

      shānshuǐ   landscape

      shānshuǐ-huàr   landscape painting

37. Zhèizhāng-shānshuǐ-huàr 'duōshao-qián? How much is this landscape painting?

      búdàn   not only

      érqiě   but also

38. Tā-búdàn-piàoliang, érqiě hén-yǒu-qián. She's not only attractive, but also very rich.

      niàndao   reach [in studying]

      niàndao-dì-'jǐkè?   reach what lesson?

39. Wǒmen-jīntian niàndao-dì-'jǐkè?   What lesson have we reached to-day?

      niànbudào   unable to reach [in studying]

      niànbudào-dì-èrshikè   unable to reach the 20th lesson

40. Wǒmen-xià-xīngqī niànbu-dào-dì-èrshikè. We can't get to Lesson 20 by next week.

pǎodào
pǎodào-nǎr-qu?
41. Tā-pǎodào-nǎr-qu-le?

run to
run away to where?
Where's he run off to?

bǎ
bǎ-'suóyǒude-shū
42. Qíng-ní-bǎ 'suóyǒude-shū
dōu-gěi-ta.

take
take all the books
Please give him all the books.

cuò
cuò-le
43. Wǒ-zhīdao-wǒ-cuò-le.

wrong
made a mistake
I know I made a mistake.

bú-cuò
hěn-bú-cuò
44. Nèige-diànyǐngr hěn-bu-cuò.

not bad
very good
That movie is very good.

cuò
niàncuò
45. Zhèige-zì nǐ-niàncuò-le.

wrong
read incorrectly
You've read this character in-correctly.

xiěcuò-le
zài-xiě-yícì
46. Bá-xiěcuò-le-de-zì 'zài-xiě-yícì.

wrote incorrectly
write once more
Write once more the characters that you wrote incorrectly.

jièshao
nǐmen-liǎngwèi
47. Wó-géi-nǐmen-liǎngwèi
'jièshao-jièshao.

introduce
the two of you
I'll introduce the two of you (to each other).

jièshao-'Wàn-Jiàoshòu

gěi-'Bái-Xiānsheng
48. Qíng-ní-gěi-'Bái-Xiānsheng
jièshao-jièshao-'Wàn-Jiào-shòu.

introduce Professor Wana-maker
to Mr. White
Please introduce Professor Wanamaker to Mr. White.

lián
lián-'Wàn-Jiàoshòu
49. Lián-'Wàn-Jiàoshòu yě-bù-dǒng.

even
even Professor Wanamaker
Even Professor Wanamaker doesn't understand.

lián-Niǔyue
50. Wǒ-lián-Niǔyue dōu-méi-qù-guo.

even New York
I haven't even been to New York.

yìfēn-qián
51. Wǒ-'yìfēn-qián dōu-méi-you.

one cent
I don't even have a cent.

jiúyǎng
52. Liǎngge-rén-dōu-shuō: "Jiú-yǎng."

pleased to meet you
Both persons said: "Pleased to meet you."

	tiāntáng	heaven
	shàngbuliǎo	unable to go up
53.	Tā-'yídìng shàngbuliǎo-tiāntáng!	He certainly can't go to heaven!

	yóu-'jǐkuài-qián?	have how many dollars?
54.	Ní-yóu-'jǐkuài-qián?	How many dollars do you have?

	'yóu-jǐkuài-qián	have a few dollars
55.	Wǒ-'zhí-yóu-jǐkuài-qián.	I have only a few dollars.

	shéi-shuō?	who says?
	'shéi-dōu-shuō	everyone says
56.	'Shéi-dōu-shuō tā-'hén-yǒu-qián.	Everyone says he's very wealthy.

	yào-shénmo?	want what?
	'shénmo-yě-bú-yào	want nothing
57.	Wǒ-'shénmo-yě-bú-yào.	I want nothing.

	tā-xiě-shū	he writes books
58.	Shū-shi-'tā-xiě-de.	The books were written by him.

PATTERN DRILLS

Pattern 16.1.   Verbs of Motion   (Note 1 below)

S	V	O
Subject	Verb	Object
Tā	shàng	shān.

'He is climbing the hill.'

1. 'Jiàoyuán duì-xuésheng-shuō: "Shàng-kè-de-shíhou bié-wàngle-ná-shū."

The teacher said to the students: "When you go to class don't forget to take (your) books."

2. Míngtian tā-xiǎng-chū-chéng-kàn-péngyou.

Tomorrow he plans to leave the city to see (some) friends.

3. 'Bái-Xiānsheng-jìn-chéng mǎi-le-hěn-duō-dōngxi.

Mr. White went to the city and bought a lot of things.

4. Wó-měitiān-wǎnshang 'bādiǎn-zhōng-huí-jiā.

I return home every evening at eight o'clock.

5. 'Máo-Xiānsheng míngtian-zǎochen-shàng-chuán.

Mr. Mao will go aboard tomorrow morning.

6. Tā-zhùzai-shānshang. Měi-tiān-dōu-yào 'shàng-shān 'xià-shān.

He lives on a hill. Every day he goes up and down the hill.

7. Xuéxiào zài-hú-zuǒbiar. Wǒ-
   jiā zài-hú-yòubiar. Měitiān-
   yào-guò-hú.

The school is to the left of the
lake. My home is to the right of
the lake. I have to cross the
lake every day.

8. Wǒmen-jīntian 'shénmo-shíhou-
   xià-kè?

When do we leave class today?

9. 'Wáng-Xiānsheng hái-yǒu-'sānge-yuè jiu-huí-guó-le.

Mr. Wang still has three months
before returning to his own
country.

10. 'Máo-Xiānsheng jīntian-wǎn-
    shang 'jiúdiǎn-zhōng-shàng-
    fēijī.

Mr. Mao boards the plane this
evening at nine.

Pattern 16.2.   Directive Postverbs   (Notes 2–3 below)

S	V	-PV
Subject	Verb	Postverb
Tā	shàng	-qu.

'He is going up.'

1. 'Shū-mǎi-le, kěshi-méi-nálai.

The books have been bought, but
not brought (here).

2. Wǒ-nèiren hái-méi-huílai-ne.

My wife hasn't come back yet.

3. Zuótian wǒ-qu-zhǎo-'Gāo-
   Xiānsheng. Wǒ-hái-méi-jìn-
   qu, tā-jiu-chūlai-le.

Yesterday I went to visit Mr.
Gao. Just as I was about to go
in, he came out.

4. Ní-'zěnmo-lái-de? . . . Wó-
   zǒulai-de.

How did you come? . . . I came
on foot.

5. Wǒ-jīntian 'jiā-lǐtou-yǒu-shì.
   Wǒ-'xiànzài-jiu-huíqu.

I have something to do at home
today. I'm going back (there)
right now.

6. Wó-yǒu-yìběn 'hén-hǎode-zìdiǎn. 'Wàn-Jiàoshòu jièqu-le.

I have an excellent dictionary.
Professor Wanamaker borrowed
it [and took it away].

7. Nèige-zì wǒ-wàngle. Xiǎng-
   lái-xiǎngqù 'hái-bu-rènshi.

I've forgotten that character.
I've thought and thought and still
don't recognize it.

8. Kèren-lái-le, nèige-háizi pǎo-
   lái-pǎoqù.

When the guests came the child
ran back and forth.

9. Jīntian-lùshang guòlái-guòqù-
   de-rén hěn-duō.

Today there are a lot of people
going back and forth on the road.

10. 'Bái-Xiānsheng bú-zài-jiā.
    Chūqu-le.

Mr. White isn't at home. He's
gone out.

Pattern 16.3.   Objects and Postverbs   (Notes 4–5 below)

S	V	O	(PV)
Subject	Verb	Object	(Postverb)
Tā	shàng	shān	qu.

'He is going up the hill.'

1. Wǒ-shàng-shān qu-bàifang-
   'Gāo-Xiānsheng.

   I'm going up the hill to visit Mr. Gao.

2. Wǒ-fùqin chū-chéng-qu-le.

   My father has gone out of town.

3. Wǒ-shi-zuótian jìn-chéng-lái-de.

   I came into town yesterday.

4. Mā! 'Qíng-nǐ shàng-'zhèr-lai.

   Mom! Please come here.

5. 'Bái-Xiānsheng 'Qián-Xiānsheng tāmen-'dōu-shàng-shān-
   lái-le.

   Mr. Bai and Mr. Qian both came up the hill.

6. Wó-hěn-xīwang shàng-'Háng-
   zhou-qu-lǚxíng.

   I hope very much to go to Hang-chow for a trip.

7. Wó-yǒu-jīhui yě-shàng-'Sū-
   zhou-qu-kànkan.

   (If) I have an opportunity I will also go to Soochow to have a look.

8. Nèige-háizi xiànzài-'hái-méi-
   huí-jiā-lai-ne. Bù-zhīdào tā-
   shàng-nǎr-qu-le.

   That child still hasn't come home. I don't know where he's gone.

9. Yǐjing-'shídiǎn-le. Wǒ-yào-
   huí-jiā-qu-le.

   It's already ten. I'm going back home.

10. 'Wáng-Jiàoshòu jīnnian-jiǔ-
    yue-huí-guó-qu.

    Professor King is going back to his own country this September.

Pattern 16.4.   Compound Verbs   (Note 6 below)

S	V_1	(bu/de)	V_2	PV
Subject	Verb$_1$	(bu/de)	Verb$_2$	Postverb
Tā	pǎo		shang	lai.

'He is running up(ward).'

1. Yǒude-háizi pǎoshanglai-le,
   yǒude-háizi pǎoxiaqu-le.

   Some children ran up, some (children) ran down.

2. Shān-'tài-gāo, zǒubushàngqù.

   The hill is too high, (one) can't walk up it.

3. Nèige-shān-'tài-gāo. Suóyǒu-
   de-rén 'dōu-zǒubushàngqù.

   That hill is too high. Nobody
   can walk up it.

4. Wǒde-shū nábuhuílái-le.

   I can't get my book back.

5. Zuótian wǒ-cóng-shūdiàn
   'zǒuhuíqu-de.

   I walked back from the bookstore yesterday.

6. Nèige-háizi 'zǒuhuílai-de.

   That child came back on foot.

7. Nèige-mén 'tài-xiǎo. Méi-
   yǒu-fázi 'zǒujìnqu.

   That door is too small. There's
   no way of going in.

8. Zhèige-dōngxi 'tài-dà. Ná-
   bujìnqù.

   This thing is too big. It can't be
   carried in.

9. Nèitiáo-lù yóu-shuǐ, zǒubu-
   guòqù.

   There's water on the road, (you)
   can't walk across.

10. Nèige-dōngxi bú-tài-dà.
    'Yídìng-nádejìnqù.

    That thing isn't too big. It can
    certainly be taken in.

Pattern 16.5. Compound Verbs with Objects (Notes 6–7)

S	V₁	V₂	O	PV
Subject	Verb₁	Verb₂	Object	Postverb
Tā	pǎo	shàng	shān	lái.

'He is running up the hill (toward us).'

1. **Tā-kāi-mén zǒujìn-fángzi-qu-**
   le.

   He opened the door and went into
   the house.

2. Yǒude-náhuí-shūdiàn-qu, yǒu-
   de-náhuí-túshūguǎn-qu.

   Take some back to the bookstore, and [take] some back to
   the library.

3. 'Nèige-dōngxi yīngdāng-nájìn-
   fángzi-lai.

   That thing should be brought into
   the house.

4. Tā-zuótian-wǎnshang 'shíyī-
   diǎn-bàn-zhōng cái-zǒuhuí-jiā-
   qu-de.

   Yesterday evening (it was) elev-
   en-thirty before he walked back
   home.

5. 'Zuótian-tāmen-sānge-rén yí-
   kuàr-zǒushang-shān-qu-le.

   Yesterday the three of them
   walked up the mountain together.

6. Wǒ-'wàngle-ná-běnzi-le. Wó-
   déi-'pǎohuí-jiā-qu-ná.

   I forgot to bring (my) notebook.
   I must hurry back home to get
   it.

7. Ní-yǐqián-jiè-de-shū qǐng-
   'náhui-túshūguǎn-lai.

   Please bring back to the library
   the books that you borrowed earlier.

8. Zuótian wǒ-kàn-diànyǐngr-yǐ-
   hòu, wǒ-shi-'zǒuhuí-jiā-qu-de.

   Yesterday I walked (back) home
   after I saw the movie.

9. Ní-mǎi-de-shū 'dōu-yào-ná-
    huí-Měiguo-qu-ma?

Are you taking all the books you
bought back to America?

10. Lùyīnjī míngtian-nǐ-yào-
     'náhui-xuéxiào-lai.

You must bring the recorder
back to school tomorrow.

Pattern 16.6.   Compound Verbs with <u>dào</u>   (Notes 8–9)

S	V	-dào	P	(lai/qu)
Subject	Verb	'to'	Place	('come'/'go')
Tā	huí	-dào	shānshang	qu.

'He went back to the top of the hill.

1. 'Xiān-nádao-zhèr-lai, 'hòu-
    nádao-wàitou-qu.

First bring it here, and then
take it outside.

2. Zhèibén-shū yǐjing-xuédao
    dì-shíliùkè-le.

We've already studied this book
up to Lesson 16.

3. Wǒmen-'xià-xīngqī xuédedào-
    xuébudào dì-shíjiǔkè?

By next week can we study up to
Lesson 19?

4. Wó-mǔqin huídào-Měiguo-qu-
    le.

My mother has gone back to
America.

5. Tā-xiěde-nèibén-shū yǐjing-
    'xiědào-nǎr-le?

How far has he gotten in that
book he's writing?

6. 'Gāo-Xiānsheng 'méi-zuò-chē,
    shi-'zǒudào-chénglǐ-qu-de.

Mr. Gao didn't go by car, he
went to town on foot.

7. Wǒde-shū dōu-nádào-jiā-qu-
    le.

My books have all been taken
home.

8. Nǐmen-tīng-lùyīn 'yídìng-yào-
    tīngdào dì-shíliùkè.

In listening to the recordings,
you must be sure to listen up
to Lesson 16.

9. Qǐng-wèn, wǒmen-jīntian xué-
    dào-nǎr-le?

May I ask, where have we gotten
to [lit. studied to] today?

10. Chē kāidào-nǎr-qu-le?

Where has the car been driven
to?

Pattern 16.7.   Definite Objects with the Coverb <u>bǎ</u>   (Note 10 below)

S	bǎ	O₁	V	(O₂)
Subject	'take'	Object₁	Verb	(Object₂)
Wó	bǎ	zìdiǎn	gěi	ta.

'I gave him the dictionary.'

1. 'Bái-Xiānsheng bǎ-tāde-shū
   'dōu-nádào-xuéxiào-qu-le.

   Mr. White took all his books to
   school.

2. Wó-bǎ-tāmende-míngzi 'dōu-
   wàng-le.

   I've forgotten all their names.

3. Ní-bǎ-nèibĕn-shū 'dōu-kàn-
   wán-le-ma?

   Have you finished reading all of
   that book?

4. Wǒ-rúguó-yǒu-qián, bǎ-nèige-
   shūdiànde-shū 'dōu-mǎilai.

   If I had the money, I'd buy all
   the books in that bookstore.

5. Tā-bǎ-lùyīnjī-mài-le.

   He sold the recorder.

6. 'Bái-Xiānsheng bǎ-jīntian-
   xué-de-zì 'dōu-xiězài-bĕn-
   zi-shang.

   Mr. White wrote in his notebook
   all the words (he) studied today.

7. Qíng-ni-bǎ xué-yǔyán-de-
   'fāngfǎ gàosu-wo.

   Please tell me about the way to
   study languages.

8. Nèige-xuésheng-'zhēn-bèn.
   Bǎ-'zuì-jiǎndānde-zì dōu-
   xiěcuò-le.

   That student is really stupid. He
   wrote all the simplest characters wrong.

9. Jīntian wó-bá-biǎo kàncuò-
   le.

   I looked at my watch wrong today.

10. 'Máo-Xiānsheng bǎ-shūdiàn-
    lide-Zhōng-Yīng-zìdiǎn 'dōu-
    náchulai géi-wǒ-kànkan.

    Mr. Mao brought out all the
    Chinese-English dictionaries in
    the bookstore for me to look at.

11. Ní-bǎ-shū 'dōu-mǎi-le-ma?

    Did you buy all the books?

12. 'Wáng-Xiānsheng bǎ-shān-
    shang-nèisuǒr-fángzi-mài-le.

    Mr. King sold that house on the
    hill.

13. Tā-bá-wǒde-shū dōu-náqu-le.

    He took away all my books.

14. 'Bié-bǎ-zhèibĕn-shū-gĕi-ta.
    Wǒ-hái-kàn-ne.

    Don't give him this book. I'm
    still reading it.

15. Nǐ-bù-bǎ-qián-gĕi-ta tā-zĕn-
    mo-mǎi-ne?

    (If) you don't give him the money
    how will he buy it?

Pattern 16.8. The Coverb <u>lián</u> (Note 11 below)

Pattern 16.8 a.   <u>lián</u>   S   <u>yě</u>/<u>dōu</u>   V

                    'even'   Subject   'also'   Verb

                    Lián   tā   yě   qù-le.

                    ' Even <u>he</u> went.'

Pattern 16.8 b.

(S)	(<u>lián</u>)	O	(S)	(<u>yě</u>/<u>dōu</u>)	V
(Subject)	('even')	Object	(Subject)	('also')	Verb
	Lián	'tā	wǒ	yě	bù qǐng.

                    'I'm not even inviting <u>him</u>.'

1. Jīntian wǒ-zhí-qíng-nǐ-'yíge-
    rén. Lián-'Bái-Xiānsheng wǒ-
    dōu-bù-qǐng.

    Today I'm inviting only you. I'm
    not even inviting Mr. White.

2. Nèige-zì búdàn-'wǒmen-bú-
    rènshi, lián-'jiàoyuán yě-bú-
    rènshi.

    Not only do WE not recognize
    that character, even the teacher
    doesn't recognize it.

3. Zuótian wǒmen-qu-kàn-diàn-
    yǐngr. Lián-'fùqin-dōu-qù-
    le.

    Yesterday we went to see a
    movie. Even father went.

4. Ní-zěnmo-'zènmo-bèn-a?
    'Zhèige-zì yě-bú-rènshi.

    How come you're so stupid? You
    don't even recognize this char-
    acter.

5. Wǒ-jīntian-'tài-máng-le.
    Lián-'fàn-dōu-méi-chī.

    I'm too busy today.   I haven't
    even eaten.

6. Wǒ-jīntian 'yì máo-qián-dōu-
    méi-yǒu.

    I don't have a dime today.

7. Wǒ-jīntian-zǎochen dào-xué-
    xiào-de-shíhou, xuéxiàoli 'yí-
    ge-rén-yě-méi-yǒu.

    When I went to school this morn-
    ing, there wasn't a single person
    there [lit. in school].

8. 'Wáng-Xiānsheng tài-cōng-
    ming-le. Xuéle-liǎngniánde-
    'Zhōngwén búdàn-huì-shuō-
    Zhōngwén lián-'shū-dōu-néng-
    kàndǒng-le.

    Mr. King is awfully intelligent.
    After studying Chinese for two
    years, he can not only speak
    Chinese but can even read [and
    understand].

9. Nèige-rén 'yíge-péngyou-dōu-
    méi-yǒu.

    That man doesn't have even one
    friend.

10. Zhèige-zì 'tài-róngyi-le. Ní-
    zěnmo-lián-'zhèige-zì dōu-bú-
    huì-xiě?

    This character is very easy.
    How come you can't even write
    it [lit. this character]?

Pattern 16.9. Question Words as Indefinites (Note 12 below)

Pattern 16.9a.

(S)	V	QW
(Subject)	Verb	Question Word
Wó	'yǒu	jíběn shū.

'I have a few books.'

Pattern 16.9b.

QW	yě/dōu	V
Question Word	yě/dōu	Verb
Shéi	dōu	méi-lái.

'Nobody came.'

1. Nǐ-dào-nǎr-qu? Wǒ-'bú-dào-nǎr-qu.

   Where are you going? I'm not going anywhere (in particular).

2. Nǐ-xué-'Zhōngguo-huà xuéle-'jǐnián-le? Wǒ-xué-le yǐjing-'yóu-jǐnián-le.

   How many years have you been studying the Chinese language? I've been studying it for a few years.

3. Ní-yǒu-'duōshao-shū? Wǒ-'méi-you-duōshao-shū.

   How many books do you have? I don't have many books.

4. 'Gāo-Xiáojie jīntian-dào-nǎr-qu-le? Tā-jīntian-'nár-yě-méi-qù.

   Where did Miss Gao go today? She didn't go anywhere today.

5. Nǐ-yào-mǎi-'shénmo-shū? Wǒ-'shénmo-shū-dōu-bù-mǎi.

   What books do you want to buy? I'm not buying any books.

6. Jīntian-wǎnshang nǐ-jiāli-yǒu-'jǐge-kèren? Jīntian-wǎnshang 'méi-jǐge-rén.

   How many guests are there at your house this evening? There aren't many [people] this evening.

7. 'Wáng-Jiàoshòu 'hén-yǒu-xué-wen-ma? Tā-'méi-shénmo-xuéwen.

   Is Professor King very learned? He doesn't have much learning.

8. Nǐ-zài-zhèr-zhùle-'jǐnián-le? Wǒ-zài-zhèr 'méi-zhù-jǐnián.

   How many years have you been living here? I haven't been living here long [lit. many years].

9. Ní-xiǎng-shàng-nǎr-qu? Wó-'nár-yě-bù-xiǎng-qù.

   Where are you planning to go? I'm not thinking of going anywhere.

10. 'Qián-Xiáojie zěnmo-'nènmo-piàoliang? Wǒ-shuō-ta 'bù-zěnmo-piàoliang.

    How is it that Miss Qian is so pretty? I say she isn't so pretty.

Pattern 16.10.   Passives with <u>shi</u> . . . <u>de</u>   (Note 13 below)

S	shi	(N)	V	de
Subject	shi	(Noun)	Verb	de
Zhèibǎn-shū	shi	tā	xiě	de.

'This book was written by him.'

1. Zhèizhāng-shānshuǐ-huàr shi-'Gāo-Xiáojie-huà-de.

   This landscape painting was painted by Miss Gao.

2. 'Nèige-péngyou shi-'Gāo-Xiānsheng-jièshao-de.

   That friend was introduced by Mr. Gao.

3. Nèibǎn-shū hǎojíle. Shi-'Zhāng-Xiānsheng-mǎi-de.

   That book is excellent. It was bought by Mr. Johnson.

4. Mǎi-'shū-de-qián shi-'wó-
    gěi-de.

The money for buying books was given by me.

5. Nèiběn-zìdiǎn shi-'Bái-Xiān-
    sheng-jiè-de.

That dictionary was borrowed by Mr. White.

6. Zhè-'suóyǒude-zì dōu-shi-
    'Gāo-Xiānsheng-xiě-de-ma?

Were all these characters written by Mr. Gao?

7. Jīntian-wǎnshang wǒmen-qu-
    kàn-diànyǐngr. Piào-shi-
    'Máo-Xiānsheng-mǎi-de. Tā-
    'qíng-wǒmen.

This evening we're going to see a movie. The tickets were bought by Mr. Mao. He is inviting us.

8. Nèige-'Zhōngwen-xìn xiě-de-
    zhēn-hǎo. Shi-'Wáng-Xiān-
    sheng-xiě-de-ma?

That Chinese letter is very well written. Was it written by Mr. King?

9. Zuótian wǒ-tīngle-yìhuěr-
    lùyīn. Nèige-lùyīn shi-
    'Wáng-Xiānsheng-lù-de.
    Zhōngwén shuōde-hǎo-jíle.

I listened to a recording for a while yesterday. That recording was done by Mr. Wang. The Chinese was spoken exceedingly well.

10. 'Shānshang-nèisuǒr-fángzi
    'zhēn-piàoliang. Shi-'Gāo-
    Xiānsheng-zhù-de-ma?

That house on the hill is very attractive. Is it occupied by Mr. Gao?

SUBSTITUTION TABLES

I: 32 sentences   (Note 1)

nǐmen	—	shàng	chuán	—
tāmen	xiǎng	xià	shān	ma

II: 96 sentences   (Notes 2–3)

nán-rén	huí	-lai	—
nü-rén	guò	-qu	le
tāmen	pǎo		
	ná		
	jìn		
	chū		
	shàng		
	xià		

III: 72 sentences (Notes 4–5)

xiānsheng	shàng	shān	—	—
háizi	xià	chē	lái	ma
tāmen			qù	

IV: 90 phrases (Notes 6–7)

pǎo	—	shàng	lái
zǒu	bu	guò	qù
ná	de	huí	
		jìn	
		chū	

V: 72 sentences (Note 6)

háizi	—	shàng	shān	—
tāmen	pǎo	xià	chuán	lái
	zǒu			qù

VI: 64 phrases (Note 8)

pǎo	dào	túshūguǎn	lái	—
zǒu		shūdiàn	qù	le
huí		Hángzhou		
ná		Sūzhou		

PRONUNCIATION DRILLS

Contrasts of Initials in Two-Syllable Pairs

This exercise consists of pairs of expressions which are distinguished in meaning solely by the differences of tone on the first syllable. Blank spaces indicate phrases involving a shift from 3 3 to 2 3, that is a shift from third tone to second tone.

1 0, 2 0	zhuōzi, zhuózi		1 1, 2 1	fēijī, féi-jī
1 0, 3 0	Shānxi, Shǎnxi		1 1, 3 1	mā-chī, mǎ-chī
1 0, 4 0	zhuīzi, zhuìzi		1 1, 4 1	shāng-fēng, shàng-fēng
1 2, 2 2	fēi-é, féi-é		1 3, 2 3	huī-shǒu, huí-shǒu
1 2, 3 2	zōng-zé, zǒng-zé		(1 3, 3 3)	
1 2, 4 2	yǒng-rén, yòng-rén		1 3, 4 3	jūn-zhǔ, jùn-zhǔ

1 4, 2 4 tōu-piào, tóu-piào

1 4, 3 4 xiāng-jiàn, xiǎng-jiàn

1 4, 4 4 jiē-dào, jiè-dào

20, 10 zhuózi, zhuōzi	21, 11 féi-jī, fēi-jī
20, 30 yízi, yǐzi	21, 31 wú-yī, wǔ-yī
20, 40 máde, màde	21, 41 huá-bīng, huà-bīng
22, 12 féi-é, fēi-é	23, 13 huí-shǒu, huī-shǒu
22, 32 hú-lái, hǔ-lái	(23, 33)
22, 42 huí-lái, huì-lái	23, 43 xíng-lǐ, xìng-lǐ

24, 14 tóu-piào, tōu-piào
24, 34 wú-shì, wǔ-shì
24, 44 dádào, dà-dào

30, 10 Shǎnxi, Shānxi	31, 11 mǎ-chī, mā-chī
30, 20 mǎde, máde	31, 21 wǔ-yī, wú-yī
30, 40 mǎide, màide	31, 41 huǒ-chē, huò-chē
32, 12 zǒng-zé, zōng-zé	(33, 13)
32, 22 hǔ-lái, hú-lái	(33, 23)
32, 42 mǎi-fáng, mài-fáng	(33, 43)

34, 14 xiǎng-jiàn, xiāng-jiàn
34, 24 wǔ-shì, wú-shì
34, 44 zuǐ-huài, zuì-huài

40, 10 zhuìzi, zhuīzi	41, 11 shàng-fēng, shāng-fēng
40, 20 màde, máde	41, 21 huà-bīng, huá-bīng
40, 30 màide, mǎide	41, 31 huò-chē, huǒ-chē
42, 12 yòng-rén, yōng-rén	43, 13 jùn-zhǔ, jūn-zhǔ
42, 22 huì-lái, huí-lái	43, 23 xìng-lǐ, xíng-lǐ
42, 32 mài-fáng, mǎi-fáng	(43, 33)

44, 14 jiè-dào, jiē-dào
44, 24 dà-dào, dádào
44, 34 zuì-huài, zuǐ-huài

ANSWERING QUESTIONS

1. Rúguǒ ní-géi-liǎngge-rén-jièshao, shi-'yíge-rén-shuō-Jiúyǎng háishi-'liǎngge-rén-shuō-Jiúyǎng-ne?

2. Tā-rènshi 'èrbǎige-Zhōngguo-zì. Wǒ-rènshi 'sānbái-wǔshige-Zhōngguo-zì. 'Shéi-rènshi-de-zì-duō?

3. 'Wáng-Xiānsheng qùguo-Hángzhou. 'Zhāng-Xiānsheng qùguo-Sūzhou. Tā-men-liǎngge-rén 'shéi-qùguo-Hángzhou?

4. 'Qián-Xiānshengde-tàitai hěn-piàoliang. 'Wáng-Xiānshengde-tàitai bú-piàoliang. Nǐ-shuō 'shéide-tàitai-hǎokàn?

5. 'Wáng-Tàitai cóng-Gāo-jia-dào-shūdiàn-qu. 'Gāo-Tàitai zài-jiā-lǐtou. Shi-shéi-zài-lùshang?

6. 'Gāo-Xiáojie xǐhuan-huà-huàr. 'Wáng-Xiáojie hén-xǐhuan-huàr. Tā-men-liǎngge-rén 'shéi-huì-huà-huàr?

7. 'Bái-Xiānsheng lái-Zhōngguo-'yìnián. 'Wàn-Jiàoshòu lái-Zhōngguo-'èr-nián. Tāmen-liǎngge-rén 'shéi-xiān-dào-Zhōngguo-de?

8. Wáng-Xiānsheng zuótian-kāile-'sānge-zhōngtóude-chē. Wáng-Tàitai 'bú-huì-kāi-chē. 'Shéi-huì-kāi-chē?

9. Wáng-Xiānsheng huídào-Yīngguo-qu-le. Wáng-Tàitai 'hái-zài-Zhōng-guo-ne. 'Shéi-dào-Yīngguo-qu-le?

10. Gāo-Xiānsheng zǒuhuilai-de. Gāo-Tàitai zuò-'chē-huílai-de. Zǒu-lù-de-shi-shéi?

NOTES

1. In Chinese, as in English, verbs of motion sometimes indicate direction relative to the speaker (e.g. go in, come in), and sometimes have no such indication (e.g. enter). Thus Tāmen-jīntian-jìn-chéng 'They're entering the city today' gives no clue to whether the speaker is himself inside or outside the city.

2. Postverbs of direction indicate the direction of a motion relative to the speaker. Two of these are lai 'come [toward me]' and qu 'go [away from me]':

> Qǐng-jìnlai. 'Please come in.' (Spoken by someone already inside to someone outside.)

> Qǐng-jìnqu. 'Please go in.' (Spoken by someone outside to another person who is also outside.)

3. A verb said twice, first with postverb <u>lái</u> 'come' and immediately after with postverb <u>qù</u> 'go' (both with tones) means 'do V back and forth':

zǒulái-zǒuqù 'walk back and forth'

Sometimes the meaning is figurative:

xiǎnglái-xiǎngqù 'rack one's brains' [lit. 'think back and forth']

4. When a verb with a directional verb after it has an object, the object is either placed in front of the verb, as the topic, or is inserted between the verb and the postverb:

Nèiběn-shū qíng-nǐ-nálai.
    or   } 'Please bring that book.'
Qíng-nǐ-ná-nèiběn-shū-lai.

5. Some compound verbs consist of two verbs of motion or action:

pǎoshàng 'run up'	náshàng 'carry up'
pǎojìn 'run in'	nájìn 'carry in'
pǎohuí 'run back'	náhuí 'carry back'

Such verbs are further compounded with directional postverbs:

pǎoshànglai 'run up (toward the speaker)'
pǎoshàngqu 'run up (away from the speaker)'
náhuílai 'bring back'
náhuíqu 'take back'

6. If the compound verbs mentioned in the preceding note have a place word as object, this is inserted before the postverb:

pǎoshàng-shān-lai 'run up the mountain (toward the speaker)'
pǎoshàng-shān-qu 'run up the mountain (away from the speaker)'
náhuí-shūdiàn-lai 'bring back to the bookstore'
náhuí-shūdiàn-qu 'take back to the bookstore'

7. The compound verbs with directional postverbs described in Note 5 are resultative verbs. This means they have special forms to express 'be able to' and 'be unable to':

náhuílai 'bring back'
nádehuílái 'able to bring back'
nábuhuílái 'unable to bring back'

8. The verb <u>dào</u> 'to' is often suffixed to other verbs to mean 'to' or 'toward' or 'up to, as far as,' forming expressions parallel to English 'walk to,' 'run to,' 'take [something] to,' 'read as far as.' Use of <u>lai</u> 'come' or <u>qu</u> 'go' at the end shows whether the direction is toward or away from the speaker:

Wǒmen-míngtian xuédào-dì-sānkè. 'We study to the third lesson tomorrow.'
Tā-pǎodào-shānshang-lai. 'He is running up the mountain (toward the
speaker).'

The last sentence is almost the same in meaning as:

Tā-pǎoshang-shān-lai.

The former gives somewhat greater emphasis to the destination (shān-shang), the latter to the action (pǎoshang).

9. Compound verbs with dào, discussed in the preceding note, are resultative verbs, so that de and bu are inserted between the main verb and dào to make the phrase mean 'able to' and 'unable to' respectively:

> xuédào 'study as far as'
> xuédedào 'able to study as far as'
> xuébudào 'unable to study as far as'
> Wǒmen-míngtian xuébudào dì-sānkè.   'We can't get to the third lesson by tomorrow.'

10. The coverb bǎ, literally 'take,' introduces the direct object of a verb. It is used—

(a) When a definite thing is referred to. Compare:

> Tā-géi-wǒ-shū. 'He gave me a book.'
> Tā-bǎ-shū-géi-wǒ. 'He gave me the book.'

(b) When the main verb is followed by another object, verb, or suffix, e.g. :

> Wó-bǎ-zì dōu-xiěwán-le. 'I've finished writing all the characters.'

A useful way to drill this construction is for the teacher to present an ordinary SVO sentence and request students to transform it into the bǎ construction. For example:

> Teacher: Tā-géi-wǒ-shū.
> Student: Tā-bǎ-shū-géi-wǒ.

11. The adverb yě 'also,' if used with a stressed object placed before the verb, means 'even':

> Wǒ-'yìběn-shū yé-méi-yǒu.
>   or   } 'I don't have even one book.'
> 'Yìběn-shū wǒ-yé-méi-yǒu.

(The subject comes either before or after the transposed object.)

The adverb dōu, literally 'all,' is also used in this way:

> Wǒ-'yìběn-shū dōu-méi-yǒu.
>   or   } 'I don't have even one book.'
> 'Yìběn-shū wǒ-dōu-méi-yǒu.

The preceding examples are also expressed with the coverb lián 'even' before the object:

> Wǒ-lián-'yìběn-shū yě-méi-yǒu. or
> Wǒ-lián-'yìběn-shū dōu-méi-yǒu. or
> Lián-'yìběn-shū wó-yě-méi-yǒu. or
> Lián-'yìběn-shū wǒ-dōu-méi-yǒu.

If yě or dōu are used in reference to the subject, the coverb lián is generally used also:

Lián-'tā yě-bú-rènshi-zhèige-zì.   or
Lián-'tā dōu-bú-rènshi-zhèige-zì.
   'Even he doesn't recognize this character.'

A useful way to drill this construction is for the teacher to present an
ordinary SVO sentence and request students to transform it into the foregoing construction. For example:

   Teacher: Tā-bú-rènshi-zhèige-zì.
   Student: Lián-tā-dōu-bú-rènshi-zhèige-zì.

12. The meanings of question words (shénmo 'what?' shéi 'who?' nǎr
     'where?' etc.) shift to indefinite meanings ('few,' 'everything,' 'noth-
     ing,' 'everywhere,' 'nowhere,' and the like) under the following con-
     ditions:

   (a) When they occur in constructions containing dōu 'all' or yě 'also' plus
        a verb:

        Wǒ-'shénmo-dōu-bú-yào. ⎫   'I want nothing.' or 'I don't want any-
             or   ⎬   thing.'
        Wǒ-'shénmo-yě-bú-yào.   ⎭

        'Shéi-dōu-huì. 'Everybody knows how.'

        'Shéi-dōu-bú-huì. 'Nobody knows how.'

   (b) When some word other than the question word receives the chief
        stress. Compare:

        Tā-yóu-'jǐběn-shū? 'How many books does he have?'
           (stress on jǐ 'how many?')

        Tā-'yóu-jǐběn-shū. 'He has a few books.'
           (stress on yǒu 'have')

13. Sentences of the type (S) V O (Subject-Verb-Object) when transformed into
     the pattern O shi (S) V de cause shifts in the connotation of the Chinese
     sentence which correspond to the following English processes: (a) the
     object changes from indefinite to definite; (b) the tense becomes past;
     (c) the voice becomes passive; (d) the portion of the utterance between shi
     and de receives the chief emphasis. Thus:

        Wǒ-mǎi-shū. 'I'm buying books.'
        but—
        Shū shi-wǒ-mǎi-de. 'The books were bought by me.'

        Nǎr-mǎi-shū? 'Where (does one) buy books?'
        but—
        Shū shi-nǎr-mǎi-de? 'Where were the books bought?'

        Shénmo-shíhou mǎi-shū? 'When does one buy books?'
        but—
        Shū shi-shénmo-shíhou-mǎi-de? 'When were the books bought?'

A useful way to drill this construction is for the teacher to present the SVO form and request students to transform it into O shi S V de. For example:

Teacher: Wó-mǎi-shū.
Student: Shū-shi-'wó-mǎi-de.

14. Girls' names frequently include the word měi 'beautiful,' as in Měiyīng—literally 'beautiful (and) brave.'

15. The word mā 'mother' is most often used in direct address. Occasionally one hears wǒ-mā for 'my mother,' but mā is not used in reference to another person's mother.

16. The word for 'wife' is nèiren if spoken by a man in reference to his own wife, and tàitai in direct address (i.e. 'Wife!') or if the reference is to another person's wife. (See also Supplementary Lesson 16, Note 2)

17. The verb shi 'be' is frequently used to join verbal phrases as well as noun phrases:

Xiě-Zhōngguo-zì shi-hěn-bu-róngyi-de.   'Writing characters is (something which is) not at all easy.'
Xué-xiě-zì shi-bìděi-yònggōng.   'Studying the writing of characters is (a matter of) having to be industrious.'
Xué-yǔyánxué jiù-shi-yánjiu-wàiguo-huà.   'To study linguistics is to investigate foreign languages.'

18. The verb cuò 'wrong' preceded by bu 'not' has the special meaning 'not bad' or 'that's right.' Hěn-bu-cuò, literally 'quite not bad,' is much like English 'not at all bad,' actually meaning 'pretty good.' Cuò is also suffixed to a few verbs to mean '[do] wrong or incorrectly':

Wó-bǎ-shū-mǎicuò-le. 'I bought the wrong book.'   [lit. 'I incorrectly bought the book.']

Here are some other compounds formed with cuò:

niàncuò 'read incorrectly'   xiěcuò 'write incorrectly'
kàncuò 'look at incorrectly'   zuòcuò 'do incorrectly'
shuōcuò 'say incorrectly'   mǎicuò 'buy incorrectly'
tīngcuò 'hear incorrectly'   nácuò 'take incorrectly'

19. Yìdiǎr yě and yìdiǎr dōu are used with negative verbs to express the idea 'not at all':

Wǒ-yìdiǎr dōu-bù-dǒng. 'I don't understand anything at all.'
Wǒ-yìdiǎr-qián yě-méi-yǒu. 'I don't have any money at all.'
Yīngwén-yìdiǎr-yě-bù-nán. 'English isn't at all difficult.'

Lesson 17 PLAYING 'GUESS-FINGERS'

"Qīge-qīge-qīge-a! . . . Bā-a!"

Dialogue: Mr. Gao, Professor Wanamaker, and Mr. White converse as Mrs. Gao and Miss Gao put the finishing touches on dinner.

Gāo-Xiānsheng, Wàn-Jiàoshou, Bái-Xiānsheng tāmen-sānge-rén hē-chá-de-shíhou, tāmen-tán-Sūzhou-Hángzhou.

While Mr. Gao, Professor Wanamaker, and Mr. White are drinking tea, they talk of Soochow and Hangchow.

Gāo : Nǐmen-tándào   5

(Since) you've mentioned

    Shàng-yǒu-tiāntáng
    Xià-yǒu-Sū-Háng

    Above is Heaven
    Below are Soochow and Hangchow

    wǒ-xiànzài-gēn-nǐmen-tányitan wǒde-lǎo-jiā-Hángzhou.   10

I'll tell you now about my old home, Hangchow.

Bái : Nín-shi-zài-Hángzhou zhǎng-dà-de-ma?

Did you grow up in Hangchow?

Gāo : Wǒ-shi-zài-Hángzhou-shēng-de. Wǒ-'èrshi-jǐsuì cái-líkai-Háng-zhou.   15

I was born in Hangchow. I didn't leave there [lit. Hangchow] until I was in my twenties.

270

Wàn: Wǒ-zài-Yīngguo jiù-tīngshuō   (Even while) I was in England, I
      'Hángzhou-hén-hǎo. 'Yīng-   heard that Hangchow is very
      guo-rén dào-'Zhōngguo-lǚ-   nice. Englishmen who travel to
      xíng yídìng-yào-dào-Háng-   20   China feel it is a must to go
      zhou-qu. Huílai-'dōu-shuō   there [to Hangchow]. When they
      Hángzhou-hǎode-bùdéliǎo.   come back, they all say that
                                        Hangchow is wonderful.

Gāo: Nǐ-méi-qùguo-Hángzhou-ma,   You haven't been to Hangchow,
      Lǎo-Wàn?   [Old] Wan?

Wàn: Wǒ-méi-qùguò.   25   I never have.

Gāo: Hángzhou-yǒu-ge-hú jiào-   Hangchow has a lake called West
      Xī-Hú shi-'hén-yǒu-míng-   Lake that's very famous. Peo-
      de. Cóngqiánde-rén bǎ-   ple of earlier days compared
      Xī-Hú bǐzuò-yíge-'zuì-   West Lake to Xi Shi, one of the
      piàoliàngde-nǚ-rén Xī-Shī.* 30   most beautiful of women.* You
      Nènmo-nǐ-jiù-zhīdao zhèi-   can tell from this how beautiful
      ge-hú shi-zěnmoyàngde-   the lake is.
      piàoliàng-le.

Wàn: Wǒ-láiguo-Zhōngguo-'jǐcì   I've been to China several times
      dōu-méi-qùguo-Hángzhou.   35   but have never been to Hang-
      Xīwang-jiānglái qù-yícì.   chow. I hope to go there some
                                        day [lit. once in the future].

Gāo: Tiānqi-nuǎnhuode-shíhou   When the weather's warm a lot
      yóu-hǎoxiē-rén dào-Háng-   of people make trips to Hang-
      zhou-lǚxíng.   chow.

Bái: Wǒ-xīwang jiānglái-yǒu-jī-   40   I hope [in the future] I'll have an
      hui dào-Hángzhou-lǚxíng.   opportunity to make a trip to
      'Sūzhou-zěnmoyàng? Sū-   Hangchow. What's Soochow like?
      zhou gēn-Hángzhou-yíyang-   Is Soochow like Hangchow?
      ma?

Gāo: Sūzhou méi-yǒu-Hángzhou-   45   Soochow isn't as big as Hang-
      nènmo-dà. Shānshuǐ-bù-   chow. The scenery is different,
      yíyàng, kěshi-yé-hěn-piào-   but also very beautiful.
      liàng.

Bái: Nín-fǔshang-zhèige-dìfang   This area around your home is
      'yé-hěn-piàoliang. Chàbu-   50   very beautiful too. It's almost
      duō-gēn-Gāo-Xiáojie huà-   as beautiful as that painting of
      de-nèizhāng-huàr yíyàng-   Miss Gao's.
      piàoliang.

Gāo: Yīnwei-wó-xǐhuan-Háng-   Since I like Hangchow, I used to
      zhou, suóyi-cóngqian-jiu-   55   think that at some future time I
      xiǎng, jiānglái-wǒ-'yídìng-   would make it a point to look for
      zhǎo-yíge-dìfang xiàng-   a place as nice as Hangchow to
      'Hángzhou-yíyàng-hǎo wǒ-   settle down. Later, friends in-
      cái-zhù-ne. Hòulai-péng-   troduced me to this place. Al-
      you jièshao-zhèige-dìfang.   60   though it's not as nice as Hang-

---

* Xī-Shī, one of the greatest beauties in Chinese history, lived during the
Warring Kingdoms Period (B.C. 403–221).

Suírán-méi-you-'Hángzhou-
nènmo-hǎo, kěshi-yǒu-yì-
diǎr-xiàng-Hángzhou. Wǒ-
jiù-zài-zhèr mǎile-zhèi-
suǒr-fángzi.   65

chow, still it resembles Hangchow a bit. So I bought this
house here.

Bái : Tīngshuō Sūzhou-nǔ-rén-
piàoliang.* Shì-zhēnde-
ma?

I hear the women of Soochow are
beautiful.* Is that so?

Gāo : Bù-yídìng. Yǒude-piào-
liang, yǒude-yé-hěn-nán-   70
kàn.

Yes and no. Some are beautiful,
some are ugly.

Wàn: Shì. Sūzhou-nǔ-rén 'shì-
piàoliang. Nǐ-kàn-Gāo-
Xiáojie duómo-piàoliang.

It is so. Soochow women are
beautiful. You see how attractive Miss Gao is.

Bái : Gāo-Xiáojie shi-'Sūzhou-   75
rén-a?

Is Miss Gao a native of Soochow?

Wàn: Gāo-Xiáojie shi-zài-'Sūzhou-shēng-de. Gāo-'Tài-
tai-shi-Sūzhou-rén. Lǎo-
Gāo zài-Sūzhou-rènshi-de-   80
Gāo-Tàitai. Tāmen-liǎng-
ge-rén zài-'Sūzhou-jiēhūn,
Gāo-Xiáojie shi-zài-'Sū-
zhou-shēng-de. Gāo-'Xiáojie-zhǎngde gēn-Gāo-'Tài-   85
tai-yíyàng-piàoliang.

Miss Gao was born there. Mrs.
Gao comes from Soochow. [Old]
Gao met Mrs. Gao there. They
were married in Soochow, and
Miss Gao was born there. Miss
Gao has grown up as attractive
as Mrs. Gao.

Bái : Oh, suóyi-Gāo-Tàitai Gāo-
Xiáojie nènmo-piàoliang-
ne!

Oh, so that's why Mrs. Gao and
Miss Gao are so attractive !

Wàn: Hángzhou-shānshuí-yǒu-   90
míng. Sūzhou-nǔ-rén-yǒu-
míng.

Hangchow is famous for its
scenery, and Soochow is famous
for its women.

Gāo : Wǒmen-zhǐ-shuō-huà-le.
Wǒ-wàngle qíng-nǐmen-
liǎngwèi-hē-jiǔ-le. Lǎo-   95
Wàn, 'Bái-Xiānsheng,
qǐng.

All we're doing is talking. I've
forgotten to ask you to have
some wine. [Old] Wan, Mr.
White, please.

Wàn: Zhèi-jiǔ-'zhēn-hǎo. Shi-
shénmo-jiǔ-a?

This wine is really nice. What
is it?

---

* China has its geographical stereotypes comparable to the thrifty Scotch-
man and the hard-bargaining New Englander. Natives of Shansi are supposed
to be penny-pinching, southerners cunning, and Soochow women beautiful.

Gāo : Shi-Méigui-Lù.* Lǎo-   100   It's Rose Dew.* [Old] Wan, what
Wàn, zěnmoyàng, wǒmen-   do you say, after this cup shall
hēle-zhèibēi huá-'quán-   we play 'guess-fingers'.? **
hǎo-bu-hǎo? **

Wàn : Hǎo.   Fine.

Gāo : 'Bái-Xiānsheng, nǐ-kàn-   105   Mr.White, have you seen 'guess-
jianguo-huá-quán-de-ma?   fingers' played?

Bái : Wǒ-hái-méi-kànjianguo-   No, I haven't.
ne.

Gāo : Lǎo-Wàn, lái, wǒmen-huá-   [Old] Wan, come on, let's play.
quán-ba.   110

Gāo : Sìge-a!   Wàn: Qī-a!   (Gao:) Four!   (Wan:) Seven!

Wàn : Nǐ-yíng-le. Wǒ-hē.   You win. I drink.

Gāo : Shíge-shíge-a! Wàn: Wǔ-   (Gao:) Ten!   (Wan:) Five!
a!

Gāo : Wǒ-yíng-le. Nǐ-hē.   115   I win. You drink.

Gāo : Wǔge-wǔge-a! Wàn: Lìu-a.   (Gao:) Five!   (Wan:) Six!

                                         (No one wins.)

Gāo : Qīge-qīge-qīge-a! Wàn: (Gao:) Seven!   (Wan:) Eight!
Bā-a!

Wàn : Nǐ-yíng-le. Wǒ-'yòu-hē.   You win. I drink again.

Gāo : 'Bái-Xiānsheng, nǐ-kàn.   120   Mr. White, what do you think, is
Yǒu-yìsi-ma?   it interesting?

Bái : 'Hén-yǒu-yìsi. Wó-hěn-   Very interesting. I'm puzzled
qíguài wèi-shénmo-'yíng-   about why the winner doesn't
de-rén bu-hē-jiǔ-ne?   drink.

---

* Méigui-Lù 'Rose Dew' is the name of a popular light wine which is taken in tiny cups holding only a few thimblefuls.

** The game of 'guess-fingers' is widely played in China by people of all ages. There are several versions. In one, especially popular with children, two opponents simultaneously extend the right hand in the form of a fist or an open palm or with the first and second fingers spread apart, the others being held against the palm. The fist represents a stone, the open palm represents cloth, and the spread fingers represent scissors. Cloth wins over stone, stone wins over scissors, and scissors win over cloth (since cloth covers stone, stone breaks scissors, scissors cut cloth). In another version, the two contestants simultaneously extend none to five fingers while calling out their guesses as to the total number of fingers extended by the two contestants. The numbers are often called out over and over again at a very rapid pace; sometimes the numbers are called in fixed phrases with such auspicious connotations as 'four happinesses' and 'six successes.' These latter versions are especially popular with men who like to play the game while having wine as a prelude to dinner.

Gāo : Ní-'děng-yìhuěr jiù-míng-   125   Wait a moment and you'll under-
       bai-le.   stand.

Gāo : Qīge-qīge-a! Wàn: Jiǔ-a!   (Gao:) Seven!   (Wan:) Nine!

Gāo : Wǒ-'yòu-yíng-le. Nǐ-'yòu-   I win again.   You drink again.
       hē.

Wàn : Lǎo-Gāo, nǐ-kàn, jiǔ-bēi-   130   [Old] Gao, see, the wine cups
       zhēn-bù-xiǎo-a.   aren't so small after all.

Gāo : Lǎo-Wàn, 'zài-huá.   [Old] Wan,   let's play again.

Wàn : Gòu-le. Zài-huá jiù-hēde-   Enough. If I play again I'll have
       'tài-duō-le.   too much wine.

Bái : Oh, 'xiànzài-wǒ-cái-míng-   135   Oh, now I understand why the
       bai wèi-shénmo 'yíng-de-   winner doesn't drink.
       rén bù-hē-jiǔ.

VOCABULARY

bēi	cup (M) (Note 8)
bēi(zi)	cup (N) (Note 8)
bǐ	compare (TV)
bùdéliǎo	awfully [lit. not reach end] (Note 10)
chá	tea (N)
cóngqián	formerly, in the past (TW) [lit. from before]
děng	wait (IV)
gòu	be enough (IV)
hǎoxiē	good many, a lot (Note 9)
hē	drink (TV)
huá-quán	play guess-fingers (See Supplementary Lesson 17, Note 1)
jiéhūn, jiéhūn	marry (IV)
jiǔ	wine (N)
lù	dew (N)
méigui	rose (N)
míngbai	understand (TV) [lit. clear white]
nuǎnhuo	warm (SV)
quán	fist (N)
shēng	be born (IV); give birth to (TV)
tiānqi	weather (N)
wèi-shénmo?	why? [lit. for what?]
xiàng	resemble (EV) (Notes 1, 2, 4)

xiē	few (M) (Note 9)
yàng	kind (M)
yíng	win (TV)
yíyàng	same (SV) (Notes 2–3, 5)
yǒu-míng	famous (VO) [lit. have name]
zěn(mo)yàng? zěn(me)yàng?	like what? how about it? well? [lit. how kind?]
zhǎng	grow (IV)
zuò	as (Note 7)

SENTENCE BUILD-UP

xiàng xiàng-tāde-fùqin	resemble resemble his father
1. Tā-hěn-xiàng tāde-fùqin.	He looks a lot like his father.
yǒu-yìdiǎr yǒu-yìdiǎr-xiàng	have a little resemble a little
2. Tā-yǒu-yìdiǎr xiàng-tāde-mǔqin.	He resembles his mother a little.
yàng zhèiyàng	kind this kind
3. Zhèiyàng-rén hén-shǎo.	This sort of person is quite rare.
nèiyàng nèiyàngde	that kind that kind (of)
4. Wó-xiáng-mǎi 'nèiyàngde-bǐ.	I'd like to buy that kind of pen.
yíyàng	one kind, same
5. Zhèi-liǎngge-dōngxi-yíyàng.	These two things are alike.
yíyàng bù-yíyàng	the same not the same, different
6. Zhèi-liǎngge-lùyīnjī bù-yíyàng.	These two recorders are not the same.
zhèige gēn-nèige	this with that
7. Zhèige-gēn-nèige-yíyàng.	This and that are the same.
xiàng-nèiběn-shū xiàng-nèiběn-shū-yíyàng	resemble that book be the same as that book
8. Zhèiběn-shū xiàng-nèiběn-yíyàng.	This book is the same as that one.
tiānqi	weather

zhèrde-tiānqi	the weather here
9. Zhèrde-tiānqi bù-gēn-nèrde-tiānqi-yíyàng.	The weather here is not the same as the weather there.
Húnánde-tiānqi gēn-Dōngběide-tiānqi	the weather in Hunan and the weather in Manchuria
10. Húnánde-tiānqi gēn-Dōngběide-tiānqi bù-yíyàng.	The weather in Hunan is different from the weather in Manchuria.
Húběide-tiānqi chàbuduō	the weather in Hupei almost
11. Húběide-tiānqi chàbuduō-gēn-Húnánde-tiānqi-yíyàng.	The weather in Hupei is almost the same as the weather in Hunan.
bú-xiàng bú-xiàng-wǒde-yíyàng	does not resemble is not like mine
12. Nǐde-bǐ bú-xiàng-wǒde-yíyàng.	Your pen is not like mine.
jiǔ	wine
13. Zhèige-jiǔ hén-hǎo.	This wine is excellent.
bēi jiǔ-bēi	cup wine cup
14. Zhōngguo-jiǔ-bēi hén-xiǎo.	Chinese wine cups are very small.
bēizi sānge-bēizi	cup three cups
15. Ná-sānge-bēizi-lai.	Bring three cups.
bēi sānbēi-jiǔ	cup three cups of wine
16. Qíng-ni-ná sānbēi-jiǔ-lai.	Please bring three cups of wine.
gēn-nèige-bēizi-yíyàng gēn-nèige-bēizi yíyàng-xiǎo	the same as that cup as small as that cup
17. Zhèige-bēizi gēn-nèige-yíyàng-xiǎo.	This cup is as small as that one.
nuǎnhuo gēn-Húnán yíyàng-nuǎnhuo	warm as warm as Hunan
18. Húběi-gēn-Húnán yíyàng-nuǎnhuo-ma?	Is Hupei as warm as Hunan?
nuǎnhuo gēn-Húnán yíyàng-nuǎnhuo bù-gēn-Húnán yíyàng-nuǎnhuo	warm as warm as Hunan not as warm as Hunan

19. Shāndong bù-gēn-Húnán yí-
    yàng-nuǎnhuo.

     Shantung is not as warm as Hu-
nan.

       xiàng-Shānxi-yíyàng
       xiàng-Shānxi-yíyàng-dà
20. Shāndong chàbuduō-xiàng-
    Shānxi-yíyàng-dà.

       like Shansi
       as big as Shansi
Shantung is almost as large as
Shansi.

       méigui
       yǒude-méigui
21. Yǒude-méigui shi-hóngde,
    yǒude-shi-báide.

       rose
       some roses
Some roses are red, some are
white.

       lù
       Méigui-Lù
       xiàng-Méigui-Lù
22. Zhèige-jiǔ xiàng-Méigui-Lù
    yíyàng-hǎo.

       dew
       Rose Dew
       resemble Rose Dew
This wine is as nice as Rose
Dew.

       xǐhuan-kàn-diànyǐngr
       yíyàng-xǐhuan kàn-
        diànyǐngr
23. Wǒ-gēn-nǐ-yíyàng xǐhuan-
    kàn-diànyǐngr.

       like to see movies
       equally like to see movies
I like to see movies as much as
you do.

       xǐhuan-chī-'Zhōngguo-
        fàn
       yíyàng-xǐhuan-chī-
        'Zhōngguo-fàn
24. Wǒ-bù-xiàng-tā-yíyàng xǐ-
    huan-chī-'Zhōngguo-fàn.

       like to eat Chinese food
       equally like to eat Chinese
        food
I don't like to eat Chinese food
as much as he does.

       nǐ-xiàng-tā
       nènmo-cōngming
25. Nǐ-xiàng-'tā-nènmo-cōng-
    ming.

       you resemble him
       that intelligent
You are as intelligent as he is.

       tā-xiàng-nǐ
       zhènmo-cōngming
26. Tā-xiàng-'nǐ-zhènmo-cōng-
    ming.

       he resembles you
       this intelligent
He is as intelligent as you are.

       nènmo-yònggōng
27. Ní-yǒu-tā-nènmo-yònggōng.

       so hard-working
You work as hard as he does.

       nènmo-xǐhuan-chī-
        'Zhōngguo-fàn
28. Nǐ-méi-yǒu-tā nènmo-xǐ-
    huan-chī-'Zhōngguo-fàn.

       like to eat Chinese food as
        much
You don't like to eat Chinese
food as much as he does.

       chá
       ná-chá-lai
29. Qǐng-ná-chá-lai.

       tea
       bring tea
Please bring some tea.

       hē

       drink

xǐhuan-hē-chá   like to drink tea
30. Wǒ-xiàng-nǐ-yíyàng xǐhuan-   I like to drink tea as much as
hē-chá.   you do.

hē   drink
hǎo-hē   nice to drink
31. Zhèige-chá-'zhēn-hǎo-hē.   This tea is really nice to drink.

míng   name
yǒu-míng   be famous or well known
32. Sūzhou-méi-yǒu-Hángzhou   Soochow isn't as well known as
nènmo-yǒu-míng.   Hangchow.

jiēhūn   marry
33. Tāmen-shi-'qùnian-jiēhūn-   They were married last year.
de.

Wáng-Xiānsheng gēn-   Mr. and Mrs. King
Wáng-Tàitai
shi-qùnian-jiēhūn-de   were married last year
34. Wáng-Xiānsheng gēn-Wáng-   Mr. and Mrs. King were married
Tàitai shi-qùnian-jiēhūn-de.   last year.

zhǎng   grow
zhǎng-dà   grow up
35. Tā-shi-zài-'Zhōngguo-zhǎng-   He grew up in China.
dà-de.

zhǎng-gāo   grow tall
36. Nèige-háizi xiànzài-zhǎng-   That child has grown tall now.
gāo-le.

gòu   enough
'gòu-bu-gòu   enough or not
37. Fàn-'gòu-bu-gòu?   Is there enough food?

huá-quán   play 'guess-fingers'
38. Nǐ-huì-huá-quán-ma?   Can you play 'guess-fingers'?

gēn-ta-fùqin   with his father
yíyàng-gāo   equally tall
39. Tā-zhǎngde gēn-ta-fùqin   He's grown as tall as his father.
yíyàng-gāo.

gēn-ta-yíyàng-hǎo   as good as he
40. Nǐ-huá-quán-huá-de gēn-   You play 'guess-fingers' as well
ta-yíyàng-hǎo.   as he does.

cóngqián   formerly
gēn-ta-yíyàng-duō   as much as he
41. Wǒ-cóngqián-chī-de gēn-   I used to eat as much as he does.
tā-yíyàng-duō.

xiàng-tā-nènmo-duō   as much as he
42. Nǐ-mǎi-shū-mǎi-de xiàng-   You buy as many books as he
'tā-nènmo-duō.   does.

méi-yǒu-'tā-nènmo-duō
not as many as he
43. Ní-mǎi-shū-mǎi-de méi-
    yǒu-'tā-nènmo-duō.
You don't buy as many books as
he does.

yíng
win
yíng-le-sāncì
won three times
44. Wó-yě-yíngle-sāncì.
I also won three times.

shēng
be born
45. Tā-shi-zài-Húnán-shēng-de.
He was born in Hunan.

shēngzài
be born in
46. Tā-shēngzài-Húnán.
He was born in Hunan.

míngbai
understand
míngbai-nǐde-yìsi
understand your meaning
47. Wǒ-bù-míngbai-nǐde-yìsi.
I don't understand what you
mean.

wèi-shénmo?
why?
48. Nǐ-wèi-'shénmo-bú-qù?
Why aren't you going?

děng
wait
'děngyiděng
wait a while
49. Qǐng-ni-'děngyiděng.
Please wait a while.

nǐ-kàn
you see or you think
zěnmoyàng?
like what?
50. Nǐ-kàn-nèiběn-shū zěnmo-
    yàng?
What do you think of that book?

zěnmoyàng?
like what?
'bù-zěnmoyàng
nothing much
51. Nèiběn-shū 'bù-zěnmoyàng.
That book isn't anything much.

xiē
a few
zhèixiē-shū
these books
52. Zhèixiē-shū 'dōu-shi-nǐde-
    ma?
Are all these books yours?

nèixiē
those
nèixiē-rén
those men
53. Nèixiē-rén dōu-shi-'shén-
    mo-rén?
Who are those men?

hǎoxiē
a good many, a lot
54. Hǎoxiē-fángzi 'dōu-shi-yí-
    yàngde.
A lot of homes are alike.

yǒu-xiē
there are some
yǒu-xiē-rén
there are some people
55. Yǒu-xiē-rén 'xǐhuan-lǚxíng,
    yǒu-xiē-rén 'bù-xǐhuan-
    lǚxíng.
There are some people who like
to travel, and some people who
don't [like to travel].

bǐ   compare
'bǐyibǐ   make a comparison
56. Nèi-liǎngge-xuésheng 'bǐ-   Compare those two students.
yìbǐ.

bǎ-zhèige-xuésheng   take this student
gēn-nèige-xuésheng   with that student
57. Bǎ-'zhèige-xuésheng gēn-   Compare this student with that
'nèige-xuésheng 'bǐyìbǐ.   student.

bǐdeshàng   comparable
bǐbushàng   not comparable
58. 'Tāde-xuéwen bǐdeshàng-   Can his learning compare with
bǐbushàng 'Wàn-Jiàoshòu?   Professor Wanamaker's?

bǐzuò   compare with, equate with
bǐ-sìniánjíde-xuésheng   equate with senior students
59. Jiàoshòu 'dōu-bǎ-ta bǐzuò-   The professors all rank him
'sìniánjíde-xuésheng.   with the senior students.

kànzuò   view as, take for, mistake
                                                    for
kànzuò-yíge-'Zhōngguo-   view as a Chinese, (mis)-
rén   take for a Chinese
60. Wó-bǎ-nèige-'Rìběn-rén kàn-   I mistook that Japanese for a
zuò-yíge-'Zhōngguo-rén.   Chinese.

hǎo-kàn   pretty
hǎo-kànde-hěn   very pretty
61. Méigui-hǎo-kànde-hěn.   Roses are very pretty.

bùdéliǎo   awfully
dàde-bùdéliǎo   awfully big
62. Tāde-fángzi dàde-bùdéliǎo.   His house is awfully big.

méi-yǒu-rén   there isn't anyone
xǐhuan-mǎi   like to buy
63. Nèisuǒr-fángzi-dàde méi-   That house is so big that no one
yǒu-rén-xǐhuan-mǎi.   wants to buy it.

nènmo   since that's the case
wǒmen-yíkuàr-qù   we go together
64. Nènmo-wǒmen-'yíkuàr-qù   Then how about our going to-
'hǎo-bu-hǎo?   gether?

PATTERN DRILLS

Pattern 17.1. Similarity and Disparity (Note 2 below)

N_1	gēn/xiàng	N_2	yíyàng
Noun$_1$	'with'/'resemble'	Noun$_2$	'alike'
Zhèige-yánse	gēn	nèige-yánse	yíyàng.

'This color is like that color.'

1. Wǒde-biǎo gēn-nǐde-biǎo-yí-yàng.

My watch is like your watch.

2. Nèizhī-bǐ gēn-zhèizhǐ-yí-yàng.

That pen is like this one.

3. 'Jīntiande-tiānqi gēn-'zuó-tiānde-tiānqi-yíyàng.

Today's weather is like yesterday's weather.

4. Shāndong bù-gēn-Shānxi-yí-yàng.

Shantung is not like Shansi.

5. Rìběn-fàn bú-xiàng-'Zhōng-guo-fàn-yíyàng.

Japanese food is not like Chinese food.

6. 'Zhèrde-tiānqi chàbuduō-gēn-'nèrde-tiānqi-yíyàng.

The weather here is almost the same as the weather there.

7. 'Zhōngguo-bǐ bú-xiàng-'Měi-guo-bǐ-yíyàng.

Chinese pens are not like American pens.

8. 'Dàxué bú-xiàng-'zhōngxué-yíyàng.

College isn't like middle school.

9. Zǎofàn-gēn-wǎnfàn bù-yí-yàng.

Breakfast is different from dinner.

10. 'Rìběn-zì gēn-'Zhōngguo-zì yǒude-yíyàng yǒude-'bù-yí-yàng.

Some Japanese and Chinese characters are the same and some are different.

Pattern 17.2. Similarity and Disparity (Note 3 below)

N₁	gēn/xiàng	N₂	yíyàng	V
Noun₁ 'with'/'resemble'		Noun₂	'alike'	Verb
Tā	gēn	nǐ	yíyàng	yònggōng.

'He is as diligent as you are.'

| Tā | gēn | nǐ | yíyàng | xǐhuan-kàn-shū. |

'He likes to read as much as you do.'

1. Wáng-Tàitai xiàng-Wáng-Xiān-sheng yíyàng-yònggōng.

Mrs. Wang is as hard-working as Mr. Wang.

2. Niàn-Zhōngguo-shū gēn-xiě-Zhōngguo-zì yíyàng-nán.

Reading Chinese is as hard as writing Chinese.

3. Zhèige-fàn gēn-wó-mǔqin-zuò-de yíyàng-hǎo-chī.

This food is as delicious as my mother's.

4. Húnánde-shānshuǐ gēn-Húběide yíyàng-hǎo-kàn.

The scenery in Hunan is as beautiful as that in Hupei.

5. Gāo-'Xiáojie-xiě-de-zì gēn-Gāo-'Xiānsheng-xiě-de-zì yí-yàng-hǎo-ma?

Are the characters written by Miss Gao as nice as the characters done by Mr. Gao?

6. 'Zhèige-chá-bēi gēn-'nèige-yí-
    yàng-dà.

This teacup is as big as that
one.

7. Nǐde-zìdiǎn gēn-wǒde-yíyàng-
    xiǎo.

Your dictionary is as small as
mine.

8. 'Wáng-Xiáojie xiàng-ta-mǔ-
    qin yíyàng-piàoliang.

Miss King is as attractive as
her mother.

9. Tā-shuōde-Zhōngwén gēn-
    'Zhōngguo-rén-shuō-de
    yíyàng-hǎo.

The Chinese that he speaks is as
good as that spoken by a Chinese.

10. Tā-niàn-shū xiàng-nǐ-niàn-
    shū yíyàng-hǎo.

He studies as well as you do.

11. Húběi bù-gēn-Shāndong yí-
    yàng-dà-ma?

Isn't Hupeh as large as Shantung?

12. Diànchē bú-xiàng-gōnggòng-
    qìchē yíyàng-kuài.

Streetcars aren't as fast as buses.

13. 'Wǒde-qián bú-xiàng-'nǐde-
    qián yíyàng-duō.

I don't have as much money as
you do.

14. 'Wáng-Tàitai-huà-de-huàr
    xiàng-'Qián-Tàitai-huà-de yí-
    yàng-hǎo.

The paintings done by Mrs. Wang
are as good as those done by
Mrs. Qian.

15. 'Wáng-Xiānsheng bú-xiàng-
    'Zhāng-Xiānsheng yíyàng-
    cōngming.

Mr. King is not as intelligent as
Mr. Johnson.

16. 'Zhōngguo-rén gēn-'wàiguo-
    rén yíyàng-xǐhuan-wár.

Chinese like to have fun as much
as foreigners do.

17. Wǒ-xiàng-tā-yíyàng xīwang-
    dào-'Zhōngguo-qu.

I'm as eager as he is to go to
China.

18. 'Qián-Xiānsheng bú-xiàng-
    'Gāo-Xiānsheng yíyàng-xǐhuan-
    lǚxíng.

Mr. Qian does not like to travel
as much as Mr. Gao does.

19. 'Máo-Xiānsheng xiàng-'Gāo-
    Xiānsheng yíyàng-xǐhuan-kàn-
    shū.

Mr. Mao likes to read as much
as Mr. Gao does.

20. Wǒ-gēn-ta-yíyàng xīwang-dào-
    'Zhōngguo-qu-niàn-shū.

I'm as eager as he is to go to
China to study.

Pattern 17.3. Similarity and Disparity (Note 4 below)

N₁	yǒu/xiàng	N₂	nènmo	V
Noun₁	'have'/'like'	Noun₂	'as'	Verb
Wǒ	yǒu	tā	nènmo	gāo.

'I'm as tall as he is.'

| Wǒ | yǒu | tā | nènmo xǐhuan-kàn-shū. |

'I like to read as much as he does.'

.

1. Wáng-Tàitai yǒu-Wáng-'Xiān-
   sheng-nènmo-cōngming.

   Mrs. King is as smart as Mr.
   King.

2. 'Nèizhāng-dìtú méi-yǒu-zhèi-
   zhāng-zhènmo-hǎo.

   That map isn't as good as this
   one.

3. Zuò-chuán méi-yǒu-zuò-fēijī-
   nènmo-kuài.

   Going by boat isn't as fast as
   going by plane.

4. 'Qián-Xiānsheng-xiě-de-zì
   méi-yǒu-'Gāo-Xiānsheng-xiě-
   de-nènmo-hǎo.

   The characters that Mr. Qian
   writes aren't as nice as those
   written by Mr. Gao.

5. 'Zhèiběn-zìdiǎn méi-yǒu-'nèi-
   běn-nènmo-hǎo.

   This dictionary isn't as good as
   that one.

6. 'Nèiběn-shū méi-yǒu-'zhèiběn-
   shū-zhènmo-róngyi.

   That book isn't as easy as this
   one.

7. 'Qián-Xiáojie méi-yǒu-'Wáng-
   Xiáojie-nènmo-piàoliang.

   Miss Qian is not as attractive as
   Miss Wang.

8. Wǒ-dìdi xiàng-'Bái-Xiānsheng-
   nènmo-yònggōng.

   My younger brother works as
   hard as Mr. Bai.

9. 'Zhèrde-rén méi-yǒu-'nèrde-
   nènmo-duō.

   There aren't as many people
   here as there are there.

10. 'Niàn-Zhōngguo-zì méi-yǒu-
    'xiě-Zhōngguo-zì-nènmo-nán.

    Reading Chinese characters is-
    n't as hard as writing them.

11. Wǒ-bú-xiàng-nǐ nènmo-xīwang-
    dào-'wàiguo-qù.

    I'm not as eager as you are to
    go abroad.

12. 'Wáng-Xiānsheng méi-yǒu-
    'Bái-Xiānsheng nènmo-xǐhuan-
    chī-Zhōngguo-fàn.

    Mr. King does not like to eat
    Chinese food as much as Mr.
    White does.

13. Wǒ-xiàng-nǐ-nènmo-xǐhuan-lǚ-
    xíng.

    I like to travel as much as you
    do.

14. Gāo-Tàitai bú-xiàng-Gāo-'Xiān-
    sheng-nènmo-xīwang Měiyīng-
    dào-'wàiguo-qu-niàn-shū.

    Mrs. Gao is not as eager as Mr.
    Gao for Meiying to go abroad to
    study.

15. Wǒ-bú-xiàng-nǐ nènmo-xīwang-
    jiēhūn.

    I'm not as eager as you are to
    get married.

Pattern 17.4. Similarity and Disparity (Note 5 below)

S	V₁	O₁	V₁	-de	gēn	O₂	yíyàng	SV
Subject	Verb₁	Object₁	Verb₁	-de	'with'	Object₂	'equally'	Stative Verb
Nǐ	niàn	shū	niàn	-de	gēn	tā	yíyàng	hǎo.

'You study as well as he does.'

1. Tā-xiǎng-de gēn-nǐ-yí-
   yàng-kuài.

   He thinks as fast as you do.

2. 'Wàn-Jiàoshòu shuō-de-gēn-   Professor Wanamaker speaks as
    'Zhōngguo-rén yíyàng-hǎo.   well as a Chinese.

3. Tā-niàn-shū niànde-gēn-nǐ-   He studies as well as you do.
    yíyàng-hǎo.

4. Tā-zǒu-lù gēn-nǐ-yíyàng-kuài.   He walks as fast as you do.

5. Tā-chī-fàn gēn-nǐ-yíyàng-duō.   He eats as much as you do.

6. 'Gāo-Xiānsheng-mǎi-shū mǎi-   Mr. Gao buys as many books as
    de-gēn-wǒ-yíyàng-duō.   I do.

7. Tā-kǎoshì-kǎo-de xiàng-wǒ-   He's as busy with exams as I
    yíyàng-máng.   am.

8. 'Gāo-Xiáojie-huà-shānshuǐ   Miss Gao paints landscapes as
    huà-de gēn-'tā-yíyàng-hǎo.   well as he does.

9. Tā-huá-quán-huá-de gēn-nǐ-yí-   He plays 'guess-fingers' as well
    yàng-hǎo.   as you do.

10. Tā-shuō-huà gēn-nǐ-yíyàng-   He talks as slowly as you do.
    màn.

Pattern 17.5.   Similarity and Disparity   (Note 6 below)

S	V₁	O₁	V₁	-de	yǒu/xiàng	O₂	nènmo	SV

S   V$_1$ O$_1$ V$_1$ -de   yǒu/xiàng   O$_2$ nènmo   SV
Subject Verb$_1$ Object$_1$ Verb$_1$ -de   'have'/'like'   Object$_2$ 'as'   Stative Verb
Nǐ   niàn   shū   niàn   -de   yǒu   tā   nènmo   hǎo.
'You study as well as he does.'

1. 'Zhāng-Xiānsheng-xiě-zì-xiě-   Mr. Johnson does not write
    de méi-yóu-nǐ-zhènmo-hǎo.   characters as well as you do.

2. 'Wáng-Xiānsheng shuō-'Zhōng-   Mr. King speaks Chinese as well
    wén-shuō-de xiàng-'nǐ-   as you do.
    zhènmo-hǎo.

3. Tā-kǎoshì-kǎo-de méi-'nǐ-   He isn't as busy with exams as
    zhènmo-máng.   you are.

4. Tā-chī-de xiàng-nǐ-zhènmo-   He eats as fast as you do.
    kuài.

5. 'Máo-Xiānsheng rènshi-zì-   Mr. Mao does not know as many
    rènshide méi-'nǐ-zhènmo-duō.   characters as you do.

6. 'Máo-Xiānsheng-kàn-shū xiàng-   Mr. Mao reads as many books as
    'Gāo-Xiānsheng-nènmo-duō.   Mr. Gao does.

7. 'Qián-Xiānsheng-shuō-Yīng-   Mr. Qian speaks English as well
    wén shuō-de-xiàng-'Yīngguo-   as an Englishman.
    rén-nènmo-hǎo.

8. Sān-Yǒu-Shūdiàn-mài-shū-mài-   The Three Friends Bookstore
    de xiàng-'Wáng-Xiānsheng-   sells as many books as Mr.
    shūdiàn-nènmo-duō.   Wang's bookstore.

9. Tā-jiè-shū-jiè-de méi-yǒu-
    'nǐ-zhènmo-duō.

He doesn't borrow as many
books as you do.

10. Tā-tīng-lùyīn bú-xiàng-'nǐ-
    zhènmo-duō.

He doesn't listen to recordings
as much as you do.

Pattern 17.6. Qualification of Stative Verbs (Note 10 below)

S	SV	-de	A*	
Subject	Stative Verb	-de	A*	
Tā	hǎo	-de	hěn.	'He's very good.'
Tā	hǎo	-de	bùdéliǎo.	'He's awfully good.'
Tā	piàoliang	-de	rén-dōu-xǐhuan-ta.	'She's so attractive every-one likes her.'

1. Shānshang-nèisuǒr-fángzi
    dàde-hěn.

That house on the hill is huge.

2. Nèige-dìfang piàoliangde-
    bùdéliǎo.

That area is awfully attractive.

3. Niǔyue-rén duōde-bùdéliǎo.

New York has a terrific number
of people.

4. Zhèige-chá hǎo-hēde-bùdé-
    liǎo.

This tea is awfully good.

5. Wǒ-mángde méi-jīhui-kàn-
    diànyǐngr.

I'm so busy I don't have time to
see movies.

6. Nèige-xiáojie-piàoliangde hěn-
    duō-rén xiǎng-gēn-ta-jiēhūn.

That young lady is so pretty that
she has lots of suitors.

7. 'Hángzhou-shānshuǐ hǎo-kànde-
    méi-fázi-shuō.

The scenery at Hangchow is in-
describably beautiful.

8. Nèige-xuésheng-'tài-bèn,
    bènde-lián-'yíge-zì-dōu-bu-
    rènshi.

That student is very stupid, so
much so that he doesn't recognize a single character.

9. Nèige-dìfang-piàoliangde chà-
    buduō-'suóyǒude-rén 'dōu-
    xiǎng-dào-nèr-qu-lüxíng.

That place is so beautiful that
almost everyone wants to make
a trip there.

10. Nèige-fángzi-'tài-dà, dàde-
    méi-rén-yào-mǎi.

That house is too big, so much
so that no one wants to buy it.

---

* Where A is hěn 'very,' bùdéliǎo 'extremely,' or else a sentence.

SUBSTITUTION TABLES

I: 32 sentences (Note 2)

(The asterisks here and in Table II below indicate that only
items in the same row may be taken together — zhèrde-tiānqi
with nèrde-tiānqi, Sānfánshì with Niǔyue, etc.)

*				*	
zhèrde-tiānqi	—	xiàng	nèrde-tiānqi	yíyàng	—
Sānfánshì	bu	gēn	Niǔyue		ma
dàxué			zhōngxué		
gāngbǐ			máobǐ		

II: 32 sentences (Note 3)

*			*		
zhèiběn-shū	—	xiàng	nèiběn-shū	yíyàng	—
wǒde-bǐ	bu	gēn	nǐde-bǐ		hǎo
Sūzhou			Hángzhou		
zhèige-yánse			nèige-yánse		

III: 72 sentences (Note 4)

Húnán	(méi) yǒu	Húběi	zhènmo	yuǎn
	(bú) xiàng	Dōngběi	zènmo	dà
			nènmo	hǎo

IV: 72 sentences (Note 5)

(The asterisks here and in Table V below indicate that only
items from the same row may be taken together. Also, either
one of the asterisked columns may be omitted altogether.)

	*	*				
wǒ	shuō-huà	shuō-de	xiàng	tā	yíyàng	—
	niàn-shū	niàn-de	gēn			hǎo
	xiě-zì	xiě-de				kuài
	zuò-shì	zuò-de				màn

V: 64 sentences (Note 6)

	*	*				
wǒ	shuō-huà	shuō-de	(méi) yǒu	tā	zhènmo	hǎo
	xiě-zì	xiě-de·	(bú) xiàng		nènmo	kuài

PRONUNCIATION DRILLS

I. Contrast of Finals in Two-Syllable Pairs

This exercise consists of pairs of expressions which are distinguished in meaning solely by differences in tone on the second syllable. Digits represent tone sequences; 10, for example, means first tone followed by neutral tone.

10 vs. 11–14

dōngxi, dōng-xī
fāde, fādá
xiāzi, xiāzǐ
tāde, tā-dà

11 vs. 10–14

dōng-xī, dōngxi
sānshī, sānshí
fēnfā, fēnfǎ
shān-dōng, shān-dòng

12 vs. 10–14

fādá, fāde
sānshí, sānshī
gāi-mái, gāi-mǎi
gōng-rén, gōng-rèn

13 vs. 10–13

xiāzǐ, xiāzi
fēnfǎ, fēnfā
gāi-mǎi, gāi-mái
gāi-mǎi, gāi-mài

14 vs. 10–13

tā-dà, tāde
shān-dòng, shān-dōng
gōng-rèn, gōng-rén
gāi-mài, gāi-mǎi

20 vs. 21–24

méimao, méi-māo
méi-ne, méi-ná
xíngli, xíng-lǐ
yíge, yígè

21 vs. 20–24

méi-māo, méimao
méi-qiān, méi-qián
qígān, qígǎn
bái-huā, báihuà

22 vs. 20–24

méi-ná, méi-ne
méi-qián, méi-qiān
méi-lí, méi-lǐ
méi-qián, méi-qiàn

23 vs. 20–24

xíng-lǐ, xíngli
qígǎn, qígān
méi-lǐ, méi-lí
qiánjǐn, qiánjìn

24 vs. 20–23

yígè, yíge
báihuà, bái-huā
méi-qiàn, méi-qián
qiánjìn, qiánjǐn

30 vs. 31—34   31 vs. 30—34   32 vs. 30—34

huǒji, huǒjī   huǒjī, huǒji   mǎi-má, mǎi-ma
mǎi-ma, mǎi-má   běifāng, běi-fáng   běi-fáng, běifāng
hǎode, hǎo-dà   wǔ-yī, wǔyì   wǔshí, wǔshì

              (33 vs. 30—34)   34 vs. 30—33

                                          hǎo-dà, hǎode
                                          wǔyì, wǔ-yī
                                          wǔshì, wǔshí

40 vs. 41—44   41 vs. 40—44   42 vs. 40—44

dà-ma, dà-mā   dà-mā, dà-ma   dàodé, dàode
dàode, dàodé   yì-tīng, yì-tíng   yì-tíng, yì-tīng
kuàide, kuài-dǎ   huìzhāng, huìzhǎng   xià-xué, xià-xuě
kuàile, kuàilè   huì-fēi, huì-fèi   xìngmíng, xìngmìng

              43 vs. 40—44   44 vs. 40—43

              kuài-dǎ, kuàide   kuàilè, kuàile
              huìzhǎng, huìzhāng   huì-fèi, huì-fēi
              xià-xuě, xià-xué   xìngmìng, xìngmíng
              kuài-mǎi, kuài-mài   kuài-mài, kuài-mǎi

II.   Tonal Shifts in Three-Syllable Expressions

A.   Changes of Third Tone to Second Tone

If two third-tone syllables occur together, the first changes to second tone. If
three third-tone syllables occur together, the first two change to second tone.
These changes are shown in our transcription.

              330 > 230   331 > 231

        nǐ mǔqin > ní-mǔqin   hěn jiǎndān > hén-jiǎndān
        wǒ xǐhuan > wó-xǐhuan   yě hǎo chī > yé-hǎo-chī
        qǐng wǔge > qíng-wǔge   wǒ mǎi shū > wó-mǎi-shū
        mǎi jiǔge > mái-jiǔge   yě yǒu chē > yé-yǒu-chē

332 > 232		333 > 223	
wǒ lǚxíng	> wó-lǚxíng	wǒ yě yǒu	> wó-yé-yǒu
hěn yǒu míng	> hén-yǒu-míng	nǐ mǎi bǐ	> ní-mái-bǐ
zhǐ yǒu qián	> zhí-yǒu-qián	yě hěn hǎo	> yé-hén-hǎo
yě děi lái	> yé-děi-lái	mǎi wǔběn	> mái-wúběn

334 > 234

yě kǎoshì	> yé-kǎoshì
wǒ xiě zì	> wó-xiě-zì
yě hǎokàn	> yé-hǎokàn
wǔlǐ lù	> wúlǐ-lù

B. Change of Second Tone to First Tone

If a second-tone syllable with light stress occurs as the middle of three tonal syllables and follows a first or second tone, it changes to a first tone when spoken at rapid conversational speed. Since this change does not always take place, however, we do not show it in our writing.

121 > 111	122 > 112	123 > 113	124 > 114
Zhōngwén-shū	sānmáo-qián	dōu-méi-mǎi	sāntiáo-lù
dōu-méi-shuō	tā-méi-yíng	jiānglái-xiě	tā-hái-zuò
tā-néng-fēi	dōu-nán-xué	tā-lái-zhǎo	dōu-méi-kàn
tā-cháng-chī	sānniánjí	xīnán-yǒu	Sānfánshì

221 > 211	222 > 212	223 > 213	224 > 214
shéi-néng-shuō	xué-wénxué	yuánlái-yǒu	Húnán-huà
nín-hái-chī	hái-méi-lái	hái-nán-xiě	lái-xuéxiào
shéi-méi-hē	cóng-Húnán	suírán-yǒu	shéi-tán-huà
cái-néng-jiāo	bié-ná-qián	cái-lái-mǎi	bié-lái-kàn

C. Change of Third Tone to First Tone

If a third-tone syllable with light stress occurs in the middle of a three-syllable expression after a first or second tone and before another third tone, it changes to a first tone in rapid speech. (Note that this change is a combination of the two changes mentioned in A and B.) We show in our transcription only the A change, since the B changes do not always occur.

133 > 123 > 113   233 > 223 > 213

tā yě yǒu   > tā-yé-yǒu   nín děi zǒu   > nín-déi-zǒu

dōu mǎi bǐ   > dōu-mái-bǐ   shéi xiǎng mǎi > shéi-xiáng-mǎi

shū yě hǎo   > shū-yé-hǎo   méi yǒu bǐ   > méi-yóu-bǐ

tā hěn lǎo   > tā-hén-lǎo   ná wǔběn   > ná-wúběn

EXPANSION DRILLS

I

tā

gēn-tā

gēn-tā-yíyàng

gēn-tā-yíyàng-hǎo

bù-gēn-tā-yíyàng-hǎo

nǐ-bù-gēn-tā-yíyàng-hǎo

nǐ-bù-gēn-tā-yíyàng-hǎo-ma

II

kuài

nènmo-kuài

chīde-nènmo-kuài

chīde-yóu-nǐ-nènmo-kuài

tā-chīde-yóu-nǐ-nènmo-kuài

tā-chīde méi-yóu-nǐ-nènmo-kuài

tā-chī-fàn-chīde méi-yóu-nǐ-nènmo-kuài

III

yíyàng

yíyàng-màn

gēn-tā-yíyàng-màn

nǐ-gēn-tā-yíyàng-màn

nǐ-zuò-shì gēn-tā-yíyàng-màn

nǐ-zuò-shì-zuòde gēn-tā-yíyàng-màn

SENTENCE CONVERSION

The Chinese sentences below are converted step by step into quite different sentences.

I. From: Mrs. Gao is very fond of visiting foreign friends.
    To: Professor Wanamaker can't read Chinese books.

1. 'Gāo-Tàitai-hén-xǐhuan bàifang-wàiguo-péngyou.

2. 'Wàn-Tàitai-hén-xǐhuan bàifang-wàiguo-péngyou.

3. 'Wàn-Jiàoshòu-hén-xǐhuan bàifang-wàiguo-péngyou.

4. 'Wàn-Jiàoshòu-hén-xǐhuan kàn-wàiguo-péngyou.

5. 'Wàn-Jiàoshòu-bù-xǐhuan kàn-'wàiguo-péngyou.

6. 'Wàn-Jiàoshòu-bù-xǐhuan kàn-'wàiguo-shū.

7. 'Wàn-Jiàoshòu-bù-xǐhuan kàn-'Zhōngwén-shū.

8. 'Wàn-Jiàoshòu bú-huì-kàn-'Zhōngwén-shū.

II. From: I'm also buying a five-dollar pen tomorrow.
    To: He reads only ten minutes a day.

1. Wǒ-míngtian yé-mái-wǔkuài-qiánde-bǐ.

2. Wǒ-míngtian yé-mái-wǔfēn-qiánde-bǐ.

3. Wǒ-míngtian yé-mái-wǔfēn-qiánde-shū.

4. Wǒ-míngtian jiù-mái-wǔfēn-qiánde-shū.

5. Tā-míngtian jiù-mái-wǔfēn-qiánde-shū.

6. Tā-měitiān jiù-mái-wǔfēn-qiánde-shū.

7. Tā-měitiān jiù-kàn-wǔfēn-zhōngde-shū.

8. Tā-měitiān jiù-kàn-shífēn-zhōngde-shū.

ANSWERING QUESTIONS

1. Qián-Xiānsheng hēle-'sānbēi-chá. Qián-Tàitai hēle-'sìbēi-chá. Tāmen-yígòng-hēle-'jǐbēi-chá?

2. Gāo-Xiānsheng shuō-'Hángzhou-huà. Gāo-Tàitai Gāo-Xiáojie dōu-shuō-'Sūzhou-huà. Shuō-'Hángzhou-huà-de-rén-duō háishi-shuō-'Sūzhóu-huà-de-rén-duō?

3. 'Wáng-Xiānsheng-huá-quán yíngle-liùcì. 'Zhāng-Xiānsheng yíngle-sān-cì. 'Shéi-yíng-le?

4. 'Máo-Xiānsheng qùguo-Hángzhou-wǔcì. 'Bái-Xiānsheng qùguo-sìcì. 'Shéi-qùde-duō?

5. Wáng-Xiānsheng hē-Méigui-Lù. Wáng-'Tàitai-hē-chā. 'Shéi-hē-jiǔ?

6. 'Gāo-Xiáojie huàle-'wǔzhāng-shānshuǐ-huàr.   'Wàn-Xiáojie huà-le-
    'liǎngzhāng.   Huà-wǔzhāng-de-shi-shéi?

7. 'Zhāng-Xiānsheng jiēhūn-wǔnián-le. 'Wáng-Xiānsheng jiēhūn-qīnián-le.
    Shéi-'xiān-jiēhūn?

8. Wǒ-qùguo-Xī-Hú-liǎngcì.   Tā-qùguo-Xī-Hú-yícì.   Tā-qùguo-'jǐcì?

9. Wǒ-líkai-Hángzhou shí-wǔnián. Tā-líkai-Hángzhou shí'èrnián.   Shéi-
    'xiān-líkai-Hángzhou?

10. Tā-xǐhuan-nuǎnhuode-tiānqi. Wó-xǐhuan-bù-nuǎnhuode-tiānqi.   'Shéi-
     xǐhuan-nuǎnhuode-tiānqi?

NOTES

1. The expression yǒu yìdiǎr—literally 'have a little'—is used in the meaning
    'somewhat' before verbs:

    Wǒ-zhèi-jǐtiān yǒu-yìdiǎr-máng.   'I've been somewhat busy these
        few days.'
    Tā-yǒu-yìdiǎr xiàng-ta-mǔqin. 'He somewhat resembles his moth-
        er.'

2. The expression yíyàng—literally 'one kind'—as a verb means 'be alike,'
    'be like,' 'similar to':

    Zhèi-liángběn-shū yíyàng. 'These two books are alike.'
    Zhèi-liángběn-shū bù-yíyàng. 'These two books are not alike.' or
        'These two books are different.'

    If the things being compared are mentioned separately, they are con-
    nected by gēn 'with' or xiàng 'resemble':

    Wǒde-bǐ gēn-tāde-bǐ yíyàng.
        or   } 'My pen is like his pen.'
    Wǒde-bǐ xiàng-tāde-bǐ yíyàng.

    (See also Supplementary Lesson 17, Note 2)

3. Yíyàng used adverbially before a verb means 'equally' or 'as':

    Wǒde-bǐ gēn-tāde-bǐ yíyàng-hǎo. or
    Wǒde-bǐ xiàng-tāde-bǐ yíyàng-hǎo.
        'My pen is as good as his.' [lit. 'My pen and his pen are equally
        good.']

    In this construction, bu 'not' and other adverbial modifiers are placed
    before either gēn 'with, and' or xiàng 'resemble':

    Wǒde-bǐ bù-gēn-tāde-bǐ yíyàng-hǎo. or
    Wǒde-bǐ bú-xiàng-tāde-bǐ yíyàng-hǎo.
        'My pen isn't as good as his pen.'

    In sentences with gēn 'with, and' it is possible also to put an adverbial
    modifier before yíyàng:

    Wǒde-bǐ gēn-tāde-bǐ bù-yíyàng-hǎo. 'My pen isn't as good as his
        pen.'

A few verbs other than stative verbs (e.g. hǎo 'good') are used in this construction. Note xǐhuan in the following example:

Wǒ-gēn-nǐ yíyàng-xǐhuan-kàn-diànyǐngr. 'I like to see movies as much as you do.' [lit. 'I and you equally like to see movies.']

(See also Supplementary Lesson 17, Note 2)

4. An alternative way of expressing similarity and disparity is to use yǒu 'have' or xiàng 'resemble' in the coverb position before a verb which is itself preceded by any of the adverbs nènmo, zhènmo, or zènmo 'so':

Ní-yǒu-tā-nènmo-hǎo.
or
Nǐ-xiàng-tā-nènmo-hǎo. } 'You are as good as he is.'

Tā-yóu-nǐ-zhènmo-hǎo.
or
Tā-xiàng-nǐ-zhènmo-hǎo. } 'He is as good as you are.'

The negative forms of these sentences use méi before yǒu and bú before xiàng:

Nǐ-méi-yǒu-tā-nènmo-hǎo.
or
Nǐ-bú-xiàng-tā-nènmo-hǎo. } 'You're not as good as he is.'

In sentences containing yǒu the adverbs nènmo, zhènmo, and zènmo can be omitted:

Nǐ-méi-yǒu-tā-nènmo-hǎo.
or
Nǐ-méi-yǒu-tā-hǎo. } 'You're not as good as he is.'

5. The constructions described in Note 3 are also used in sentences comparing how an action is performed:

Nǐ-xiě-zì xiěde-gēn-tā-yíyàng-hǎo. 'You write as well as he does.'

In such sentences, xiě-zì and xiěde are optional:

Ní-xiěde gēn-tā-yíyàng-hǎo.
or
Ní-xiě-zì gēn-tā-yíyàng-hǎo. } 'You write as well as he does.'

(See also Supplementary Lesson 17, Note 2)

6. The constructions discussed in Note 4 are also used in sentences comparing how an action is performed:

Ní-xiě-zì xiěde-méi-yǒu-tā-nènmo-hǎo. 'You don't write as well as he does.'

Here also, xiě-zì and xiěde are optional.

7. The verb zuò 'do' is used as a postverb in kànzuò 'regard as,' bǐzuò 'rank as, equate with':

Wó-bǎ-ta kànzuò-wǒde-péngyou. 'I regarded him as my friend.'
Wó-bǎ èr-zì kànzuò-sān-zì. 'I took the character two to be the character three.'
Wó-bǎ-nèige-'zhōngxuéde-xuésheng bǐzuò-'dàxuéde-xuésheng. 'I rank that high-school student as a college student.'

8. The Chinese tendency to use two-syllable expressions as full forms and monosyllables as combining forms is illustrated by the contrast of <u>bēi</u> and <u>bēizi</u>. The latter is a fully independent word for 'cup':

    Zhèige-bēizi-tài-dà-le. 'This cup is too large.'

    <u>Bēi</u> is used as a combining nominal form (<u>chá-bēi</u> 'teacup,' <u>xiǎo-bēi</u> 'small cup') as well as a measure (<u>sānbēi-chá</u> 'three cups of tea').

9. The measure <u>xiē</u> is used as a general pluralizing form:

    Zhèibĕn-shū-shi-wŏde. 'This book is mine.'
    Zhèixiē-shū-shi-wŏde. 'These books are mine.'

    <u>Xiē</u> is not used if a specific number is mentioned (except in the expression <u>yìxiē</u> 'a few'):

    Zhèi-sānbĕn-shū-shi-wŏde. 'These three books are mine.'

    <u>Xiē</u> 'few' combines with <u>hǎo</u> 'good' in <u>hǎoxiē</u> 'a good many, a good deal':

    Mǎi-yìsuŏr-fángzi yào-hǎoxiē-qián. 'Buying a house requires quite a lot of money.'

    <u>Hǎoxiē</u> is often used after <u>yǒu</u> 'have' in the shared-object-subject construction described in Lesson 9 (Note 7, p. 118):

    Zuótian-yóu-hǎoxie-xuésheng lái-kǎoshì. 'Yesterday there were quite a few students who came to take the exams.'

    <u>Xiē</u> is also used in the combination <u>yǒu-xiē</u> meaning 'some':

    Nèige-shūdiàn-mǎi-de-shū, yǒu-xiē-shi-hǎo-de, yǒu-xiē-shi-bú-hǎo-de. '(Of) the books sold by that bookstore, some are good, some are bad.'

10. The most common type of qualifier for a stative verb is a preceding adverb:

    hĕn-dà 'quite large'

    Stative verbs can also be qualified by the suffix <u>de</u> plus a following qualifying expression:

    dàde-hĕn 'very large'
    dàde-bùdéliǎo 'awfully big'
    dàde-méi-rén-yào 'so big that no one wants (it)'

Lesson 18 REVIEW

PRONUNCIATION REVIEW

All the possible tonal combinations of three syllables are here illustrated with vocabulary from the first three Units. The digits to the left indicate the tone of the first syllables, those at the top the tones of the second and third syllables. Asterisks indicate expressions which have undergone tonal shifts. (See Lesson 17, Pronunciation Drill II, pp. 288–90, for these and other possible changes in tone.)

	0 0	0 1	0 2	0 3	0 4
1	zhīdaole	xiānsheng-shuō	tāmen-lái	chībuliǎo	shuōde-màn
2	háizide	xuésheng-tīng	róngyi-xué	xuéde-hǎo	fángzi-dà
3	xǐhuan-ma	zěnmo-shuō	xǐhuan-lái	xiěde-hǎo	pǎode-kuài
4	tàitaide	màide-duō	wàngle-ná	niànbuliǎo	kànbujiàn

	1 0	1 1	1 2	1 3	1 4
1	gāozhōngde	sānfēn-zhōng	yīngdāng-xué	xīngqīwǔ	fēijī-kuài
2	rén-duō-le	méi-tīngshuō	xué-Zhōngwén	shízhí-bǐ	néng-chī-fàn
3	wǒ-shuōde	wǒ-jiāo-shū	xiě-Yīngwén	mǎi-gāngbǐ	yě-chī-fàn
4	kuài-chī-ba	lùyīnjī	niàn-kēxué	sìzhībǐ	dào-shūdiàn

	2 0	2 1	2 2	2 3	2 4
1	dōu-lái-le	tā-huí-jiā	zhēn-nán-xué	gōngyuán-yuǎn	tā-méi-kàn
2	shéi-lái-le	hái-méi-chī	xué-wénxué	méi-qián-mǎi	Húnán-huà
3	wǒ-xuéde	yě-méi-shuō	qǐng-nín-lái	yǒu-qián-mǎi	hěn-nán-niàn
4	tài-róngyi	zuì-nán-shuō	dào-Húnán	zuì-nán-zhǎo	shàng-xuéxiào

	3 0	3 1	3 2	3 3	3 4
1	shū-mǎi-le	zhēn-hǎo-chī	tā-yǒu-qián	gāngbǐ-hǎo*	xiān-mǎi-piào
2	nán-zǒu-ma	shíběn-shū	Húběi-rén	qián-hén-shǎo*	shíjiǔsuì
3	mái-běnzi*	hén-hǎo-chī*	jiúbǎi-rén*	wó-yóu-bǐ*	hén-hǎo-kàn*
4	tài-hǎo-le	qù-mǎi-shū	yào-wǔmáo	wàng-béi-guǎi*	zuì-hǎo-kàn

	4 0	4 1	4 2
1	dōu-mài-le	tīng-lùyīn	dōu-tài-nán
2	hái-zuò-ma	néng-shàng-shān	shíkuài-qián
3	kǎoshì-le	yě-yònggōng	mǎi-dìtú
4	zuì-dà-de	zì-tài-duō	màipiàoyuán

	4 3	4 4
1	shān-tài-xiǎo	tā-zuì-dà
2	rén-tài-shǎo	lí-zhèr-jìn
3	yǒu-sìběn	yě-tài-dà
4	jiè-zìdiǎn	sìwànkuài

ANALOGY DRILL

The drills below consist of three parts: (1) a statement, (2) a question, and (3) an answer. In Section A, all three are given; in Section B, only the statement is given. To perform Section B, the teacher says the statement, one student asks an appropriate question on the analogy of those in Section A, and another student makes an appropriate response, again on the foregoing analogy. Examples:

Ta-'bú-xìng-Wáng. 'His name isn't King.'
Ta-bú-xìng-Wáng xìng-shénmo? 'If his name isn't King, what is his name?'
Ta-xìng-Zhāng. 'His name is Johnson.'

Jīntian bú-shi-xīngqīyī. 'Today isn't Monday.'
Jīntian bú-shi-xīngqīyī shi-xīngqījǐ? 'If today isn't Monday what day of the week is it?'
Jīntian shi-xīngqī'èr. 'Today is Tuesday.'

Zhèi-bú-shi-'gāngbǐ. 'This isn't a fountain pen.'
Zhèi-bú-shi-'gāngbǐ shi-shénmo? 'If this isn't a fountain pen what is it?'
Zhèi-shi-'qiānbǐ. 'This is a pencil.'

Wǒ-bú-niàn-shū. 'I don't study.'
Nǐ-bú-niàn-shū zuò-shénmo? 'If you don't study what do you do?'
Wǒ-zuò-shì. 'I work.'

Section A

1. Wǒ-bù-chī-'Zhōngguo-fàn. Nǐ-bù-chī-'Zhōngguo-fàn chī-shénmo? Wǒ-chī-'Měiguo-fàn.

2. Zhèi-bú-shi-wǒde-shū. Zhèi-bú-shi-'nǐde-shū shi-'shéide-shū?   Shi-'Zhāng-Xiānshengde-shū.

3. Wǒ-bú-huà-huàr. Nǐ-bú-huà-huàr zuò-shénmo? Wó-xiě-zì.

4. Wǒ-jīntian bù-tīng-lùyīn. Nǐ-bù-tīng-lùyīn zuò-shénmo? Wǒ-niàn-shū.   .

5. Wǒ-bú-shàng-Hángzhou. Nǐ-bú-shàng-'Hángzhou shàng-nǎr? Wǒ-shàng-Sūzhou.

6. Wǒ-míngtian 'bú-qù-lǔxíng. Nǐ-bù-lǔxíng zuò-shénmo? Kàn-diànyǐngr.

7. Wǒ-bù-hē-jiǔ. Nǐ-bù-hē-jiǔ hē-shénmo? Wǒ-hē-chá.

8. Tā-xiě-xìn bú-yòng-máobǐ. Tā-bú-yòng-'máobǐ yòng-shénmo?   Tā-yòng-'gāngbǐ.

9. Wǒ-bú-shàng-xuéxiào. Nǐ-bú-shàng-xuéxiào shàng-nǎr?   Shàng-túshū-guǎn.

10. 'Qián-Xiānsheng jīnnian-bú-dào-'Měiguo-qu.   Tā-bú-dào-'Měiguo dào-nǎr-qu? Tā-dào-'Rìběn-qu.

11. 'Gāo-Xiānsheng 'wúdiǎn-zhōng-bù-lái. Tā-'wúdiǎn-zhōng-bù-lái 'jídiǎn-zhōng-lái? Tā-'liùdiǎn-zhōng-lái.

12. Wó-mǔqin sìyue-'bú-dào-Měiguo-lái. Tā-'sìyue-bù-lái 'shénmo-shíhou-lái? Tā-'báyue-lái.

13. 'Qián-Xiānsheng jīnnian-bú-dào-Yīngguo-qu. Tā-jīnnian bú-dào-'Yīng-guo-qu dào-nǎr-qu? Tā-dào-Měiguo-qu.

14. Wǒ-jīntian-bù-mǎi-shū-qu. Nǐ-jīntian-bù-mǎi-shū mǎi-shénmo?   Wó-mǎi-mòshuǐ-qu.

15. Wǒ-bú-zài-'Yuǎndōng-Dàxué-niàn-shū. Nǐ-bú-zài-'Yuǎndōng-Dàxué-niàn-shū zài-'nǎr-niàn-shū? Wǒ-zài-'zhōngxué-niàn-shū.

16. Wǒ-fùqin bù-xǐhuan-chī-'Zhōngguo-fàn. Tā-bù-xǐhuan chī-'Zhōngguo-fàn xǐhuan-chī-'shénmo-fàn? Tā-xǐhuan-chī-'Měiguo-fàn.

17. Tā-bú-xiàng-ta-mǔqin. Tā-bú-xiàng-ta-mǔqin xiàng-shéi?   Tā-xiàng-tā-fùqin.

18. Wǒ-'bù-xiáng-mǎi-biǎo. Nǐ-bù-mǎi-biǎo mǎi-shénmo? Wó-xiáng-mǎi-shū.

19. Tā-bú-zài-'zhōngxué-jiāo-shū. Tā-bú-zài-zhōngxué-jiāo-shū   zài-'nǎr-jiāo-shū? Tā-zài-'xiǎoxué-jiāo-shū.

20. 'Wǒmen-bù-huānying-ta. 'Nǐmen-bù-huānying-ta   'shéi-huānying-ta? 'Méi-rén-huānying-ta.

21. Wǒ-jīntian-bú-shàng-kè. Nǐ-bú-shàng-kè zuò-shénmo? Wǒ-tīng-lùyīn.

22. Wǒ-bú-zài-sìniánjí. Nǐ-bú-zài-'sìniánjí zài-'jǐniánjí? Wǒ-zài-'sān-
     niánjí.

23. Wǒ-duì-'kēxué-méi-yǒu-xìngqu. Nǐ-duì-'kēxué-méi-yǒu-xìngqu duì-
     'shénmo-yǒu-xìngqu? Wǒ-duì-'yǔyánxué-yǒu-xìngqu.

24. Wǒ-bù-xǐhuan 'zhèige-fāngfǎ. Nǐ-bù-xǐhuan 'zhèige-fāngfǎ xǐhuan-'něi-
     ge-fāngfǎ? Wó-xǐhuan-'nèige-fāngfǎ.

25. Wǒ-bù-shífēn-xǐhuan chī-'Zhōngguo-fàn. Nǐ-bù-xǐhuan chī-'Zhōngguo-
     fàn xǐhuan-chī-'shénmo-fàn? Wó-xǐhuan chī-'Rìběn-fàn.

26. Wǒ-bú-yòng-'Zhōngwén-xiě-xìn. Nǐ-bú-yòng-'Zhōngwén-xiě-xìn yòng-
     'shénmo-wén-xiě-xìn? Wǒ-yòng-'Yīngwén-xiě-xìn.

27. Nèige-háizi 'zuì-bù-xǐhuan-kàn-shū. Tā-bù-xǐhuan-kàn-shū xǐhuan-
     zuò-shénmo? Tā-xǐhuan-wár.

28. Wǒmen-jīntian xuébuwán-dì-'sānkè. Nǐmen-xuébuwán-dì-'sānkè xué-
     dewán-dì-jǐkè? Wǒmen-xuédewán-dì-'èrkè.

29. Wǒ-jīntian-bù-xiǎng-tīng 'liǎngge-zhōngtóude-lùyīn. Nǐ-bù-xiǎng-tīng
     'liǎngge-zhōngtóude-lùyīn xiǎng-tīng-'jǐge-zhōngtóude-lùyīn? Wó-xiǎng-
     tīng 'yíge-zhōngtóude-lùyīn.

30. Tā-méi-bǎ-zìdiǎn-géi-wo. Tā-méi-ba-'zìdiǎn-géi-ni bǎ-'shénmo-géi-
     ni-le? Tā-bǎ-'dìtú-géi-wo-le.

31. 'Zhèige-fázi bù-hǎo. 'Zhèige-fázi-bù-hǎo 'shénmo-fázi-hǎo?   'Méi-
     you-hǎo-fázi.

32. Wó-géi-ni-'jièshao-de-nèiwèi-péngyou bú-shi-jiàoshòu. Tā-bú-shi-'jiào-
     shòu shi-shénmo? Tā-shi-'zhōngxué-jiàoyuán.

33. Bié-bǎ-zhèxiē-dōngxi nájìn-fángzi-qu. Bù-nájìn-fángzi-qu nádào-nǎr-
     qu? Nádào-shūdiàn-qu.

34. Bú-shi-'wǒ-gàosu-xiānsheng-de. Bú-shi-'nǐ-gàosu-xiānsheng-de shi-
     shéi-gàosu-xiānsheng-de? Shi-'tā-gàosu-xiānsheng-de.

35. Tā-bú-shi-zài-'Zhōngguo-zhǎng-dà-de. Tā-bú-shi-zài-'Zhōngguo-zhǎng-
     dà-de shi-zài-'nár-zhǎng-dà-de? Tā-shi-zài-'Měiguo-zhǎng-dà-de.

36. Jīntian-bú-shi-'wǔhào. Jīntian-bú-shi-'wǔhào shi-'jǐhào? Jīntian-shi-
     'liùhào.

37. Xī-Shān bú-zài-xīnánbiar. Xī-Shān bú-zài-xīnánbiar zài-něibiar? Xī-
     Shān-zài-xīběibiar.

38. Wǒmen-bú-zài-'zhèr-xià-chē. Wǒmen-bú-zài-'zhèr-xià-chē zài-'nǎr-
     xià-chē? Wǒmen-zài-gōngyuán-mén-kǒur-xià-chē.

39. Wǒmen-bú-mài 'hóng-mòshuǐ. Nǐmen-bú-mài 'hóng-mòshuǐ mài-'shén-
     mo-yánse-mòshuǐ? Wǒmen-jiù-mài-'hēi-mòshuǐ, 'lán-mòshuǐ.

40. Wǒ-bú-shi-děng-Gāo-Xiáojie. Nǐ-bú-shi-děng-Gāo-Xiáojie děng-shéi?
    Wǒ-děng-Gāo-Xiānsheng.

41. Tā-bú-shi-'qùnian-jiēhūn-de. Tā-bú-shi-'qùnian-jiēhūn-de shì-'shénmo-
    shíhou-jiēhūn-de? Tā-shì-'jīnnian-jiēhūn-de.

42. Tiānqi-bù-hǎode-shíhou wǒ-bú-dào-gōngyuán-qu. Nǐ-bú-dào-gōngyuán-
    qu dào-nǎr-qu? Wǒ-'bú-dào-nǎr-qu.

43. Tā-huá-quán bú-shi-yíngle-'sāncì. Tā-bú-shi-yíngle-'sāncì yíngle-'jǐ-
    cì? Tā-yíngle-'liǎngcì.

44. Chī-de-dōngxi bú-shi-'wǒ-mǎi-de. Bú-shi-'nǐ-mǎi-de shi-'shéi-mǎi-
    de? Shi-'tā-mǎi-de.

45. 'Liǎngge-běnzi-bú-gòu. 'Liǎngge-běnzi-bú-gòu 'jǐge-běnzi-gòu-ne?
    'Sānge-běnzi-cái-gòu-ne.

Section B

1. Wǒ-jīntian bú-dào-túshūguǎn-qu.

2. Wǒ-méi-yǒu-yìbǎikuài-qián.

3. Wǒ-bù-gěi-ta-qián.

4. Tā-yuánlái bù-xǐhuan-yánjiu-kēxué.

5. Wǒ-jiānglái bú-niàn-dàxué.

6. Tā-bù-xǐhuan-jiāo-shū.

7. Wǒ-jīntian bù-xiǎng-chūqu.

8. Wǒ-bù-xǐhuan zhùzai-shānshang.

9. Tā-bù-xǐhuan kāi-diànchē.

10. Wǒ-bù-xiáng-mǎi-chá-bēi.

11. Wǒ-bù-xǐhuan-lǚxíng.

12. Tā-bú-shi-zài-'Húnán-shēng-de.

13. Tā-bú-shi-'zǎochen-lái-de.

14. Tā-bú-niàn-'yìniánjí.

15. Tā-bú-duì 'Gāo-Xiānsheng-shuō-huà.

16. Wǒ-bù-géi-wǒ-mǔqin-mǎi-shū.

17. Zhèige-bú-jiào-qiānbǐ.

18. Wǒmen-jīntian bú-niàn-dì-shíjiǔkè.

19. Zhèige-zì bú-shi-wǒ-xiě-de.

20. Wǒ-bú-zuò-fēijī-qù.

21. Zhèige-zìdiǎn bú-shi-wǒde.

22. Wǒmen-bú-wàng-béi-guǎi.

23. Tā-bú-xìng-Bái.

24. Tā-bú-zhù-Niǔyue.

25. Bú-shi-'tā-gàosu-wǒ-de.

REPLACEMENT DRILL

Replace some element in each sentence with the parenthesized expression to
the right.

1. Tāde-Zhōngguo-huà bú-cuò.   (hén-hǎo)

2. Wǒmen-zuì-hǎo déng-jǐfēn-zhōng.   (yìhuěr)

3. Wǒmen-bìděi-dào-biéde-dìfang-qu.   (děi)

4. Nǐ-wèi-shénmo méi-dài-biǎo?   (mǎi)

5. **Nǐ-kàn zhèizhāng-shānshuǐ-huàr 'hǎo-bù-hǎo?   (zěnmoyàng)**

6. Nǐmen-yīngdāng měitiān-tīng 'liǎngge-zhōngtóu-lùyīn.   (gāi)

7. Tā-shuō-de-huà wo-'dōu-dǒng.   (míngbai)

8. Tā-qǐngle-hěn-duō-kèren, kěshi-lián-'yíge-rén dōu-méi-lái.   (yě)

9. 'Zhèige-dōngxi gēn-'nèige-dōngxi-yíyàng.   (xiàng)

10. Nèige-lǎo-xiānsheng hén-yǒu-qián.   (míng)

11. Yìqiānkuài-qián 'gòu-bu-gòu?   (wàn)

12. Wǒmen-chī-fàn-yǐqián xiān-hē-chá.   (huá-quán)

13. Wó-zhí-yǒu-sānkuài-qián.   (jiù)

14. Rúguó-wó-yǒu-jīhui wǒ-yídìng-dào-nèr-qu-lǚxíng.   (gōngfu)

15. Wǒmen-dōu-mángde-hěn.   (bùdéliǎo)

16. Wó-bǎ-ta kànzuò-yíge-xuésheng.   (jiàoyuán)

17. Wǒmen-kuài-yào-kǎo-shū-le.   (kǎoshì)

18. Wǒ-yìdiǎr-dōu-bù-míngbai.   (shénmo)

19. Zhèiyàng bú-xiàng-nèiyàng nènmo-hǎo.   (méi-yǒu)

20. Tāmen-dāngrán chī-'Zhōngguo-fàn.   (yídìng)

INSERTION DRILL

Insert into the following items the material in parentheses. This may require
you to combine the two sentences into one. For example:

Wǒ-máng. Lián-'fàn-dōu-bù-néng-chī. (de)
'I'm busy. I can't even eat.'

Insertion of <u>de</u> into these sentences gives a single sentence: '

Wǒ-mángde lián-'fàn-dōu-bù-néng-chī.
'I'm so busy I can't even eat.'

1. Wǒ-méi-gōngfu, bù-néng-qu-kàn-diànyǐngr. (yīnwei . . . suóyi)

2. Tā-bìyè-le. Dào-'Rìběn-qu-le. (yǐhòu . . . jiu)

3. Nèige-xuéxiào yǒu-'Zhōngguo-xuésheng, yǒu-'wàiguo-xuésheng. (yě. . . yě)

4. Tā-méi-yǒu-qián. Hái-yào-qu-kàn-diànyǐngr. (suírán . . . kěshi)

5. Tāmen-dōu-bèn. Méi-yǒu-rén-xǐhuan-tāmen. (de)

6. Tā-huì-shuō-'Zhōngguo-huà, huì-xiě-'Zhōngguo-zì. (yě . . . yě)

7. Nǐ-méi-yǒu-qián. Bù-néng-mǎi-shū. (rúguǒ . . . jiu)

8. Tā-chī-fàn. Dào-túshūguǎn-qu. (xiān . . . hòu)

9. Wó-xiǎng-qu-bàifang-péngyou. Méi-yǒu-gōngfu. (kěshi)

10. Wǒ-yào-kǎoshì-le, bù-néng-qu-wár. (yīnwei . . . suóyi)

11. Wǒ-jīntian-méi-niàn-shū, yě-méi-xiě-zì. (búdàn . . . érqiě)

12. Bái-Xiānsheng-cōngming, érqiě-yònggōng. (yòu . . . yòu)

13. Wó-yǒu-gōngfu. Yídìng-dào-nín-jiā-qu. (rúguǒ)

14. Nèige-xuésheng-hěn-bèn, yě-bú-yònggōng. (búdàn . . . érqiě)

15. Wǒ-néng-kàn-Zhōngwén-shū, bù-néng-xiě-Zhōngguo-zì. (suírán . . . kěshi)

16. Wǒ-xué-yǔyán. 'Měitiān-tīng-lùyīn. (de-shíhou)

17. Wǒ-méi-yǒu-gōngfu-qu-wár. Méi-yǒu-qián. (búdàn . . . érqiě)

18. Tā-niànguo-dàxué. Méi-bìyè. (kěshi)

19. Tā-xuéle-yìniánde-'Zhōngguo-huà-le. Yíjù-'Zhōngguo-huà yě-bù-néng-shuō. (suírán . . . kěshi)

20. Wǒ-zuòwán-le-shì. Wǒmen-kéyi-zǒu. (yǐhòu . . . jiu)

TRANSFORMATION DRILL

A. Transformation from Affirmative to Negative.

Note that there are several possible types of transformation, depending on the form of the affirmative sentence.

1. Tā-zuótian-lái-le. Tā-zuótian-'méi-lái.

2. Tā-shi-zài-Dōngběi-shēng-de. Tā-'bú-shi-zài-Dōngběi-shēng-de.

3. Tā-zài-Húnán-zhǎng-dà-de. Tā-'bú-shi-zài-Húnán-zhǎng-dà-de.

4. Tā-kǎodeshàng-dàxué. Tā-kǎobushàng-dàxué.

5. Nǐ-déi-zǒu. Nǐ-'bú-bǐ-zǒu.

6. Tā-dào-nǎr-qu? Tā-'bú-dào-nǎr-qu.

7. Tāde-xuéwen-hén-hǎo. Tāde-xuéwen-'bù-hén-hǎo.

8. Tā-zài-'Gāo-Xiānsheng-jiā-chī-fàn. Tā-'bú-zài-Gāo-Xiānsheng-jiā-
    chī-fàn.

9. Tā-shuō-'Zhōngguo-huà shuōde-hén-hǎo.   Tā-shuō-'Zhōngguo-huà
    shuōde-'bù-hén-hǎo.

10. Wǒmen-xià-xīngqī niàndedào-dì-'èrshikè. Wǒmen-xià-xīngqī niàn-
     budào-dì-'èrshikè.

B. Transformation from Indefinite Active to Definite Passive.

In the first of each pair of sentences below, the object is either definite or
indefinite, the verb is active, and the time is immaterial. In the second,
the object is always definite, the time is past, and the translation can be
expressed as a passive. For example:

> Tāmen-mài-shū. 'They sell books.'
> Shū-shi-'tāmen-mài-de. 'The books were sold by them.'

1. Gāo-Xiáojie huà-huàr. Huàr shi-'Gāo-Xiáojie-huà-de.

2. 'Wàn-Jiàoshòu xiěle-zhèibén-shū. Zhèibén-shū shi-'Wàn-Jiàoshòu-
    xiě-de.

3. Tā-mǎile-nèige-'zìdiǎn-méi-yǒu? Nèige-zìdiǎn shi-'tā-mǎi-de-ma?

4. Tā-mǎi-piào. Piào-shi-'tā-mǎi-de.

5. 'Gāo-Tàitai zuò-'Zhōngguo-fàn. 'Zhōngguo-fàn   shi-'Gāo-Tàitai-
    zuò-de.

6. Tā-xiěle-sānbén-shū-le. Sānbén-shū shi-'tā-xiě-de.

7. Tā-zài-túshūguǎn-jiè-shū. Shū-shi-tā-zài-'túshūguǎn-jiè-de.

8. Wó-géi-tā-qián. Qián-shi-'wó-géi-ta-de.

9. 'Wáng-Xiānsheng jiāo-wo-Zhōngwén. Zhōngwén shi-'Wáng-Xiān-
    sheng-jiāo-wo-de.

10. Wó-xiě-xìn. Xìn-shi-'wó-xiě-de.

MISCELLANEOUS SENTENCES

(Read aloud and translate)

1. Xià-kè-yǐhòu wǒ-jiù-huí-jiā.

2. 'Gāo-Xiáojie zuótian-mǎile-yíge-biǎo.

3. Tā-'gāozhōng-hái-méi-niànwán jiù-yào-kǎo-dàxué.

4. Wǒ-xīngqīliù xiǎng-qu-kàn-diànyǐngr.

5. Nèiwèi-jiàoyuán-hén-hǎo. Wǒmen-'dōu-huānying-ta.

6. Qíng-nǐ-kàn wó-xiě-de-zhè-jǐge-'Zhōngguo-zì 'duì-bu-duì.

7. Xué-yǔyán yǒu-'yídìngde-fāngfǎ.

8. Nǐ-chīguo-'Zhōngguo-fàn-ma? Wǒ-chīguo-hěn-duō-cì-le.

9. Wó-yóu-wǔqiānkuài-qián wǒ-jiù-dào-Yīngguo-Měiguo qù-lǚxíng.

10. 'Gāo-Xiáojie zhǎngde-'shífēn-piàoliang.

11. 'Qián-Xiānsheng yòng-wǔwànkuài-qián mǎile-yìsuǒr-fángzi.

12. Jīntian wǒ-hái-méi-géi-wo-nǔ-péngyou-xiě-xìn-ne.

13. 'Máo-Xiānsheng duì-kēxué-'hén-yǒu-xìngqu.

14. 'Gāo-Xiānsheng-láile-yìhuěr jiù-zǒu-le.

15. 'Bái-Xiānsheng yuánlái-shi-xué-'kēxué-de. Hòulái yòu-xué-wénxué-le.

16. Wó-měitiān děi-tīng yíge-zhōngtóude-lùyīn.

17. Yīnwei-tā-bìng-le, suóyi-jīntian-bú-dào-xuéxiào-lái.

18. Nǐ-míngtian-sāndiǎn-zhōng 'yídìng-dào-túshūguǎn-qù-ma? Wǒ-dāng-rán-qù-le.

19. 'Kuài-yào-kǎoshì-le. Wó-děi-yònggōng-niàn-shū-le.

20. Wǒ-xīwang-jiānglái néng-shàng-'Zhōngguo-qu-niàn-shū.

21. Wǒmen-'dōu-xǐhuan nèiwèi-jiàoyuán. Tā-jiāo-shū jiāode-hǎojíle.

22. Wǒ-jiānglái-yǒu-jīhui yě-dào-wàiguo-qu-lǚxíng.

23. 'Bái-Xiānsheng rènshi-'Máo-Xiānsheng. Shi-'Qián-Xiānsheng-jièshao-de.

24. Zuótian gēn-jǐge-péngyou yíkuàr-shàng-shān-le.

25. Wǒmen-xué-yǔyán yīngdāng-měitiān-tīng-lùyīn.

26. Wáng-Xiānsheng-bìng-le. Wǒ-yīnggai-qu-kànkan-ta.

27. Tā-jiā-zhùzai-shānshang. Mǎi-dōngxi-hěn-máfan.

28. 'Bái-Xiānsheng búdàn-'shū-niànde-hǎo, érqiě-zì yé-xiěde-hǎo.

29. Yuǎndōng-Dàxué kǎoshì-xiě-Zhōngguo-zì. Yígòng-kǎole èrbǎi-duō-ge-zì. 'Bái-Xiānsheng lián-'yíge-zì dōu-méi-xiěcuò.

30. Xué-yǔyán, tīng-lùyīn-zhèige-fāngfǎ zhēn-hǎo.

31. Liǎngge-rén-kāishǐ-rènshi yídìng-děi-shuō "Jiúyǎng, jiúyǎng."

32. Nèige-háizi sìsuì-le. Lián-yíjù-huà yě-bú-huì-shuō.

33. Gāo-Tàitai gěi-Gāo-Xiáojie-kāi-mén.

34. Nèige-háizi-bènjíle. Niànle-yìnián-shū lián-yíge-zì yě-bú-rènshi.

35. Tā-bǎ-jiā-lǐtou 'suóyǒude-shū 'dōu-nádào-xuéxiào-qu-le.

36. Yǒude-rén-xǐhuan-lǚxíng, yǒude-rén xǐhuan-kàn-diànyǐngr.

37. 'Wàn-Jiàoshòu 'zhēn-yǒu-xuéwen. Tā-xiěde-shū-hǎojíle.

38. Tā-dài-ta-fùqinde-biǎo.

39. 'Máo-Xiānsheng 'bú-zài-jiā. Tā-chūqu-le.

40. Nín-qǐng-'jìnlai-zuò-yìhuěr.

DIALOGUE

'Wàn-Jiàoshòu yào-huí-'Yīngguo-qu-le.   Tāde-xuésheng, 'Zhāng-Dōngshēng, xiáng-qǐng-tā-chī-fàn. Tāmen-liǎngge-rén-tán-huà.

Zhāng: 'Wàn-Jiàoshòu, nín-hǎo-ma?

Wàn : Oh, Dōngshēng, wó-hǎo. Ní-hǎo-ma?

Zhāng: Wó-hǎo, xièxie-nín. Wǒ-tīngshuō nín-yào-huí-'Yīngguo-qu-le.

Wàn : Duì-le. Wǒ-èrshiwǔhào jiù-zǒu-le. Ní-kǎoshì-yǐhòu dào-Yīngguo-qu-wárwar.

Zhāng: Wó-hěn-xīwang dào-'Yīngguo-qu, kěshi-tài-máng. Kǎoshì-yǐhòu yě-bìděi-yònggōng-niàn-shū. Wó-xiáng-děi-bìyè-yǐhòu cái-yǒu-jīhui dào-'Yīngguo-qu-ne.

Wàn : Xīwang-nǐ-bìyè-yǐhòu dào-Yīngguo-qu. Wǒmen-zài-'Yīngguo-jiàn.

Zhāng: Hǎo. Wó-yě-shi zènmo-xīwang. 'Wàn-Jiàoshòu, nín-kuài-zǒu-le. Wó-xiǎng-zhèige-xīngqī-lǐtou qǐng-nín-chī-fàn. Wǒ-hái-qíng-jǐge-'biéde-péngyou. Nín-shénmo-shíhou-yǒu-gōngfu-ne?   Qǐng-nín-'shuō-yíge-shíhou.

Wàn : Nǐ-tài-kèqi.

Zhāng: Nín-bié-kèqi.

Wàn : Nènmo xìngqī'wú-hǎo-bu-hǎo?

Zhāng: Hǎo. Wó-xiǎng-qǐng-nín dào-wǒ-'jiā-lǐtou-lái.   Qǐng-nín-chī-'Zhōngguo-fàn 'hǎo-bù-hǎo?

Wàn : Hǎojíle. Wǒ-zuì-xǐhuan chī-'Zhōngguo-fàn.   Kěshi-tài-máfan-le.

Zhāng: Nín-bié-kèqi.

Wàn : Ní-fǔshang-zài-nǎr-a?

Zhāng: Wǒ-jiā-jiù-zài-Zhōngshān-Lù, yìbái-wǔshibáhào. Lí-Sān-Yǒu-Shū-diàn-bù-yuǎn. Qǐng-nín-xīngqīwǔ wǎnshang-qīdiǎn-zhōng dào-wǒ-jiā-lái.

Wàn : Hǎo. Wǒmen-xīngqīwǔ-jiàn.

Zhāng: Xīngqīwǔ wǎnshang-jiàn.

Wàn : Xièxie-ni.

NARRATIVE

Zuótian-tiānqi hén-nuǎnhuo. Wǒmen-xuéxiào bú-shàng-kè, suóyi-wo-
zhǎole-jǐge-péngyou. Yé-yǒu-'Gāo-Měiying-Xiáojie. Wǒmen-yígòng-qíge-rén
qu-lǚxíng. Wǒmen-jiù-xiǎng: "Dào-nǎr-qu-hǎo-ne?"   'Gāo-Xiáojie-shuō:
"Wǒmen-shàng-Běi-Hú-nèibiar, nèige-dà-shānshang-qu-wár-ba."   Tā-shuō-
nèige-shānshang piàoliang-jíle. Tā-shuō-nèige-shānshang zuì-gāode-dìfang
jiù-shi-yíge-dà-gōngyuán. Nèr-yóu-hěn-duō-méigui. Yīnwei-tā-hén-xǐhuan-
méigui, tā-shuō-dào-nèr-qu. Suóyi-wǒmen-jiù-qù-le.

   'Qù-de-shíhou, wǒmen-xiān-zuò gōnggòng-qìchē.   Yīnwei-wǒmen-shi-
lǚxíng, suóyi-wǒmen-zuòdào-Zhōngshān-Lù jiù-xià-chē-le.   Zhōngshān-Lù
lí-nèige-dà-shān hái-yǒu-hén-yuǎn-ne. Wǒmen-qíge-rén yíkuàr-zǒu-lù-tán-
huà, hén-yǒu-yìsi. Wǒmen-wàng-shānshang-zǒu-de-shíhou, yùjian-le-Máo-
Xiānsheng Máo-Tàitai gēn-tāmen-liǎngge-háizi 'yě-lái-shàng-shān.   Yǒude-
péngyou bú-rènshi-Máo-Xiānsheng、 Máo-Tàitai.   Wó-gěi-tāmen-jièshao-le-
yǐhòu, jiù-dōu-rènshi-le. Wǒmen-jǐge-rén 'dōu-xǐhuan-tāmen - nèi-liǎngge-
háizi. 'Dōu-hěn-piàoliang. Xiànzai-yòu-yǒu-'Máo-Xiānsheng tāmen - sìge-
rén, wǒmen-yígòng-shi shíyīge-rén-le.

   Wǒmen-dào-shānshang yǐjing-chàbuduō-shí'èrdiǎn-le.   Dōu-xiǎng-chī-
dōngxi-le. Bá-wǒmen-zài-shānxià-mǎi-de-dōngxi dōu-náchulai. Wǒmen-zài-
yíkuàr-chī. Suírán-wǒmen-'chī-de-dōngxi mǎile-bù-shǎo,   kěshi-wǒmen-
wàngle-ná-shuǐ. Wǒmen-méi-yóu-shuǐ-hē. 'Máo-Tàitai-tāmen ná-shuǐ-lái-le.
Wǒmen-měige-rén dōu-hēle-yìdiár-shuǐ.

   Chīwanle-dōngxi-yǐhòu, 'Máo-Xiānsheng-shuō: "Xiànzài-wǒmen-kāishǐ-
wár-le."   'Gāo-Xiáojie-huà-huàr.   Wǒmen-jǐge-rén yǒude-zóuzou, yǒude-
kàn-méigui, yǒude-tántan. 'Zuì-yǒu-yìside hái-shi-nèi-liǎngge-háizi pǎolái-
pǎoqù-de.

   Jīntian-wǒmen-wárde-hén-hǎo.   Yǐjing-kuài-dào-wúdiǎn-zhōng-le, 'Máo-
Xiānsheng-shuō: "Wǒmen-gāi-xià-shān-huí-jiā-le." Kěshi-nèi-liǎngge-xiǎo-
háizi 'hái-bù-xiáng-zǒu.

ANSWERING QUESTIONS

1. 'Zhāng-Xiānsheng méi-yǒu-qián, suóyi-tā-bù-néng-qu-kàn-diànyǐngr.
    'Wáng-Xiānsheng yě-bù-néng-qù, yīnwei-ta-méi-yǒu-gōngfu. 'Zhāng-
    Xiānsheng-wèi-shénmo bù-néng-qu-kàn-diànyǐngr?

2. Wó-xiáng-mǎi-liùběn-shū. Yǐjing-mǎile-sìběn-le. Wǒ-hái-yào-mái-jí-
   běn?

3. Wǒ-yòng-'gāngbí-xiě-zì. Tā-yòng-'máobí-xiě-zì. 'Shéi-yòng-máobí-
   xiě-zì?

4. 'Wáng-Xiānsheng-chīle-fàn jiù-dào-túshūguǎn-qu-le. Tā-'jièle-shū-yǐhòu
   jiù-huí-jiā. Tā-'xiān-zuò-shénmo?

5. Niàn-'wénxué-de-xuésheng dōu-shi-nǚ-ren. Niàn-kēxuéde 'dōu-shi-nán-
   ren. Nǚ-xuésheng-niàn-shénmo?

6. 'Wáng-Xiānsheng 'Wáng-Tàitai shàng-xīngqī-bìng-le. Wáng-Xiānsheng
   xiànzai-hǎo-le, Wáng-Tàitai hái-méi-hǎo-ne. 'Shéi-hái-yǒu-bìng?

7. Xiànzài-yǐjing-sāndiǎn-le. Wǒ-yào-zǒu-le. Xiànzài-jídiǎn-zhōng-le?

8. Wǒ-dìdi méi-niànguo-kēxué. Tā-shuō kēxué-méi-yǒu-yìsi. Tā-duì-kē-
   xué yǒu-xìngqu-ma?

9. 'Wáng-Xiānsheng dào-'Zhōngguo-lái-yǐhòu jiù-kāishǐ-xué-'Zhōngwén. Tā-
   zài-'Měiguo-de-shíhou xué-le-'Zhōngwén-méi-you?

10. Méi-yǒu-xuéguo-'Zhōngguo-huà-de-xuésheng kàndedǒng-kànbudǒng
    'Zhōngwén-shū?

11. Yígòng-yǒu yíwànwàn-'zhōngxuéde-xuésheng, yìqīanwàn-'dàxuéde-xué-
    sheng. Shi-'zhōngxuéde-xuésheng-duō háishi-'dàxuéde-xuésheng-duō?

12. 'Gāo-Xiānsheng bú-zài-túshūguǎn-le. Tā-huí-jiā-le. 'Gāo-Xiānsheng
    hái-zài-túshūguǎn-ma?

13. 'Bái-Xiānsheng zuótian-niànle-wǔge-zhōngtóu-shū. 'Gāo-Xiáojie cóng-
    liángdiǎn-dào-wúdiǎn-zhōng niàn-shū. 'Shéi-niànde-duō?

14. 'Wàitou-yóu-liǎngge-rén. Wó-qǐng-tāmen-jìnlai. Wǒ-zài-lǐtou háishi-
    zài-wàitou?

15. Tā-bǎ-'Zhōngwén-shū dōu-nádào-túshūguǎn-qu-le,   bǎ-'Yīngwén-shū
    dōu-náhuí-jiā-lái-le. 'Zhōngwén-shū-zài-nǎr?

16. Wǒ-xìng-Wáng. Wǒ-bú-huì-zuò-'Zhōngguo-fàn. Lián-wǒ-'nèiren yě-
    bú-huì-zuò. Wáng-Tàitai huì-bú-huì-zuò-'Zhōngguo-fàn?

17. Tā-'shénmo-dōu-méi-mǎi. Tā-mǎile-'shū-méi-you?

18. Wǔge-zì shi-wó-xiě-de. Shíge-shi-'tā-xiě-de. 'Shéi-xiěde-duō?

19. Tā-shuō-'Zhōngguo-huà shuōde-bí-ní-hǎo. Wǒ-shuōde méi-yóu-nǐ-
    zhènmo-hǎo. Wǒmen-sānge-rén 'shéi-shuōde-hǎo?

20. Yǒude-'Rìběn-zì gēn-'Zhōngguo-zì-yíyàng, yǒude-'bù-yíyàng. Suóyǒu-
    de-'Rìběn-zì dōu-gēn-'Zhōngguo-zì yíyàng-ma?

21. Tā-zuótian-jièle-'liángběn-shū. Jīntian-yòu-jièle-'sānběn. Tā-yígòng-
     jièle-'jíběn-shū?

22. 'Dìdi-niàn-dàxué-'sìniánjí. Mèimei-niàn-'èrniánjí. 'Shéi-xiān-bìyè?

23. Yīnwei-tā-méi-yǒu-qián, suóyi-bù-néng-qu-kàn-diànyǐngr. Tā-wèi-
     shénmo bú-qu-kàn-diànyǐngr?

24. Wáng-Xiānsheng hén-xǐhuan-yánjiu-kēxué. Wáng-Xiáojie hén-xǐhuan-
     yánjiu-wénxué. Wáng-Xiānsheng duì-shénmo-yǒu-xìngqu?

25. 'Zhāng-Xiānsheng zài-Zhōngguo-xuéle liǎng-niánde-'Zhōngguo-huà. Zài-
     'Yīngguo-xuéle-yìnián-Zhōngwén. Tā-zài-'Yīngguo-xuéguo-méi-you?

26. 'Wàn-Jiàoshòu zài-Zhōngguo yánjiule-wǔnián-yǔyán, èrnián-wénxué. Tā-
     yánjiu-'shénmo-de-shíhou zuì-duō?

27. Qián-'Xiānsheng-hěn-máng. Tā-méi-gōngfu-kàn-diànyǐngr. Qián-'Tài-
     tai-cháng-kàn-diànyǐngr. 'Shéi-bú-kàn-diànyǐngr?

28. Wǒ-shi-zài-'Zhōngguo-zhǎng-dà-de. Tā-zài-'Rìběn-zhǎng-dà-de. 'Shéi-
     shi-Zhōngguo-rén?

29. Wǒ-fùqin-géi-wo-'wǔkuài-qián. Wó-mǔqin-géi-wo-'sānkuài-qián.   Tā-
     men-liǎngge-rén 'yígòng-géi-wo-duōshao-qián?

30. Zhèizhī-bǐ bú-shi-'wó-mǎi-de. Shi-'Wáng-Xiānsheng-mǎi-de. Zhèizhī-
     bǐ shi-'shéi-mǎi-de?

CROSSWORD PUZZLE

Cóng-zuǒ-wàng-yòu

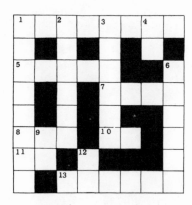

1. Zhōngguo-zuì-piàoliangde-
    chéng.
5. Wǒ-méi-yǒu-tā ——cōngming.
7. Fāngfǎ.
8. Xiānsheng、 tàitai、 xiáojie、 xuésheng、
    háizi 'dōu-shi-shénmo?
10. Bǎ.
11. Yī-gēn-sān-de-zhōngjiàr.
13. Yǒude-rén yòng-zhèige-xiě-zì.

Cóng-shàng-wàng-xià

1. Cóng-Húnán-lái-de-rén.
2. Tāmen-bú-shi-nǔ-rén shi-shénmo?
3. Ní-měitiān-zǎochen chī-shénmo?
4. Míngbai-le-yǐhòu, cháng-yòng-
    zhèige-zì.

6. Wǒ-bù-néng-qu-kàn-diàn-
    yǐngr, —— wǒ-méi-yǒu-
    qián.
9. Gēn-shàngtou-shíyī-yíyàng.
12. Mǔqin.

UNIT IV

Lesson 19 EATING FAMILY STYLE

"Biàn-fàn, hén-jiǎndān."

Dialogue: Mr. White and Professor Wanamaker have dinner at the Gao home.

Gāo-Tàitai: Fàn-hǎo-le. 'Wàn-Xiānsheng 'Bái-Xiānsheng, qǐng-chī-fàn-ba.

Dinner's ready. Mr. Wanamaker, Mr. White, please (come and) eat.

Gāo-Xiānsheng: Lǎo-Wàn Bái-Xiānsheng, wǒmen-chī-fàn.   5

[Old] Wan, Mr. White, let's have dinner.

Wàn: Gāo-Tàitai, jīntian-'tài-máfan-nín-le.

Mrs. Gao, we've put you to too much trouble today.

Gāo-Tàitai: Méi-shénmo. Biàn-fàn,* hén-jiǎndān.

It's nothing. It's plain food,* very simple.

---

* The Chinese dinner at the Gaos', though not precisely biàn-fàn 'plain food' in the American sense, is not an elaborate dinner such as one might have in a restaurant. The courses are as follows:

Shīzi-tóu 'lion's head' (large meatballs made of ground pork, fried with cabbage and stewed for several hours)

Hóng-shāo-jī 'red-cooked chicken' (chicken first seared in hot fat and then simmered in soy sauce until the meat is very soft)

Táng-cù-yú 'sweet-and-sour fish' [lit. sugar and vinegar fish] (fish cooked

311

Gāo-Xiānsheng: Qǐng-zuò, qǐng-   10   Please sit down, please sit down.
    zuò. Wǒmen-suíbiàn-zuò.   Let's sit down anywhere we like.

Bái : Gāo-Tàitai Gāo-Xiáojie,   Mrs. Gao, Miss Gao, please
    qǐng-lái-yíkuàr-chī-ba.   come and eat with us.

Gāo-Xiānsheng: Měiyīng-lái. Wǒ-   Meiying (can) come. My wife
    nèiren déi-bǎ-cài-zuòwán.   15   has to finish preparing the (re-
    Wǒmen-xiān-chī. Tā-yì-   maining) dishes. Let's start
    huěr-jiu-lái.   eating. She'll come in a mo-
                                         ment.

Wàn: He! Bùdéliǎo! Zěnmo-   My! There's no end (of food).
    'zhènmo-duōde-cài-a!   How is it that there are so many
                                         courses!

Gāo-Xiānsheng: Biàn-fàn, 'méi-   20   It's plain food, nothing in partic-
    yǒu-shénmo-cài. Nǐmen-   ular. [Both of you] sit and eat
    liǎngwèi suíbiàn-zuò, suí-   as you please. My wife isn't
    biàn-chī. Wǒ-nèiren yě-   such a good cook. If it isn't fish
    'bù-zěnmo-huì-zuò-cài.   then it's meat. There aren't any
    Bú-shi-yú jiù-shi-ròu.   25   fine dishes.
    'Méi-shénmo-hǎo-cài.

Bái : Gāo-Tàitai, cài-'tài-duō-   Mrs. Gao, there are too many
    le. Nín-bié-máng-le.   courses. Don't do so much.
    Qǐng-lái, wǒmen-yíkuàr-   Please come, let's eat together.
    chī-fàn-ba.   30

Gāo-Tàitai: Nǐmen-jǐwèi-xiān-   (All of) you start eating. There's
    qǐng. Hái-yǒu-'yíge-cài   still one more dish and then I'll
    wǒ-jiù-lái-le.   come.

Gāo-Xiānsheng: Wǒmen-'xiān-   Let's start eating.
    chī.   35

Bái : Cài-zhēn-piàoliang. Dōu-   Everything is [lit. The dishes
    jiào-shénmo?   are] very attractive. What are
                                         they all called?

Gāo Xiānsheng: Zhèige-jiào-shī-   This one is called lion's head.
    zi-tóu.

Bái : 'Zěnmo-jiào-shīzi-tóu-ne?   40   How come it's called lion's
    Míngzi-hěn-qíguài.   head? It's an odd name.

―――――――――

    with sugar and vinegar)
  Chǎo-dòufu 'fried bean curd' (bean curd fried in a very hot pan while being
    constantly stirred, with soy sauce, ginger, and scallions, and beef, pork,
    or shrimp)
  Chǎo-báicài 'fried cabbage' (cabbage fried with soy sauce, ginger, scal-
    lions, and meat)
  Niú-ròu-tāng 'beef soup' (beef with scallions and ginger)
Note that the soup is usually taken toward the end of the meal. A soup is not
reckoned as a course, so that in a restaurant one might say: Yào-sìge-cài
yíge-tāng 'Order four dishes and a soup.'

Gāo-Xiānsheng: Wó-xiǎng-huòzhě
  shi-yīnwei-měi-yíge-dōu-
  hěn-dà, suóyi-jiào-shīzi-
  tóu.   45

I think perhaps it's because each
(of the meatballs) is quite large,
[so it's called lion's head].

Bái : 'Zhèige-cài-shi-shénmo?

What is this dish?

Gāo Xiānsheng: Zhèi-shi-chǎo-
  báicài.

[This is] fried cabbage.

Bái : Zhèige-ne?

And what about this?

Gāo Xiānsheng: Zhèi-shi-hóng-   50
  shāo-jī.*

[This is] red-cooked chicken.*

Bái : 'Zhèige-wǒ-zhī dao. Shi-
  chǎo-dòufu.

This I know.   It's fried bean
curd.

('Gāo-Tàitai bǎ-cài-zuòhǎo-le
názhe-cài-chūlai-le.)   55

(Mrs. Gao, having finished the
[last] dish, brings it out.)

Gāo-Tàitai: 'Méi-shénmo-hǎo-
  cài. Qǐng-'duō-chī-yì-
  diǎr. Wó-xiǎnglái-xiǎngqù yé-xiǎngbuchū tèbiéde-
  cài-lai.   60

There aren't any fine dishes.
Please eat a little more.   I
thought and thought but couldn't
think of anything special.

Wàn: Nín-tài-kèqi-le. Cài-'tài-
  hǎo-le, bǐ-fànguǎrde-cài-
  dōu-hǎo.

You're too polite.   The food is
excellent, better than any restaurant food.

Gāo-Tàitai: Guòjiǎng, guòjiǎng.

You flatter me.

Wàn: Shīzi-tóu zuòde-hǎojí le.   65
  Wǒ-tèbié-xǐhuan-chī.

The lion's head is awfully well
done.   I'm particularly fond of
it.

Gāo-Tàitai: Bái-Xiānsheng, nǐ-
  dōu-xǐhuan chī-'shénmo-
  cài?

Mr. White, what dishes do you
like?

Bái : Wó-xǐhuan chī-hóng-shāo-   70
  de, xiàng-hóng-shāo-ròu,
  hóng-shāo-jī, hóng-shāo-
  yú—wǒ-'dōu-xǐhuan-chī.

I like red-cooked things, such as
[red-cooked] meat, [red-cooked]
chicken, [red-cooked] fish — I
like them all.

Gāo-Xiānsheng: 'Bái-Xiānsheng,
  nǐ-zài-Měiguo yě-cháng-   75
  chī-'Zhōngguo-fàn-ma?

Mr. White, did you often have
Chinese food in America too?

Bái : Cháng-chī. Wó-hén-xǐ-
  huan-chī, cháng-gēn-péng-
  you-yíkuàr qu-chī-Zhōng-
  guo-fànguǎr.   80

I often did.   I liked [to eat] it
very much, and often went with
friends to eat in Chinese restaurants.

---

* 'Red-cooked,' so called from the coloring imparted by the liberal use of
soy sauce, is the rendering for <u>hóng-shāo</u> given by Buwei Yang Chao in her
delightful book, <u>How to Cook and Eat in Chinese</u>, New York, John Day, 1945.
(Her introduction, incidentally, contains a wealth of information on Chinese
table manners.)

Gāo-Tàitai: Suóyi-nǐ-yòng-kuàizi
    yòngde-nènmo-hǎo-ne.

That's why you use chopsticks
so well.

Gāo-Xiáojie: Zài-Měiguo-de-
    'Zhōngguo-fànguǎr duō-
    ma?   85

Are there many Chinese restaurants in America?

Bái : Bù-shǎo.

Quite a few.

Gāo-Xiáojie: Měiguo-de-Zhōng-
    guo-fàn hǎo-chī-ma?

Is the Chinese food in America
good?

Bái : Zài-Měiguo-de-'Zhōngguo-
    fànguǎr chàbuduo-dōu-shi-   90
    Guǎngdong-fànguǎr. Tāmen-
    zuò-de hǎo-shi-hǎo, kěshi-
    méi-yǒu-Gāo-Tàitai-zuò-
    de zhènmo-hǎo-chī. Shī-
    zi-tóu-zài-Měiguo chúle-   95
    Sānfánshì-Niǔyue jǐge-dà-
    chéng-yǐwài, jiu-chību-
    zháo.

The Chinese restaurants in
America are almost all Cantonese restaurants. Their cooking is good all right, but it isn't
as good as Mrs. Gao's. Apart
from a few big cities (like) San
Francisco and New York, lion's
head just can't be had in America.

Wàn: Zhèige-táng-cù-yú hén-hǎo-
    chī.   100

This sweet-and-sour fish is delicious.

Bái : Gāo-Tàitai, qǐng-wen, zhèi-
    ge-táng-cù-yú-lǐtou dōu-
    yǒu-shénmo?

May I ask, Mrs. Gao, what's in
it [lit. what's in this sweet-and-
sour fish]?

Gāo-Tàitai: Táng-cù-yú-lǐtou
    yǒu-bái-táng-yǒu-cù. Yīn-   105
    wei-yòu-yǒu-táng-yòu-yǒu-
    cù, suóyi-yòu-tián-yòu-
    suān.

It [lit. the sweet-and-sour fish]
has white sugar and vinegar [in
it]. Since it has both sugar and
vinegar, it's both sweet and
sour.

Bái : Báicài bì děi-yòng-'zhū-ròu-
    chǎo-ma?   110

Does cabbage have to be fried
with pork?

Gāo-Tàitai: Bù-yídìng. Rúguó-
    ní-xǐhuan chī-niú-ròu, jiù-
    yòng-niú-ròu-chǎo.

Not necessarily. If you like to
eat beef, make it with beef.

Bái : Nènmo-chǎo-dòufu-ne?

Then how about fried bean curd?

Gāo-Tàitai: Suíbiàn-zhū-ròu niú-   115
    ròu dōu-kéyi.

Whatever you like—pork and beef
will both do.

Bái : Gāo-Xiáojie, nǐ-huì-zuò-
    fàn-ma?

Miss Gao, can you cook?

Gāo-Xiáojie: Wǒ-bú-huì-zuò-fàn.

I don't know how to.

Gāo-Tàitai: Tā-yě-huì-zuò jǐ-   120
    yàng-cài, zuòde-hái-bú-
    cuò.

She can make a few [kinds of]
dishes too, and she doesn't do
them badly at all.

Bái : Nín-cài zuòde-zhènmo-
    hǎo, wó-xiǎng-Gāo-Xiáo-
    jie yídìng-zuòde-yě-bú-   125
    cuò.

You've done these dishes so well
I'm sure Miss Gao also is a
good cook.

Gāo-Tàitai: Xīwang-nǐ-cháng-lái,   I hope you will come often and
        jiù-zài-zhèr chī-biàn-fàn.   have our simple cooking here.

Bái : Xièxie-nin.   Thank you.

Gāo-Tàitai: Nǐ-xià-cì-lái wǒ-   130   Next time you come I'll have
        jiào-Měiyīng-zuò.   Meiying cook.

Gāo-Xiānsheng: Qǐng-chī-cài.   Please eat. (To his wife:) You
        Tàitai, gāi-ná-tāng-le.   should bring the soup.

Gāo-Tàitai: Wǒ-gēn-'Bái-Xiān-   I've been talking with Mr. White
        sheng shuō-huà-shuōde   135   so much that I've forgotten to
        wàngle-ná-tāng-le.   get it.   (She brings the soup.)
        (Tā-bǎ-tāng-nálai.)

Bái : Zhèi-shi-'shénmo-tāng?   What (kind of) soup is this?

Gāo-Tàitai: 'Niú-ròu-tāng.   Beef soup.

Bái : Tāng-'zhēn-hǎo.   140   It's really nice.

Gāo-Xiānsheng: Qǐng-duō-chī-   Please have some more food.
        cài.

Wàn: Wǒmen-yǐjing-chībǎo-le,   We've already eaten our fill, and
        yòu-hē-hěn-duō-tāng.   we've had a lot of soup too.

Gāo-Xiānsheng: Lǎo-Wàn, Bái-   145   [Old] Wan, Mr. White, have a bit
        Xiānsheng, zài-chī-yì-   more.   You've eaten too little.
        diǎr. Chīde-'tài-shǎo.

Wàn: Wǒ-yìdiǎr-yě-méi-kèqi.   I haven't been the least bit po-
        Chīde-hén-bǎo. Xièxie.   lite.   I've eaten until I'm quite
                                        full.   Thank you.

Bái : Xièxie. Chīde-'tài-duō-   150   Thank you.   I've eaten too much.
        le.

Gāo-Tàitai: 'Zhēn-chībǎo-le-   Are you really full?
        ma?

Wàn: Bǎo-le. Xièxie.   Yes, thank you.

Gāo-Xiānsheng: Nènmo jiù-qǐng- 155   Then please have some tea.
        hē-chá-ba.

VOCABULARY

báicài	cabbage (N) [lit. white vegetable]
bǎo	full, satiated (SV)
biàn-fàn	plain food (N) [lit. convenient food]
cài	dish, course; vegetable (N)
chǎo	sauté, fry (TV)
chúle	except for (MA) (Note 5 below)

cù	vinegar (N)
dòufu	bean curd (N) [lit. legume curd]
fànguǎn/r	restaurant (N) [lit. food establishment]
Guǎngdong	(city of) Canton, (province of) Kwangtung (PW) [lit. broad east]
guòjiǎng	(you) flatter (me) [lit. pass praise] (See Supplementary Lesson 19, Note 1)
he!	Gosh! My!
jī	chicken (N)
kuàizi	chopsticks (N)
niú	cow, ox (N)
ròu	meat (N)
shāo	roast, braise (N)
shīzi	lion (N)
suān	sour (SV)
suíbiàn	as you please, any way one likes (MA) [lit. follow convenience] (Note 13 below)
tāng	soup (N)
táng	sugar (N)
tèbié	special (SV) [lit. special other]
tián	sweet (SV)
tóu	head (N)
yǐwài	besides, except for [lit. take outside] (Note 5 below)
yú	fish (N)
-zháo	(suffix indicating accomplishment: Note 8 below)
-zhe	(suffix indicating progressive action: Note 2 below)
zhū	pig (N)

SENTENCE BUILD-UP

	cài	dish, course
	jǐge-cài	how many courses?
1.	Wǒmen-jīntian chī-'jǐge-cài?	How many courses shall we have today?

	tāng	soup
	yíge-tāng	one soup
2.	Wǒmen-yào sìge-cài-yíge-tāng.	We want four dishes and a soup.

| | táng | sugar |

bái-táng
white sugar

3. Zuì-hǎode-táng shi-bái-táng.
The best sugar is white sugar.

kuàizi
chopsticks

yòng-kuàizi-chī-fàn
eat with chopsticks

4. Nǐ-huì-yòng-'kuàizi-chī-fàn-ma?
Can you eat with chopsticks?

hē-yìdiǎr
drink a little

duō-hē-yìdiǎr
drink a little more

5. Duō-hē-yìdiǎr-táng-ba.
Have a little more soup.

'màn-yìdiǎr
a little slower

shuō-'màn-yìdiǎr
speak a little slower

6. Wǒ-bù-dǒng. Qǐng-nín-shuō-'màn-yìdiǎr.
I can't understand. Please speak a little more slowly.

'màn-yìdiǎr
a little slower

'màn-yìdiǎr-shuō
speak a little slower

7. Wǒ-bù-míngbai. Qǐng-nín-'màn-yìdiǎr-shuō.
I don't understand. Please speak a little more slowly.

dòufu
bean curd

yòng-kuàizi-chī-dòufu
eat bean curd with chopsticks

8. Yòng-kuàizi-chī-dòufu bù-róngyì.
It's not easy to eat bean curd with chopsticks.

báicài
cabbage

xǐhuan-chī-báicài
like to eat cabbage

9. Zhōngguo-rén hén-xǐhuan-chī-báicài.
Chinese are very fond of cabbage.

fànguǎr
restaurant

zài-fànguǎr-chī-fàn
eat in a restaurant

10. Wó-hén-xǐhuan zài-fànguǎr-chī-fàn.
I like to eat in restaurants very much.

fànguǎr
restaurant

chī-fànguǎr
eat in a restaurant

11. Nǐ-bù-xǐhuan chī-fànguǎr-ma?
Don't you like to eat in restaurants?

Guǎngdong
Canton

chī-Guǎngdong-fànguǎr
eat at a Cantonese restaurant

12. Wǒmen-chī-Guǎngdong-fànguǎr kéyi-ma?
Can we eat at a Cantonese restaurant?

tīng
listen

tīngzhe
listening

13. Wǒ-tīngzhe-lùyīn-ne.
I'm listening to a recording.

chīzhe-fàn
eating

tīng-lùyīn
14. Wǒ-chīzhe-fàn tīng-lùyīn.

listen to recordings
I listen to recordings while eating.

chǎo
chǎo-báicài
chǎo-dòufu
15. Chǎo-báicài chǎo-dòufu dōu-
hěn-róngyi-zuò.

sauté, fry
fried cabbage
fried bean curd
Fried cabbage and fried bean
curd are both very easy to make.

ròu
yòng-shénmo-ròu?
16. Zuò-chǎo-báicài yòng-shénmo-ròu?

meat
use what meat?
What meat is used in (making)
fried cabbage?

zhū
zhū-ròu
zhū-ròu-chīde-duō
17. Zhōngguo-rén zhū-ròu-chīde-
duō.

pig
pork
eat more pork
Chinese eat more pork.

niú
niú-ròu
niú-ròu-chīde-duō
18. Měiguo-rén niú-ròu-chīde-
duō-ne háishi-zhū-ròu-chī-
de-duō-ne?

cow
beef
eat more beef
Do Americans eat more beef or
pork?

shīzi
méi-yǒu-shīzi
19. Zhōngguo-yǒu-láohu méi-yǒu-
shīzi.

lion
there are no lions
There are tigers but not lions in
China.

tóu
shīzi-tóu
20. Zhèige-cài jiào-'shīzi-tóu.

head
lion's head
This dish is called lion's head.

bú-shi-Yīngguo-rén
jiù-shi-Měiguo-rén
21. Nèige-'wàiguo-rén bú-shi-
'Yīngguo-rén jiù-shi-'Měiguo-rén.

isn't an Englishman
then is an American
That foreigner — if he isn't English, he's American.

bù-chī-zhū-ròu
jiù-chī-niú-ròu
22. Wǒmen-bù-chī-'zhū-ròu jiù-
chī-'niú-ròu.

not eat pork
then eat beef
If we don't eat pork then we eat
beef.

bú-shi-chī-zhū-ròu
jiù-shi-chī-niú-ròu
23. Wǒmen-bú-shi-chī-zhū-ròu
jiù-shi-chī-niú-ròu.

not eat pork
then eat beef
If we don't eat pork then we eat
beef.

shāo
24. Zhèige-ròu shi-shāo-de.

roast, braise
This meat is roasted.

hóng-shāo
hóng-shāo-ròu
25. Ní-xǐhuan-chī hóng-shāo-ròu-ma?

red-cooked
red-cooked meat
Do you like red-cooked meat?

mǎi
mǎizhao
26. Ní-'mǎizhao-le-méi-you?

buy
succeed in buying
Did you succeed in buying it?

mǎizhao
mǎibuzháo
27. Zhèige xiànzài-mǎibuzháo.

succeed in buying
unable to succeed in buying
This can't be bought nowadays.

wó-děngle-bàntiān
tā-yě-méi-lái
28. Wó-děngle-bàntiān, tā-yě-méi-lái.

I waited a long time
yet he did not come
Although I waited a long time, he didn't come.

wó-děngle-bàntiān
tā-dōu-méi-lái
29. Wó-děngle-bàntiān, tā-dōu-méi-lái.

I waited a long time
yet he didn't come
Although I waited a long time, he didn't come.

náchulai
náchu-shūdiàn-lai
30. Bǎ-shū dōu-náchu-shūdiàn-lai.

bring out
bring out of the bookstore
Bring all the books out of the bookstore.

náchulai
náchu-huàr-lai
31. Qǐng-nín náchu-huàr-lai, wǒ-yào-kànkan.

bring out
bring out the paintings
Please bring out the paintings, I want to look at them.

tèbié
32. Nèige-rén hěn-tèbié.

special, peculiar
That man is quite peculiar.

tèbié-xǐhuan
33. Wǒ-tèbié-xǐhuan chī-shīzi-tóu.

especially like
I especially like to eat lion's head.

yú
34. Zhèi-shi-yú-shi-ròu-ne?

fish
Is this fish or meat?

cù
yòngwán-le
35. Cù-yòngwán-le-ma?

vinegar
use up
Is the vinegar all used up?

chúle
chúle-chá

except for, besides
except for tea

36. Chúle-chá ta-'shénmo-dōu-bù-   He doesn't drink anything but
     hē.   tea.

          yǐwài   except for
          chá-yǐwài   except for tea
37. Chá-yǐwài tā-'shénmo-dōu-   He doesn't drink anything but
     bù-hē.   tea.

          chúle-chá-yǐwài   except for tea
38. Tā-chúle-chá-yǐwài 'shénmo-   He doesn't drink anything but
     dōu-bù-hē.   tea.

          tián   sweet
          tiánde   sweet thing
39. Wǒ-bù-xǐhuan-chī-tiánde.   I don't like to eat sweet things.

          suān   sour
40. Cù-shi-suānde.   Vinegar is sour.

          guòjiǎng   you flatter me
          kèqi-huà   polite expression
41. "Guòjiǎng" jiu-shi-kèqi-huà.   "You flatter me" is a polite ex-
                                         pression.

          bǎo   full, satiated
          tài-bǎo-le   too full
42. Wǒ-tài-bǎo-le.   I'm too full.

          chībǎo   eat until full
43. Nǐ-'chībǎo-le-méi-you?   Have you had enough to eat?

          chībǎo   eat until full
          chībubǎo   unable to eat until full
44. Fàn-tài-shǎo, wǒ-chībubǎo.   There isn't enough food, I can't
                                         get filled.

          hǎo   good
          xiéhǎo   finish writing
45. Zì-dōu-xiéhǎo-le-ma?   Did you finish writing all the
                                         characters?

          xiéhǎo   finish writing
          xiěbuhǎo   unable to finish writing
46. Wǒ-yíge-zhōngtóu xiěbuhǎo.   I can't finish writing it in an
                                         hour.

          hǎo-shi-hǎo   good all right
          méi-yǒu-'nèige-nènmo-   not as good as that
          hǎo
47. Zhèige-hǎo-shi-hǎo, kěshi-   This is good all right, but it's
     méi-yǒu-'nèige-nènmo-hǎo.   not as good as that.

          biàn-fàn   plain food
          hǎo-chī-shi-hǎo-chī   is appetizing all right

48. Biàn-fàn hǎo-chī-shi-hǎo-
    chī, kěshi-wǒ-bù-xǐhuan-
    chī.

    Plain food is appetizing all right,
    but I don't like to eat it.

    suíbiàn
49. Wǒmen-'suíbiàn-zuò, hǎo-
    bù-hǎo?

    as one pleases
    Shall we sit as we please?

    suíbiàn
    kéyi
50. 'Suíbiàn-shénmo-shíhou-dōu-
    kéyi.

    as one pleases
    all right
    Any time you please is all right.

    'suíbiàn-shénmo-shíhou
    kéyi-lái
51. Nǐ-'suíbiàn-shénmo-shíhou
    'dōu-kéyi-lái.

    any time you please
    may come
    You may come any time you
    please.

    jī
52. Ní-xǐhuan-chī-jī-ma?

    chicken
    Do you like to eat chicken?

    he!
53. He! Zěnmo-'zhènmo-duōde-
    rén-ne?

    my!
    My! How come there are so
    many people?

    yào
    yào-cài
54. Wǒmen-zài-fànguǎr yàole-
    sānge-cài.

    want
    order dishes
    We ordered three dishes in the
    restaurant.

PATTERN DRILLS

Pattern 19.1. Stative Verbs Expressing Manner (Note 1 below)

Pattern 19.1 a.

duō/ shǎo	V	A	(O)
'more'/'less'	Verb	Amount	(Object)
Duō	hē	(yì)diǎr	chá.

'Drink a little more tea.'

Sháo	gěi	yíkuài	qián.

'Give a dollar less.'

Pattern 19.1 b.

V	SV	(yì)diǎr
Verb	Stative Verb	'a little'
Zǒu	màn	yìdiǎr.

'Walk a little slower.'

Pattern 19.1 c.

SV	(yì)diǎr	V
Stative Verb	'a little'	Verb
Màn	yìdiǎr	zǒu.

'Walk a little slower.'

1. Nǐ-yīnggāi-'shǎo-yào-yìdiǎr.

   You should order a little less.

2. Qíng-ní-zǒu-'kuài-yìdiǎr.

   Please walk a little faster.

3. Nǐ-xiě-de-zì 'tài-xiǎo-le. Qíng-ni-zài-xiě-'dà-yìdiǎr.

   The characters you've written are too small. Please rewrite (them) a little bigger.

4. Qíng-ni 'duō-mǎi-yìxiē-bǐ.

   Please buy a few more pens.

5. 'Duō-ná-diar-qián.

   Take a little more money.

6. Yào-kǎoshì-le. Wó-děi-'duō-niàn-yìdiǎr-shū.

   I'm about to have exams. I'm going to study a bit more.

7. Zhèizhāng-huàr wó-děi-huà-'hǎo-yìdiǎr.

   I must do this painting a little better.

8. Nǐ-shuō-de-huà tā-bù-dǒng. Nǐ-děi-'màn-yìdiǎr-shuō.

   He doesn't understand what you say. You must speak a little slower.

9. Wǒ-bù-hē-tāng. Wǒ-yào-duō-hē-diar-chá.

   I'm not having soup. I want to drink a little more tea.

10. Zài-'nèige-shūdiàn mǎile-yì-běn-zìdiǎn. Tāmen-shǎo-yào-wǔmáo-qián.

    I bought a dictionary in that bookstore. They reduced the price by fifty cents.

11. Kuàizi-bù-róngyi-yòng. Wó-děi-'màn-diar-chī.

    Chopsticks are not easy to use. I have to eat a little slowly.

12. Ní-děi-'duō-géi-jǐkuài-qián.

    You should give a few dollars more.

13. Mǎi-zhèibén-shū ní-kéyi-'sháo-géi-jǐmáo-qián.

    (If) you buy this book you can take a few dimes off the price.

14. Jīntian-wǒ-bìngle. 'Shǎo-niàn-yìdiǎr-shū.

    I'm sick today. I'm going to study a little less.

15. Wǒ-méi-dǒng. Qíng-ni shuō-'màn-yìdiǎr.

    I didn't understand. Please speak a little more slowly.

Pattern 19.2. Progressive Action (Note 2 below)

Pattern 19.2 a.

S	V	-zhe	(O)	(ne)
Subject	Verb	-zhe	(Object)	(ne)
Wǒ	chī	-zhe	fàn	ne.

'I'm eating.'

Pattern 19.2 b.

S	V₁	-zhe	(O)	V₂	(O₂)
Subject	Verb₁	-zhe	(Object)	Verb₂	(Object₂)
Wǒ	chī	-zhe	fàn	kàn	shū.

'I read while eating.'

1. Xiànzài-bù-néng-qù-le. Wǒ-gēn-péngyou shuōzhe-huà-ne.

   I can't go now. I'm talking with a friend.

2. Tā-lái-zhǎo-wo-de-shíhou, wǒ-chīzhe-fàn-ne.

   When he came to visit me I was having dinner.

3. Wǒ-tīngzhe-lùyīn-ne, tā-jiào-wǒ-qu-kàn-diànyǐngr.

   (As) I was listening to recordings he asked me to go see a movie.

4. Wǒ-huí-jiā-de-shíhou wó-mǔqin-zuòzhe-fàn-ne.

   When I returned home my mother was cooking dinner.

5. Zuótian wǒ-gēn-'Máo-Xiānsheng dào-túshūguǎn-qu. Zǒuzhe-lu shuōzhe-huà, hén-yǒu-yìsi.

   Yesterday I went to the library with Mr. Mao. It was very pleasant to walk and talk.

6. Háizi-xǐhuan kànzhe-diànyǐngr-chī-dōngxi.

   Children like to eat things while seeing a movie.

7. Wǒmen-gēn-péngyou shuōzhe-huà-hē-chá.

   We drank tea while talking with friends.

8. Nèige-háizi názhe-zhǐ, názhe-bǐ, yào-xiě-zì.

   That child is holding paper and pen. He wants to write characters.

9. 'Gāo-Xiáojie dàizhe-yígè 'hěn-piàoliangde-biǎo.

   Miss Gao is wearing a very attractive watch.

10. 'Wáng-Xiáojie názhe-hěn-duō-méigui.

    Miss Wang is holding a lot of roses.

11. Nǐ-dào-túshūguǎn-lái, zuò-'chē-lái-de háishi-'zǒuzhe-lái-de?

    When you came to the library, did you come by car or on foot?

12. Zuótian-wǎnshang zài-fànguǎr-chīzhe-fàn-de-shíhou, 'Wáng-Xiānsheng yě-lái-chī-fàn.

    Yesterday evening while I was eating in the restaurant, Mr. Wang also came to eat.

13. Zuótian-gēn-péngyou dào-túshūguǎn-qu. Zǒuzhe-lù, shuōzhe-huà, yìhuěr-jiu-dào-le.

    Yesterday I went to the library with friends. Walking and talking, we arrived in a moment.

14. Wǒ-bìngzhe-ne hái-déi-kǎoshì.

    I'm sick (but) I still have to take the exam.

15. Tā-méi-yǒu-qián. Zuòzhe-shì niàn-dàxué.

    He doesn't have any money. He's working his way through college.

Pattern 19.3. A Special Type of 'if Sentence (Note 3 below)

bu	V₁	jiù	V₂
'not'	Verb₁	'then'	Verb₂
Bú	shi zhū-ròu	jiù	shi niú-ròu.

' (If) it isn't pork then it's beef.'

| Bú | (shi) chī-zhū-ròu | jiù | (shi) chī-niú-ròu. |

' (If he) doesn't eat pork then (he) eats beef.'

1. Wǒ-bù-zhīdào tā-shi-'něiguó-rén. Bú-shi-'Měiguo-rén jiù-shi-'Yīngguo-rén.

   I don't know what country he's a native of. He's either American or English.

2. Nèige-háizi hěn-yònggōng. Měitiān bú-shi-kàn-shū jiù-shi-xiě-zì.

   That child works hard. Every day he either reads or writes characters.

3. 'Gāo-Xiānsheng-měitiān bú-dào-shūdiàn jiù-dào-túshūguǎn.

   Every day if Mr. Gao doesn't go to the bookstore then he goes to the library.

4. 'Máo-Xiānsheng hén-xǐhuan-chī-chǎo-de-cài. Bú-shi-chī-chǎo-dòufu jiù-shi-chī-chǎo-báicài.

   Mr. Mao likes to eat fried things. He has fried bean curd or fried cabbage, one or the other.

5. 'Wàn-Jiàoshòu hén-xǐhuan-chī-ròu. Bú-shi-zhū-ròu jiù-shi-niú-ròu.

   Professor Wanamaker likes to eat meat. If it isn't pork then it's beef.

6. Wó-xiǎode-shíhou hén-xǐhuan-lǚxíng. Bú-shi-dào-Hángzhou jiù-shi-dào-Sūzhou.

   When I was young I was very fond of traveling. If I didn't go to Hangchow then I went to Soochow.

7. Wó-měitiān bú-shi-tīng-lùyīn jiù-shi-xiě-zì.

   Every day I either listen to recordings or write characters.

8. Wó-xiě-zì bú-shi-yòng-'máobǐ jiù-shi-yòng-'gāngbǐ.

   In writing characters I use either a brush or a pen.

9. 'Máo-Xiānsheng bù-chī-'Zhōng-guo-fàn jiù-chī-'Měiguo-fàn.

   If Mr. Mao doesn't eat Chinese food then he has American food.

10. Wǒ-bù-xué-kēxué jiù-xué-yǔ-yánxué.

    If I don't study science then I'll study linguistics.

Pattern 19.4. A Special Type of 'although' or 'but' Sentence   (Note 4 below)

V₁	yě/dōu	bù/méi	V₂
Verb₁	'still'	'not'	Verb₂
Zhǎolái-zhǎoqù	yě	méi	zhǎodào.

'Although I searched and searched I still didn't succeed in finding (it).'

1. 'Wáng-Xiáojie xuéle-bànnián-Yīngwén yě-bú-huì-shuō-Yīngguo-huà.

   Although Miss Wang studied English for half a year she can't speak it.

2. Tā-shuōle-'hěn-duōde-huà, wó-yě-bù-dǒng.

   He talked a lot but I didn't understand (what he said).

3. 'Zhāng-Xiānsheng xiáng-zhǎo-'Bái-Xiānsheng. Tā-bú-rèn-shi-lù. Zhǎole-bàntiān dōu-méi-zhǎozháo.

   Mr. Johnson wanted to visit Mr. White. He didn't know the way. Although he hunted for a long time [lit. half a day], he didn't succeed in finding (him).

4. Zhèige-zì-wǒ-wàngle. Xiǎng-lái-xiǎngqù dōu-xiǎngbuchūlái.

   I've forgotten this character. I've racked my brains but can't recall it.

5. Wǒ-shuōle-'hǎoxie-cì, tā-yě-bù-dǒng.

   Although I said it a good many times, he didn't understand.

6. Wó-děngle-bàntiān, tā-yě-méi-lái.

   I waited for a long time but he didn't come.

7. Wó-zhǎo-ta-sì-wǔcì, ta-'dōu-bú-zài-jiā.

   I went to see him four or five times, but he wasn't at home.

8. Wǒ-zài-dàxué xuéle-'èrnián-le, yě-bù-néng-xiě hén-hǎode-Zhōngguo-zì.

   Although I studied for two years in college I can't write very good Chinese characters.

9. Wǒ-zuótian qu-kàn-'Wáng-Xiānsheng. Wó-děngle-bàntiān tā-yě-méi-chū-lai.

   Yesterday I went to see Mr. Wang. I waited for a long time but he didn't come out.

10. Wǒ-wàngle-wèn-Máo-Xiānsheng zài-'nǎr-zhù-le. Zhǎolái-zhǎo-qù dōu-zhǎobuzháo.

    I forgot to ask Mr. Mao where he lives. I searched and searched but wasn't able to find (him).

Pattern 19.5. Expressing 'besides,   except for,   apart from' (Note 5 below)

(chúle)	N/V	(yǐwài)
chúle	Noun/Verb	yǐwài
chúle	nǐ	yǐwài

   except for you, besides you'

| chúle | zǒu | yǐwài |

   except for walking'

1. Zài-Měiguo chúle-chīdezháo-'Zhōngguo-fàn yě-chīdezháo-'Rìběn-fàn.

   In America, besides being able to eat Chinese food, you can also eat Japanese food.

2. Chúle-'Máo-Xiānsheng-yǐwài, wǒmen-dōu-xǐhuan-chī-hóng-shāo-yú.

   Except for Mr. Mao, we all like to eat red-cooked fish.

3. Chúle-tiánde-yǐwài, wǒ-hái-xǐhuan-chī-suānde.

Besides sweet things I also like to eat sour things.

4. 'Wàn-Jiàoshou chúle-tèbié-xǐhuan-chī 'Gāo-Tàitai-zuò-de-fàn, Zhōngguo-fàn tā-'bù-zěnmo-xǐhuan-chī.

Professor Wanamaker, apart from a special liking for Mrs. Gao's cooking, isn't that fond of Chinese food.

5. 'Wàn-Jiàoshòu xǐhuan-táng-cù-yú-yǐwài yé-xǐhuan-chī hóng-shāo-yú.

Professor Wanamaker, besides liking sweet-and-sour fish, also likes [to eat] red-cooked fish.

6. Wǒ-chúle-tīng jiàoyuán-jiāo-'Zhōngwén, hái-měitiān tīng-lùyīn.

In addition to listening to the teacher teach Chinese, I also listen to recordings every day.

7. Wǒmen-shuō 'Gāo-Tàitai-zuò-de-cài-hǎo. Tā-chúle-shuō-"Guòjiǎng"-yǐwài, hái-shuō-hěn-duō-biéde-kèqi-huà.

We said that the dishes Mrs. Gao made were excellent. Besides saying "You flatter me," she said a lot of other polite things.

8. Wǒ-xué-shuō 'Zhōngwén-yǐwài, yòu-xué-xiě-'Zhōngguo-zì.

Besides learning to speak Chinese, I'm also learning to write Chinese characters.

9. Tā-chúle yánjiu-'Zhōngguo-yǔyán-yǐwài, yě-yánjiu-'Rì-běn-yǔyán.

Besides doing research on the Chinese language, he is also studying Japanese.

10. Chúle-tā-yǐwài biéde-xuésheng 'dōu-duì-wǒ-hén-hǎo.

Apart from him, the rest of the students are all very nice to me.

Pattern 19.6. Concessive Construction (Note 6 below)

V₁	shi	V₁
Verb₁	'is'	Verb₁
lái	shi	lái

' came all right'

1. Yòng-kuàizi-chī-fàn, nán-shi-nán, kěshi-chī-'Zhōngguo-cài 'bìděi-yòng.

Eating with chopsticks is hard all right, but you have to use them when you eat Chinese food.

2. 'Zhōngguo-cài hǎo-chī-shi-hǎo-chī, jiù-shi-róngyi chīde-'tài-bǎo-le.

Chinese food is delicious, to be sure. The only thing is, it's easy to overstuff oneself.

3. Shīzi-tóu dà-shi-dà kěshi-wó-děi-chī-liǎngge.

The lion's head is big all right, but I must eat two.

4. Wǒ-jīntian-qǐng-'Gāo-Xiáojie chī-biàn-fàn. Tā-chī-shi-chī-le, wó-xiǎng tā-méi-chībǎo.

I invited Miss Gao to have some ordinary food today. She ate, to be sure, but I don't think she had enough to eat.

5. Zuótian wǒ-dào-'Gāo-Xiānsheng-jiā qù-shi-qù-le, kěshi-
   méi-kànjian-ta.

I <u>did</u> go to Mr. Gao's home today, but I didn't see him.

6. Wǒ-gàosu-ta-shi-gàosu-ta-le.
   Tā-dǒng-bu-dǒng wǒ-jiù-bù-
   zhīdào-le.

I told him, to be sure, but I
don't know if he understood.

7. Jīntian-'Wáng-Xiáojie lái-shi-
   lái-le. Zuò-yìhuěr-jiù-zǒu-le.

Miss King did come today. She
stayed a while and then left.

8. Nèige-fànguǎrde-cài hǎo-shi-
   hǎo, kěshi-gěide-'hén-shǎo.

The food in that restaurant is
good, yes—but the servings are
small.

9. Zhèibén-shū wǒ-kàn-shi-kàn-
   guo-le. Xiànzài-'dōu-wàng-
   le.

I did read this book, but now I've
forgotten it all.

10. Shū-mǎi-shi-mǎi-le, kěshi-
    mǎicuò-le.

I bought the book all right, but I
bought the wrong one.

SUBSTITUTION TABLES

I: 16 sentences (Note 1)

(In the columns marked by asterisks, only items from
the same row may be taken together: hē with tāng, gěi
with qián, etc.)

	*		*
duō	hē	diar	tāng
shǎo	gěi	yìdiǎr	qián
	chī		táng
	mǎi		dòufu

II: 16 sentences (Note 1)

(One or the other, but not both, of the columns marked
with asterisks may be used.)

	*		*
chī	kuài	diar	chī
hē	màn	yìdiǎr	hē
zǒu			zǒu
zuò			zuò

III: 55 phrases (Note 5)

——	——	shī zi-tóu	——
chúle	chī	chǎo-dòufu	yǐwài
	zuò	hóng-shāo-yú	
		chǎo-báicài	
		táng-cù-yú	

PRONUNCIATION DRILLS

Review of Four-Syllable Expressions (I)

This and similar exercises in subsequent lessons provide practice in the pronunciation of four-syllable expressions using vocabulary encountered in previous lessons. Items marked with asterisks have undergone a shift from third tone to second tone.

	0 0 0	1 0 0	2 0 0
1	tāmende-ne	kāi-chē-le-ma	tā-lái-le-ma
2	xuéguo-le-ma	nín-chī guo-le	nín-xuéguo-le
3	wǒmende-ne	wǒ-zhīdao-le	yǒu-fázi-ma
4	gàosu-le-ma	zuì-duōde-ne	zuì-nánde-ma

	3 0 0	4 0 0
1	dōngběide-ne	Gāo-Tàitaide
2	ná-wǒmende	méi-yìside
3	yóu-hǎode-ma*	yǒu-xìngqu-ma
4	kuài-hǎo-le-ma	tài-kèqi-le

	0 1 0	1 1 0	2 1 0
1	xiānsheng-shuō-le	tā-dōu-chī-le	tā-méi-shuōguo
2	róngyi-shuō-ma	shéi-dōu-zhīdao	hái-néng-chī-ma
3	nǐmen-chī-ba	wǒ-xiān-shuō-de	nǐ-cái-zhīdao
4	zhùzai-shānshang	zài-jiā-chī-ma	tài-nán-shuō-le

	3 1 0	4 1 0
1	tā-yǒu-shū-ma	tā-zhù-Sūzhou
2	méi-yǒu-tāde	shéi-lù-yīn-ne
3	hén-hǎo-chī-de*	nǐ-huì-shāo-ma
4	yào-mǎi-shū-ma	mài-qìchē-ma

0 2 0

1 tāde-fángzi
2 biéde-fázi
3 wŏmen-míngbai
4 sìge-péngyou

1 2 0

tā-shuō-shénmo
shéi-chīwán-le
měitiān-lái-ma
dào-Xī-Hú-le

2 2 0

dāngrán-lái-le
hái-méi-lái-ne
hěn-nán-xué-ma
dà-bái-fángzi

3 2 0

1 dōu-yŏu-fángzi
2 shéi-yŏu-qián-ne
3 ní-xiăng-shénmo*
4 zuì-yŏu-qián-le

4 2 0

tā-jiào-shénmo
nín-yào-xué-ma
wŏ-jiù-lái-le
màipiàoyuán-ne

0 3 0

1 tāmen-măi-le
2 nínde-mŭqin
3 wŏmen-zŏu-ba
4 tài-bu-hăo-le

1 3 0

fēijī-hăo-ma
shífēn-hăo-ma
nĭ-jiā-yuăn-ma
lùyīn-hăo-ma

2 3 0

tā-hái-yŏu-ma
hái-néng-xiě-ma
yŏu-rén-zhăo-ta
zuì-nán-măi-le

3 3 0

1 dōu-hén-hăo-ma*
2 shéi-xiáng-zŏu-le*
3 ní-mái-bĭ-ma*
4 jiè-jíběn-le*

4 3 0

tā-tài-hăo-le
yídìng-zŏu-le
yě-yào-măi-le
wàng-nèr-zŏu-ma

0 4 0

1 chībuxià-le
2 shéide-fùqin
3 zăochen-qù-le
4 kànbujiàn-le

1 4 0

fēijī-kuài-ma
xué-shuō-huà-ma
wŏ-chī-fàn-le
zuò-chē-kuài-ma

2 4 0

tā-néng-huà-ma
shéi-ná-zhèige
nĭ-néng-mài-ma
zuì-nán-mài-le

3 4 0

1 tā-kăoshì-le
2 nín-yŏu-fùqin
3 wó-yŏu-dìdi*
4 yào-măi-sìge

4 4 0

chē-tài-dà-ma
nín-huì-huà-ma
nĭ-wèn-mèimei
Wàn-Jiàoshòude

SENTENCE CONVERSION

I. <u>From</u>: Does he also want a little tea?
    <u>To</u>: Give one dollar more.

    1. Tā-yě-yào-yìdiǎr-chá-ma?

    2. Tā-yě-yào-yìdiǎr-qián-ma?

    3. Tā-yě-yào-yíkuài-qián-ma?

    4. Tā-yé-gěi-yíkuài-qián-ma?

    5. Tā-duō-gěi-yíkuài-qián-ma?

    6. Nǐ-duō-gěi-yíkuài-qián-ma?

    7. Nǐ-duō-gěi-yíkuài-qián-ba.

II. <u>From</u>: Who requested you all to come and borrow books?
    <u>To</u>: I said they don't have any good friends.

    1. 'Shéi-jiào-nǐmen dōu-lái-jiè-shū?

    2. 'Shéi-jiào-tāmen dōu-lái-jiè-shū?

    3. 'Shéi-shuō-tāmen dōu-lái-jiè-shū?

    4. Wǒ-shuō-tāmen dōu-lái-jiè-shū.

    5. Wǒ-shuō-tāmen 'méi-lái-jiè-shū.

    6. Wǒ-shuō-tāmen 'méi-you-jiè-shū.

    7. Wǒ-shuō-tāmen 'méi-you-hǎo-shū.

    8. Wǒ-shuō-tāmen 'méi-you-hǎo-péngyou.

III. <u>From</u>: Anyone can cook fried cabbage.
    <u>To</u>: We don't like to eat in restaurants.

    1. 'Shéi-dōu-huì-zuò chǎo-báicài.

    2. Wǒmen-dōu-huì-zuò chǎo-báicài.

    3. Wǒmen-bú-huì-zuò chǎo-báicài.

    4. Wǒmen-bù-xǐhuan-zuò chǎo-báicài.

    5. Wǒmen-bù-xǐhuan-chī chǎo-báicài.

    6. Wǒmen-bù-xǐhuan-chī fànguǎr.

ANSWERING QUESTIONS

1. 'Wàn-Jiàoshou chīde-hěn-duō. 'Bái-Xiānsheng chīde-'bù-duō. 'Shéi-
chīde-tài-bǎo?

2. Bái-táng shi-tiánde, cù shi-suānde. 'Shénmo-shi-tiánde?

3. 'Gāo-Xiānsheng tèbié-xǐhuan-chī-yú. 'Wàn-Jiàoshòu tèbié-xǐhuan-chī-ròu. Shéi-bù-xǐhuan-chī-yú?

4. 'Wáng-Xiānsheng shi-'Guǎngdong-rén. 'Zhāng-Xiānsheng shi-'Shāndong-rén. Nèige-Guǎngdong-rén xìng-shénmo?

5. Shíge-rén yào-hē-tāng. Sìge-rén yào-hē-chá. Xǐhuan-hē-tāngde-rén-duō-ne, háishi-xǐhuan-hē-chá-de-rén-duō-ne?

6. Táng-shi-tiánde, cù-shi-suānde. Nǐ-shuō-'duì-bu-duì?

7. Fànguǎrde-cài méi-you-'Gāo-Tàitai zuòde-hǎo-chī. Shi-'fànguǎr-zuò-de-hǎo háishi-'Gāo-Tàitai-zuòde-hǎo-ne?

8. Péngyou-shuō: "'Gāo-Tàitai, nǐde-xiáojie yòu-piàoliang-yòu-cōngming." 'Gāo-Tàitai yīnggāi-duì-péngyou shuō-shénmo-kèqi-huà?

9. 'Wàn-Jiàoshòu-hē-tāng, 'Bái-Xiānsheng-hē-chá. Hē-'tāng-de-rén shi-shéi?

10. 'Gāo-Xiáojie-shuō ta-bú-huì-zuò-fàn. 'Gāo-Tàitai-shuō Měiyīng-huì-zuò-fàn. Nǐ-shuō-ta-huì-zuò-fàn bú-huì-zuò-fàn?

WHAT WOULD YOU SAY?

Imagine that you and a Chinese friend, Zhang, are having dinner in a restaurant.

You ask your friend what he would like to eat. He replies that he likes everything, and asks about your preference. You reply that you also like everything. Zhang then asks if it is O.K. to order two dishes and one soup. You say this is fine, and you tell him to speak up first. He says he'd like red-cooked meat. You say you want fried bean curd, and ask what soup to order. Your friend suggests that the two of you should order one cabbage soup. You say this is fine, as you are very fond of cabbage. Zhang remarks that the food in this restaurant is delicious. You say you think you should order one more dish. He asks you to say what more should be ordered. You ask if he likes sweet-and-sour fish. He says he does, but that he prefers to eat red-cooked things. You suggest that in that case you should order a red-cooked fish. To your friend's question whether you can use chopsticks or not, you reply that you can, but that you don't use them very well. He asks if you often eat Chinese food. You say you do, adding that the places where you eat are almost all Cantonese restaurants, and that this is the first time you've come to this restaurant. He suggests that hereafter when you eat Chinese food you should come here to eat.

NOTES

1. When stative verbs are modified by expressions of amount ('more, a lit-
    tle,' etc.), the following patterns occur:

    (a) Duō 'more' and shǎo 'less' come before the main verb, while yìdiǎr
         (or diar) 'a little' and number-measure-noun phrases (e.g. yíkuài-
         qián 'one dollar') follow the main verb:

         'Duō-gěi-ta-yìdiǎr. ⎫
               or   ⎬ 'Give him a little more.'
         'Duō-gěi-ta-diar. ⎭

         'Duō-gěi-ta-yíkuài-qián. 'Give him a dollar more.'

    (b) When yìdiǎr (or diar) is combined with kuài 'fast' or màn 'slow,' the
         phrase may appear either before or after the main verb:

         Zǒu-'màn-yìdiǎr. (Zǒu-'màn-diar.) ⎫
                or   ⎬ 'Walk a little slower.'
         'Màn-yìdiǎr-zǒu. ('Màn-diar-zǒu.) ⎭

    (c) In other cases, the stative verb and yìdiǎr come after the main verb:

         Nǐ-kéyi-zuò-'hǎo-yìdiǎr-ma? 'Can you do it a little better?'

2. The verb suffix -zhe forms expressions which correspond to certain -ing
    phrases in English. A main verb with -zhe attached, and frequently with
    the sentence particle ne at the end, means 'is (am, are) [do]ing':

         Wǒ-chīzhe-ne. 'I'm eating.'
         Wǒ-kànzhe-shū-ne. 'I'm reading.'

    A phrase consisting of two verbs, A and B, with -zhe attached to the first
    (A-zhe B) means '[The subject] while doing A, does B':

         Wǒ-chīzhe-fàn kàn-shū. 'I read while eating.'
         Wǒ-zuòzhe-chī-fàn. 'I eat sitting down.'

3. There is a sentence pattern for mentioning two alternative actions and in-
    dicating that if the first is not true, the second automatically is true. The
    pattern consists of two short verb expressions, the first negative; the
    second, which is affirmative, is introduced by jiù 'then, it follows
    (that)':

         Tā-měitiān bù-chī-'Zhōngguo·cài jiù-chī-'Rìběn-càì. 'If he doesn't
         eat Chinese food every day, then he eats Japanese food.' [lit. 'He
         doesn't eat Chinese food every day, then (it follows that) he eats
         Japanese food.' (The implication is that he eats one or the other.)

         Tā-bú-shi-'Zhōngguo-rén jiù-shi-'Rìběn-rén. 'If he isn't Chinese
         then he's Japanese.'

    Often shi 'am, is, are' is added before the verbs if these are not them-
    selves shi. Thus, shi can be added to the first of the two sentences just
    above, but not to the second:

         Tā-měitiān bú-shi-chī-'Zhōngguo-cài jiù-shi-chī-'Rìběn-càì.

4. If the second of two related verbal clauses has a negative verb which is preceded by yĕ 'also' or dōu 'all,' the construction is equivalent to 'although . . . yet' or 'but' in English. Thus if you have lost a book and are hunting for it, you might say:

> Wó-zhăolái-zhăoqù yé-zhăobuzháo.   or
> Wó-zhăolái-zhăoqù dōu-zhăobuzháo.
> 'I've looked and looked but can't find it.'

5. The expression chúle A yĭwài '[lit.] removing A apart,' in which A is a noun or verb expression, has two different meanings depending on what follows:

(a) It means 'besides A' if the following clause contains hái, yĕ, or yòu, all meaning 'also':

> Chúle-ròu-yĭwài wŏ-hái-xĭhuan-chī-yú.   'Besides meat I also like to eat fish.'
> Chúle-Zhōngwén-shū-yĭwài wó-yé-yŏu-Yīngwén-shū. 'Besides Chinese books I also have English books.'
> Chúle-tā-yĭwài yòu-yŏu-sānge-rén-lái-le.   'Besides him three other men came.'
> Chúle-bù-xĭhuan chī-ròu-yĭwài wŏ-hái-bù-xĭhuan-chī-yú.   'Besides not liking to eat meat, I also don't like to eat fish.'

(b) It means 'except for A' if the following clause contains the adverb dōu 'all' or some other expression meaning 'all' or 'more':

> Chúle-tā-yĭwài wŏmen-dōu-shuō-Zhōngwén. 'Except for him, we all speak Chinese.'
> Chúle-tā-yĭwài méi-yŏu-rén-huì-shuō-Zhōngwén. 'Except for him, there is no one who can speak Chinese.'

In this construction, either chúle or yĭwài may be omitted:

> Chúle-ròu-yĭwài wŏ-hái-xĭhuan-chī-yú.   or
> Ròu-yĭwài wŏ-hái-xĭhuan-chī-yú.   or
> Chúle-ròu wŏ-hái-xĭhuan-chī-yú.
> 'Besides meat I also like to eat fish.'

6. Repetition of a verb (or verb phrase), with shi 'be' inserted between the two occurrences, means '[verb] may be true' or '[verb] is true, to be sure.' The construction is often followed by a 'but' clause:

> Nèige-nŭ-xuésheng piàoliang-shi-piàoliang, kĕshi-ta-bènjíle.   'That girl (student) is beautiful all right, but she's awfully dumb.'

In this construction the second occurrence of the verb can take a suffix as an additional element:

> Tā-lái-shi-lái-le, kĕshi-wŏ-méi-zài-jiā.   'He came all right, but I wasn't at home.'

7. The expression náchu A lai 'bring out A' (or náchu A qu 'take out A') is ambiguous in that A may be the object of either ná 'take' or chu 'go out':

> Náchu-shū-lai.   'Bring the books out.'
> Náchu-fángzi-lai.   'Bring (them) out of the house.'

Náchu-shū-qu. 'Take the books out.'
Náchu-fángzi-qu. 'Take (them) out of the house.'

8. The postverb zháo meaning 'succeed in [do]ing' is used to form resultative verbs (see Lesson 14, Note 6, p. 217):

zhǎozhao 'succeed in finding'
mǎizhao 'succeed in buying'
zhǎobuzháo 'be unable to find' (= 'not succeed in finding')

9. The verb bǎo 'be full (in the stomach)' is used to form resultative compounds:

chībǎo 'eat until full, be satiated'
chībubǎo 'be unable to eat one's fill'
chīdebǎo 'be able to eat one's fill'

10. The verb hǎo 'good' is used as an independent verb meaning 'finished'
(fàn-hǎo-le 'food's ready') and as a postverb to form resultative compounds meaning 'finish [do]ing':

zuòhǎo 'finish doing'
zuòbuhǎo 'be unable to finish doing'
zuòdehǎo 'be able to finish doing'

Observe the significance of the particle -de in distinguishing this construction from the otherwise identical one meaning 'do badly' (Lesson 10,
Note 2, p. 136):

zuòbuhǎo 'be unable to finish doing'
zuòde-bu-hǎo 'do badly'

The parallel expressions meaning 'be able to finish doing' and 'do well'
are distinguished in speech only by context (in our transcription, we set
off -hǎo with a hyphen in the meaning 'do well'):

zuòdehǎo 'be able to finish doing'
zuòde-hǎo 'do well'

11. The verb xiàng 'resemble' has the extended meaning 'such as' (cf. English 'like'):

Wǒ-jiù-huì-xiě jǐge-jiǎndānde-zì, xiàng yī, èr, sān. 'I can write
only a few simple characters, such as one, two, three.'

12. The expression bùdéliǎo, which we have encountered in the meaning 'awfully' after a stative verb (piàoliangde-bùdéliǎo 'awfully attractive'), is
used independently as an exclamation having approximately the value of
English ' My!' or ' Gosh!'

13. The expression suíbiàn, literally 'follow (one's) convenience,' is often

used with <u>kéyi</u> 'permit' or <u>hǎo</u> 'good' in the construction <u>suíbiàn . . . dōu kéyi</u> 'as you please':

Suíbiàn-shénmo-dōu-kéyi. 'Anything will do.'
Suíbiàn-máobi-qiānbi dōu-hǎo. 'Either brush or pencil is O. K.'

14. The verb <u>yào</u> 'want' also means 'order (food, in a restaurant)':

Wǒmen-'zài-yào-yíge-cài. 'We are ordering another dish.'

Lesson 20 CALLING A FRIEND

"Měiyīng, zěnmoyàng?"

Dialogue: Several months after his first visit to the Gaos', Mr. White, who has since been a frequent guest in their home, calls and speaks to Miss Gao.

Bái : Wai, shi-yī-liù-qī-bā-ma?

Hello, is this 1-6-7-8?

Gāo-Tàitai : Shì. Ní-zhǎo-shéi?

It is. Who are you calling?

Bái : Wǒ-shi-Wénshān-ne.* Nín-shi-Gāo-Tàitai-ma? Nín-hǎo?   5

This is Vincent.* Is this Mrs. Gao? How are you?

Gāo-Tàitai : Oh, Wénshān-a. Ní-hǎo-ma?

Oh, Vincent. How are you?

Bái : Hǎo, xièxie-nin. Měiyīng-zài-jiā-ma?

Fine, thank you. Is Meiying at home?

Gāo-Tàitai : Zài-jiā. Nǐ-yào-gēn-ta-shuō-huà-ma?   10

Yes. Do you want to talk to her?

---

* Mr. White is now on sufficiently familiar terms with the Gaos so that he is addressed by them as Wenshan. (See Lesson 10, Note 10.) Note also that Miss Gao has dropped the formal nín for the more familiar nǐ in addressing him.

Bái : Shì.

Yes.

Gāo-Tàitai: Hǎo. Qíng-ni-'děng-yiděng.

All right. Please wait a moment.

Gāo-Xiáojie: Wai, Wénshān. Wǒ-yìcāi jiù-shi-nǐ. Wó-xiáng-nǐ-jīntian-zǎoshang yídìng-géi-wó-dǎ-diànhuà.

15

Hello, Vincent. I guessed it was you right away. I thought you would surely call me this morning.

Bái : Zhēn-cōngming. Nǐ-yìcāi jiù-cāiduì-le. Měiyīng, zěnmoyàng? Kǎowán-le-ma? Kǎode-'hǎo-bu-hǎo?

20

You're really sharp. You guessed right on the first try. Meiying, how are things? Have you finished taking your exams? Did they go well?

Gāo: Hai, bié-tí-le. Yīngwén guó-wén kǎode-hái-hǎo, kěshi-shùxué kǎode-zāogāo-jíle. Wǒ-kàncuò-le-tímu.

25

Gosh, don't bring that up. I did rather well in English and Chinese, but I messed up the math exam terribly. I misread a question.

Bái : Zhèi-yě-shi-kǎoshì 'cháng-yǒu-de-shìqing.

This is something that happens often in examinations.

Gāo: Zài-kǎoshì de-shíhou wǒ-yìdiár-yě-bù-zhīdào shi-cuò-le. Kǎowán-le-yǐhòu, yíkàn-tímu cái-zhīdao-shi-cuò-le. 'Nǐ-kǎode-zěnmo-yàng-ne?

30

When I was taking the exam I wasn't at all aware of my mistake. After I finished [with the exam], as soon as I looked at the question I realized it was wrong. How did you make out?

Bái : 'Yīngwén-kǎode wó-xiáng-hái-kéyi. 'Zhōngwén-kǒng-pà-bú-tài-hǎo.

35

I think the English exam came off all right. I'm afraid the Chinese wasn't too good.

Gāo: Yǔyánxué-ne?

How about linguistics?

Bái : Dàgài-yě-'bù-zěnmoyàng.

Most likely not so good either.

Gāo: Xiànzài-wǒ-gàosu-nǐ-yíjiàn-shìqing. Zuótian-wǒ-fùqin-mǔqin-shuō-le, xiànzài-wǒ-fàngjià-le, xià-xīngqī jiào-wǒ-gēn-tāmen-yíkuàr qu-lǚ-xíng. Nǐ-cāi wǒmen-dào-nǎr-qu.

40

45

I have something to tell you now. Yesterday my father and mother said that since I'm having vacation, next week I'm to go on a trip with them. Guess where we're going.

Bái : Dào-'Rìběn-qu.

To Japan.

Gāo: 'Nǐ-zěnmo-zhīdao-ne?

How did you know?

Bái : Gāo-Xiānsheng-Gāo-Tàitai tāmen-liǎngwèi-'dōu-xǐhuan-Rìběn-me. Suóyi-nǐ-yì-shuō-lǚxíng wǒ-jiù-zhīdao shi-dào-Rìběn-qu.

50

Mr. and Mrs. Gao both like Japan, you see. So as soon as you mentioned a trip, I knew it was to Japan.

Gāo: Nǐ-zhēn-cōngming.

You're really sharp.

Bái : Qù-duōshao-shíhou? 'Shén-mo-shíhou-huílai-ne?

55

How long will you be gone? When are you coming back?

Gāo : Wǒ-fùqin-mǔqin-tāmen-xiǎng
zài-nèr-zhù-liǎngge-yuè,
kěshi-wǒ-bù-gāoxìng zhù-
'nènmo-duō-de-shíhou. Wǒ-   60
xiǎng-gēn-tāmen-shuō 'yíge-
yuè-jiù-huílai.

My father and mother plan to
stay there for two months, but
I'm not happy about staying that
long. I'm going to tell them that
I'd like to come back in one
month.

Bái : Hǎojíle. Nènmo-wó-déi-
qíng-ni-chī-fàn.

Fine. So I must ask you to dinner.

Gāo : Zěnmo-'nènmo-kèqi-ne?   65

Why so polite?

Bái : Nǐ-'shénmo-shíhou yǒu-
gōngfu? Wǒmen-yíkuàr-
chī-fàn. Chī-fàn-yǐhòu
wǒmen-zài-qu-kàn-diàn-
yǐngr, 'hǎo-bu-hǎo?   70

When are you free? Let's have
dinner together and [after eat-
ing] go see a movie, O.K.?

Gāo : Hǎo. Wǒmen-yǐjing-fàng-
jià-le. Wó-něitiān-dōu-
yǒu-gōngfu.

Fine. We're already on vacation. I'm free every day.

Bái : Háishi-nǐ-shuō shénmo-
shíhou-hǎo.   75

It would be better for you to set
a time.

Gāo : Xīngqīsān 'hǎo-bu-hǎo? Ní-
yǒu-gōngfu-ma?

Is Wednesday all right? Are you
free?

Bái : Hǎo. Ní-xǐhuan-chī-shén-
mo-ne?

Fine. What would you like to
eat?

Gāo : Wǒ-'shénmo-dōu-xǐhuan-chī.   80
'Zhōngguo-fàn 'wàiguo-fàn
wǒ-'dōu-xǐhuan. Wó-xiáng-
qilai-le—shūdiān-fùjìn yǒu-
yíge-'běifāng-fànguǎr jiào-
Wànnián-Fànguǎr. Nǐ-zhī-   85
dao-ma?

I like (to eat) everything. Chinese food, foreign food — I like
them both. It's just occurred to
me—near the bookstore there's
a Northern restaurant called the
Ten Thousand Years Restaurant.
Do you know it?

Bái : Zài-shūdiàn-něibiar?

On which side of the bookstore?

Gāo : Zài-shūdiàn-dōngbiar.

East of the bookstore.

Bái : Oh, nǐ-shuō-wó-xiángqilai-
le. Kěshi-wǒ-méi-qu-chī-   90
guo. Tīngshuō-nèrde-cài
zuòde-hén-hǎo.

Oh, I realized it as you were
speaking. But I've never gone
there to eat. I hear their food is
very good.

Gāo : Wǒmen-dào-Wànnián-Fàn-
guǎr chī-běifāng-cài 'hǎo-
bu-hǎo?   95

Shall we go to the Ten Thousand
Years Restaurant and have
Northern Chinese food?

Bái : Hǎojíle. Wó-hén-xǐhuan
chī-běifāng-fàn. Wǒmen-
jiù-dào-nèr-qu-chī.

Fine. I like Northern food very
much. So let's go there for dinner.

Gāo : Hǎo-ba.

Fine.

Bái : Wǒmen-dào-nǎr kàn-diàn-   100
yǐngr-qu-ne?

Where shall we (go) see a
movie?

Gāo : Tīngshuō Zhōngguo-Diàn-

I hear the movie being shown at

yǐngryuàn yǎn-de-nèibù-
piānzi bú-cuò. Shi-yíbù-lì-
shǐ-piānzi. Gùshi-xiěde-   105
hǎo, yǎnyuán-yǎnde-hǎo. Ní-
xǐhuan-lìshǐ-piānzi-ma?

the China Theater isn't bad. It's
a historical movie. The story is
well written, and the actors do
their parts well. Do you like
historical movies?

Bái : Wó-xǐhuan. Wǒmen-jiù-dào-
Zhōngguo-Diànyǐngryuàn qu-
kàn-ba.   110

I do.   So let's go to the China
Theater.

Gāo: Tīngshuō-nèibù-piānzi hěn-
duō-rén-kàn. Pà-mǎibuzháo-
piào-ba.

I hear a lot of people are seeing
that movie. I'm afraid we may
not be able to buy tickets.

Bái : Wǒ-xiān-qu-mǎi-piào. Wǒ-
men-kàn-jiúdiǎn-nèichǎng   115
hǎo-ma?

I'll buy the tickets ahead of time.
Let's take in the nine o'clock
show, O.K.?

Gāo: Kéyi.

O.K.

Bái : Xīngqīsān-wǎnshang liùdiǎn-zhōng wǒ-dào-fǔshang-
qu-jiē-ni.   120

I'll come to your home for you
Wednesday at six.

Gāo: Hǎo, xièxie-ni.

Fine, thank you.

Bái : Yídìng-le.

That's definite.

Gāo: Yídìng. Zàijiàn.

Sure.   Good-bye.

Bái : Zàijiàn, zàijiàn.

Good-bye.

VOCABULARY

běifāng	the North; northern region (PW)
bù	(measure for movies and sets of things, e.g. books)
cāi	guess (that), figure out (that) (TV)
chǎng	(measure for showings of movies)
dǎ	hit, strike (TV) (Note 3 below)
dǎkai	open (RV) [lit. strike open] (Note 3 below)
dàgài	likely, probable; probably, in all probability; approximately (MA) [lit. big outline]
diànhuà	telephone (N) [lit. electric speech]
diànyǐng(r)yuàn	movie theater (N) [lit. electric shadow hall]
fàngjià	have vacation (IV) [lit. release leave]
fùjìn	vicinity (PW) [lit. join near]
gāoxìng	be happy (SV) [lit. high spirits]
guówén	Chinese (N) [lit. national language] (Note 6 below)
gùshi	story, narrative (N) [lit. old matter]
hai	(sigh of dejection, regret, etc.)

jiàn	(measure for matters, tasks, etc.)
jiē	greet, meet; receive (guests, ships, letters) (TV)
kǒngpà	fear (that), be afraid (of), be afraid (to) (TV)
lìshǐ	**history (N)**
me	**(particle indicating obviousness) (Note 8 below)**
nánfāng	the South; southern region (PW)
pà	**fear, be afraid of (V)**
piānzi	reel, movie (N)
qǐlái	get up (IV) [lit. rise come] (Note 2 below)
shìqing	**affair, matter (N)**
shùxué	mathematics (N) [lit. number study]
tí	carry, lift, take, bring (up), mention (TV)
tímu	topic (N)
yǎn	act (in); put on (a performance) (TV)
yǎnyuán	actor (N) [lit. act person]
yí, yì	as soon as (AD) (Note 1 below)
zāogāo	**messed up (SV) (Note 7 below)**

SENTENCE BUILD-UP

yì

wǒ-yì-tīng-ta-shuō-
  huà

jiù-zhīdao ta-bú-shi-
  Zhōngguo-rén

1. Wǒ-yì-tīng-ta-shuō-huà, jiù-
zhīdao ta-bú-shi-'Zhōngguo-
rén.

once, as soon as

as soon as I heard him
  speak

then I knew he wasn't Chinese

As soon as I heard him speak I
knew he wasn't Chinese.

nǐ-yì-shuō

wǒ-cái-zhīdao

2. Nǐ-yì-shuō wǒ-cái-zhīdao.

as soon as you spoke

I only then knew

I only found out about [lit. knew
of] it when you mentioned it.

wǒ-yì-chī

zhēn-shi-Guǎngdong-fàn

3. Wǒ-yì-chī zhēn-shi-Guǎngdong-fàn.

I took a taste

it really was Cantonese food

I took a taste and sure enough it
really was Cantonese food.

gùshi

yì-tīng-tā-yào-shuō-
  gùshi

4. Yì-tīng-tā-yào-shuō-gùshi
háizi-'dōu-pǎolai-le.

story

on hearing he was going to
  tell a story

As soon as they heard he was
going to tell a story the children
all came running.

fàngjià

have a vacation

dàxué-yí-fàngjià

as soon as college vacation starts

wǒ-jiù-huí-guó

I'll go back to my own country

5. Dàxué-yí-fàngjià wǒ-jiù-huí-guó.

As soon as college vacation starts I'll go back to my own country.

guówén

Chinese (literature)

gēn-Yīngwén

and English

6. Guówén-gēn-Yīngwén yíyàng-nán-ma?

Is Chinese as hard as English?

pà

fear

xuésheng-dōu-pà-ta

students all fear him

7. Nèige-xiānsheng xuésheng-dōu-pà-ta.

The students are all afraid of that teacher.

kǒngpà

fear or be afraid that

8. Kǒngpà chībuwán-nènmo-duō-cài.

I'm afraid we can't finish so many courses.

qǐlai

get up

'shénmo-shíhou-qǐlai?

get up at what time?

9. Ní-zǎochen-'shénmo-shíhou-qǐlai?

When do you get up in the morning?

ná

grasp

náqilai

lift up

10. Wǒmen-yíkuàr-náqilai-ba.

Let's lift it together.

náqilai

lift (up)

náqi-shū-lai

take up your book

11. Náqi-shū-lai-niàn-yící.

Pick up your book and take a turn reading.

náqilai

lift up

nábuqilái

unable to lift (up)

12. Nènmo-duōde-dōngxi wǒ-ná-buqilái.

I can't lift so many things.

jiàn

(measure for matters, tasks, etc.)

zhèijiàn-shì

this task

13. Zhèijiàn-shì 'hěn-róngyi-zuò.

This job is easy to do.

shì

affair, task

shìqing

affair, task

14. Zhèijiàn-shìqing hěn-nán-zuò.

This job is hard to do.

diànyǐngr

movie

diànyǐngryuàn

movie theater

15. Fànguǎr lí-diànyǐngryuàn-   The restaurant is close to the
    hěn-jìn.   movie theater.

        dǎ   hit, strike
16. Bié-dǎ-ta.   Don't hit him.

        diànhuà   telephone
        dǎ-diànhuà   make a phone call
        gěi-ta-dǎ-diànhuà   call him on the phone
17. Wó-déi-gěi-ta-dǎ-diànhuà.   I have to phone him.

        dǎ   from
        dǎ-fànguǎr   from the restaurant
18. Dǎ-fànguǎr-dào-shūdiàn   It's three miles from the restau-
    yǒu-sānlǐ-lù.   rant to the bookstore.

        dǎkai   open
19. Qíng-nǐmen-bǎ-shū-dǎkai.   Please open your books.

        dǎdao   fight up to
        fùjìn   vicinity
20. Yǐjing-dǎdao-chéngde-fùjìn.   The fighting has already reached
                                     the vicinity of the city.

        tímu   topic, problem
        wèn-tímu   pose a problem
21. Xiānsheng-wèn-ni 'shénmo-   What problem did the teacher
    tímu?   put to you?

        lìshǐ   history
        xué-Zhōngguo-lìshǐ   study Chinese history
22. Wǒmen-jīntian kāishǐ-xué   Today we begin the study of Chi-
    Zhōngguo-lìshǐ.   nese history.

        bù   set (of books)
        zhèibù-shū   this set of books
23. Zhèibù-shū yígòng-yǒu-sān-   Altogether there are three vol-
    běn.   umes in this set of books.

        piānzi   movie
        nèibù-piānzi   that movie
24. Nèibù-piānzi hǎode-bùdé-   That movie is terrific.
    liǎo.

        yǎn   put on a performance
        yǎn-diànyǐngr   show a movie
25. Wǒmen-xuéxiào jīntian-yǎn-   Our school is showing a movie
    diànyǐngr.   today.

        yǎnyuán   actor
        yǎnde-hén-hǎo   act very well
26. Nèige-yǎnyuán yǎnde-hén-hǎo.   That actor performs very well.

        chǎng   showing of a movie

yănle-sānchăng
27. Nèibù-piānzi jīntian-yănle-
'sānchăng.

        shown three times
That movie was shown three
times today.

nèichăng
bādiăn-nèichăng
28. Wŏmen-kàn 'bādiăn-nèichăng
'hăo-bu-hăo?

        that showing
the eight o'clock show
How about our seeing the eight
o'clock show?

dàgài
dàgài-bù-lái
29. Tā-míngtian dàgài-bù-lái.

        probably
probably isn't coming
He probably isn't coming tomorrow.

dàgài
dàgài-yŏu-yìlĭ-lù
30. Fànguăr-lí-zhèr dàgài-yŏu-
yìlĭ-lù.

        approximately
about one mile
The restaurant is about a mile
from here.

cāi
31. Nĭ-cāi tā-shi-'nĕiguó-rén.

        guess
Guess what nationality he is.

shùxué
32. Zhōngguo-rén duì-shùxué-
hén-hăo.

        mathematics
Chinese are very good at mathematics.

tí
tíqilai
tíqilai-nèige-rén
33. Nĭ-tíqilai-nèige-rén 'wó-yĕ-
rènshi.

        lift, raise; mention
mention
mention that man
(Now that) you mention that man,
I also know him.

jiē
34. Wó-dĕi-dào-chē-zhàn qu-jiē-
ta.

        meet, greet
I have to go to the bus station to
meet him.

jiēdào
35. Nĭ-jiēdàole-nĭ-péngyoude-
'xìn-méi-you?

        receive (a letter)
Did you get a letter from your
friend?

jiēzhao
méi-jiēzháo
36. Wŏ-láiwăn-le. Méi-jiēzháo-
ta.

        succeed in meeting
failed to meet
I came late and missed him.

bĕifāng
37. Wŏ-zuì-xĭhuan-chī-de shi-
bĕifāng-cài.

        northern region
What I like to eat most is Northern cooking.

nánfāng
38. Guăngdong-rén dāngrán-shi-
nánfāng-rén.

        southern region
Cantonese of course are Southerners.

zāogāo
39. Nèige-piānzi zāogāo-jíle.

        messed up, confused
That movie was a mess.

        hai   (a sigh)
40. Hai, wǒ-xuébuhuì-Zhōngwén.   Gosh, I can't learn Chinese.

        me   you see
        kǎodeshàng   able to pass the entrance
                                                exams
        tā-hěn-cōngming-me   he's intelligent, you see
41. Wó-xiǎng tā-yídìng-kǎode-   I think he can certainly pass the
      shàng, yīnwei-tā-hěn-cōng-   entrance exams since he's in-
      ming-me.   telligent, you see.

        gāoxìng   happy
        gāoxìng-nín-néng-lái   happy that you can come
42. Wó-hěn-gāoxìng nín-néng-   I'm very happy that you can
      lái.   come.

PATTERN DRILLS

Pattern 20.1.   Use of yí as an Adverb   (Note 1 below)

S	yí/yì	V	(O)
Subject	yí/yì	Verb	(Object)
nǐ	yí	gàosu	ta

        as soon as you tell him'

1. Nèige-xuésheng 'zhēn-cōng-   That student is really bright.
     ming. Shàng-kè-de-shíhou,   When he goes to a class, as soon
     xiānsheng-yì-jiāo tā-jiu-   as the teacher teaches (some-
     míngbai.   thing) he immediately under-
                                       stands.

2. Wǒ-xué-'Yīngwén, 'zěnmo-   I can't master English no matter
     xué-yě-bú-huì. Wǒ-xué-   how I study.   But whenever I
     'Zhōngwén 'yì-xué-jiù-huì-le.   study Chinese, I get it right
                                       away.

3. Wǒ-yí-kàn-biǎo, yǐjing-bā-   When I looked at my watch it was
     diǎn-zhōng-le. Kǒngpà-ta-bù-   already eight o'clock. I'm afraid
     lái-le.   he isn't coming after all.

4. Wó-mǔqin-shuō-le, wǒ-yí-fàng-   My mother said that as soon as I
     jià wǒmen-jiu-dào-Húnán-qu-le. go on vacation we will go to Hu-
                                       nan.

5. Jīntian wǒ-yì-chūqu jiu-yùjian-   Today I had no sooner gone out
     'Bái-Xiānsheng-le.   than I met Mr. White.

6. Nèizhī-bǐ wǒ-yí-kàn jiu-zhī-   As soon as I saw that pen I knew
     dao-shi-'Gāo-Xiáojiede.   it was Miss Gao's.

7. Guǎngdong-cài tài-hǎo-chī-le.   Cantonese food is too delicious.
     Wǒ-yì-chī jiu-chīde-tài-bǎo-le. Whenever I eat it I overstuff my-
                                       self.

8. 'Qián-Xiānshengde-nèi-jǐge-
    háizi 'hén-xǐhuan-tīng-gùshi.
    Wǒ-yí-qù tāmen-jiu-jiào-wǒ-
    shuō-gùshi.

    Mr. Qian's children love to lis-
    ten to stories. Whenever I go
    there they ask me to tell a story.

9. Zuótian kànjian-nèige-nǔ-háizi.
    Wǒ-yí-kàn-ta jiu-shi-Yīngguo-
    rén.

    I saw that girl yesterday. I took
    one look and sure enough she
    was English.

10. 'Gāo-Tàitai-hǎojíle. Wǒ-yí-qù
    ta-jiu-qíng-wo zài-tā-jiā-chī-
    fàn. Pà-tài-máfan-ta-le.

    Mrs. Gao is very nice. When-
    ever I go (there) she invites me
    to eat at her home. I'm afraid
    it's too much trouble for her.

11. Wó-hén-xǐhuan yánjiu-kēxué.
    Wǒ-yí-dào-túshūguǎn jiu-kàn-
    kēxué-shū.

    I love to study science. When-
    ever I go to the library I read
    science books.

12. 'Zhōngguo-zì hěn-nán-xiě.
    Wǒ-yì-xiě jiu-xiěcuò-le.

    Chinese characters are hard to
    write. Whenever I write them I
    do it wrong.

13. Nèige-xuésheng-hěn-qíguài.
    Yì-kǎoshì tā-jiu-bìng.

    That student is pretty queer.
    Whenever there are exams he
    gets sick.

14. Wó-kǒngpà yòng-kuàizi-yòng-
    de-bú-tài-hǎo. Wǒ-yí-yòng-
    'kuàizi-chī-fàn, biéde-rén-
    dōu-kàn-wo.

    I'm afraid I don't use chopsticks
    too well. Whenever I eat with
    chopsticks everyone looks àt me.

15. Wǒ-yì-chī, zhēn-hǎo-chī-
    jíle.

    I took a taste, and sure enough it
    really was delicious.

Pattern 20.2. Use of qǐlai as a Postverb (Note 2 below)

V	-qǐlai	
Verb	'up'	
ná	-qilai	'take up'
xiáng	-qilai	'recall'

1. Zuótian xiǎng-kàn-diànyǐngr.
    Dàole-diànyǐngryuàn cái-xiáng-
    qilai wàngle-ná-qián-le.

    Yesterday I planned to go to a
    movie. Only after reaching the
    theater did I remember that I'd
    forgotten to bring any money.

2. Nèige-háizi 'hén-xǐhuan-huà-
    huàr. Yì-náqi-bǐ-lai jiu-huà-
    huàr.

    That child loves to draw. When-
    ever he picks up a pen he makes
    a drawing.

3. Kànqilai zhèijiàn-shìqing hěn-
    máfan.

    On examination, this matter is
    quite a nuisance.

4. Yǔyánxué yánjiuqilai 'hén-yǒu-
    yìsi.

    Studying linguistics is very in-
    teresting.

5. Zuò-chē-hěn-jìn. Zóuqilai-   It's close if you go by car. It's
    hén-yuǎn.   quite far if you walk.

6. Nèige-rén wǒ-jiànguo, kěshi-   I've seen that man, but I can't
    wǒ-xiǎngbuqǐlái tā-xìng-shén-   remember what his name is.
    mo-le.

7. Shuōqilai wó-yé-déi-zǒu-le.   Speaking (of it), I have to go too.

8. Shīzi-tóu hén-hǎo-chī. Kěshi-   Lion's head is delicious.   But
    zuòqilai-hěn-máfan.   making it is a lot of trouble.

9. Wó-xiǎngqilai-le. Jīntian shi-   It has occurred to me that today
    xīngqīliù. Wǒmen-děi-qu-kàn-   is Saturday. We must go see a
    diànyǐngr.   movie.

10. Nèige-zì wǒ-wàngle-niàn-shén-   I've forgotten how that character
    mo-le. 'Zěnmo-xiǎng yé-   is read.   No matter how (hard) I
    xiǎngbuqilái.   think of it, I still can't recall it.

11. Nèiběn-shū wǒ-náqilai-   I took up the book and glanced at
    yíkàn shi-yìběn-gùshi-shū.   it, and sure enough it was a
                                        story book.

12. Zuò- Zhōngguo-cài xuéqilai-   Learning how to cook Chinese
    hěn-róngyı.   food is very easy.

13. Nèige-háizi nǐ-yì-shuōqi-láo-   As soon as you mention a tiger
    hu-lai tā-jiu-pà.   to that child, he gets scared.

14. Wǒ-nábuqi nèige-dōngxi-lai.   I can't lift (up) that thing.

15. Nèige-háizi tài-xiǎo. Ta-ná-   That child is too small.   He
    buqi nèiběn-dà-shū-lai.   can't lift that big book.

Pattern 20.3.   Expressions with <u>dǎ</u>   (note 3 below)

Pattern 20.3a.

dǎ	Noun	
dǎ	mén	'knock on the door'
dǎ	diànhuà	'make a phone call'

Pattern 20.3b.

| dǎ | Place Word | |
| dǎ | zhèr | 'from here' |

Pattern 20.3c.

| dǎ | Verb | |
| dǎ | -kai | 'open up' |

1. Zuótian wǒ-huí-jiā-dǎ-mén.   Yesterday I returned home and
    Dǎle-yǒu-yíge-zhōngtóu, yě-   knocked on the door. I knocked
    méi-rén-kāi-mén.   for an hour, but no one opened
                                        the door.

2. Wǒ-'jiù-pà-wǒ-mèimei dǎ-
   diànhuà. Yì-dǎ jiu-shuō-
   liǎngge-zhōngtóu.

   The only thing I'm afraid of is
   my younger sister making a
   phone call. Whenever she calls
   she talks for a couple of hours.

3. Shàng-kè-de-shíhou, jiàoyuán-
   shuō: "Qǐng-nǐmen-bǎ-shū
   xiān-dǎkai.".

   When we go to class, the teacher
   says: " Please first open your
   books."

4. Zuótian-'Gāo-Xiáojie géi-wó-
   dǎle-'sāncì-diànhuà.

   Yesterday Miss Gao phoned me
   three times.

5. Liǎngge-háizi dáqilai-le.

   The two children have begun to
   fight.

6. Rén-'dōu-pǎo-le, yīnwei-yǐ-
   jing-dǎdào Nán-Hú-fùjìn-le.

   Everyone has fled, as the fighting has already reached the
   vicinity of South Lake.

7. Nèige-jiàoyuán jiāo-shū-de-
   fázi 'zhēn-hǎo. Jiāo-lìshǐ-
   de-shíhou ta-bú-jiào-wǒmen-
   dǎkai-shū. Tā-xiān-wèn-wǒ-
   men-tímu.

   That teacher's method of teaching is really good. When teaching history he doesn't tell us to
   open our books. He first poses
   us problems.

8. Dá-Niǔyue-dào-Sānfánshì zuò-
   chuán bu-zhīdào-yào-jǐtian.

   I don't know how many days it
   takes from New York to San
   Francisco by boat.

9. Jīntian wó-géi-'Gāo-Xiáojie-
   dǎ-diànhuà. Dǎle-sìcì, ta-
   dōu-bú-zài-jiā.

   Today I called Miss Gao. I
   called four times, but she was
   never at home.

10. Dǎ-zhèr wàng-béi-guǎi jiu-
    dào-'Gāo-Xiānsheng-jiā.

    Turn north from here and
    you'll get to Mr. Gao's home.

Pattern 20.4.   More Resultative Verb Compounds

V₁	(bu/de)	V₂
Verb₁	(bu/de)	Verb₂
tīng	bu	míngbai

' unable to understand (aurally)'

1. Bú-yào-shuō-huà. Qǐng-
   nǐmen-bǎ-shū-dǎkāi.

   Don't talk. Please open your
   books.

2. Zhèige-mén kāibukāi-le.
   'Zěnmo-dǎ yé-dǎbukāi.

   This door can't be opened. No
   matter how (hard) you try, you
   can't open it.

3. Wǒ-shuōle-bàntian. Nǐ-tīng-
   'míngbai-le-méi-you?

   I've been talking for a long time.
   Have you been understanding?

4. Tā-hěn-cōngming. Yì-'xué-
   jiu-xuéhuì.

   He's very bright. As soon as he
   studies (something) he gets it.

5. Wǒ-chīgòu-le. Bù-néng-duō-   I've eaten enough. I can't eat
    chī-le.   very much.

6. Nèige-xuésheng zhēn-bu-cōng-   That student is really not very
    ming. 'Nèige-zì-dōu-méi-   bright. He didn't write any char-
    xiěduì.   acters correctly.

7. Nèige-xiānsheng cháng-bá-wǒ-   That teacher often writes my
    de-míngzi xiěcuò-le.   name wrong.

8. Qǐng-ni bǎ-chē-mén-dǎkai.   Please open the car door.

9. Xuéxiàode-fàn bù-hǎo-chī. Wǒ-   The school food is unappetizing.
    měitiān dōu-chībubǎo.   Every day I can't get filled (up).

10. Ní-bá-wǒde-shìqing gēn-ta-   Did you reach an agreement with
    'shuōhǎo-le-méi-you?   him on that business of mine?

11. Tā-shuō wǒ-'zuótian-qu-kàn-   He said I went to the movies
    diànyǐngr-le. Tā-zhēn-cāi-   yesterday. He really guessed
    duì-le.   right.

12. Tā-shuō-de-huà wǒ-yìdiár-yě-   I can't understand the least bit
    tīngbumíngbai.   of what he's saying.

13. Kāi-qìchē 'zěnmo-xué wó-yě-   No matter how (hard) I study
    xuébuhuì.   driving, I can't learn.

14. Wó-hén-xǐhuan chī-Zhōngguo-   I love [to eat] Chinese food. No
    fàn. Wó-'zěnmo-chī yě-chī-   matter how (much) I eat I can't
    bugòu.   eat enough.

15. Nèige-jiàoyuánde-tímu hěn-   That teacher's questions are
    tèbié. Ní-'zěnmo-cāi yě-cāi-   pretty peculiar. No matter how
    buzháo.   you guess you can't guess them.

16. Nǐ-wèi-'shénmo láiwǎn-le-ne?   Why have you come late?

17. Ní-xiáng-wǒ-xué-Zhōngwén   Do you think I can learn Chi-
    'xuédehuì-xuébuhuì?   nese?

18. Tā-jīntian dào-xuéxiào qùwǎn-   He was late (in going) to school
    le.   today.

19. Wǎnfàn 'liùdiǎn-zhōng 'zuò-   Can you finish cooking dinner by
    dehǎo-zuòbuhǎo?   six o'clock?

20. Wǒ-zuò-'qìchē-lái. Yídìng-   I'm coming by car. I certainly
    láibuwǎn.   can't be late.

SUBSTITUTION TABLES

I: 48 phrases (Note 1)

jiàoyuán	yí	kànjian	wǒ
jiàoshòu		gàosu	nǐ
xiānsheng		wèn	tā
tàitai		jiào	

PRONUNCIATION DRILLS

Review of Four-Syllable Expressions (II)

(Asterisks mark expressions which have undergone a change of third tone to second tone.)

001

1 tāmende-shū
2 xuéshengde-chē
3 nǐmende-jiā
4 màile-de-chē

101

tā-hē-de-tāng
nín-kāide-chē
nǐ-chīde-jī
tài-duōde-chē

201

tīng-xuésheng-shuō
nín-xuéde-duō
wǒ-náde-shū
zuì-róngyi-shuō

301

1 dōu-xǐhuan-chī
2 Húběide-duō
3 wó-xiǎngbuchū *
4 tài-hǎode-shū

401

xiān-xiàle-shān
shéi-kànde-duō
wǒ-niànle-shū
zuì-dàde-shān

011

1 tāmen-jiēhūn
2 shéide-shū-duō
3 nǐmen-duō-chī
4 niànde-zhēn-duō

111

yīnggāi-duō-chī
nín-hē-sānbēi
yǒu-sānqiān-duō
dà-shān-zhēn-gāo

211

tā-huí-jiā-chī
Húnán-shān-duō
wǒ-méi-tīngshuō
jiào-shéi-xiān-chī

311

1 tā-yě-tīngshuō
2 shídiǎn-duō-zhōng
3 wó-mǎi-sānzhī *
4 bìděi-jiēhūn

411

tā-niàn-gāozhōng
shéi-zuò-fēijī
mǎi-lùyīnjī
zuì-huì-jiāo-shū

021

1 tāmen-hái-shuō
2 xuésheng-méi-tīng
3 wǒmen-hái-chī
4 wàngle-ná-shū

121

tā-dāngrán-hē
nín-xiān-lái-chī
wǒ-gāi-huí-jiā
qìchē-shéi-kāi

221

Zhōngwén-nán-shuō
shéi-néng-lái-chī
wǒ-xué-shítiān
zuò-chuán-huí-jiā

321

1 tā-qǐng-shéi-chī
2 shéi-xiǎng-huí-jiā
3 ní-hěn-néng-chī *
4 zuì-hǎo-rén-duō

421

tā-jiào-shéi-shuō
shéi-zuì-néng-chī
nǐ-yào-ná-shū
xiànzài-hái-chī

0 3 1	1 3 1	2 3 1
1 shuōde-hěn-duō	tā-jiāo-Měiyīng	tā-néng-xiě-shū
2 tiánde-hǎo-chī	nín-kāishǐ-shuō	nín-méi-mǎi-zhōng
3 yǒude-yě-shuō	bǐ-jī-hǎo-chī	yǒu-rén-kǎo-shū
4 rènshi-hěn-duō	qìchē-hěn-duō	tèbié-hǎo-chī

3 3 1	4 3 1
1 tā-xiáng-mǎi-shū *	tā-yào-mǎi-shū
2 hái-yóu-hěn-duō *	nín-zhù-wǔtiān
3 wó-hén-xiǎng-shuō *	yě-tài-jiǎndān
4 fàn-hén-hǎo-chī *	sìwàn-jiǔqiān

0 4 1	1 4 1	2 4 1
1 tāmen-yào-chī	fēijī-zuì-duō	tā-méi-zài-jiā
2 fángzi-tài-gāo	cháng-shuō-yào-chī	nín-xué-sìtiān
3 nǐmen-huì-shuō	wǒ-gāi-lù-yīn	yǒu-rén-yào-chē
4 dàde-qìchē	dì-sānhào-chē	jiào-shéi-lù-yīn

3 4 1	4 4 1
1 kāishǐ-niàn-shū	gōnggòng-qìchē
2 nín-yě-yònggōng	shéi-huì-lù-yīn
3 wó-xiǎng-mài-shū *	nǐ-yào-jiè-shū
4 sì-wǔ-liù-qī	jiàoshòu-kàn-shū

A CONVERSATION

Translate the following conversation between Mr. White and Mr. Mao.

Máo: 'Bái-Xiānsheng, nín-hǎo-ma? 'Háo-jiǔ-bú-jiàn-le.

Bái : Oh, Máo-Xiānsheng, ní-hǎo. Wǒmen-'háo-jiǔ-bú-jiàn-le.

Máo: Zěnmoyàng, tài-máng-ma?

Bái : Duì-le. Yǒu-yìdiǎr-máng.

Máo: Nín-yào-dào-nǎr-qu?

Bái : Wǒ-'bú-dào-nǎr-qu. Wǒ-zài-zhèr děng-péngyou.

Máo: Nín-děng-shéi?

Bái : Wó-děng-'Gāo-Xiáojie. Tā-jiào-wo-'sìdiǎn-zhōng zài-zhèr-děng-ta.

      Xiànzài-yǐjing kuài-wúdiǎn-le. Tā-hái-méi-lái-ne.

Máo: 'Gāo-Xiānsheng-tāmen yào-dào-'Rìběn-qu-le. Shì-ma?

Bái : Duì-le. Dàgài-tāmen xià-xīngqī jiu-zǒu-le.

Máo: 'Gāo-Xiānsheng zuì-gāoxìng dào-'Rìběn-qu-le. Tāmen-zài-'Rìběn
        yào-zhù-'duōshao-shíhou-ne?

Bái : Kǒngpà-yào-zhù 'yì-liǎngge-yuè-ba.

Máo: Kěshi-nín-gēn-Gāo-Xiáojie yào-'háo-jiǔ-bu-jiàn-le.

Bái : Duì-le.

Máo: Nín-yǐhòu qǐng-'cháng-dào-shūdiàn-lai.

Bái : Wǒ-xiànzài yǐjing-kǎowán-le. Bú-tài-máng-le. Kéyi-cháng-dào-shū-
        diàn-qu. 'Máo-Xiānsheng, qǐng-wèn-ni. Zhè-fùjìn yǒu-diànhuà-ma?
        Wó-xiáng-gěi-Gāo-jia dǎ-ge-diànhuà, wènwen-'Gāo-Xiáojie yǐjing-
        'chūlai-le-méi-you.

Máo: Gōngyuán-lǐbiar, wàng-'zuó-guǎi nèige-xiǎo-fángzi jiu-shi-dǎ-diàn-
        huà-de-dìfang.

Bái : Xièxie-ni.

Máo: Zàijiàn.

Bái : Zàijiàn.

ENGLISH TO CHINESE

Put yourself in the role of Mr. White narrating the following to a Chinese
friend.

Our school has now begun its vacation. Vacation will last about two
months. Some students have returned home, some have gone to other places
on trips. I plan to do some more studying during vacation. When I left home,
my father and mother hoped I would be a good student, so I must work hard.
It will soon be almost a year since I've come to China. I've made a number of
friends, and they have been very nice to me. Mr. and Mrs. Gao are awfully
nice to me. Every time I go to their home they insist on my eating with them.
Mrs. Gao knows I like red-cooked dishes. Then there's Miss Gao, who is
also a good friend of mine. We often talk together, or study a little language
and literature. She is both intelligent and attractive. They are going on a
trip soon and I won't be able to see them for a month or two.

ANSWERING QUESTIONS

1. 'Gāo-Xiáojie měi-yíge-xīngqī kàn-liǎngcì-diànyǐngr. 'Wàn-Xiáojie
   liǎngge-xīngqī kàn-yícì-diànyǐngr. 'Shéi-zuì-xǐhuan kàn-diànyǐngr?

2. Kǎoshì-de-shíhou, lìshǐ-tímu wǒ-yí-kàn-jiu-dǒng. Shùxué-tímu wǒ-
   kànle-bàntiān yě-méi-dǒng. Nǐ-shuō-'shénmo-róngyi?

3. 'Wáng-Xiānsheng yí-fàngjià jiu-kàn-diànyǐngr. 'Zhāng-Xiānsheng suí-
   rán-fàngjià, 'háishi-**kàn-shū-xiě-zì.** Nǐ-shuō tāmen-liǎngge-rén 'shéi-
   shi-hǎo-xuésheng?

4. Zhèige-háizi xǐhuan-dǎ-rén. Nèige-háizi 'bù-dǎ-rén. Nǐ-shuō 'něige-
   háizi-hǎo?

5. Yǎn-diànyǐngr shi-zài-'nár-yǎn-ne?

6. 'Qián-Xiānsheng-jiā lí-nǐ-jiā-hěn-jìn. Tā-fùjìn jiù-shi-túshūguǎn. Nǐ-
   jiā lí-túshūguǎn-yuǎn-ma?

7. Ní-xǐhuan-kàn-diànyǐngr. Nǐ-zhīdao-yǎn-diànyǐngr-de-rén jiào-shénmo?

8. 'Bái-Xiānsheng kàn-'wúdiǎn-nèichǎng-diànyǐngr. 'Máo-Xiānsheng kàn-
   'qīdiǎn-nèichǎng-diànyǐngr. Nǐ-shuō-shéi-'xiān-huí-jiā, shéi-'hòu-huí-
   jiā?

9. Rúguó-nǐ-péngyou 'sāndiǎn-zhōng zuò-chuán-dào-zhèr-lái, nǐ-'sìdiǎn-
   zhōng cái-qu-jiē-ta, nǐ-'jiēdezháo-jiēbuzháo?

10. Wǒmen-kàn-diànyǐngr zài-'nǎr-kàn? Shi-zài-'jiā-lǐtou-kàn-ma?

NOTES

1. Yí or yì 'one' as an adverb means 'as soon as.' The second clause is
   commonly introduced by jiù 'then':

   > Wǒ-yí-kàn-ta jiu-zhīdao tā-shi-'wàiguo-rén. 'As soon as I saw him,
   > I knew he was a foreigner.'

   Or, the second clause may be introduced by cái 'then and only then,' 'then
   for the first time':

   > Wǒ-yí-kàn-ta cái-zhīdao tā-shi-'wàiguo-rén. 'As soon as I saw him,
   > then (for the first time) I realized he was a foreigner [though I had
   > previously thought he was the same nationality as myself].'

   The connection between the second clause and the yī + verb in the first
   clause is often implied rather than stated:

   > Wǒ-yí-kàn, tā-'zhēn-shi-wàiguo-rén. 'The minute I saw him (I
   > knew) he was a foreigner.'

2. The verb qǐlai 'get up' is also used as a postverb, in two separate senses. First, it can correspond to 'up' in expressions like náqilai 'take up.' The object of such a verb is either introduced by the coverb bǎ 'take,' or inserted between the parts of the combination:

> Bǎ-shū-náqilai. 'Pick up your book.'
> Náqi-shū-lai. 'Pick up your books.'

In a second sense, qǐlai as a postverb means 'begin to [do or be]':

> Nèige-háizi chīqǐ-fàn-lai jiu-yào-shuō-huà. 'When that child begins to eat he immediately wants to talk.'

> Cóng-nèige-shíhou wǒde-Zhōngwén jiù-hǎoqilaile. 'From that time my Chinese began to improve [lit. began to be good].'

Verbs compounded with qǐlai are resultative verbs:

> xiángqilai 'recall'
> xiǎngbuqǐlái 'unable to recall'

3. The basic meaning of dǎ is 'strike':

> dǎ-mén 'knock on a door'
> dáqilai 'begin to strike [each other]' — i.e. 'fight'

Dǎ in addition enters into phrases with nouns, with a variety of English equivalents:

> dǎ-piào 'buy tickets'
> dǎ-quán 'box' (i.e. 'have a boxing contest')
> dǎ-diànhuà 'make a phone call'

Before a place word, dǎ means 'from,' synonymous here with cóng:

> Dǎ-zhèr-dào-fànguǎr yǒu-duō-yuǎn? 'How far is it from here to the restaurant?'

Note also the following special combination:

> dǎkai 'open [a book, box, etc.]' — lit. 'hit open'

4. The stative verb duì 'correct, right' is used as a postverb to form resultative compounds:

> shuōduì 'say correctly'
> shuōbuduì 'unable to say correctly'
> shuōdeduì 'able to say correctly'

The following sentences illustrate the last two forms given above:

> Tā-hěn-bèn, yídìng-shuōbuduì. 'He's very stupid. He certainly can't say it right.'
> Tā-hěn-cōngming. Yídìng-shuōdeduì. 'He's very bright. He can certainly say it right.'

Note the difference (in the written form only) between shuōdeduì 'able to say correctly' and shuōde-duì 'says correctly.' The former is a resultative verb, the latter a construction involving an adverb of manner (see Lesson 10, Note 2). A similar overlapping occurs when hǎo 'good' is used as a postverb:

> shuōhǎo 'agree on (something)'
> shuōbuhǎo 'unable to agree'
> shuōdehǎo 'able to agree'

(Do not confuse shuōdehǎo with shuōde-hǎo 'speak well'; cf. Lesson 19, Note 10.)

5. Háishi . . . hǎo (see Dialogue, p. 338, lines 74–75) is the second part of the construction shi-A-hǎo háishi-B-hǎo? 'is A or B better?' (Lesson 7, Note 12); but the A is implied rather than expressed. Another example: if a friend who likes walking suggests going on foot to a movie some distance away, one might say—

Háishi-zuò-chē-hǎo. 'It's better (to go) by car.

6. Guówén 'national literature' means 'Chinese' [as an academic subject]. (See also Supplementary Lesson 20, Note 1)

7. The stative verb zāogāo 'confused, messed up' is also used as a mild exclamation comparable to English 'Darn!'

8. The sentence particle me has about the force of 'You see?' or 'Don't you see?':

Tā-'zěnmo-néng-mǎi nènmo-dàde-fángzi?   'How come he can buy such a large house?'
Tā-yǒu-qián-me! 'He has money, don't you see?'

Lesson 21   EATING IN A RESTAURANT

"Qíng-ni-bāngzhu-wǒmen xiáng-liǎngge-cài."

Dialogue: Mr. White takes Miss Gao out to dinner.

Huǒji :	Xiānsheng, Xiáojie, liǎng- wèi-zuò-nǎr?	Sir, Miss, where would you like to sit?
Bái :	Wǒmen jiù-zài-'zhèr-zuò- ba. Géi-wǒmen xiān-lái- yìhú-chá. 5	We'll sit right here. First bring us a pot of tea.
Huǒji :	Shì, xiānsheng.	Yes, sir.
Bái :	Qíng-bǎ-cài-'dār-nálai.	Please bring the menu.
Gāo :	Wǒmen-jiǎndān-yìdiǎr-chī. Yàoburán diànyǐngr-gāi- wǎn-le. 10	Let's have a simple meal. Oth- erwise we're bound to be late for the movie.
Huǒji :	Géi-nín-cài-dār.	Here's the menu.
Bái :	Qíng-ni-bāngzhu-wǒmen xiáng-liǎngge-cài.	Please help us order a couple of dishes.
Huǒji :	Hǎo. Wǒ-jièshao-nín-jǐ- yàng wǒmen-zhèr-'zuì- 15 hǎode-cài. Wǒmen-zhèr hóng-shāo-yú, chǎo-xiā- rér, kǎo-yāzi, dōu-hǎo. Yóuqí shi-nèige-kǎo-yāzi	Fine. I'll introduce you to a few of our best dishes. Our red- cooked fish, fried shrimp, and roast duck are all fine. The roast duck, in particular, we can say is the best in the whole

355

dàgài-wǒmen-kéyi-shuō   20   country.
shi-quán-guó-dì-yī-le.

Bái : Wǒmen-liǎngge-rén yào-   The two of us would like two
        liǎngge-cài-yíge-tāng-chī-   dishes and a soup, and rice. Do
        fàn. Nǐ-kàn 'gòu-chī-ba?   you think that's enough (to eat)?

Huǒji: Chàbuduō. Wǒmen-zhèrde-   25   Just about. Our dumplings and
        jiǎozi, chǎo-miàn yě-bú-   fried noodles are also not bad.
        cuò. Hái-yóu-chǎo-dòufu.   We also have fried bean curd.

Bái : Hǎo. Měiyīng, nǐ-yào-   Fine. Meiying, what would you
        shénmo?   like?

Gāo : Wǒ-suíbiàn.   30   Anything.

Huǒji: Xiáojie, wǒmen-zhèr-chǎo-   Miss, our fried shrimp is awful-
        xiārér hǎode-hěn. Nín-   ly good. You might order one.
        yào-ge-chǎo-xiārér-ba.

Gāo : Kéyi. Wǒ-yào-chǎo-xiārér.   O.K.   I'll order fried shrimp.
        Wénshān, 'nǐ-yào-shénmo?   35   Vincent, what would you like?

Bái : Wǒ-yào hóng-shāo-yú.   I'd like red-cooked fish.

Huǒji: Liǎngwèi-lái-ge-shénmo-   What soup do you want?
        tāng-ne?

Bái : Měiyīng, 'nǐ-shuō yào-   Meiying, what do you say to
        shénmo-tāng-hǎo-ne?   40   soup?

Gāo : Niú-ròu-báicài-tāng 'hǎo-   How's beef and cabbage soup?
        bu-hǎo?

Bái : Hǎojíle. Géi-wǒmen-lái   Excellent. Bring us some beef
        niú-ròu-báicài-tāng. Měi-   and cabbage soup. Meiying, how
        yīng, wǒmen-zài-yào-diar- 45   about our also ordering a few
        jiǎozi, 'hǎo-bu-hǎo?   dumplings?

Gāo : Wó-xiǎng-gòu-le. Yào-duō-   I think (this) is enough. If we
        le wǒmen-chībuliǎo.   order too much we won't be able
                                           to eat it.

Bái : Huǒji, 'jiǎozi-zěnmo-yào?   Waiter, how does one order
        Mài-duōshao-qián?   50   dumplings? How much do they
                                           sell for?

Huǒji: Jiǎozi nín-chī-duōshao   Dumplings you order by the
        jiù-yào-duōshao. Yíkuài-   number you eat. They're $1.20
        liǎngmáo-qián-shíge.   for ten.

Bái : Hǎo, wǒmen-bú-gòu-zài-   Fine. If we don't have enough,
        shuō-ba.   55   we'll speak up again.

Gāo : Chīwán-le wǒmen-yào-ge-   After we've finished we'd like a
        'tián-diǎnxin.   [sweet] dessert.

Bái : 'Shénmo-tián-diǎnxin?   What [sweet] dessert?

Gāo : Xìngrér-dòufu.   Almond bean curd.

Bái : Huǒji, xìngrér-dòufu-yǒu-   60   Waiter, do you have almond bean
        ma?   curd?

Huǒji:	Duìbuqǐ, 'gāng-màiwán. Nín-yào-diar-biéde-ba?	I'm sorry, we're just sold out. Would you like something else?
Gāo :	Yǒu-xìngrér-chá-ma?	Do you have almond tea?
Huǒji:	Yǒu. 65	Yes.
Bái :	Qǐng-lái-liángwǎn. . . . (Cài-lái-le.)	Please bring two bowls. . . . (The food arrives.)
Bái :	Měiyīng, nǐ-kàn, cài- zuòde-bú-cuò.	Meiying, look, the food's very nice.
Gāo :	Nǐ-kàn, zhèige-chǎo- 70 xiārér duó-piàoliang.	See how attractive this fried shrimp is.
Bái :	Zhèige-hóng-shāo-yú yě- bú-cuò, kěshi-wǒ-chī- fànguǎrde-cài dōu-méi- you-fǔshangde-cài-hǎo- 75 chī.	This red-cooked fish isn't bad either, but none of the food I've had in restaurants is as deli- cious as what I've had in your home.
Gāo :	Yīnwei-wǒ-fùqin-xǐhuan- chī, wó-mǔqin-yě-méi- shì-zuò, tā-měitiān jiù- yánjiu zěnmo-zuò-fàn. 80 Tā-hái-shuō jiānglái tā- bǎ-zuò-fàn-de-jīngyan yào-xiě-yìběn-shū-ne. Zuò-'Zhōngguo-fàn méi- yǒu-kēxuéde-fāngfǎ, jiù- 85 shi-yì zhǒng-jīngyan.	Since my father likes to eat and my mother doesn't have a job, every day she experiments with (new ways of) cooking. She also says that [in the future] she's going to write a book about her experiences in cooking. There are no scientific procedures in cooking Chinese food, it's just a matter of experience.
Bái :	"Hóng-shāo-yú" zhèige- míngzi wèi-shénmo-jiào- hóng-shāo-yú?	Why is "red-cooked fish" called that?
Gāo :	Hóng-shāode jiù-shi-duō- 90 fàng-jiàngyóu, shāo-de- 'shíhou-cháng-yìdiǎr. Yīnwei-hóng-shāo-de-cài shi-jiàngyóu-yánse, suóyi- jiào-hóng-shāo-de. 95	Red-cooking is just putting in a lot of soy sauce and cooking for a long time. [Because] red- cooked dishes are the color of soy sauce, so they're called red- cooked.
Bái :	Zài-Měiguo-de-'Zhōngguo- fànguǎr chàbuduō-'dōu-shi- Guǎngdong-fànguǎr.	Almost all the Chinese restau- rants in America are Cantonese restaurants.
Gāo :	Ní-xǐhuan-chī-Guǎngdong- cài-ma? 100	Do you like [to eat] Cantonese food?
Bái :	Wó-yé-xǐhuan, kěshi-wǒ- juéde háishi-běifāng-fàn bíjiáo-hǎo-'chī-yìdiǎr. 'Nǐ-dōu-xǐhuan-nǎrde- cài-ne? 105	I [also] like it, but I think that Northern cooking is a little bet- ter. What kind of food do you like?
Gāo :	Dāngrán-'wó-yé-xǐhuan chī-běifāng-cài-le. Wǒ-	Naturally I also like Northern cooking. I don't much care for

	duì-ròu bú-dà-xǐhuan. Wǒ-tèbié-xǐhuan chī-yú, xiā, jī.	110	meat. I especially like fish, shrimp, and chicken.
Bái :	'Zhōngguo-fàn zhēn-hǎo-chī. Jiù-shi-zuòqilai-máfan.		Chinese food is really delicious. The only thing is that it's a bother to cook it.
Gāo :	Yě-'bù-zěnmo-máfan. . . . Jīntian-cài hái-bú-cuò.	115	It's not such a bother. . . . This food [lit. the food today] is not bad.
Bái :	Měiyīng, nǐ-chībǎo-le-ma? Zài-yào-diar-shén-mo?		Meiying, have you had enough [to eat]? What else should we have?
Gāo :	Wǒ-chībǎo-le. 'Shénmo-yě-bú-yào-le.	120	I'm stuffed. I don't want anything more.
Bái :	Zài-lái-diar-jiǎozi 'hǎo-bu-hǎo?		How about ordering a few dumplings?
Gāo :	Wǒ-chīde-'tài-bǎo-le. Jiù-shi-nǐ-yào wó-yě-bù-chī-le.	125	I've eaten too much. Even if you order them I can't eat any more.
Bái :	Nènmo wǒmen-zài-hē-diar-chá. Huǒji, zài-lái-diar-chá.		Then let's have a little more tea. Waiter, some more tea.
Huǒji:	Lái-le.		Coming.
Gāo :	Bādiǎn-bàn-le. Wǒmen-gāi-zǒu-le.	130	It's eight-thirty. We should be leaving.
Bái :	Huǒji, suàn-zhàng.		Waiter, the bill.
Huǒji:	Shì. Yígòng-sìkuài-sān-máo-liù.		Yes. Altogether, four thirty-six.
Bái :	Zhè-shi-wǔkuài. Bú-bì-zhǎo-le. Shèngxia-de géi-xiǎofèi-le.	135	Here's five dollars. You don't need to make change. The rest is your tip.
Huǒji:	Xièxie-nín. Liǎngwèi-màn-zǒu. Zàijiàn.		Thank you. Don't be in a hurry to leave. Good-bye.

VOCABULARY

bāngzhu	help (TV) [lit. help assist]
bíjiǎo, bǐjiào	relatively (AD) [lit, compare compare]
cháng	long (SV)
dān, dār	list, bill (N)
dǎsuan	plan to (V)

diǎnxin	dessert, pastry, cakes, etc. (N) [lit. bit heart]	
duìbuqǐ	sorry, excuse me [lit. face not begin]	
fàng	put (TV)	
gāng(cái)	just (now), just a moment ago (AD)	
hú	pot (N, M)	
huǒji	waiter, clerk (N) [lit. partner plan] (See Supplementary Lesson 21, Note 1)	
jiàngyóu	soy sauce (N) [lit. soy-sauce oil]	
jiǎozi	dumplings (N)	
jīngyan	experience (N, V) [lit. pass verify]	
jiùshi	even (if) (MA) [lit. exactly is]	
juéde	have the feeling that (TV)	
kǎo	roast, cook by roasting (TV)	
miàn	noodles (N)	
quán	the whole	
shèng(xia)	have left over, be left over (V)	
suàn	reckon (as), calculate (TV)	
wǎn	bowl, cup (N, M)	
xiā	shrimp (N)	
xiārér	shelled shrimp (N) [lit. shrimp kernel]	
xiǎofèi	tip (N) [lit. small spend] (See Supplementary Lesson 21, Note 2)	
xìngrér	almond (N)	
yā(zi)	duck (N)	
(yào)bùrán	otherwise (MA) (bùrán is more common)	
yóuqí(shi)	especially, above all (MA)	
zhàng	bill (N)	
zhǒng	kind of, sort of, variety of (M)	

SENTENCE BUILD-UP

jiàngyóu   soy sauce

1. Zhèr mǎibuzháo-jiàngyóu.   Soy sauce can't be bought here.

fàng   put
néng-fàng-ròu   can put in meat

2. Zhèige-càili néng-fàng-ròu-ma?   Is it possible to put meat in this dish?

fàng   put

         fàngzài   put (at)
3. Bǎ-shū fàngzài-zhèr.   Put the books here.

         fàng   put
         fàngxia   put down
4. Bǎ-dōngxi-fàngxia.   Put the things down.

         nǐ-yào-chī-shénmo?   what do you want to eat?
         fàng-shénmo?   put in what?
5. Nǐ-yào-chī-shénmo jiù-fàng-   Put in whatever you want to eat.
    shénmo.

         shéi-yào-yòng-máobǐ?   who wants to use a brush?
         shéi-jiù-mǎi-máobǐ?   who then buys a brush?
·6. Shéi-yào-yòng-máobǐ shéi-   Whoever wants to use a brush
     jiù-mǎi-máobǐ.   (should) buy one.

         xìngrér   almond
         xìngrér-chá   almond tea
7. Wǒ-méi-hēguo-xìngrér-chá.   I've never had almond tea.

         diǎnxin   dessert
8. Nǐ-bù-chī-diǎnxin-ma?   Aren't you eating any dessert?

         xiǎofèi   tip
9. Xiǎofèi-suíbiàn-gěi.   Give whatever tip you want.

         jiùshi   even, even if
         jiùshi-tā-géi-wo   even if he gives it to me
         wó-yě-bú-yào   I still don't want it
10. Jiùshi-tā-géi-wo wó-yě-bú-   Even if he gives it to me I don't
     yào.   want it.

         jiùshi   even, even if
         jiùshi-lián   even, even if
11. Jiùshi-lián-tā-géi-wo wó-   Even if he gives it to me I don't
     yě-bú-yào.   want it.

         jiùshi-tā   even he
         bú-rènshi-zhèige-zì   does not recognize this
                                                       character
12. Jiùshi-tā yě-bú-rènshi-zhèige-   Even he does not recognize this
     zì.   character.

         xiā   shrimp
13. Ní-xǐhuan-chī-xiā-ma?   Do you like (to eat) shrimp?

         xiārér   shelled shrimp
14. Chǎo-xiārér hén-hǎo-chī.   The fried shrimp is delicious.

         hú   pot
         sānhú-chá   three pots of tea
15. Wǒmen-liǎngge-rén hēle-   The two of us drank three pots
     sānhú-chá.   of tea.

hú

chá-hú

pot

teapot

16. Zhèige-chá-hú shi-Rìběn-
    zuò-de.

This teapot was made in Japan.

zhàng

17. Zhèige-zhàng-cuò-le.

bill

This bill is in error.

suàn

suàn-zhàng

reckon, figure

figure out a bill

18. Shūdiàn hái-méi-suàn-zhàng-
    ne.

The bookstore hasn't yet figured
out the bill.

suàn

suàn-hǎo

be reckoned as

be considered good

19. Tāde-'Zhōngwén bú-
    suàn-hǎo.

His Chinese can't be considered
good.

suàn

suàn-shi

reckoned as

reckoned to be

20. Shīzi-tóu suàn-shi-běifāng-
    cài-ma?

Is lion's head considered a
Northern dish?

suàn

dǎsuan

reckon, plan to

plan to

21. Wó-dǎsuan míngtian-qu-kàn-
    ta.

I plan to go see him tomorrow.

bíjiǎo

22. Yīngwén bíjiǎo-róngyi.

relatively

English is relatively easy.

wǎn

liángwǎn-fàn

bowl

two bowls of rice

23. Wǒ-yíge-rén kéyi-chī-liáng-
    wǎn-fàn.

I can eat two bowls of rice by
myself.

wǎn

zhèige-wǎn

bowl

this bowl

24. Zhèige-wǎn shi-'nár-mǎi-de?

Where was this bowl bought?

cháng

yìtiáo-bíjiǎo-chángde-lù

long

a relatively long road

25. Zhōngshān-Lù shi-yìtiáo-bí-
    jiǎo-chángde-lù.

Sun Yatsen Avenue is a relatively long road.

dār

kāi-yìzhāng-dār

list

make a list

26. Ní-bá-nǐ-yào-mǎi-de-dōngxi
    kāi-yìzhāng-dār.

Make a list of the things you
want to buy.

dār

cài-dār

list

menu

27. Nǐ-néng-kàn 'Zhōngguo-cài-
    dār-ma?

Can you read a Chinese menu?

	bāngzhu	help
	bāngzhu-wo	help me
28.	Qíng-ni bāngzhu-wo-zhǎo-shū.	Please help me find the book.

	yǒu-bāngzhu	be helpful
	duì-xué-yǔyán hén-yǒu-bāngzhu	be very helpful in studying languages
29.	Tīng-lùyīn duì-xué-yǔyán hén-yǒu-bāngzhu.	Listening to recordings is very helpful in studying languages.

	gāng	just (now)
	gāng-zǒu-le	has just left
30.	'Bái-Xiānsheng gāng-zǒu-le.	Mr. White has just left.

	gāng	just (now)
	gāngcái	just (now)
31.	Wǒ-gāngcái-chīwán-le-fàn.	I've just finished eating.

	duìbuqǐ	sorry, excuse me
32.	Duìbuqǐ, wó-zhǎobuzháo-dār-le.	I'm sorry, I can't find the list.

	dà	big
	bú-dà-xǐhuan	not much like
33.	Wǒ-bú-dà-xǐhuan-chī-xiā.	I don't much like [to eat] shrimp.

	lǎo	old; always
	lǎo-kèqi	always polite
34.	Ní-lǎo-zènmo-kèqi.	You are always so polite.

	bái	white; uselessly
	bái-lái-le	come uselessly
35.	Tā-zuótian-bái-lái-le. Wǒ-méi-zài-jiā.	He came in vain yesterday. I wasn't at home.

	yā	duck
36.	Yā-bǐ-jī-dà.	Ducks are bigger than chickens.

	yāzi	duck
37.	Yāzi-méi-you-jī-hǎo-chī.	Duck isn't as tasty as chicken.

	kǎo	roast
	kǎo-yāzi	roast duck
38.	Běifāngde-kǎo-yāzi 'tèbié-hǎo.	Northern roast duck is especially good.

	huǒji	waiter
39.	Zhèixiē-huǒji jiù-huì-shuō-Guǎngdong-huà.	These waiters can speak only Cantonese.

	miàn	noodles
	fàn	rice
40.	Ní-chī-fàn-chī-miàn?	Are you having rice or noodles?

juéde
feel (that), think (that)
41. Wǒ-juéde zhèige-cài-tài-suān.
I think this dish is too vinegary.

jīngyan
experience
42. Wǒ-juéde tāde-jīngyan-bú-gòu.
I think he doesn't have enough experience.

quán
the whole
quán-xuéxiào
the whole school
43. Wǒmen-quán-xuéxiào dōu-kǎo-shì.
Our whole school is having exams.

zhǒng
kind of
zhèizhǒng-cài
this kind of food
44. Wǒ-juéde-'zhèizhǒng-cài bù-hǎo-chī.
I think this kind of food is un-appetizing.

yóuqí
especially
yóuqíshi
especially
45. Wǒmen-dōu-chīde-hěn-duō, yóuqíshi-wǒ.
We all ate a lot, especially I.

yóuqíshi-děi
especially have to
46. Nǐmen-yóuqíshi-děi duō-tīng-lùyīn.
You especially have to listen to recordings more.

shèng
be left over
shèngle-hěn-duō-cài
a lot of food was left over
47. Zuótian shèngle-hěn-duō-cài.
Yesterday a lot of food was left over.

shèng
have left over
shèng-wǔmáo-qián
have fifty cents left
48. Wǒ-jiù-shèng wǔmáo-qián.
I have only fifty cents left.

shèngxia
be left over
shèngxia-hěn-duō-cài
a lot of food is left over
49. Jīntian méi-shèngxia-hěn-duō-cài.
There isn't much food left over today.

mài
sell or sell for
mài-'duōshao-qián?
sell for how much?
50. Zhèige-chá-hú mài-'duōshao-qián?
How much does this teapot sell for?

(yào)bùrán
otherwise
51. Kuài-zǒu-ba. (Yào)bùrán-wǎn-le.
Let's hurry. Otherwise we'll be late.

PATTERN DRILLS

Pattern 21.1.   Repetition of Question Words   (Note 1 below)

Pattern 21.1 a.

V_1	QW	<u>jiu</u>	V_2	QW
Verb$_1$	Question Word	'then'	Verb$_2$	Question Word
Yào	shénmo	jiu	mǎi	shénmo.

'Buy whatever you want.'

Pattern 21.1 b.

QW	V_1	(QW)	<u>jiu</u>	V_2
Question Word	Verb$_1$	(Question Word)	'then'	Verb$_2$
Shéi	yào-chī-fàn	shéi	jiu	chī-fàn.

'Whoever wants to eat, eat.'

1. Ní-xiǎng wǒ-chī-'shénmo-hǎo-ne? . . . Nǐ-'yào-chī-shénmo jiu-'chī-shénmo.

   What do you think (it) would be best for me to eat? . . . Eat whatever you want.

2. Zuótian-wǒ-fùqin-shuō wǒ-bìyè-yǐhòu 'xiǎng-dào-nǎr-niàn-shū jiu-dào-nǎr-niàn-shū.

   Yesterday my father said that after I graduate I'm to go anywhere I like, to study.

3. Wǒ-míngtian-fàngjià-le. Nǐ-shuō wǒ-dào-'nǎr-qu-lǔxíng-ne? . . . Nǐ-'yào-dào-nǎr-qu jiu-dào-nǎr-qu.

   I'm going on vacation tomorrow. Tell me where I should go on a trip. . . . Go anywhere you want.

4. Wǒ-jīntian shuō-huà-de-tímu bù-yídìng. Wǒ-'yào-shuō-shénmo jiu-shuō-shénmo.

   I have no definite topic to talk about today.   I'll speak of whatever I want.

5. Wó-xiǎng-chī-jiǎozi. Nǐ-ne? . . . Nǐ-'chī-shénmo 'wǒ-jiu-chī-shénmo.

   I'd like to eat dumplings. What about you? . . . I'll eat whatever you eat.

6. Wǒ-fùqin zuì-xǐhuan-wǒ-dìdi-le. Wǒ-dìdi-'yào-mǎi-shénmo tā-jiu-mǎi-shénmo.

   My father likes my younger brother best.   Whatever my younger brother wants to buy he buys.

7. Nǐ-shuō wǒ-yào-'duōshao-jiǎo-zi-ne? . . . Nǐ-'chī-duōshao jiu-'yào-duōshao.

   Tell me how many dumplings I should order. . . . Order as many as you're going to eat.

8. Wǒ-yīnggāi gěi-duōshao-xiǎo-fèi-ne? . . . Zhè-bù-yídìng.

   How much of a tip should I give? . . . There's no fixed amount.

'Yào-gěi-duōshao jiu-'gěi-
duōshao.

Give as much as you want to.

9. Zhèige-cài yào-fàng-'duōshao-
jiàngyóu-ne? . . . Bù-yídìng.
'Yào-fàng-duōshao jiu-'fàng-
duōshao.

How much soy sauce should I put
into this dish? . . . No fixed
amount. Put in as much as you
want.

10. Zhèige-tián-diǎnxin hén-hǎo-
chī. Wǒ-duō-chī-'yìdiǎr
kéyi-ma? . . . Kéyi. Nǐ-
'yào-chī-duōshao jiu-'chī-
duōshao.

This sweet dessert is delicious.
May I have a little more? . . .
Yes. You may have as much as
you want.

11. Zhèijiàn-shìqing nǐ-shuō-
zěnmo-zuò-hǎo-ne? . . . Nǐ-
'yào-zěnmo-zuò jiù-zěnmo-
zuò.

What do you think would be the
best way to do this? . . . Do it
whatever way you want.

12. Zhèi-jíbén-shū nǐ-shuō wǒ-
jiè-néibén-hǎo-ne? . . . Nǐ-
'yào-jiè-néibén jiu-'jiè-néi-
bén.

Which of these books do you
think it would be best for me to
check out? . . . Take out whichever one you want.

13. Nǐ-shuō wǒ-kàn-něige-diàn-
yíngr-hǎo-ne? . . . Nǐ-'yào-
kàn-něige jiu-'kàn-něige.

What movie would it be best for
me to see? . . . See whichever
one you want.

14. Nǐ-shuō wǒ-xué-Zhōngwén-hǎo-
ne háishi-xué-lìshǐ-hǎo-ne?
. . . Nǐ-'yào-xué-shénmo
jiu-'xué-shénmo.

Do you think it would be better
for me to study Chinese or history? . . . Study whatever you
want.

15. 'Shéi-huì-zuò-jiǎozi 'shéi-
jiu-zuò-jiǎozi.

Whoever knows how to make
dumplings, do so.

16. 'Něige-hǎo jiu-'géi-wo-něi-
ge.

Give me whichever one is better.

17. Nǐmen-shéi-huì-shuō-'Zhōng-
wén jiu-shuō-'Zhōngwén.
Rúguǒ-bú-huì-shuō-
'Zhōngwén jiu-shuō-'Yīngwén.

Those of you who can speak Chinese, do so. If you are not able
to speak Chinese, then speak
English.

18. Ní-yǒu-duōshao jiu-'géi-wo-
duōshao.

Give me as much as you have.

19. Něiwèi-xuéde-zuì-hǎo jiu-bú-
bì-kǎoshì.

Whoever studies best doesn't
need to take the exam.

20. Něige-xiānsheng-jiāode-hǎo
wǒ-jiu-gēn-tā-xué.

I'll study with whichever teacher
is best.

Pattern 21.2. Sentences with <u>jiùshi</u> 'even (if)'   (Note 2 below)

Pattern 21.2 a. (Sentences 1–10)

<u>jiùshi</u>	S_1	V_1	S_2	<u>dōu/yě</u>	V_2
<u>jiùshi</u>	Subject$_1$	Verb$_1$	Subject$_2$	<u>dōu/yě</u>	Verb$_2$
Jiùshi	nǐ	qù	wó	yě	bú qù.

'Even if you go, I'm not going.'

Pattern 21.2 b. (Sentences 11–15)

<u>jiùshi</u>	S	<u>dōu/yě</u>	V
<u>jiùshi</u>	Subject	<u>dōu/yě</u>	Verb
Jiùshi	tā	yě	qù.

'Even he is going.'

1. Nèiběn-shū wǒ-bù-xǐhuan. Jiùshi-'ní-mǎi wó-yě-bù-mǎi.

   I don't like that book. Even if you buy it, I'm not going to (buy it).

2. 'Wǒ-'zuì-bù-xǐhuan chī-xìngrér-dòufu. Jiùshi-nǐ-yào-le wó-yě-bù-chī.

   I very much dislike [eating] almond bean curd. Even if you ordered it I wouldn't eat it.

3. Nèijiàn-shìqing wǒ-shi-'bú-huì gàosu-bié-rén-de. Jiùshi-'nǐ-shuō wǒ-dōu-bù-shuō.

   I can't tell anyone about that matter. Even if you speak of it, I won't.

4. Wǒ-jīntian-hěn-máng. Jiùshi-wǒ-'fùqin-lái wó-yě-bù-néng-qu-jiē.

   I'm very busy today. Even if my father comes I won't be able to go and meet (him).

5. Nèige-xiǎo-chá-hú 'tài-xiǎo-le. Jiùshi-'ní-mǎi wó-yě-bù-mǎi.

   That little teapot is too small. Even if you buy one, I'm not going to.

6. Zhèijiàn-shìqing 'tā-yě-bù-zhīdào. Jiùshi-tā-zhīdao tā-yě-bú-huì-shuō.

   Even he doesn't know about this matter. Even if he knew, he wouldn't be able to speak of it.

7. Wǒ-zuì-xǐhuan chī-chǎo-xiārér. Jiùshi-nǐ-bù-chī wó-yě-yào.

   I like fried shrimp best. Even if you don't eat it I'm going to order some.

8. Tā-shuō nèige-biáo-hén-hǎo. Jiùshi-nǐ-bú-jiào-wó-mǎi wó-yě-yào-mǎi.

   He said that watch is very good. Even if you tell me not to buy it I'm going to (buy it).

9. Zhèi-jǐtiān bù-xiǎng-kàn-shū. Jiùshi-'nǐ-kàn wǒ-dōu-bú-kàn.

   For a few days now I don't plan to read. Even if you read I'm not going to.

10. Tāde-nèige-chá-hú 'tài-

    That teapot of hers is awfully

piàoliang-le. Jiùshi-nǐ-yào
tā-yě-bù-géi-ni.

pretty. Even if you asked for it
she wouldn't give it to you.

11. Zhèige-xuéxiào zhēn-nán-kǎo.
Jiùshi-'dàxué-bìyè-de-xué-
sheng yé-kǎobushàng.

This school gives very tough exams. Even students who have
graduated from college can't
pass the entrance exams.

12. Zhèibén-shū hěn-nán-niàn.
Jiùshi-wǒ-'fùqin yě-bù-dōu-
dǒng.

This book is very hard to read.
Even my father doesn't understand it all.

13. Chǎo-xiārér hén-hǎo-chī.
Jiùshi-'bù-xǐhuan-chī-yú-de-
rén dōu-xǐhuan-chī.

Fried shrimp are delicious.
Even people who don't like fish
like [to eat] them.

14. Zhèige-xuéxiào jiāo-Zhōngwén
jiāode-hén-hǎo. Jiùshi-lián-
yìniánjíde-xuésheng dōu-néng-
shuō hén-hǎode-Zhōngguo-huà.

This school teaches Chinese
very well. Even first-year students can speak very good Chinese.

15. Wǒ-dìdi zì-xiěde-zhēn-hǎo.
Jiùshi-'dà-xuéde-xuésheng yě-
méi-yǒu-tā-xiěde-hǎo.

My younger brother writes characters very well. Even college
students don't write as well as
he does.

Pattern 21.3.   Transformation of V-O to O-V   (Note 3 below)

V	O	>	O	V
Verb	Object	>	Object	Verb
chī	fàn	>	fàn	chī
'eat food'		>	'food to eat'	

1. Nǐ-yìhuěr qíng-wǒ-hē-chá,
'hǎo-bu-hǎo? . . . Bié-tí-
hē-chá-le. Yīnwei-méi-you-
shuǐ, wǒmen-jīntian-'dōu-
méi-chá-hē.

How about inviting me to have
some tea in a little while? . . .
Don't mention drinking tea.
Since we haven't any water, none
of us has any tea to drink today.

2. Wǒmen-méi-yǒu-jiàngyóu
fàngzài-chǎo-cài-lǐtou.

We don't have any soy sauce to
put into the fried dishes.

3. Wó-yǐjing-gēn-ta shuōle-
hěn-duō-huà. Xiànzài méi-
yǒu-huà-shuō-le.

I've already talked a lot with
him. Now I don't have anything
more to say.

4. Xiànzài xuéxiào-fàngjià-le.
Dǎsuan-kàn-diar-shū. Kěshi-
túshūguǎn shū-tài-shǎo, méi-
shū-jiè.

School's gone on vacation now. I
had planned to read some books.
But there are too few books in
the library, and there are no
books to take out.

5. Nèige-háizi shíwǔsuì-le hái-

That child is fifteen and has not

méi-niàn-shū. Yīnwei-jiāli
méi-yǒu-qián, suóyi-méi-yǒu-
shū-niàn.

yet read any books.   Since his
family doesn't have any money,
he has no books to read.

6. Xiànzài fángzi-'tài-shǎo. Mǎi-
buzháo-hǎo-fángzi-zhù.

Houses are in short supply now.
One can't buy a good house to
live in.

7. 'Qián-Xiānsheng yǒu-chē-zuò.
Bú-bì-zǒu-lù.

Mr. Qian has a car [to travel by].
He doesn't have to walk.

8. Qíng-ní-gěi-ta-wǔkuài-qián.
. . . Wó-méi-qián-gěi-ta.

Please give him five dollars. . . .
I don't have any money to give
him.

9. Wó-xiáng-mǎi-lùyīnjī. Yǒu-
lùyīnjī-mài-ma?

I'm thinking of buying a recorder. Do you have any recorders
to sell?

10. Xiànzài rén-'tài-duō, shì-'tài-
shǎo. Wó-zhǎobuzháo-shì-
zuò.

Nowadays there are too many
people, too few jobs. I can't find
any work to do.

Pattern 21.4   Stative Verbs as Adverbs

SV	V
Stative Verb	Verb
lǎo	chī

'always eat'

1. Diànyǐngryuàn lí-zhèr-hěn-
jìn. Wǒmen-zài-hē-yìdiǎr-
chá-ba. Wǒmen-kéyi-màn-
zǒu.

The movie theater is quite near
here. Let's drink some more
tea. We can take our time about
leaving.

2. Wǒ-bù-xǐhuan-nèige-rén. Měi-
tiān-'lǎo-shuō-huà.

I don't like that man. He jabbers
constantly [every day].

3. Zhèitiáo-lù chē-bù-róngyi-zǒu.
Qíng-nǐ-màn-kāi.

Cars can't get over this road
easily. Please drive slowly.

4. Nǐ-shuōde-huà wǒ-bú-dà-míng-
bai.

I don't fully understand what
you're saying.

5. Wǒmen-zhèr lí-chéng-'tài-
yuǎn. 'Sháo-yǒu-rén-lái.

We're too far from the city here.
People rarely come (here).

6. Zhèiběn-shū wǒ-bái-xué-le.
Xiānsheng-méi-kǎo.

I studied this book for nothing.
The teacher didn't test (us on it).

7. 'Zhāng-Xiānsheng xǐhuan-chī-
yāzi. Tā-'lǎo-chī-kǎo-yāzi.

Mr. Zhang likes (to eat) duck.
He's always eating roast duck.

8. Tā-yí-dào-fànguǎr jiu-dà-
    chī. Bú-shi-hóng-shāo-ròu
    jiù-shi-shīzi-tóu.

Whenever he goes to the restaurant, he eats enormously. If it
isn't red-cooked meat then it's
lion's head.

9. Duìbuqǐ, wǒ-yào-kǎoshì-le.
    Wó-déi-'wǎn-huíqu.

Sorry, I'm going to have an
exam. I'll have to go back
(home) late.

10. Wǒ-bú-dà-xǐhuan kàn-diàn-
    yǐngr.

I don't much like to see movies.

SUBSTITUTION TABLES

I: 36 sentences (Note 1)

(Identical items in the 'A' columns are to be used together; similarly
for the 'B' columns.)

		A	B		A	B
wǒ	xiǎng	chī	duōshao	jiu	chī	duōshao
nǐ	yào	mǎi	shénmo		mǎi	shénmo
tā		gěi			gěi	

II: 48 sentences (Note 2)

(Only identical items in the asterisked columns may be used together.)

		*				*	
jiùshi	nǐ	—	qù	wǒ	yě	—	qù
	tā	bù	lái		dōu	bù	lái
			gěi				gěi

PRONUNCIATION DRILLS

Review of Four-Syllable Expressions (III)

(Asterisks indicate changes of third tone to second tone.)

0 0 2

1 xiānshengde-qián

2 láile-de-rén

3 wǒmende-chá

4 zuòle-de-chuán

1 0 2

tā-chīdewán

nín-hē-de-chá

děng-tāmen-lái

jiào-sānge-rén

2 0 2

hē-chá-de-rén

cóng-chéngli-lái

yě-róngyi-xué

tèbiéde-rén

3 0 2

1 dōu-xǐhuan-xué

2 nín-xiědewán

3 wó-zhǎobuzháo*

4 tài-xiǎode-hú

4 0 2

tā-zuòdewán

Máo-Tàitai-lái

nǐ-mài-de-chá

jiào-tàitai-lái

0 1 2

1 tāmen-chī-yú

2 shíge-zhōngtóu

3 wǒmen-dōu-lái

4 dàde-gōngyuán

1 1 2

xīngqīsān-lái

nín-yīnggāi-xué

yǒu-sānbēi-chá

xià-xīngqī-lái

2 1 2

chī-tián-suān-yú

shéi-xué-Yīngwén

zhǎo-shéi-kāi-mén

zuò-hóng-shāo-yú

3 1 2

1 tā-yǒu-sānmáo

2 nín-xiě-Zhōngwén

3 qíng-Měiyīng-lái*

4 jiù-yǒu-sānshí

4 1 2

dōu-niàn-Zhōngwén

yígòng-sānmáo

yě-niàn-Yīngwén

dàgài-tā-néng

022

1 tāmen-lái-wár
2 biéde-méi-ná
3 zěnmo-méi-lái
4 wàngle-ná-qián

122

fēijī-méi-lái
shéi-shuō-bié-ná
yǒu-sānmáo-qián
niàn-sānniánjí

222

shuō-nín-méi-lái
cóngqián-méi-xué
yě-xué-wénxué
kàn-shéi-néng-lái

322

1 tā-yě-néng-lái
2 nín-jǐniánjí
3 yóu-wǔmáo-qián *
4 niàn-yǔyánxué

422

tā-niàn-wénxué
shéi-niàn-guówén
kǒngpà-méi-lái
màipiàoyuán-néng

032

1 xiānsheng-yě-lái
2 tímu-hěn-nán
3 xǐhuan-lǚxíng
4 nèige-xiǎo-hú

132

tā-shuō-yǐqián
rén-dōu-hěn-máng
měitiān-mǎi-táng
kàn-shū-yǐqián

232

tā-xué-yǎnyuán
bái-táng-hěn-tián
yǎnyuán-yǒu-míng
jiàoyuán-dǎ-mén

332

1 dōu-hén-yǒu-míng *
2 nín-yé-yǒu-qián *
3 wó-yé-hěn-máng *
4 lì shí-hěn-nán *

432

chī-fàn-yǐqián
hái-niàn-xiǎoxué
yě-qù-lǚxíng
dàgài-yě-lái

042

1 tāmen-tài-máng
2 nínde-jiàoyuán
3 xǐhuan-shùxué
4 nèige-dà-chéng

142

tā-shuō-xìng-Máo
ná-sānkuài-qián
wǒ-kāi-dà-mén
dì-sāncì-lái

242

shū-shíkuài-qián
lái-xué-shùxué
yě-néng-zuò-chuán
jiàoyuán-xìng-Máo

342

1 dōu-hěn-tèbié
2 hái-qǐng-jiàoyuán
3 wó-mǎi-dìtú *
4 yìhuěr-jiù-lái

442

tā-huà-dìtú
shéi-pà-shùxué
bǎ-cài-zuòwán
jiào-màipiàoyuán

CHINESE MENU

This isn't exactly the way a Chinese menu would look, but the names of the dishes are authentic. Translate the names and practice them until you feel confident enough to order a full-course dinner for yourself and several friends.

CÀI DĀR

Tāng

zhū-ròu-tāng
niú-ròu-tāng
báicài-tāng
dòufu-tāng
jī-tāng
báicài-jī-tāng

zhū-ròu-báicài-tāng
báicài-dòufu-tāng
zhū-ròu-báicài-dòufu-tāng
niú-ròu-báicài-tāng
zhū-ròu-dòufu-tāng

Chǎo-Cài

chǎo-dòufu
chǎo-báicài
chǎo-jī
chǎo-xiārér
chǎo-niú-ròu

niú-ròu-chǎo-dòufu
zhū-ròu-chǎo-dòufu
zhū-ròu-chǎo-báicài
niú-ròu-chǎo-báicài
chǎo-zhū-ròu

Fàn

bái-fàn
chǎo-fàn
jī-chǎo-fàn
xiārér-chǎo-fàn

niú-ròu-chǎo-fàn
zhū-ròu-chǎo-fàn
niú-ròu-báicài-chǎo-fàn
zhū-ròu-báicài-chǎo-fàn

Jiǎozi

xiārér-jiǎozi
zhū-ròu-jiǎozi
niú-ròu-jiǎozi

xiārér-zhū-ròu-jiǎozi
zhū-ròu-báicài-jiǎozi
niú-ròu-báicài-jiǎozi

Kǎo

kǎo-yāzi
kǎo-jī

kǎo-zhū-ròu
kǎo-niú-ròu

Hóng-Shāo

hóng-shāo-yú
hóng-shāo-jī
hóng-shāo-ròu
hóng-shāo-yāzi

hóng-shāo-niú-ròu
hóng-shāo-dòufu
shīzi-tóu

Táng-Cù

táng-cù-yú
táng-cù-báicài

táng-cù-ròu

Miàn

chǎo-miàn
jī-chǎo-miàn
xiārér-chǎo-miàn
zhū-ròu-báicài-chǎo-miàn

niú-ròu-chǎo-miàn
zhū-ròu-chǎo-miàn
niú-ròu-báicài-chǎo-miàn

Diǎnxin

xìngrér-dòufu

xìngrér-chá

Chá

hóng-chá*

(a) báicài tāng

(b) hóng shāo yú

(c) chǎo xiārér

(d) liángwǎn fàn

---

* <u>Hóng-chá</u>, literally 'red tea,' is 'black tea' to speakers of English. <u>Xìngrér-chá</u>, literally 'almond tea,' is not tea at all, but a porridge-like dessert made of rice meal, almonds, sugar, and cinnamon.

ANSWERING QUESTIONS

1. Chīwánle-fànguǎr-yǐhòu, shèngde-qián-géi-huǒji, nà-jiào-'shénmo-qián?

2. Wáng-Xiānsheng kāi-chē-de-jīngyan-hěn-duō. 'Zhāng-Xiānshengde-jīng-yan-bú-gòu. Shéi-kāi-chē-kāide-hǎo?

3. Máo-Xiáojie shèngle-hěn-duō-chǎo-xiārér.   Máo-Xiānsheng bǎ-hóng-shāo-yú-'dōu-chīwán-le. Shéi-méi-shèng-cài-ne?

4. Rúguó-liǎngge-rén qù-chī-fàn, nǐ-yào-shīzi-tóu, chǎo-báicài, wǒ-yào-hóng-shāo-yú, kǎo-yāzi, nǐ-shuō-shèngdeliǎo-ma?

5. 'Wáng-Xiānsheng xǐhuan-chī-jiǎozi. 'Zhāng-Xiānsheng xǐhuan-chī-chǎo-miàn. Tāmen-liǎngge-rén shéi-chī-jiǎozi?

6. 'Gāo-Xiáojie chī-chǎo-xiārér, 'Bái-Xiānsheng chī-hóng-shāo-yú. Něi-ge-cài-lǐtou fàng-de-jiàngyóu fàngde-duō?

7. Wǒmen-dào-fànguǎr chīwánle-fàn-yǐhòu, jiào-'shéi-lái géi-wǒmen-suàn-zhàng?

8. 'Bái-Xiānsheng yào-xìngrér-dòufu. Huǒji-shuō-gāng-màiwán. Nèige-fànguǎr hái-yǒu-xìngrér-dòufu-ma?

9. 'Máo-Xiáojie hěn-cōngming. Tā-dìdi-niàn-shū-niànde méi-tā-nènmo-hǎo. 'Máo-Xiáojie 'néng-bu-néng-bāngzhu-tā-ne?

10. Zhèige-xuéxiào jiàoyuán dōu-shi-nǚ-de, xuésheng dōu-shi-nǚ-xuésheng. Nǐ-shuō-quán-xuéxiào yǒu-'nán-de-méi-you?

WHAT WOULD YOU SAY?

Imagine that you and a friend, Mr. Johnson, are both talking with a waiter in a North Chinese restaurant in the United States. Make up an appropriate dialogue along the following lines:

The waiter greets the two of you and asks where you want to sit. You suggest a place, and Johnson agrees to it. The waiter asks if you would both like some tea; you say you would, and tell him to bring a pot. Johnson adds that he should bring a menu, too. You ask about the specialties of the house. The waiter wants to know whether you're eating dumplings or rice, and Johnson says he wants to study the menu.

The waiter says you both speak Chinese very well, and asks where you studied and whether you have ever been to China. You answer that you haven't been, adding that your Chinese was studied in America. You ask whether your Chinese is really good or whether he's just being polite. The waiter says he's telling the truth, not being polite.

You ask Johnson what should be ordered, and Johnson suggests ordering ten dumplings, pork and fried bean curd, and fried shrimp. The waiter asks what soup you want, and Johnson asks for beef and cabbage soup. The waiter asks if you often eat Chinese food. You say you often do, that you like to very much, but that this is the first time you've come here.

Johnson asks the waiter if he's a Northerner. The waiter says all of them here are. Johnson wants to know how long the waiter has been in America, and the waiter tells him twenty-odd years. You say the food is not bad. The waiter hopes you will come often.

NOTES

1. Question words in pairs have meanings like 'whatever,' 'whoever,' 'whichever,' etc. They occur in paired phrases the second of which usually contains the word jiù 'then':

Ní-xǐhuan-shénmo (nǐ-) jiù-'chī-shénmo. 'Eat whatever you like.' [lit. 'You like what, then eat what.']

Mǔqin-zuò-shénmo nǚ-háizi-jiù-'zuò-shénmo. 'Girls do whatever their mothers do.'

If the subject is the same for both verbs, its mention before the second verb is optional (see also the first sentence above):

'Shéi-yào-lǚxíng 'shéi-jiù-qù-lǚxíng. or
'Shéi-yào-lǚxíng jiù-qù-lǚxíng.
'Whoever wants to make a trip can go on a trip.'

Sometimes the question word in the second phrase occurs in a different usage from that of the first phrase. Thus in the following sentence the first néiběn is the subject of the sentence, and the second is the object:

'Néiběn-shū-róngyi-kàn wǒ-jiu-yào-'néiběn. 'I want whichever book is easiest to read.'

Sometimes the question in the second phrase is interchangeable with some other word:

'Shéi-huì-zuò-Zhōngguo-cài jiu-qǐng-shéi-zuò. or
'Shéi-huì-zuò-Zhōngguo-cài jiù-qǐng-ta-zuò.
'Whoever can cook Chinese food is invited to do so.'

2. The adverbs yě 'also' and dōu 'all' are used in the patterns A yě B and A dōu B, in which B is a verb phrase and A is either a noun or a verb phrase. If A is a noun phrase, the construction means 'even A does B':

Wáng-Xiānsheng yě-bu-lái. or
Wáng-Xiānsheng dōu-bu-lái.
'Even Mr. Wang isn't coming.'

If A is a verb phrase, the construction means 'even if A (still) B':

Nǐ-lái Wáng-Xiānsheng-yě-bu-lái. or
Nǐ-lái Wáng-Xiānsheng-dōu-bu-lái.
'Even if you come, Mr. Wang isn't coming.'

The 'even' meaning can be made more explicit by using lián (lit. 'join') or jiùshi (lit. 'precisely is') or jiùshi lián before A:

      Lián-'Wáng-Xiānsheng yě-bu-lái. <u>or</u>
      Jiùshi-'Wáng-Xiānsheng yě-bu-lái. <u>or</u>
      Jiùshi-lián-'Wáng-Xiānsheng yě-bu-lái.
      'Even Mr. Wang isn't coming.'

      Lián-nǐ-lái Wáng-Xiānsheng-yě-bu-lái. <u>or</u>
      Jiùshi-nǐ-lái Wáng-Xiānsheng-yě-bu-lái. <u>or</u>
      Jiùshi-lián-nǐ-lái Wáng-Xiānsheng-yě-bu-lái.
      'Even if you come, Mr. Wang isn't coming.'

3. The transformation of the verb-object sequence into the inverted order of object-verb changes the meaning from 'do X' to 'X to do':

      Tā-chī-fàn. 'He eats food.'
      Tā-méi-yǒu-fàn-chī. 'He has no food to eat.'

      Tā-zuò-shì. 'He is working.'
      Tā-méi-yǒu-shì-zuò. 'He has no work to do.'

<u>Kéyi</u> 'can' may be inserted between the two elements of these phrases:

      Tā-méi-yǒu-fàn-kéyi-chī. 'He has no food (which he) can eat.'

The inverted phrase is most often used with a preceding <u>yǒu</u> or <u>méi-yǒu</u>, as in the examples above.

4. We have seen (Lesson 8, Note 1, p. 100) that some stative verbs combine with transitive verbs to form compound descriptive phrases, such as <u>hǎochī</u> 'good to eat.' Another of these is <u>gòu</u> 'enough':

      Fàn-gòu-chī-ma? 'Is there enough food to eat?'

We have also seen (Lesson 13, Note 6, p. 188) that <u>kuài</u> 'fast' means 'soon' when used before another verb:

      Wǒmen-kuài-zǒu-ba. 'Let's leave right away.'

<u>Màn</u> 'slow' in a similar usage means 'not (so) soon'; a common phrase <u>màn-zǒu</u> [lit. 'go not (so) soon'] is said to departing guests — 'Don't be in a hurry to go.' <u>Màn</u> in this usage also means 'slow,' 'slowly,' according to the context:

      màn-zǒu 'go slowly'
      màn-kāi 'drive slowly'

Other stative verbs acquire further shades of meaning when used adverbially:

<u>Lǎo</u> 'old' becomes 'always':

      Wó-lǎo-chī-'Zhōngguo-fàn. 'I always eat Chinese food.'

<u>Dà</u> 'big' becomes 'much' or 'very':

      Wǒ-bu-dà-huì-shuō-Zhōngguo-huà. 'I can't speak Chinese very well.'

<u>Bái</u> 'white' becomes 'uselessly':

      Wǒ-bái-qù-le. Tā-méi-zài-jiā. 'I went to no purpose. He wasn't at home.'

5. <u>Shi</u> 'be' is added to a number of expressions, especially adverbs, to make them more emphatic:

        yóuqí   <u>or</u> yóuqíshi   'especially'
        tèbié   <u>or</u> tèbiéshi   'especially'
        hái   <u>or</u> háishi   'still'

    Wǒ-shuōle-hěn-duō-cì. Tā-'háishi-bù-dǒng. 'I said it several times. He <u>still</u> didn't understand.'

6. The verb <u>lái</u> 'come' is also used in restaurants in the sense of 'cause to come, bring':

    Lái-yìhú-chá-ba. 'Bring a pot of tea.'

Lesson 22 DISCUSSING CHINESE

"Nǐ-shuō-pīnyīnde-fāngfǎ 'zěnmo-hǎo-ne?"

Dialogue: Mr. Gao and Mr. White exchange views on Chinese.

Gāo-Xiānsheng、 Gāo-Tàitai、 Gāo-Xiáojie dào-Rìběn-qù-lǚxíng-huílai-yǐhòu, 'Bái-Xiānsheng lái-kàn-tāmen. 'Gāo-Xiānsheng hěn-gāoxìng, qǐng-'Bái-Xiānsheng zài-tāmen-jiā-lǐ-tou chī-wǎnfàn, gēn-ta-tán guān-yú-Zhōngguo-yǔyán gēn-wénxué-de-yìxiē-wèntí.

After Mr. and Mrs. Gao and Miss Gao return from traveling in Japan, Mr. White comes to see them. Mr. Gao is delighted, and invites Mr. White to have dinner at their home and to chat with him about some problems concerning Chinese language and literature.

(Bái-Xiānsheng-dǎ-mén.)

(Mr. White knocks on the door.)

Gāo-Xiáojie: Shéi-a?

Who is it?

Bái: Shi-wǒ, Měiyīng.

It's me, Meiying.

(Měiyīng-kāi-mén.)

(Meiying opens the door.)

Gāo-Xiáojie: Wénshān, hǎo-ma? Nǐ-zǎochen-dǎ-diànhua shuō-jīntian-lái wǒ-fùqin-hěn-gāoxìng, děngzhe-nǐ-lái-ne.

Vincent, how are you? When you called this morning and said you were coming today my father was very happy. He's been waiting for you [to come].

Bái: Měiyīng, nǐ-zuò-shénmo-ne? Huà-huàr-ne, háishi-niàn-shū-ne?   20

Meiying, what are you doing? Are you painting or reading?

Gāo-Xiáojie: Yě-méi-huà-huàr yě-méi-niàn-shū. Bāngzhu-mǔ-qin-zuò-fàn-ne.

Neither. I'm helping my mother cook dinner.

Gāo-Xiānsheng: Wénshān, nǐ-lái-le. Hǎo-ma?   25

Vincent, welcome [lit. you've come]! How are you?

Bái: Gāo-Xiānsheng, nín-hǎo? Jīntian-méi-chūqu-ma?

Hello, Mr. Gao. You haven't been out today?

Gāo-Xiānsheng: Méi-you. Qǐng-zuò. Wǒmen-hē-chá, chī-diǎnxin. Měiyīng, ná-diar-'Rìběn-diǎnxin-lái. Zài-géi-wo-yìbēi-chá. Wǒ-zài-Rìběn mǎile-jíběn-guānyú-yǔyánxué-de-shū. Wǒ-kàn-guole, 'hěn-bú-cuò. Duì-ni-hén-yǒu-yòng. Sònggei-ni.   30 ... 35

No, I haven't. Sit down. Let's have some tea and cakes. Meiying, get some Japanese pastry. Give me a cup of tea too. In Japan I bought several books dealing with linguistics. I've read them. They're not bad at all. They'll be useful to you. I'm presenting them to you.

Bái: Xièxie-nín.

Thank you.

Gāo-Xiānsheng: Wǒ-zhèng-xīwang-nǐ-lái. Wǒmen-tántan zhè-jíběn-shū-lǐtóu guānyú-yǔ-yán-gēn-wénxué-de-wèntí.   40

I was just hoping you would come. Let's talk about some problems in these books concerning language and literature.

Bái: Hǎojíle. Nín-zài-Rìběn wárde-hěn-gāoxìng-ba?

Excellent. I take it you were happy with your Japanese holiday.

Gāo-Xiānsheng: Hén-hǎo. 'Rìběn-hén-yǒu-yìsi. Yuánlái-xiǎng 'duō-zhù-jǐtiān, Měi-yīng-láo-xiǎng-huílai.   45

It was fine. Japan is very interesting. I had originally planned to stay a few more days, but Meiying kept wanting to come back.

Bái: Měiyīng, nǐ-zài-'Rìběn-huà-de-huàr náchulai-wǒ-kànkan.   50

Meiying, bring out the paintings you did in Japan so I can see them.

Gāo-Xiáojie: Nǐ-máng-shénmo? Děng-yìhuěr mànmārde-kàn. Wó-yě-méi-huà-jǐzhāng. Měitiān-gēnzhe-fùqin-mǔqin-qu-wár.   55

What's the hurry? Wait a while and take your time looking. I didn't make many paintings. Every day I went around with my father and mother having fun.

Bái: Gāo-Xiānsheng, nín-zài-Rì-běn hái-tiāntiān-xiě-zì-ma?

Mr. Gao, when you were in Japan did you still practice calligraphy every day?

Gāo-Xiānsheng: Méi-you. Měitiān-dōu-chūqu-wár. Nár-yǒu-gōngfu-xiě-zì-ne? Wǒmen-zài-Rìběn-de-shíhou nǐ-dōu-   60

No. I spent every day having a good time. Where would I find time to write characters? When we were in Japan what did you

	zuò-xiē-shénmo-ne? Kéyi- gàosu-wǒmen-ma?	do all the time? Can you tell us?
Bái:	Wó-'nár-yě-méi-qù. Měitiān- kànkan-shū-zháozhao-péngyou, 65 kànle-'jǐcì-diànyǐngr, zài- gěi-fùqin-mǔqin-péngyou xié- xie-xìn.	I didn't go anywhere. I read a bit and visited friends every day, saw a few movies, and wrote to my father and mother and friends.
Gāo:	Nǐ-zhēn-shi-yíge-hǎo-xué- **sheng. Zì-xiěde-nènmo-hǎo,** 70 huà-shuōde-sìshēng-nènmo- zhǔn. Rúguǒ-méi-hǎohǎorde- xué nǎr-néng-'zhènmo-hǎo- ne?	You really are a good student. You write so well, and speak with such accurate tones. If you hadn't studied so well how could you be so good?
Bái:	Nín-guòjiǎng. 75	You flatter me.
Gāo:	Xiànzài-wǒ-gàosu-ni wó-mǎi- de-nèi-jíběn-shū-lǐtou yǒu- yìběn shi-yíwèi-'Rìběn- jiàoshòu Zhōngshān*-Xiān- sheng-xiě-de. Tándào-pīn- 80 yīn**-gēn-Hànzìde-wèntí. Nǐ- kāishǐ-xué-Zhōngwén shi-'zěn- mo-xué-de-ne? Zài-Měiguo- **xuéxiàolǐ** jiāo-de-fāngfǎ dōu-yíyàng-ma? 85	I want to tell you now that among the books I bought there's one written by a Japanese professor, Mr. Nakayama.* It discusses the problem of alphabetic writ- ing** and Chinese characters. When you began to study Chinese how did you study? Is there a uniform method of teaching in American schools?
Bái:	Měiguo-xuéxiào-lǐtou jiāo- de-fázi-bù-yíyàng. 'Yǒude- kāishǐ-jiù-xué-Hànzì, 'yǒu- de-yòng-pīnyīn-xué.	The teaching methods in Ameri- can schools are not uniform. Some begin with studying Chi- nese characters, some use transcription.
Gāo:	Nǐ-juéde néizhǒng-fāngfǎ-hǎo? 90	Which method do you think is better?
Bái:	Wǒ-juéde pīnyīnde-fázi-bǐ- jiáo-hǎo.	I think the transcription method is better.
Gāo:	Wó-xiǎng guānyú-Zhōngguo- yǔyán wǒ-bù-xǐhuan-yòng- pīnyīnde-fāngfǎ. Rúguǒ-yòng- 95	I don't think I like using a ro- manization in connection with the Chinese language. If you use

---

* The characters for the Chinese name <u>Zhōngshān</u>, which means 'middle mountain,' are read by the Japanese as <u>Nakayama</u> (<u>naka</u> 'middle,' <u>yama</u> 'mountain'), so that the name Nakayama is the Japanese equivalent of Chinese <u>Zhōngshān</u>. (Nakayama is a common Japanese name, and this is why Sun Yat-sen adopted the corresponding Chinese name <u>Zhōngshān</u>—by which most Chinese know him—while he was a political exile in Japan. The practice of giving Chinese readings for Japanese words and expressions is a common one, and the reverse practice is common in Japan.

** The term <u>pīnyīn</u> [lit. 'spell sounds'] is used in two senses: (1) as a general term for transcription or romanization, and (2) as the designation for a specific system of transcription, that used in this book.

pínyīn-fāngfǎ nà-bú-shi-niàn-
Yīngwén-le-ma? Nǎr-shi-
xué-Zhōngwén-ne?

romanization isn't that reading
English?   Where is there any
studying of Chinese?

Bái: Nín-'bù-xǐhuan-pīnyīnde-
fázi-ma? Wǒ-juéde yòng-
pīnyīnde-fázi bíjiáo-hǎo.
Yòu-kuài-yòu-róngyi.

100

You don't like the transcription
method?   I think it's better to
use this method. It's faster as
well as easier.

Gāo: Nǐ-shuō-pīnyīnde-fāngfǎ 'zěnmo-hǎo-ne?

Tell me how transcription is
better.

Bái: Xiān-xué-huì-shuōle yǐhòu-
zài-niàn-shū-xiě-zì jiù-bù-
nán-le.

105

(If you) first learn to speak and
afterwards go on to reading and
writing, then it is no longer difficult.

Gāo: Nǐ-shuō-'zěnmo-bù-nán?

How   come   it's   not difficult?

Bái: Huì-shuō-le-yǐhòu zhīdao-
tāde-yìsi-le, zài-niàn-shū
jiù-bíjiǎo-róngyi-míngbai-
le.

110

After mastering speech you've
learned what it means and so in
going on to reading it's relatively easier to understand.

Gāo: Kěshi-nǐ-xué-pīnyīn bú-
rènshi-Zhōngguo-zì, hái-
děi-'zài-xué-Zhōngguo-zì.

115

But in learning romanization you
don't become familiar with Chinese characters, and you still
have to study them.

Bái: Kěshi-zìde-yìsi rúguó-yǐ-
jing-xuéguo-le, xué-Hànzì-
de-shíhou zhǐ-xué-Hànzì,
jiù-bú-bì-xué-yìsi-le.

But if the meanings of the characters have been learned already, when you study characters you just study characters,
and so it's no longer necessary
to study meanings.

Gāo: Nǐ-nènmo-yì-shuō huòzhě-
pīnyīnde-fāngfǎ yé-yǒu-tāde-
hǎochu.

120

From what you say, perhaps the
transcription method has some
advantages.

Bái: Wó-xiǎng-'shì-hén-hǎo.
Yǔyán-shi-yǔyán, wénxué-
shi-wénxué, shi-liǎng-bù-
fen.

125

I believe it is very good. Language is language, literature is
literature, and they're two different things [lit. two parts].

Gāo: Nǐ-kāishǐ-xué yídìng-hěn-
yònggōng-le.

When you began your studies you
must have been very diligent.

Bái: Nèige-shíhou wó-hěn-yònggōng. Měitiān-tīng-lùyīn,
zìjǐ-gēn-zìjǐ-shuō-huà,
liànxi-fāyīn, bá-měitiān-
xué-de dōu-jìzhu. Yuè-xué-
yuè-yǒu-xìngqu.

130

At that time I did work hard.
Every day I listened to recordings, carried on monologues,
practiced pronunciation, and
fixed in my memory all that we
studied every day. The more I
studied the more interested I became.

Gāo: Nǐ-kāishǐ shi-xiān-xué-
shuō-huà-ma?

135

At the beginning did you first
study speaking?

Bái: Shì, wǒ-xiān-xué-shuō-huà.

Gāo: Nǐ-xiān-xué-shuō-huà shi-
'zěnmo-xué-ne?

Bái: Wǒ-kāishǐ-xué-sìshēng gēn-   140
qīngzhòngyīn, yǐhòu-xué-
cér (bǐfang-shuō shū, tàitai
jiù-shi-cér) gēn-duǎn-jùzi,
zài-xué-huìhuà.

Gāo: Xué-yǔyán 'tèbié-yīnggāi-   145
zhùyì-de shi-shénmo?

Bái: Tèbié-yào-zhùyì-de shi-fāyīn-gēn-yúfǎ.

Gāo: Pīnyīn-duì-fāyīn yǒu-bāng-
zhu-ba.   150

Bái: Pīnyīnde-fázi-duì-fāyīn
hén-yǒu-bāngzhu. Zhōngguo-
huà zuì-yào-zhùyì-de shi-
sìshēng. Bǐfang-shuō tài-
tai-zhèige-cér jiù-shi-liǎng-   155
ge-yīnjié. Dì-yíge-yīnjié
shi-yǒu-shēng-de, dì-sì-
shēng. Dì-èrge-yīnjié shi-
qīng-shēng, jiù-shi-méi-
you-shēng.   160

Gāo: Rúguǒ-yòng-Hànzì 'duǎnchu-
zài-nǎr?

Bái: Bǐfang-shuō tàitai-zhèige-
cér. Rúguǒ-yòng-Hànzì-xiě,
jiù-yòng-liǎngge-yíyàngde-   165
zi. Yòng-Hànzì yě-bù-zhī-
dào zhèi-liǎngge-zi zài-yí-
kuàr-niàn háishi-'bú-zài-yí-
kuàr-niàn. Shi-'jǐshēng yě-
bù-zhīdào. Rúguó-liǎngge-   170
zì yíyàng-niàn jiù-shi-tài-
tài, nà-jiu-'bú-shi-shuō-
huà-le.

Gāo: Nǐ-shuōde-yě-bú-cuò, kěshi-
bù-'dōu-duì. Nǐ-yòng-Hànzì-   175
xué yídìng-yǒu-ge-Zhōngguo-
xiānsheng-jiāo-ni. Bù-
rán-ní-'zěnmo-xué? Xiān-
sheng yídìng-gàosu-nǐ zěnmo-niàn. Tā-yídìng-gàosu-   180
nǐ-niàn-tàitai. Tā-bú-huì-
jiāo-nǐ-niàn-tài-tài.

Yes, I first learned to speak.

When you began with speech, how
did you study?

I began by studying the four
tones and stress. Afterwards I
studied words (for example, shū
and tàitai are words) and
phrases, and then studied conversation.

In studying languages what must
you pay special attention to?

What needs most attention is
pronunciation and grammar.

I take it transcription is helpful
in pronunciation.

The transcription method is very
helpful in pronunciation. In Chinese what needs the most attention is the four tones. For
example, the word tàitai is two
syllables. The first syllable has
a tone, the fourth tone. The
second syllable is a neutral tone,
that is, it has no tone.

If you use Chinese characters
where are the disadvantages?

Take this word tàitai for example. If you write it in Chinese
characters, you use two identical
characters. If you use Chinese
characters you don't know
whether these two characters
are read together or not. Neither can you tell what tones they
are. If the two characters are
read in the same way, it becomes tài tài, and that's no
longer a spoken form.

Your ideas aren't bad, but they
aren't entirely correct. If you
study by means of Chinese characters you will certainly have a
Chinese teacher to teach you.
Otherwise how would you study?
The teacher would certainly tell
you how to read it. He would
[certainly] tell you to read it
tàitai. He couldn't tell you to
read it tài tài.

Bái: Rúguǒ-yòng-Hànzì xué-
Zhōngguo-yǔyán, méi-xué-
guo-de-zì nǐ-méi-fázi zì-   185
jǐ-huì-niàn. Xiàng-tā-
zhèige-zì, zuǒbiār-shi-rén,
yòubiār-shi-yě. Méi-yǒu-
tā-zìde-yīn. Rúguǒ-zìjǐ-
liànxi-de-shíhou wǒmen-yí-   190
kàn-pīnyīn jiù-huì-niàn-le.
Suóyi-pīnyīn shi-zuì-hǎode-
fāngfǎ-le.

If you use Chinese characters to study the Chinese language, there is no way of knowing by yourself how to read a character which you have not previously studied. For example, the character for tā is rén on the left and yě on the right. There is no sound of the character tā. When we practice by ourselves, as soon as we see the transcription then we're able to read it. That's why a transcription is the best system.

$$亻 + 也 = 他$$

rén + yě ≠ tā

Gāo: Néng-bù-néng Hànzì-gēn-
pīnyīn yí-'kuàr-xué-ne?   195

Would it be possible to study Chinese characters together with the romanization?

Bái: Yòng-pīnyīnde-fázi-xué,
kéyi-xiān-xué-fāyīn, cérde-
yìsi, gēn-yúfǎ. Yǐhòu-zài-
xué-Hànzì. Rúguǒ-tóngshí
yòu-xué-fāyīn, cér, Hànzì,   200
wénfǎ, xué-de-dōngxi-'tài-
duō-le, jiù-xuéde-bíjiǎo-
màn-le.

If you study using the transcription method, you can first study pronunciation, the meaning of words, and the grammar of the language. Later you also study characters. If you study pronunciation, vocabulary, characters, and grammar at (one and) the same time, there are too many things to learn, and so progress is relatively slow.

Gāo: Xué-Hànzì yé-bu-tài-nán-
ne. Jiù-shi-duō-liànxi-me.   205

Learning characters is not too hard. It's just a matter of practicing more, of course.

Bái: Xué-Hànzì yóu-liǎngge-nán-
chu. Yíge shi-wǒ-gāngcái-
shuōguo méi-fázi-zhīdao-
zěnmo-niàn. Yíge-shi-bì-
děi-jìzhu zěnmo-xiě, yóu-   210
jǐhuá. Bǐfang-tā-zhèige-zì
yóu-wǔhuá, shi-liǎng-bùfen.
Xiān-xié-zuǒbiar hòu-xiě-
yòubiar. Bìděi-jìzhu xiěde-
fázi. Nín-kàn xiān-xué-   215
Hànzì bǐ-xiān-xué-pīnyīn
nánde-duō.

There are two difficulties in studying Chinese characters. One, as I've just mentioned, is that there is no way to know how to read them. Another is that one must memorize how to write them, how many strokes they have. For example, the character for tā has five strokes and consists of two parts. First you write the left and then you write the right. You must memorize how to write. You see that studying characters first is a lot harder than studying transcription first.

Gāo: Pīnyīnde-fāngfǎ hǎo-shi-hǎo,   Alphabetic writing is good, all
      kěshi-kànqilai háishi-Hànzì-   right; but still to the eye the
      piàoliang.   220   Chinese characters are more
                                               beautiful.

VOCABULARY

bǐfang	example (N) (Note 12 below)
bùfen	section, part, member (M) [lit. section part]
cí, cér	word (N)
duǎn	short (SV)
duǎnchu	disadvantage, shortcoming (N) (Note 5)
fā	put out, emit (TV)
fāyīn	pronunciation (N) [lit. emit sound]
guānyú	concerning, regarding (CV)
Hàn	**China, Chinese (N) (Note 13)**
Hànzì	Chinese characters (N) (Note 14)
hǎochu	advantage (N) (Note 5)
huá, huà	stroke (in a character) (M)
huìhuà	dialogue, conversation (N) [lit. assembly speech]
jì(zhu)	remember, memorize (TV) (Note 5)
jùzi	sentence (N)
liànxi	practice, learn how to (TV) [lit. practice practice]
nánchu	difficulty (N) (Note 5)
pīn	spell (out), write in alphabetic script (TV)
pīnyīn	alphabetic writing, spelling, transcription, romanization (N)
qīng	light (in weight) (SV)
qīngzhòngyīn	stress (N) (Note 9)
shēng	sound, tone (N, M) (Note 10)
shēngyin	noise, sound (N) (Note 5)
sìshēng	(four) tones (N) (Note 11)
sòng	escort, send, give (TV)
tóngshí	same time, simultaneously (TW) (Note 5)
wénfǎ	grammar (N) (Note 14)
wèntí	problem, question, theme (N) [lit. ask topic]
yīn	sound (N)

yīnjié	syllable (N) [lit. sound joint]
yúfǎ	grammar (N) (Notes 5, 14)
yuè	the more (AD) (Note 1)
zhèng	just (now), precisely, exactly (AD) (Note 11)
zhòng	heavy (SV)
zhǔn	accurate (SV)
zhùyì	pay attention to (TV) [lit. note idea]
zìjǐ	self (lit. self self]

SENTENCE BUILD-UP

yuè... yuè
the more... the more
1. Yuè-duō-yuè-hǎo.
The more the better.

yuè-chī-Zhōngguo-cài
the more I eat Chinese food
yuè-xǐhuan-chī
the more I like to eat
2. Wǒ-yuè-chī-Zhōngguo-cài yuè-xǐhuan-chī.
The more I eat Chinese food the more I like [to eat] it.

yuè-lái-yuè
more and more
3. Rén-yuè-lái-yuè-duō.
People are becoming more and more numerous.

zhǔn
accurate
4. Nǐde-biǎo 'zhǔn-bu-zhǔn?
Is your watch accurate?

shēng
sound, tone
sìshēng
four tones
5. Zhōngwén yǒu-sìshēng.
Chinese has four tones.

yīn
sound, pronunciation
yīn-hěn-duì
pronunciation quite correct
6. Tā-shuō-huà yīn-hěn-duì.
[In speaking] his pronunciation is quite correct.

shēngyin
sound, noise
shēngyin-tài-dà
noise is too great
7. Zhèr-shēngyin-tài-dà.
There's too much noise here.

pīn
spell alphabetically
8. Zhèige-yīn-zěnmo-pīn?
How is this sound spelled?

pīnyīn
spelling, alphabetic writing
9. Pīnyīn hěn-róngyi-niàn.
Alphabetic writing is easy to read.

fā
put out, emit

fā-yīn   utter sounds, pronounce
10. Tā-fā-de-yīn hěn-duì.   The sounds he makes are quite
                                          correct.

fāyīn   pronunciation
fāyīn-bú-cuò   pronunciation is not bad
11. Tā-shuō-Zhōngwén fāyīn-   (When) he speaks Chinese his
     bú-cuò.   pronunciation isn't bad.

zhùyì   pay close attention to
12. Kāishí-děi-zhùyì-fāyīn.   At the beginning one must pay
                                          close attention to pronunciation.

liànxi   practice
13. Ní-děi-duō-liànxi-fāyīn.   You should practice pronuncia-
                                          tion more.

wèntí   problem, question
wèn-wèntí   ask a question
14. Wǒ-xiànzài wèn-nǐmen-jǐge-   Now I'll put several problems to
     wèntí.   you.

hǎo   good, well
hǎohāorde   well
15. Ní-déi-hǎohāorde-niàn-shū.   You must study well.

wén   literature, language
wénfǎ   grammar
'Zhōngwénde-wénfǎ   grammar of Chinese
16. Zhōngwénde-wénfǎ gēn-Yīng-   Chinese grammar is not the
     wénde-wénfǎ bù-yíyàng.   same as English grammar.

yúfǎ   grammar
17. 'Wénfǎ-gēn-yúfǎ yìsi-yíyàng.   Wénfǎ and yúfǎ mean the same
                                          thing.

jùzi   sentence
dì-sìge-jùzi   the fourth sentence
18. Qíng-nǐ-niàn dì-sìge-jùzi.   Please read the fourth sentence.

cér   word
jǐge-cér?   how many words?
19. Zhèige-jùzili yóu-jǐge-cér?   How many words are there in
                                          this sentence?

sòng   see [a person] off
sòng-péngyou   see a friend off
sòng-péngyou-shàng-   see a friend off on the boat
     chuán
20. Wǒ-míngtian sòng-péngyou-   I'm seeing him off on the boat
     shàng-chuán.   tomorrow.

sòng-qián   send money
sòng-ta-yìdiǎr-qián   send him a little money

21. Wǒ-míngtian sòng-tā-yìdiǎr-   I'll send him a little money to-
    qián.   morrow.

      sòng-qián   send money
      sòng-qián-gěi-ta   send money to him
22. Wǒ-míngtian sòng-qián-gěi-   I'll send him some money to-
    ta.   morrow.

      sònggei   send to
23. Nǐ-míngtian bǎ-qián-sònggei-   Send him the money tomorrow.
    ta.

      yuè   month
      yuèyuer   every month
24. Wǒ-yuèyuer-qù-Hángzhou.   I go to Hangchow every month.

      yíge-cér   one word
      gège-cér   every word
25. Nǐ-gège-cér dōu-shuōcuò-   You've said every word wrong.
    le.

      rén   person
      'rénrén   everyone
26. 'Rénrén-dōu-děi-chī-fàn.   Everybody has to eat.

      bú-shi-'rénrén   it isn't everybody
27. Bú-shi-'rénrén dōu-xǐhuan-   Not everybody likes to study
    xué-Zhōngwén.   Chinese.

      qīng   light (in weight)
      qīng-shēng   neutral tone
28. Chúle-sìshēng-yǐwài hái-   Apart from the four tones there
    yǒu-qīng-shēng.   is also a neutral tone.

      zhòng   heavy
      zhòng-yīn   heavy sound, stress
29. Zhèige-cérde-zhòng-yīn zài-   Where is the stress in this
    nǎr?   word?

      qīngzhòngyīn   stress
30. Xué-yǔyán děi-zhùyì-qīng-   In studying a language one must
    zhòngyīn.   pay attention to stress.

      bùfen   part
      yíbùfen   one part
31. Wǒde-shū yíbùfen-zài-Zhōng-   Part of my books are in China.
    guo.

      huá   stroke (of a character)
      jǐhuá?   how many strokes?
32. Zhèige-zì-yóu-jǐhuá?   How many strokes are there in
                                         this character?

      duǎn   short

hén-duǎnde-lù
33. Nà-shi-yìtiáo hén-duǎnde-lù.

a very short road
That is a very short road.

huìhuà
liànxi-huìhuà
34. Ní-déi-hǎohāorde-liànxi-huì-
huà.

conversation
practice conversation
You must carefully practice conversation.

Hàn
Hàn-Yīng
35. Xué-Zhōngwén déi-yǒu-Hàn-
Yīng-zìdiǎn.

Chinese
Chinese-English
In studying Chinese one must
have a Chinese-English dictionary.

Hànzì
36. Hànzì bù-róngyì-xiě.

Chinese characters
Chinese characters are not easy
to write.

zìjǐ
wǒ-zìjǐ
37. Fàn wǒ-zìjǐ-zuò zìjǐ-chī.

self
I myself
I make and eat the food by my-
self.

guānyú
guānyú-tāde-shìqing
38. Guānyú-tāde-shìqing bié-gēn-
wǒ-shuō.

regarding
regarding his affairs
Don't speak to me regarding his
affairs.

yīnjié
39. Zhèige-duǎn-jùzi yóu-jǐge-
yīnjié?

syllable
How many syllables are there in
this phrase?

zhèng
40. Wǒ-zhèng-xiě-zì-ne.

just now, at this moment
I'm just now writing characters.

zhèng
zhèng-zài
41. Wǒ-zhèng-zài-xiě-zì-ne.

just now, at this moment
just in the act of
I'm just now writing characters.

duǎn
duǎnchu
42. Tāde-duǎnchu 'tài-duō-le.

short
shortcoming, inadequacy
He has too many shortcomings.

jì
43. Hànzìde-xiéfǎ hěn-nán-jì.

remember
It's difficult to remember the
way to write Chinese characters.

jì
jìzhu
44. Xué-'Zhōngwén yào-jì-
zhu-sìshēng.

remember
fix in mind
In studying Chinese one must fix
the tones in mind.

bǐfang

example

zuò-ge-bǐfang   make up an example
45. Yòng-zhèige-zì zuò-ge-bǐ-   Make up an example using this
    fang.   word.

máng   busy
máng-shénmo?   in a hurry over what?
46. Nǐ-máng-shénmo?   What are you in a hurry about?

tóngshí   same time
47. Tāmen-liǎngge-rén tóngshí-   They both came at the same
    lái-le.   time.

PATTERN DRILLS

Pattern 22.1. Expressing 'the more . . . the more . . .' (Note 1 below)

yuè	V₁	yuè	V₂
'the more'	Verb₁	'the more'	Verb₂
yuè	gāo	yuè	hǎo

'the higher the better'

1. Wǒ-yuè-yánjiu-'Zhōngguo-   The more I study the Chinese
   yǔyán yuè-juéde-yǒu-xìng-   language the more interested I
   qu.   become.

2. Wǒ-yuè-chī-'Zhōngguo-cài   The more Chinese food I eat the
   yuè-juéde-hǎo-chī.   more delicious I consider it to
                                      be.

3. Xué-pīnyīn-zì yuè-xué-yuè-   When you study transcription,
   róngyi.   the more you study the easier it
                                      gets.

4. Měiguo-qìchē yuè-lái-yuè-   American cars are becoming
   duō.   more and more numerous.

5. Zuótian-wǒ-jiè-de-nèiběn-   That book I borrowed yesterday,
   shū, yuè-kàn-yuè-xiǎng-kàn.   the more I read the more I want
                                      to read.

6. Wǒ-'yuè-bu-xǐhuan-ta ta-yuè-   The more I dislike him the more
   gēn-wǒ-shuō-huà.   he talks to me.

7. Nǐ-Zhōngwén yuè-lái-   You're speaking Chinese better
   yuè-shuōde-hǎo.   and better.

8. 'Gāo-Xiáojie-shuō ta-huà-   Miss Gao says that the more
   de-huàr yuè-huà-yuè-bù-hǎo.   paintings she does the worse
                                      they get.

9. 'Gāo-Xiānsheng yuè-gāoxìng   The happier Mr. Gao gets the
   yuè-xǐhuan-shuō-huà.   more he likes to talk.

10. Kāishǐ-xué-sì shēng-de-shí-   When you first study the four
     hou, yuè-xué-yuè-zhǔn.   tones, the more you study the
                                          more correct they become.

Pattern 22.2. Reduplicated Stative Verbs (Note 2 below)

        SV₁   SV₁   (-r)   (-de)

        hǎo   hāo   -r   -de

        = hǎohāorde 'well'

1. Wó-déi-hǎohāorde niàn-shū-   I must study hard, otherwise I
    le, bùrán-kǎobushàng.   can't pass the exam.

2. Nǐmen-jǐge-rén dōu-xǐhuan-   (Since) you all like to eat lion's
    chī-shīzi-tóu, xià-cì wǒ-   head, next time I'll make a few
    duōduōrde-zuò-diar.   more.

3. Wǒmen-děi-kuàikuārde-zǒu.   We must hurry. Otherwise the
    Bùrán diànyǐngr-yào-kāi-   movie will have started.
    yǎn-le.

4. Wó-yuǎnyuārde jiù-kànjian-   From far off I saw him coming
    ta wàng-zhèr-lái-le.   here.

5. Rúguó-yǒu-yíge-wèntí děi-   If there is a problem you must
    mànmārde-yánjiu.   take your time in studying it.

6. Nǐ-xiáng-bǎ-'Zhōngwén   If you want to speak Chinese
    shuō-de-hén-hǎo, děi-duō-   very well, you must do a lot of
    duōrde-liànxi-fāyīn.   practicing of pronunciation.

7. Liànxi-xiě-'Zhōngguo-zì   In learning how to write Chinese
    déi-hǎohāorde-zhùyì xiě-de-   characters, you must pay care-
    fāngfǎ.   ful attention to the way of writing
                                         (them).

8. Wǒ-chībǎo-le.   Qǐng-nín-   I'm full. Please take your time
    mànmārde-chī-ba.   eating.

9. Qíng-nǐmen-bié-shuō-huà.   Please don't talk. Listen care-
    Hǎohāorde-tīng-lùyīn.   fully to the recording.

10. Qíng-nǐ-kuàikuār-gàosu-wo,   Please tell me quickly how to
     zhèige-zì shi-shénmo-yīn.   pronounce this character.

Pattern 22.3. Reduplication of Measures (Note 3 below)

        M   M
        Measure   Measure (-r)
        běn   běn/běr
        = běnběr 'every volume'

1. 'Wáng-Xiānsheng yǒu-sìge-
   háizi. Gèger dōu-nènmo-
   yònggōng-niàn-shū.

   Mr. King has four children.
   Each one studies so diligently.

2. 'Zhāng-Tàitai zuì-xǐhuan-
   lǚxíng. Tā-niánniár dōu-
   dào-biéde-dìfang-qu-yícì.

   Mrs. Johnson likes most to travel. Once every year she goes
   somewhere [else].

3. 'Máo-Xiānsheng zuótian-
   sònggei-wo-wúběn-shū. Bén-
   běr-dōu-hǎo-kàn.

   Mr. Mao sent me five books yesterday. Every volume was beautiful.

4. Xué-yǔyán děi-zhùyì-gège-
   cérde-fāyīn.

   When you study a language, you
   must pay attention to the pronunciation of every word.

5. Wǒ-tiāntiār bāngzhu-wó-mǔ-
   qin-zuò-fàn.

   Every day I help my mother
   cook.

6. Wǒ-yuèyuer dōu-qu-Niǔyue-
   wár-yícì.

   I go to New York to have fun
   once every month.

7. Nèige-háizi hén-hǎo. 'Rénrén dōu-xǐhuan-ta.

   That child is very nice. Everyone likes him.

8. 'Wáng-Xiānsheng-xué-'Zhōngwén fāyīn, jùzi, wénfǎ
   yàngyàngr-dōu-hǎo.

   In studying Chinese, Mr. King is
   good in every aspect of pronunciation, sentences, and grammar.

9. 'Wáng-Xiáojie-huà-de-huàr
   zhāngzhāngr-dōu-hén-hǎo.

   Every one of the paintings that
   Miss Wang has painted is excellent.

10. Nèige-dàxuéde-jiàoshòu gè-
    ger-dōu-hén-yǒu-míng.

    Every one of the professors in
    that university is famous.

SUBSTITUTION TABLES

I: 12 phrases (Note 1)

yuè	róngyi	yuè	—	hǎo
	nán		bu	
	duō			
	kuài			
	màn			
	lái			

II : 36 sentences   (Note 1)

(In the columns marked by asterisks, only items from
the same row may be used together : chī with chī, hē
with hē, etc.)

		*			*
wǒ	yuè	chī	yuè	xǐhuan	chī
nǐ		hē		xiǎng	hē
tā		kàn		yào	kàn
		mǎi			mǎi

PRONUNCIATION DRILLS

Review of Four-Sýllable Expressions (IV)

(Asterisks mark forms which have undergone changes of third to second tone.)

0 0 3	1 0 3	2 0 3
1 tāmende-jiǔ	tā-shuōde-hǎo	tā-huódeliǎo
2 máfande-hěn	Wáng-Xiānsheng-yǒu	ná-biéde-bǐ
3 mǎile-de-zhǐ	jiǎndānde-hǎo	nǔ-háizi-xiǎo
4 kèrende-bǐ	wàng-xībiar-zǒu	yìzhíde-zǒu

3 0 3	4 0 3
1 dōu-mǎibuliǎo	tā-zuòde-hǎo
2 nín-dǒng-bu-dǒng	nán-kàn-de-hěn
3 hén-hǎode-shuǐ *	wǒ-kànbudǒng
4 gèng-hǎode-jiǔ	tài-dàde-bǐ

0 1 3	1 1 3	2 1 3
1 bēizi-dōu-xiǎo	xīngqīyī-zǒu	jiānglái-dōu-mǎi
2 shénmo-fāngfǎ	shízhī-gāngbǐ	chá-shífēn-hǎo
3 nǐmen-xiān-qǐng	mǎi-sānzhī-bǐ	qǐng-shéi-hē-jiǔ
4 gùshi-shū-shǎo	yào-sānzhāng-zhǐ	zài-túshūguǎn

3 1 3	4 1 3
1 tā-mǎi-qiānbǐ	tā-huì-hē-jiǔ
2 lí-wǒ-jiā-yuǎn	yígòng-sānběn
3 wúdiǎnzhōng-zǒu *	bǐ-ròu-dōu-hǎo
4 jiù-yǒu-sānběn	kuài-dào-sāndiǎn

0 2 3

1 bēizi-nán-mǎi
2 juéde-hái-hǎo
3 yǒude-méi-dǒng
4 tàitai-méi-mǎi

1 2 3

tīngshuō-hái-yǒu
hóng-shāo-yú-hǎo
kǎo-yā-méi-yǒu
qìchē-nán-mǎi

2 2 3

tā-huí-Húběi
quán-guó-méi-yǒu
yǎnyuán-méi-zǒu
jiàngyóu-hái-yǒu

3 2 3

1 tā-yǒu-chá-wǎn
2 érqiě-nán-xiě
3 wó-yǒu-máobǐ *
4 zhèiběn-hái-hǎo

4 2 3

chē-zài-mén-kǒur
táng-cù-yú-hǎo
kǒngpà-méi-yǒu
hòu-dào-Húběi

0 3 3

1 tīanqi-hén-hǎo *
2 názhe-bí-xiě *
3 běnzi-yé-yǒu *
4 zuòde-hén-hǎo *

1 3 3

tā-chī-liángwǎn *
ná-gāngbí-xiě *
wǒ-jiā-hén-yuǎn *
cài-dār-hén-xiǎo *

2 3 3

xiārér-yé-yǒu *
cóngqián-yé-yǒu
yǒu-qián-mái-bǐ *
jiàngyóu-hén-hǎo *

3 3 3

1 tā-yé-hén-lǎo *
2 érqié-hén-shǎo *
3 wó-yé-yóu-bǐ *
4 fàn-yé-hén-hǎo *

4 3 3

zhōngjiàr-yé-yǒu *
niú-ròu-yé-hǎo *
nǐ-wàng-béi-guǎi *
zhèiyàng-hén-hǎo *

0 4 3

1 Zhōngguo-lìshǐ
2 yánjiu-lìshǐ
3 yǎnde-tài-hǎo
4 wàngle-dài-biǎo

1 4 3

tā-chī-fànguǎr
lí-jiā-tài-yuán
wǒ-chī-fànguǎr
yào-sān-sìběn

2 4 3

tiāntáng-zài-nǎr
wénxué-tài-hǎo
yě-lí-zhèr-yuǎn
jiàngyóu-zài-nǎr

3 4 3

1 sāndiǎn-nèichǎng
2 shéi-yǒu-zìdiǎn
3 ní-děng-yìhuěr *
4 guòjiǎng-guòjiǎng

4 4 3

tā-dào-fànguǎr
Wáng-Jiàoshòu-hǎo
wǒ-niàn-lìshǐ
qù-kàn-diànyǐngr

COMBINING FORMS

This exercise contains a number of expressions which are not included in the Vocabulary but are made up from the combining forms discussed in Note 5 below.

1. Wàiguo-rén-xué-Hànyǔ 'zuì-dàde-nánchu shi-xué-fāyīn.

   When foreigners study the Chinese language, the biggest difficulty is learning pronunciation.

2. Wǒ-zuì-dàde-duǎnchu shi-xué-yǔyán bù-tīng-lùyīn.

   My biggest shortcoming is that when I study a language I don't listen to recordings.

3. Zhōngwénde-'xiéfǎ gēn-Yīng-wénde-'xiéfǎ bù-yíyàng. Zhōng-wén shi-cóng-shàngtou-wàng-xià-xiě, Yīngwén shi-cóng-zuǒbiar-wàng-yòu-xiě.

   The way of writing Chinese and the way of writing English are not the same. Chinese is written from top to bottom, English is written from left to right.

4. Xué-wénxué bìděi-xiān-xué-wénfǎ. Tóngyàngde xué-yǔyán bìděi-xiān-xué-yúfǎ.

   When you study literature, you must first learn the grammar. Similarly, when you study a language, you must first learn its grammar.

5. Qǐng-wèn, zhèige-cérde-'niàn-fǎ shi-shénmo?

   I'd like to ask how this word is read.

6. Zhōngwén-gēn-Yīngwén shuō-fǎ-bù-yíyàng.

   The way of speaking Chinese and English is not the same.

7. Lùyīnjīde-hǎochu shi-yíjù-huà kéyi-'suíbiàn-tīng-jǐcì.

   The advantage of a recorder is that you can hear a sentence as many times as you please.

8. Xué-wénxué gēn-xué-shùxué-de-'xuéfǎ bù-yíyàng.

   The way to study literature and mathematics is not the same.

9. Huà-shānshuǐ-de-fázi gēn-huà-rén-de-fázi huàfǎ-bu-yíyàng.

   With respect to [the technique of] painting landscapes and [the technique of painting] portraits, the methods of painting are not the same.

10. 'Wáng-Xiānsheng màigei-wo-hěn-duō-shū. Dōu-hén-yǒu-yòngchu.

    Mr. King sold me a lot of books. They are all very useful.

11. Xièxie-ni. Qǐng-ní-bǎ-nèiběn-shū nágei-wo.

    [Thank you.] Please hand me that book.

12. Xué-Zhōngguo-yǔyán bá-měige-

    When you study the Chinese lan-

cérde-sìshēng-jìzhu. Bié-
shuōcuò.

guage, fix in mind the tones of
every word. Don't say them
wrong.

13. Nǐ-shuō-tā-yóu-hěn-duō-
chángchu. Tā-yìdiár-duǎn-
chu-dōu-méi-yǒu-ma?

You say he has a lot of good
points. Doesn't he have any
shortcomings at all?

14. Nèijiàn-shìqing wǒde-kànfǎ
gēn-nǐde-kànfǎ bù-yíyàng.

In that matter, your way of looking at it and my way of looking
at it differ.

15. Nǐde-wènfǎ-bú-duì.

Your way of asking the question
is not right.

16. Táng-cù-yú gēn-hóng-shāo-
yú-de-zuòfǎ bù-yíyàng.

The way of making sweet-and-
sour fish and red-cooked fish is
not the same.

17. Ní-bǎ-nèige-wǎn názhù-le.

Take a firm hold on that bowl.

18. Ní-bǎ-nèijiàn-shìqing xiě-
zai-běnzishang. Yàoburán-
jìbuzhù.

Write that business in your
notebook. Otherwise you won't
be able to remember it.

19. Wǒ-gàosu-nǐ-de-shìqing 'jì-
dezhù-jìbuzhù?

Can you bear in mind that
business I told you about?

20. Shuō-huà yídìng-děi-zhùyì-
qīngzhòng-yīn. Yàoburán
jiù-xiàng-niàn-shū-le.

When you speak, you must be
sure to pay attention to stress.
Otherwise it will be like reading
a book (aloud).

21. Yíge-rén tóngshí-zuò-liǎng-
jiàn-shìqing yídìng-zuòde-
bu-hǎo.

If a person does two things at
the same time he will certainly
do them badly.

22. 'Gāo-Xiáojie gēn-'Qián-Xiáojie tāmen-shi-tóngxué.

Miss Gao and Miss Qian are
fellow students.

23. Xué-wénxué gēn-xué-yǔyán-
xué tóngyàngde-nán.

Studying literature and linguistics is equally difficult.

24. 'Gāo-Xiānsheng 'Máo-Xiānsheng dōu-zài Sān-Yǒu-Shū-
diàn-zuò-shì. Tāmen-shi-
tóngshì.

Mr. Gao and Mr. Mao both work
in the Three Friends Bookstore.
They are fellow workers.

25. 'Wàn-Jiàoshòu gēn-'Gāo-
Xiānsheng tāmen-liǎngwèi-
tóngsuì.

Professor Wanamaker and Mr.
Gao are both the same age.

MONOLOGUE

Wǒ-shi-yíge-Měiguo-xuésheng.   Wǒ-zài-zhōngxué-de-shíhou jiu-kāishǐ-
xué-Zhōngguo-yǔyán-le.   Wó-hén-xiǎode-shíhou jiu-tīngshuō-Zhōngguo, suó-
yi-jiu-xiǎng zhǎng-dà-le dào-'Zhōngguo-qu-niàn-shū. Zài-gāozhōng niàn-shū-
de-shíhou wó-yǐjing-shíjǐsuìle, yé-dǒngle-hěn-duō-de-shìqing. Wǒ-jiu-xiǎng
rén-gēn-rén-zuò-péngyou bìděi-yòng-yǔyán cái-néng-míngbai-liǎngge-rénde-
yìsi.   Wǒ-rúguǒ-dào-Zhōngguo-qu wǒ-jiu-děi-rènshi-'Zhōngguo-péngyou, nèn-
mo-wǒ-bìděi-xué-Zhōngguo-huà, suóyi-zài-zhōngxué jiu-kāishǐ-xué.   Suírán-méi-xuéhǎo kěshi-yòngle-bù-shǎode-gōngfu.

Zài-kāishǐ-xué-de-shíhou hěn-bu-róngyi, kěshi-wǒ-duì-ta hén-yǒu-xìngqu. Wǒ-kāishǐ-xiān-xué-sìshēng, fāyīn, pīnyīn.   Wàiguo-rén kāishǐ-xué-
Zhōngguo-yǔyán duì-fāyīn shi-hěn-bu-róngyide-yíjiàn-shì.   Yīnwei-Zhōng-
guo-huà gēn-Yīngguo-huà-de-fāyīn yìdiár-yě-bù-yíyàng, suóyi-hěn-bù-róng-
yi. Yǐhòu-mànmārde-liànxi bíjiǎo-róngyi-duō-le.

Wǒ-kāishǐ-xué-Zhōngguo-huà shi-yòng-pīnyīnde-fāngfǎ-xué-de.   Zhèige-
fázi-hǎojíle. Xuéhuì-le-pīnyīn yí-kàn-jiù-huì-niàn-le.   Yǒude-rén-shuō
Zhōngguo-yǔyán bìděi-yòng-Hànzì-xué, rúguǒ-yòng-pīnyīn xué-le-bàntiān
háishi-bú-rènshi-Zhōngguo-zì; xué-Zhōngguo-yǔyán-gēn-wénxué bìděi-yòng-
Hànzì-xué-cái-duì. Wǒ-juéde-shuō-de bù-hěn-duì. Wó-xiǎng xiān-xuéhuì-
le-pīnyīn, fāyīn, sìshēng yě-míngbai-tāde-yìsi-le   yě-huì-shuō-yǐhòu,
zài-kāishǐ-xué-Hànzì bíjiǎo-róngyide-duō. Yàoburán Hànzì-shi-měige-yīn-
jié dōu-yǒu-shēng-de.

Rúguǒ yíge-kāishǐ-xué-Zhōngguo-huà-de-wàiguo-rén jiù-yòng-Hànzì-xué
nènmo-sìshēng-qīngzhòngyīn dōu-bù-zhīdào. Měige-yīnjié-fāyīn méi-yǒu-
qīngzhòngyīn, dōu-yíyàng. Nà-nǎr-shi-shuō-huà-ne? Shi-niàn-zì-ne. Bǐ-
fang-shuō-<u>cér</u> wǒmen-shuō-huà-shi-'yíge-yīnjié. Pīnchulai yě-shi-yíge-yīn-
jié. Hànzì shi-liǎngge-zì liǎngge-yīnjié, jiù-shi-<u>cí</u>, ér. Zhè-bú-shi-shuō-
huà-ne. Zhè-shi-niàn-zì.

ANSWERING QUESTIONS

1. Bái-Wénshān-dǎ-mén. Gāo-Xiáojie-kāi-mén. Shéi-dào-Gāo-jiā-lái-le?

2. Gāo-Xiānsheng Gāo-Tàitai dōu-xǐhuan-zài-Rìběn-'duō-zhù-jǐtiān. Měi-
    yīng-láo-xiǎng-huílai. Shéi-bu-xǐhuan zài-Rìběn-duō-zhù-ne?

3. 'Bái-Xiānsheng-shuō xué-yǔyán zuì-hǎode-fázi shi-yòng-pīnyīnde-fázi.

'Gāo-Xiānsheng-shuō pīnyīnde-fāngfǎ-bù-hǎo. Shéi-xǐhuan-pīnyīnde-fāng-fǎ-ne?

4. 'Gāo-Xiānsheng-shuō Bái-Xiānsheng-sìshēng-hén-zhǔn. 'Bái-Xiānsheng-de-Zhōngwén shuōde-'hǎo-bu-hǎo?

5. 'Zhāng-Xiānsheng-shuō xué-Zhōngwén xiān-xué-Hànzì zuì-róngyi. 'Wáng-Xiānsheng-shuō xiān-xué-pīnyīn zuì-róngyi. 'Wáng-Xiānsheng-shuō pīnyīn-zuì-róngyi háishi-'Zhāng-Xiānsheng-shuō pīnyīn-zuì-róng-yi?

6. 'Máo-Xiānsheng-shuō yīnggāi-xiān-liànxi-xiě-jùzi. 'Bái-Xiānsheng-shuō xiān-xué-yúfǎ. 'Bái-Xiānsheng-shuō yīnggāi-xiān-zuò-shénmo?

7. Qǐng-ni-shuō nǐ-xiànzài-niànde-zhèige-jùzi shi-yòng-pīnyīn-xiě-de hái-shi-yòng-Hànzì-xiě-de?

8. Gāoxìng-zhèige-cér shi-jǐge-yīnjié?

9. Hànzì-de-Hàn shi-dì-jǐshēng?

10. Zìjǐ-zhèige-cér něige-yīnjié-shi-dì-sìshēng?

NOTES

1. The adverb yuè 'more' is used twice, before successive verb expressions, to mean 'the more . . . the more . . .':

   Diǎnxin-yuè-tián-yuè-hǎo. 'As for desserts, the sweeter the better.'
   Tā-yuè-shuō wǒ-yuè-bù-dǒng. 'The more he talks the less I understand.'

   Similarly, yuè-lái-yuè means '(become) more and more':

   Tā-yuè-lái-yuè-yònggōng. 'He's becoming more and more diligent.'
   Tā-yuè-lái-yuè chīde-duō. 'He's eating more and more.'

2. Stative verbs expressing manner (Lesson 10, Note 2) sometimes occur in reduplicated form (that is, doubled) before the verb. The second occurrence is always in the first tone (e.g. mànmān); the whole expression often has the Pekingese r suffix, which may modify the syllable to which it is attached (e.g. mànmār); and the suffix de is generally attached at the end (e.g. mànmārde). Here are some examples:

   hǎo : hǎohāorde 'well,' 'diligently,' 'carefully'
   kuài : kuàikuārde 'quickly'
   duō : duōduōrde 'in a large quantity'
   màn : mànmārde 'slowly'

3. Measures are often reduplicated, with or without the suffix r at the end, to mean 'every [occurrence of the measure]':

   tiāntiān 'every day'

> bénběr 'every volume'
> Wǒ-tiāntiān-chī-Zhōngguo-fàn. 'I eat Chinese food every day.'
> Zhèixiē-shū bénběr-dōu-hěn-nán-niàn. 'Every one of these books is
>   hard to read.'

The noun rén reduplicated means 'everyone, everybody':

> Rénrén-dōu-xǐhuan-ta. 'Everybody likes him.'

Dōu 'all' is often used with these expressions, reinforcing the all-in-
clusive meaning.

4. Nearly all Chinese characters (zì) represent single syllables of Chinese
    speech. Because so many Chinese words are monosyllabic, zì is also
    often used in the meaning 'word' as well as 'syllable,' so that it overlaps
    in meaning with cí and cér, both of which mean 'word [monosyllabic or
    polysyllabic].'

5. The syllabic units of Chinese have varying degrees of freedom. Wǒ 'I' is
    a FREE FORM — for example, it can occur alone (as in answer to the
    question 'Who's there?'). The syllable men in wǒmen, on the other hand,
    is a COMBINING FORM — it never occurs by itself but is always suffixed
    to something, and is always neutral in tone. Both free forms and com-
    bining forms are used with a great deal of freedom to form compound
    words and phrases. In this lesson we see the following examples:

(a) The combining form fǎ 'method' occurs as an initial syllable, with
     second tone, in fázi 'method'; it also occurs as a suffixed element, in
     third tone, in combinations:

fāngfǎ	'method'	wénfǎ	'grammar (of
huàfǎ	'way of painting'		writing)'
kànfǎ	'way of looking (at	wènfǎ	'way of asking'
	something)'	xiéfǎ	'way of writing'
niànfǎ	'way of reading	xuéfǎ	'way of studying'
	or studying'	yúfǎ	'grammar (of
shuōfǎ	'way of speaking		speech)'
	or saying'	zuòfǎ	'way of doing'

(On the term fāngfǎ see also Supplementary Lesson 22, Note 1)

(b) The combining form chu, a neutral-toned syllable, is suffixed to a few
     verbs, chiefly stative, to form related noun expressions:

> hǎo 'good'   : hǎochu 'benefit'
> duǎn 'short'   : duǎnchu 'shortcoming'
> nán 'difficult'   : nánchu 'difficulty'
> cháng 'long'   : chángchu 'advantage'
> yòng 'use [verb]'   : yòngchu 'use [noun]'

(On the term nánchu see also Supplementary Lesson 22, Note 2)

(c) Gěi 'give' in its neutral form gei is suffixed to some verbs in the
     meaning 'to':

> nágei   'bring to'
> sònggei 'send to'
> màigei   'sell to'

(d) The neutral syllable <u>zhu</u>, which is derived from the free form <u>zhù</u> 'live (in a place),' is suffixed to verbs in the meaning 'firmly':

názhu   'hold firmly'
jìzhu   'bear firmly in mind'

Expressions with <u>zhu</u> are resultative compounds:

nábuzhù   'unable to hold firmly'
jìdezhù   'able to bear firmly in mind'

(Note that in these last forms the tone reappears on <u>zhù</u>.)

(e) The syllable <u>tóng</u> 'same' is joined as a prefix to various elements to form special phrases:

with <u>shí</u> (short for <u>shíhou</u>) 'time' :

   tóngshí 'at the same time'

with <u>shì</u> 'job' :

   tóngshì 'co-worker'

with <u>suì</u> 'year of age' :

   tóngsuì 'be of the same age'

with <u>yàng</u> 'kind' :

   tóngyàng 'be similar,' '(be) equal (to)'

(f) The syllable <u>yǔ</u> 'speech,' which we have encountered in <u>yǔyán</u> 'speech,' occurs also in the combination <u>yúfǎ</u> 'grammar (of speech)' and in the names of specific spoken languages:

Hànyǔ   'Chinese'
Yīngyǔ   'English'

6. The suffix <u>zi</u>, which has the function of signaling a noun, is attached to a number of syllables, most of them combining forms. The following are the nouns we have had so far with this ending :

fázi	'method'	kuàizi	'chopsticks'
háizi	'child'	shīzi	'lion'
fángzi	'house'	piānzi	'movie'
běnzi	'notebook'	jiǎozi	'dumpling'
míngzi	'name'	yāzi	'duck'
bēizi	'cup'	jùzi	'sentence'

7. The Pekingese suffix <u>r</u> is attached to various kinds of words:

infrequently to verbs :

   wán, wár 'have fun'

more often to measures :

   běn, běr 'volume'

and most often to nouns :

   mén, mér 'door'
   cí, cér 'word'
   dān, dār 'list'

The process of suffixing an r often alters or modifies the spelling of a syllable. (See pp. xxvii—xxviii.)

8. Reduplication of xiě 'write' and zhǎo 'seek' results in the forms xiéxie 'write (a bit)' and zháozhao 'look (for a while),' in which the original third tone shifts to second under the influence of the second syllable—the latter also having been third tone originally but here occurring in the neutral tone. Another example of this sort of shift is fǎ becoming fá in fázi 'method.'

9. The term zhòng-yīn—literally 'heavy sound'—means '[a specific instance of] stress or emphasis'; qīngzhòngyīn, literally 'light and heavy sound,' means 'stress [in general, and of any degree].'

10. The term sìshēng, literally 'four tones,' refers either specifically to the four full tones of Chinese, or to the tones of the language in general.

11. The adverb zhèng 'just (now)' modifies verbs whose action is in progress at the time of speaking. Zhèng is often combined with zài 'at' and followed at the end of the sentence by the particle ne:

Wǒ-zhèng-chī-fàn-ne. 'I'm eating right now.'
Tā-zhèng-zài-kàn-shū-ne. 'He's [just in the act of] reading.'

12. Bǐfang 'example' combined with shuō 'say' results in the phrase bǐfang-shuō 'for example.'

13. From the Han dynasty (B.C. 206—220 A.D.), one of the periods of greatest Chinese grandeur, comes Hàn, a slightly more literary name for China and the Chinese than Zhōngguo. The phrase Zhōngguo-rén has a broader application than Hànrén: Zhōngguo-rén refers to a citizen of China of whatever national origin, while Hànrén refers specifically to a Chinese person (as against a Mongol or any other member of a minority nationality).

14. The expressions wénfǎ and yúfǎ, both meaning 'grammar,' are sometimes used in the senses 'grammar of the written language' and 'grammar of the spoken language' respectively. Many people use them synonymously, however, and that is the practice we have adopted in this textbook. In actual practice yúfǎ is used more often than wénfǎ.

Lesson 23 LEAVING CHINA

"Yílù-píng'ān!"

Dialogue: Mr. and Mrs. Gao and Miss Gao see Mr. White off at the airport.

'Bái-Xiānsheng yào-huí-guó-le.
Tā-shi-zuò-fēijī-huíqu. Zǎochen Gāo-Xiānsheng, Gāo-Tàitai,
Měiyīng sānge-rén dōu-dào-Bái-
Xiānsheng-zhù-de-dìfang qu-jiē-   5
ta, bāngzhu-ta yíkuàr-dào-fēijī-
chǎng-qu.

Mr. White is about to return to
the United States. He is going
back by plane. In the morning
Mr. Gao, Mrs. Gao, and Meiying
all go to the place where Mr.
White lives to meet him, help
him, and go to the airport together.

Bái: Zǎo! 'Tài-láojià-le. Zhēn-
bùgǎndāng.

Good morning! I've put you to
too much trouble. I really don't
deserve this.

Gāo-Xiānsheng: Nǎrde-huà-ne.   10
Wǒmen-yīnggāi-lái-de-me.
Dōngxi dōu-shōushihǎo-le-
ma?

Nonsense. Of course we should
come. Are your things all
packed?

Bái: 'Méi-shénmo-dōngxi-le. Wǒde-shū qián-jǐtiān yǒu-ge-   15
péngyou-zuò-chuán-huíqu
'dōu-ràng-ta-dàizǒu-le.

I don't have anything much left
any more. A few days ago I had
a friend who is returning by boat
take all my books.

401

Gāo-Tàitai: Zǒu-ba. Wǒmen-xiān-
　　dào-fēijīchǎng-cāntīng zài-
　　nèr-mànmārde-tán-ba.　　　　20

Let's go. Supposing we go to the
airport cafeteria first and have
a leisurely talk there.

Gāo-Xiáojie: Dào-Rìběn-yào-'jǐ-
　　ge-zhōngtóu?

How many hours does it take to
Japan?

Bái: Dàgài-sān-sìge-zhōngtóu.
　　Chàbuduō-xiàwǔ liángdiǎn-
　　zhōng kéyi-dào-le. Měiyīng,　25
　　yíkuàr-dào-Měiguo-qu 'hǎo-
　　bu-hǎo?

About three or four hours. We
will [lit. can] get there about two
P.M. Meiying, how about our
going to America together?

Gāo-Xiáojie: Zènmo-máng nǐ-hái-
　　shuō-xiàohuar.

Even being in a hurry doesn't
keep you from joking.

Gāo-Xiānsheng: Wǒmen 'zǎo-yì-　30
　　diǎr-dào-fēijīchǎng-yé-hǎo.
　　(Tāmen-zài-mén-kǒur-shàng-
　　qìchē.) Nǐmen-sānge-rén
　　zài-'hòubiar-zuò. Wǒ-zuò-
　　qiánbiar.　　　　　　　　　35

It's not a bad idea for us to get
to the airport a little early.
(They get in the car at the door.)
You three sit in back. I'll sit in
front.

Bái: Háishi-ràng-wǒ zài-qiánbiar-
　　zuò-ba.

Let me sit in front.

Gāo-Xiānsheng: Yíyàng, yíyàng.

It's all the same.

Gāo-Tàitai: Wénshān, zhè-jǐtiān-
　　shōushi-dōngxi yídìng-　　　40
　　mángde-bùdéliǎo. Hěn-lèi-
　　ba.

Vincent, you must have been
terribly busy these days packing
your things. I suppose you're
very tired.

Bái: Méi-shénmo. Wǒde-dōngxi-
　　shǎo, suóyi-'hěn-róngyi-
　　shōushi.　　　　　　　　　45

Not particularly. I don't have
many things, so it was quite easy
to pack.

Gāo-Xiānsheng: Xīwang-nǐ-míng-
　　nián-bì yè-yǐhòu 'zài-dào-
　　Zhōngguo-lái.

I hope after you graduate next
year you will come to China
again.

Bái: Wó-hěn-xīwang 'zài-huílai.

I hope very much to come back
again.

Gāo-Xiānsheng: Nǐ-huídào-Měi-　50
　　guo háishi-jìxu-xué-Zhōng-
　　guo-yǔyán gēn-wénxué-ma?

When you return to America will
you go on studying Chinese language and literature?

Bái: Shì. Búdàn-'jìxu-xué, wǒ-
　　hái-děi hǎohāorde-xué-ne.

Yes. I'll keep on with it, and I'll
have to study hard too.

Gāo-Xiānsheng: Xué-yìzhǒng-xué-　55
　　wen rúguǒ-xīwang-xuédehǎo,
　　zuì-yàojǐn-de shi-yào-yóng-
　　yuǎn-xuéxia-qu.

When you study anything [lit. any
branch of learning], if you hope
to [be able to] master it, the
most important thing is to keep
on studying all the time.

Bái: Nín-shuōde-hěn-duì. Nínde-
　　huà dōu-shi-yǒu-'jīngyan-de-　60
　　huà.

What you say is quite right.
Your words are the words of experience.

Gāo-Xiānsheng: Dào-'Rìběn dǎ-
suan-zhù-jǐtiān-ne?

Bái: Dàgài-bú-dào-yíge-xīngqī.
Zài-Dōngjīng-Dàxué wó-   65
yǒu-yíwèi-lǎoshī wǒ-
děi-qu-kànkan-ta. Nèi-wèi-
lǎoshī shi-yíwèi-hén-yǒu-
míng-de-yǔyánxuéjiā. Guān-
yú-yǔyánxué-zhèi-fāngmiàn   70
wǒ-gēn-ta-dédào-bù-shǎo-
de-xuéwen.

That's right. You should go see

How many days do you plan to
stay in Japan?

Perhaps less than a week. At
Tokyo University I have a teacher I must see. He's a famous
linguist. I've acquired quite a
lot of knowledge from him about
linguistics.

Gāo-Xiānsheng: Duì-le. Yīng-
gāi-qu-kànkan-ta.

That's right. You should go see
him.

Bái: Wǒ-zhèicì-dào-Zhōngguo-   75
lái-niàn-shū, péngyoumen-
duì-wǒ-dōu-hén-hǎo. Yóu-
qíshi-nǐmen-liǎngwèi. Zhè-
shi-wó-yóngyuǎn bù-néng-
wàng-de.   80

On this (occasion of my) coming
to China to study, (my) friends
have been very good to me. Especially you two. This is something I can never forget.

Gāo-Xiānsheng: Bié-kèqi.

Don't mention it.

Bái: Měiyīng-sòng-wǒ-de-nèi-
zhāng Hángzhōu-shānshuǐ-
huàr, wǒ-dào-jiā-yǐhòu
bǎ-ta-guàqilai, qíng-wǒde-   85
péngyoumen-kànkan.

That Hangchow landscape that
Meiying presented to me—after
I get back home I'm going to
hang it up and invite my friends
to take a look at it.

Gāo-Xiáojie: Déle, déle. Bié-
guà. Huàde-bù-hǎo.

[Enough, enough.] Don't hang it
up. It's no good.

Bái: 'Hén-hǎo.

It's very good.

Gāo-Xiānsheng: Cóng-'Rìběn   90
jǐge-zhōngtóu-jiù-dào-
Měiguo-le. Bǐ-zuò-chuán
kuàide-duō.

From Japan you'll be getting to
America in just a few hours.
It's a lot faster than traveling by
boat.

Gāo-Tàitai: Wénshān, Gāo-Xiānsheng hén-xǐhuan-lǚxíng.   95
Shuōbudìng wǒmen-huòzhe-
dào-Měiguo-qu-zháo-ni.

Vincent, Mr. Gao loves to travel. Perhaps we might be going
to America to see you.

Bái: Nà-huānyíng-jíle. Wǒ-fùqin-mǔqin-tāmen 'hěn-xī-
wang rènshi-nǐmen-liǎngwèi. 100
Wó-gěi-fùqin-mǔqin-tāmen-
xiě-xìn, cháng-tídao-nǐmen-
jǐwèi. Rúguǒ-jiàndao-nǐmen-
jǐwèi tāmen-'yídìng-huān-
yíngde-bùdéliǎo.   105

Then you'd be most welcome.
My father and mother hope very
much to get to know both of you.
In (writing) letters to them, I
have often spoken of you. If they
did manage to see you they would
welcome you most cordially.

Gāo-Tàitai: Wénshān, jiānglái-
nǐ-dìdi-mèimei yě-dào-
'Zhōngguo-lái-niàn-shū-
ma?

Vincent, will your younger
brother and sister also come to
China later to study?

Bái: Bù-zhīdào jiānglái-tāmen-   110
       xué-shénmo. Rúguǒ-tāmen-
       xué 'Dōngfāng-wénhuà
       tāmen-kěnéng-dào-Zhōng-
       guo-lái.

I don't know what they'll study
[later]. If they study Oriental
civilization there's a possibility
that they will come to China.

Gāo-Xiānsheng: Dào-le. Shíhou-   115
       zǎode-hěn. Wǒmen-xiān-
       dào-cāntīng.

Here we are. It's quite early.
Let's go first to the cafeteria.

Bái: Hǎo-ba.

Very good.

Gāo-Xiānsheng: Wénshān, nǐ-chī-
       shénmo?   120

Vincent, what would you like to
eat?

Bái: Wǒ-shénmo-yě-bù-chī. Wǒ-
       yǐjing-chīguo-zǎofàn. Nǐmen-
       liǎngwèi-gēn-Měiyīng 'chī-
       diar-shénmo.

I'm not having anything. I've
already had breakfast. You two
and Meiying have something.

Gāo-Xiānsheng: Wǒmen-chīguo-   125
       zǎofàn cái-dào-nǐ-nèr-qù-
       de. Nènmo-wǒmen 'dōu-hē-
       chá-ba.

We didn't go to your place until
after we'd had breakfast. Then
let's all have tea.

(Gāo-Xiānsheng、 Gāo-Tàitai kàn-
jian-tāmende-lǎo-péngyou Wáng-   130
Xiānsheng Wáng-Tàitai xià-fēijī,
zǒuguoqu-gēn-tāmen-tán-huà.)

(Mr. and Mrs. Gao, seeing some
old friends of theirs, Mr. and
Mrs. Wang, getting off a plane,
walk over and chat with them.)

Bái: Měiyīng, nèi-liǎngwèi-shi-
       shéi?

Meiying, who are those two?

Gāo-Xiáojie: Shi-Wáng-Xiānsheng   135
       Wáng-Tàitai. Tāmen-gēn-
       fùqin-mǔqin shi-lǎo-péng-
       you. Tāmen-qùnián-chūqu-
       lǚxíng. Xiànzài-bu-zhīdào
       cóng-'nǎr-huí lai-le.   140

They're Mr. and Mrs. Wang.
They're old friends of father and
mother. They went on a trip last
year. I don't know where they're
coming back from now.

Bái: Měiyīng, zài-zhèi-yìnián-
       lǐtou wǒmen-liǎngge-rén
       shi-zuì-hǎode-péngyou-le.
       Chàbuduō wǒmen-měi-xīng-
       qī dōu-yào-jiàndao liǎng-   145
       sāncì. Xiànzài-wǒmen-yào-
       hěn-'chángde-shíhou bú-jiàn-
       le. Xīwang-nǐ-cháng-géi-
       wo-xiě-xìn.

Meiying, (in) this year the two of
us have become very good
friends. We've seen each other
almost two or three times a
week. Now we won't be seeing
each other any more for a long
time. I hope you will write me
often.

Gāo-Xiáojie: Dāngrán-géi-ni-xiě-   150
       xìn-le.

Of course I'll write you.

Bái: Ní-'jǐtian géi-wo-xiě-yì-
       fēng-xìn?

How often will you write me?

Gāo-Xiáojie: Ní-géi-wo-xiě-xìn,
       wó-mǎshàng-jiù-géi-ni-huí-   155
       xìn.

Whenever you write me, I'll
send you a return letter immediately.

Bái: Hǎo-ba.

You said a moment ago it was possible that you would come back again. I hope you really will come back.

Gāo-Xiáojie: Nǐ-gāngcái-shuō kěnéng-zài-huílai. Xī-wang-nǐ-'zhēnde-huílai.   160

Bái: Zhēnde. Wǒ-xīwang-bù-jiǔ jiu-huílai.

I really will. I hope I can come back before long.

(Gāo-Xiānsheng Gāo-Tàitai huí-lai-le.)

(Mr. and Mrs. Gao return.)

Gāo-Xiānsheng: Wénshān, shí-hou-chàbuduō-le. Gāi-shàng-fēijī-le.   165

Vincent, it's just about time. You should get on the plane.

Gāo-Xiáojie: Nǐ-zài-dào-Zhōng-guo-lái shi-zuò-fēijī-shi-zuò-chuán?   170

When you come to China again, will you travel by plane or by boat?

Gāo-Xiānsheng: Zhèi-háizi! Tā-hái-méi-zǒu-ne, nǐ-jiu-wèn-ta zuò-shénmo-huílai. Tā-xiànzài-'zěnmo-zhīdao-ne? Wénshān, xīwang-ni-zǎo-yìdiǎr-huílai.   175

This child! He hasn't left yet, and you ask him how he's returning. How could he know now? Vincent, I hope you will be coming back soon.

Bái: Hǎo.

Yes.

Gāo-Xiānsheng: Zhù-ni-yílù-píng'ān.

I wish you a pleasant trip.

Bái: Xièxie. Zàijiàn.   180

Thank you. Good-bye.

Gāo-Tàitai: Yílù-píng'ān. Huí-jiā-wèn-hǎo.

Have a nice trip. When you get back home give my best.

Bái: Xièxie-nín.

Thank you.

Gāo-Xiáojie: Xiě-xìn. Zàijiàn. Yílù-píng'ān!   185

Write me. Good-bye! Bon voyage!

Bái: Zàijiàn, zàijiàn.

Good-bye!

Wó-mǎshàng-jiu-lái!

VOCABULARY

bùgǎndāng	(I'm) not equal to the honor, I don't deserve it (Note 12)
cāntīng	cafeteria (N) [lit. meal room]
dài	carry; take along (a thing or person) (TV)
dé	get, attain (TV) (Note 10)
Dōngfāng	Orient, the East (PW) [lit. east region] (See Supplementary Lesson 23, Note 1)
'fāngmiàn	side (figurative), aspect (M) [lit. side face]
fēijīchǎng	airport, airfield (N)
fēng	(measure for letters, i.e. mail)
guà	hang (TV)
-jīng	capital (N) (Note 5)
jìxu	continue (doing something) (AV)
kěnéng	possible (SV) [lit. may able]
láojià	I've caused you trouble. Sorry to trouble you. (Note 13)
lǎoshī	teacher, tutor (N) [lit. old teacher] (Note 4)
lèi	tired; tiring (SV)
mǎshàng	immediately (AD) [lit. on horseback] (Mǎ is also a surname)
míngnian	next year (TW)
píng'ān	peaceful, at peace, safe (SV) [lit. even peace] (Note 11)
qiántian	day before yesterday (TW) [lit. front day]
ràng	let, request (TV); by (CV) (Note 7)
shōushi	straighten up, put in order, pack (TV) [lit. collect gather]
wénhuà	culture, civilization (N) [lit. literature change]
wǔ	noon (TW) (Note 8)
xiào	laugh (at) (V)
xiàohua(r)	joke (N) [lit. laugh speech]
xíngli	baggage (N)
yàojǐn	important (SV) [lit. important urgent]
yóngyuǎn	forever, always (AD) [lit. eternal far]
zǎo	early (SV) (Note 9); long since (AD) (Note 9)
zhù	wish (someone something) (TV)

SENTENCE BUILD-UP

yì	the whole
yì-gōngyuánde-rén	the people in the whole park

1. Yì-gōngyuánde-rén dōu-zǒu-le. — Everyone in the park has left.

yì-tiān	the whole day
yì-tiān-dào-wǎn	the whole day until late

2. Tā-yì-tiān-dào-wǎn zuò-shì. — He works all day long until late.

fēijī	airplane
fēijīchǎng	airfield

3. Fēijīchǎng 'zěnmo-méi-yǒu-fēijī? — How come there are no planes at the airfield?

cāntīng	cafeteria
yì-cāntīngde-rén	people in the whole cafeteria

4. Yì-cāngtīngde-rén dōu-shi-'wàiguo-rén. — Everyone in [the whole] cafeteria is a foreigner.

shōushi	put in order

5. Zhèi-jǐtiān túshūguǎn yào-shōushi-shū. — For these few days the library will be putting books in order.

xíngli	baggage
shōushi-xíngli	put baggage in order, pack

6. Wǒ-jīntian-yì-tiān shōushi-xíngli. — I've been packing the whole day.

yóngyuǎn	forever
yóngyuǎn-bú-huì-shuō	never able to speak

7. Wó-xiǎng wó-yóngyuǎn-bú-huì-shuō-Zhōngwén. — I think I shall never be able to speak Chinese.

kēxué	science
kēxuéjiā	scientist

8. Wó-xīwang-zuò-kēxuéjiā. — I hope to become a scientist.

lǎoshī	teacher
shi-kēxuéjiā	is a scientist
shi-huàjiā	is a painter

9. Tāde-lǎoshī yòu-shi-kēxuéjiā yòu-shi-huàjiā. — His teacher is both a scientist and an artist.

háizi	child
háizimen	children

10. Háizimen 'dōu-xǐhuan-wár. — All children like to play.

xiào	laugh

11. Nǐ-xiào-shénmo? — What are you laughing at?

xiào	laugh

xiàohua	joke
shuō-xiàohua	tell jokes
12. Wǒde-lǎoshī hěn-huì-shuō-xiàohua.	My teacher is very good at telling jokes.
wénhuà	culture
xīfāng-wénhuà	Western civilization
13. 'Xīfāng-wénhuà méi-yǒu-'Dōngfāng-wénhuà nènmo-lǎo.	Western civilization isn't as old as Oriental civilization.
kěnéng	be possible
14. Zhèijiàn-shì hén-kěnéng.	This matter is quite possible.
kěnéng	possibility
zuò-huàjiā-de-kěnéng	possibility of being an artist
15. Wǒ-méi-yǒu zuò-huàjiā-de-kěnéng.	There's no possibility of my becoming an artist.
jìxu	continue (to do something)
16. Qíng-nǐ-jìxu-niàn.	Please continue reading (aloud).
lèi	tired
17. Nǐ-yídìng-hěn-lèi-le-ba.	You must be very tired.
ràng	let
18. Ràng-tā-zuò.	Let him do it.
ràng	by
ràng-wǒ	by me
19. Shū-ràng-wó-mǎilai-le.	The books were bought by me.
ràng-tā	by him
ràng-tā-máizǒu	bought by him
ràng-tā-géi-máizǒu-le	bought by him
20. Shū-dōu-ràng-tā géi-máizǒu-le.	The books were all bought by him.
guà	hang
guàqilai	hang up
21. Zhèizhāng-huàr shi-'shéi-guàqilai-de?	By whom was the painting hung up?
fēng	(measure for letters)
zhèifēng-xìn	this letter
22. Zhèifēng-xìn shi-'shéi-xiě-de?	By whom was this letter written?
dài	carry, bring, take
dài-bǐ	bring a pen
23. Zāogāo! Wǒ-wàngle-dài-bǐ-le.	Darn! I forgot to bring a pen.
zǎo	early

hén-záo-qǐlai
24. Wǒ-tiāntian hén-záo-qǐlai.

get up early
I get up early every day.

zǎo
zǎo-huí-jiā-le
25. Tāmen-dōu-zǎo-huí-jiā-le.

long ago
long since returned home
They have all long since returned home.

míngnian
míngnian-kāishǐ-niàn
26. Wǒ-míngnian kāishǐ-niàn-
dàxué.

next year
begin studying next year
I'll begin studying at the university next year.

nán
Nánjīng
27. Nǐ-qùguo-Nánjīng-ma?

south
Nanking (southern capital)
Have you ever been to Nanking?

běi
Běijīng
28. Nánjīng-méi-you-Běijīng-dà.

north
Peking (northern capital)
Nanking isn't as big as Peking.

Běijīng
Běijīng-huà
29. Tāde-Běijīng-huà shuōde-
hǎojíle.

Peking
Peking dialect
He speaks excellent Pekingese.

dōng
Dōngjīng
30. Xiànzài-Dōngjīng bí-Niǔyue-
rén-duō.

east
Tokyo (eastern capital)
There are now more people in
Tokyo than New York.

-wǔ
zhōngwǔ
31. Wǒ-míngtian-zhōngwú-zǒu.

noon
noon
I'm leaving at noon tomorrow.

shàngwǔ
32. Chuán shàngwǔ-shídiǎn-zhōng-
kāi.

forenoon, A.M.
The boat leaves at ten A.M.

xiàwǔ
33. Qǐng-nín xiàwǔ-sāndiǎn-bàn-
lái.

afternoon, P.M.
Please come at three-thirty P.M.

wǔfàn
34. Wǒmen-wǔfàn bù-chī-ròu.

lunch
We don't have meat at lunch.

yàojǐn
zuì-yàojǐnde
35. Zuì-yàojǐnde shi-fāyīn.

important
the most important thing
The most important thing is pronunciation.

bú-yàojǐn
36. Tā-'qù-bu-qù dōu-bú-yàojǐn.

not important
It doesn't matter whether he
goes or not.

zhù	wish, hope
37. Zhù-ní-kǎo-dì-yī.	I hope you get first on the exams.
píng'ān	peaceful, safe and sound
píng'ān-huí-jiā	return home safe and sound
38. Xīwang-nǐ-píng'ān-huí-jiā.	I hope you return home safe and sound.
fāngmiàn	side, aspect
39. Zhèige-wèntí yóu-'liǎngfāng-miàn.	There are two sides to this question.
jǐfāngmiàn	several aspects
40. Zhōngguo-wénhuà 'yóu-jǐfāng-miàn.	There are several aspects to Chinese civilization.
yìfāngmiàn	one aspect
duì-yǔyán-yìfāngmiàn	regarding the one aspect of language
41. Wǒ-duì-'yǔyán-yìfāngmiàn hén-yǒu-xìngqu.	I am very much interested in the linguistic aspect.
dé	get, obtain
42. Èr-sì-dé-bā.	Two fours are eight.
déle	finished, ready
43. Fàn-déle-ma?	Is the food ready?
déle	finished
xiědéle	finished writing
44. Ní-xiědéle-ma?	Have you finished writing?
dédào	obtain, receive, get
dédào-tāde-xìn	receive a letter from him
45. Wǒ-zuótian dédào-le-tāde-xìn.	I received a letter from him yesterday.
láojià	I trouble you
46. Láojià ní-géi-wo mǎi-yìzhī-bǐ-lai.	May I trouble you to buy a pen for me?
bùgǎndāng	I don't deserve it
47. Xièxie-ni, wǒ-bùgǎndāng.	Thank you, I don't deserve it.
qián	front
qiántian	day before yesterday
48. Tā-shi-'qiántian-zǒu-de.	He left day before yesterday.
'qián-jǐtiān	a few days ago
49. Tā-shi-'qián-jǐtiān-zǒu-de.	He left a few days ago.
mǎshàng	immediately

50. Wó-mǎshàng-jiù-lái.   I'm coming right away.

      Dōngfāng   Orient
      Dōngfāng-lìshǐ   Oriental history
51. Wǒ-xué-Dōngfāng-lìshǐ.   I'm studying Oriental history.

PATTERN DRILLS

Pattern 23.1. Use of yī 'one' as 'the whole' (Note 1 below)

yī	N/M	
'whole'	Noun/Measure	
yì	xuéxiào	'the whole school'
yì	tiān	'the whole day'

1. Yì-chéng-rén dōu-pǎo-le.   Everyone in the city has fled.

2. Yì-fēijīchǎngde-rén dōu-shi-   Everyone in the airport is meet-
    jiē-péngyou-de.   ing friends.

3. Yì-cāntīngde-rén dōu-hē-chá   Everyone in the cafeteria is hav-
    chī-diǎnxin.   ing tea and dessert.

4. Yì-túshūguǎnde-rén 'dōu-shi-   Has everyone in the library
    lái-kàn-shū-de-ma?   come to read?

5. Yì-fángzi-rén dōu-shi-bāng-   Everyone in the house is helping
    zhu-ta shōushi-xíngli-de.   him pack.

6. Wǒ-yì-tiān méi-chū-mér.   I haven't been out of the house
                                             [lit. door] the whole day.

7. Yì-jiā-rén yóngyuǎn-nènmo-   The whole family is always so
    hǎo.   nice.

8. Tā-yì-bēizi-shuǐ 'dōu-hē-le.   He drank the whole cup of water.

9. Yì-xuéxiàode-xuésheng dōu-   All the students in the school
    zǒu-le.   have left.

10. Yì-lùshangde-rén dōu-shi-   Everyone on the avenue has gone
    dào-'gōngyuán-qù-de.   to the park.

11. Wǒ-yì-nián yě-méi-zuò-shì-   I haven't worked all year.
    le.

12. Nèige-xuésheng yì-'xīngqī-   That student hasn't studied all
    dōu-méi-niàn-shū-le.   week.

13. Wǒ-yì-tiān shénmo-shì-yě-   I do nothing but read the whole
    bù-zuò 'jiù-kàn-shū.   day long.

14. Yì-chuánde-rén yì-tiān-dōu-   Everyone on the ship has gone
    méi-chī-fàn-le.   all day without eating.

15. Yì-běnzide-zì dōu-shi-'Bái-   All the characters in the note-
    Xiānsheng-xiě-de.   book were written by Mr. White.

Pattern 23.2.   Use of Suffixes <u>jiā</u> and <u>men</u>   (Notes 2–3 below)

Pattern 23.2 a.

N	-jiā	
Noun	-jiā	
lì shǐ 'history'	-jiā	'historian'

Pattern 23.2 b.

N	-men	
Noun	-men	
háizi 'child'	-men	'children'

1. Tāde-lǎoshī shi-yíwèi 'zuì-   His teacher is a very famous
   yǒu-míngde-yǔyánxuéjiā.   linguist.

2. Tā-shi-yíge yánjiu-Dōngfāng-   He is a historian who does re-
   wénhuàde-lì shǐjiā.   search in Oriental civilization.

3. 'Wáng-Xiānsheng suírán-shi-   Although Mr. Wang is a famous
   yíge-hén-yǒu-míng-de-huàjiā-   artist, he continues to study.
   le, kěshi-tā-hái jìxu-xué.

4. Nèiwèi-wénxuéjiā zuì-xǐhuan-   That literary man delights in
   shuō-xiàohua.   telling jokes.

5. Nèiwèi-kēxuéjiā zhēn-cōng-   That scientist is really brilliant.
   ming. Yánjiuchu-hěn-duō-   He has discovered [lit. searched
   dōngxi.   out] a lot of things.

6. Nèige-háizi shùxué-hén-hǎo.   That youngster is very good in
   Yóngyuǎn-shi-tā-kǎo-dì-yī.   math. He always scores first in
   Jiānglái kěnéng-shi-yíge-shù-   exams. It's possible that in the
   xuéjiā.   future he will be a mathemati-
                                     cian.

7. Jīntian-wǒmen xià-kè-hén-   Today we left class very early.
   zǎo. Xiānshengmen-yǒu-shì.   The teachers had something to
                                     do.

8. Gēn-péngyoumen-zài-yíkuàr   It is a great pleasure to be with
   shi-'zuì-gāoxìngde-yíjiàn-   friends.
   shì.

9. Háizimen-zuì-xǐhuan tīng-   Children delight in hearing peo-
   rén-shuō-xiàohua.   ple tell jokes.

10. Xuéshengmen-'dōu-xǐhuan   All the students like to go to the
    dào-'Gāo-Xiānsheng-kāi-de-   bookstore run by Mr. Gao to buy
    nèige-shūdiàn qu-mǎi-shū.   books.

Pattern 23.3.   Passive with <u>ràng</u> and <u>jiào</u>   (Note 7 below)

S	<u>ràng</u>/<u>jiào</u>	O	(<u>gěi</u>)	V	(<u>le</u>)
Subject	<u>ràng</u>/<u>jiào</u>	Object	(<u>gěi</u>)	Verb	(<u>le</u>)
Fàn	ràng	tā		chī	le.

' The food was eaten by him.'

1. Nǐ-sòng-wǒde-nèizhāng-huàr ràng-tā-gěi-guàqilai-le.

That painting that you presented to me was hung up by him.

2. Xiǎo-háizi jiào-dà-háizi géi-dǎ-le.

The little child was beaten by a big child.

3. Nèixiē-diǎnxin ràng-wǒ-dìdi gěi-chī-le.

Those cakes were eaten by my little brother.

4. Nèifēng-xìn hěn-yàojǐn. Ràng-ta-gěi-wàngle-sòng-le.

That letter is very important. (And) he forgot to send it.

5. Zhèiběn-shū shūdiànli zhí-yǒu-zhèi-yìběn-le. Jiào-tā-géi-mǎilai-le.

The bookstore had only one copy of this book (left). It was bought by him.

6. Nèixiē-shū jiào-'Wáng-Xiān-sheng gěi-dàiqu-le.

Those books were carried away by Mr. King.

7. Nǐde-bǐ jiào-'tā-náqu-le.

Your pen was taken away by him.

8. Nèiběn-shū yǐjing-ràng-yí-ge-xuésheng jièqu-le.

That book has already been taken out by a student.

9. Nèisuǒr-fángzi záo-yǐjīng-jiào-bié-rén mǎiqu-le.

That house has long since been purchased by someone else.

10. Nǐde-zìdiǎn ràng-wǒ-dìdi géi-názǒu-le.

Your dictionary was taken away by my [younger] brother.

SUBSTITUTION TABLE

I: 64 sentences   (Note 7)

huàr	ràng	shéi	—	mǎiqu	le
shū	jiào	tā	gěi	jièqu	
				názǒu	
				dàiqu	

PRONUNCIATION DRILLS

Review of Four-Syllable Expressions (V)

(Asterisks indicate changes of third tone to second tone.)

	0 0 4	1 0 4	2 0 4
1	tāmende-piào	tā-cāibuduì	gēn-xuésheng-qù
2	róngyide-shì	shéi-shuōde-huà	nán-háizi-dà
3	nǐmende-huàr	nǐ-chīde-màn	nǐ-xuéde-kuài
4	kèqide-huà	tài-duōde-cài	tèbiéde-cài

	3 0 4	4 0 4
1	tā-xiěde-xìn	shuō-kèqi-huà
2	nín-zěnmoyàng	nín-suànde-zhàng
3	ní-zěnmoyàng*	wǒ-kànbujiàn
4	yào-wǔge-cài	yào-sìge-cài

	0 1 4	1 1 4	2 1 4
1	tāmen-chī-fàn	tā-chī-zhū-ròu	chī-hóng-shāo-ròu
2	fángzi-zhōngjiàn	lí-Zhōngshān-Lù	nín-méi-cāiduì
3	wǒde-dōu-duì	nǐ-gāi-shuō-huà	nǐ-lái-chī-fàn
4	shèngxia-sānkuài	xià-xīngqīliù	zuò-tián-suān-ròu

	3 1 4	4 1 4
1	dōu-hěn-gāoxìng	tā-zài-zhōngjiàr
2	érqiě-dōu-huì	yíkuàr-chī-fàn
3	wó-yǒu-sānkuài*	yě-yòng-zhū-ròu
4	liùdiǎn-zhōng-jiàn	kuài-dào-shūdiàn

0 2 4

1 xiānsheng-bié-wèn
2 lánde-shéi-yào
3 xǐhuan-niú-ròu
4 kuàizi-nán-yòng

1 2 4

tā-dōu-néng-zuò
cháng-chī-báicài
wǒ-shuō-nán-zuò
dào-Sānfánshì

2 2 4

dāngrán-néng-zuò
cóngqián-cháng-qù
dǒng-Húnán-huà
shùxué-méi-niàn

3 2 4

1 chī-chǎo-báicài
2 méi-yǒu-shíkuài
3 yé-hěn-qíguài *
4 zài-nǎr-tán-huà

4 2 4

gēn-huàr-yíyàng
yígòng-shíwàn
wǒ-yào-báicài
xiànzài-lái-kàn

0 3 4

1 duōshao-xiǎofèi
2 yíngle-wǔcì
3 zǒude-hěn-màn
4 zhèige-yǐwài

1 3 4

fēijī-hěn-kuài
lí-jiā-hěn-jìn
yǒu-sānlǐ-lù
huà-shānshuǐ-huàr

2 3 4

jiānglái-yě-zuò
bié-tí-kǎoshì
zǒu-shílǐ-lù
dàxué-yǐwài

3 3 4

1 tā-yé-xiě-zì *
2 nín-láo-xiě-xìn *
3 wó-yóu-wǔkuài *
4 bìdéi-kǎoshì *

4 3 4

chī-fàn-yǐhòu
lí-zhèr-hěn-jìn
fǔshàng-jǐhào
dào-diànyǐngryuàn

0 4 4

1 xiānsheng-guìxìng
2 róngyi-huà-huàr
3 wǒmen-fàngjià
4 nánchu-zài-zhèr

1 4 4

pīnyīn-huìhuà
nín-jiā-fùjìn
yě-dōu-bìyè
zài-shuō-sìcì

2 4 4

guānyú-zhèijiàn
nín-suíbiàn-zuò
qǐng-shéi-zuò-shì
pà-Wáng-Jiàoshòu

3 4 4

1 tā-yě-fàngjià
2 nín-yě-bìyè
3 yé-děi-zhùyì *
4 fànguǎr-fùjìn

4 4 4

jiē-Wàn-Jiàoshòu
tí-zhèijiàn-shì
hěn-huì-zuò-cài
dàgài-zài-zhèr

MISCELLANEOUS SENTENCES

1. Zuótian-mǎi-de-diànyǐngr-
   piào wǒ-jìcuò-shíhou-le.
   Piào shi-'wúdiǎn-nèichǎng-
   de-piào. Wǒ-qīdiǎn-zhōng
   cái-qù.

   I made a mistake about [lit. remembered incorrectly] the tickets I bought yesterday. The
   tickets were for the five o'clock
   show. I didn't go until seven
   o'clock.

2. Cóng-xiànzài-kāishǐ, wó-děi-
   jìxu-xiě Hànzì-le.

   Beginning [from] now, I must
   keep on writing Chinese characters.

3. Guānyú-xué-**Zhōngwén-yì**-
   fāngmiàn, 'zuì-yàojǐnde shi-
   fāyīn.

   With respect to studying Chinese, what is most important is
   pronunciation.

4. Wǒmen mǎshàng-zǒu-bā.
   Liángdián-chǎng-diànyǐngr
   kuài-kāi-yǎn-le.

   Let's leave right away. The two
   o'clock show will start soon.

5. Wǒ-zuì-jìn duì-Rìběn-wén-
   huà-yìfāngmiàn hén-yǒu-
   xìngqu.

   Quite recently I've become very
   interested in Japanese culture.

6. Qián-jǐtian wǒ-dédào-le
   'Wáng-Jiàoshòu géi-wǒ-de-
   yìfēng-xìn.

   A few days ago I received a letter from Professor King.

7. Wó-yǐjing-gēn-wǒ-fùqin shuō-
   hǎo-le, míngnian-dào-Yīng-
   guo-qu-niàn-shū.

   I've already reached an agreement with my father to go to
   England next year to study.

8. Zuótian-'Zhāng-Xiānsheng
   zài-diànhuà-lǐtou gēn-wǒ-
   shuōle-'hěn-duōde-shìqing.

   Yesterday Mr. Johnson discussed a lot of things with me on
   the telephone.

9. Zuótian-yí-xià-kè 'Wàn-
   Jiàoshòu mǎshàng-jiu-pǎo-
   dào-fēijīchǎng qu-jiē-péng-
   you.

   As soon as he left class yesterday Professor Wanamaker immediately hurried to the airport
   to meet a friend.

10. Nèige-xuésheng hěn-huì-
    shuō-xiàohua. Tā-shuō-de-
    xiàohua 'zhēn-kě-xiào.

    That student is awfully good at
    telling jokes. His jokes are
    really funny.

11. Nèige-lǎoshī bìngle-hén-jiǔ.
    Hǎobuliǎo-le. Tā-wán-le.

    That teacher was sick for a long
    time. He couldn't get well. He
    died [lit. he's finished].

12. Zài-hén-záo-yǐqián Zhōng-
    guo-jiu-kāishǐ yǒu-le-wén-
    huà.

    Very early in the past China
    began to become civilized.

13. Rúguó-nǐ-zuì-hǎode-péng-
    you yǒngyuǎn-kànbujiàn-le,
    ní-zěnmoyàng-ne?

    If you could never see your best
    friend again, how would you
    feel?

14. Wǒ-zuótian dài-wǒ-dìdi dào-
fēijīchǎng-qu-kàn-fēijī.

Yesterday I took my younger brother to the airport to see the planes.

15. Wǒ-zhèi-jǐge-yuè shì-'tài-
duō-le. Mángde-bùdéliǎo.
Suóyi-wǒ-lèijíle.

These (past) few months I've had too much to do. I've been terribly busy. So I'm awfully tired.

16. Zhèrde-shānshuǐ 'duómo-
piàoliang! Wó-déi-bǎ-tā-
huàxialai.

How beautiful the scenery here is! I must paint it [down].

17. Guòqude-yíge-xīngqī-lǐtou
wǒ-dōu-bāngzhu-péngyou
shōushi-dōngxi.

I've spent the whole of the past week helping a friend put things in order.

18. Guò-yì-liǎngtiān wó-děi-láo-
jià-ni bāngzhu-wǒ-shōushi-
xíngli.

After a day or two I must trouble you to help me pack my baggage.

19. Tiān-bu-zǎo-le. Wǒmen-déi-
zǒu.

The day's getting on. We must go.

20. Zuótian-nèige-háizi gēn-tā-
fùqin yào-wǔkuài-qián-mǎi-
shū.

Yesterday that youngster asked his father for five dollars to buy a book.

21. Wǒde-yìsi-shi xiān-xué-xiě-
zì, hòu-xué-niàn-shū. 'Nǐ-
de-yìsi-zěnmoyàng?

My idea is first to study writing and then to study reading. What do you think?

22. Wǒmen-zài-cāntīng-hē-chá-
de-shíhou tánde-hén-yǒu-
yìsi.

We had a very interesting conversation while having tea in the cafeteria.

23. Tā-jiàole-bàntiānde-mén yě-
méi-rén-kāi. Tā-háishi-jì-
xude-jiào.

He knocked [lit. called] at the door for a long time but no one came. He continued to knock.

24. Zhèrde-shānshuǐ rúguǒ-huà-
chulai hěn-piàoliang.

If you paint [lit. paint out] the landscape here it will be very beautiful.

25. Yīnwei-wǒmen-shi-lǎo-péng-
you, bú-yòng-tài-kèqi. 'Suí-
biàn-chī-yìdiǎr.

Since we're old friends, there's no need to be too formal. Let's have a little snack.

26. Wǒ-tài-máng. Zhí-háo-qǐng-
péngyou bāngzhu-wǒ-shōushi-
xíngli.

I'm too busy. The only thing I can do [lit. only good] is to ask a friend to help me pack.

27. Wǒde-lǎoshī xiěle-yìběn shuō-
Zhōngguo-wénhuà-de-shū.

My teacher has written a book on Chinese culture.

28. Wǒ-ràng-cāntīngde-huǒji géi-
wǒ-ná-càidār-lai.

I asked the waiter in the cafeteria to bring me a menu.

29. Wǒ-dào-'Rìběn-qu, kěnéng-
bú-dào-'liǎngge-xīngqī jiù-
huílai.

I'm going to Japan, and it's possible I'll return in less than two weeks.

30. Wǒ-míngnian dào-'Zhōngguo-   I shall begin the study of Chi-
     lǚxíng huílai-yǐhòu jiù-kāi-   nese next year after I get back
     shǐ-xué-Zhōngwén.   from my trip to China.

MONOLOGUE

Miss Gao, shortly after leaving the airport, meets a friend and tells her
about Mr. White.

Wǒ-gēn-fùqin-mǔqin gāng-cóng-fēijīchǎng-huílai. Shi-sòng-yíge-péngyou-
huí-guó. Zhèige-péngyou míngzi-jiào-Bái-Wénshān. Shi-Měiguo-rén. Tā-
de-Zhōngwén hén-hǎo. Tā-shuō-de-Zhōngguo-huà gēn-Zhōngguo-rén-yíyàng.
Nǐ-gēn-ta-zài-yíkuàr yídiár-yě-bù-juéde tā-shi-yíge-'wàiguo-rén. Wǒmen-
kāishǐ-rènshi shi-zài-wǒmen-nèige-shūdiàn-lǐtou. Yǒu-yìtiān, wǒ-gēn-fùqin-mǔqin wǒmen-dào-shūdiàn-qu-le. Zhèng-yùjian-Bái-Wénshān 'yě-qu-
mǎi-shū. Fùqin-jiù-gēn-ta-shuō-huà, érqié-yě-jièshao-mǔqin-gēn-wǒ rèn-
shi-ta.

Yǒu-yícì fùqin-qǐng-ta dào-wǒmen-'jiā-lǐtou-lái-chī-fàn. Zhèng-hǎo wǒ-
zài-gōnggòng-qìchēshang yùjian-ta. Wǒmen-liǎngge-rén yíkuàr-huídào-jiā-
lǐtou-lái. Cóng-zhèige-shíhou, wǒmen-mànmārde jiù-shi-hén-hǎode-péng-
you-le.

Cóng-nèige-shíhou-kāishǐ, guānyu-'shùxué-yìfāngmiàn rúguó-wó-yǒu-wèntí huòzhě-bù-míngbai-de-dìfang, tā-'dōu-néng-gàosu-wo.

Tā-láidào-Zhōngguo-yìnián-le. Zài-zhèi-yìnián-lǐtou, qián-jǐge-yuè wǒ-
men-'bù-zěnmo-cháng-jiàn. Kěshi-yǐhòu měige-xīngqī wǒmen-dōu-jiàn-
liǎng-sāncì. Yǒude-shíhou wǒmen-yíkuàr dào-túshūguǎn-qù-kàn-shū, huò-
zhě-yíkuàr qu-kànkan-diànyǐngr.

Tā-shi-yíge-hěn-yònggōng, érqiě yé-hěn-cōngming-de-rén. Fùqin-hén-xǐ-
huan-ta. Tā-'yí-dào-wǒmen-jiā-lǐtou-lái, fùqin-hěn-gāoxìng. Fùqin-hén-xǐ-
huan-gēn-tā-tán guānyu-'Zhōngguo-yǔyán gēn-wénxué-de-wèntí. Tóngshí-
mǔqin duì-tā-yé-hén-hǎo. Tā-xǐhuan-chī-hóng-shāo-cài. Měicì-dào-wǒ-
men-jiā, mǔqin-chàbuduō 'dōu-shi-zuò-hóng-shāo-cài gěi-ta-chī.

Xiànzài-tā-huí-guó-le. Yíge-'zuì-hǎode-péngyou-zǒu-le, ní-xiǎng shi-
zěnmoyàng-ne? Tā-suírán-zǒu-de-shíhou-shuō tā-huíqu-bìyè-yǐhòu hái-
huílai, kěshi-tā-shì-bu-shi 'zhēnde-néng-huílai-ne?

ANSWERING QUESTIONS

1. Lǎoshī dōu-shi-lǎo-rén-ma? Yíge-èrshi-duō-suìde-xiānsheng 'kéyi-bu-kéyi suàn-shi-lǎoshī?

2. Dài-biǎo-de-dài gēn-dài-dōngxi-de-dài yòng-Hànzì-xiě shi-bu-yíyàng-de. Rúguǒ-yòng-pīnyīn-xiě yíyàng-ma?

3. Zhōngguo yǒu-sānqiān-duō-niánde-wénhuà. Měiguo-ne?

4. Yíge-péngyou shi-sānhào-líkai-Dōngjīng liùhào-dàode-Niǔyue. Nǐ-shuō-shi-zuò-fēijī-lái-de háishi-zuò-chuán-lái-de-ne?

5. Rúguó-wǒ-shuō míngtiān shi-míngniánde-dì-yītiān, nènmo-jīntiān shi-jǐyuè-jǐhào?

6. Chuán shi-shàngwǔ-qīdiǎn-zhōng-kāi-de, xiàwǔ-sìdiǎn-zhōng-dào-de. Yígòng-zǒule-'jǐge-zhōngtóu?

7. Měiguo-zuì-dàde-chéng shi-Niǔyue. 'Rìběn-ne?

8. Rúguó-nǐ-yào-dài-hěn-duō-xíngli, shi-zuò-fēijī-hǎo háishi-zuò-chuán-hǎo?

9. Wǒde-xíngli ràng-yíge-péngyou gěi-shōushihǎo-le. Wǒ-yīngdāng-duì-ta-shuō "Nǐ-tài-kèqi" háishi-"Tài-láojià"-ne?

10. Zhèiběn-shū nǐ-kuài-yào-niànwán-le. Niànwán-le-yǐhòu, nǐ-hái-jìxu-niàn-Zhōngwén-ma?

NOTES

1. Yī 'one' is used before a noun or measure in the meaning 'the whole of.' In this meaning, the yī expression comes before the verb and is often accompanied by the adverb dōu 'all':

   Yì-jiā-rén dōu-hěn-cōngming. 'The whole family is very intelligent.'
   Tā-yì-tiān jiùshi-niàn-shū. 'He does nothing but study the whole day long.'

2. The pluralizing suffix -men, which we have encountered attached to pronouns (as in wǒmen 'we'), is also attached to nouns relating to people:

   háizimen 'children'
   péngyoumen 'friends'

   The resulting form has a general collective meaning. Hence the suffix is never attached to a noun that is specifically quantified; note wǔshige háizi 'fifty children.'

3. The suffix -jiā, derived from jiā 'house,' is attached to nouns, and more rarely to verbs, to form a noun relating to a profession:

lìshǐ 'history'	:	lìshǐjiā 'historian'
shùxué 'mathematics'	:	shùxuéjiā 'mathematician'
huà 'paint'	:	huàjiā 'painter'

4. The term <u>lǎoshī</u>, literally 'old teacher,' is applied to teachers of any age, but is a more honorific term than <u>xiānsheng</u> 'teacher.'

5. The syllable <u>jīng</u> 'capital' is a combining form which enters into the names of many capital cities:

> Nánjīng 'Nanking' [lit. 'Southern Capital']
> Běijīng 'Peking' [lit. 'Northern Capital']
> Dōngjīng 'Tokyo' [lit. 'Eastern Capital']

The city known to English speakers as Peking or Peiping has been called <u>Běijīng</u> 'Peking' [Northern Capital] at various times when governments have designated it the capital: during the Ch'ing Dynasty (1644–1911); during the years 1912–1928 of the Republic of China; and since the establishment of the Chinese People's Republic in 1949. In 1928, Chiang Kai-shek's government established Nanking as the capital, renaming the former capital <u>Běipíng</u> 'Peiping' [Northern Peace]. In spite of political fluctuations, many fixed phrases—for example, <u>Běijīng Dàxué</u> 'Peking University'—have retained the original name continuously.

6. The verb <u>ràng</u> 'permit,' 'let,' like <u>qǐng</u> 'invite' and <u>jiào</u> 'tell,' can have a sentence as a direct object:

> Wó-qǐng-ta-lái. 'I invited him to come.'
> Wǒ-jiào-ta-lái. 'I told him to come.'
> Wǒ-ràng-ta-lái. 'I let him come.'
> Wǒ-ràng-ta-xiě-zì. 'I let him write characters.'

7. An active sentence of the pattern S-V-O (Subject-Verb-Object) can be transformed into a passive sentence of the pattern O-<u>ràng</u>-S-V, with <u>ràng</u> 'by' as the coverb of agent:

> Wó-dǎ-ta-le. 'I hit him.'
> Tā-ràng-wó-dǎ-le. 'He was hit by me.'

<u>Ràng</u> may here be replaced by <u>jiào</u>, and the main verb may be preceded by <u>gěi</u> 'give' (cf. English 'He was given a beating by me'). Hence, 'He was beaten by me' can be expressed in the following ways:

> Tā-ràng-wó-dǎ-le.
> Tā-ràng-wó-géi-dǎ-le.
> Tā-jiào-wó-dǎ-le.
> Tā-jiào-wó-géi-dǎ-le.

The passive is used most often to refer to completed (past) activity. In general, it is far less common in Chinese than in English.

8. The syllable <u>wǔ</u> 'noon,' a combining form, joins with <u>shàng</u> 'up,' <u>xià</u> 'down,' <u>zhōng</u> 'middle,' and <u>fàn</u> 'food' to make the following expressions:

> shàngwǔ 'forenoon, morning, A.M.'
> xiàwǔ 'afternoon, P.M.'
> zhōngwǔ 'noon'
> wǔfàn 'lunch'

9. The word <u>zǎo</u> is used as a stative verb meaning 'early,' as an adverb meaning 'long ago,' 'long since,' and as a conventional greeting meaning 'Good morning.'

10. The verb dé 'get' is used in reciting the multiplication table when the product is an expression of one syllable, as in sān-sān-dé-jiǔ 'three times three is nine.' With the perfective suffix le it becomes déle and means 'finished, ready,' as:

> Fàn-déle. 'The food is ready.'

Déle is frequently used by itself:

> Déle-ma? 'Ready?'
> Déle. 'Finished.'

It also occurs by itself as a sort of exclamation, usually in answer to excessive praise ('Stop!' 'That's enough!'), as in the Dialogue (line 87); this usage is very informal, restricted to conversations between close friends.

11. Yílù-píng'ān, literally '(may things) be peaceful the whole way,' is a conventional expression equivalent to Bon Voyage!

12. Bùgǎndāng, literally 'not dare undertake,' is a conventional response to praise. It means something like 'You do me too much honor' or 'I don't deserve (your praise, attention, etc.).'

13. Láojià is a conventional expression used when one has caused trouble to someone, or expects to do so. In the former case, it is about equivalent to English 'Sorry to have troubled you' or 'Much obliged.' In the latter, it has the force of 'Sorry to trouble you,' 'Excuse me,' 'May I trouble you?'

14. The conventional phrase nǎrde-huà 'where (is there any such) talk?' often corresponds to the phrase 'Not at all' as a response to expressions of thanks:

> A. Nǐ-tài-kèqi. 'You're too polite.' 'You're too kind.'
> B. Nǎrde-huà. 'Not at all.'

15. Shuōbudìng has the form of a resultative verb phrase and means 'unable to say for sure'; but no corresponding form exists with de replacing bu. Besides its literal meaning, 'one can't say for sure,' it often means simply 'perhaps.'

16. The place word qián 'front' occurs in the following combinations:

> qiántian 'day before yesterday'
> qiánnian 'year before last'
> qián-jǐtiān 'a few days ago,' 'the first few days'
> qián-jǐge-xīngqī 'a few weeks ago,' 'the first few weeks'
> qián-jǐge-yuè 'a few months ago,' 'the first few months'
> qián-jǐnián 'a few years ago,' 'the first few years'

Lesson 24 REVIEW

PRONUNCIATION REVIEW

I. Sentences Distinguished Only by Context

In Chinese, as in English, sentences occur which are pronounced exactly alike but have different meanings. In isolation, such sentences are ambiguous; but people do not say things in isolation. The context of an utterance almost always makes its meaning clear.

The following sentences are examples. Invent suitable contexts for both members of each pair.

1. Nǐ-zuò-shénmo?

    (a) What are you doing?
    (b) What [conveyance] are you taking?

2. Nèige-hú-hěn-dà.

    (a) That lake is quite large.
    (b) That pot is quite large.

3. Wǒ-jiào-Měiyīng.

    (a) I'm calling Meiying.
    (b) I'm called Meiying.

4. Zhǐ-yǒu-sānzhāng.

    (a) There are only three sheets.
    (b) (Of) paper, there are three sheets.

5. Wǒ-míngtian-sòng-ta.

    (a) I'll see him off tomorrow.
    (b) I'll present it to him tomorrow.

6. Tāmen-kǎode-zhēn-bú-cuò.

    (a) They roasted it really well.
    (b) They did really well in the exams.

II. Sentences Distinguished by Tonal Contrasts

In contrast to the sentences presented in the foregoing exercise, which are capable of two different interpretations as determined by context, the exercise below gives pairs of sentences which are almost identical, differing only with respect to a single tone. (The first pair, for example, are identical except for mǎi in the first and mài in the second.) A tone distinction like this is as significant to Chinese ears as a vowel or consonant difference is to ours: each pair below is as different as the English pair Bake the pie and Take the pie.

Practice the following by pronouncing ONE sentence from each pair, testing yourself by asking the Chinese teacher to identify what you think you said by giving the English for what he thinks he heard. When you have had a perfect score on every sentence at least twice, reverse the process and try to identify the meanings of the sentences pronounced one at a time by the Chinese teacher.

1.	Tāmen-mǎi-shū.	They buy books.
	Tāmen-mài-shū.	They sell books.
2.	Wǒ-míngtian-qu-jiē.	I'm going to meet (him) tomorrow.
	Wǒ-míngtian-qu-jiè.	I'm going to borrow (it) tomorrow.
3.	Nǐmen-yǒu-tāng-ma?	Do you have soup?
	Nǐmen-yǒu-táng-ma?	Do you have sugar?
4.	"Dōng-xī" zěnmo-xiě?	How do you write "East-West"?
	"Dōngxi" zěnmo-xiě?	How do you write "thing"?
5.	Tāmen-bu-dǎ.	They're not hitting.
	Tāmen-bu-dà.	They're not big.
6.	Tā-xiǎng-ta-fùqin.	He's thinking of his father.
	Tā-xiàng-ta-fùqin.	He resembles his father.
7.	Tā-yào-nèizhāng-dìtú.	He wants that map.
	Tā-yào-'něizhāng-dìtú?	What map does he want?
8.	Tā-wán-le.	He's done for.
	Tā-wǎn-le.	He's late.
9.	Jiǔ-zài-zhèr.	The wine is here.
	Jiù-zài-zhèr.	It's right here.
10.	Yígòng-yǒu-shíwǎn.	Altogether there are ten bowlfuls.
	Yígòng-yǒu-shíwàn.	Altogether there are 100,000.
11.	Chá-sānkuài-qián.	The tea is three dollars.
	Chà-sānkuài-qián.	(I'm) short three dollars.
12.	Wǒ-jiāo-Měiyīng.	I'm teaching Meiying.
	Wǒ-jiào-Měiyīng.	I'm calling Meiying.

PATTERN REVIEW

Each of the patterns studied in this book is reviewed below, generally in a more complicated form and with different vocabulary than when first presented. If you have difficulty with any pattern, go back to the lesson in which it first appeared and review it. (For this purpose, each pattern is identified by lesson and drill number: 2.4, for example, means Lesson 2, Pattern Drill 4.

Unit I

1.1.   Xíngli-bú-tài-duō.

1.2.   Wǒmen-dōu-chī-xìngrér-dòufu.

1.3.   Fēijīchǎng bú-'tài-yuǎn-ma?

2.1.   'Zhāng-Jiàoshòu bú-shi-Nánjīng-rén-ma?

2.2.   Wǒmen-yīngdāng-yánjiu-zhèijiàn-shìqing.

2.3.   Nǐ-'huì-bu-huì yòng-kuàizi chī-Zhōngguo-fàn?

2.4.   'Wáng-Xiānsheng shì-nǐde-lǎoshī-bu-shi?

3.1.   Yìwǎn-fàn 'gòu-bu-gòu?

3.2.   Zhèisuǒr-fángzi mài-'duōshao-qián?

3.3.   Zhèi-sānzhāng-huàr dōu-shi-'tā-huà-de.

5.1.   Tāde-xuéwen yě-bú-cuò.

5.2.   Zuì-cōngmingde-xuésheng shi-shéi?

Unit II

7.1.   Fànguǎr zài-túshūguǎn gēn-shūdiàn-de-zhōngjiàr.

7.2.   'Zhāng-Xiānsheng zài-Yuǎndōng-Dàxué **xué-kēxué**.

7.3.   Zài-tā-jiā-fùjìn yǒu-yíge-xiǎo-fēijīchǎng.

7.4.   Zài-nèr-niàn-shū-de-rén chàbuduō-dōu-shi-'wàiguo-rén.

7.5.   Wǒmen-xiě-Hànzì háishi-xiě-pīnyīn?

8.1a.   Tā-jiā-lí-fēijīchǎng 'tài-jìn.

8.1b.   Diànyǐngryuàn lí-Sān-Yǒu-Shūdiàn yǒu-yìlǐ-duō-lù.

8.2.   Yóu-hěn-duō-yǎnyuán yǎnde-bù-hǎo.

8.3.   Shīzi-tóu bù-róngyi-zuò.

8.4.   Shi-'zìjǐ-zuò-hǎo háishi-qǐng-'biéde-rén-zuò-hǎo?

9.1.   Wó-měitiān dào-Sān-Yǒu-Shūdiàn-qu.

9.2a.   Wǒmen-'shénmo-shíhou qu-jiē-ta?

9.2b.   Tāmen-liùdiǎn-zhōng kàn-diànyǐngr-qu.

9.3.   Tā-'xiàwǔ wúdiǎn-bàn cóng-túshūguǎn-lái.

9.4.   Cóng-zhèr-**yìzhí wàng-xībéi-zǒu-sānlǐ**-lù jiù-dào-le.

9.5.   Rúguó-wǒ-zuò-chuán-qù wǒ-jiu-zǎo-yìdiár-zǒu.

10.1.   Zhèi-xīngqīde-piānzi bǐ-shàng-xīngqīde-hǎo.

10.2.   Nǐ-shuōde-hěn-duì.

10.3a. Nán-háizi bí-nǚ-háizi chīde-duō.

10.3b. Tā-láide bí-wó-wǎn.

10.4.   Tā-shuō-xiàohua shuōde-zhēn-hǎo.

10.5 a. Wǒ-kàn-diànyǐngr bǐ-tā-kànde-duō.

10.5 b. Tā-dài-xíngli dàide-bí-nǐ-duō.

11.1.   Tā-dǎsuan míngnian-èryue-sānhào líkai-Zhōngguo.

11.2.   'Wáng-Xiānsheng shi-qùnian-liùyue bìyè-de.

11.3 a. Tā-shi-zài-'Rìběn niàn-shū-de.

11.3 b. Wǒ-shi-zài-'fànguár-mǎi-de-chá.

Unit III

13.1 a. Wó-bá-suóyǒude-xíngli dōu-shōushihǎo-le.

13.1 b. Zuótian-wǎnshang wǒmen-kàn-le-diànyǐngr-le.

13.2 a. Wǒmen-chīwánle-fàn jiù-qu-kàn-diànyǐngr.

13.2 b. Wó-'mǎile-shū jiù-huí-jiā-le.

13.3 a. Wǒ-chīde-tài-bǎo-le.

13.3 b. Xiànzài-yǐjing wǔyue-báhào-le.

13.4 a. Wǒmen-yàole-wǔge-cài yíge-tāng.

13.4 b. Wó-yǐjing-xiěle wǔfēng-xìn-le. Hái-yào-xiě-sānfēng.

13.5.   Xiànzài tiānqi-nuǎnhuo-le.

13.6 a. Xué-kàn-shū-yǐqián děi-xiān-xué-shuō-huà.

13.6 b. Wǒ-zài-Zhōngguo-de-shíhou cháng-qu-kàn Zhōngguo-diànyǐngr.

13.7.   Cóng-yī-jiǔ-liù-èr-nián-kāishǐ tā-jiù-bú-xué-Zhōngwén-le.

14.1.   Wǒde-lǎoshī duì-Rìběn-lìshǐ hén-yǒu-yánjiu.

14.2 a. Wàn-Jiàoshòu-xiě-de-shū dōu-hěn-nán-dǒng.

14.2 b. Néng-yòng-Hànzì-xiě-xìn-de-wàiguo-rén hén-shǎo.

14.3 a. Nǐ-méi-tīngshuōguo zhèige-xiàohua-ma?

14.3 b. Wǒde-nèijiàn-shì tā-zuótian-tíguo-le-ma?

14.4.   Wǒ-yídìng-jìbuzhù nènmo-duō-Hànzì.

14.5 a. Měiguo-zuì-dàde-dàxué yóu-liǎngwàn-sānqiān-duō-xuésheng.

14.5 b. Nèige-túshūguǎn chàbuduō-yǒu-yìbái-wǔshi-wàn-běn-shū.

15.1.   Wǒ-hái-děi-xué liǎngniánde-shùxué.

15.2.   Cóng-Měiguo wǒ-zuòle-liǎngge-xīngqī-chuán cái-dào-'Rìběn.

15.3.   Wǒ-shōushile-'liùge-zhōngtóude-xíngli-le, 'hái-méi-shōushihǎo.

15.4.   Tāmen-zài-diànhuàli-shuō-huà yǐjing-yǒu-'yíge-duō-zhōngtóu-le.

15.5.   Wǒ-kànle-liǎngcì 'Zhōngguo-diànyǐngr.

16.1.   Xiǎo-háizi-guò-lù yào-zhùyì-chē.

16.2.   Wó-měitiān qīdiǎn-zhōng-qǐlai.

16.3.   Rúguó-wó-yǒu-jīhui wǒ-yídìng shàng-Guǎngdong-qu-lǚxíng.

16.4.   Wó-xiángqilai-zhèige-zìde-yìsi-le.

16.5.   Qíng-nǐmen dōu-náqi-shū-lai.

16.6.   Wǒde-xíngli dōu-nádao-nǎr-qu-le?

16.7.   Bú-yào-bǎ-zhèijiàn-shìqing gàosu-ta.

16.8 a.   Lián-wǒde-lǎoshī yě-bú-rènshi-zhèige-zì.

16.8 b.   Zhèige-jùzi lián-yíge-zì wǒ-dōu-bú-rènshi.

16.9.   Wó-xiáng-mǎi-zhèi-jíběn-shū sònggei-ta.

16.10.   Jiǎozi yě-shi-nǐ-zuò-de-ma?

17.1.   Zhōngguo-kuàizi gēn-Rìběn-kuàizi yíyàng-ma?

17.2.   Guǎngdong-cài gēn-běifāng-cài yíyàng-hǎo-chī-ma?

17.3.   'Gāo-Xiáojie méi-yǒu-tā-fùqin nènmo-xǐhuan-xiě-zì.

17.4.   Nǐ-zuò-táng-cù-yú zuòde-gēn-tā-yíyàng-hǎo.

17.5.   Wǒ-chī-jiǎozi-chīde yóu-nǐ-zhènmo-duō.

17.6.   Wǒ-lèide-lián-fàn yě-bù-xiǎng-chī.

Unit IV

19.1 a.   Nǐ-yīngdāng duō-liànxi-xiě-Hànzì.

19.1 b.   Wǒmen-zǒu-'kuài-yìdiǎr, yàoburán-wǒmen-qùwǎn-le.

19.1 c.   Qíng-nǐ-míngtian zǎo-yìdiǎr-lái.

19.2 a.   Tāmen-zài-cāngtīngli tánzhe-huà-ne.

19.2 b.   Tā-dàizhe-xíngli shàng-chuán-qu-le.

19.3.   Tā-bú-shi-'Hànrén jiù-shi-'Rìběn-rén.

19.4.   Tā-shuōle-hǎoxiē-xiàohua yě-méi-yǒu-rén-xiào.

19.5.   Chúle-fāyīn-yǐwài tāde-'Zhōngwén-bú-cuò.

19.6.   Tā-sìshēng liànxi-shi-liànxi, kěshi-hái-shuōde-bù-zhǔn.

20.1.   Tā-yí-dào-fēijīchǎng jiù-shàng-fēijī-le.

20.2.   Zhèizhāng-huàr nǐ-'shénmo-shíhou-guàqilai?

20.3 a.   Wó-dǎle-bàntiān-mén dōu-méi-rén-kāi.

20.3 b.   Dǎ-'Gāo-Xiānsheng-jiā dào-fēijīchǎng yǒu-bālǐ-duō-lù.

20.3 c.   Qíng-nǐmen-dǎkai-shū yíkuàr-niàn.

20.4.   Zhèi-liǎngge-zì ní-xiěcuò-le.

21.1 a.   Ní-'yǒu-duōshao jiu-'gěi-duōshao.

21.1 b.   'Shéi-yào-míngtian-qù 'shéi-jiu-míngtian-qù.

21.2 a.   Jiùshi-nǐ-'bù-xiě-xìn wó-yé-xiě.

21.2 b.   Jiùshi-'wàiguo-rén duì-Hànzì yé-yǒu-xìngqu.

21.3.   Rúguó-wó-yǒu-qián wǒ-yídìng-gěi-ta, kěshi-wǒ-méi-yǒu-qián-gěi-ta.

21.4.   Tā-tiāntian-dà-chī-dà-hē.

22.1.   Wǒ-yuè-xué-Zhōngguo-huàde-fāyīn yuè-juéde-nán.

22.2.   Ní-hǎohāorde tīng-wǒde-huà.

22.3.   Ní-xiě-de-zì gèger-dōu-shi-cuò-de.

23.1.   Yì-jiā-rén dōu-duì-wó-hén-hǎo.

23.2 a. Měiguo-wénxuéjiā bú-tài-zhùyì 'Zhōngguo-wénxué.

23.2 b. 'Zhōngguo-háizimen 'wàiguo-háizimen dōu-shi-yíyàngde-xǐhuan-wár.

23.3.   Wǒde-shū ràng-'shéi-gěi-názǒu-le?

FOREIGN CORRESPONDENCE

After returning to America, Mr. White starts corresponding with Miss Gao.
Here is his first letter and her reply. Note the format of Chinese letters:
salutation at the beginning, body of the letter, complimentary close set off as
indicated, signature at the end, and date after the name.

Měiyīng:

   Zhèi-shi-wó-géi-nǐ-de-dì-yìfēng-xìn. Wǒ-dàole-'Rìběn xiàle-fēijī jiù-
qu-kàn-wǒde-lǎoshī. Tā-hěn-gāoxìng, qíng-wǒ-chīle-yí cì-fàn, hái-géi-wo-
jièshaole liǎngwèi-'Rìběn-péngyou, yíwèi-'Měiguo-péngyou.   Zhèi-sānge-
péngyou duì-wǒ-dōu-hén-hǎo. Wǒ-shi-dì-èrcì lái-'Rìběn-le. Wǒ-juéde-Rì-
běn hén-yǒu-yìsi. Nǐ-ne? Chúle-zhèige-yǐwài zài-'Rìběn   yě-méi-yǒu-
shénmo-tèbié-yǒu-yìside-shìqing gàosu-ni.

   Wǒ-xiànzài yǐjing-dàole-jiā. Wǒ-kànjian-fùqin-mǔqin, bá-ni-sònggei-wǒ-
de nèizhāng-shānshuǐ-huàr náchulai-gěi-tāmen-kàn.   Fùqin-mǔqin-dōu-shuō
nǐ-huà-de-hǎo. Wó-yě-gàosu-tāmen nǐ-shi-wǒ-zuì-hǎode-péngyou. Tāmen-
dōu-hěn-gāoxìng, shuō-xīwang-nǐ-néng-dào-'Měiguo-lái.   Wó-yé-bǎ-Gāo-
Xiānsheng Gāo-Tàitai duì-wǒ-nènmo-hǎo gàosu-tāmen.   Fùqin-mǔqin dōu-
shuō xièxie-tāmen-liǎngwèi.

   Wǒ-líkai-jiā-yìnián. Fùqin-mǔqin hái-gēn-qùnian-yíyàng,   kěshi-dìdi-
mèimei zhǎnggāo-le-hěn-duō. Dìdi-gēn-wǒ-yíyàng-gāo. Mèimei-yuè-zhǎng
yuè-piàoliang. Fùqin-mǔqin yīnwei-wǒ-líkai-tāmen-yìnián-le   wǒ-huílai-le
tāmen-gāoxìngde-bùdéliǎo. Mǔqin-měitiān zuò-hén-hǎode-cài géi-wǒ-chī.

   Wó-yě-qu-kànguo-jǐge-péngyou. Dōu-gēn-yǐqián-chàbuduō. Wǒ-zhèi-jǐ-
tiān-hěn-lèi. Guò-yì-liǎngtiān wǒ-dào-dàxué-qu-kànkan 'shénmo-shíhou-
shàng-kè, yīnggāi-mǎi-'shénmo-shū yìxiē-wèntí. Wó-xiǎng-zài-zhèi-yìnián-
lǐtou wǒ-bìděi-yònggōng-niàn-shū.

Wǒ-cóng-shàng-fēijī dào-xiànzài dōu-hén-hǎo, kěshi-kànbujiàn-nǐ-le. Bù-
zhīdào 'shénmo-shíhou wǒmen-zài-jiàn. Xīwang-nǐ-cháng-géi-wó-xiě-xìn.
Zài-tán. Zhù-nǐ
Píng'ān

                                        Wénshān

                                            jiǔyue-báhào

Wénshān:

   Zuótian-jiēdào-nǐde-xìn gāoxìng-jíle. Zhīdao-ní-yǐjing píng'ān-huídào-
jiā-le. Wó-bá-ní-zǒule-yǐhòu-de-yìxiē-shìqing gàosu-nǐ-yìdiǎr.

   Qián-jǐtiān wǒ-dào-Yuǎn-Dà-qùguo-le.   Wǒmen-xià-xīngqī jiù-kāishǐ-
shàng-kè-le. Wǒmen 'yìniánjíde-xuésheng hái-děi-xué yì niánde-shùxué.
Zāogāo! Wǒde-shùxué bú-tài-hǎo. Nǐ-shi-zhīdao-de. Érqiě wǒde-shùxué-
lǎoshī yǐjing-huídào-hén-yuǎnde-Měiguo-le. Rúguó-wó-yǒu-wèntí, 'shéi-
gàosu-wo? Wǒ-duì-shùxué-méi-xìngqu. Ràng-wǒ-zài-xué-yìnián-shùxué wǒ-
zhēn-bù-gāoxìng-xué. Wǒ-bù-míngbai xué-wénxué wèi-shénmo hái-yào-xué-
yìnián-shùxué-ne? Shì-bu-shi-měi-yíge-dàxué dōu-shi-yíyàng-ne?

   Wó-xiǎng-shàng-kè-yǐhòu wǒ-bìdéi-hǎohāorde yònggōng-niàn-shū-le.
Yóuqíshi-duì-'xiě-zì-yìfāngmiàn.   Wó-xiěde-'tài-bù-hǎo-le.   Fùqin-cháng-
jiào-wó-xiě-zì. Kěshi-láo-yě-méi-hǎohāorde yònggōng-xiěguo.

   Qián-jǐtiān yǒu-yíwèi-péngyou ràng-wó-gěi-ta-huà-yì zhāng-huàr. Xiǎng-
lái-xiǎngqù gěi-ta-huà-'shénmo-hǎo-ne? Xiángqilai-le bǎ-túshūguǎn-huàxia-
lai. Nǐ-kàn-túshūguǎn duómo-piàoliang-a!   Huàxialai yídìng-'hén-hǎo-kàn.
Nǐ-shuō-shì-bu-shi?

   Ní-zǒule-yǐhòu fùqin-mǔqin-tāmen měitiān-tídao-ni.   Tāmen-shuō nǐ-
shi-cōngmingde-hǎo-xuésheng. Xīwang-bù-jiǔ nǐ-'zài-dào-Zhōngguo-lái.

   Guòqude-yìnián-lǐtou hén-yǒu-yìsi. Nǐ-duì-wǒ-de-shùxué bāngzhu-hěn-
duō. Wó-hěn-xièxie-ni. Wó-xiǎng-yǐhòu měi-xīngqīliù-xiě-xìn, bǎ-yíge-
xīngqīde-shìqing xiěchulai. Nǐ-juéde-zěnmoyàng? Zhù
Hǎo.

                                        Měiyīng

                                            jiǔyue shísān

DIALOGUE SUMMARIES

The Dialogues are summarized below, lesson by lesson. They are told in narrative style here, and provided with background material and explanations, but do not exceed the vocabulary and grammar presented in the book.

Unit I

Dì-yīkè

'Gāo-Xiānsheng kāile-yíge-Sān-Yǒu-Shūdiàn, lí-Yuǎndōng-Dàxué-bù-yuǎn. 'Bái-Xiānsheng cóng-Měiguo-dào-Zhōngguo-yǐhou, zài-shūdiànli-mǎi-shū jiù-rènshi-'Gāo-Xiānsheng-le. Tóngshí-yě-rènshi-le-Gāo-Tàitai Gāo-Xiáojie. Yǒu-yìtiān 'Bái-Xiānsheng-chūqu suíbiàn-zài-lùshang-zóuzou, yùjian-le-'Gāo-Xiānsheng. 'Bái-Xiānsheng wèn-'Gāo-Xiānsheng zuì-jìn-hǎo-ma. 'Bái-Xiānsheng yòu-wèn-Gāo-Tàitai Gāo-Xiáojie dōu-hǎo-ma. Gāo-Xiān-sheng-xièxie-ta, gàosu-'Bái-Xiānsheng Gāo-Tàitai-Gāo-Xiáojie dōu-hǎo.

Dì-èrkè

Yǒu-yícì yíge-'Zhōngguo-rén qíng-hěn-**duō**-péngyou dào-ta-jiā-lǐtou qu-hē-chá. Tā-qǐng-de-péngyou-lǐtou yǒu-'Zhōngguo-rén yé-yǒu-'wàiguo-rén. 'Bái-Xiānsheng gēn-'Qián-Xiānsheng tāmen-liǎngge-rén zài-yíkuàr-zuòzhe. Yīnwei-rén-tài-duō yě-méi-yǒu-rén gěi-tāmen-liǎngge-rén-jièshao, 'Bái-Xiānsheng xiǎng-gēn-Qián-Xiānsheng-shuō-huà, tā-jiù-wèn-Qián-Xiānsheng-guìxìng. Qián-Xiānsheng-gàosu-tā-xìng-Qián. Kěshi 'Qián-Xiānsheng jìcuò-le. Tā-xiǎng-'Bái-Xiānsheng shi-'Wáng-Xiānsheng. 'Bái-Xiānsheng-shuō ta-'bú-shi-Wáng-Xiānsheng, tā-xìng-Bái. Qián-Xiānsheng-yòu-wèn-ta shi-'Yīngguo-rén-bú-shi. Bái-Xiānsheng-yòu-gàosu-ta 'bú-shi-Yīngguo-rén, ta-shi-Měiguo-rén. 'Bái-Xiānsheng wèn-'Qián-Xiānsheng huì-shuō-'Yīngguo-huà-bú-huì. 'Qián-Xiānsheng-shuō ta-bú-huì, zhǐ-huì-shuō-'Zhōngguo-huà.

Dì-sānkè

'Bái-Xiānsheng xiáng-mǎi-jǐzhī-Zhōngguo-bǐ, suóyi-tā-jiù-dào Gāo-Xiān-shengde-shūdiàn-qu-le. Tā-kànjian-yǒu-yìběn-<u>Zhōngguo-Wénxué</u>. Shi-yíwèi-Yuǎn-Dà-jiàoshòu-xiě-de. Yīnwei-tā-yánjiu-Zhōngguo-wénxué ta-xiáng-mǎi, tā-jiù-wèn-shūdiànli mài-shū-de-rén 'Máo-Xiānsheng zhèiběn-shū-'duōshao-

qián. Máo-Xiānsheng-gàosu-ta yíkuai-èrmáo-qián-yìběn.   Tā-yào-mái-
liángběn. Tā-juéde-zhèiběn-shū hén-hǎo. Tā-xiǎng-sònggei-péngyou-yìběn,
suóyi-mái-liángběn.

   Tā-yòu-wèn máobǐ-duōshao-qián-yìzhī.   Tā-xiǎng-tā-niàn-Zhōngwén bì-
déi-xiě-Hànzì. 'Máo-Xiānsheng-shuō liǎngmáo-qián-yìzhī.   Tā-mǎile-wǔ-
zhī-bǐ, liángběn-shū. Yígòng-yòngle wǔkuài-sìmáo-qián. Máihǎo-le-yǐhòu
tā-názhe-shū-gēn-bǐ jiù-huíqu-le.

<h2 align="center">Dì-sìkè</h2>

   Yuǎndōng-Dàxué yǐjing-shàng-kè-le. 'Bái-Xiānsheng yīnggāi mǎi-de-dōngxi
hěn-duō, bǐfang-běnzi, dìtú, zìdiǎn, mòshuǐ, gāngbǐ, qiānbǐ tā-dōu-déi-mǎi.
Tā-yòu-pǎodào-shūdiàn-qu. Tā-xiànzài gēn-'Máo-Xiānsheng   jiànguo-hěn-
duō-cì. 'Máo-Xiānsheng-wèn-ta yào-mǎi-shénmo-dōngxi. Tā-yào-mǎi-'hóng-
mòshuǐ, kěshi-shūdiàn-lǐtou 'hóng-mòshuǐ-dōu-màiwán-le.   Zhí-yǒu-'lán-
mòshuǐ, 'hēi-mòshuǐ-le. Tā-mǎi-zìdiǎn, dìtú, gāngbǐ, qiānbǐ, zhǐ. Tā-bǎ-
dōngxi-máihǎo-le-yǐhòu, Máo-Xiānsheng-gěi-ta-suànsuan-zhàng. Yígòng-shí-
liùkuài-jiǔmáo-èrfēn-qián. Tā-gēn-Máo-Xiānsheng shuō-zàijiàn, názhe-dōng-
xi jiù-zǒu-le.

<h2 align="center">Dì-wǔkè</h2>

   'Bái-Xiānsheng láidào-Zhōngguo yǐjing-chàbuduō-bànnián-le.   Tā-cháng-
dào-shūdiàn-qu-mǎi-shū, suóyi-cháng-kànjian-'Gāo-Xiānsheng. Tā-gēn-Gāo-
Xiānsheng mànmārde-jiù-shi-hén-hǎode-péngyou-le.   Gāo-Xiānsheng tèbié-
xǐhuan-ta. Gāo-Xiānsheng yǒu-yíwèi-Yīngguo-péngyou, 'Wàn-Jiàoshòu. Hén-
záo-yǐqián Gāo-Xiānsheng jiù-xiáng-qǐng-'Wàn-Jiàoshòu gēn-'Bái-Xiānsheng
dào-tāmen-jiā-lǐtou-chī-fàn, kěshi-Wàn-Jiàoshòu-tài-máng, lǎo-méi-gōngfu.
Yǒu-yìtiān 'Wàn-Jiàoshòu xiàwǔ-sāndiǎn-duō-zhōng tā-gěi-Gāo-Xiānsheng-
dǎ-diànhuà shuō-ta-jīntian-wǎnshang yǒu-gōngfu, kéyi-dào-Gāo-jia-chī-wǎn-
fàn.

   'Wàn-Jiàoshòu gěi-'Gāo-Xiānsheng-dǎle-diànhuà-yǐhòu, 'Gāo-Xiānsheng
mǎshàng-jiù-gěi-Bái-Xiānsheng-dǎ-diànhuà, qǐng-ta-jīntian-wǎnshang   lái-
chī-wǎnfàn. Érqiě-gàosu-ta jīntian-wǎnshang   hái-qǐngle-yíwèi-'Yīngguo-
péngyou. Qǐng-'Bái-Xiānsheng wǎnshang-qīdiǎn-zhōng-yídìng-lái.

Unit II

Dì-qīkè

'Bái-Xiānsheng jīntian-'yòu-dào-shūdiàn-qu-le.   Tā-bú-shi-qu-mǎi-shū.
Tā-shi-wèn-'Máo-Xiānsheng 'Gāo-Xiānsheng-qǐng-chī-fàn shi-zài-nǎr, shi-
zài-shūdiàn shi-zài-ta-'jiā-lǐtou. Yīnwei-'Gāo-Xiānsheng gěi-ta-dǎ-diàn-
huà-de-shíhou ta-wàngle-wèn, suóyi-ta-lái-wèn-'Máo-Xiānsheng. 'Máo-Xiānsheng-gàosu-ta shi-zài-jiāli. Yòu-gàosu-ta Gāo-Xiānsheng-jiā zài-chéng-
'wàitou yíge-xiǎo-shānshang. Nèige-shānshang yǒu-sānsuǒr-fángzi.   Gāo-
Xiānsheng-jiā shi-zhōngjiàr-nèisuǒr-fángzi. Shān-xiàtou shi-Zhōngshān-Lù,
fùjìn-hái-yǒu-yíge-hú, yǒu-gōngyuán. 'Bái-Xiānsheng-tīngmíngbaile-yǐhòu
jiù-zǒu-le.

Dì-bākè

'Bái-Xiānsheng gēn-'Máo-Xiānsheng wènle-Gāo-Xiansheng-jiā-zài-nár-yǐ-
hòu, ta-zǒu-le. Kěshi-ta-'yòu-xiángqilai-le. Ta-xiǎng ta-'xiān-dào-túshūguǎn-
jiè-shū 'hòu-zài-dào-Gāo-jia-qu, yīnwei-ta-xiǎng-jiè-de-shū Yuǎn-Dàde-tú-
shūguán-lǐtou-méi-yǒu. Zhèrde-túshūguǎn ta-yě-méi-qùguo, háishi-děi-wèn-
'Máo-Xiānsheng. Yòu-huídào-shūdiàn.
  Máo-Xiānsheng-gàosu-ta túshūguǎn-lí-shūdiàn-hén-yuǎn, lí-Gāo-jia-yě-bú-
jìn. Máo-Xiānsheng-wèn-ta yào-jiè-'shénmo-shū. Tā-shuō tā-yào-jiè liáng-
běn-'Yīngwén-shū. Máo-Xiānsheng-hái-wèn-ta zài-dàxué-xué-shénmo. Tā-
gàosu-'Máo-Xiānsheng Zhōngguo-wénxué Yīngguo-wénxué ta-'dōu-xué.

Dì-jiŭkè

  Suírán-'Bái-Xiānsheng wènle-'Máo-Xiānsheng túshūguǎn-zài-nǎr, kěshi-
ta-méi-'gàosu-Bái-Xiānsheng 'zěnmo-zǒu, wàng-'něibiar-zǒu.   Bái-Xiānsheng-yòu-wèn cóng-shūdiàn-dào-túshūguǎn 'zěnmo-zǒu.   Máo-Xiānsheng-
gàosu-ta wàng-nán-zǒu, zài-wàng-xī-guǎi, guò-báge-lù-kǒur jiù-shi-túshūguǎn.
Túshūguǎnde-fángzi-hěn-dà, hěn-róngyi-kànjian.
  Bái-Xiānsheng-yòu-wèn zuò-'shénmo-chē.   Yīnwei-shūdiàn-fùjìn yǒu-
gōnggòng-qìchē-zhàn kéyi-zuò-gōnggòng-qìchē-qu. Máo-Xiānsheng-gàosu-ta
zuò-gōnggòng-qìchē, túshūguǎn-fùjìn yǒu-gōnggòng-qìchē-zhàn, xià-chē jiù-
shi-túshūguǎn.

Bái-Xiānsheng yòu-wèn-'Máo-Xiānsheng dào-Gāo-jia-qu-yǒu-gōnggòng-
qì chē-ma. Máo-Xiānsheng-gàosu-ta cóng-túshūguǎn-fùjìn-de-chē-zhàn
shàng-chē dào-Zhōngshān-Lù, zài-gōngyuán-mén-kǒur-xià-chē, shàng-yíge-
xiǎo-shān jiù-dào-le.

Dì-shíkè

'Bái-Xiānsheng wènwánle-Máo-Xiānsheng-yǐhòu, tā-jiù-zài-shūdiàn-fùjìn
nèige-gōnggòng-qì chē-zhàn shāng-le-chē yào-dào-túshūguǎn-qù-le. Nèige-
gōnggòng-qì chēshangde-màipiàoyuán hěn-kèqi. Tā-ràng-Bái-Xiānsheng-
mǎi-piào, kěshi-'Bái-Xiānsheng bù-zhīdào-duōshao-qián, jiù-wèn-ta. Tā-
jiù-gēn-'Bái-Xiānsheng shuōqi-huà-lai-le.

Tā-yí-kàn-'Bái-Xiānsheng shi-yíge-'wàiguo-rén kěshi-shuō-nènmo-hǎo-
de-Zhōngguo-huà, ta-shuō-'Bái-Xiānshengde-Zhōngguo-huà shuōde-'zhēn-hǎo.
Hái-wèn-'Bái-Xiānsheng shi-'něiguó-rén, zuò-shì-háishi-niàn-shū. Bái-Xiānsheng-gàosu-ta zài-Yuǎndōng-Dàxué-niàn-shū. Tā-yòu-wèn-'Bái-Xiānsheng
Yuǎn-Dàde-wàiguo-xuésheng 'duō-bu-duō. Ta-wèn-'Bái-Xiānsheng zài-Měiguo
yǒu-méi-yǒu-'wàiguo-xuésheng. Bái-Xiānsheng-gàosu-ta Měiguode-dàxué-lǐ-
tou wàiguo-xuésheng-'gèng-duō.

Bái-Xiānsheng-wèn-màipiàoyuán dào-túshūguǎn děi-'duōshao-shíhou. Mài-
piàoyuán-gàosu-'Bái-Xiānsheng chàbuduō-'èrshifēn-zhōng jiù-dào-le. Tā-wèn-
Bái-Xiānsheng jiā-zài-nǎr. Bái-Xiānsheng-gàosu-ta jiā-zài-Měiguo, jiā-lǐtou yǒu-fùqin-mǔqin dìdi-mèimei. Màipiàoyuán yòu-wèn-Bái-Xiānsheng fù-
qin-zuò-'shénmo-shì. Bái-Xiānsheng-gàosu-ta fùqin-mǔqin-dōu-shi-jiào-
yuán.

Bái-Xiānsheng-yě-wèn-tā jiā-lǐtou-dōu-yǒu-'shénmo-rén. Màipiàoyuán-
shuō yǒu-tàitai hái-yǒu-liǎngge-háizi. Nán-háizi jiào-Láohu. Bái-Xiānsheng-juéde zhèige-míngzi-hěn-qíguài, kěshi-ta-méi-'shuō-shénmo. Nǚ-háizi jiào-Xiǎomèi. Màipiàoyuán gàosu-'Bái-Xiānsheng nǚ-háizi 'yísuì-jiu-
huì-zǒu-lù. Ta-zìjǐ-juéde yísuìde-háizi-huì-zǒu-lù-hěn-qíguài, kěshi-yí-
suìde-háizi-huì-zǒu-lù 'yìdiár-yě-bù-qíguài.

Dì-shíyīkè

'Bái-Xiānsheng xiàle-gōnggòng-qì chē-yǐhòu jiù-dào-túshūguǎn-lái-le.
Gāng-yí-jìnqu tā-tīngjian-yǒu-rén gēn-ta-shuō-huà. Yí-kàn jiù-shi-qián-jǐ-
ge-yuè zài-péngyou-nèr-hē-chá-yùjian-de nèiwèi-'Qián-Xiānsheng. Qián-

Xiānsheng-wèn-ta shì-bu-shi-dào-túshūguǎn-lái-kàn-shū.　Tā-gàosu-'Qián-
Xiānsheng ta-'bú-kàn-shū, ta-xiǎng-'jiè-shū.　Qián-Xiānsheng-wèn-ta dá-
'nǎr-lái, shì-bu-shi-zuò-'chē-lái-de.　Tā-gàosu-'Qián-Xiānsheng zuò-gōng-
gòng-qì chē-lái-de.　Qián-Xiānsheng-hái-wèn-ta shì-bu-shi-'cháng-lái-túshū-
guǎn.　Ta-gàosu-'Qián-Xiānsheng zhè-shi-dì-'yícì.　'Qián-Xiānsheng suí-
rán-'qián-jǐge-yuè 'jiànguo-Bái-Xiānsheng,　kěshi-méi-jīhui gēn-ta-'duō-
tántan.　Jīntian-zài-túshūguǎn-yùjian-le, jiù-wèn-'Bái-Xiānsheng 'shénmo-
shíhou-lái Zhōngguo-de, zuò-'chuán-lái-de háishi-zuò-'fēijī-lái-de.　'Bái-
Xiānsheng-dōu-gàosu-ta-le.　'Bái-Xiānsheng yě-wèn-Qián-Xiānsheng 'shén-
mo-shíhou-líkai-túshūguǎn.　Qián-Xiānsheng-shuō ta-yǒu-yídiǎr-shì, ta-'jiù-
yào-zǒu.　Tā-hái-gàosu-'Bái-Xiānsheng zhèrde-shū-hěn-duō, kéyi-suíbiàn-
jiè.　Tā-hái-shuō yùjian-'Gāo-Xiānsheng-le.　Gāo-Xiānsheng-gàosu-ta jīntian-wǎnshang qǐng-Bái-Xiānsheng-chī-fàn.　Qián-Xiānsheng-shuō rúguó-
wǎnshang Bái-Xiānsheng-yǒu-gōngfu, yé-qǐng-dào-ta-jiā-lǐtou 'zuòyizuò,
yīnwei-ta-jiā lí-Gāo-jia hěn-jìn.

Unit III

Dì-shísānkè

'Bái-Xiānsheng zài-túshūguǎn jièhǎo-le-shū-yǐhòu, yòu-dào-gōnggòng-qì-
chē-zhàn qu-děng-chē.　Gāng-yí-shàng-qìchē kànjian-Gāo-Xiáojie zài-chē-
shang-ne.　Tā-jiù-gēn-Gāo-Xiáojie-shuō-huà.

Gāo-Xiáojie-gàosu-ta jīntian-xuéxiào-yǒu-shìqing, suóyi-huí-jiā wǎn-le-
yìdiǎr.　Gāo-Xiáojie-wèn-ta shì-bu-shi-dào-tāmen-jiā-lǐtou-qu.　Tā-gàosu-
Gāo-Xiáojie-shì.　'Bái-Xiānsheng hái-wèn-'Gāo-Xiáojie zài-'nǎr-niàn-
shū.　Gāo-Xiáojie-gàosu-ta zài-'zhōngxue-niàn-shū, jīnnian-jiù-bìyè-le.　Gāo-
Xiáojie-wèn-ta zài-dàxué-'jǐniánjí.　Tā-gàosu-Gāo-Xiáojie tā-zài-'sānniánjí.　Tāmen-liǎngge-rén-shuōhǎo-le kǎoshì-yǐhòu 'Bái-Xiānsheng qǐng-'Gāo-
Xiáojie kàn-diànyǐngr.　Gāo-Xiáojie-zài-chēshang gàosu-'Bái-Xiānsheng ta-
fùqin-jīntian-wǎnshang hái-qǐngle-yíwèi-'Yīngguo-péngyou.　Yīnwei-'Gāo-
Xiānsheng méi-gàosu-'Bái-Xiānsheng shi-nán-de-shi-nǚ-de,　Gāo-Xiáojie-
gàosu-ta shi-yíwèi-xiānsheng. Tāmen-liǎngge-ren zai-chēshang-tánde-hěn-
gāoxìng.

Dì-shísìkè

'Bái-Xiānsheng yòu-wèn-'Gāo-Xiáojie xuéxiào-lǐtou yǒu-'duōshao-xué-

sheng. Tóngshí-'Gāo-Xiáojie yě-wèn-'Bái-Xiānsheng Yuǎn-Dà-yǒu-duōshao-
xuésheng. Tā-hái-wèn-Gāo-Xiáojie jiānglái-bìyè-yǐhòu xué-shénmo?   Gāo-
Xiáojie-kǒngpà zìjǐ-kǎobushàng-dàxué.   Bái-Xiānsheng-xīwang-Gāo-Xiáojie
'yě-xué-wénxué, kěshi-Gāo-Xiáojie-shuō rúguó-kǎobushàng-dàxué jiù-xué-
huàr, yīnwei-ta-duì-huà-huàr hén-yǒu-xìngqu.

    Tāmen-liǎngge-rén hái-tándào-xué-yǔyán-de-wèntí, yīnwei-Bái-Xiānsheng
shi-xué-Zhōngguo-yǔyán gēn-wénxué-de.   Gāo-Xiáojie-jiù-wèn-ta xué-yǔyán
'zěnmo-xué.   Bái-Xiānsheng-gàosu-ta xué-yǔyán-de-'fāngfǎ, érqiě-gàosu-ta
xué-yǔyánxué shi-yòng-kēxuéde-fázi yánjiu-yǔyán.   Tāmen-yòu-shuōdao xiě-
'zì-yìfāngmiàn. 'Bái-Xiānsheng néng-yòng-máobí-xiě-zì. Gāo-Xiáojie-gàosu-ta xiànzài-'Zhōngguo-rén dōu-'bú-zěnmo-yòng-máobí-xiě-zì-le.

    'Gāo-Xiānsheng zì-xiěde-hén-hǎo, kěshi-ta-měitiān 'háishi-jìxude-xiě-
zì. Tā-xiěde-zì cháng-sònggei-péngyou. Yé-yóu-hěn-duō-rén gēn-ta-yào-
ta-xiě-de-zì. Gāo-Xiānsheng-péngyou-'jiā-lǐtou, chàbuduō-dōu-guàzhe Gāo-
Xiānsheng-xiě-de-zì.

Dì-shíwǔkè

    'Gāo-Xiáojie cháng-tīng-ta-fùqin-shuō Bái-Xiānsheng-hěn-cōngming, shū-
niànde-bú-cuò. Tā-jīntian-gēn-Bái-Xiānsheng zài-chēshang-tánle-hěn-duō-
huà zhīdao-'Bái-Xiānsheng 'shì-hén-hǎo, suóyi-tā-wèn-'Bái-Xiānsheng niàn-
'duōshao-nián Zhōngguo-shū-le. Bái-Xiānsheng-gàosu-ta yǐjing-niànguo-wǔ-
nián-le. Tā-hái-gàosu-'Gāo-Xiáojie zài-'zhōngxué-zěnmo-xué, zài-'dàxué-
zěnmo-xué. Tā-hái-shuō xué-de-shíhou yòng-lùyìnjī tīng-lùyīn. 'Bái-Xiānsheng yòu-gàosu-'Gāo-Xiáojie xué-yǔyán shi-hén-yǒu-yìsi-de.   Kāishǐ-nán,
yǐhòu-jiu-bíjiǎo-róngyi-le.

    Gāo-Xiáojie-wèn-ta cóng-Měiguo-zěnmo-lái-de.   Tā-shuō shì-cóng-Niǔ-
yue-zuò-qìchē-dào-Sānfánshì, zuò-chuán-dào-'Rìběn, yǐhòu-zuò-fēijī dào-
Zhōngguo-lái-de. Gāo-Xiáojie-gēn-Bái-Xiānsheng-shuō ta-méi-zuòguo-fēijī.
Fùqin-mǔqin-hén-xǐhuan-qù-Rìběn-wár. Huòzhě-ta-bìyè-yǐhòu gēn-ta-fùqin-
mǔqin zuò-fēijī-dào-'Rìběn-qu. Bái-Xiānsheng-shuō huàjiā-bìděi-dào-bié-
de-dìfāng qu-kàn-shānshuǐ, duì-huà-huàr hén-yǒu-bāngzhu.

Dì-shíliùkè

    'Gāo-Xiáojie 'Bái-Xiānsheng tánde-hén-yǒu-yìsi. Zài-chēshang-yuǎnyuǎr-
de jiù-kànjian-shānshang Gāo-jia-nèisuǒr-fángzi-le. Bái-Xiānsheng-yí-kàn

Gāo-jia-zhù-de-zhèige-dìfang hén-hǎo. Yǒu-shān-yóu-shuǐ. 'Gāo-Xiáojie gàosu-'Bái-Xiānsheng ta-fùqin-hén-xǐhuan-zhèige-dìfang, suóyi-tāmen jiù-zài-zhèr-zhù-le.

Liǎngge-rén xià-chē-le, zǒuzhe-lù-tánzhe-huà, yìhuěr-jiù-dàole-Gāo-jia-mén-kǒur-le. Gāo-Xiáojie-jiu-jiào-mén. Gāo-Tàitai-chūlai-kāi-mén. Tā-kànjian-Bái-Xiānsheng-lái-le hěn-gāoxìng. Zhèige-shíhou Gāo-Xiānsheng-yě-chūlai-le gēn-Bái-Xiānsheng-shuō-huà hái-gěi-ta-jièshao zhèiwèi-Yīng-guo-rén. Yīngguo-rén shi-yíwèi-jiàoshòu, shi-Gāo-Xiānshengde yíwèi-lǎo-péngyou. Tāde-Zhōngguo-xuéwen hén-hǎo, érqiě yě-néng-shuō 'hén-hǎode-Zhōngguo-huà. Gāo-Xiānsheng-juéde jīntian-hén-yǒu-yìsi. Suírán-qíng-liǎngwèi-'wàiguo-péngyou lái-chī-fàn, kěshi-'dōu-shuō-Zhōngguo-huà.

Zhèige-shíhou 'Wàn-Jiàoshòu gēn-'Bái-Xiānsheng liǎngge-rén-tánqilai-le. Wàn-Jiàoshòu-wèn-'Bái-Xiānsheng shénmo-shíhou-láide, hái-tán-yìxiē-guān-yú-xuéxiào-de-wèntí. Yòu-wèn-ta shi-xué-shénmo-de. 'Wàn-Jiàoshòu shi-yíwèi-wénxuéjiā. Tā-xiěle-hěn-duō-shū. Tā-xiě-de-Zhōngguo-Wénxué-Yán-jiu nèiběn-shū 'Bái-Xiānsheng yǐjing-kànguo-le. Bái-Xiānsheng-shuō tā-xiě-de-hǎo, tā-hěn-gāoxìng. Yīnwei-'Gāo-Xiānsheng hén-xǐhuan-'Bái-Xiān-sheng, tā-gàosu-'Bái-Xiānsheng Wàn-Jiàoshòude-xuéwen-hǎo, ràng-ta-yǐhòu cháng-gēn-Wàn-Jiàoshòu zài-yíkuàr-'yánjiu-yánjiu.

'Bái-Xiānsheng zhīdao-'Gāo-Xiáojie néng-huà-huàr, suóyi-ta-xiǎng-kàn-kan. Kěshi-'Gāo-Xiáojie shi-yíge-nǚ-háizi, tā-bù-xiǎng-ràng-tāmen-kàn ta-huàde-huàr, suóyi-Gāo-Xiānsheng yídìng-jiào-ta-náchulai, qǐng-tāmen-kàn-kan. Tóngshí-'Gāo-Xiānsheng hái-gàosu-tāmen Gāo-Xiáojie hén-xiǎode-shí-hou jiù-xǐhuan-huà-huàr. Tā-yě-méi-xué duōshao-shíhou. Huàr-lǐtou-yǒu-yìzhāng Hángzhou-shānshuǐ-huàr. Hángzhoude-shānshuǐ shi-'hén-yǒu-míng-de, suóyi-huàchulai hěn-piàoliang. 'Bái-Xiānsheng hén-xǐhuan-nèizhāng-huàr.

Dì-shíqīkè

Tāmen-zhèng-zài-kànzhe Gāo-Xiáojie-huàde nèizhāng-Hángzhou-shānshuǐ-huàr-de-shíhou, 'Gāo-Xiānsheng jiù-gàosu-'Wàn-Jiàoshòu gēn-'Bái-Xiān-sheng tā-yuánlái-shi-'Hángzhou-rén, èrshijǐsuì tā-líkai-tāde-lǎo-jiā-Háng-zhou. Wàn-Jiàoshòu-shuō Hángzhou-yǒu-míng, Yīngguo-rén-dōu-zhīdao. Gāo-Xiānsheng-'gàosu-tāmen Hángzhou-yǒu-yíge-hú jiào-Xī-Hú, hěn-piào-liang. Tā-shuō-cóngqián-yǒu-rén ná-Xī-Hú-bǐ-zuò-Xī-Shī. Xī-Shī zài-

Zhōngguo-lìshǐshang-xiěde shi-zuì-piàoliangde-nǔ-rén. Suírán-'Wàn-Jiàoshòu dàoguo-Zhōngguo-hěn-duō-cì, kěshi-tā-méi-qùguo-Hángzhou. 'Bái-Xiānsheng tīng-tāmen-bǎ-Hángzhou shuōde-nènmo-hǎo, suóyi-tā-shuō jiānglái rú-
guó-yǒu-jīhui tā-yě-dào-Hángzhou-qu-lǔxíng.

   'Bái-Xiānsheng kànjian-Gāo-Xiáojie-huà-de-nèizhāng-Hángzhou-huàr gēn-
tāmen-xiànzài-zhù-de-dìfang-chàbuduō, tā-hěn-qíguài jiu-wèn-'G ā o -X i ā n-
sheng. Gāo-Xiānsheng-xiào-le, gàosu-ta yīnwei-tā-xǐhuan-tāde-lǎo-jiā tā-
kànjian-zhèige-dìfang hěn-xiàng-Hángzhou jiu-zài-zhèr mǎile-zhèisuǒr-fáng-
zi-le.

   'Bái-Xiānsheng tīng-rén-shuōguo Sūzhou-nǔ-rén-piàoliang tā-jiu-wèn-
'Gāo-Xiānsheng 'duì-bu-duì. Wàn-Jiàoshòu-shuō-shi-zhēnde, hái-gàosu-ta
Gāo-'Tàitai-shi-Sūzhou-rén, suóyi-Gāo-'Xiáojie-nènmo-piàoliang.

   'Wàn-Jiàoshòu hén-xǐhuan-hē-jiǔ-huá-quán. Zhèige-shíhou tā-gēn-'Gāo-
Xiānsheng huáqi-quán-lai-le. 'Bái-Xiānsheng yǐqián-méi-kànjianguo. Tā-
kànle-bàntiān tā-hěn-qíguài wèi-shénmo-yíngle bù-hē-jiǔ-ne. Tā-kàn-tāmen-
huále-jǐcì ta-cái-míngbai.

Unit IV

Dì-shíjiǔkè

   'Gāo-Xiānsheng 'Wàn-Jiàoshòu zhèng-zài-huá-quán-de-shíhou, Gāo-Tàitai bǎ-fàn-zuòhǎo-le, ràng-tāmen-chī-fàn. Gāo-Tàitai zuòle-hěn-duōde-cài.
'Wàn-Jiàoshòu shi-Gāo-Xiānshengde-lǎo-péngyou, 'Bái-Xiānsheng shi-xuésheng, suóyi-bú-yòng-zěnmo-kèqi.   Tāmen-suíbiàn-zuòzhe suíbiàn-chī.
Gāo-Tàitai-děi-zuò-cài, bù-néng-gēn-tāmen yíkuàr-chī-fàn. Kèren-dāngrán-
déi-qǐng-Gāo-Tàitai-lái yíkuàr-chī-le.

   Gāo-Tàitai-cài zuòde-zhēn-hǎo.   'Wàn-Jiàoshòu gēn-'Bái-Xiānsheng tāmen-liǎngge-rén, suírán-cháng-chī-Zhōngguo-fàn, kěshi-yǒude-cài tāmen-
hái-bù-zhīdao jiào-shénmo. Jǐ-zuòde-hén-hǎo-chī.   Tāmen-wèn nèige-jǐ-
shi-zěnmo-zuòde, jiào-shénmo-míngzi. Gāo-jia-jīntian-zuò-le wǔge-cài-yí-
ge-tāng. Yóu-chǎo-báicài, shīzi-tóu, táng-cù-yú, chǎo-dòufu, hóng-shāo-jī,
niú-ròu-tāng. Tāmen-'dōu-hén-xǐhuan-chī, érqiě zhèi-liǎngwèi-wàiguo-péng-
you yòng-kuàizi-yòngde-hén-hǎo.

   Jǐge-rén chīzhe-fàn tánzhe-huà, dōu-hěn-gāoxìng. 'Bái-Xiānsheng wèn-
'Gāo-Xiáojie huì-zuò-'fàn-bú-huì. 'Gāo-Xiáojie dāngrán-shuō-ta-bú-huì-le,
kěshi-Gāo-Tàitai-shuō tā-huì-zuò.

Dì-èrshikè

Cóng-Gāo-jia-qǐng-'Bái-Xiānsheng chī-fàn-yǐhòu, Gāo-Xiáojie mànmār-de-gēn-'Bái-Xiānsheng tāmen-liǎngge-rén-hén-hǎo. Liǎngge-rén chàbuduō-měige-xīngqī dōu-jiàn-liǎng-sāncì. Érqiě 'Bái-Xiānsheng cháng-gěi-Gāo-Xiáojie-dǎ-diànhuà.

Liùyuede-kǎoshì-wánle-yǐhòu, yǒu-yìtiān 'Bái-Xiānsheng gěi-Gāo-Xiáojie-dǎ-diànhuà. Gāo-Xiáojie zài-diànhuà-lǐtou gàosu-Bái-Xiānsheng tā-zhèicì-kǎode-bú-dà-hǎo. Tā-yě-wèn-'Bái-Xiānsheng kǎode-zěnmoyàng. 'Bái-Xiān-sheng dāngrán-yé-děi-shuō zìjí-kǎode-'bù-zěnmoyàng-le.

Gāo-Xiáojie-yòu-shuō fùqin-mǔqin yào-dài-ta dào-Rìběn-qu-lǚxíng-le. Tā-fùqin-mǔqin-xiǎng-zài-'Rìběn zhù-liǎngge-yuè-cái-huílai, kěshi-tā-bù-xiǎng-zhù-nènmo-jiǔ. Tā-xiǎng-gēn-fùqin-mǔqin-shuō zhù-'yíge-yuè-jiù-huí-lai. Bái-Xiānsheng-dāngrán-xīwang Gāo-Xiáojie-kuài-huílai-le.

Bái-Xiānsheng-shuō xiáng-qǐng-ta chī-fàn-kàn-diànyǐngr, wèn-tā-shén-mo-shíhou-yǒu-gōngfu. Gāo-Xiáojie-shuō 'měitiān-dōu-kéyi, yīnwei-yǐjing-fàngjià-le. Bái-Xiānsheng-xiǎng háishi-ràng-'Gāo-Xiáojie shuō-yíge-shíhou bíjiáo-hǎo, suóyi-Gāo-Xiáojie-shuō xīngqīsān. Tā-yòu-wèn-Gāo-Xiáojie xǐ-huan-chī-shénmo. Gāo-Xiáojie-zhīdao Bái-Xiānsheng-yé-hén-xǐhuan chī-běifāng-fàn, tā-gàosu-'Bái-Xiānsheng shūdiàn-fùjìn yǒu-ge-běifāng-fànguǎr, dào-nèige-fànguǎr-chī 'hǎo-bu-hǎo. 'Bái-Xiānsheng 'dāngrán-xǐhuan-qù-le.

Tāmen-yòu-yánjiu zài-nǎr-kàn-diànyǐngr. 'Gāo-Xiáojie tīng-biéde-péng-you-shuō Zhōngguo-Diànyǐngryuàn-yǎn-de-nèibù-piānzi bú-cuò, shi-yíbù-lì-shǐ-piānzi. Tāmen-shuōhǎole chīle-wǎnfàn qù-kàn-'jiúdiǎn-nèi-yìchǎng. Kě-shi-bìděi-xiān-qu-mǎi-piào, yīnwei-piānzi-hǎo, kàn-de-rén-tài-duō.

Dì-èrshiyīkè

Bái-Wénshān-Xiānsheng xīngqīsān-xiàwǔ-liùdiǎn-zhōng jiù-dào-Gāo-jia qù-jiē-Gāo-Měiyīng-Xiáojie. Liǎngge-rén yíkuàr-dào-fànguǎr-qu-le. Dàole-fànguǎr-yǐhòu huǒji-guòlai wèn-tāmen-yào-chī-shénmo.   'Bái-Xiānsheng qǐng-huǒji bǎ-càidār-gěi-ta-nálai. Gāo-Xiáojie-gàosu-ta bú-yào-tài-duōde-cài, jiǎndān-yìdiǎr-chī, yàoburán diànyǐngr-kāi-yǎn-le, jiu-kànbujiàn gùshi-de-kāishǐ-shi-shénmo. Huǒji-'gàosu-tāmen zhèige-fànguǎr-zuì-hǎode-cài yǒu-shīzi-tóu, hóng-shāo-yú、kǎo-yāzi, chǎo-xiārér. Tā-hái-shuō yóuqíshi-tāmen-zhèrde-kǎo-yāzi shi-quán-guó-dì-yī-le.

Tāmen-liǎngge-rén xiǎng-yào-liǎngge-cài-yíge-tāng. Huǒji-gēn-Gāo-Xiáo-

jie-shuō, tāmende-chǎo-xiārér-hǎojíle. 'Gāo-Xiáojie jiu-yàole-ge-chǎo-xiā-
rér. 'Bái-Xiānsheng yào-yíge-hóng-shāo-yú. Tā-yòu-wèn-'Gāo-Xiáojie yào-
shénmo-tāng. Gāo-Xiáojie-shuō yào-zhū-ròu-báicài-tāng.   Bái-Xiānsheng-
hái-xiǎng zài-yào-yìdiár-jiǎozi. Gāo-Xiáojie-juéde liǎngge-rén liǎngge-cài-
yíge-tāng yídìng-gòu-chī-le. Tā-bú-ràng-'Bái-Xiānsheng zài-yào-jiǎozi-
le. Kěshi-'Gāo-Xiáojie xiǎng-chī-fàn-yǐhòu chī-diar-tián-diǎnxin. Tā-zhī-
dao-běifāng-fànguǎr chàbuduō-dōu-yǒu-xìngrér-dòufu.   Yí-wèn huǒji-shuō-
yǐjing-màiwán-le.

    Huǒji-bǎ-cài-nálai. Liǎngge-rén-yí-kàn zhèrde-cài zuòde-zhēn-piàoliang.
Kěshi-Bái-Xiānsheng-juéde háishi-'Gāo-jiade-cài-hǎo-chī.   Gāo-jiade-cài
zuòde-hǎo-shi-zhēnde, yīnwei-Gāo-Tàitai tā-tiāntian-yánjiu-zuò-fàn.   'Gāo-
Xiáojie gàosu-'Bái-Xiānsheng tā-mǔqin-xiáng-bǎ-zuò-fàn-de-jīngyan xiě-yì-
běn-shū-ne. Bái-Xiānsheng-juéde Zhōngguo-fàn hǎo-chī-shi-hǎo-chī, kěshi-
zuòqilai-tài-máfan-le. Gāo-Xiáojie-juéde yě-bù-zěnmo-máfan.

    Nèige-shíhou yǐjing-bādiǎn-bàn-le. Tāmen-liǎngge-rén hēle-yìdiǎr-chá,
ràng-huǒji-bǎ-zhàng-suàn-le, gěile-qián yé-gěile-huǒji-yìdiár-xiǎofèi, jiù-
zǒu-le.

                                    Dì-èrshi'èrkè

    Gāo-Xiānsheng, Gāo-Tàitai, Gāo-Xiáojie dào-Rìběn-lǚxíng-huílai-de-shí-
hou, suírán-'Bái-Xiānsheng dào-fēijīchǎng-qu-'jiē-tāmen, kěshi-méi-shuō-
hěn-duōde-huà. Dì-èrtiān-zǎochen 'Bái-Xiānsheng gěi-Gāo-jia-dǎ-ge-diàn-
huà, shuō-xiàwǔ dào-Gāo-jia-qu-'kàn-tāmen.   Gāo-Xiānsheng-hěn-gāoxìng
gàosu-Gāo-Tàitai ràng-'Bái-Xiānsheng zài-tāmen-jiā-lǐtou-chī-wǎnfàn.

    Bái-Xiānsheng-'lái-de-shíhou, Gāo-Xiáojie-kāi-de-mén. Yí-kànjian-'Bái-
Xiānsheng jiu-gàosu-ta Gāo-Xiānsheng-děng-ta-ne. 'Gāo-Xiānsheng tīngjian-
'Bái-Xiānsheng-lái-le, yě-chūlai-le. Tā-ràng-Gāo-Xiáojie bǎ-Rìběn-mǎilai-
de-diǎnxin náchulai, qǐng-Bái-Xiānsheng-chī.

    'Gāo-Xiānsheng zài-Rìběn-jiu-xiǎng mǎi-yìdiǎr-dōngxi huílai-sònggei-
'Bái-Xiānsheng. Tā-zài-shūdiàn-mǎi-shū kànjian-yìběn shuō-pīnyīn-gēn-
Hànzì-wèntí-de-shū, tā-jiu-mǎi-le dǎsuan-huílai-jiù-sònggei-'Bái-Xiānsheng.
Tā-jiànle-'Bái-Xiānsheng wèn-ta-zhèixiē-shíhou dōu-zuò-xiē-shénmo. Bái-
Xiānsheng-gàosu-ta 'nár-yě-méi-qù, tiāntian-kàn-shū, kànkan-péngyou, gěi-
fùqin-mǔqin-péngyoumen-xiě-xìn, hái-kànle-jǐcì-diànyǐngr.

    Gāo-Xiānsheng-gàosu-'Bái-Xiānsheng Rìběn-jiàoshòu-Zhōngshān-Xiānsheng
xiě-de-yìběn-shū-lǐtou shuō-guānyú-Hànzì gēn-pīnyīn-de-wèntí. Tā-wèn-

'Bái-Xiānsheng kǎishǐ-xué-Zhōngwén shi-zěnmo-xuéde, Měiguo-xuéxiào-jiāo-Zhōngwén dōu-yòng-shénmo-fāngfǎ, jiào-Bái-Xiānsheng-gàosu-ta.

Bái-Xiānsheng-gàosu-ta měige-xuéxiào-bù-yíyàng. Kāishǐ-xuéde-shíhou yǒude-yòng-'Hànzì-jiāo yǒude-yòng-'pīnyīn-jiāo. Gāo-Xiānsheng-juéde xué-'Zhōngwén yīnggāi-yòng-'Hànzì-jiāo, rúguǒ-yòng-pīnyīn gēn-niàn-'Yīngwén-chàbuduō-le, nà-jiù-'bú-shi-xué-Zhōngwén-le.

Kěshi-'Bái-Xiānsheng-juéde yòng-pīnyīn-fázi-hǎo. Xiān-huì-shuō-le-yǐ-hou, zài-xué-Hànzì jiù-róngyi-le. 'Gāo-Xiānsheng-xiǎng 'Bái-Xiānsheng-shuōde-bú-duì. Tā-shuō xuéle-'bàntiānde-pīnyīn lián-'yíge-Zhōngguo-zì yě-bu-rènshi. Rúguǒ-niàn-Zhōngguo-shū hái-děi-zài-kāishǐ-xué-Hànzì. Bái-Xiānsheng-gēn-tā-shuō xiān-míngbai-le cér-gēn-jùzi-de-yìsi-yǐhou, zài-xué-Hànzì-jiu-róngyi-duō-le. Bú-bì-jì-yìsi-le, zhǐ-jì-Hànzì jiu-kéyi-le.

'Gāo-Xiānsheng tīng-'Bái-Xiānsheng-shuōde yé-yǒu-yìdiǎr-duì tā-yòu-wèn Bái-Xiānsheng-kāishǐ-xué shi-zěnmo-xuéde. Bái-Xiānsheng-gàosu-ta kāishǐ-xué shi-tīng-lùyīn zìjǐ-liànxi-fāyīn. Gāo-Xiānsheng-yòu-wèn-ta xué-shuō-huà shi-zěnmo-xué. Bái-Xiānsheng-gàosu-ta xiān-xué-sìshēng zài-xué-cér, jùzi, qīngzhòngyīn-zài-nǎr yǐhòu-zài-xué-huìhuà. Tā-shuō xué-yǔyán-zuì-yàojǐnde shi-zhùyì-fāyīn. Pīnyīn-duì-fāyīn yǒu-bāngzhu. Zuì-yàojǐn-de-shi sìshēng-yào-zhǔn. Bái-Xiānsheng-shuō yòng-Hànzì-xué, nǐ-bú-rèn-shi-de-zì (bǐfang-shuō-zhèige-tā-zì), nǐ-jiu-méi-fázi zhīdao-zěnmo-niàn. Rúguǒ-yòng-pīnyīn yí-kàn-jiù-zhīdao tāde-yīn-shi-shénmo, jiù-huì-niàn-le. Gāo-Xiānsheng-juéde Bái-Xiānsheng-shuōde yé-yǒu-yìdiǎr-duì. Tā-méi-fá-zi-le. Zhí-hǎo-shuō pīnyīnde-fázi hǎo-shi-hǎo, kànqilai kěshi-méi-yǒu-Hànzì-piàoliang.

Dì-èrshisānkè

'Bái-Xiānsheng zài-Zhōngguo-niànle-yìnián-shū, xiànzài-yào-huídao-Měi-guo-qu niàn-dàxué-sìniánjí. Gāo-Xiānsheng Gāo-Tàitai Gāo-Xiáojie zài-zǒu-de-nèi-yìtiān zǎochen-hén-zǎo jiu-dào-ta-zhù-de-dìfang-qù-le, bāngzhu-ta-shōushi-dōngxi, érqiě xīwang-gēn-ta-duō-tán-yihuěr. Yǐhòu bù-zhīdào-shén-mo-shíhou cái-néng-zài-kànjian-ta.

'Bái-Xiānsheng kànjian-tāmen-hén-zǎo-jiu-lái-le, hěn-'xièxie-tāmen. Gāo-Tàitai-juéde yīnggāi-zǎo-yìdiǎr-dào-fēijīchǎng. Tāmen-zuòzhe-chē jiù-dào-fēijīchǎng-qù-le.

Gāo-Xiānsheng-tāmen dōu-hěn-xīwang Bái-Xiānsheng-'zài-huílai. Gāo-Xiānsheng-wèn-ta huíqu-yǐhòu shì-bu-shi jìxu-xué-yǔyánxué-gēn-wénxué.

Bái-Xiānsheng-gàosu-ta hái-jìxu-xué. Tā-hái-yào-yònggōng-xué. Gāo-Xiānsheng-wèn-ta zài-Rìběn-zhù-'jǐtiān. Tā-dǎsuan-zài-nèr-zhù bú - dào - yíge-
xīngqī jiù-huí-Měiguo. Tā-zài-Rìběn yào-qu-kàn-tāde-lǎoshī. Tā-zài-Měi-
guo-de-shíhou gēn-nèiwèi-lǎoshī dédao-bù-shǎo-de-xuéwen. Tā - gēn - Gāo-
Xiānsheng-shuō hěn-xièxie-Gāo-Xiānsheng-Gāo-Tàitai tāmen-duì-ta-nènmo-
hǎo. Tāmen-zhèng-zai-cāntīng zuòzhe-hē-chá-de-shíhou,   'Gāo-Xiānsheng
kànjian-tāmende-péngyou Wáng-Xiānsheng-Wáng-Tàitai xià-fēijī. Gāo-Xiānsheng-Gāo-Tàitai gēn-tāmen-shuō-huà-qu-le.

   Zhèr-zhí-yǒu Bái-Xiānsheng-gēn-Gāo-Xiáojie tāmen-liǎngge-rén-le.'Bái-
Xiānsheng jiù-gēn-Gāo-Xiáojie-shuō ta - zǒule - yǐhòu yǎo-hén-jiǔ-bú-jiàn-le,
xīwang-Gāo-Xiáojie gěi-ta-duō-xiě-xìn. Gāo-Xiáojie-wèn-ta zǒule - yǐhòu,
shì-bu-shi-'zhēnde-néng-huílai. Tā-shuō xīwang-'zhēnde-néng-huílai.

   Tāmen-liǎngge-rén zhèng-shuōzhe-huà-ne, Gāo-Xiānsheng-Gāo-Tàitai huí-
lai-le. Gāo-Xiānsheng-shuō shíhou-dào-le.   'Bái-Xiānsheng jiu-shàng-le-
fēijī.

UNIT V

Lesson 25 INTRODUCTION TO CHINESE CHARACTERS

I. Introductory Remarks

The earliest specimens of Chinese writing which have come down to us consist of characters written on bones, tortoise shells, and bronze vessels which were used in connection with certain ritual practices of the Shang Dynasty (about 1500–1028 B.C.).   In the 3,500 years since then the characters have been modified and formalized, but the basic principles have remained unaltered, so that the contemporary Chinese script is more closely related to the literary past than any other writing system.   One of the most stimulating aspects of the study of Chinese is the feeling of continuity and of contact with the past which is provided by a knowledge of the characters.

The evolution of the Chinese script through the past three and a half millenia is a fascinating but complicated subject.   Relationships between the written symbols and the spoken words of the Chinese language present even more complex problems.   Perhaps as your study of Chinese progresses, you will want to pursue some of these matters further.   Here, we give you only a brief introduction to the Chinese characters.

Some contemporary Chinese characters are formalized pictographs whose origins can be traced back to antiquity.   Two examples of these are the characters for <u>mǎ</u> 'horse' and <u>yú</u> 'fish,' for which we give below the evolution from the Shang Dynasty to the present.   Some contemporary characters are obscure in origin and others have a complex history.   A few characters with varied origins are illustrated below (III, "Examples of Chinese Characters"). In Section IV, "Explanation of Chinese Characters," a few notes are provided, including the modern pronunciation.

Although the characters with a clearly pictographic origin are perhaps of greatest interest, they now form only a small part of the total.   As the Chinese script developed and became more complex,   various new devices were intro-

duced into it. One device was to combine two or more characters to form a
new one whose meaning was related to that of the original characters. No. 18
in the "Examples of Chinese Characters" illustrates this sort of character
compounding. Another device was to assign additional extended meanings to
a character; this is illustrated in the "Explanations" for character No. 14
(yīn). Hardly anyone reading the characters for yīnwei 'because' would now
associate yīn with a man resting on a mat.

Indeed, sometimes there is no connection at all between the original significance of a character and a meaning it has subsequently acquired. Characters were often borrowed to represent sounds rather than meanings; an
analogous English example would be to write the word 'too' with the figure '2.'
Borrowings like these overloaded some characters to the point where it became necessary to suggest specific areas of meaning by adding another
element, called a radical; thus, character No. 16 (mén 'door' or 'gate')
is taken (in neutral tone) for its phonetic value and combined with a variant
form of No. 2 (rén 'man'), to form a new character (No.17) which is pronounced men and has a meaning connected with 'man' or 'person': it functions
as the pluralizing suffix for personal pronouns, as well as a few nouns denoting
persons.

All this would be complicated enough if this were the end of the story. The
fact, however, is that in the past three and a half millenia, so many changes
have occurred in the ways characters are pronounced and written that many of
them are now inconsistent and ambiguous, and others are shrouded in mystery.
The origin of No. 19 (yě 'also'), for example, is unknown; there is no indication in the symbol itself of its sound or its meaning. In the case of No. 20
(tā 'he'), although the left-hand part (a variant of rén 'man') tells us that the
character probably has something to do with human beings, the right-hand
part—a character which when used independently means 'also' and is pronounced yě—not only fails to identify a meaning more specifically but adds an
element of confusion regarding pronunciation.

As a result of these factors, although it is a stimulating and pleasurable
experience to learn some of the Chinese characters, learning many others involves a great deal of hard work.

One aspect of writing Chinese characters is learning the order in which the
strokes are written. The general rule is : top before bottom, left before right,
and inside before outside. There are so many exceptions to this, however,
that we have provided a table entitled "Stroke Order of Chinese Characters"
(Section V below) to show the sequence of strokes for each of the characters
discussed in Section III, as well as for the numbers from one to ten.

If one does not write the strokes in the proper sequence, the characters
will simply not look right. Pleasing appearance of characters is very important to the Chinese, who have elevated calligraphy to the rank of a fine art.
Some Chinese, like Mr. Gao, practice calligraphy the way a musician practices
his music. (This applies, of course, only to characters written with a brush;
those written with a pencil or fountain pen, as in ordinary usage, lack altogether the aesthetic appeal of characters done with a Chinese writing brush.)

There are several styles of writing Chinese characters. In the regular
style, each character is written deliberately and each stroke is made distinctly. In another style, the Running Hand, some of the strokes are run
together, but the relationship of these characters to the regular forms is
usually fairly clear. A still more cursive style, sometimes called Grass
Writing or Grass Characters, departs widely from the original. It is in this
latter form that Chinese writing has been most highly developed into an art in

which flow of line, relative thickness of strokes, and other elements give scope for the diverse talents of Chinese calligraphists.

Handwritten characters, in whatever style, differ in appearance from printed characters. There are also several styles of the latter, including some which are analogous to our italic, boldface, and even the distorted forms used in advertisements.

The various styles of writing Chinese, together with one printed version, are illustrated in this and the next lesson. In Lesson 26 (which repeats the contents of Lesson 1, so that you can study in characters the same material you learned the first time in transcription), the Dialogue is shown in a printed version and the rest in handwritten form. In the present lesson, the table "Styles of Writing Chinese Characters" (Section VII below) presents a group of characters each written in various styles: the regular form (written first with a fountain pen and again with a brush), the Running Hand, and the Grass Characters. The latter style also appears in "The Art of the Character-Scroll" (Section VIII below).*

---

* The brush-written characters in "Styles of Chinese Writing" below were done by Dr. John C. H. Wu, who—besides being a noted jurist—is also a poet and a calligraphist. Dr. Wu also contributed the character-scroll to illustrate this distinctively Chinese art form. The remaining characters in this lesson and the following one were written by Mrs. Teng Chia-yee. A former student of Professor Tung Tso-pin, one of China's leading authorities on the early script, Mrs. Teng also contributed to the analysis of the characters presented here.

II.   Evolution of m<u>ă</u> 'horse' and y<u>ú</u> 'fish'

mă   yú

      Shang Dynasty (about 1500–1028 B.C.). Earliest known form, found on bronze vessels and oracle bones.

      About 200 B.C. "Small Seal" characters developed in the Ch'in Dynasty (221–206 B.C.)

      About 200 B.C. A scribal script developed as a simplification of the "Small Seal" and other complex forms.

      About 100 A.D. "Model Script," a standardized form which replaced the previous variety of styles and has continued in use to the present.

III. Examples of Chinese Characters

(The first form shown is the modern form; the second is the
earliest known form.)

1. 馬 㣉		11. 車 車	
2. 魚 𩵋		12. 上 二	
3. 人 人		13. 下 二	
4. 大 大		14. 囚 囚	
5. 天 天		15. 黑 黑	
6. 水 水		16. 門 朋	
7. 山 山		17. 門 門	
8. 日 日		18. 明 明	
9. 月 月		19. 也 也	
10. 中 中		20. 他 他	

' IV. Explanations of Chinese Characters

1. Mǎ 'horse.'   Pictograph showing an eye, body and four legs, and a tail.

2. Yú 'fish.'   Pictograph showing scales and flippers.

3. Rén 'man.'   This is a sort of stick drawing of a man, showing only the two legs and a simple line for the rest of the body.

4. Dà 'big.'   Drawing of a man with arms.

5. Tiān 'heaven; deity.'   Drawing of a deity in the form of a man. From this comes the meaning 'heaven,' and from the latter the meaning of 'day.'

6. Shuǐ 'water.'   Pictograph of flowing water.

7. Shān 'mountain.'   Drawing of mountain peaks.

8. Rì 'sun.'   Pictograph of the sun. The character is used to represent the first syllable of Rìběn 'Japan.'

9. Yuè 'moon' or 'month.'   Early Chinese chronology was based on the lunar calendar.   The solar calendar used in the West was officially adopted after the establishment of the Chinese Republic in 1911.

10. Zhōng 'middle.'   Picture of a target being pierced by an arrow.

11. Chē 'cart, vehicle.'   Bird's-eye view showing two wheels, the axle, and the body.

12. Shàng 'above.'   A somewhat more abstract pictograph showing the earth as a straight line and a dot or stroke above it.

13. Xià 'below.'   Based on the same principle as No. 12.

14. Yīn. Pictograph of a man lying sprawled on a square mat. The character had an original meaning of 'rest upon.'   From this come the extended meanings 'rely on; based on, owing to, because of.'   The character is used to represent the first syllable of yīnwei 'because.'

15. Hēi 'black.'   Pictograph of a man with face and body covered with spots, perhaps black war paint.

16. Mén 'door, gate.'   Pictograph reminiscent of the doors in old-style saloons of America's West.

17. Men. Pluralizing suffix for pronouns. The right-hand part, mén 'gate,' is used here for its phonetic value. The left-hand part, a variant form of rén 'man,' indicates that the character has to do with human beings.

18. Míng 'bright.'   Compounded from the pictographs for rì 'sun' and yuè 'moon' to represent the somewhat more abstract idea of 'bright.'   As in

the corresponding English word, <u>míng</u> has acquired a figurative meaning in addition to its literal one. It is used to represent the first syllable of <u>míngbai</u> 'understand, be clear about' and the second syllable of <u>cōng-ming</u> 'bright, clever.'

19. <u>Yě</u> 'also.'   Origin unknown.

20. <u>Tā</u> 'he, she.'   Character compounded from <u>rén</u> on the left and <u>yě</u> on the right.   The pronunciation <u>tā</u> is related to neither of the components.

V. Stroke Order of Chinese Characters

	1	2	3	4	5	6	7	8	9	10	11	12
1. 馬	一	⺲	三	三	厗	馬	馬	馬	馬	馬		
2. 魚	ノ	ク	ク	각	뎡	甬	魚	魚	魚	魚	魚	
3. 人	ノ	人										
4. 大	一	ナ	大									
5. 天	一	二	于	天								
6. 水	亅	才	水	水								
7. 山	丨	山	山									
8. 日	丨	冂	日	日								
9. 月	ノ	刀	月	月								
10. 中	丶	冖	口	中								
11. 車	一	𠂉	斤	甘	亘	亘	車					
12. 上	丨	卜	上									
13. 下	一	丁	下									
14. 囚	丨	冂	冂	冈	冈	囚						
15. 黑	丶	冂	四	四	日	旦	甲	里	里	黑	黑	黑
16. 門	丨	𠃌	𠃌	𠃌	門	門	門					
17. 們	ノ	亻	门	伊	伊	伊	们	们	們	們		
18. 明	丶	刀	日	日	日	明	明	明				
19. 也	𠃌	力	也									
20. 他	ノ	亻	仢	仲	他							

VI.   The Numbers from One to Ten

	1	2	3	4	5
1.	一	一			
2.	二	ー	二		
3.	三	ー	三	三	
4.	四	㇑	冂	帀	四
5.	五	ー	丁	丆	五
6.	六	丶	二	六	六
7.	七	一	七		
8.	八	丿	八		
9.	九	丿	九		
10.	十	一	十		

VII. Styles of Writing Chinese Characters

Columns 1 and 5. Regular characters written with a fountain pen.

Columns 2 and 6. Regular characters written with a brush.

Columns 3 and 7. Running Hand characters written with a brush.

Columns 4 and 8. Grass characters written with a brush.

1	2	3	4		5	6	7	8
馬	馬	馬	馬		車	車	車	車
魚	魚	魚	魚		上	上	上	上
人	人	人	人		下	下	下	下
大	大	大	大		因	因	因	因
天	天	天	天		黑	黑	黑	黑
水	水	水	水		門	門	門	門
山	山	山	山		們	們	们	们
日	日	日	日		明	明	明	明
月	月	月	月		也	也	也	也
中	中	中	中		他	他	他	他

VIII.   The Art of the Character-Scroll

The following example of Grass Characters illustrates how they might appear
on a scroll hung on a wall for decorative purposes.

Lesson 26 LESSON 1 IN CHARACTER FORM

VOCABULARY

I. Transcription

The following transcriptions represent the sounds of the characters as they occur in actual usage in Lesson 1. Those in parentheses show their sounds as spoken in isolation, when this is different.

1. a	7. jiàn	13. nín	19. xiáo (xiǎo)
2. bái	8. jie (jiě)	14. sheng (shēng)	20. xiè, xie
3. dōu	9. ma	15. tā	21. yě
4. gāo	10. men	16. tài	22. zài
5. hǎo	11. ne	17. wǒ	
6. hěn	12. nǐ	18. xiān	

II. Stroke Order

1   2   3   4   5   6   7   8   9   10   11   12

1. 啊   丶 口 口 叮 阿 阿 阿 阿 阿 啊
2. 白   丿 亻 白 白 白
3. 都   一 十 土 耂 考 者 者 者 都 都
4. 高   丶 二 亠 古 古 盲 高 高 高 高
5. 好   乚 女 女 女 好 好
6. 很   丿 彳 彳 彳 彳 彳 很 很 很
7. 見   丨 刀 刀 月 月 見 見
8. 姐   乚 女 女 如 如 如 姐 姐
9. 嗎   丶 口 口 口 叩 叩 叩 嗎 嗎 嗎 嗎 嗎

454

	1	2	3	4	5	6	7	8	9	10	11	12
10. 們	ノ	亻	亻	们	伊	伊	伊	們	們	們		
11. 哪	丶	叮	口	叮	叨	叩	叨	哪	哪			
12. 你	ノ	亻	亻	伙	价	你	你					
13. 您	ノ	亻	亻	们	价	你	你	你	您	您	您	
14. 生	ノ	㇒	仁	牛	生							
15. 他	ノ	亻	伂	仲	他							
16. 太	一	ナ	大	太								
17. 我	ノ	二	于	手	扎	我	我					
18. 先	ノ	丿	屮	生	失	先						
19. 小	亅	小	小									
20. 謝	丶	二	六	言	言	言	言	訁	訃	訃	訃	訃
	訃	謝	謝	謝謝								
21. 也	フ	也	也									
22. 再	一	冂	冂	冄	再	再						

DIALOGUE

白：高先生，你好啊？

高：我很好，你呢？

白：好，謝謝您．高太太，高小姐也好嗎？

高：他們都好，謝謝．

白：再見，高先生．

高：再見，再見．

SENTENCE BUILD-UP

你
好
1. 你好。

您
2. 您好。

你
你們
3. 你們好?

好啊?
4. 你好啊?

好嗎?
5. 你好嗎?

白
先生
白先生
6. 白先生、您好嗎?

高
高先生
7. 高先生、您好嗎?

小姐
高小姐
8. 高小姐、您好嗎?

太太
高太太
9. 高太太您好嗎?

謝謝
10. 謝謝你、

我
我們
11. 我們謝謝你、

他
他們
12. 他們謝謝你、

很
很好
13. 我很好。

也
也很好
14. 他也很好、

都
都高
15. 他們都高嗎?

我好
你哪
16. 我好、你哪?

再見
17. 再見高太太、

PATTERN DRILLS

Pattern 1.1.

1. 好

2. 很好

3. 也好

4. 我好

5. 我很好

6. 也很高

7. 他們都好

8. 他們都很高

9. 高小姐也好

10. 白先生白太太都很高

Pattern 1.2.

1. 我謝謝他

2. 他謝謝我

3. 他謝謝你

4. 我也謝謝他

5. 他們都謝謝你

Pattern 1.3.

1. 你好嗎？

2. 他們都高嗎？

3. 白先生也好嗎？

4. 白太太白小姐都好嗎？

5. 你們都好嗎？

SUBSTITUTION TABLES

I

你　　好　　⋯
您　　　　　啊
你們　　　　嗎

II

白　先　生　⋯　好　⋯
高　太　太　你　　　啊
　　小　姐　您　　　嗎

III

白　先　生　謝謝　我　⋯
高　太　太　　　　你　們
　　小　姐　　　　他

IV

白　先　生　也　好　⋯
高　太　太　很　高　嗎
　　小　姐

BOY MEETS GIRL

白。　高小姐你好?
高。　好。您好嗎?
白。　很好。高先生，高太太都好嗎?
高。　都好。謝謝您。
白。　再見，再見。
高。　再見。白先生。

SUPPLEMENTARY MATERIALS AND INDEXES

MEMORIZATION EXERCISES (CHINESE)

The following exercises consist of Basic Sentences, some but not all of which are identical with the pattern sentences, and Dialogues, which consist chiefly of excerpts from the dialogues in the text. The two types of exercises together include all of the new structural patterns and vocabulary introduced in each lesson. Hence these exercises, despite their brevity, are of fundamental importance and should be thoroughly memorized to the point where the student has complete mastery over the material and can recite it with near-perfect pronunciation and fluency.

Tape recordings of these exercises are available from the Institute of Far Eastern Studies, Seton Hall University.* The dialogues are recorded four times: once at ordinary conversational speed; once with pauses for repetition; once to present the part of speaker A, followed by pauses in which the student responds with the part of speaker B; once with the roles reversed so that the student takes the part of speaker A in the pauses provided for this purpose and the recording takes the part of speaker B. In the English versions of the dialogues, given below, the two parts are separated to facilitate the dialogue between the student and the tape recorder.

LESSON 1

Basic Sentences

1. Tā-hén-hǎo.

2. Xièxie-ni.

3. Ní-yé-hǎo-ma?

Dialogue

Bái: 'Gāo-Xiānsheng, nín-hǎo-a?

Gāo: Wó-hén-hǎo. Ní-ne?

Bái: Hǎo, xièxie-nin. Gāo-Tàitai Gāo-Xiáojie yé-hǎo-ma?

Gāo: Tāmen-'dōu-hǎo, xièxie.

Bái: Zàijiàn, 'Gāo-Xiānsheng.

Gāo: Zàijiàn, zàijiàn.

---

* In South Orange, New Jersey, 07079.

LESSON 2

Basic Sentences

1. Tā-shi-'Yīngguo-rén.

2. Tā-huî-shuō-'Yīngguo-huà.

3. Tā-shî-bu-shi-'Yīngguo-rén?

4. Tā-shi-'Yīngguo-rén-bu-shi?

Dialogue

Bái: Qǐng-wèn-Xiānsheng, 'nín-quìxìng?

Qián: Wǒ-xìng-Qián. Nín-shi-'Wáng-Xiānsheng-ba?

Bái: Bú-shi. Wǒ-xìng-Bái.

Qián: Oh, nín-shi-'Bái-Xiānsheng. Nín-shi-'Yīngguo-rén-ma?

Bái: Bú-shi. Wǒ-shi-'Měiguo-rén. Qǐng-wèn, nín-huî-shuō-'Yīngguo-huà-
        bu-huî?

Qián: Wǒ-'bú-huî. 'Jiù-huî-shuō 'Zhōngguo-huà.

LESSON 3

Basic Sentences

1. Yìběn-shū-'duōshao-qián?

2. Zhèiběn-shū wǔkuài-èrmáo-qián.

3. Zhèi-sānběn-shū yígòng-liǎngkuài-sî.

Dialogue

Máo: Xiānsheng, nín-mǎi-shénmo?

Bái: Wǒ-yào-mǎi-shū. 'Nèiběn-shū 'duōshao-qián?

Máo: 'Néiběn?

Bái: Nèiběn-'Zhōngguo-shū.

Máo: 'Zhèiběn-shū shi-liǎngkuài-èrmáo-qián.

Bái: Hǎo, wó-mái-'liángběn.

Máo: Nín-'hái-yào mǎi-shénmo-ne?

Bái: Nǐmen-mài-'máobǐ-bu-mài?

Máo: Mài. Nín-yào-mái-jǐzhī-bǐ?

Bái: Sān-sîzhī.

LESSON 4

Basic Sentences

1. Zhèizhāng-zhǐ-liùfēn-qián.

2. Shíge-běnzi-jiǔmáo-bā.

3. Tā-yǒu-'qíběn-Zhōngwén-zìdiǎn, jiù-yǒu-'yìběn-Yīngwén-zìdiǎn.

4. 'Zhōngguo-dìtú, 'wàiguo-dìtú wǒmen-'dōu-mài.

5. Wǒmen-yé-yǒu-shū, yé-yóu-bǐ. Shū, bǐ wǒmen-'dōu-yǒu.

Dialogue

Bái: Yǒu-'mòshuǐ-ma?

Máo: Nín-mǎi-'shénmo-yánse-mòshuǐ?

Bái: Yǒu-'hóng-mòshuǐ-ma?

Máo: 'Méi-yǒu. Yǒu-'hēi-mòshuǐ, 'lán-mòshuǐ.

Bái: Yǒu-'qiānbǐ-méi-you?

Máo: Qiānbǐ, gāngbǐ, máobǐ— wǒmen-'dōu-yǒu.

Bái: Nǐmen-yǒu-dìtú-ma?

Máo: Yǒu. Nín-mǎi 'něiguó-dìtú?

Bái: Wó-mǎi-'Zhōngguo-dìtú.

Máo: 'Zhèige-dìtú-hén-hǎo. Nín-'mǎi-yìzhāng-ba.

Bái: Hǎo. Wǒ-hái-yào-yìběn-Zhōng-Yīng-zìdiǎn.

LESSON 5

Basic Sentences

1. Wáng-Xiānsheng-de-shū dōu-shi-Zhōngwén-shū.

2. Zhèi-shi-hén-hǎo-de-shū.

3. Tā-yě-shi-wó-hén-hǎo-de-péngyou.

4. Zhèiběn-shū-bú-shi-tāde, shi-wǒde.

Dialogue

Gāo: Wai! Wai! Ní-nǎr? Shi-'Bái-Xiānsheng-jiā-ma?

Bái: Shì. Nín-zháo-'něiwèi-shuō-huà?

Gāo: Qǐng-'Bái-Xiānsheng-shuō-huà.

Bái: Wǒ-jiù-shì. Qǐng-wèn, 'nín-shi-shéi?

Gāo: Wǒ-xìng-Gāo.

Bái: Oh, 'Gāo-Xiānsheng, 'háo-jiǔ-bú-jiàn. 'Nín-hǎo-ma?

Gāo: 'Hén-hǎo. 'Jīntian-wǎnshang ní-yǒu-gōngfu-ma? Wó-xiǎng qíng-ni-chī-
        fàn. 'Qǐdiǎn-zhōng-kéyi-ma?

Bái: Qǐng-wèn, xiànzài-shi-'shénmo-shíhou?

Gāo: Xiànzài-'sìdiǎn-zhōng.

Bái: Hǎo. Xièxie-nin. Qǐdiǎn-zhōng-jiàn.

LESSON 7

Basic Sentences

1. Tā-zài-Húběi háishi-zài-Húnán?

2. Nǐ-zài-'nǎr-chī-fàn?

3. Zài-Dōngběi-yǒu-dà-shān-ma?

4. Tā-yòubiārde-nèiwèi-xiānsheng shi-'Shāndong-rén, tā-zuǒbiār-de-shi-
   'Shānxi-rén.

Dialogue

Bái: 'Gāo-Xiānsheng jīntian-wǎnshang qíng-wǒ-chī-fàn.   Nǐ-'zhīdao-bu-
        zhídào shi-zài-zhèr-ne háishi-zài-ta-jiā-ne?

Máo: Zài-ta-'jiā-chī-fàn.

Bái: Tā-jiā-zài-nǎr? Shi-zài-chéng-lǐtou háishi-zài-chéng-wàitou?

Máo: Gāo-Xiānsheng-jiā zài-chéngwài, jiù-zài-zhèitiáo-lùde-běibiar, yíge-
        xiǎo-shānshang.

Bái: Zài-nèige-shānshang yóu-'jísuǒr-fángzi?

Máo: Nèr-yígòng jiù-yǒu-'sānsuǒr-fángzi.   Xībiar yǒu-yìsuǒr-'dà-fángzi.
        Dōngbiar yǒu-yìsuór-'xiǎo-fángzi.   Zhōngjiàrde-fángzi jiù-shi-Gāo-
        Xiāsheng-jiā.   Nánbiar-shānxià shi-Zhōngshān-Lù.   Zhōngshān-Lù-
        qiánbiar yǒu-yíge-dà-gōngyuán.   Shān-hòutou yǒu-yíge-xiǎo-hú.

LESSON 8

Basic Sentences

1. Túshūguǎn-lí-zhèr-yuǎn-ma?

2. Túshūguǎn-lí-zhèr-yǒu-sānlǐ-lù.

3. Tā-zài-túshūguǎn-kàn-shū.

4. Zhōngguo-zì-tài-nán-xiě. Wǒ-jiù-néng-xiě hén-jiǎndānde-zì.

5. Shi-'nǐ-duì háishi-'tā-duì?

Dialogue

Bái: 'Zhèr-yǒu-túshūguǎn-méi-yǒu?

Máo: Yǒu. Zhèrde-túshūguǎn hěn-dà, shū-bù-shǎo. Měitiān yóu-hěn-duō-xuésheng zài-nèr-kàn-shū. Nín-yào-jiè-shū-ma?

Bái: Wó-xiǎng-jiè-'Zhōngwén-shū.

Máo: Nín-zài-dàxué xué-shénmo?

Bái: Wǒ-niàn-wénxué. .

Máo: Nín-xǐhuan-'Zhōngguo-wénxué-ma?

Bái: Wó-hén-xǐhuan-'Zhōngguo-wénxué.

Máo: 'Zhōngguo-wénxué-róngyi háishi-'Yīngguo-wénxué-róngyi-ne?

Bái: 'Dōu-hěn-nán-xué. Túshūguǎn-zài-nǎr? Lí-zhèr-yuǎn-ma?

Máo: Túshūguǎn-hén-yuǎn.

Bái: Lí-zhèr-duó-yuǎn?

Máo: Lí-zhèr-yǒu-qílǐ-duō-lù.

Bái: Oh, qī-bālǐ-lù bú-'tài-yuǎn.

Máo: Yě-bú-jìn.

LESSON 9

Basic Sentences

1. Wǒ-xiān-dào-túshūguǎn, hòu-dào-nǐ-jiā-qu.

2. Wǒ-míngtian-zuò-chē-qu-kàn-ta.

3. Cóng-zhèr-dào-túshūguǎn-'zěnmo-zǒu?

4. Cóng-gōngyuán-mén-kǒur-wàng-béi-guǎi.

5. Qǐng-nín-'zài-shuō.

Dialogue

Bái: Cóng-shūdiàn-dào-túshūguǎn 'zěnmo-zǒu?

Máo: Nín-cóng-zhèr wàng-nán-yìzhí-zǒu, wàng-xī-guǎi, guò-báge-lù-kǒur, jiù-shi-túshūguǎn.

Bái: Cóng-zhèr-dào-túshūguǎn-nèr yǒu-'shénmo-chē-kéyi-zuò-ne?

Máo: Gōnggòng-qìchē diànchē 'dōu-yǒu. Nín-xiǎng-zuò-'shénmo-chē-ne?

Bái: Wó-xiǎng-zuò-gōnggòng-qìchē-qu. Gōnggòng-qìchē-zhàn-zài-nǎr?

Máo: Lí-shūdiàn-bù-yuǎn.

Bái: Zuò-'jǐhào-chē-ne?

Máo: Zuò-'sānhào-chē. Yìzhí-jiù-dào-túshūguǎn.

Bái: Cóng-túshūguǎn dào-'Gāo-Xiānsheng-jiā 'zěnmo-zǒu?

Máo: Nín-shàng-chē dào-Zhōngshān-Lù. Zài-gōngyuán-mén-kǒur-xià-chē.

Bái: Xièxie-ni.

Máo: Nín-míngtian-'lái-bu-lái?

Bái: Huòzhě-wǒ-míngtian-'hái-lái-mǎi-shū.

LESSON 10

Basic Sentences

1. Màipiàoyuán-bǐ-wǒ-gāo-yìdiǎr, ní-bǐ-tā-'gèng-gāo.

2. Xiànzài-chàbuduō-bādiǎn-sānkè.   Wó-jiúdiǎn-chà-wǔfēn jiù-yào-zuò-chē
   dào-Yuǎndōng-Dàxué-qu.

3. Tā-mǎi-shū mǎide-bǐ-wǒ-duō.

4. Tāmen-zài-gōnggòng-qìchēshang-tán-huà.

Dialogue

MPY: Nín-Zhōngwén-shuōde-'zhēn-hǎo.

Bái: Wǒ-shuōde-'bù-hǎo. Shuōde-tài-màn. Yóu-hěn-duō-wàiguo-rén shuōde-
        bǐ-wó-hǎo-de-duō.

MPY: Nín-jiāli dōu-yǒu-'shénmo-rén?

Bái: Wǒ-jiāli-yǒu-fùqin-mǔqin, hái-yǒu-yíge-dìdi, yíge-mèimei.

MPY: Nín-fùqin-zuò-'shénmo-shì?

Bái: Wǒ-fùqin shi-'zhōngxué-jiàoyuán.   Mǔqin shi-'xiǎoxué-jiàoyuán.   'Nǐ-
        jiāli dōu-yǒu-'shénmo-rén?

MPY: Wó-yǒu-tàitai, hái-yóu-liǎngge-háizi.

Bái: Nán-háizi háishi-nǚ-háizi-ne?

MPY: Yíge-'nán-háizi, yíge-'nǚ-háizi.

Bái: Tāmen-duó-dà?

MPY: Nán-háizi-qīsuì, nǚ-háizi-liǎngsuì.

Bái: Tāmen-míngzi-dōu-jiào-shénmo?

MPY: Nán-háizi-jiào-Láohu. Nǚ-háizi-jiào-Xiǎomèi.

Song

Sānge-láohu,	Yíge-méi-you-wěiba,
Sānge-láohu,	Yíge-méi-you-wěiba,
Pǎode-kuài,	Zhēn-qíguài,
Pǎode-kuài.	Zhēn-qíguài.

LESSON 11

Basic Sentences

1. Wǒ-shi-zuótian-wǎnshang-bādiǎn-bàn 'yùjian-tā-de.

2. Tā-shi-jīnnian-èryue-sānhào líkāi-de-Měiguo.

3. Shéi-gàosu-ni wǒ-bú-shi-zài-jiā-chī-de-wǎnfàn?

4. Nǐ-zài-'nǎr-kànjian-ta-de?

Dialogue

Qián: Nín-cháng-dào-túshūguǎn-lái-ma?

Bái: Bù. Wǒ-jīntian shi-dì-yícì-lái. Nín-ne?

Qián: 'Wó-yě-bù-cháng-lái. Nín-shi-'shénmo-shíhou dào-Zhōngguo-lái-de?

Bái: Wǒ-shi-qùnian-báyue-qīhào-lái-de.

Qián: Nín-zuò-'chuán-lái-de háishi-zuò-'fēijī-lái-de?

Bái: Wǒ-dào-Rìběn shi-zuò-chuán, cóng-Rìběn-dào-Zhōngguo shi-zuò-'fēijī-lái-de.

Qián: 'Chuán-zǒude-hěn-màn-ba.

Bái: Suírán-hěn-màn, kěshi-zuò-chuán hén-yǒu-yìsi. Kéyi-rènshi hěn-duō-péngyou.

Qián: Rúguǒ-nín-jīntian-wǎnshang yǒu-gōngfu, qǐng-dào-wǒ-jiā-lái zuòyizuò-tántan.

Bái: Hǎo. Xièxie-nín. Rúguó-wǎnshang-yǒu-gōngfu, wǒ-'yídìng-dào-fǔshang-bàifang.

Qián: Xīwang-nín-wǎnshang 'yídìng-néng-lái.

LESSON 13

Basic Sentences

1. Nǐ-chīle-fàn-le-ma?

2. Wǒmen-chīle-zǎofàn-jìu-zǒu-le.

3. Tā-xiànzài-'hǎole-méi-you?

4. Wǒ-jīntian-yǐjing-kànle-'liángběn-shū-le. Wǒ-bú-zài-kàn-le.

5. Wǒmen-xià-xīngqī 'yòu-kǎo-shū-le.

Dialogue

Bái: Nǐ-cóng-xuéxiào huí-jiā-hén-wǎn-ne.

Gāo: Yīnwei-xià-kè-yǐhòu wǒmen-xuéxiào-yǒu-yìdiǎr-shì, suóyi-'wǎn-le-yìdiǎr. Jīntian-wǎnshang wǒ-fùqin-qǐng-nín-chī-fàn, 'duì-bu-duì?

Bái: Duì-le. Tài-'máfan-nǐmen-le.

Gāo: 'Bù-máfan. Huānyíng-nín-lái.

Bái: Wǒ-hái-bu-zhīdào nǐ-zài-'nèige-xuéxiào-niàn-shū-ne.

Gāo: Wǒ-zài-Dì-'yī-Zhōngxué-niàn-shū.

Bái: 'Jǐniánjí?

Gāo: Gāozhōng-'sānniánjí. Jīnnián-wǒ-jiù-bìyè-le.

Bái: Wó-xiǎng nǐ-'yídìng-hén-cōngming.

Gāo: Wǒ-'bù-cōngming.

Bái: Nǐ-kèqi-ne. Nǐ-xǐhuan-kàn-diànyǐngr-ma? Nǐ-kǎoshì-yǐhòu, wó-qǐng-ni-kàn-diànyǐngr, hǎo-ma?

Gāo: Xièxie-nin. 'Bái-Xiānsheng, qǐng-wèn xiànzài-'jídiǎn-zhōng-le? Wó-zǎochen-hěn-máng. Chīle-zǎofàn-jiù-zǒule, wàngle-dài-biǎo-le.

Bái: Xiànzài chà-yíkè-qīdiǎn.

LESSON 14

Basic Sentences

1. Tā-xiěde-nèibén-shū nǐ-kànguo-le-ma?

2. Nǐ-chīguo-'Zhōngguo-fàn-méi-you?

3. Tā-Zhōngguo-huà-'dōu-tīngdedǒng, yě-shuōde-shífēn-hǎo.

4. Wàn-Xiānsheng-duì-nǐ-shuōde-huà nǐ-'dōu-tīngdedǒng-ma?

5. Yìhuěr-wǒ-jiu-kéyi-kànjian nǐ-huàde-huàr-le.

Dialogue

Gāo: Nǐmen-Yuǎn-Dà yǒu-'duōshao-xuésheng?

Bái: Yǒu-'sānqiān-wúbǎi-duō-rén.   'Gāo-Xiáojie, nǐ-zhōngxué-bìyè-yǐhòu xiǎng-xué-shénmo-ne?

Gāo: Wó-xiǎng-xué-wénxué, kěshi-wó-xiǎng wǒ-yídìng-kǎobushàng-dàxué. Rúguó-wó-kǎobushàng-dàxué wǒ-jiù-xué-huà-huàr. 'Bái-Xiānsheng, 'nín-shi-xué-shénmo-de?

Bái: Wǒ-yuánlái shi-xiǎng-xué-'kēxué-de, kěshi-wǒ-duì-'wàiguo-huà hén-yǒu-xìngqu, 'gèng-xǐhuan-Zhōngguo-huà, suóyi-wǒ-zài-Měiguo jiù-xué-Zhōngguo-huà, niàn-Zhōngguo-shū. Xiànzài-wǒ-dào-Zhōngguo-lái xué-Zhōngguo-wénxué, yě-xué-yǔyánxué.

Gāo: Xué-yǔyánxué-'zěnmo-xué-ne?

Bái: Xué-yǔyánxué shi-yòng-'kēxuéde-fāngfǎ yánjiu-yǔyán.

Gāo: Nín-xǐhuan-xiě-Zhōngguo-zì-ma? Nín-yòng-Zhōngwén-xiě-xìn xiědeliǎo-xiěbuliǎo?

Bái: Suírán-xiĕdeliăo, kĕshi-xiĕ-de-bu-hăo. Wó-gĕi-Zhōngguo-péngyou-xiĕ-
        xìn xǐhuan-yòng-Zhōngwén-xiĕ. Nǐ-fùqin-zì xiĕde-hén-hăo.

Gāo: Tā-chàbuduō-mĕitiān-xiĕ-zì.

Bái: Nǐ-méi-tīngshuō-ma:

                    Huó-dào-lăo,
                    Xué-dào-lăo,
                    Hái-yóu-sānfēn
                    Xuébudào.

Gāo: Bù-zhí-yŏu-'sānfēn-ba!

                        LESSON 15

                       Basic Sentences

1. Wŏ-xiànzài-gāi-zŏu-le, kĕshi-nǐ-bú-bì-zŏu.

2. Wŏ-jīntian-dĕi-kànwán-zhèibĕn-shū.

3. Wŏ-dāngrán-yīngdāng-gēn-ta-yíkuàr-qù-yícì.

4. Wŏ-xué-Zhōngwén yǐjing-yŏu-sānnián-le. Hái-yào-xué liăng-sān-niánde-
    Zhōngwén.

5. Tā-kànle-yíge-zhōngtóude-shū-le.

                         Dialogue

Gāo: 'Bái-Xiānsheng, nín-xuéle-'jǐniánde-Zhōngwén-le?

Bái: Wŏ-niàn-'Zhōngwén chàbuduō-yǐjing-yóu-'wŭnián-le.

Gāo: Suóyi-nínde-Zhōngwén-nènmo-hăo-ne. Nín-zài-Mĕiguo-xué-Zhōngwén
        'zĕnmo-xué-ne?

Bái: Wŏmen-kāishǐ-'xué-de-shíhou mĕitiān-shàng-'yíge-zhōngtóude-kè. Jiào-
        yuán-jiāo-wŏmen-shuō. Xià-kè-yǐhòu wŏmen-jiu-tīng-lùyīnjīde-lùyīn.

Gāo: Nín-dào-Zhōngguo zuò-'fēijī háishi-zuò-'chuán-lái-de-ne?

Bái: Wŏ-xiān-cóng-Niŭyue zuò-qìchē-dào-Sānfánshì. Wŏ-zuòle-'liùtiān-de-
        qìchē cái-dào-ner. Zài-Sānfánshì-zhùle-bātiān. Wŏ-yòu-zuòle-shítiānde-
        chuán dào-Rìbĕn. Zài-Rìbĕn-zhùle-yíge-xīngqī, jiù-zuò-fēijī-dào-
        'Zhōngguo-lái-le.

Gāo: Wŏ-hái-méi-zuòguo-fēijī-ne. Yŏu-jīhui wó-dĕi-'zuò-yícì.

Bái: Jiānglái nǐ-bìyè-yǐhòu yīnggāi-zuò-fēijī dào-biéde-dìfang-qu-wárwar.

Gāo: Wŏ-fùqin-mŭqin dōu-qùguo-Rìbĕn. Tāmen-zài-nèr zhùle-liăngge-duō-
        yuè-ne, hái-măile-hĕn-duō Rìbĕn-dōngxi.

LESSON 16

Basic Sentences

1. Yǒude-shi-zài-'Hángzhōu-mǎide, yǒude-shi-zài-'Sūzhou-mǎide.

2. 'Shéi-dōu-shuō tā-hén-yǒu-xuéwen.

3. Ní-bǎ-zhèi-jǐge-dōngxi dōu-nájin-fángzi-qu.

4. Wǒ-nèiren-búdàn-huî-shuō-Zhōngguo-huà, érqiě-shuōde-shífēn-hǎo.

5. Lián-wǒ-dōu-méi-fázi-gēn-tā-shuō-huà-le.

Dialogue

Bái:　　　Fúshang-zhèige-dìfang hén-hǎo-a.

Gāo-Xiáojie:　Suóyi-wǒ-fùqin 'měitiān-dōu-yào-chūqu-zóuzou. Lián-xīngqítiān tā-méi-shì dōu-yào-chūqu. Chūqu-huílai dōu-shi-zǒu-lù.

Bái:　　　Ní-fùqin 'yé-xǐhuan-lǚxíng-ma?

Gāo-Xiáojie:　Tā-'zuì-xǐhuan-lǚxíng-le. . . . Dào-le. Mā! Kāi-mén! 'Kèren-lái-le.

Bái:　　　Gāo-Tàitai, 'háo-jiǔ-bú-jiàn. Nín-hǎo?

Gāo-Tàitai:　Oh, 'Bái-Xiānsheng-lái-le. 'Háo-jiǔ-bú-jiàn. Ní-hǎo-ma?

Bái:　　　Gāo-Xiānsheng, nín-hǎo?

Gāo-Xiānsheng:　'Bái-Xiānsheng, hǎo-ma? Lái-lái. Wó-géi-nǐmen-liǎngwèi-'jièshao-jièshao. Zhèiwèi-shi-Wàn-Jiàoshòu. Zhèiwèi-shi-'Bái-Xiān-sheng.

Bái:　　　Jiúyǎng.

Wàn:　　　Ní-hǎo. . . . Gāo-Xiáojie cōngming-piàoliang. Shū-niànde-hǎo, huàr-huà-de-hǎo.

Bái:　　　Duì-le. 'Gāo-Xiáojie, wǒmen-děi-'kànkan-nǐde-huàr-le.

Gāo-Xiáojie:　Bié-kàn-le. Wǒ-huà-de-bù-hǎo.

Bái:　　　Qíng-ní-bǎ-huàr-dōu-náchulai wǒmen-kànkan.

Gāo-Xiānsheng:　Měiyīng, bá-ní-'suóyǒu-de-huàr dōu-náchu-lai. Qǐng-tāmen-liǎngwèi-kànkan.

Bái:　　　Zhèizhāng-shānshuǐ-huàr-'zhēn-hǎo. Huà-de-shi-nǎr-a?

Gāo-Xiáojie:　Zhèi-jiu-shi-Hángzhou-a.

Bái:　　　Oh, zhè-jiu-shi-Hángzhou-a. 'Zhēn-piàoliang.

Wàn:　　　Zhōngguo yǒu-yíjù-huà-shuō:

'Shàng-yǒu-tiāntáng,
'Xià-yǒu-Sū-Háng.

Shuōde-yì-'diár-yě-bú-cuò.

LESSON 17

Basic Sentences

1. Jīntiande-tiānqi méi-yǒu-zuótiande-nènmo-nuǎnhuo.

2. Zhèiyàngde-chá gēn-nèiyàngde-yíyàng-hǎo.

3. Yóu-hǎoxiē-jiàoshòu dōu-bǎ-ta-kànzuò sìniánjíde-xuésheng.

4. Nèisuǒ-fángzi-dàde-bùdeliǎo, dàde-méi-rén-yào-mǎi.

5. Wǒ-měiyuè-de-qián shǎode-bùdeliǎo, bú-gòu-mǎi-fángzi.

6. Zhèixiē-Zhōngguo-xuésheng shuō-Yīngwén shuōde-gēn-Měiguo-rén-yíyàng-hǎo.

Dialogue

Bái: Gāo-Xiáojie shi-'Sūzhou-rén-a?

Wàn: Lǎo-Gāo zài-Sūzhou-rènshi-de-Gāo-Tàitai.   Tāmen-liǎngge-rén zái-'Sūzhou-jiēhūn, Gāo-Xiáojie shi-zài-'Sūzhou-shēng-de.   Gāo-'Xiáojie-zhǎngde gēn-Gāo-'Tàitai-yíyàng-piàoliang.

Bái: Oh, suóyi-Gāo-Tàitai Gāo-Xiáojie nènmo-piàoliang-ne!

Wàn: Hángzhou-shānshuí-yǒu-míng. Sūzhou-nǔ-rén-yǒu-míng. . . . Zhèi-jiǔ-'zhēn-hǎo.

Bái: Shi-shénmo-jiǔ-a?

Gāo: Shi-Méigui-Lù. Lǎo-Wàn, zěnmoyàng, wǒmen-hēle-zhèibēi huá-'quán-hǎo-bu-hǎo? . . . 'Bái-Xiānsheng, nǐ-kàn. Yǒu-yìsi-ma?

Bái: 'Hén-yǒu-yìsi. Wó-hěn-qíguài wèi-shénmo-'yíng-de-rén bu-hē-jiǔ-ne?

Gāo: Ní-'děng-yìhuěr jiù-míngbai-le.

LESSON 19

Basic Sentences

1. Tā-zuòde-táng-cù-yú bú-shi-tài-tián jiù-shi-tài-suān.

2. Wó-hén-xiǎng-duō-hē-yìdiǎr-niú-ròu-tāng, kěshi-wó-yǐjing-chī-bǎo-le.

3. Tāmen-chīzhe-fàn-shuō-huà.

4. Chúle-shuō-"Guòjiǎng"-yǐwài tā-hái-shuō-shénmo-ne?

5. Kuàizi-zài-nǎr? Wó-zhǎolai-zhǎoqù-dōu-zhǎobuzháo.

6. Hóng-shāo-zhū-ròu gēn-hóng-shāo-yú wǒ-chī-shi-chīguo, kěshi-wǒ-bù-xǐhuan.

Dialogue

Bái: He! Bùdéliǎo! Zěnmo-'zhènmo-duōde-cài-a!

Gāo: Biàn-fàn, 'méi-yǒu-shénmo-cài. Nǐmen-liǎngwèi suíbiàn-zuò, suíbiàn-
        chī.

Bái: 'Zhèige-cài-shi-shénmo?

Gāo: Zhèi-shi-chǎo-báicài.

Bái: Zhèige-ne?

Gāo: Zhèi-shi-hóng-shāo-jī.

Bái: 'Zhèige-wǒ-zhīdao. Shi-chǎo-dòufu.

Gāo: 'Bái-Xiānsheng, nǐ-zài-Měiguo yě-cháng-chī-'Zhōngguo-cài-ma?

Bái: Cháng-chī.

Gāo: Měiguo-de-Zhōngguo-cài hǎo-chī-ma?

Bái: Zài-Měiguo-de-'Zhōngguo-fànguǎr chàbuduo-dōu-shi-Guǎngdong-fànguǎr.
        Tāmen-zuò-de hǎo-shi-hǎo, kěshi-méi-yǒu-Gāo-Tàitai-zuò-de zhènmo-
        hǎo-chī. Shízi-tóu-zài-Měiguo chúle-Sānfánshì-Niǔyue jǐge-dà-chéng-
        yǐwài, jiu-chībuzháo.

LESSON 20

Basic Sentences

1. Nǐ-yì-géi-wó-dǎ-diànhuà wǒ-jiu-gāoxìng-jíle.

2. Tā-shi-běifāng-rén shi-nánfāng-rén wǒ-dōu-cāibuzháo.

3. Kǒngpà-nènmo-dàde-dōngxi tā-nábuqǐlái.

4. Tā-Zhōngwén-zěnmo-shuōde-nènmo-hǎo-a? . . . Tā-shēngzài-Zhōngguo-
   me.

5. Xiānsheng-dàgài-bú-yào-wǒmen-bǎ-shū-dǎkai.

6. Wǒ-xiángqǐlai-le, wǒ-jīntian-bìděi-dào-chē-zhàn-qu jiē-Gāo-Xiānsheng.

Dialogue

Bái: Měiyǐng, zěnmoyàng? Kǎowán-le-ma? Kǎode-'hǎo-bu-hǎo?

Gāo: Hai, bié-tí-le. Yīngwén Zhōngwén kǎode-hái-hǎo, kěshi-shùxué kǎode-
        zāogāo-jíle. Wǒ-kàncuò-le-tímu.

Bái: Zhèi-yě-shi-kǎoshì 'cháng-yǒu-de-shìqing.

Gāo: Xiànzài-wǒ-gàosu-ni-yíjiàn-shìqing. Xiànzài-wǒmen-fàngjià-le, wǒ-
        fùqin-mǔqin jiào-wǒ-gēn-tāmen-yíkuàr-dào-Rìběn-qu.

Bái: Nènmo-wó-déi-qíng-ni-chī-fàn. Chī-fàn-yǐhòu wǒmen-zài-qu-kàn-
        diànyǐngr, 'hǎo-bu-hǎo? Nǐ-xǐhuan-chī-shénmo-ne?

Gāo: Wǒ-'shénmo-dōu-xǐhuan-chī. Wó-'xiángqǐlái-le— shūdiàn-fùjìn yǒu-
        yíge-běifāng-fànguǎr jiào-Wànnián-Fànguǎr. Nǐ-zhīdao ma?

Bái: Nǐ-shuō-wó-'xiángqǐlái-le. Wǒmen-jiu-dào-nèr-qù-chī. Wǒmen-dào-
        nǎr-kàn-diànyǐngr-qu-ne?

Gāo: Tīngshuō Zhōngguo-Diànyǐngryuàn yǎn-de-nèibù-piānzi bú-cuò.   Shì-
        yíbù-lìshǐ-piānzi. Gùshi-xiěde-hǎo, yǎnyuán-yǎnde-hǎo.

Bái: Wǒmen-kàn-jiúdiǎn-nèichǎng-hǎo-ma?

Gāo: Kéyi.

LESSON 21

Basic Sentences

1. Nǐ-dǎsuan-mái-'néizhǒng-chá-wǎn jiù-mái-'néizhǒng.

2. Tā-lǎo-shuō-wǒde-jīngyan-bú-gòu,   kěshi-wǒ-juéde wǒde-jīngyan-bǐ-tā-
   duōde-duō.

3. Zěnmo-méi-yǒu-jiàngyóu fàngzài-chǎo-cài-lǐtou?

4. Nǐ-gāngcái-mǎide-nèige-chá-hú jiùshi-zài-Zhōngguo-yě-mǎibudào.

5. Wǒ-bú-dà-xǐhuan kàn-hěn-chángde-piānzi.

6. Nǐ-duō-gěi-ta-yìdiǎr-qián, yàoburán-tā-bú-mài.

Dialogue

Huǒji: Gěi-nín-cài-dār.

Bái: Qǐng-ni-bāngzhu-wǒmen xiáng-liǎngge-cài.

Huǒji: Hǎo. Wǒ-jièshao-nín-jǐyàng wǒmen-zhèr-'zuì-hǎode-cài. Wǒmen-zhèr
        hóng-shāo-yú、 chǎo-xiā-rér、 kǎo-yāzi, dōu-hǎo. Yóuqíshi-nèige-kǎo-
        yāzi dàgài-wǒmen-kéyi-shuō shi-quán-guó-dì-yī-le.   Wǒmen-zhèrde-
        jiǎozi、 chǎo-miàn yě-bú-cuò.

Bái: 'Jiǎozi-zěnmo-yào? Mài-duōshao-qián?

Huǒji: Jiǎozi nín-chī-duōshao jiù-yào-duōshao. Yíkuài-liǎngmáo-qián-shíge.

Bái: Hǎo, wǒmen-bú-gòu-zài-shuō-ba. Chīwán-le wǒmen-yào-ge-'tián-diǎnxin.
        Xìngrér-dòufu-yǒu-ma?

Huǒji: Duìbuqǐ, 'gāng-màiwán. Nín-yào-diar-biéde-ba?

Bái: Yǒu-xìngrér-chá-ma?

Huǒji: Yǒu.

Bái: Qǐng-lái-liángwǎn. . . . Huǒji, suàn-zhàng.

Huǒji: Shì. Yígòng-sìkuài-sānmáo-liù.

Bái: Zhè-shi-wǔkuài. Bú-bì-zhǎo-le. Shèngxia-de-géi-xiǎofèi-le.

Huǒji: Xièxie-nín. Liǎngwèi-màn-zǒu. Zàijiàn.

LESSON 22

Basic Sentences

1. "Shēngyīn"-de-"shēng"-zì yóu-jǐhuá?

2. Guānyu-nèige-wèntí, wǒ-zhèng-zài-yánjiu-ne.

3. Rénrén-dōu-zhīdao, rúguǒ-tóngshí-yòu-xué-fāyīn, yòu-xué-Hànzì, yòu-xué-wénfǎ, nánchu-duō-hǎochu-shǎo.

4. Yíge-jùzi yīnjié-yuè-duō yuè-nán-shuō.

5. Zhèixiē-shū yíbùfen-sònggei-nǐ, yíbùfen-sònggei-tā.

6. Nǐ-déi-hǎohāorde-xué-sìshēng. Sìshēng-bù-zhǔn, Zhōngwén-yídìng-shuōde-bù-hǎo.

Dialogue

Gāo: Zài-Měiguo-xuéxiàolǐ jiāo-de-fāngfǎ-dōu-yíyàng-ma?

Bái: Měiguo-xuéxiào-lǐtou jiāo-de-fázi-bù-yíyàng. 'Yǒude-kāishǐ-jiù-xué-Hànzì, 'yǒude-yòng-pīnyīn-xué.

Gāo: Nǐ-kāishǐ-xué yídìng-hěn-yònggōng-le.

Bái: Nèige-shíhou wó-hěn-yònggōng. Měitiān-tīng-lùyīn, zìjǐ-gēn-zìjǐ-shuō-huà, liànxi-fāyīn, bá-měitiān-xué-de dōu-jìzhu. Yuè-xué-yuè-yǒu-xìngqu.

Gāo: Nǐ-kāishǐ shi-xiān-xué-shuō-huà-ma?

Bái: Shì, wǒ-xiān-xué-shuō-huà. Wǒ-kāishǐ-xué-sìshēng gēn-qīngzhòngyīn, yǐhòu-xué-cér (bǐfang-shuō shū、tàitai jiù-shi-cér) gēn-duǎn-jùzi, zài-xué-huìhuà.

Gāo: Xué-yǔyán 'tèbié-yīnggāi-zhùyì-de shi-shénmo?

Bái: Tèbié-yào-zhùyì-de shi-fāyīn-gēn-yúfǎ.

Gāo: Rúguǒ-yòng-Hànzì 'duǎnchu-zài-nǎr?

Bái: Rúguǒ-yòng-Hànzì xué-Zhōngguo-yǔyán, méi-xuéguo-de-zì nǐ-méi-fázi-zìjǐ-huì-niàn.

Gāo: Xué-Hànzì yé-bu-tài-nán-ne. Jiù-shi-duō-liànxi-me.

LESSON 23

Basic Sentences

1. Míngnián-wó-xiǎng yìnián-dōu-yánjiu-Dōngfāng-wénhuà-nèi-fāngmiande-dōngxi.

2. Qǐng-bǎ-zhèifēng-xìn mǎshàng-sònggei-Wáng-Lǎoshī.

3. Qiántian-zhōngwǔ péngyoumen-sòng-wǒ-dào-Dōngjīngde-fēijichǎng.

4. Déle! Déle! Zhèizhāng-huàr-huàde-bù-hǎo. Bié-guà.

5. Tā-shuōde-xiàohua-hěn-néng-ràng-rén-xiào.

6. Shū kěnéng-dōu-ràng-tā-gěi-názǒu-le.

Dialogue

Bái: Zǎo! 'Tài-láojià-le. Zhēn-bùgǎndāng.

Gāo: Nǎrde-huà-ne. Wǒmen-yīnggāi-lái-de-me. Dōngxi dōu-shōushihǎo-le-ma?

Bái: 'Méi-shénmo-dōngxi-le. Wǒde-shū qián-jǐtiān yǒu-ge-péngyou-zuò-chuán-huíqu 'dōu-ràng-ta-dàizǒu-le.

Gāo: Zǒu-ba. Wǒmen-xiān-dào-fēijīchǎngde-cāntīng zài-nèr-mànmārde-tán-ba. Nǐ-huídào-Měiguo háishi-jìxu-xué-Zhōngguo-yǔyán gēn-wénxué-ma?

Bái: Shì. Búdàn-'jìxu-xué, wǒ-hái-děi hǎohāorde-xué-ne.

Gāo: Xué-yìzhǒng-xuéwen rúguǒ-xīwang-xuédehǎo, zuì-yàojǐn-de shi-yào-yóngyuǎn-xuéxiaqu. Wénshān, jiānglái-nǐ-dìdi-mèimei yě-dào-'Zhong-guo-lái-nián-shū-ma?

Bái: Bù-zhīdào jiānglái-tāmen-xué-shénmo. Rúguǒ-tāmen-xué-'Dōngfāng-wénhuà tāmen-kěnéng-dào-Zhōngguo-lái.

Gāo: Wénshān, shíhou-chàbuduō-le. Gāi-shàng-fēijī-le.

Bái: Hǎo.

Gāo: Zhù-ni-yílù-píng'ān.

Bái: Xièxie. Zàijiàn, zàijiàn!

MEMORIZATION EXERCISES (ENGLISH)

LESSON 1

Basic Sentences

1. He's very well.

2. Thank you.

3. Are you also well?

Dialogue A

Bai: . . .

Gao: I'm fine. And you?

Bai: . . .

Gao: They're both well, thanks.

Bai: . . .

Gao: See you again.

Dialogue B

Bai: Mr. Gao, how are you?

Gao: . . .

Bai: Fine, thank you. And how are Mrs. Gao and Miss Gao?

Gao: . . .

Bai: Good-bye, Mr. Gao.

Gao: . . .

LESSON 2

Basic Sentences

1. He is an Englishman.

2. He can speak English.

3. Is he an Englishman?

4. Is he an Englishman?

Dialogue A

Bai: . . .

Qian: My name is Qian. I take it you're Mr. King?

Bai: . . .

Qian: Oh, you're Mr. White. Are you English?

Bai: . . .

Qian: No. I can only speak Chinese.

Dialogue B

Bai: May I ask your name, Sir?

Qian: . . .

Bai: No, my name is White.

Qian: . . .

Bai: No, I'm American. [May I ask] do you speak English?

Qian: . . .

LESSON 3

Basic Sentences

1. How much is one book?

2. This book is $5.20.

3. These three books are $2.40 in all.

Dialogue A

Mao: . . .

Bai: I'd like to buy (some) books. How much is that book?

Mao: . . .

Bai: That Chinese book.

Mao: . . .

Bai: Fine, I'll buy two copies.

Mao: . . .

Bai: Do you sell Chinese writing brushes?

Mao: . . .

Bai: Three or four.

Dialogue B

Mao: What will you have, sir?

Bai: . . .

Mao: Which one?

Bai: . . .

Mao: This book is two dollars and twenty cents.

Bai: . . .

Mao: What else do you want to buy?

Bai: . . .

Mao: Yes. How many brushes do you want?

Bai: . . .

LESSON 4

Basic Sentences

1. This sheet of paper is six cents.

2. Ten notebooks are ninety-eight cents.

3. He has seven Chinese dictionaries (but) only one English dictionary.

4. We sell both Chinese and foreign maps.

5. We have books and also have pens. We have both books and pens.

Dialogue A

Bai: . . .

Mao: What color ink do you want?

Bai: . . .

Mao: No. We have black ink and blue ink.

Bai: . . .

Mao: Pencils, fountain pens, writing brushes—we have them all.

Bai: . . .

Mao: What country do you want a map of?

Bai: . . .

Mao: This map is excellent. I suggest you buy one.

Bai: . . .

Dialogue B

Bai: Do you have any ink?

Mao: . . .

Bai: Do you have red ink?

Mao: . . .

Bai: Do you have pencils?

Mao: . . .

Bai: Do you have any maps?

Mao: . . .

Bai: I'd like to buy a map of China.

Mao: . . .

Bai: O.K. I'd also like to buy a Chinese-English dictionary.

LESSON 5

Basic Sentences

1. Mr. Wang's books are all Chinese books.

2. This is an excellent book.

3. He's also a very good friend of mine.

4. This book isn't his; it's mine.

Dialogue A

Gao: . . .

Bai: Yes. Who are you calling?

Gao: . . .

Bai: Speaking. Who's calling, please?

Gao: . . .

Bai: Oh, Mr. Gao, I haven't seen you for a long time. How are you?

Gao: . . .

Bai: Could you tell me, please, what time is it now?

Gao: . . .

Bai: Fine. Thank you. See you at seven o'clock.

Dialogue B

Gao: Hello, hello. Who's this? Is this Mr. White's home?

Bai: . . .

Gao: I'd like to speak to Mr. White.

Bai: . . .

Gao: This is Gao.

Bai: . . .

Gao: I'm fine. Are you free this evening? I'd like to ask you to dinner. Can
        (you manage it) at seven o'clock?

Bai: . . .

Gao: It's now four o'clock.

Bai: . . .

LESSON 7

Basic Sentences

1. Is he in Hupeh or Hunan?

2. Where do you eat?

3. Are there big mountains in Manchuria?

4. That gentleman on his right is a Shantungese, the one on his left is a native
   of Shansi.

Dialogue A

Bai: . . .

Mao: The dinner is at his home.

Bai: . . .

Mao: Mr. Gao's home is outside the city, south of this road, on a small hill.

Bai: . . .

Mao: There are only three houses [in all] there. To the west there's a big
        house. To the east is a small house. The house in between is Mr. Gao's
        home.   To the south below the hill is Sun Yatsen Road. In front of Sun
        Yatsen Road is a big park. Behind the hill is a small lake.

Dialogue B

Bai: Mr. Gao asked me to dinner this evening. Do you know whether it's here
        or at his home?

Mao: . . .

Bai: Where is his home? Is it inside the city or outside the city?

Mao: . . .

Bai: How many houses are there on the hill?

Mao: . . .

LESSON 8

Basic Sentences

1. Is the library far from here?

2. The library is three (Chinese) miles from here.

3. He's reading in the library.

4. Chinese characters are too hard to write. I can write only very simple characters.

5. Are you right or is he right?

Dialogue A

Bai: . . .

Mao: Yes. The library here is pretty big and has quite a few books. Every day there are a lot of students reading there. Do you want to borrow some books?

Bai: . . .

Mao: What are you studying in college?

Bai: . . .

Mao: Do you like Chinese literature?

Bai: . . .

Mao: Which is easier, Chinese or English literature?

Bai: . . .

Mao: The library is quite far.

Bai: . . .

Mao: It's seven-odd (Chinese) miles from here.

Bai: . . . .

Mao: It's not close either.

Dialogue B

Bai: Is there a library here?

Mao: . . .

Bai: I'm planning to take out some Chinese books.

Mao: . . .

Bai: I'm studying literature.

Mao: . . .

Bai: I like Chinese literature very much.

Mao: . . .

Bai: Both are very difficult to study.   Where is the library?   Is it far from
       here?

Mao: . . .

Bai: How far is it from here?

Mao: . . .

Bai: Oh, seven or eight miles isn't too far.

Mao: . . .

LESSON 9

Basic Sentences

1. I'm going first to the library and then to your home.

2. I'm going by car to see him tomorrow.

3. How does one get from here to the library?

4. Turn north from the entrance of the park.

5. Please say it again.

Dialogue A

Bai: . . .

Mao: You go straight south from here, turn west, pass eight intersections,
       and there's the library.

Bai: . . .

Mao: There are both busses and streetcars. What would you like to take?

Bai: . . .

Mao: Not far from the bookstore.

Bai: . . .

Mao: Take a No. 3 bus. It goes directly to the library.

Bai: . . .

Mao: You get on the bus and go to Sun Yatsen Avenue.   Get off the bus at the
       park gate.

Bai: . . .

Mao: Are you coming tomorrow?

Bai: . . .

Dialogue B

Bai: How do I get from the bookstore to the library?

Mao: . . .

Bai: From here to the library what car do I take?

Mao: . . .

Bai: I'd like to go by bus. Where's the bus stop?

Mao: . . .

Bai: What [number] bus do I take?

Mao: . . .

Bai: How do I go from the library to Mr. Gao's home?

Mao: . . .

Bai: Thanks.

Mao: . . .

Bai: Perhaps I'll come again tomorrow to buy some books.

LESSON 10

Basic Sentences

1. The ticket-seller is a little taller than I am. You're even taller than he is.

2. It's now almost 8:45. At five minutes of nine I'm going by car to Far Eastern University.

3. He buys more books than I do.

4. They're chatting on the bus.

Dialogue A

MPY: . . .

Bai: I don't speak it well. I speak too slowly. There are lots of foreigners who speak much better than I do.

MPY: . . .

Bai: In my family there's my father and my mother, and also a younger brother and a younger sister.

MPY: . . .

Bai: My father's a high-school teacher. My mother is a grade-school teacher. Who's in your family?

MPY: . . .

Bai: Boys or girls?

MPY: . . .

Bai: How old are they?

MPY: . . .

Bai: What are their names?

MPY: . . .

Dialogue B

MPY: You speak Chinese really well.

Bai: . . .

MPY: What family do you have?

Bai: . . .

MPY: What does your father do?

Bai: . . .

MPY: I have a wife and two children.

Bai: . . .

MPY: One boy, one girl.

Bai: . . .

MPY: The boy is seven, the girl two.

Bai: . . .

MPY: The boy is called Tiger, the girl is called Little Sister.

Song

Three tigers,	One's without a tail,
Three tigers,	One's without a tail,
Running fast,	Really strange,
Running fast.	Really strange.

LESSON 11

Basic Sentences

1. I encountered him yesterday at 8:30 in the evening.

2. He left the United States on February third of this year.

3. Who told you I didn't have dinner at home?

4. Where did you see him?

Dialogue A

Qian: . . .

Bai: No. Today is the first time I've come. How about you?

Qian: . . .

Bai: I came on August seventh of last year.

Qian: . . .

Bai: I came by boat to Japan, and by plane from Japan to China.

Qian: ...

Bai: [Although] it was very slow, but traveling by boat is quite interesting.
        One can make a lot of friends.

Qian: ...

Bai: How nice. Thank you. If I have time this evening I'll certainly stop in
        at your home to visit.

Qian: ...

Dialogue B

Qian: Do you come to the library often?

Bai: ...

Qian: I don't come often either. When was it that you came to China?

Bai: ...

Qian: Did you come by boat or by plane?

Bai: ...

Qian: I suppose the boat traveled very slowly.

Bai: ...

Qian: If you have time this evening I'd like to invite you to drop in at my home
        to sit a while and chat.

Bai: ...

Qian: I hope you really will be able to come this evening.

LESSON 13

Basic Sentences

1. Have you eaten?

2. After eating breakfast, we left.

3. Is he well now?

4. I've already read two books today. I'm not going to read any more.

5. We're having another exam next week.

Dialogue A

Bai: ...

Gao: After class we had something to do at school, so I'm a little late. My
        father invited you to dinner this evening, isn't that so?

Bai: ...

Gao: It's no trouble; we're glad you're coming.

Bai: . . .

Gao: I'm studying at No. 1 Middle School.

Bai: . . .

Gao: Third year higher middle. I'll be graduating this year.

Bai: . . .

Gao: No, I'm not.

Bai: . . .

Gao: Thank you. Mr. White, [may I ask] what time is it? I left right after breakfast and forgot to wear my watch.

Bai: . . .

Dialogue B

Bai: You're returning home from school very late, (aren't you)?

Gao: . . .

Bai: Yes. It puts you to too much trouble.

Gao: . . .

Bai: [I still don't know] at what school are you studying?

Gao: . . .

Bai: What year?

Gao: . . .

Bai: [I think] you must be very bright.

Gao: . . .

Bai: You're being polite. Do you like to see movies? After your exams may I invite you to see a movie?

Gao: . . .

Bai: It's now quarter of seven.

LESSON 14

Basic Sentences

1. Have you read the book he's written?

2. Have you ever eaten Chinese food?

3. He understands everything in Chinese, and also speaks it very well.

4. Do you understand everything that Mr. Wan says to you?

5. In a little while I'll be able to see the paintings you've done.

Dialogue A

Gao: . . .

Bai: There are over 3,500. Miss Gao, what do you plan to study after graduating from middle school?

Gao: . . .

Bai: I originally planned to study science, but I'm very much interested in
foreign languages, especially Chinese, so in America I studied (spoken)
Chinese and read Chinese books. Now I've come to China to study Chinese literature, and also to study linguistics.

Gao: . . .

Bai: [Studying] linguistics is analyzing languages by scientific means.

Gao: . . .

Bai: I can [do so], but I write badly. (When) I write letters to Chinese friends,
I like to write in Chinese. Your father writes [characters] very well.

Gao: . . .

Bai: Haven't you heard it said:

> Live to old age,
> Study to old age,
> There's still three-tenths
> That one can't learn.

Gao: . . .

Dialogue B

Gao: How many students do you have at Far Eastern?

Bai: . . .

Gao: I'd like to study literature, but I'm sure that I can't pass the college
exams. If I can't pass the exams for college, then I'll study painting.
What are you studying, Mr. White?

Bai: . . .

Gao: How does one study linguistics?

Bai: . . .

Gao: Do you like to write Chinese characters? Can you use Chinese in writing letters?

Bai: . . .

Gao: He practices calligraphy almost every day.

Bai: . . .

Gao: It's not just three-tenths!

LESSON 15

Basic Sentences

1. I have to go now, but you don't need to go.

2. I have to finish reading this book today.

3. Of course I should go with him once.

4. I've [already] been studying Chinese for three years. I'll study another two or three years of Chinese.

5. He's been reading for an hour.

Dialogue A

Gao: . . .

Bai: I've been studying Chinese for almost five years.

Gao: . . .

Bai: At the beginning we went to class one hour a day. The teacher taught us to speak. After leaving class we listened to recordings on a tape recorder.

Gao: . . .

Bai: First I went by car from New York to San Francisco, arriving there after a six-day drive. I stayed in San Francisco for eight days. Then I traveled for ten days by boat to Japan. I stayed in Japan for a week, and then came to China by plane.

Gao: . . .

Bai: In the future after you graduate you should take a plane somewhere and go have fun.

Gao: . . .

Dialogue B

Gao: Mr. White, how many years have you been studying Chinese?

Bai: . . .

Gao: That's why your Chinese is so good. How did you study Chinese in America?

Bai: . . .

Gao: Did you come to China by plane or by boat?

Bai: . . .

Gao: I haven't been on a plane yet. If I have a chance I must take one once.

Bai: . . .

Gao: My father and mother have both been to Japan. They stayed there for more than two months, and bought a lot of Japanese things.

LESSON 16

Basic Sentences

1. Some were bought in Hangchow, some [were bought] in Soochow.

2. Everyone says he's very learned.

3. Carry all these things into the house.

4. Not only can my wife speak Chinese, but she speaks it very well.

5. Even I have no way of speaking to him.

Dialogue A

Bai: . . .

Miss Gao: That's why my father likes to go out for a walk every day.   Even on Sundays when he doesn't have to work he always goes out. [Going and returning] he always walks.

Bai: . . .

Miss Gao: He likes nothing better than traveling. . . . Here we are.   Mom! Open the door. The guest has come.

Bai: . . .

Mrs. Gao: Oh, Mr. White, you're here.   I haven't seen you for a long time. How are you?

Bai: . . .

Mr. Gao: Mr. White, how are you?   Come (in), come (in).   I'll introduce the two of you. This is Professor Wanamaker. This is Mr. White.

Bai: . . .

Wan: Pleased to meet you. . . . Miss Gao is intelligent and attractive.   She studies well, she paints well.

Bai: . . .

Miss Gao: Don't look (at them). I paint badly.

Bai: . . .

Mr. Gao: Meiying, bring all your paintings out. Let [both of] them have a look.

Bai: . . .

Miss Gao: Why, this is Hangchow.

Bai: . . .

Wan: China has a saying:

> Above is heaven,
> Below are Soochow and Hangchow.

The saying is not at all an exaggeration.

Dialogue B

Bai: The area around your home is very nice.

Miss Gao: . . .

Bai: Does your father also like to travel?

Miss Gao: . . .

Bai: Mrs. Gao, haven't seen you for a long time. How are you?

Mrs. Gao: . . .

Bai: Mr. Gao, how are you?

Mr. Gao: . . .

Bai: Pleased to meet you.

Wan: . . .

Bai: That's right. Miss Gao, we must look at your paintings.

Miss Gao: . . .

Bai: Please bring out all the paintings for us to look at.

Mr. Gao: . . .

Bai: This landscape painting is really nice. What place is it?

Miss Gao: . . .

Bai: Oh, so this is Hangchow. It's really attractive.

Wan: . . .

LESSON 17

Basic Sentences

1. The weather today isn't as warm as yesterday's.

2. This kind of tea is as nice as that kind.

3. There are a good many professors who compare him (as equal) to a fourth-year student.

4. That house is awfully big, so big that no one wants to buy it.

5. My monthly salary is very small, not enough (for me) to buy a house.

6. These Chinese students speak English as well as Americans do.

Dialogue A

Bai: . . .

Wan: [Old] Gao met Mrs. Gao in Soochow. They were married in Soochow, and Miss Gao was born there. Miss Gao has grown up to be as attractive as Mrs. Gao.

Bai: . . .

Wan: Hangchow is famous for its scenery, and Soochow is famous for its wom-
        en. . . . This wine is really nice.

Bai: . . .

Gao: It's Rose Dew. [Old] Wan, what do you say, after this cup shall we play
        'guess-fingers'? . . . Mr. White, what do you think, is it interesting?

Bai: . . .

Gao: Wait a moment and you'll understand.

Dialogue B

Bai: Is Miss Gao a native of Soochow?

Wan: . . .

Bai: Oh, so that's why Mrs. Gao and Miss Gao are so attractive!

Wan: . . .

Bai: What is it?

Gao: . . .

Bai: Very interesting. I'm puzzled as to why the winner doesn't drink.

Gao: . . .

LESSON 19

Basic Sentences

1. The sweet-and-sour fish that she makes is either too sweet or too sour.

2. I'd like very much to have some more beef soup, but I'm already full.

3. They're talking while eating.

4. Apart from saying "You flatter me," what did he say?

5. Where are the chopsticks? I've looked everywhere but can't find them.

6. Red-cooked pork and fish I've eaten, to be sure, but I don't like them.

Dialogue A

Bai: . . .

Gao: It's plain food, nothing in particular.   [Both of you] sit and eat as you
        please.

Bai: . . .

Gao: This is fried cabbage.

Bai: . . .

Gao: This is red-cooked chicken.

Bai: . . .

Gao: Mr. White, did you often have Chinese food in America too?

Bai: . . .

Gao: Is the Chinese food in America good?

Bai: . . .

Dialogue B

Bai: My! There's no end (of food). How is it that there are so many courses!

Gao: . . .

Bai: What is this dish?

Gao: . . .

Bai: And what about this?

Gao: . . .

Bai: This I know. It's fried bean curd.

Gao: . . .

Bai: I often did.

Gao: . . .

Bai: The Chinese restaurants in America are almost all Cantonese restaurants. Their cooking is good all right, but it isn't as good as Mrs. Gao's. Apart from a few big cities (like) San Francisco and New York, lion's head just can't be had in America.

LESSON 20

Basic Sentences

1. As soon as you called me I was delighted.

2. I can't guess whether he's a northerner or a southerner.

3. I'm afraid he can't lift such a heavy thing.

4. How come he speaks Chinese so well? . . . (Because) he was born in China, of course.

5. The teacher probably doesn't want us to open our books.

6. I've (just) remembered, I have to go to the station today to meet Mr. Gao.

Dialogue A

Bai: . . .

Gao: Gosh, don't bring that up. I did rather well in English and Chinese, but I messed up the math exam terribly. I misread a question.

Bai: . . .

Gao: I have something to tell you now.   We're having vacation now, and my father and mother are having me go with them to Japan.

Bai: . . .

Gao: I like to eat everything.   It just occurred to me—near the bookstore there's a Northern restaurant called the Ten Thousand Years Restaurant. Do you know it?

Bai: . . .

Gao: I hear the movie being shown at the China Theater isn't bad. It's a historical movie. The story is well written, and the actors do their parts well.

Bai: . . .

Gao: O.K.

Dialogue B

Bai: Meiying, how are things?   Have you finished taking your exams?   Did they go well?

Gao: . . .

Bai: This is something that happens often in examinations.

Gao: . . .

Bai: So I must ask you to dinner. After eating let's also go see a movie, O.K.? What would you like to eat?

Gao: . . .

Bai: I remembered it as you were speaking.   So let's go there for dinner. Where shall we go see a movie?

Gao: . . .

Bai: Let's take in the nine o'clock show, O.K.?

Gao: . . .

LESSON 21

Basic Sentences

1. Buy whatever kind of teacups you planned to.

2. He's always saying I don't have enough experience, but I feel I have a lot more experience than he has.

3. How come there's no soy sauce to put into the sautéed dish?

4. That teapot you've just bought can't be bought even in China.

5. I don't care much for [seeing] very long movies.

6. Give him a little more money, otherwise he won't sell.

Dialogue A

Waiter: . . .

Bai: Please help us order a couple of dishes.

Waiter: . . .

Bai: How does one order dumplings? How much do they sell for?

Waiter: . . .

Bai: Fine. If we don't have enough, we'll speak up again. After we've finished we'd like a [sweet] dessert. Do you have almond bean curd?

Waiter: . . .

Bai: Do you have almond tea?

Waiter: . . .

Bai: Please bring two bowls. . . . Waiter, the bill.

Waiter: . . .

Bai: Here's five dollars. You don't need to make change. The rest is your tip.

Waiter: . . .

Dialogue B

Waiter: Here's the menu.

Bai: . . .

Waiter: Fine. I'll introduce you to a few of our best dishes. Our red-cooked fish, fried shrimp, and roast duck are all fine. Our dumplings and fried noodles are also not bad.

Bai: . . .

Waiter: Dumplings you order by the number you eat. They're $1.20 for ten.

Bai: . . .

Waiter: I'm sorry, we're just sold out. Would you like something else?

Bai: . . .

Waiter: Yes.

Bai: . . .

Waiter: Yes. Altogether, four thirty-six.

Bai: . . .

Waiter: Thank you. Don't be in a hurry to leave. Good-bye.

LESSON 22

Basic Sentences

1. How many strokes are there in the character shēng of shēngyīn?

2. With regard to that problem, I'm just in the process of investigating it.

3. Everyone knows that if one simultaneously studies pronunciation, Chinese characters, and grammar, the disadvantages will outweigh the advantages.

4. The more syllables there are in a sentence the more difficult it is to say.

5. I'm presenting a portion of these books to you, and a portion to him.

6. You must thoroughly master the four tones. If the [four] tones are not accurate, you certainly won't (be able to) speak Chinese well.

Dialogue A

Gao: . . .

Bai: The teaching methods in American schools are not uniform. Some begin with studying Chinese characters, some use transcription.

Gao: . . .

Bai: At that time I did work hard. Every day I listened to recordings, carried on monologues, practiced pronunciation, and fixed in my memory all that we studied every day. The more I studied the more interested I became.

Gao: . . .

Bai: Yes, I first learned to speak. I began by studying the four tones and stress. Afterwards I studied words (for example, shū and tàitai are words) and phrases, and then studied conversation.

Gao: . . .

Bai: What needs most attention is pronunciation and grammar.

Gao: . . .

Bai: If you use Chinese characters to study the Chinese language, there is no way of knowing by yourself how to read a character which you have not studied previously.

Gao: . . .

Dialogue B

Gao: Is there a uniform method of teaching in American schools?

Bai: . . .

Gao: When you began your studies you must have been very diligent.

Bai: . . .

Gao: At the beginning did you first study speaking?

Bai: . . .

Gao: In studying languages what must you pay special attention to?

Bai: . . .

Gao: If you use Chinese characters where are the disadvantages?

Bai: . . .

Gao: Learning characters is not too hard.   It's just a matter of practicing more, of course.

LESSON 23

Basic Sentences

1. Next year I plan to spend the whole year studying [things of] Oriental culture [that aspect].

2. Please give this letter to Teacher Wang right away.

3. Yesterday noon friends saw me off at the Tokyo airport.

4. Enough! Enough! This painting is badly done. Don't hang it up.

5. The jokes he tells are very funny.

6. It's possible that all the books have been carried off by him.

Dialogue A

Bai: . . .

Gao: Nonsense. Of course we should come. Are your things all packed?

Bai: . . .

Gao: Let's go. Supposing we go to the airport cafeteria first and have a leisurely talk there. When you return to America will you go on studying Chinese language and literature?

Bai: . . .

Gao: When you study any branch of learning, if you hope [to be able] to master it, the most important thing is to keep on studying all the time. Vincent, will your younger brother and sister also come to China later to study?

Bai: . . .

Gao: Vincent, it's just about time. You should get on the plane.

Bai: . . .

Gao: I wish you a pleasant trip.

Bai: . . .

Dialogue B

Bai: Good morning! I've put you to too much trouble. I really don't deserve this.

Gao: . . .

Bai: I don't have anything much left any more. A few days ago I had a friend
       who is returning by boat take all my books.

Gao: . . .

Bai: Yes. I'll keep on with it, and I'll have to study hard too.

Gao: . . .

Bai: I don't know what they'll study [later]. If they study Oriental civilization
       there's a possibility that they will come to China.

Gao: . . .

Bai: Yes.

Gao: . . .

Bai: Thank you. Good-bye!

LESSON 1

New Vocabulary

lǎo	old (chiefly of animate things) (SV)
xiǎo	small, little, young (SV)
tóngzhì	comrade (N) [lit. same determination] (See Note 1)
lǎoshī	teacher (N) [lit. old teacher] (See Note 1)

Exercises

tóngzhì	comrade
'Gāo-Tóngzhì	Comrade Gao
1. 'Gāo-Tóngzhì, ní-hǎo-ma?	Comrade Gao, how are you?
lǎoshī	teacher
'Xiè-Lǎoshī	Teacher Xie
2. 'Xiè-Lǎoshī, ní-hǎo-a?	Teacher Xie, how are you?
3. Gāo: 'Xiè-Tóngzhì, nín-hǎo-a?	Comrade Xie, how are you?
Xiè: Hǎo. Nín-ne, 'Gāo-Tóngzhì?	Fine. And you, Comrade Gao?
Gāo: Wó-yé-hǎo.	I'm fine too.
4. Bái: 'Xiè-Lǎoshī hén-lǎo-ma?	Is Teacher Xie quite old?
Gāo: Tā-hén-lǎo.	He's very old.
5. Gāo: Nǐmen dōu-hǎo-ma?	Are you all well?
Bái: Wǒmen dōu-hén-hǎo. Nǐmen-ne?	We're all fine. And you?
Gāo: Wǒmen yě-dōu-hén-hǎo.	We're also all well.
Bái: Zàijiàn, 'Gāo-Lǎoshī.	Good-bye, Teacher Gao.
Gāo: Zàijiàn, zàijiàn.	Good-bye.
6. Xiè: Lǎo-Gāo, ní-hǎo-ma?	How are you, (Old) Gao?
Gāo: Hǎo.	Fine.

Xiè:	Xiăo-Bái yé-hăo-ma?	And how's (Young) Bai?
Gāo:	Tā-yé-hăo.	He's fine too.

7. Bái: 'Xiè-Lăoshĭ, nín-hăo-a?   Teacher Xie, how are you?

   Xiè: Wó-hén-hăo. Nĭ-ne?   I'm fine. And you?

   Bái: Wó-yé-hăo. Zàijiàn, 'Xiè-   I'm fine too. Good-bye, Teacher Xie.
   Lăoshĭ.

   Xiè: Zàijiàn, zàijiàn.   See you again.

8. 'Bái-Xiānsheng, 'Gāo-Tóngzhĭ   Mr. White and Comrade Gao are both
   'dōu-hěn-gāo. 'Xiè-Lăoshĭ yé-   quite tall. Teacher Xie is also quite
   hěn-gāo.   tall.

Note

1. The problem of forms of address, a traditionally complex matter in Chinese (as indeed it is in most languages), has acquired an added dimension of complexity and uncertainty owing to the rapid but uneven changes that have been taking place in the People's Republic of China. There are considerable variations stemming from differences in age, in dialect, in nationality (i.e., Chinese versus non-Chinese), and in individual preferences for one or another form of address. In general the tendency is in the direction of greater simplicity, but the present situation, which is likely to last for some time, is one of transition, and it is therefore difficult to prescribe simple clear usage for all situations.

In the PRC among Chinese themselves the Government has expressed official preference for the generalized use of tóngzhĭ 'Comrade,' as in Gāo Tóngzhĭ 'Comrade Gao,' a form which is used in reference to both men and women. Many Chinese, however, prefer to be addressed by terms expressing their position or status, such as 'Delegation Head Gao, Party Secretary Gao,' etc. Some of the older forms of address still persist, especially among older people and in rural areas (where traditional linguistic usages are particularly persistent) or in special situations. Xiānsheng is still used as a respectful designation for important people (non-Party members, famous professors and writers, etc.). Even more than xiānsheng, the terms tàitai and xiăojie have fallen into disfavor in general usage in the PRC since they are considered to reflect respect for the élite status of the former privileged classes.

Chinese men and women sometimes address each other by their full names (e.g., Gāo Měiyĭng), that is surname plus given name, without the use of any title. A more familiar form of address is to precede the surname with Xiăo (literally 'small') when addressing a smaller or younger person or Lăo (literally 'old') when addressing an older person, though considerations of relative size or age are not strictly followed. These terms, which are used for both men and women, should not be translated literally since they merely convey a degree of familiarity similar to English usage of personal name or surname, e.g., Hi, John! Hi, Smith!

Among some Chinese in the PRC the term àirén, literally 'loved person,' is used for both 'wife' and 'husband' and for 'fiancé' and 'fiancée.'

Coming now to usage between Chinese and non-Chinese, the situation is complicated by the fact that contacts between the two are seldom very extensive, at least rarely so extensive as to reach the degree of intimacy that non-Chinese, especially Americans, are accustomed to in their social contacts. Thus the familiarity with which the American student White greets his Chinese friend Gao in Lesson 1 is more likely to characterize situations in Chinese communities outside the PRC than in it.

In the PRC Chinese still often address foreigners by using xiānsheng for males and xiáojie for unmarried women. More rarely, tàitai is sometimes used in reference to foreign married women. A more common familiar usage is to address both men and women by the Chinese equivalent of their surname plus given name.

Insofar as foreigners addressing Chinese is concerned, perhaps the safest procedure is to call them by their titles of position or rank, such as 'Delegation Head Gao.' Tóngzhì may sometimes be used by foreigners in addressing Chinese who are their social equals, but the term should be handled with caution, as some Chinese may resent its indiscriminate use by foreigners. However, the term can be used widely for information or help, as illustrated in Supplementary Lesson 3 and subsequent lessons. In some situations foreigners may also use the title xiānsheng, but careful attention should be paid as to whether the usage is appropriate in the given situation.

In situations of great familiarity, but only in such situations, foreigners may address Chinese by using their surname plus given name (e. g., Gāo Měiyīng) or only their given name (e. g., Měiyīng) or by prefixing Xiǎo or Lǎo to the surname (e. g., Lǎo-Gāo, Xiǎo-Bái). The latter would be particularly appropriate among students who are on quite friendly and familiar terms.

The term àirén has struck the fancy of many Western observers, but it should be used by non-Chinese only with the greatest caution, as it involves delicate problems of degree of familiarity. It should never be used as a title. Special care should also be exercised in using it in speaking with Chinese outside the PRC since it retains for them its original connotation of an extra-marital lover or mistress.

Students will have frequent contact with Chinese teachers and can address them (both in the PRC and elsewhere) as lǎoshī 'teacher.'

In addressing Chinese outside the PRC, which will probably be the situation in which students of the language will most often find themselves, the older forms of address can of course still be used (unless of course the Chinese in question are visitors from the PRC). It would usually not be appropriate to use such terms as tóngzhì and àirén in speaking with Chinese not connected with the PRC.

The respectful pronoun nín 'you' is used by many Chinese in the PRC among themselves and in addressing foreigners and can be used by foreigners in addressing Chinese, though some of the latter disapprove of it as being overly polite.

In view of the fact that usage in these matters is not yet completely standardized, students are advised to take careful note of what is said in specific situations in which they find themselves. In classroom situations the best procedure would be to observe the preference of one's teacher as to forms of address. They should not hesitate to ask what forms they as foreigners should use in a given situation. Indeed this approach should be generalized to language usage in general. In view of the wide variations in individual language usage, students are particularly cautioned to observe specific language usage themselves and not to accept uncritically such sweeping statements as "We always say such-and-such" or "We never say so-and-so."

LESSON 2

Exercises

1. Nín-shì-bu-shi 'Qián-Tóngzhǐ?   Are you Comrade Qian?

2. 'Wáng-Lǎoshǐ shi-'Měiguo-rén-   Is Teacher Wang an American?
   bú-shi?

3. Xiǎo-Gāo-Lǎo-Bái dōu-huì-   (Little) Gao and (Old) Bai can both
   shuō-'Yīngguo-huà. Wǒ-bú-huì.   speak English. I can't.

4. 'Xiè-Tóngzhǐ wèn-tāmen: "Nǐmen   Comrade Xie asked them: "Are you
   'dōu-shi-Měiguo-rén-ma?"   all Americans?" They said they were
   Tāmen-shuō tāmen-'dōu-shi-   all Americans.
   Měiguo-rén.

5. Qián: Qǐng-wèn, nín-guìxìng?   May I ask your name?

   Gāo: Wǒ-xìng-Gāo. Nín-ne?   My name is Gao. And you?

   Qián: Wǒ-xìng-Qián.   My name is Qian.

6. Bái: Nín-shi-'Gāo-Tóngzhǐ-   Are you Comrade Gao?
        ma?

   Qián: Bú-shi. Wǒ-xìng-Qián.   No. My name is Qian.

7. Qián: Nín-shi-'Gāo-Lǎoshǐ-ba?   I take it you're Teacher Gao?

   Wáng: Bú-shi. Wǒ-xìng-Wáng.   No, my name is Wang.

8. Gāo: Qǐng-wèn-Tóngzhǐ, 'nín-   May I ask, Comrade, what is your
        guìxìng?   name?

   Xiè: Wǒ-xìng-Xiè. Nín-ne?   My name is Xie. And yours?

   Gāo: Wǒ-xìng-Gāo. Zàijiàn,   My name is Gao. Good-bye, Comrade
        'Xiè-Tóngzhǐ.   Xie.

   Xiè: Zàijiàn, zàijiàn.   Good-bye.

Note

1. There are differences of opinion among PRC informants regarding the use
   of the polite expression Nín-guìxìng? 'What is your (honorable) surname?'
   Some speakers have abandoned it for the more straightforward Nín (or
   Nǐ)-xìng-shénmo?, literally 'You are surnamed what?' (An exercise on
   this is provided in Lesson 3, where shénmo? 'what?' is introduced.) However, the polite form is still widely used in conversations involving non-
   Chinese.

LESSON 3

New Vocabulary

yuán   yuan; dollar (M) (See Note 1)

jiǎo   dime (M) (See Note 1)

Exercises

1. Gāo: Nǐ-yóu-'jǐzhī-bǐ?   How many pens do you have?

   Bái: Wǒ-jiù-yǒu 'yìzhī-bǐ.   I have only one pen.

2. Máo: Qǐng-wèn, nín-guìxìng?   May I ask, what is your name?

   Qián: Wǒ-xìng-Qián. 'Nín-xìng-   My name is Qian. What is your name?
          shénmo?

   Máo: Wǒ-xìng-Máo.   My name is Mao.

3. 'Wáng-Lǎoshī-shuō tā-yào-   Teacher Wang says he wants these
   'zhèi-liǎngzhī-máobǐ.   two writing brushes.

4. Wáng: Tā-wèn nǐ-huì-bu-huì-   He asks whether you can speak Chi-
          shuō 'Zhōngguo-huà?   nese.

   Bái: Huì. Tā-'hái-wèn-wǒ-   I can. What else is he asking?
          shénmo?

   Wáng: Tā-hái-wèn nǐ-shì-bu-   He also asks whether you are an Amer-
          shì-Měiguo-rén?   ican.

5. Máo: Nǐ-hái-yào-mǎi-shénmo?   What else would you like to buy?

   Bái: Wǒ-hái-yào-mái-bǐ.   I also want to buy a pen.

   Máo: Yào-mái-'jǐzhī?   How many do you want to buy?

   Bái: 'Yìzhī   One.

   Máo: Yìzhī liǎngkuài-qián.   One (is) two dollars.

6. Xiè: Tóngzhì, zhèizhī-máobǐ   Comrade, how much does this writing
          mài-duōshao-qián?   brush sell for?

   Qián: Mài-yíkuài-èr.   It sells for a dollar twenty.

Xiè:	Hǎo, wó-mǎi-liǎngzhǐ.	Fine, I'll buy two.
Qián:	Hǎo.	O.K.

7. Máo: Nín-mǎi-shénmo?   What would you like to buy?

   Bái: Wǒ-yào-mǎi-shū. Nèiběn-   I'd like to buy a book. How much is
          shū duōshao-qián?   that book?

   Máo: Zhèiběn-shū liǎngyuán-   This book is $2.40.
          sìjiǎo.

   Bái: Hǎo, wó-mǎi-yìběn.   Fine, I'll buy one.

Note

1. On banknotes and in other printed materials the written equivalent of <u>kuài</u> is <u>yuán</u> and óf <u>máo</u> is <u>jiǎo</u>. In the PRC these forms are beginning to enter into the spoken language, especially in Common Speech as spoken by Southerners, but <u>kuài</u> and <u>máo</u> are still used more frequently in everyday speech. (Some readers may prefer to render <u>kuài</u> and <u>yuán</u> as 'yuan' instead of as 'dollar' in order to avoid confusion with American currency.)

LESSON 4

Exercises

1. 'Yán-Lǎoshǐ yào-mǎi yíge-   Teacher Yan wants to buy a Chinese
   Zhōngguo-dìtú, yìzhǐ-gāngbǐ,   map, a pen, and two pencils. He also
   liǎngzhǐ-qiānbǐ. Hái-yào-mǎi   wants to buy fifty sheets of paper.
   wǔshizhāng-zhǐ.

2. 'Wáng-Tóngzhǐ yào-mǎi-máobǐ. Comrade Wang wants to buy a Chinese
   'Zhāng-Tóngzhǐ yào-mái-běnzi. pen. Comrade Zhang wants to buy a
                                  notebook.

3. Bái: Ní-yóu-jǐge-běnzi?   How many notebooks do you have?

   Lán: Wǒ-jiù-yǒu zhèi-yìběn.   I have only this one.

4. Máo: Nǐmen-mǎi shénmo-   What color ink are you buying?
         yánse-de-mòshuǐ?

   Xiè: Wó-mǎi-'hóng-mòshuǐ.   I'm buying red ink. He's buying blue
         Tā-mǎi-'lán-mòshuǐ.   ink.

5. Bái: Zhèige-dìtú mài-duōshao- How much is this map?
         qián?

   Máo: Liǎngkuài-èr.   Two-twenty.

   Bái: Liǎngkuài-èr bú-guì. Wó- Two-twenty isn't expensive. I'll buy
         mǎi-yìzhāng.   one.

6. Xiè: 'Lán-Tóngzhǐ, nín-hǎo-   How are you, Comrade Lan?
         ma?

Lán:	Hǎo. Nǐ-ne, Xiǎo-Xiè?	Fine, and you, (Little) Xiè?
Xiè:	Hǎo. Zàijiàn, 'Lán-Tóngzhǐ.	Fine. Good-bye, Comrade Lan.
Lán:	Zàijiàn, zàijiàn.	Good-bye.
7. Bái:	Zhèibén-Yǐngwén-shū mài-duōshao-qián?	How much does this English book sell for?
Máo:	Liǎngyuán-qījiǎo.	$2.70.
Bái:	Zhèibén-Zhōng-Yǐng-zìdiǎn-ne?	And this Chinese-English dictionary?
Máo:	Bāyuán-èrjiǎo.	$8.20
Bái:	Hǎo, wó-mǎi-yìběn.	Good, I'll buy one.

LESSON 5

New Vocabulary

shíjiān   (period of) time (N) [lit. time interval] (See Note 1)

Exercises

shíjiān	time
yǒu-shíjiān	have time

1.	Nǐmen-xiànzài dōu-yǒu-shíjiān-ma?	Do you all have time now?
2.	Xiè-Lǎoshǐ-shuō zhèige-Zhōngguo-dìtú hén-hǎo, yě-bù-hěn-guì, jiù-mài-wǔmáo-qián.	Teacher Xie says this map is very good, and it's not very expensive, selling for only fifty cents.
3. Qián:	Tóngzhǐ, yǒu-shénmo-yánse-de-zhǐ?	What color paper do you have, Comrade?
Máo:	Jiù-yǒu-hóng-zhǐ.	We just have red paper.
4. Xiè:	Zhāng-Lǎoshǐ huì-shuō-wàiguo-huà-bú-huì?	Can Teacher Zhang speak a foreign language?
Wáng:	Huì. Tā-huì-shuō-Yǐngwén.	Yes. He can speak English.
5. Bái:	Wai, wai, nín-nǎr? Shi-'Gāo-jiā-ma?	Hello, hello. Who's this? Is this the Gao home?
Gāo:	Shì. Qǐng-wèn, nín-shi-néiwèi?	Yes. Who's this, please?
Bái:	Wǒ-shi-Bái-Wénshān.	I'm Vincent White.

6. Gāo: Ní-wǎnshang yǒu-shíjiān-   Are you free this evening? I'd like to
         ma? Wó-xiáng-qǐng-ni   ask you to dinner.
         chī-fàn.

   Bái: Hǎo. Xièxie-ni. 'Jídiǎn-   (How) nice. Thank you. At what time?
         zhōng?

   Gāo: 'Qīdiǎn kéyi-ma?   Is seven o'clock O. K.?

   Bái: Kéyi, kéyi.   Fine.

7. Lán: Zhèizhī-gāngbǐ shi-shéi-   Whose pen is this? Is it Teacher
         de? Shi-Qián-Lǎoshī-de-   Qian's?
         ma?

   Bái: Bú-shi. Gāngbǐ shi-   No. The pen is Comrade Zhang's. The
         Zhāng-Tóngzhì-de. Qiānbǐ   pencil is Teacher Qian's.
         shi-Qián-Lǎoshī-de.

Note

1. In the PRC the expression <u>Ní-yǒu-gōngfu-ma?</u> for 'Do you have time?' or
   'Are you free?' is considered by some speakers as too colloquial. They
   prefer instead <u>Ní-yǒu-shíjiān-ma?</u>

LESSON 6

Exercises

1. Xiè: Xiànzài jídiǎn-zhōng?   Bái: Zhèizhī-'hóng-bǐ.

   Bái: Xiànzài qīdiǎn-zhōng.   Xié: Shi-'Lán-Tóngzhì-de.

2. Qián: Zhèizhāng-dìtú mài-
         duōshao-qián?   5. Zhè shi-shénmo-shū? Shi-Zhōng-
                                            Yīng-zìdiǎn-ma?   Mài-duōshao-
   Gāo: Mài-liǎngyuán-sānjiǎo.   qián? Mài - liǎngkuài - qián - ma?
                                           Liǎngkuài-qián-bú-guì. Hǎo, wó-
3. Yán: Wai! Wai! Ní-nǎr? Shi-   mǎi-yìběn. Wǒ-hái-yào-mǎi yìzhī-
         Wáng-Tóngzhì-jiā-ma?   gāngbǐ. Nǐmen-bú-mài-gāngbǐ-ma?

   Wáng: Shì. Ní-shi-něiwèi?

   Yán: Wǒ-xìng-Yán.   6. Zhāng-Lǎoshī wèn-wǒ jīntian-wǎn-
                                            shang yǒu-méi-yǒu-shíjiān. Tā-
4. Bái: Zhè-shi-shéi-de-bǐ?   shuō   tā-xiáng-qǐng-wǒ-chī-fàn.
                                           Wǒ-shuō-yǒu-shíjiān. Tā-bādiǎn-
   Xiè: 'Něizhī-bǐ?   zhōng qǐng-wǒ-chī-fàn.

LESSON 7

New Vocabulary

xiǎode   know (V) [lit. know get] (See Note 2)

Exercises

1. Zhāng: Nǐ-yào-shénmo-yánse-
   de-bǐ?

   What color pen do you want?

   Wáng: Wǒ-yào yìzhǐ-hóng-
   gāngbǐ, yìzhǐ-lán-qiānbǐ.

   I'd like a red pen and a blue pencil.

2. Bái: Fángzi-wàibiar-de-nèige-
   rén shi-shéi, nǐ-'xiǎode-
   bu-xiǎode?

   Who's that person outside the house,
   do you know?

   Xiè: Shi-'Gāo-Tóngzhì.

   It's Comrade Gao.

3. Lán: Zhè-shi-nǐde-zhǐ-ma?

   Is this your paper?

   Xiè: Bú-shi.

   No.

   Lán: Zhèizhāng-dìtú-ne?

   What about this map?

   Xiè: Yě-bú-shi-wǒde.

   It's not mine either.

4. Wáng: Nǐ-jiā-zài-nǎr? Zài-
   chénglǐ háishi-zài-
   chéngwài?

   Where is your home? Is it inside or
   outside the city?

   Zhāng: Zài-chéngwài.

   It's outside the city.

   Wáng: 'Gāo-Lǎoshǐ-jiā-ne?

   How about Teacher Gao's home?

   Zhāng: Wǒ-bù-xiǎode.

   I don't know.

5. Gāo: Nǐ-jīntian-wǎnshang yǒu-
   shíjiān-ma? Wó-xiǎng
   qíng-nǐ-chī-fan.

   Are you free this evening? I'd like to
   ask you to dinner.

   Bái: Xièxie-ni. Yǒu-shíjiān.
   Shénmo-shíhou?

   Thank you. I'm free. At what time?

   Gāo: Qīdiǎn.

   Seven.

   Bái: Hǎo. Qīdiǎn-zhōng-jiàn.

   Fine. See you at seven.

6. Xiè: 'Zhāng-Tóngzhì jiā-zài-
   nǎr, nǐ-'xiǎode-bu-
   xiǎode?

   Where is Comrade Zhang's home, do
   you know?

   Bái: Zài-zhèitiáo-lù-de-dōngbiar. Jiù-zài-Zhōngshān-
   Gōngyuán-de-hòubiar.

   It's to the east of this road. It's behind Sun Yatsen Park.

7. Wáng: Fángzi-wàitou-de-nèi-
   sānge-rén shi-shéi, nǐ-
   xiǎode-ma?

   Who are those three people outside
   the house, do you know?

   Máo: Zài-zuǒbiar-de shi-'Xiè-
   Lǎoshǐ, zài-yòubiar-de
   shi-'Qián-Lǎoshǐ. Zhōng-
   jiàr-de shi-'Bái-Xiānsheng.

   The one on the left is Teacher Xie,
   the one on the right is Teacher Qian.
   The one in the middle is Mr. White.

8. Bái: Zhōngshān-Gōngyuán zài-   Do you know where Sun Yatsen Park
         năr, ní-xiăode-bu-xiăode?   is?

   Zhāng: Wŏ-bù-xiăode.   I don't know.

Notes

1. In the Common Speech of the PRC the suffixed placeword <u>bian</u> or <u>biar</u> occurs more often than <u>tou</u>, which is more typical of the Peking dialect.
   Thus <u>lĭbian</u> or <u>lĭbiar</u> is used more often than <u>lĭtou</u>, and <u>shàngbian</u> or
   <u>shàngbiar</u> more often than <u>shàngtou</u>, etc. However, the forms with <u>tou</u> do
   occur in Common Speech and are presented in PRC materials along with
   the forms <u>bian</u> and <u>biar</u>.

2. The Central China and rather colloquial expression <u>xiăode</u> 'know' is entering into Common Speech along with <u>zhĭdao</u>, though the latter is still more
   widely used.

LESSON 8

New Vocabulary

xuéxí   study (N/V) [lit. study practice] (See Note 1)

Exercises

   xuéxí   study

   xuéxí-Zhōngwén   study Chinese

1. Wŏmen-xuéxí-Zhōngwén.   We are studying Chinese.

2. Wŏ-hén-xĭhuan-Zhōngwén. Wŏ-   I like Chinese a lot. I can speak Chi-
   xiànzài néng-shuō-Zhōngwén,   nese now, can read simple Chinese
   néng-kàn jiăndānde-Zhōngwén-   books, and can also write Chinese
   shū, yě-huì-xiě Zhōngguo-zì.   characters.

3. Xiè: Nín-zài-dàxué xué-shénmo?   What are you studying in college?

   Bái: Wŏ-xué-wénxué.   I'm studying literature.

   Xiè: Nín-xué-'Zhōngguo-wénxué-   Are you studying Chinese literature?
        ma?

   Bái: 'Zhōngguo-wénxué, 'Yīng-   I'm studying both Chinese and English
        guo-wénxué wŏ-'dōu-xuéxí.   literature.

4. Máo: Zhōngguo-wénxué nán-xué-   Is Chinese literature hard (to study)?
        ma?

   Xiè: Hĕn-nán-xué.   It's very hard (to study).

   Máo: Yīngguo-wénxué-ne?   How about English literature?

   Xiè: Yé-hĕn-nán-xué.   It's also hard (to study).

5. Bái: Fángzi-qiántou-de-nèige-   Who is that man in front of the house?
          rén shi-shéi?

   Gāo: Shi-'Zhāng-Tóngzhì.   It's Comrade Zhang.

   Bái: Tā-shì-bu-shi 'Dōngběi-   Is he a Northeasterner?
          rén?

   Gāo: Bú-shi. Tā-shi-'Shāndong- No. He's from Shantung.
          rén.

6. Xiè: Qíng-nǐ-kàn-wǒ-xiè-zì.   Please watch me write characters.

   Máo: Wǒ-xiànzài méi-shíjiān.   I don't have time now.

   Xiè: Wǎnshang yǒu-shíjiān-ma? Will you have time (this) evening?

   Máo: Wǎnshang-yǒu.   Yes.

7. Bái: Nǐ-fángzi-nánbiar-de-   Is that street south of your house East
          nèitiáo-lù shi-Dōng-Hú-   Lake Road?
          Lù-ma?

   Xiè: Bù. Shi-'Xī-Hú-Lù.   No. It's West Lake Road.

8. Wáng: Nín-zài-'něige-dàxué-   At what college are you studying?
           xuéxí?

   Qián: Wǒ-zài-Zhōngshān-   I'm studying at Sun Yatsen Univer-
           Dàxué-xuéxí.   sity.

9. Bái: Túshūguǎn zài-nǎr, nǐ-   Where is the library, do you know?
          xiǎode-ma?

   Máo: Lí-zhèr hén-yuǎn. Zài-   It's quite far from here. It's behind
          Zhōngshān-Gōngyuán-   Sun Yatsen Park.
          hòubiar-ne.

10. Wáng: Zhōngguo-zì 'tài-nán-xiě. Chinese characters are too difficult
                                 (to study).

   Zhāng: Nǐde-huà hěn-duì.   You're quite right.

11. Gāo: Nǐ-wǎnshang jídiǎn-zhōng At what hour do you eat in the eve-
          chī-fàn?   ning?

   Bái: Wó-měitiān-wǎnshang   I eat at seven (in the evening) every
          qídiǎn-zhōng chī-fàn. Nǐ- day. And you?
          ne?

   Gāo: Wǒ-liùdiǎn-zhōng-chī.   I eat at six.

Note

1. In the PRC xuéxí is in common use for the generalized concept of 'to study'
and xué or xuéxí are used in reference to studying specific subjects. (Note
that xué is generally used with an object.) These terms have largely displaced niàn, which is now mainly used in its original meaning 'read aloud.'

For silent reading, especially for pleasure (i.e., not in the sense of 'studying'), the verb <u>kàn</u> is used, as in <u>kàn shū</u> 'to read [a book].' Note the following usages:

Tā-xuéxí   'He studies' (i.e., is studying rather than working at a job).
Tā-xué-wénxué   ⎱
Tā-xuéxí-wénxué ⎰ 'He is studying literature.'
Tā-zài-dàxué-xuéxí   'He is studying at the university.'

The term <u>xuéxí</u> is derived from a classical expression meaning 'learn and often practice.' It thus suggests one of the constant themes in the PRC, namely that study should involve a combination of theory and practice.

LESSON 9

New Vocabulary

yéxǔ   probably (MA) [lit. also permit] (Xǔ is also a surname) (See Note 1)

Exercises

yéxǔ   perhaps

yéxǔ-míngtian-lái   perhaps come tomorrow

1. Tāmen-yéxǔ-míngtian-lái.   Perhaps they'll come tomorrow.

2. Zhāng: Tā-shuō shénmo?   What did he say?

   Wáng: Tā-shuō zài-chéng-mén-   He said to get off (the bus) at the city
   nèr xià-chē.   gate.

3. Xǔ: Zhèiběn-shū 'guì-bu-guì?   Is this book expensive?

   Máo: Bù-hěn-guì. Yíkuài-qián.   It's not very expensive. One dollar.

4. Gāo: Nǐ-xiǎng-xué-shénmo?   What are you thinking of studying?

   Bái: Wǒ-xiǎng-xué 'Zhōngguo-   I'm thinking of studying Chinese or
   wénxué huòzhě-'Yīngguo-   English literature.
   wénxué.

   Gāo: 'Měiguo-wénxué-ne?   What about American literature?

   Bái: 'Yé-xiǎng-xué.   I'm also thinking of studying (it).

5. Máo: Wǒmen-něitian qù-kàn-   What day shall we go see Comrade
   Qián-Tóngzhì?   Qian?

   Gāo: Huòzhě-jīntian huòzhě-   Either today or tomorrow are (both)
   míngtian 'dōu-kéyi.   O.K.

6. Wáng: Qǐng-wèn, cóng-zhèr dào-   May I ask, how does one get from
   túshūguǎn zěnmo-zǒu?   here to the library?

   Qián: Nǐ-cóng-zhèr yìzhí-wàng-   You go straight north from here.
   běi-zǒu.

Wáng:	Shūdiàn-ne?	What about the bookstore?
Qián:	Yě-yìzhí-wàng-béi-zǒu. Lí-túshūguǎn-bù-yuǎn.	Also go straight north. (It's) not far from the library.
7. Bái:	Hào-zì zěnmo-xiě?	How is the character for "number" written?
Wáng:	Bù-xiǎode. Wǒ-hái-méi-yǒu-xuéxí xiě-zì.	(I) don't know. I haven't studied writing characters yet.
8. Xiè:	Nǐ-xìng-shénmo?	What is your name?
Xǔ:	Wǒ-xìng-Xǔ.	My name is Xu.
Xiè:	Nǐ-shi-'Yīngguo-rén shi-Měiguo-rén?	Are you English or American?
Xǔ:	Wǒ-shi-'Měiguo-rén.	I'm American.
9. Máo:	Nǐ-huì-kàn 'Zhōngwén-shū-ma?	Can you read Chinese books?
Bái:	Wǒ-jiù-huì-kàn hén-jiǎndān-de-shū.	I can only read very simple books.
10. Bái:	Qǐng-wèn, cóng-zhèr dào-túshūguǎn zuò-jǐlù-chē?	Excuse me, what bus (or car) do I take from here to the library?
Xiè:	Zuò-liùlù-jiǔlù 'dōu-kéyi.	You can take either Route 6 or Route 9.
Bái:	Bálù-chē-ne?	What about Route 8?
Xiè:	Bù-xiǎode. Yéxǔ 'yé-kéyi.	I don't know. Perhaps it's also O. K.
11. Wáng:	Zhèitiáo-lù-shang-de-chē 'tài-duō. Guò-lù hěn-nán.	There are too many cars on this street. It's hard to cross the street.
Zhāng:	Nǐde-huà hěn-duì.	You're quite right.
12. Gāo:	Nǐ-xǐhuan zuò-diànchē-ma?	Do you like to ride streetcars?
Bái:	Wó-hén-xǐhuan. Zuò-diànchē hén-yǒu-yìsi.	I like to very much. Riding streetcars is very interesting.
13. Bái:	Zhōngshān-Gōngyuán zài-chénglǐ háishi-zài-chéngwài?	Is Sun Yatsen Park inside or outside the city?
Máo:	Zài-chéngwài. Lí-chéng-mén-bù-yuǎn.	It's outside the city. It's not far from the city gate.
14. Bái:	Zhè-shi-'jǐlù-chē?	What route is this bus?
Xiè:	Shi-'wǔlù-chē.	It's Route 5.

Notes

1. In the PRC yéxǔ is competing with huòzhě in the meaning 'perhaps,' as in

   Tā-yéxǔ-míngtian-lái.   'Perhaps he'll come tomorrow.'

2. In the PRC the designation for the number of a bus line uses lù 'road, route' in place of hào 'number.'

   Sānlù-chē   'Route 3 bus, No. 3 bus'

LESSON 10

New Vocabulary

shòupiàoyuán	ticket-seller (N) [lit. sell-ticket person] (See Note 1)
gōngzuò	work (N/V) [lit. work do] (See Note 2)

Exercises

shòupiàoyuán	ticket-seller
shòupiàoyuán-tóngzhì	comrade ticket-seller

1. Tā-shi-shòupiàoyuán-tóngzhì.   He's the (comrade) ticket-seller.

gōngzuò	work
shénmo-gōngzuò?	what work?

2. Tā-zuò-shénmo-gōngzuò?   What work does he do?

3. Bái: Shòupiàoyuán-tóngzhì xìng-shénmo, ní-'xiǎode-bu-xiǎode?   What's the comrade ticket-seller's name, do you know?

   Xiè: Tā-xìng-Wáng.   His name is Wang.

   Bái: Tā-míngzi jiào-shénmo?   What's his given name?

   Xiè: Wǒ-bù-xiǎode.   I don't know.

4. Bái: Nǐ-fùqin yě-gōngzuò-ma?   Does your father also work?

   Xiè: Tā-yě-gōngzuò.   Yes, he does.

   Bái: Tā-zuò-shénmo-gōngzuò?   What work does he do?

   Xiè: Tā-shi-shòupiàoyuán.   He's a ticket-seller.

5. Bái: Nín-dào-gōngyuán-qù, zuò-chē háishi-zǒu-lù?   In going to the park, will you go by bus (or streetcar) or will you walk?

   Qián: Wǒ-xiǎng zuò-chē-qu.   I'm thinking of going by a vehicle.

   Bái: Nín-zuò-diànchē háishi-zuò-gōnggòng-qìchē?   Will you take the streetcar or the bus?

Qián: Wó-yéxǔ zuò-gōnggòng-   Perhaps I'll take the bus.
       qìchē.

6. Bái: Tāmen-zài-nèr zuò-   What are they doing there?
        shénmo?

   Gāo: Tāmen-zài-nèr-tántan.   They're talking there.

7. Xiè: 'Xǔ-Lǎoshī jiā-zài-nǎr,   Where is Teacher Xu's home, do you
        ní-xiǎode-ma?   know?

   Gāo: Tā-jiā zài-zhèitiáo-lù-de- His home is on the eastern side of
        dōngbiar wǔhào.   this street, No. 5.

   Xiè: Shì-bu-shi dōngbiar-nèige- Is it that big house (lit. gate) to the
        dà-mén?   east?

   Gāo: Shì.   Yes.

8. Bái: Nèige-nǔ-tóngzhì zuò-   What kind of work does that woman
        shénmo-gōngzuò?   comrade do?

   Máo: Wǒ-bù-xiǎode.   I don't know.

9. Bái: Zhōngguode-shòupiàoyuán   Are all the ticket-sellers in China
        'dōu-shi-nán-de-ma?   men?

   Xiè: Bù-'dōu-shì. Yǒu-bù-shǎo   Not all are. There are quite a few
        shi-'nǔ-tóngzhì.   who are women (comrades).

10. Xǔ: Nǐ-cóng-nǎr-lái?   Where are you coming from?

    Máo: Wǒ-cóng-jiāli-lái.   I'm coming from home.

    Xǔ: Nǐ-jiā zài-nǎr?   Where is your home?

    Máo: Wǒ-jiā zài-gōngyuán-   My house is behind the park.
         hòutou.

    Xǔ: Lí-zhèr yuǎn-bu-yuǎn?   Is it far from here?

    Máo: Bù-yuǎn. Guò-sānge-lù-   Not far. Go past three intersections.
         kǒur.

11. Wáng-Tóngzhì yóu-liǎngge-háizi,   Comrade Wang has two children, a
    yíge-nán-háizi, yíge-nǔ-háizi.   boy and a girl. The boy is seven, the
    Nán-háizi 'qīsuì, nǔ-háizi 'liù- girl six. Both children study in ele-
    suì. Liǎngge-háizi dōu-zài-   mentary school.
    xiǎoxué-xuéxí.

Notes

1. The syllable shòu 'to sell,' once used mainly in the written style, is now
   entering more and more into Common Speech. Thus shòupiàoyuán is preferred over màipiàoyuán for 'ticket-seller.' (The previously used suffix
   yuán is increasingly appended to the names of certain types of workers to
   form somewhat more respectful designations. The contrast is somewhat
   like that represented by English janitor versus custodian.)

2. The expression <u>zuò-shì</u> 'to work, to make a living' implies earning money and has therefore acquired a somewhat pejorative connotation in the PRC. On the other hand, <u>gōngzuò</u> 'work' (used as a noun or a verb), has a more positive connotation in that it implies providing a service or working for the benefit of others. It is therefore preferred over <u>zuò-shì</u> in Common Speech.

> Nǐ-xuéxí-ne háishi-gōngzuò-ne?   'Are you studying or working?'

LESSON 11

Exercises

1. Gāo: Rúguó-wǎnshàng yǒu-shíjiān qǐng-dào-wǒ-jiā-lai zuòyizuo-tántan.

If you're free this evening please come to my home to (sit a while and) talk.

   Xiè: Hǎo. Xièxie-ni. Rúguó-yǒu-shíjiān yídìng-dào-nǐ-jiā-qù kàn-ni.

O.K. Thank you. If I have time I'll certainly go to your home to see you.

2. Zhāng: 'Xiè-Tóngzhì-de-jiā zài-nǎr, nǐ-xiǎode-ma?

Where is Comrade Xie's home, do you know?

   Máo: Wǒ-fùqin-rènshi-ta. Nǐ-zhǎo-wǒ-fùqin, tā-yídìng-gàosu-ni.

My father knows him. Ask (lit. seek) my father, he'll certainly (be able to) tell you.

   Zhāng: Duì! Wǒ-dào-nǐ-jiā wèn-nǐ-fùqin.

Right! I'll go to your home to ask your father.

3. Qián: 'Wáng-Xiānsheng, nǐ-shi-shénmo-shíhou líkai-Měiguo-de?

Mr. King, when did you leave the United States?

   Wáng: Wǒ-shi-jīnnián-báyue.

August of this year.

   Qián: Nǐ-shi-zuò-fēijī-lái-de, háishi-zuò-chuán-lái-de?

Did you come by plane or by boat?

   Wáng: Wǒ-zuò-fēijī-lái-de.

I came by air.

   Qián: Nǐ-dào-zhèr-lái-xuéxí háishi-gōngzuò?

Did you come here to study or to work?

   Wáng: Wǒ-shi-lái-xuéxí.

I've come to study.

   Qián: Nǐ-Zhōngwén shuōde-hén-hǎo. Nǐ-huì-xiě-Zhōng-guo-zì-ma?

You speak Chinese very well. Can you write Chinese characters?

   Wáng: Xiě-Zhōngguo-zì hěn-nán. Wǒ-jiù-huì-xiě jiǎndānde-Zhōngguo-zì.

Writing Chinese characters is very difficult. I can only write simple Chinese characters.

4. Bái: 'Máo-Lǎoshī, nín-cháng-dào túshūguǎn lái-kàn-shū-ma?

Teacher Mao, do you often come to the library to read?

Máo: Shì. Wǒ-chàbuduō-měitiān   Yes. I come almost every day (to the
      dōu-dào-túshūguǎn-lái.   library).

Bái: Nín-xǐhuan-kàn-shénmo-   What books do you like to read?
      shū?

Máo: Wǒ-xǐhuan-kàn wénxuéde-   I like reading literary works.
      shū.

Bái: Nín-jiā-lí-túshūguǎn 'yuǎn- Is your home far from the library?
      bu-yuǎn?

Máo: Bù-hén-yuǎn. Rúguó-yǒu-   Not very far. If you have time please
      shíjiān qǐng-dào-wǒ-jiā-   come to my home for a chat.
      lái-tántan.

Bái: Hǎo. Wǒ-yǒu-shíjiān   Fine. (If) I have time (I will) certainly
      yídìng-qù-bàifang.   go and call (on you).

5. 'Wáng-Tóngzhì jīnnián sānshisuì.   Comrade Wang is thirty years old this
   Tā-shi-gōnggòng-qìchē-shang-   year. He is a ticket-seller on a bus.
   de-shòupiàoyuán. Tā-suírán-   Although he works every day, he still
   měitiān-gōngzuò, kěshi tā-měi-   studies every evening. His home is
   tiān-wǎnshang hái-xuéxí. Tā-jiā   not far from the library. He also often
   lí-túshūguǎn-bù-yuǎn. Tā-yě-   goes to the library to borrow books
   cháng-dào-túshūguǎn-qù jiè-shū,   to read at home.
   zài-jiāli-kàn.

Note

1. The honorific expression <u>fǔshang</u> 'your home' is no longer popular in the
   PRC, where it has been superceded by <u>nǐ-jiā</u>. On the other hand the very
   polite form <u>bàifang</u> 'to visit' is still used, though <u>kàn</u> 'see' is used more
   often.

LESSON 12

Exercises

1. Máo: Nǐ-suírán-shi-'wàiguo-
         rén, Zhōngwén-shuōde-
         'hén-hǎo.

   Bái: Wǒ-shuōde-'bù-hǎo.

2. Xǔ: Nǐ-shénmo-shíhou líkai-
         zhèr?

   Xiè: Wǒ-míngtian jiù-líkai-
         zhèr, dào-Rìběn-qù.

   Xǔ: Nǐ-zuò-'jídiǎn-zhōng-de-
         fēijī?

   Xiè: Wǒ-zuò-'sāndiǎn-zhōng-
         de-fēijī.

3. Qián: Zhèiběn-shū duōshao-qián?

   Máo: Zhèiběn-shū sānkuài-jiǔ-
          máo-qián.

   Qián: Wǒ-mǎi-yìběn.   Nǐmen-
          yǒu-Zhōngguo-dìtú-ma?

   Máo: Yǒu. Nǐ-yào-'dà-zhāng-de,
          yào-'xiǎo-zhāng-de?

   Qián: Wǒ-yào-'dà-zhāng-de.

   Máo: Dà-zhāng-de liǎngkuài-èr.

4. Xiè: Cóng-zhèr dào-Zhōngshān-
         Lù yǒu-diànchē-ma?

Bái: Gōnggòng-qìchē, diànchē
dōu-yǒu. Nǐ-yào-zuò-gōng-
gòng-qìchē, háishi-yào-zuò-
diànchē?

Xiè: Bù-yídìng. Yéxǔ zuò-gōnggòng-qìchē, yéxǔ zuò-
diànchē.

5. Lán: Zhèiběn-shū mài-duōshao-
qián?

Xǔ: 'Néiběn-shū?

Lán: Zhèiběn-'Zhōngwén-shū.

Xǔ: Oh! Nèiběn-Zhōngwén-shū
mài-liǎngyuán-wújiǎo.

Lán: Wǒ-yào-yìběn.

Xǔ: Nín-hái-mǎi-shénmo?

Lán: Wǒ-hái-mǎi-máobǐ.

Xǔ: Nín-yào-jǐzhī-máobǐ?

Lán: Wó-mǎi-liǎngzhī.

6. Zuótian wǒ-qù-bàifang-Lǎo-Zhāng,
kànjian-tāde-dà-nán-háizi. Tāde-
dà-nán-háizi-rènshi-wǒ. Tā-gàosu-wǒ, tā-fùqin-bú-zài-jiā.

LESSON 13

Exercises

1. Dài: Nǐ-zài-nǎr-xuéxí?

   Where are you studying?

   Gāo: Wǒ-zài-zhōngxué-xuéxí.
   Nǐ-ne?

   I'm studying in middle school. And you?

   Dài: Wó-yě-shàng-zhōngxué.

   I'm also going to middle school.

2. Máo: Nǐ-shàng-dàxué-'jǐniánjí?

   What year of college are you in?

   Wáng: Wǒ-shàng-'èrniánjí. Nǐ-
   ne?

   I'm in the second year. How about you?

   Máo: Wǒ-shàng-'sānniánjí.

   I'm in the third year.

3. Bái: Nǐ-xǐhuan-kàn-diànyǐng-
   ma?

   Do you like to see movies?

   Gāo: Wó-hén-xǐhuan.

   I like to very much.

   Bái: Kǎoshì-yǐhòu wǒmen-qu-
   kàn diànyǐng, 'hǎo-bu-
   hǎo?

   Let's go see a movie after the exams, O.K.?

   Gāo: Hǎojíle.

   Fine.

4. Zhāng: Qián-Lǎoshī, wǒmen-
   jīntian xué-dì-jǐkè?

   Teacher Qian, what lesson are we studying today?

   Qián: Wǒmen-jīntian yào-xué-
   dì-sānkè-le.

   We'll study lesson three today.

5. Bái: Wǒmen-lí-nǐ-jiā hái-yǒu-
   duō-yuǎn?

   How much farther is it to your home?

   Gāo: Yǐjing-kuài-dàole. Hái-
   yóu-liǎng-sānfēn-zhōng.

   We'll soon be there, in another two or three minutes.

6. Qián: Dài-Tóngzhì zhēn-cōngming Tā-shíbāsuì dàxué-
jiù-bìyè-le.

Comrade Dai is very bright. He graduated from college at eighteen.

Máo: Tā-fùqin yě-shi-shíbā-jiǔ-
suì dàxué-bìyè-de.

His father also graduated from college at eighteen or nineteen.

7. Dài: Xiè-Lǎoshī, hǎo-jiǔ-bú-
jiàn. Nín-dào-nǎr-qu?

Teacher Xie, haven't seen you for a
long time. Where are you going?

Xiè: Wǒ-dào-túshūguǎn-qu-jiè-
shū. Nǐ-xiànzài zài-nǎr-
xuéxí?

I'm going to the library to borrow
(some) books. Where are you studying
now?

Dài: Wǒ-bìyèle. Wǒ-xiànzài-
gōngzuò.

I've graduated. I'm working now.

8. Wáng: Máo-Tóngzhì, nǐ-dào-
nǎr-qù?

Comrade Mao, where are you going?

Máo: Wǒ-dào-shūdiàn-qù mǎi-
qiānbǐ, gāngbǐ, zhǐ. Nǐ-
dào-'nǎr-qù?

I'm going to the bookstore to buy
(some) pencils, pens, and paper.
Where are you going?

Wáng: Wǒ-dào-túshūguǎn-qù-jiè-
shū, jièle-shū jiù-huí-jiā.

I'm going to the library to borrow
(some) books, (and) after borrowing
the books I'll return home.

Máo: Kǎoshìle-yǐhòu yǒu-shíjiān
dào-wǒ-jiā-lái-tántan.

After exams if you have time come to
my home for a chat.

Wáng: Hǎo. Zàijiàn.

Fine. Good-bye.

9. Xiè: Lán-Tóngzhì, nǐ-xiànzài-
zài-'nǎr-xuéxí?

Comrade Lan, where are you studying
now?

Lán: Wǒ-zài-Zhōngshān-Dàxué-
xuéxí. Nǐ-xiànzài-gōngzuò-
ne, háishi-xuéxí-ne?

I'm studying at Sun Yatsen University.
Are you working or studying now?

Xiè: Wǒ-xiànzài-bù-xuéxí-le.
Wǒ-xiànzài-shi-yíge-
shòupiàoyuán.

I'm not studying any longer now. I'm
a ticket-seller now.

10. Máo: Bì-Lǎoshī, xīngqǐ-wú-
wǎnshang wó-qǐng-nín-
chī-fàn, yǒu-shíjiān-ma?

Teacher Bi, Friday evening I (would
like to) invite you to dinner. Do you
have time?

Bì: Nǐ-tài-kèqi. Tài-máfan-le.

You're too kind. It's too much trouble.

Máo: Bù-máfan. Hén-jiǎndān.

No trouble. It will be very simple.

11. Wáng: Yán-Tóngzhì, Zhāng-
Tóngzhì-láile-yǐhòu wǒ-
men-dào-túshūguǎn-qù
xuéxí-jīntian-de-kè, 'hǎo-
bu-hǎo?

Comrade Yan, after Comrade Zhang
comes let's go to the library to study
today's lesson, O.K.?

Yán: Yīnwei-Zhāng-Tóngzhǐ-   Because Comrade Zhang says he will
       shuō tā-lái-de-hén-wǎn,   be very late in coming, we won't be
       wǒmen-bù-néng-zài-   able to study anymore.
       xuéxí-le.

LESSON 14

New Vocabulary

gǎn   to feel (emotion) (V) (See Note 1)

gǎn-xìngqu   be interested (in) (See Note 1)

Exercises

gǎn   feel

gǎn-xìngqu   be interested (in)

1. Tā-duì-wénxué hén-gǎn-xìngqu.   He is very much interested in litera-
                                        ture.

2. Wáng: Nǐ-duì-huà-huàr gǎn-   Are you interested in painting?
          xìngqu-ma?

   Zhāng: Wǒ-duì-huà-huàr bù-gǎn-   I'm not interested in painting.
          xìngqu.

3. Gāo: Wǒ-duì-yǔyánxué hén-   I'm greatly interested in linguistics.
          gǎn-xìngqu. Nǐ-ne?   What about you?

   Xiè: Wó-yé-hén-xǐhuan yǔyán-   I also like linguistics. Studying (lit.
          xué. Yánjiu-yǔyánxué   researching) linguistics is very in-
          hén-yǒu-yìsi.   teresting.

4. Máo: Lǎo-Wàn, tīngshuō nǐ-   (Old) Wan, I hear you've done a lot of
          duì-yǔyánxué hén-yǒu-   research in linguistics.
          yánjiu.

   Wàn: Méi-yǒu. Wǒ-yuánlái shi-   No, I haven't. I originally studied sci-
          xué-kēxué-de. Yīnwei wǒ-   ence. Because I became interested in
          duì-yǔyánxué gǎn-xìngqu,   linguistics, afterwards I studied lin-
          suóyǐ yǐhòu xuéxí-yǔyán-   guistics.
          xué-le.

5. Xiè: Dài-Tóngzhǐ, nǐ-'rènshi-   Comrade Dai, are you acquainted with
          bu-rènshi Gāo-Sīcōng?   Gao Sicong?

   Dài: Wǒ-rènshi-ta. Tā-shi-   I know him. He's my friend.
          wǒde-péngyou.

   Xiè: Hǎojíle. Nǐ-yǒu-shíjiān   Wonderful. (When) you have time in-
          géi-wǒ-'jièshao-jièshao   troduce (him) to me, O.K.?
          'hǎo-bu-hǎo?

Dài: Wǒ-míngtian-zǎochén-jiǔ-   I have time tomorrow morning at 9:00.
diǎn-zhōng yǒu-shíjiān.

Xiè: Míngtian-zǎochén-jiǔdiǎn-   Can we go call on him tomorrow
zhōng wǒmen-qu-bàifang-ta   morning at 9:00?
kéyǐ-ma?

Dài: Kéyǐ.   (We) can.

6. Máo: Zhèibén-shū shi-shéide?   Whose book is this?

Bái: Shi-Bì-Tóngzhì-de.   It's Comrade Bì's.

Máo: Máfan ni, qǐng-nǐ-gàosu Bì- Could I trouble you to inform Com-
Tóngzhì tāde-shū-zài-zhèr. rade Bì that his book is here.

7. Xiè: Nǐ-shi-shénmo-shíhou   When did you leave the United States?
líkai-Měiguo-de?

Máo: Wǒ-shi-jiǔyuè-báhào líkai- I left on September ninth.
de.

Xiè: Nǐ-shi-zuò-'fēijī-lái-de,   Did you come by plane or by boat?
shi-zuò-'chuán-lái-de?

Máo: Wǒ-shi-zuò-'chuán-lái-de. I came by boat.

Xiè: Zuò-chuán bú-shi-hěn-màn- Isn't traveling by boat very slow?
ma?

Máo: Zuò-chuán-suírán-hěn-màn, Although traveling by boat is quite
kěshi-shífēn-yǒu-yìsi.   slow, it's very interesting.

Xiè: Nǐ-dào-zhèr-lái xuéxí-   What did you come here to study?
shénmo?

Máo: Wǒ-lái-xuéxí Zhōngguo-   I've come to study Chinese language
yǔyán.   and literature.

Xiè: Jīntian-wǎnshang-liùdiǎn- This evening at 6:00 I'd like to ask
zhōng wó-qǐng-nǐ-chī-fàn   you to dinner. Can you manage it?
'hǎo-bu-hǎo?

Máo: Xièxie, nǐ-tài-kèqi.   Thank you, you're too kind.

8. Lǎoshī: Zhèibén-shū yǐjing-   We've already studied fifteen lessons
xuéxí-shíwǔ-kè-le.   in this book.

Xuésheng: Zhèige-xīngqī shì-bu- Will we have an exam this week?
shi-yào-kǎoshì?

Lǎoshī: Bù. Xià-xīngqī wǒmen-   No. We'll have an exam next week.
kǎoshì.

9. Wǒ-shi-yíge dàxué-sìniánjí-de- I'm a senior in college. Because I'll
xuésheng. Yīnwei wǒ-míngnián be graduating next year, I'm very
jiù-yào-bìyè-le, suóyǐ wǒ-   busy now.
xiànzài-hěn-máng.

Note

1. In Common Speech both <u>duì . . . gǎn-xìngqu</u> and <u>duì . . . yǒu-xìngqu</u> are used for 'to be interested in . . .' The former is somewhat closer to the written style.

LESSON 15

New Vocabulary

xiǎoshí	hour (N/M) [lit. little time] (See Note 1)
bìxū	must, have to (AV) [lit. must must] (See Note 2)
Jiùjīnshān	San Francisco (PW) [lit. old gold mountain] (Jīn is also a surname) (See Note 3)

Exercises

xiǎoshí   hour

liǎngge-xiǎoshí   two hours

1. Wó-měitiān xué-liǎngge-   I study Chinese two hours every day.
   xiǎoshíde-Zhōngwén.

bìxū   must

bìxū-kànwán   must finish reading

2. Wǒ-jīntian bìxū-kànwán-zhèiběn-   I must finish reading this book today.
   shū.

jiāo-kè   teach (classes)

jiāo-yíge-xiǎoshí-de-kè   teach one hour (of classes)

3. Wǒ-xiànzài yào-jiāo-yíge-   I will teach for one hour now.
   xiǎoshí-de-kè.

jiāo-sìge-xiǎoshí-kè   teach for four hours

jiāole-sìge-xiǎoshí-kè   taught for four hours

4. Wǒ-zuótian jiāole-sìge-xiǎoshí-kè.   I taught for four hours yesterday.

5. Xiè: Wǒ-míngtian děi-jiāo-sìge-   I have to teach four hours tomorrow.
           xiǎoshí-de-kè. Nǐ-ne?   How about you?

   Bái: Wó-yě-bìxū-jiāo sìge-   I also have to teach four hours.
           xiǎoshí.

6. Máo: Nǐ-dào-Jiùjīnshān shi-zuò-   When you went to San Francisco did
           fēijī háishi-zuò-chuán-qù-   you go by plane or by boat?
           de?

   Wáng: Wǒ-shi-zuò-fēijī-qù-de.   I went by plane.

7. Gāo: Nǐ-xià-kè-yǐhòu zuò-   What do you do after class?
         shénmo?

   Bái: Xià-kè-yǐhòu wǒ-jiù-tīng-   After class I listen to tape record-
         lùyīn.   ings.

   Gāo: Tīng-duōshao-shíjiān-   How long do you listen (to tape re-
         lùyīn?   cordings)?

   Bái: Wó-měitiān tīng-yì-   I listen one or two hours every day.
         liǎngge-xiǎoshí.

8. Gāo: Bái-Xiānsheng, nǐ-xuéle   Mr. White, how many years have you
         jǐniánde-Zhōngwén-le?   been studying Chinese?

   Bái: Wǒ-zài-zhōngxué jiù-kāishǐ-   I began studying Chinese in high
         xué-Zhōngwén. Gāozhōng-   school. I began to study Chinese in
         'èrniánjí wǒ-jiù-xué-   the second year of senior high school.
         Zhōngwén-le.

   Gāo: Nǐ-Zhōngwén xuéde-zhēn-   You've really studied a lot of Chinese.
         bú-shǎo-le.

   Bái: Wǒ-xué-Zhōngwén chàbu-   I've already been studying Chinese
         duō yǐjing-yóu-'wǔnián-le.   for almost five years.

9. Xiè: Nǐ-zài-nǎr-gōngzuò?   Where do you work?

   Bái: Wǒ-zài-Zhōngshān-Dàxué-   I work at Sun Yatsen University. I
         gōngzuò, jiāo-Zhōngguo-   teach English to Chinese students.
         xuésheng-Yīngwén.

10. Wáng: Jiùjīnshān-lí-Niǔyue 'yuǎn- Is San Francisco far from New York?
          bu-yuǎn?

    Qián: 'Hén-yuǎn. Cóng-Niǔyue-   Quite far. It takes five hours by plane
          dào-Jiùjīnshān zuò-fēijī   from New York to San Francisco.
          yào-wǔge-xiǎoshí.

    Wáng: Cóng-Jiùjīnshān-dào-Rìběn   It's also five hours from San Fran-
          yě-yào-wǔge-xiǎoshí, shì-   cisco to Japan, isn't that so?
          bu-shi?

    Qián: Bù. Yào-bā-jiǔge-xiǎoshí.   No. It takes eight or nine hours.

11. Gāo: Nǐmen-měitiān shàng-jǐge-   How many hours of class do you have
          xiǎoshíde-kè?   every day?

    Bái: Wǒmen-měitiān shàng-   We attend classes five hours every
          wǔge-xiǎoshíde-kè.   day.

    Gāo: Xīngqiliù yě-shàng-kè-ma?   Do you also attend classes on Satur-
                                        day?

    Bái: Xīngqiliù méi-yǒu-kè.   We don't have classes on Saturday.

12. Xiè: Nǐ-dào-Jiùjīnshān-yǐhòu   After going to San Francisco where
          zài-dào-nǎr-qù?   else are you going?

Bái: Wǒ-zài-dào-Niǔyue-qù.   I'll also go to New York.

13. Dài: Nǐ-jiā lí-zhèr-yuǎn-ma?   Is your home far from here?

    Yán: Bù-yuǎn. Zuò-gōnggòng-   Not far. You can get there in half an
           qìchē bànge-xiǎoshí jiù-   hour by bus.
           kéyi-dào-le.

    Dài: Zǒu-lù-ne?   And on foot?

    Yán: Zǒu-lù yào-liǎng-sānge-   If you walk it will take two or three
           xiǎoshí.   hours.

14. Xiè: Tīngshuō Jiùjīnshān   I hear there are a lot of Chinese in
           Zhōngguo-rén-hěn-duō.   San Francisco. Is that true?
           Shì-zhēnde-ma?

    Bái: Jiùjīnshān Zhōngguo-rén   There really are a lot of Chinese in
           zhēn-bù-shǎo.   San Francisco.

     Xiè: Shì-Jiùjīnshānde-Zhōng- Are there more Chinese in San Fran-
           guo-rén-duō háishi-Niǔ- cisco or in New York?
           yuede-Zhōngguo-rén-duō?

    Bái: Háishi-Niǔyuede-Zhōng- There are more Chinese in New York.
           guo-rén-duō.

15. Dài: Nǐ-jīntian tīng-lùyīn-le-   Have you listened to tape recordings
           méi-yǒu?   today?

    Bái: Tīngle-yíge-duō-xiǎoshí. I've listened for over an hour.

    Dái: Nǐ-hái-xiǎng-tīng-ma?   Do you plan to listen some more?

    Bái: Wǒ-hái-xiǎng-tīng bànge- I plan to listen for another half hour.
           xiǎoshí.

16. Bái: Nǐ-měitiān jiāo-jǐge-   How many hours do you teach each
           xiǎoshíde-kè?   day?

    Bì: Xīngqiyī, sān, wǔ jiāo-   On Mondays, Wednesdays, and Fri-
           sānge-xiǎoshí. Xīngqièr, days I teach three hours. On Tues-
           sì jiāo-liǎngge-xiǎoshí. days and Thursdays I teach two hours.

    Bái: Xīngqiliù yǒu-méi-yǒu-kè? Do you have classes on Saturday?

    Bì: Xīngqiliù méi-yǒu-kè.   I don't have classes on Saturday.

17. Zhāng: Nèige-Yīngguo-rén huì- Can that Englishman speak Chinese?
           shuō-Zhōngwén-ma?

    Wáng: Huì-shuō. Tā-yǐjing-   Yes. He's already studied it for three
           xuéxí-le sānnián-le.   years.

    Zhāng: Tā-zài-'nǎr-xuéxí-de?   Where did he study?

    Wáng: Tā-zài-'Yīngguo-xuéxí-de. He studied in England.

18. Gāo: Zuótian Jīn-Xiānsheng   Yesterday Mr. Gold bought a paint-
           mǎile-yìzhāng-huàr.   ing.

Xiè: Tīngshuō nèizhāng-huàr   I hear that painting was very expen-
      hěn-guì.   sive.

Gāo: Shì. Tīngshuō wúbǎikuài-   Yes. I hear it was $500.
      qián.

19. Bì: Nǐ-jiānglái zhōngxué-bìyè-   In the future after graduating from
          yǐhòu xuéxí-shénmo?   middle school what will you study?

    Dài: Wǒ-duì-huà-huàr hěn-gǎn-   I'm very much interested in painting.
          xìngqu. Wó-xiǎng-xué-huà-   I think I'll study painting. How about
          huàr. Nǐ-ne?   you?

    Bì: Wǒ-duì-yǔyánxué hěn-gǎn-   I'm very much interested in linguis-
          xìngqu. Yéxǔ yánjiu-   tics. Perhaps I'll study (lit. research)
          yǔyánxué.   linguistics.

20. Jīn: Lǎo-Xiè, nǐ-kànjian-Wàn-   (Old) Xie, have you seen Comrade
          Tóngzhì-le-ma?   Wan?

    Xiè: Wó-háo-jiǔ-méi-kànjian-ta. I haven't seen him for a long time. I
          Tīngshuō tā-xiànzài-bù-   hear he's not studying anymore, he's
          xuéxí-le, yǐjing-gōngzuò-le. already working.

    Jīn: Tā-yīnggāi zài-túshūguǎn-   He should work in a library.
          gōngzuò.

    Xiè: Tā-gōngzuò 'shì-zài-   His work is in a library.
          túshūguǎn.

21. Zuótian-wǒ-dào-shūdiàn-qu géi-   Today I went to the bookstore to buy
    wó-liǎngge-háizi-mǎi-shū. Zài-   some books for my two children. On
    lùshang yùjian-Yán-Xiānsheng.   the street I met Mr. Yan. He said
    Tā-shuō tā-xià-xīngqī bìxū-dào- next week he has to go to San Fran-
    Jiùjīnshān-qu, yīnwei tā-mǔqin- cisco, as his mother is sick. This
    bìngle. Jīntian-wǎnshang yīng-   evening (he) should go to school, but
    dāng-dào-xuéxiào-qu, kěshi-tā-   he doesn't have time, so he can't go.
    méi-shíjiān, suóyǐ tā-bù-néng-
    qù-le.

Notes

1. In Common Speech <u>xiǎoshí</u> 'hour' appears to be gaining ascendancy over
   <u>zhōngtóu</u>. It appears to be increasingly used as a noun, i.e., with a measure, but it also occurs without: <u>yí(ge) xiǎoshí</u> 'one hour.'

2. In Common Speech <u>bìxū</u> 'must' is used more often than <u>bǐděi</u>. However,
   the single syllable <u>děi</u> 'must' is still widely used.

3. In the PRC <u>Jiùjīnshān</u> is preferred over <u>Sānfánshì</u> for 'San Francisco.'
   The latter is considered typical of overseas and Kuomintang usage.

4. In expressions of teaching for certain lengths of time, the form <u>jiāo . . .
   kè</u> appears to be somewhat more frequently used than <u>jiāo . . . shū</u> in the
   PRC:

      Wǒ-jīntian-jiāole wǔge-xiǎoshí (de)-kè. 'I taught for five hours today.'

LESSON 16

New Vocabulary

àirén   husband, wife, fiancé, fiancée; lover (N) [lit. loved person] (See Note 1)

Exercises

àirén	husband (or wife)
wǒ-àirén	my husband (or wife)

1. Wǒ-àirén shi-Sūzhou-rén.   My husband (or wife) is from Soochow.

2. Lián: Wàn-Lǎoshī, nín-jiā zài-zhèitiáo-lù-de-dōngbiar háishi-xībiar?   Teacher Wan, is your home on the east or west side of this road?

   Wán: Zài-dōngbiar.   On the east side.

   Lián: Wǒ-jīntian-xiàwǔ dào-nín-jiā-qu bàifang-nín.   I'd like to go to your home this afternoon to call on you.

   Wán: Nǐ-tài-kèqi.   You're too kind.

   Lián: Yīnggāi-de.   I should.

   Wàn: Zuì-hǎo nǐ-míngtian-qu, yīnwei jīntian wǒ-àirén-bú-zài-jiā.   It would be best if you went tomorrow, as my wife (or husband) is not at home today.

3. Gāo: Wó-géi-nǐmen-liǎngwèi 'jièshao-jièshao. Zhèiwèi shi-'Wàn-Jiàoshou. Zhèiwèi shi-'Bái-Xiānsheng.   Let me introduce the two of you. This is Professor Wan. This is Mr. White.

   Bái: Nǐ-hǎo.   Pleased to meet you.

   Wàn: Nǐ-hǎo.   How do you do.

4. Xuésheng: Nín-kàn-wó-xiěde-zì 'duì-bu-duì?   Would you look to see if the characters I've written are right or not.

   Lǎoshī: Nǐ-zhēn-cōngming. Xiěde-yìdiár-yě-bú-cuò.   You're very smart. You've written them with no mistakes at all.

   Xuésheng: Zhèige-xīngqī kéyǐ-xuéxí dào-dì-èrshi-kè-ma?   Will be we able to study up to the twentieth lesson this week?

   Lǎoshī: Xuéxí-bu-dào dì-èrshi-kè. Yéxǔ kéyǐ-xuéxí dào-dì-shíjiǔ-kè.   We won't be able to study up to the twentieth lesson. Perhaps we'll be able to study up to the nineteenth lesson.

5. Zuótiān-wǒ-jìn-chéng. Dàole-
chéng-lǐtou-yǐhòu, wǒ-jiù-dào-
Qián-Tóngzhì-jiā-qù-le. Tā-jiā-
zhèige-dìfang hén-hǎo, yòu-yǒu-
shān yòu-yóu-shuǐ. Wǒ-jìn-chéng-
yǐhòu Qián-Tóngzhì gēn-wǒ-tán-
de-hén-yǒu-yìsi, chàbuduō dào-
liùdiǎn-zhōng-le. Tā-shuō qǐng-
wǒ-zài-tā-jiāli chī-wǎnfàn. Wǒ-
shuō tài-máfan. Tā-shuō hén-
jiāndān-bú-kèqi.

Yesterday I went into the city. After
I arrived in the city, I went to Comrade Qian's home. This area around
his home is very nice, there are hills
and water. After I entered the city
Comrade Qian and I had a very interesting talk until almost six o'clock.
He said he wanted to invite me to have
dinner at his home. I said it was too
much trouble. He said (dinner) was
very simple and not to be polite.

6. Wǒ-jiānglái yào-dào-dàxué yánjiu-
yǔyán. Wǒ-yīngdāng-mǎi yíge-
lùyīnjǐ, yīnwei-xué-yǔyán bìxū-
yǒu yíge-lùyīnjǐ. Wǒde-péngyou
Lián-Dàwén tā-yǒu-liǎngge-
lùyīnjǐ. Tā-shuō wǒ-bú-yòng-
mǎi, kéyǐ-gēn-tā-jiè-yíge.

In the future I want to go to the university to study languages. I should
buy a tape recorder, for in studying
languages one should have a recorder. My friend Lian Dawen (he) has two
tape recorders. He says I don't need
to buy any, I can borrow one of his
(lit. with him borrow one).

7. Māma, mèimei-gēn-wǒ cóng-
Niǔyue dào-Rìběn-qù-lǚxíng.
Wǒmen cóng-Niǔyue dào-Jiùjīn-
shān shi-zuò-fēijǐ. Cóng-Jiùjīn-
shān dào-Rìběn shi-zuò-chuán.
Zài-chuán-shang yǒu-hén-duō-
shíjiān-xuéxí.

Mama, younger sister, and I took a
trip from New York to Japan. We went
by plane from New York to San Francisco and by boat from San Francisco
to Japan. On the boat there was a lot
of time to study.

8. Shàng-xīngqǐ wǒmen-kǎoshìle-
yǐhòu, wǒ-gēn-Biān-Tóngzhì,
Lián-Tóngzhì wǒmen-sānge-rén
yào-dào-gōngyuán-qù. Gōngyuán
lí-zhèr-hén-yuǎn, bìxū-kāi-chē-
qù. Nèitiān shi-Biān-Tóngzhì-
kāi-chē. Yīnwei wǒ-gēn-Lián-
Tóngzhì wǒmen-liǎngge-rén dōu-
bú-huì-kāi-chē, suóyǐ Biān-
Tóngzhì-yíge-rén kāile-sāngge-
xiǎoshí-chē, cái-dào-gōngyuán.
Nèige-gōngyuán-de-shānshuǐ
piàoliang-jíle. Wǒmen-zài-
gōngyuán-lǐtou chàbuduō-yǒu-
sìge-xiǎoshí, cái-líkai-gōngyuán.

Last week after exams I and Comrade
Bian and Comrade Lian (we three
people) wanted to go to the park. The
park was very far from here and it
was necessary to go by car. On that
day it was Comrade Bian who drove.
Because neither I nor Comrade Lian
knew how to drive, Comrade Bian
drove for three hours all by himself
and only then did we reach the park.
The scenery in that park was very
beautiful. We were in the park for almost four hours, and only then left
the park.

Notes

1. In the PRC the expression nèiren is no longer used in referring to one's
own wife. It has been partially replaced, especially among urban intellec-
tuals, by àirén. This, as mentioned in Supplementary Lesson 1, Note 1,
is used in referring to both husband and wife (or fiancé and fiancée), but
it should be used by non-Chinese only with the greatest caution.

2. In the PRC the honorific expression Jiúyǎng 'Pleased to meet you' is no longer used. When people are introduced to each other they often simply acknowledge the introduction with Nǐ-hǎo or Nín-hǎo. A more elaborate acknowledgment of an introduction is Hěn-gāoxìng-rènshi-nín-le 'Very happy to have made your acquaintance.' (See Supplementary Lesson 20, Exercise 4.)

LESSON 17

Exercises

1. Lán: Nǐde-lùyīnjī gēn-wǒde- yíyàng-ma?

Is your tape recorder the same as mine?

Yán: Bù-yíyàng. Wǒde méi-yǒu- nǐde-nènmo-hǎo.

(It's) not the same. Mine isn't as good as yours.

2. Bái: Zhèige-dìfang gēn-Háng- zhou-yíyàng-hǎo-ma?

Is this place as nice as Hangchow?

Gāo: Méi-yǒu-Hángzhou-nènmo- piàoliang.

It's not as beautiful as Hangchow.

3. Xiè: Bái-Xiānsheng xuéde- zěnmoyàng?

How is Mr. White as a student?

Gāo: Tā-hěn-yònggōng. Tā-gēn- Zhōngguo-xuésheng yíyàng- yònggōng.

He's very hard-working. He's as studious as Chinese students.

Xiè: Tā-xué-wénxué xué-de- 'hǎo-bu-hǎo?

How does he do in literature?

Gāo: Tā-xué-wénxué xué-de- gēn-Zhōngguo-xuésheng- yíyàng-hǎo.

He's as good as Chinese students (in studying literature).

4. Xuésheng: Zhèige-zì hěn-nán-xiě.

This character is hard to write.

Lǎoshī: Zhèige-zì nǐ-rènshi- ma?

Do you recognize this character?

Xuésheng: Wǒ-rènshi.

I know it.

Lǎoshī: Shì-shénmo?

What is it?

Xuésheng: Shì-jiēhūn-de hūn.

It's the hūn of jiēhūn.

Lǎoshī: Bú-cuò.

Right.

5. Māma-gàosu-wǒ, wǒ-shi-zài- Jiùjīnshān-zhǎng-dà-de, kěshi- shēng-zài-Zhōngguo. Wǒ-shēng- zài-Sūzhou. Zuótian Lán-Xiān- sheng-lái-shuō tā-hěn-xīwang dào-Zhōngguo-lǎo-jiā-qù-kàn.

Mama told me I grew up in San Francisco but was born in China. I was born in Soochow. Yesterday Mr. Lan came to say he hopes very much to go on a visit to (lit. see) his old home in China. I said I hoped as much as he

Wǒ-shuō wǒ-gēn-tā-yíyàng-
xǐwang dào-Zhōngguo-qù.

did to go to China.

6. Zuótian wǒ-qù-bàifang Zhāng-
Lǎoshǐ, tā-bú-zài-jiā, suóyǐ
wǒ-méi-jìnqu.

Yesterday I went to call on Teacher
Zhang, (but) he wasn't at home, so I
didn't go in.

7. Zuótian Dài-Tóngzhǐ géi-wǒ-
jièshào-le yíwèi-wàiguo-péngyou.
Wǒ-tīng nèiwèi-wàiguo-péngyou-
shuō-de-Zhōngwén gēn-Zhōngguo-
rén-shuō-de-yíyàng-hǎo.

Yesterday Comrade Dai introduced
me to a foreign friend. (I heard that)
the Chinese that that foreign friend
spoke is as good as that spoken by a
Chinese.

8. Xīngqītiān wǒ-gēn-wǒ-àirén cóng-
Sūzhou zuò-huǒchē dào-Hángzhou-
qù-lǚxíng, yùjianle-Lián-Tóngzhǐ
yě-gēn-tā-àirén lái-lǚxíng. Wǒ-
men-sìge-rén-zài-yíkwàr yìbiār-
tántan yìbiār-kàn-shānshuǐ, hén-
yǒu-yìsi. Wǒ-àirén gēn-Lián-
Tóngzhǐ-de-àirén liǎngge-rén
duì-huà-huàr hén-gǎn-xìngqu.
Wǒ-àirén gēn Lián-Tóngzhǐ-
àirén-shuō, huí-jiā-yǐhòu bǎ-
Hángzhoude-shānshuǐ huàchulai.

Sunday my wife and I took a trip by
train to Hangchow and met Comrade
Lian who was coming on the trip with
his wife. The four of us on the one
hand (lit. side) chatted and on the other gazed at the scenery. It was very
interesting. My wife and Comrade
Lian's wife are both very much interested in painting. My wife and Comrade Lian's wife said that on returning
home they would do some paintings of
the Hangchow scenery.

Notes

1. The game of huá-quán 'guess-fingers' is said by some strait-laced PRC
informants to be out of favor, but others report that it is still being
played in the PRC, even in public places.

2. Some PRC informants have expressed a preference, in Pattern Drills
17.1, 17.2, and 17.4, for the use of gēn rather than xiàng in combination
with yíyàng. E.g.,

Dàxué bù-gēn-zhōngxué-yíyàng.   'College isn't like middle school.'

Diànchē bù-gēn-gōnggòng-qìchē yíyàng-kuài.   'Streetcars aren't as
fast as buses.'

Tā-kǎoshǐ kǎo-de-gēn-wǒ-yíyàng-máng.   'He's as busy with exams
as I am.'

However, xiàng...zhèiyàng and xiàng...nèiyàng are still preferred.

LESSON 18

Exercises

1. Qián: Wǒ-bú-zài-Niǔyue-xuéxí.

   Xǔ: Nǐ-bú-zài-Niǔyue-xuéxí
   zài-'nǎr-xuéxí?

   Qián: Wǒ-zài-Jiùjīnshān-xuéxí.

2. Lán: Nǐ-zuótian xuéxíle-jǐge-xiǎo-
   shí?

   Bái: Wǒ-zuótian xuéxíle-wǔge-
   xiǎoshí.

Lán: Zhāng-Lǎoshī-shuō wǒmen-
      měitiān-yīngdāng-xuéxí
      báge-xiǎoshí.

3. Yán: Wǒ-duì-kēxué bù-gǎn-
        xìngqu.

   Wàn: Nǐ-duì-kēxué bù-gǎn-xìngqu
        duì-shénmo-gǎn-xìngqu?

   Yán: Wǒ-duì-yǔyánxué gǎn-
        xìngqu.

4. Bái: Wáng-Dàwén zài-dàxué
        xuéxíguo-ma?

   Zhāng: Tā-xuéxíguo, kěshi méi-
        bìyè.

5. Xiè: Qǐng-wèn, zhèiben-shū
        mài-jǐkuài-qián?

   Dài: Mài-liǎngyuán-wǔjiǎo. Nín-
        yào-mǎi-yìběn-ma?

   Xiè: Wǒ-mǎi-yìběn.

   Dài: Nín-zài-dàxué xuéxí-
        shénmo?

   Xiè: Wǒ-bù-xuéxí.

   Dài: Nǐ-bù-xuéxí zuò-shénmo?

   Xiè: Wǒ-gōngzuò.

6. Bái: Qǐng-wèn, jīntian jǐhào?

   Yán: Jīntian èryue-qīhào.

   Bái: Oh! Wǒ-chà-yìdiǎr-wàngle.
        Jīntiān-wǎnshang bìxū-qù-
        bàifang-Wàn-Lǎoshī.

   Yán: Tā-jiā-zài-nǎr?

   Bái: Tā-jiā zài-Zhōngshān-Lù-
        běibiar.

   Yán: Nǐ-zuò-shénmo-chē-qù?

   Bái: Wǒ-xiǎng-zuò-diànchē.

   Yán: Nǐ - yīnggāi - zuò gōnggòng-
        qìchē. Diànchē-zǒude-màn.

   Bái: Wǒ - yéxǔ - zuò - gōnggòng -
        qìchē.

   Yán: Wǒ - jiā lí - Wàn-Lǎoshī - jiā
        bù-yuǎn, yě-zài-Zhōngshān-
        Lù. Nǐ-kéyǐ-dào-wǒ-jiā-qu
        zuò-yìhuěr.

   Bái: Wǒ-yǒu-shíjiān yídǐng-dào-
        nǐ-jiā-qu.

7. Wǒ-gēn-wǒ-àirén jiēhūn - yìnián.
   Wǒmen - shēngle - yíge - nǚ - háizi.
   Zhèige - nǚ - háizi zhǎng - de-gen-
   wǒ-àirén-yíyàng. Xīwang-jiānglái
   zhèige - nǚ - háizi zhǎng - dà - yǐhòu
   yònggōng-xuéxí.

LESSON 19

New Vocabulary

nálǐ, náli   where?, You flatter me [lit. what inside] (See Note 1)

Exercises

       nálǐ   where?

       nálǐ, nálǐ   You flatter me

1. "Nálǐ, nálǐ" jiu-shi-kèqi-huà.   "You flatter me" is a polite expres-
                                        sion.

2. Wàn: Nǐ-zuò-de-cài bǐ-   Your dishes are better than any res-
        fànguǎnde-cài-dōu-hǎo.   taurant's.

   Gāo: Nálǐ, nálǐ.   You flatter me.

   Wàn: Shi-zhēnde!   It's the truth!

3. Dài: Tīngshuō zài-Zhōngguo   I hear that in China the polite expres-
        Guòjiǎng-zhèige-kèqi-huà   sion Guòjiǎng is no longer used now.
        xiànzài-bú-yòng-le.

   Yán: Duì-le.   That's right.

   Dài: Bù-shuō-Guòjiǎng xiànzài-   (If one) doesn't say Guòjiǎng what does
        shuō-shénmo?   one say now?

   Yán: Xiànzài-shuō-nálǐ.   One says nálǐ.

4. Xiè: Bái-Wénshān, nǐ-zài   Vincent White, how many years did
        Měiguo xuéxíle-jǐnián?   you study in America?

   Bái: Wǒ-zài-Měiguo-dàxué   (When) I was at the university in
        xuéxíle-wǔnián. Wǒ-shi-   America, I studied for five years. I
        yìbiār-gōngzuò yìbiār-   worked while I studied.
        xuéxí.

5. Wàn: Nín-shi-Qián-Jiàoshòu-ma?   Are you Professor Qian?

   Qián: Shi, wǒ-xìng-Qián. Nín-   Yes, my name is Qian. And your name
         guìxìng?   is . . . ?

   Wàn: Wǒ-xìng-Wàn. Yán-Tóngzhì   My name is Wan. Comrade Yan sug-
        jièshào-wǒ-lái-kàn-nín.   gested that I (lit. introduced me to)
                                    see you.

   Qián: Oh! Nín-shi-Wàn-Tóngzhì.   Oh! You're Comrade Wan. I and Com-
         Wǒ-gēn-Yán-Tóngzhì shi-   rade Yan are old friends. Please
         lǎo-péngyou. Qǐng-jìnlái- come in (and) sit down. Sit down as
         zuò. Suíbiàn-zuò.   you please.

   Wàn: Xièxie-nín. Wǒ-jīntian   Thank you. Today I've just come to
        jiùshi-lái-bàifang-nín gēn- call on you and have a chat with you.
        nín-tántan.

6. Yán: Nǐ-xiěde-zì zhēn-hǎo.   The characters you've written are
                                    really nice.

   Xiè: Nálǐ, nálǐ.   You flatter me.

   Yán: Nǐ-xué-xiě-zì xuéle-jǐnián? How many years did you study writing
                                    characters?

   Xiè: Wǒ-xuéle-yìnián.   I studied for one year.

   Yán: Nǐ-xiǎode-bu-xiǎode zhèr-   Do you know whether there is anyone
        yǒu-rén néng-jiāo-xiě-zì-   here who can teach writing charac-
        ma?   ters?

   Xiè: Wǒ-bù-xiǎode. Nǐ-yào-   I don't know. Do you want to study
        xuéxí xiě-zì-ma?   writing characters?

   Yán: Shì, wǒ-yào-xuéxí yòng-   Yes, I want to learn to write charac-
        máobí-xiě-zì.   ters with a brush.

7. Wǒ-māma shi-Sūzhou-rén, kěshi   My mother is a native of Soochow but
   bú-huì-shuō-Sūzhou-huà, yīnwei   can't speak the Soochow dialect, be-
   liǎngsuì-de-shíhou jiù-líkaile- cause at two years of age (she) left

Sūzhou, zài-Guǎngdong-zhǎng-dà-de, suóyǐ jiù-huì-shuō-Guǎngdong-huà.

Soochow and grew up in Canton, so (she) can only speak Cantonese.

8. Wǒ-fùqin shi-yíge-gōnggòng-qìchē-shàng-de shòupiàoyuán. Wǒ-jiāli yígòng-yǒu-sìge-rén, fùqin, mǔqin, wǒ, hái-yǒu-yíge-dìdi. Jīntian yīnwei-wǒ-bìngle, suóyǐ shǎo-xuéxí-yìdiǎr. Huí-jiā gēn-dìdi dào-shūdiàn-qu mǎi-gāngbǐ, qiānbǐ, zhǐ, běnzi. Jìnle-shūdiàn, kànjian-Lián-Lǎoshī yě-zài-nèr mǎi-shū. Tā-wèn-wǒ hǎo-yìdiǎr-ma? Wǒ-shuō-hǎole-yìdiǎr, míngtian kéyǐ-shàng-kè-xuéxí. Lián-Lǎoshī-shuō wǒ-shi-ge-hǎo-xuésheng. Wǒ-shuō: "Nálǐ, nalǐ."

My father is a ticket-collector on a bus. There are altogether four people in my family—father, mother, I, and also a younger brother. Today because I wasn't feeling well, I left school a little early (lit. studied a little less). After returning home, together with younger brother I went to the book-store to buy some pens, pencils, pa-per, and notebooks. On entering the bookstore, I saw Teacher Lian who was also buying books there. He asked me whether I was a bit better. I said I felt a little better and could go to class and study tomorrow. Teacher Lian said I was a good student. I said: "You flatter me."

9. Wǒ-zhèicì cóng-Měiguo-huílái-yǐhòu, Lián-Guóshū qǐng-wǒ zài-yíge-fànguǎn chī-fàn. Tā-yàole yíge-hóng-shāo-jī, yíge-hóng-shāo-yú, yíge-zhū-ròu-báicài-tāng. Wǒmen-liǎngge-rén chī-de-hén-bǎo. Nèige-fànguǎn-de-cài zhēn-bú-cuò. Wǒmen-liǎngge-rén yìbiār-chī yìbiār-tán. Lián-Guóshū wèn-wǒ zài-Měiguo néng-bu-néng-chīdào-Zhōngguo-cài. Wǒ-shuō zài-Měiguo chúle-néng-chīdào-Zhōngguo-cài, yě-néng-chīdào-Rìběn-cài. Tā-hái-wèn-wǒ Měiguo-rén 'xǐhuan-bu-xǐhuan chī-Zhōngguo-cài? Wǒ-shuō xiànzài hěn-duō-Měiguo-rén xǐhuan-chī-Zhōngguo-cài. Tā-yòu-wèn-wǒ, Měiguo-rén chī-Zhōngguo-cài huì-bu-huì-yòng-kuàizi. Wǒ-gàosu-tā Měiguo-rén xiànzài hěn-duō-huì-yòng-kuàizi chī-Zhōngguo-cài. Měiguo-rén yòng-kuàizi-chī-fàn nán-shi-nán, kěshi chī-Zhōngguo-cài bìxū-yòng-kuàizi.

After I returned from America this time, Lian Guoshu invited me to eat in a restaurant. He ordered a red-cooked chicken, a red-cooked fish, and a beef and cabbage soup. The two of us ate until we were quite stuffed. The food in that restaurant was really not bad. The two of us ate and talked. Lian Guoshu asked me if it was pos-sible to get to eat Chinese food in America. I said it was possible to eat Chinese food in America, and Japa-nese food as well. He also asked whether Americans liked to eat Chi-nese food. I told him nowadays a lot of Americans like to eat Chinese food. He also asked me whether Americans can eat Chinese food with chopsticks. I told him that many Americans can eat Chinese food with chopsticks now. Although it is true that for Americans to eat Chinese food with chopsticks is difficult, nevertheless Chinese food should be eaten with chopsticks.

Note

1. The expression Guòjiǎng 'You flatter me' spoken in reply to a compliment has been replaced in Common Speech by nálǐ or nalǐ (often repeated: nálǐ,

náli), Nín-tài-kèqi 'You're too kind (lit. polite),' and other expressions.
(The suffix li is a more formal equivalent of the suffix r in zhèli 'here,'
nàli 'there,' náli 'where?.')

LESSON 20

New Vocabulary

yǔwén   language and literature (N) [lit. language literature] (See Note 1)

Exercises

yǔwén	language and literature
Zhōngguo-Yǔwén	Chinese Language and Literature

1. Dàxué-túshūguǎn yǒu-Zhōngguo-   Does the university library have Chi-
   Yǔwén-ma?   nese Language and Literature?

2. Bái: Nǐ-yǔwén kǎode-'hǎo-bu-   How were the exams in Chinese?
        hǎo?

   Gāo: Wǒ-xiǎng kǎode-hái-hǎo.   I think I did rather well.

   Bái: Shùxué-ne?   How about math?

   Gāo: Kǎode-zāogāo-jíle.   I messed it up badly.

3. Lán: Nǐ-zuótian-kàn-de-nèi-   How was that movie you saw yester-
        chǎng-diànyǐng 'hǎo-bu-   day?
        hǎo?

   Xiè: Hén-hǎo, hén-yǒu-yìsi.   Fine, very interesting. If I have an
        Yǒu-jīhui zài-qù-kàn-yícì.   opportunity I'll see it (once) again.

4. Wàn: Wǒ-géi-nǐmen-liǎngwèi   Let me introduce the two of you. This
        'jièshao-jièshao. Zhèiwèi   is Teacher Qian. This is Vincent
        shi-Qián-Lǎoshi. Zhèiwèi   White
        shi-Bái-Wénshān.

   Bái: Hěn-gāoxìng-rènshi-nín-le. Very happy to have made your ac-
                                      quaintance.

   Qián: Wǒ-yé-hěn-gāoxìng.   Same here.

5. Bái: Wǒmen-dào-fànguǎn chī-   Let's go to the restaurant and have
        běifāng-cài, 'hǎo-bu-hǎo?   Northern Chinese food, O.K.?

   Gāo: Hǎojíle. Wǒ-hén-xǐhuan   Great. I like (to eat) Northern food
        chī-běifāng-cài.   very much.

   Bái: Wǒmen yě-qù-kàn-diàn-   Let's also go see a movie, O.K.?
        yǐng, 'hǎo-bu-hǎo?

   Gāo: Hǎo-ba.   Fine.

   Bái: Diànyǐngyuàn lí-nǐ-jiā   Is the theater far from your home?
        'yuǎn-bu-yuǎn?

Gāo: 'Hén-yuǎn. Wǒmen-zuì- Quite far. It would be best if we went
  hǎo zuò-chē-qù.   by bus (or streetcar).

6. Bì: Wó-qǐng-wèn-nǐ-yíge- I'd like to ask you a question.
   wèntí.

 Xiè: Shénmo-wèntí?   What question?

 Bì: Xiànzài-Zhōngguo, tīng- In present-day China, I hear the po-
   shuō kèqi-huà-de-guòjiǎng lite expression guòjiǎng is no longer
   xiànzài-bù-shuō-le. Nǐ- said now. Do you know what is said?
   xiǎode-shuō-shénmo?

 Xiè: Shuō-náli huòzhě-shuō- (They) say náli or náli, náli.
   náli, náli.

7. Zhāng: Wai! Nǐ-zhǎo-shéi? Hello, who are you calling?

 Yán: Wó-qǐng-Zhāng-Tóngzhì- I'd like to speak to Comrade Zhang.
   shuō-huà.

 Zhāng: Wǒ-xìng-Zhāng. Nǐ-shi- This is Zhang. Are you Comrade Yan?
   Yán-Tóngzhì-ma?

 Yán: Shì. Nǐ-shi-shénmo-shí- Yes. When did you come back from
   hou cóng-Rìběn-huílái-de? Japan?

 Zhāng: Wǒ-dào-Rìběn-qù-le nǐ- How did you know I went to Japan?
   zěnmo-xiǎode-de?

 Yán: Lán-Tóngzhì gàosu-wǒ- Comrade Lan told me. Whenever you
   de. Nǐ-shénmo-shíhou- have time, I'd like to go and call on
   yǒu-shíjiān, wǒ-qù- you.
   bàifang-ni.

 Zhāng: Něitiān-'dōu-yǒu-shíjiān. (I) have time any day.

8. Máo: Nǐ-shēng-zài-nǎr? Where were you born?

 Dài: Wǒ-shēng-zài-Sūzhou, I was born in Soochow and grew up in
   zài-Hángzhou-zhǎng-dà. Hangchow.

 Máo: Nǐ-dàxué zài-nǎr-bìyè-de? Where did you graduate from college?

 Dài: Wǒ-dàxué zài-Guǎngdong- I graduated from college in Canton.
   bìyè-de.

 Máo: Nǐ-shi-xué-shénmo-de? What did you study?

 Dài: Wǒ-zài-zhōngxué xuéxí- I studied mathematics in middle school
   shùxué, zài-dàxué xuéxí- and history in college.
   lìshǐ.

 Máo: Nǐ-zài-nǎr-jiēhūn-de? Where did you get married?

 Dài: Wǒ-zài-Hángzhou-jiēhūn- I was married in Hangchow.
   de.

9. Zuótian wǒ-gēn-Xǔ-Dàwén, Yán- Yesterday I and Xu Dawen, Yan Wen-
 Wénshān, hái-yǒu-Yán-Wénshān- shan, and a friend of Yan Wenshan's
 de-yíge-péngyou wǒmen-sìge- (the four of us) went to a restaurant
 rén dào-fànguǎn-qu-chī-fàn. to eat. We ordered three dishes and a

Wǒmen-yàole-sānge-cài yíge-
tāng. Sānge-cài shi-chǎo-jī,
chǎo-dòufu, hóng-shāo-yú. Tāng
shi-niú-ròu-tāng. Chī-de-hén-
bǎo. Wǒmen-sìge-rén suíbiàn-
chī, suíbiàn-tán. Yán-Wénshān-
de-péngyou wǒ-cóngqian-bú-rèn-
shi, bù-xiǎode tā-shi-Zhōngguo-
rén shi-Rìběn-rén. Jīntian yì-
tīng-tā-shuō-huà jiù-xiǎode tā-
bú-shi-Zhōngguo-rén shi-Rìběn-
rén.

soup. The three dishes were fried
chicken, fried beancurd, red-cooked
fish. The soup was beef soup. We ate
until we were quite stuffed. The four
of us ate and talked informally. I
wasn't previously acquainted with Yan
Wenshan's friend and didn't know if
he was Chinese or Japanese. Today
on hearing him speak I realized he
wasn't Chinese but Japanese.

10. Wǒ-gēn-Lán-Dàwén liǎng-sān-
nián bú-jiàn-le. Zuótian wǒ-dào-
tā-jiā-qu-kàn-ta. Yuánlái-wó-
dǎcuòle-mén. Wó-dǎ-mén-de-
shíhou yìdiǎr-yě-bù-xiǎode-shi-
cuò-le. Yíge-lǎo-tóngzhì-kāi-
mén, wèn-wó-zhǎo-shéi. Wǒ-
shuō zhǎo-Lán-Dàwén. Nèiwèi-
lǎo-tóngzhì-shuō zhèlǐ-méi-yǒu-
xìng-Lán-de. Wǒ-cái-xiǎode-shi-
cuò-le. Nèiwèi-lǎo-tóngzhì-shuō
suírán-cuò-le qǐng-jìnlai zuò-
yìhuěr. Wó-xiǎng wǒ-bú-rènshi-
nèiwèi-lǎo-tóngzhì, bú-yào-máfan.
Wǒ-shuō: "Xièxiè, bú-bì-le."

I hadn't seen Lan Dawen for two or
three years. Yesterday I went to his
home to see him. Actually I knocked
on the wrong door. When I was knock-
ing on the door I wasn't at all aware
I was wrong. An old comrade opened
the door and asked who I was looking
for. I told him I was looking for Lan
Dawen. That old comrade said there
wasn't anyone by the name of Lan
here. Only then did I realize I had
made a mistake. That old comrade
said although I had made a mistake to
please come in and sit a while. I
thought, I don't know that old comrade and don't want to trouble him, so
I said: "Thanks, it's not necessary."

Note

1. In the PRC the term Guówén 'Chinese' (as a subject of study in school) has
   been superseded by Zhōngwén or, better still, when there is no possible
   confusion with other languages, by yǔwén, literally 'language (and) literature.' The latter can be made more specific, as in Zhōngguo Yǔwén, the
   name of an important journal published from 1952–1966. Yǔwén appears to
   be used chiefly in secondary schools and Zhōngwén in universities.

LESSON 21

New Vocabulary

fúwùyuán   attendant, waiter (N) [lit. serve matters person] (See Note 1)

Exercises

fúwùyuán   waiter

fúwùyuán-tóngzhì   comrade waiter

1. Fúwùyuán-Tóngzhì, qǐng-ni-bāng-   Comrade waiter, please help us order
   zhu-wǒmen xiáng-jǐge-cài.   a few dishes.

2. Yán: Lǎo-Xiè, fúwùyuán-zài-nǎr?   (Old) Xie, where's the waiter?

   Xiè: Nǐ-kǎn, jiù-zài-nǐ-hòubiar.   Look, he's right behind you. He's
Láile.   come.

   Yán: Oh, wǒ-kànjian-le . . .   Oh, I see . . . Comrade, please bring
Tóngzhì, qǐng-bǎ-cài-dār-   the menu.
nálai.

3. Dài: Wǒmen-dōu-yīnggāi-xuéxí   We should all learn from Vincent
Bái-Wénshān xué-Zhōngwén-   White's excellent experience in study-
de-hǎo-jīngyàn.   ing Chinese.

   Lán: Duì-le! Xuéxí-tā-xué-   Right! Studying his experience in
Zhōngwén-de-jīngyàn yídìng-   learning Chinese will certainly be a
duì-wǒmen yǒu-hěn-dà-de-   big help to us.
bāngzhu.

4. Bái: Nǐmen-zhèr gěi-fúwùyuán-   Do you give the (comrade) waiters
tóngzhì-xiǎofèi-ma?   tips here?

   Gāo: 'Bù-gěi. Wǒmen-zài-Zhōng-   No. In China we don't give tips.
guo shi-méi-yǒu-xiǎofèi-de.

5. Xiè: Wàn-Tóngzhì-de-gōngzuo-   Comrade Wan has more work experi-
jīngyan bǐ-wǒmen-duō.   ence than we do.

   Bǐ: Duì-le! Wǒmen-yīnggāi-   Right! We should ask him to tell us
qǐng-ta bǎ-tāde-gōngzuo   about (lit. introduce) his work expe-
jīngyàn 'jièshao-jièshao.   rience.

6. Gāo: Qǐng-wèn-tóngzhì, dào-   May I ask you, Comrade, how does
gōngyuán-qù zěnmo-zǒu?   one get to the park?

   Yán: Cóng-zhèitiáo-lù wàng-dōng-   Go east from this street. That's a
zǒu. Nà-shi-yìtiáo-xiǎo-lù.   small road. From here it's also pos-
Cóng-zhèr zǒu-dà-lù yé-   sible to take (lit. walk) a big road, but
kéyǐ, kěshi bíjiáo-yuǎn-le-   it's a little longer (lit. farther).
yìdiǎr.

7. Máo: Nín-mǎi-shénmo?   What would you like?

   Bái: Wó-mǎi-Zhōngguo-dìtú.   I'd like a Chinese map.

   Máo: Wǒmen-yǒu-liángzhǒng,   We have two kinds, one big and one
yìzhǒng-dà-zhāng yìzhǒng-   small.
xiǎo-zhāng.

   Bái: Wǒ-yào-dà-zhāng. Duōshao-   I want the big one. How much is it?
qián?

   Máo: Liǎngkuài-wǔ.   Two-fifty.

   Bái: Wǒ-yào-yìzhāng.   I'll take one.

8. Wàn: Kuài-dào shíèrdiǎn-zhōng-   It will soon be twelve o'clock. Let's
le. Wǒmen qù-chī-fàn,   go eat, O.K.?
'hǎo-bu-hǎo?

Lán: Dào-nǎr-qù-chī-ne?

Where shall we go to eat?

Wàn: Wǒmen dào-Sānyǒu-
Fànguǎn-qù-chī-ba.

Let's go eat at the Three Friends Restaurant.

Lán: Wó-yǐjing-qùguo yícì.
Tāmende-cài-bù-hǎo. Chǎo-
xià-rér-lǐtou fàng-jiàngyóu.

I've already been (there) once. They put soy sauce in their fried shrimps.

Wàn: Dàgài nà-shi běifāng-de-
zuòfǎ.

Maybe that's the Northern way of cooking.

Lán: Kǎo-yāzi shi-hēi-de.

The roast duck is black.

Wàn: Dàgài kǎo-de-shíjiān cháng-
yìdiǎr-le.

Maybe they cook it a little too long.

Lán: Èrqiě chīwánle-yí-suàn-
zhàng hái-hěn-guì.

Moreover, after you've finished and they figure the bill, it's very expensive.

Wàn: Nènmo wǒmen-dào-Běi-Hú-
Xiáo-Guǎn-qù-chī.

Then let's go eat at the Little North Lake Restaurant.

Lán: Hǎo. Wǒmen jiǎndān-yìdiǎr-
chī. Jiù-lái yìhú-jiǔ, chī-
jiǎozi huòzhě-miàn.

O.K. Let's eat a little simply. Let's just order a pot of wine and have dumplings or noodles.

9. Zuótian wǒ-gēn-wǒ-àirén kànle-
yìchǎng-diànyǐng. Wǒ-juéde
nèibù-piānzi-de-gùshi hén-yǒu-
yìsi, kěshi wǒ-àirén-shuō
yǎnyuán-yǎn-de-bù-hǎo.

Yesterday my wife (or husband) and I went to see a movie. I thought the story (of that movie) was very interesting, but my wife (or husband) said the actors performed badly.

10. Gāngcái wǒ-dìdi mǎile-yìběn-
xiǎo-zìdiǎn. Wǒ-yí-kàn jiù-
xiǎode shi-yìběn-yǐqiánde-zìdiǎn,
yīnwei zìdiǎnshang jiù-yǒu-huǒji
méi-yǒu-fúwùyuán, yǒu-
màipiàoyuán méi-yǒu-
shòupiàoyuán.

Just now my younger brother bought a little dictionary. As soon as I looked at it I knew it was an old (lit. previous) dictionary, for it had only huǒji and not fúwùyuán, (only) màipiàoyuán and not shòupiàoyuán.

11. Yán-Wénshān zài-dàxué yǐjing-
xuéxíle-sānnián-le. Tā-hěn-
cōngming. Xuéxí shùxué. Tā-dìdi
yě-zài-dàxué-èrniánjí-xuéxí.
Xuéxí-lìshǐ. Kěshi tā-dìdi-xuéxí-
de méi-yǒu-tā-nènmo-hǎo.
Měicì-kǎoshì bú-shi-kàncuòle-
tímu jiù-shi-xiěcuòle-zì.

Yan Wenshan has already studied for three years in college. He's very bright. He studies mathematics. His younger brother is also studying in the second year. He's studying history. But his younger brother doesn't study as well as he does. At every exam if he doesn't read a topic wrong he miswrites characters.

Notes

1. In the PRC huǒji 'waiter' is used only for joking. A waiter is now referred to as fúwùyuán, a generalized term for a person (yuán) who serves (fúwù). This expression for 'to serve' embodies the well-known concept of 'serv-

ing the people.' Hence <u>fúwùyuán</u> suggests greater respect than the equivalent English terms 'waiter' or 'attendant.' A waiter is addressed directly as <u>Fúwùyuán Tóngzhì</u>, or simply as <u>Tóngzhì</u>, the latter being less formal.

2. In the PRC tipping is no longer practiced. Waiters and other personnel who provide service of one kind or another should not be offered a <u>xiǎofèi</u> 'tip.' Hence the word has largely disappeared from Common Speech in China, although Chinese of course have to use it when they travel abroad or when they discuss past or foreign tipping practices.

LESSON 22

New Vocabulary

kùnnan   difficulty, trouble (N); difficult, troublesome (SV) [lit. distress trouble] (See Note 1)

Exercises

kùnnan   difficulty

hén-yǒu-kùnnan   has many difficulties

1. Nèige-shìqing duì-wǒ hén-yǒu-kùnnan.

   That matter has many difficulties for me.

2. Bái: Nǐmen-bìyè-yǐhòu xiǎng-dào-nǎr-qu-gōngzuò?

   After you graduate where will you go to work?

   Lán: 'Nǎr-yǒu-kùnnan, wǒmen-jiù-dào-nǎr-qù.

   Wherever there are difficulties, there we will go.

3. Gāo: Wǒ-kàn xué-Hànzì bú-tài-nán-ne.

   It seems to me that learning Chinese characters isn't too hard.

   Bái: Xué-Hànzì yǒu-hěn-duó-kùnnan.

   There are a lot of difficulties in learning Chinese characters.

   Gāo: Shénmo-kùnnan?

   What difficulties?

   Bái: Xué-Hànzì yǒu-liǎngge-kùnnan. Yíge shi-méi-fázi-xiǎode zěnmo-niàn, yíge-shi bìxū-jìzhu-xiěde-fāngfǎ.

   There are the difficulties in learning Chinese characters. One is there is no way of knowing how to pronounce (lit. read aloud) them, one is you have to memorize the way they are written.

4. Zhāng: Lǎoshì, wèi-shénmo xué-de-Hànzì wǒ-bù-néng-jìzhu?

   Teacher, why can't I remember the Chinese characters we've studied?

   Wáng: Nà-jiùshi-yīnwei ní-xiě-zì xiěde-bú-gòu. Jì-Hànzì yào-duō-xiě-jǐcì. Yàoshi-xiěde-tài-shǎo, jiù-róngyi-wàng. Hái-yào-zhùyì xuéxí-fāngfǎ.

   That's because you don't write characters enough. To memorize Chinese characters you must write them a few more times. If you write too little, it's easy to forget. You must also pay attention to how to study.

5. Bái: Zhèige-zì niàn-shénmo?

    How is this character read?

   Yán: Shi-huǒji-de-huǒ.

    It's the huǒ of huǒji.

   Bái: Yóu-jǐhuá?

    How many strokes does it have?

   Yán: Yǒu-liùhuá.

    It has six strokes.

   Bái: Guòjiǎng-de jiǎng-yóu-jǐhuá?

    How many strokes does the jiǎng of Guòjiǎng have?

   Yán: Yóu-jiǔhuá.

    It has nine strokes.

   Bái: Qǐng-nín xiě-yi-xiě.

    Please write (it for me).

6. Gāo: Yǔyán-gēn-wénxué shì-bu-shi-chàbuduō?

    Are language and literature about the same?

   Bái: Bù. Yǔyán-shi-yǔyán, wénxué-shi-wénxué, shi-bù-yíyàng-de.

    No. Language is language, literature is literature. They're not the same.

7. Yán: Nǐ-huì-huá-quán-ma?

    Do you know how to play "guess-fingers"?

   Lán: Wǒ-huì.

    Yes, I know how to.

   Yán: Tīngshuō xiànzài zài-Zhōngguode-fànguǎnli bù-huá-quán-le.

    I hear that "guess-fingers" is no longer played now in Chinese restaurants.

   Lán: Yǒude-rén shuō-huá, yǒude-rén shuō-bù-huá-le.

    Some people say it's (still) played, others say it isn't.

8. Wàn: Nǐ-àirén-zuò-de-fàn zhēn-hǎo-chī.

    The food your wife made is really delicious.

   Yán: Nálǐ. Wǒ-àirén bù-zěnmo-huì-zuò-fàn, kěshi cháng-zuò, bǐjiǎo yǒu-yìdiǎr-jīngyan. Bǐfang-shuō, hóng-shāo-yú yào-fàng-duōshǎo jiàngyóu, chǎo-niú-ròu yào-fàng-duōshao, dōu-bù-yíyàng, bú-néng-suíbiàn-fàng.

    You flatter us. My wife isn't such a good cook, but she cooks frequently, and relatively (speaking) has a bit of experience. For example, how much soy sauce to put in red-cooked fish and how much in sautéed beef are not the same. You can't put it in haphazardly.

9. Bái: Guǎngdong-chǎo-miàn gēn-běifāng-chǎo-miàn yíyàng-bu-yíyàng?

    Are Cantonese fried noodles and Northern fried noodles the same?

   Gāo: Bù-yíyàng. Běifāng chǎo-miàn bǎ-ròu-gēn-cài dōu-chǎo-zài-miàn-lǐtou. Guǎng-dong-chǎo-miàn bǎ-ròu-gēn-cài dōu-fàng-zài-miàn-shàngtou.

    They're not the same. In Northern fried noodles the meat and vegetables are both fried in the noodles. In Cantonese fried noodles the meat and vegetables are placed on top of the noodles.

   Bái: Nǐ-juéde néizhǒng-hǎo-chī?

    Which do you think is tastier?

Gāo: Wǒ-juéde Guǎngdong-chǎo-miàn-hǎo-chī.

I think Cantonese fried noodles are tastier.

10. Wǒmen-xuéxí-Zhōngwén. Shàng-kè-de-shíhou, lǎoshī-shuō-Zhōngwén, wǒmen-zhùyì-tīng. Wǒmen-tiāntiān-liànxi-tīng, yě-liànxi-shuō. Wǒmen-bìxū-hǎo-hāor-xuéxí, bùrán bù-néng-bǎ-Zhōngwén-xuéhǎo.

We are studying Chinese. When we go to class, the teacher speaks Chinese, and we listen attentively. We practice listening every day, and we also practice speaking. We have to study hard, otherwise we won't be able to master Chinese.

11. Zhāng-Tóngzhì bú-shi-wǒmende-Zhōngwén-lǎoshī, kěshi tā-yě-bāngzhu-wǒmen xué-Zhōngwén. Tā-chángcháng-wèn-wǒmen xuéxí-shang yǒu-shénmo-kùnnan, hái-wèn-wǒmen-wèntí. Tā-cháng-cháng-duì-wǒmen-shuō, bú-yào-pà-kùnnan, yǒu-bù-dǒng-de-dìfang, jiù-wèn-tā. Tā-búdàn shi-wǒmende-péngyou, yě-kéyi-shuō shi-wǒmende-lǎoshī!

Comrade Zhang is not our Chinese teacher, but he still helps us study Chinese. He often asks us what difficulties we have in studying, and asks us questions. He often says to us that we shouldn't fear difficulties, and if there are things [lit. places] we don't understand just ask him. He not only is our friend, one can also say he is our teacher!

12. Wǒ-shi-yíge-wàiguo-xuésheng. Wǒ-xuéxí-Zhōngguo-yǔyán, duì-lìshǐ yě-hén-gǎn-xìngqu. Xiànzài néng-shuō jiǎndānde-Zhōngguo-huà, yě-néng-kàn jiǎndānde-Zhōngwén-shū. Zài-kāishǐ-xuéxí-de-shíhou hěn-kùnnan. Wǒde-lǎoshī kāishǐ-jiāo-wǒ-fāyīn, Hànzì, cér, yǔfǎ. Guānyú-wǒ-xuéxí, zuì-dà-de-nánchù shì-sìshēng, qīngzhòngyīn. Shénmo-jiào-qīngzhòngyīn-ne? Bǐfāng xuésheng shi-liǎngge-yīnjié. Dì-yīge-yīnjié shi-xué, shi-dì-èrshēng. Dì-èrge-yīnjié shi-shēng. Suírán shi-dì-yīshēng, kěshi yào-niàn-qīngshēng. Xiàng-zhèizhǒng-cér hěn-duō. Érqiě sìshēng hái-yào-zhǔn. Wáng-Jiàoshòu zhēn-hǎo. Tā-chúle-shàng-kè-yǐwài, měitiān hái-yòng-hěn-duō-xiǎoshí gēn-wǒ-zài-yíkuàr yánjiu-fāyīn. Wàiguo-rén-xué-Hànyǔ zuì-dà-de-kùnnan shi-xué-fāyīn. Wǒ-suírán-méi-xuéhǎo, kěshi yòngle-bu-shǎo-shíjiān.

I'm a foreign student. I'm studying the Chinese language, and I'm also very much interested in (Chinese) history. Now I can speak simple Chinese and read simple Chinese books. When I first studied Chinese it was very hard. My teacher began by teaching me pronunciation, characters, words, and grammar. In my studies, the biggest difficulty was the four tones and the neutral tone. What is the neutral tone? Xuésheng, to take an example, is two syllables. The first syllable is xué; it is second tone. The second syllable is shēng. Although it is (originally) first tone, nevertheless it must be read as neutral tone. Words like this are quite numerous. Moreover the four tones must be accurate. Professor Wang is really nice. In addition to going to class, every day he devotes many hours to work on pronunciation with me. The biggest difficulty for foreigners in studying Chinese is learning pronunciation. Although I haven't learned it well, I've devoted not a few hours (to it).

13. Wǒ-cóng-Niǔyue dào-Jiùjīnshān-lái. Zài-méi-líkai-Niǔyue-yǐqián

I came to San Francisco from New York. Before leaving New York I

wó-géi-Xǔ-Dàwén-dǎ-diànhuà,
shuō-xià-xīngqī-yī wǒ-zuò-fēijī
dào-Jiùjīnshān-qu, xīwang-tā-jiē
wǒ. Wǒ-dàole-Jiùjīnshān-yǐhòu
gāng-xià-fēijī jiù-kànjian-Láo-
Xǔ gēn-ta-àirén zài-nèr-děngzhe-
wǒ. Tā-kànjian-wǒ-dàole hěn-
gāoxìng. Nèige-shíhou shi-chī-
fàn-de-shíhou. Láo-Xǔ-shuō
wǒmen-xiān-qù-chī-fàn. Tā-wèn-
wǒ xiǎng-chī-shénmo. Wǒ-shuō
xiǎng-chī-Zhōngguo-cài. Wǒmen-
sānge-rén jiù-dàole-yíge-xiǎo-
fànguǎn. Yàole-yìhú-jiǔ, sānge-
cài, yíge-tāng: yíge-chǎo-xiārér,
yíge-hóng-shāo-jī, yíge-chǎo-
báicài. Láo-Xǔ hái-xiǎng-yào-
yíge-kǎo-yāzi. Wǒ-shuō-
chībuliǎo, bú-yào-yāzi, zài-yào-
shíge-jiǎozi-déle. Sānge-rén
chīde-hén-bǎo. Chīwánle-fàn
fúwùyuán yí-suàn-zhàng yígòng-
cái bāyuán-sìjiǎo. Gěile-yìyuán-
liùjiǎo-xiǎofèi yígòng-shíyuán.

phoned Xu Dawen to say next Monday
I was taking a plane to San Francisco
and hoped he would meet me. After
reaching San Francisco just as I got
off the plane I saw (Old) Xu and his
wife waiting for me there. He was
very glad to see me arrive. The time
was dinner time. (Old) Xu said we
should first go and eat. He asked me
what I would like to eat. I said I would
like to eat Chinese food. The three of
us then went to a small restaurant.
We ordered a pot of wine, three
dishes, and a soup: a fried shrimp, a
red-cooked chicken, and a fried cabbage. (Old) Xu also thought we should
order a roast duck. I said we couldn't
eat it, not to order a duck but to have
ten dumpling and let it go at that. The
three of us ate until we were quite
full. After we finished eating when the
waiter figured the bill it came altogether to only $8.40. We gave a tip of
$1.60, (making) altogether $10.00.

Note

1. In the PRC nánchu 'difficulty' occurs less often than kùnnan, a term of
   wider meaning and usage. The latter is used as a noun and as a stative
   verb in the meanings 'difficulty, trouble; difficult, troublesome':

   Xué-Hànzì yóu-hěn-dà-de-kùnnan.   'There are great difficulties in
   studying Chinese.'

   Xué-hànzì hěn-kùnnan.   'Studying Chinese is very difficult.'

LESSON 23

Exercises

1. Xǔ: Nǐ-shuō Lǎo-Zhāng-huà-de-
       huàr 'hǎo-bu-hǎo?

   What do you think of the painting that
   (Old) Zhang does?

   Bì: Wǒ-shuō-bú-cuò.

   I think it's not bad.

   Xǔ: Wǒ-bù-xiǎode tā-huà-de
       huàr hǎochù-zài-nǎr.

   I don't know what the good points are
   in his paintings.

   Bì: Tā-huà-de-huàr xiàng-
       zhēnde-shānshuǐ.

   His paintings look like real scenery.

   Xǔ: Huà-huàr zuì-yàojǐnde shi-
       děi-qù-lǚxíng kànkan-
       yǒumíngde-shānshuǐ.

   The most important thing in painting
   is that one must travel and see famous scenery.

2. Lán: Wǒ-zhèicì shi-dì-yīcì dào-
Rìběn-qu.

This is my first trip to Japan.

Máo: Dào-Rìběn yào-jǐge-xiǎoshí?

How many hours does it take to get to Japan?

Lán: Dàgài qī-bāge-xiǎoshí.

Approximately seven or eight hours.

Máo: Nǐ-zhèicì zài-Rìběn yào-
duōshao-shíhou?

How long will you be in Japan this time?

Lán: Dàgài yào-yìnián huòzhě-
èrnián.

Probably one or two years.

Máo: Wǒmen-yào hěn-cháng-de-
shíjiān bú-jiàn-le.

We won't be seeing each other for a long time.

Lán: Duì-le.

Right.

Máo: Nǐ-zhèicì dào-Rìběn-qù
háishi-jìxude-xuéxí Dōng-
fāng-lìshǐ-ma?

In going to Japan now will you continue to study Oriental history?

Lán: Shì. Wǒ-hái-jìxu-xuéxí
Dōngfāng-lìshǐ.

Yes, I'll continue to study Oriental history.

Máo: Zàijiàn-le. Zhù-nǐ-yílù-
píng'ān.

Good-bye. Have a nice trip.

Lán: Zàijiàn. Láojià-nǐ-lái-sòng-
wǒ.

Good-bye. Thanks for taking the trouble to come see me off.

3. Cóng-yī-jiǔ-qī-sān-nián dào-
xiànzài wǒ-dào-Zhōngguo qùle-
sāncì. Jīnnián yòu-qùle-yícì,
kěshi-zhèicì zài-Zhōngguo-de-
shíjiān-bǐjiáo-duǎn, lián-Běijīng
yě-méi-qù.

From 1973 to the present I've been to China three times. I went once again this year, but this time in China the duration was relatively short. I didn't even go to Peking.

4. Wǒ-zuótian zài-Dōngfāng-Hóng-
Shūdiàn kànjian-yìběn-guānyu-
xuéxí-yǔyán-de-shū. Shū-míngzi-
shi Zěnyàng-Xuéxí-Hànyǔ.
Zhèiběn-shū duì-wǒmen-xuéxí-
Hànyǔ-de-rén hěn-yǒu-bāngzhu.
Kāishǐ xiān-gàosu-nǐ zěnyàng-
liànxí-fāyīn, shénmo-shi-qīng-
zhòngyīn, sìshēng, shénmo-shi-
cér, shénmo-jiào-yīnjié. Rúguǒ
bǎ-zhèixiē-jìzhu-dōu-dǒng-le,
wǒ-xiǎng xuéxí-fāyīn-gēn-sìshēng
dōu-néng-bǐjiǎo-zhǔn.

Yesterday at the East is Red Bookstore I saw a book on studying the language. The title of the book was How to Study Chinese. This book is very helpful to those of us studying Chinese. To begin with it first tells you how to practice pronunciation, what the neutral tone and the four tones are, what words are, what is referred to as syllables. If one remembers and understands all these things, I think the study of pronunciation and the four tones can all be comparatively accurate.

5. Zuótian wǒ-dào-fēijīchǎng-qù
jiē-Mǎ-Dàwén. Děngle-yǒu-
liǎngge-xiǎoshí fēijī-yě-méi-lái,

Yesterday I went to the airport to meet Ma Dawen. After waiting a couple of hours the plane still hadn't ar-

suóyǐ dào-cāntíng-qu-zuò-yìhuěr. Dàole-cāntíng-yǐhòu, wǒ-ràng-cāntíngde-fúwùyuán géi-wǒ-ná-cài-dān-lái. Wǒ-yào-le-yíge-chǎo-miàn. Yìbiān-chī yìbiān-děngzhe. Bǎ-miàn-chīwán-le gāng-líkai-cāntíng kànjian-Mǎ-Dàwén-xiàle-fēijī. Wǒmen-liǎngge-rén shi-lǎo-péngyou, jiànle-miàn dāngrán-hěn-gāoxìng. Tā-gàosu-wǒ, míngnián tā-kāishǐ-shàng-dàxué-le. Wǒ-wèn-ta duì-shénmo-gǎn-xìngqu. Tā-shuō tā-duì-shùxué zhèi-fāngmian hěn-gǎn-xìngqu. Wǒ-wèn-ta Wàn-Lǎoshī duì-ta-zěnmoyàng. Tā-shuō: "Wàn-Lǎoshī hěn-hǎo. Wǒ-gēn-ta xuédào-bù-shǎo-de-dōngxi." Tā-hái-gàosu-wǒ Wàn-Lǎoshī chúle-yánjiu-xuéwen-yǐwài, hěn-xǐhuan-lǚxíng, tā-xiànzài bú-xiàng-yǐqián xǐhuan-hē-jiǔ-huá-quán. Wǒmen-liǎngge-rén líkaile-fēijīchǎng zuò-zài-chē-shang hái-jìxude-shuōxiaqu zhèi-liǎngnián-de-shìqing. Mǎ-Dàwén-shuō tā-zhèicì-lái dàiláile-yíge-hén-hǎo-de lùyīnjī shi-sònggéi-wǒ-de.

rived, so I went to the cafeteria to sit a while. After getting to the cafeteria, I had the waiter (in the cafeteria) bring me the menu. I ordered fried noodles. As I ate I waited. Just as I left the cafeteria after finishing the noodles I saw Ma Dawen getting off the plane. The two of us are old friends, so on seeing each other we were naturally very happy. He told me, he was going to start attending college next year. I asked him what he was interested in. He said he was very much interested in mathematics. I asked him what Teacher Wan's attitude toward him was. He said: "Teacher Wan is very nice. I learned a lot of things from him." He also told me that apart from acquiring knowledge Teacher Wan was very fond of traveling and now no longer liked to drink and play "guess-fingers," as he had before. After the two of us left the airport we got in the car and continued talking about matters of the past two years. Ma Dawen said that he had brought a very nice tape-recorder this time that he was presenting to me.

6. Xīngqīliù wǒ-dào-túshūguǎn-qu jiè-shū. Dàole-túshūguǎn, wǒ-duì-nèr gōngzuò-de-tóngzhì-shuō: "Tóngzhì, wó-xiǎng-jiè-yìběn wǒ-néng-kàndǒng-de-Zhōngwén-shū. Qǐng-ní-géi-wǒ zhǎo-yìběn-ba." Nèige-tóngzhì-zhǎole-yìběn-géi-wo. Wǒ-shuō: "Zhèiběn-shū 'nán-bu-nán?" Tā-shuō: "Suīrán-zhèiběn-shū yéxú-yǒu-xiē ní-bú-rènshi-de-zì, kěshi-shàngbiar-yǒu-huàr, kéyi-bāngzhu-nǐ-kàndǒng-yìsi." Jīntian wǒ-yòu-dào-túshūguǎn-qù-jiè-shū, nèige-gōngzuò-tóngzhì-wèn-wǒ: "Shàngci-jiè-de-shū nǐ-dōu-kàndǒngle-méi-yǒu?" Wǒ-shuō: "Yǒude-dìfang-méi-kàndǒng, kěshi-dàgàide-yìsi dōu-dǒngle."

Saturday I went to the library to borrow some books. When I got to the library, I said to the (work) comrade there: "Comrade I'd like to borrow a Chinese book that I can understand. Please find one for me." That comrade found one and gave it to me. I said: "Is this book difficult?" He said: "Although this book perhaps has a few characters that you don't know, still it has illustrations that can help you understand the meaning." Today I went to the library again to borrow books, and that (work) comrade asked me: "Did you understand all of the book you borrowed last time?" I said: "Some places I didn't understand, but on the whole I got the general idea."

Notes

1. Besides being the name of a popular song that is widely sung and played, Dōngfāng Hóng 'The East is Red' is also the title of a two-hour long documentary depicting the background of the People's Republic and appears in the names of many institutions (such as communes) which have taken the name because of the special aura that surrounds it.

2. Some PRC speakers have abandoned the polite expression bùgǎndāng 'I don't dare accept (your praise, assistance, etc.),' in favor of newer stereotyped phrases expressing such ideas as 'This is the merit of the people and the party (and not my own).'

LESSON 24

Exercises

1. Lán: Xiànzàide-fúwùyuán cóng-
            qián-jiào-shénmo?

   Bái: Cóngqián-jiào-huǒji.

2. Xǔ: Gāo-Lǎoshǐ, qǐng-wèn
           jīngyan-de-yàn yóu-jǐhuá?

   Gāo: Yǒu-shíhuá.

   Xǔ: Cāntīng-de-tīng yóu-jǐhuá?

   Gāo: Sìhuá.

3. Bǐ: Má-Lǎoshǐ nǐ-'máng-bu-
           máng?

   Mǎ: Xiànzài-bǐjiǎo-máng.

   Bǐ: Nǐ-yìtiān jiāo-jǐge-
           xiǎoshí-de-kè?

   Mǎ: Wǒ-yìtiān jiāo-sānge-
           xiǎoshí-de-kè. Yéxǔ
           jiānglái shǎo-jiāo yíge-
           xiǎoshí-de-kè.

4. Zhāng: Rúguó-nǐ-dào-shūdiàn-
              dài-yìběn-shū-lái 'hǎo-
              bu-hǎo?

   Wáng: Kéyǐ kéyǐ. Nǐ-yào-mǎi-
              shénmo-shū?

   Zhāng: Shi-guānyú-yǔyánxué-de-
              shū.

   Wáng: Shū-míngzi shi-shénmo?

   Zhāng: Hànyǔ-Pīnyīn-Liànxi-fǎ.

5. Dài: Zhè-jiǎozi zhēn-hǎochǐ. Lǐ-
            tou-yǒu-shénmo?

   Yán: Zhūròu-xiārér.

   Dài: Yǒu-jiàngyóu-ma?

   Yán: Yǒu. Nǐ-huì-zuò-jiǎozi-ma?

   Dài: Bú-huì. Wǒ-yīngdāng gēn-
            nǐ-xuéxí zuò-jiǎozi, kěshi
            lǎo-méi-shíjiān.

6. Wǒde-Zhōngguo-yǔwén shi-zài-
   Měiguo-xuéxí-de, yǐjing-xuéxíle-
   sìnián. Wǒ-zhèicì-dào-Zhōngguo-
   lái háishi-yào-jìxude-xuéxí. Xué-
   xí-Zhōngguo-yǔwén, zài-gāng-
   xuéxí-de-shíhou, juéde-yǒu-diǎr-
   kùnnan. Zài-kāishǐ-xuéxí-de-shí-
   hòu, zuì-yàojǐn-de shi-sìshēng,
   fāyīn, qīngzhòngyīn, cér dou-děi-
   jìzhu. Zuì-dà-de-nánchu shi-sì-
   shēng-gēn-qīngzhòngyīn, yīnwei
   bìxū-niànde-zhǔn. Bǐfāng-shuō-
   cér-ba, yíge-cér yǒu-liǎng-sānge-
   yīnjié, měige-yīnjié-de-qīng-
   zhòngyīn bù-yíyàng, bìxū-jìzhù.
   Bùrán nǐ-shuōchulái bié-rén-tīng-
   budǒng. Suóyǐ yīnggāi-hǎohāorde-
   xuéxí. Xiànzài suírán-méi-xuéhǎo,
   kěshi wǒ-gēn-Zhōngguo-péngyou-
   shuō-huà tāmen-dōu-tīngdedǒng.
   Wǒ-gěi-Zhōngguo-péngyou-xiě-xìn
   tāmen-yě-kànde-míngbai.

7. Zuótian Yán-Tóngzhǐ bāngzhu-wǒ-

qù-lùyīn. Cóng-liángdiǎn-zhōng lù-
dào-liùdiǎn-zhōng. Yǐjing-shi-chī-
wǎnfàn-de-shíhòu-le. Wǒ-shuō:
"Wǒmen-dào-fànguǎn-qù chī-kǎo-
yāzi 'hǎo-bu-hǎo?" Yán-Tóngzhǐ-
shuō: "Liǎngge-rén chī-yíge-kǎo-
yāzi zěnmo-chīdeliǎo-ne? Wǒmen-
dào-fùjìn-de-cāntīng, chī-yìdiár-
diǎnxin, yíge-rén zài-yào-yíge-

miàn jiù-gòu-le." Wǒ-shuō yě-
hǎo. Wǒmen-dàole-cāntīng, ràng-
fúwùyuán xiān - gěi-wǒmen - láile-
yìhú-chá. Chá-hén-hǎo. Yán-Tóngzhǐ wèn - wǒ zhèizhǒng - chá shi-
nǎr-de. Wǒ-shuō dàgài-shi-Háng-
zhōu-de. Chīwánle-fàn fúwùyuán-
yí-suàn-zhàng yígòng-cái-liǎng-
kuài-sìmáo-qián.

SUPPLEMENTARY VOCABULARY

Some 500 additional vocabulary items are provided here for those who wish to acquire a greater stock of words concurrently with learning the basic patterns of the language. The items fit into the grammatical patterns studied in each lesson. Many can also be used in ways not covered by the patterns, but it is not advisable to spend too much effort studying these expanded usages, as it would conflict with the emphasis this book places on rapid mastery of the basic patterns of Chinese.

For those who wish to limit the classroom language to Chinese as soon as possible, a list of useful classroom phrases is given first. (Some of these also occur elsewhere in the book but are included here for ease in reference.)

Classroom Phrases

Zǎo.   Good morning.

Qíng-nǐmen-ānjing.   Please be quiet.

Xiànzài-shàng-kè-le.   Class has begun.

Wǒmen-xià-kè-le.   Class is over.

Zuòxia.   Sit down.

Zhànqilai.   Stand up.

Zhànqilai-shuō.   Stand up and recite.

Jú-shǒu.   Raise your hand.

Wǒ-shuō, nǐmen-tīng.   Listen to what I say.

Nǐ-tīng wǒ-shuō.   Listen to me.

Wǒ-shuō, nǐmen-xiě.   Write down what I say.

Gēnzhe-wǒ-shuō.   Repeat after me.

Zài-shuō.   Repeat.

Zài-shuō-yíbiàn.   Repeat once.

Ní-dǒng-ma?   Do you understand?

Wó-dǒng.   I understand.

Wǒ-bù-dǒng.   I don't understand.

Nǐ-dōu-dǒng-ma?   Do you understand everything?

Xiānsheng, wǒ-bù-dǒng.   Teacher, I don't understand.

543

Qǐng-nín zài-shuō-yíbiàn.   Please say it again.

Qǐng-wèn. . .   May I ask . . .

Zhèige-zì shi-dì-jǐshēng?   What is the tone of this word?

Zhèige Zhōngguo-huà jiào-shénmo?   What's this called in Chinese?

Jīntian niàn-dì-jǐkè?   What lesson are we studying today?

Dǎkai-shū.   Open your books.

Bǎ-shū héqilai.   Close your books.

Kàn-dì-shíyè.   Look at page 10.

Nǐ-'tīngyitīng.   (You) listen.

Nǐ-'niànyiniàn.   (You) read.

Ní-'xiěyixiě.   (You) write.

Wǒ-shuōde-huà, nǐmen-zhùyì.   Pay attention to what I say.

Wǒ-shuō-yíjù, nǐmen-gēnzhe-shuō-yíjù.   I'll say a sentence, and you repeat
     it after me.

Zhùyì-sìshēng.   Pay attention to the four tones.

Jìzhù.   Fix in mind.

Jìzhù-le-ma?   Have you got it firmly in mind?

Zài-hēibǎnshang-xiě.   Write it on the blackboard.

Wǒmen-dàjiā yíkuàr-shuō.   Let's say it all together.

Dàjiā 'yíkuàr-shuō.   (You) say it all together.

(Qǐng)-shuō kuài-yìdiǎr.   (Please) speak more quickly.

(Qǐng)-shuō màn-yìdiǎr.   (Please) speak more slowly.

Bié-shuō-huà.   Don't talk.

Nǐmen yǒu-wèntí-ma?   Do you have any questions?

Wǒ-wèn, nǐmen-dá.   I'll ask, you answer.

Nǐmen-wèn, wǒ-dá.   You ask, I'll answer.

Qǐng-ni 'dà-shēng-shuō.   Please speak loudly.

Lesson 1

The following syllables, some of which are full words and others only combining forms, are used also as surnames:

duàn	section (N)	jiāng	(large) river (N)
fèng	phoenix (N)	kǒng	hole (N)
gǔ	ancient (SV)	lǐ	plum (N)
huáng	yellow (SV)	lì	chestnut (N)

tián	field (N)	yún	cloud (N)
xióng	bear (N)	zhū	vermilion (SV)
yáng	poplar (N)	zǔ	ancestor (N)

The following nouns are also used as titles:

bóshi	Ph.D., Dr.	tuánzhǎng	delegation head
jiāngjun	general	xiàozhǎng	principal, headmas-
lǜshi	lawyer, attorney		ter
mùshi	minister, preacher	yīsheng	doctor, M.D.
shénfù	priest, Father	zhǎngguìde	manager
tóngzhì	comrade	zhǔxí	chairman

Lesson 2

The following are additional names of countries:

Āiji	Egypt	Jiānádà	Canada
Àodalìyǎ	Australia	Měnggǔ	Mongolia
Àoguo	Austria	Miǎndiàn	Burma
Bājīsītǎn	Pakistan	Mòxīgē	Mexico
Bǐlishí	Belgium	Nuówēi	Norway
Dānmài	Denmark	Ruìdiǎn	Sweden
Déguo	Germany	Ruìshi	Switzerland
		Sūlián	Soviet Union
Éguo, Èguo	Russia	Xībānyá	Spain
Fàguo, Fǎguo	France	Yuènán	Vietnam
Gǔbà	Cuba	Yìdàlì	Italy
		Yìndu	India
Hánguó	Korea		
Hélán	Holland		

Lesson 3

For new nouns, an appropriate measure—if other than <u>ge</u>—is given in parentheses.

bǎ	(measure for chairs)	dēngpàor	light bulb (N)
chǐ	ruler (N) (gēn)	dèngzi	stool (N)
dēng	lamp (N) (zhǎn)	fénbǐ	chalk (N) (gēr)

gēn	(measure for sticks)	suànpan	abacus (N)
gēr	(measure for chalk)	táidēng	desk lamp (N)
kèběr	textbook (N)	xiàngpí	eraser (N) (kuài)
kuài	(measure for solids)	yǐzi	chair (N) (bǎ)
qiānbǐdāor	pencil sharpener (N)	yuánguī	**compasses (N)**
shǒutíbāo	briefcase (N)	zhǎn	(measure for lamps)
shūbāo	book bag (N)	zìláishuíbǐ	fountain pen (N)

Lesson 4

bào	newspaper (N) (fèr)	Xībānyá-	Spanish (language and
bàozhǐ	newspaper (N) (fèr)	wén	literature) (N)
Déwén	German (language and	Yìdàlì-wén	Italian (language and
	literature) (N)		literature) (N)
Ēwén,	Russian (language and	zázhì	periodical, magazine
Èwen	literature) (N)		(N) (běn)
Fàwén,	French (language and	Zhōng-Dé	Chinese-German, Si-
Fǎwén	literature) (N)		no-German
fěnhóng	pink (SV)	Zhōng-Ē	Chinese-Russian, Si-
fèr	(measure for news-		no-Russian
	papers)	Zhōng-Fà	Chinese-French, Si-
hēibǎn	blackboard (N) (kuài)		no-French
huàbào	illustrated journal (N)	Zhōng-	Chinese-Spanish, Si-
	(běn)	Xībānyá	no-Spanish
kǎpiàr	card (N) (zhāng)	Zhōng-Yì	Chinese-Italian, Si-
lǜ	green (SV)		no-Italian
shūzhuō	desk (N) (zhāng)	zhuōzi	table (N) (zhāng)

Lesson 5

ài	love (TV)	huítóu	a little later (MA)
báitian	daytime (TW)	jiàn	cheap (SV)
chéng	be O.K. (IV)	kěn	be willing (AV)
guì	expensive (SV)	kòngr	leisure time (N)
hèn	hate (TV)	lìngwài	additionally (MA)

piányi	cheap (SV)	yèli	night (TW)
qīnqi	relative (N)	yuànyi	be willing (AV)
shēng	not well acquainted (SV)	zǎoshang	morning (TW)
shú	well acquainted (SV)	zhái	residence (N)
xíng	be O.K. (IV)	zhōngwǔ	noon (TW)

Lesson 7

bǎihuòdiàn	department store (N)	jiē	street (N) (tiáo)
bàndǎo	peninsula (N)	jǐngchájú	police station (N)
bówuguǎn	museum (N)	lǚguǎn	hotel (N)
chéngshì	metropolis (N)	mǎlù	highway (N) (tiáo)
dàjiē	avenue (N) (tiáo)	mǎtou	dock (N)
diànbàojú	telegraph office (N)	miào	temple (N) (zuò)
dòngwuyuán	zoo (N)	pùzi	store (N)
dūshì	metropolis (N)	shì	metropolis (N)
hǎi	sea, ocean (N)	shāngdiàn	store (N)
háidǎo	island (N)	wūzi	room(s) (N) (jiān)
hé	river (N) (tiáo)	xiāngxia	the country (PW)
Héběi	Hopeh province (PW)	yīyuàn	hospital (N)
Hénán	Honan province (PW)	yínháng	bank (N)
huǒchēzhàn	railroad station (N)	yóujú	post office (N)
hútòng	alley (N) (tiáo)	záhuòdiàn	grocery store (N)
jiān	(measure for rooms in a house)	zuò	(measure for buildings)

Lesson 8

In the following names for subjects of study, the suffix xué 'study' is optional if enclosed in parentheses.

cáizhèng(xué)	finance (N)	huàxué	chemistry (N)
dìzhǐ(xué)	geology (N)	jiàoyu(xué)	education (N)
dòngwuxué	zoology (N)	jīngji(xué)	economics (N)
gōngcheng(xué)	engineering (N)	jīxiè(xué)	mechanics (N)

nóngxué	agriculture (N)	wùlǐ(xué)	physics (N)
shāngyè(xué)	business studies (N)	xīnlǐxué	psychology (N)
shèhuìxué	sociology (N)	yàoji(xué)	pharmacology (N)
shēngwu(xué)	biology (N)	yīxué	medicine (N)
shénxué	religion (N)	zhèngzhi(xué)	political science (N)
tiānwénxué	astronomy (N)	zhíwuxué	botany (N)

Lesson 9

cānjiā	take part (in) (V)	píxiédiàn	shoe store (N)
cèsuǒ	toilet (N)	rénmin	people (N)
chējiān	workshop (N)	sānlúnchē	pedicab (N) (liàng)
dàxuéshēng	college student (N)	shǒushi	jewelry, ornament
gànbù	cadre (N)		(N)
gōngchǎng	factory (N)	shǒushilóu	jewelry store (N)
gōngrén	worker (N)	shuāng	pair (M)
gúdǒng	antiques (N)	shuíguǒ	fruit (N)
gúdǒngdiàn	antique store (N)	shuíguǒdiàn	fruit store (N)
gǔwán	antiques (N)	tào	(measure for suits of
gǔwándiàn	antique store (N)		clothes)
huǒchē	train (N) (liè)	xiǎoxuésheng	elementary-school
láodòng	do physical labor (V)		student (N)
liàng	(measure for vehicles)	xīfú	Western-style cloth-
liè	(measure for trains)		ing (N) (tào)
lífǎdiàn	barber shop (N)	xīfúdiàn	clothing store (N)
màozi	hat (N) (dǐng)	yùnshūchē	truck (N) (liàng)
màozidiàn	hat store (N)	zǎotángzi	bath house (N)
nóngmín	peasant (N)	zhōngxué-	middle - school stu-
píxié	leather shoes (N)	shēng	dent (N)
	(shuāng)		

Lesson 10

| bófù | father's elder brother (N) | fùmǔ | parents (N) |
| érzi | son (N) | gēge | elder brother (N) |

gōnggong	husband's father (N)	xiūngdì	brothers (N)
gūgu	father's sister (N)	yí	mother's sister (N)
gūniang	girl (N)		
jiějie	elder sister (N)	yuèfù	wife's father (N)
jiùjiu	mother's brother (N)	yuèmǔ	wife's mother (N)
nǚ'er	daughter (N)	zhínǚ'er	brother's daughter (N)
pópo	husband's mother (N)		
shūshu	father's younger	zhízi	brother's son (N)
	brother (N)	zǐmèi	sisters (N)
wài zǔfù	mother's father (N)	zǔfù	father's father (N)
wài zúmǔ	mother's mother (N)	zúmǔ	father's mother (N)

Lesson 11

bàiwang	visit, call on (TV)	qiántian	day before yesterday (TW)
chūcì	the first time (TW)		
dà-qián-nian	year before year before last (TW)	qiáo	see, visit (TV)
		Rìwén	Japanese (language and literature) (N)
dà-qián-tian	day before day before yesterday (TW)	shòuhuò-yuán	sales person (N)
dànshi	however (MA)		
dìquè	actually (AD)	sùshè	dormitory (N)
huòchuán	freighter (N) (tiáo)	wǔfàn	lunch (N)
jìrán	since (MA)	yàoshi	if (MA)
lúnchuán	steamship (N) (tiáo)	zǎocān	breakfast (N)
pèngjian	encounter (TV)	záodiǎn	breakfast (N)
qiánnian	year before last (TW)	zhōngfàn	lunch (N)

Lesson 13

ǎi	short (SV)	héqi	congenial (SV)
bàngōngshǐ	office (N)	huài	bad (SV)
chéngshi	honest, reliable (SV)	jiāo'ào	proud, arrogant (SV)
chūzhōng	lower middle school (N)	jùyuàn	playhouse, theater (N)

kèshǐ	classroom (N)		shànliáng	kind (SV)
lǎn	lazy (SV)		shítáng	dining hall (N)
lǎoshi	honest (SV)		shòu	thin (SV)
lǐbài	week (N)		tóngyì	agree (V)
liáojiě	understand (V)		xì	drama (N)
pàng	fat (SV)		xìju	(modern) play, dra-
qióng	poor (SV)			ma (N)

Lesson 14

bànfa	method (N)		tú	drawing, sketch (N)
běnlái	originally (N)		wànyī	by chance (MA)
búguò	only (MA)		xiāngdāng	fairly, rather (AD)
dāngchū	at first (MA)		xiāngxìn	believe (TV)
jiù	old (of things) (SV)		xīn	new (SV)
liáojie	understand (TV)		xìnfēngr	envelope (N)
qīngchu	be clear, be clear about (SV)		xìnzhǐ	writing paper (N)
			yòuzhìyuán	kindergarten (N)
qùwei	interest (N)		zhìshǎo	at least (MA)
sǐ	die (IV)		zǒng(shi)	always (AD)
tǐng	very (AD)		zuìshǎo	at least (MA)

Lesson 15

Bālí	Paris (PW)		liúshēngjī	phonograph (N)
Bólín	Berlin (PW)		lìyòng	use (TV)
bù-shūfu	uncomfortable; in-disposed (SV)		Lómǎ	Rome (PW)
			Lúndun	London (PW)
diànshì	television (N)		Mòsīkē	Moscow (PW)
fēiděi	must (AV)		Shànghǎi	Shanghai (PW)
fúdǎo	to coach (V)		shèyuán	commune
gōngshè	commune (N)			member (N)
Huáshèng-dùn	Washington (PW)		shūfu	comfortable (SV)
			tàng	(measure for trips)
lǐngdǎo	to lead; leader		xūyào	require, need (TV)

yìqí   together (AD)   zìrán   naturally (AD)

Lesson 16

béng	don't (AV)	měilì	beautiful (SV)
bícǐ	mutually, among our-selves (AD)	qíngxing	situation, condition (N)
bìngqiě	but also (MA)	qíshí	(but) actually, in fact (AD)
chéngji	record (of achieve-ment) (N)	sànbù	stroll (IV)
fēngjǐng	scenery, view (N)	tǎolùn	discuss (seriously) (TV)
jiǎnzhí(de)	simply, just (AD)		
kāishuǐ	boiled water (N)	xīnshǎng	admire, enjoy (TV)
láihuí	back and forth (AD)	yùbei	prepare (TV)
liáoliao	discuss casually, chat about (TV)	zhāodài	entertain (IV)
		zhāodàishì	reception room (N)
liǔda	take a stroll	zuì jìn	most recently (AD)

Lesson 17

chūmíng	famous (SV)	kě	thirsty (SV)
dāngshí	at that time (MA)	lěng	cold (SV)
diū	lose (TV)	liángkuai	cool (SV)
duǒ	(measure for single flowers)	líhūn	divorce (IV)
		píng	bottle (N)
è	hungry (SV)	píngzi	bottle (N)
fēng	wind (N)	qìhou	climate (N)
gànmá?	why? what for?	rè	hot (SV)
guā	blow (IV)	shū	lose (IV)
guā fēng	the wind blows	xià xuě	it is snowing
háojǐ	good many (NU)	xià yǔ	it is raining
hǎoxiàng	seem as if	xuě	snow (N)
huār	flower (N)	yǔ	rain (N)
kāfēi	coffee (N)		

Lesson 19

biǎndòu	string beans (N)	lìzi	chestnut (N)
bízi	nose (N)	lóbo	turnips (N)
bōcài	spinach (N)	méimao	eyebrow (N)
bózi	neck (N)	mógu	mushroom (N)
chāzi	fork (N)	pánzi	(large) plate (N)
chízi	spoon (N)	píngguǒ	apple (N)
chúzi	cook (N)	pútao	grapes (N)
dāozi	knife (N)	qíncai	celery (N)
dàshifu	cook (N)	sháor	spoon (N)
diézi	(small) plate (N)	shìzi	persimmon (N)
dōngsǔn	bamboo shoots (N)	shǒu	hand (N) (zhī)
dòuyár	beansprouts (N)	suàn	garlic (N)
ěrduo	ear (N)	tóufa	hair (on head) (N)
gēbei	arm (N)		(gēr)
guā	melon (N)	tuǐ	leg (N) (tiáo)
huánggua	cucumber (N)	wāndòu	peas (N)
huāshēng	peanuts (N)	xiāngjiāo	banana (N)
hújiāo-	(ground) pepper	xuědòu	snow peas (N)
miàr	(N)	yán	salt (N)
jiāng	ginger (N)	yǎnjing	eye(s) (N)
jiǎo	foot (N) (zhī)	yáng	sheep (N) (zhī)
jīdàn	eggs (N)	zuǐ	mouth (N)
júzi	orange (N)		

Lesson 20

bàn	manage, do (V)	gǎnkuài	hurry up (and do something) (AV)
bìxū	necessary (SV)		
bùguǎn	no matter, don't care	gàojià	ask for leave or time off (IV)
fāngbian	convenient (SV)		
fǎnzhèng	anyway, anyhow (MA)	hūrán	suddenly (AD)
fēicháng	extremely (AD)	jiǎ	false (SV)
gǎn	dare (AV)	juédìng	decide (V)

kěxí	too bad, it's a pity (that)	mà	scold, abuse (TV)
		pèifu	admire (TV)
líng	zero	xìngkuī	fortunately (MA)
lìngwài	separately, extra (MA)	xiūxi	rest (V)
		yǐwéi	think (wrongly) that (V)
liúli	fluent (SV)		

Lesson 21

bāozi	stuffed steamed bread (N)	guāzěr	melon seeds (N)
		kètīng	living room (N)
bǐng	cake (N)	mántou	steamed bread (N)
bǐnggān	cookies (N) (kuài)	miànbāo	bread (N)
chàng	sing (V)	pángbiār	side (PW)
chōu yān	smoke (VO)	pǔtōng	ordinary (SV)
chuáng	bed (N) (zhāng)	tàiyang	sun (N)
chuānghu	window (N)	tiān	heaven (N)
chúfáng	kitchen (N)	wòfáng	bedroom (N) (jiān)
dàjiā	everybody (present)	xīngxing	star (N)
dàngāo	cake (N)	yīfu	clothes (N)
dī	low (SV)	yīshang	clothes (N)
dì	earth (N)	yuèbing	moon-cakes (N)
gē, gēr	song (N)	yuèliang	moon (N)

Lesson 22

báihuà	colloquial language (N)	cǎo zì	grass characters, cursive writing (N)
báihuàwén	vernacular literature (N)	dáying	agree (to), answer affirmatively (TV)
bàogào	report (N)	fānchéng	translate into (V)
bèi	memorize, recite by heart (TV)	fāngyán	dialect (N)
		fānyì	translate (TV)
biǎo	table, chart (N)	fēnbié	difference (N)

gēnběn	fundamentally (MA)	qiángdiào	intonation (N)	
guóyǔ	national language (N)	shàngxiàwén	context (N)	
huì	meeting (N)	tǔhuà	dialect, patois	(N)
huídá	answer (V)	wénzhāng	essay, article	(N)
jiángyǎn	lecture (N, V)	wèntí	problem (N)	
jù	according to (CV)	wényán	literary language (N)	
kāi huì	open a meeting (VO)	xíng shū	Running Hand (N)	
kǎi shū	regular characters (N)	yánjiǎng	lecture (N, V)	
kóuyǔ	spoken language (N)	yìjian	view(s) (N)	

Lesson 23

bànyè	midnight (TW)	nào	be noisy, make a noise, disturb (V)
bùhǎoyì si	embarrassed, diffi- dent (SV)	nǔlì	hard-working (SV)
chūntian	spring (season) (TW)	pī	(measure for horses)
dàlù	continent, mainland (N)	qiūtian	fall (season) (TW)
		rènao	bustling, full of life (SV)
dàodǐ	after all (MA)		
dōngtian	winter (TW)	shàng	morning (TW)
gǎndòng	be moved (V)	bàntiān	
jiěfàng	liberate (V)	wǎn bàn-	late afternoon (TW)
kèfú	overcome (V)	tiān	
kuàihuo	happy (SV)	xià bàn-	afternoon (TW)
kuàilè	happy (SV)	tiān	
lóng	dragon (N) (tiáo)	xiàtian	summer (TW)
mǎ	horse (N) (pī)	xǔ	permit (TV)
nánguò	saddened, depressed (SV)	zháojí	nervous, upset (SV)
		zhǔn	permit (TV)

INDEX OF PRONUNCIATION DRILLS

(Numbers in parentheses refer to pages)

Unit I

Unit II

GLOSSARY AND INDEX

Items both in Vocabularies (V) and in Notes (N) are included here. References after each item are to lesson and section. The notation 4 V, for example, refers to the Vocabulary of Lesson 4; 4 N 3 refers to Lesson 4, Note 3. Notations preceded by S refer to Vocabulary and Notes of the Supplementary Lessons.

Entries are arranged alphabetically by syllables. Thus jǐzhu (jǐ + zhu) precedes jìn.

The following abbreviations designate Chinese parts of speech:

AD	Adverb	NU	Number
AV	Auxiliary verb	PR	Pronoun
CV	Coverb	PW	Place word
EV	Equational verb	RV	Resultative verb
IV	Intransitive verb	SP	Specifier
M	Measure	SV	Stative verb
MA	Movable adverb	TV	Transitive verb
N	Noun	V	Verb
		VO	Verb-Object

a (question particle) 1 V, 1 N 14
abbreviated forms 4 N 2
abbreviations 10 N 9
adverbs 1 N 12, 7 N 4, 8 N 3, 10 N 2
àirén husband, wife, fiancée; lover (N) S 1 N 1, 16 V, 16 N
aspect 13 N 1–9, 19 N 6
auxiliary verbs 2 N 9, 7 N 4

bā eight (NU) 4 V
bǎ take (CV) 16 V, 16 N 10, 17 N 7, 20 N 2
ba (final particle) 2 V, 2 N 7, 5 N 8
bái white (also, a surname) (SV) 1 V; uselessly (AD) 21 N 4
bǎi hundred (NU) 14 V, 14 N 7
báicài cabbage (N) 19 V
bàifang make a call on (someone) (TV) 11 V; S 11 N 1
bàn half (M) 11 V
bāngzhu help (TV) 21 V
bǎo full, satiated (SV) 19 V, 19 N 9
bēi cup (M, N) 17 V, 17 N 8
běi north (PW) 7 V
Běi-Dà Peking University 10 N 9
běifāng the north, northern region (PW) 20 V
Běijǐng Peking (PW) 23 N 5

Běijǐng Dàxué Peking University 10 N 9
bēizi cup (N) 17 V, 17 N 8
běn volume, copy (M) 3 V, 3 N 4, 4 N 4
bèn stupid (SV) 13 V
běnzi notebook (N) 4 V
bǐ pen, pencil (N) 3 V
bǐ compare (TV); compared to (CV) 10 V, 10 N 1, 17 V
bǐ must, have to (AV) 15 V
bǐděi must, have to (AV) 15 V, 15 N 14; S 15 N 2
bǐfang example (N) 22 V, 22 N 12
bǐfang shuō for example 22 N 12
bǐjiǎo, bǐjiào relatively (AD) 21 V
bìxìng my surname is . . . 13 N 16
bìxū must, have to (AV) S 15 V, 15 N 2
bìyè graduate (IV) 13 V
biān, biār side (PW) 7 V; S 7 N 1
biàn-fàn plain food (N) 19 V
biǎo watch (N) 13 V
bìng sick (SV); sickness (N) 15 V
bié don't (AV) 16 V
bié(de) other 15 V
bù, bú, bu not, no (AD) 2 V, 7 N 4, 13 N 7, 14 N 6
bù (measure for movies, sets of books) 20 V
bú-bì don't have to 15 N 14

Dōngběi Manchuria (PW) 7 V, 7 N 11
Dōngfāng Orient, the East 23 V
Dōngfāng Hóng The East is Red S 23 N 1
Dōngjīng Tokyo 23 N 5
Dōngshēng 'East Born' 10 N 10
dōngxi (concrete) thing, object (N)
  15 V
dōu all, both, entirely (AD) 1 V,
  7 N 7, 16 N 11, 19 N 4, 21 N 2, 23 N 1
dòufu bean curd (N) 19 V
doubling see reduplication
duǎn short (SV) 22 V
duǎnchu disadvantage, shortcoming (N)
  22 V, 22 N 5
duì correct (SV) 8 V; (postverb) 20 N 4
duì (facing) toward, to, regarding (CV)
  14 V, 14 N 1
duìbuqǐ sorry, excuse me 21 V
duō numerous, many, much (SV); -odd
  8 V, 8 N 7, 10 N 1, 19 N 1
duó(mo)? how? to what degree? (AD)
  8 V, 8 N 7
duōshao? how many? how much? 3 V,
  3 N 9, 14
duration of time 15 N 3-7

enumerative comma 1 N 18
equational verbs 2 N 3
èr two (NU) 3 V, 3 N 9, 14
érqiě but, also (MA) 16 V

fā put out, emit (TV) 22 V
fǎ method, way (N) 22 N 5
fā yīn pronounce 22 V
fāyīn pronunciation (N) 22 V
fázi method, plan (N) 16 V
fàn rice, food (N) 5 V
fànguǎr restaurant (N) 19 V
fāng region, part (N) 20 V
fàng put (TV) 21 V
fāngfǎ method, technique (N) 14 V,
  22 N 5
fàngjià have vacation (IV) 20 V
fāngmian side, aspect (M) 23 V
fángzi house (N) 7 V
fēijǐ airplane (N) 11 V
fēijǐchǎng airport, airfield 23 V
fēn part, cent (M) 4 V, 4 N 7
fēn (measure for minutes) 10 V
fēn tenth 14 N 13
fēng (measure for letters) 23 V
free forms 22 N 5
fùjìn vicinity (PW) 20 V
fùqin father (N) 10 V
fǔshang (your) residence (N) 11 V; S 11 N 1

full forms 4 N 2
fúwùyuán attendant, waiter (N) S 21 V,
  21 N 1

gāi should, ought to (AV) 15 V, 15 N 15
gǎn to feel (emotion) (V) S 14 V, 14 N 1
gǎn xìngqu be interested (in) S 14 V, 14 N 1
gāngbǐ steel pen (i.e. fountain pen, ball
  point, etc.) (N) 4 V
gāng(cái) just (now), just a moment ago
  (AD) 21 V
gāo tall, high (also, a surname) (SV) 1 V
gàosu inform (TV) 11 V
gāoxìng be happy (SV) 20 V
gāozhōng higher middle school (N) 13 V
ge (general measure) 4 V, 4 N 3-4
gěi give (TV); for, to (CV) 14 V, 14 N 1;
  (suffix) 22 N 5; (in passive) 23 N 7
gēn (together) with (CV) 15 V, 15 N 16;
  S 17 N 2
gèng (still) more (AD) 10 V, 10 N 1
gōngfu (leisure) time (N) 5 V; S 5 N 1
gōnggòng public 9 V
gōngyuán park (N) 7 V
gōngzuò work (N/V) S 10 V, 10 N 2
gòu be enough (SV) 17 V, 21 N 4
gùshi story, narrative 20 V
guà hang (TV) 23 V
guǎi turn (IV) 9 V
guānyú concerning, regarding (CV) 22 V
Guǎngdong Canton, Kwangtung Province
  (PW) 19 V
guìxìng? What is your name? 2 V; S 2 N 1
guó country, nation (N) 2 V, 2 N 1, 4 N 9
guò (in time expressions) 10 N 5
guò pass (TV) 9 V
guo (verb suffix) 14 V, 14 N 5
guòjiǎng (you) flatter (me) 19 V; S 19 N 1
guówén Chinese (N) 20 V, 20 N 6; S 20 N 1

hái additionally, in addition, still more
  (AD) 3 V, 7 N 12, 10 N 1, 15 N 2, 19 N 5
hai (sigh of dejection, regret, etc.) 20 V
háishi or 7 V, 7 N 12, 8 N 6
háishi . . . hǎo better 20 N 5
háizi child (N) 10 V
Hàn China, Chinese (N) 22 V, 22 N 14
Han Dynasty 22 N 13
Hànrén Chinese (person) 22 N 13
Hànyǔ Chinese language 22 N 13
Hànzì Chinese characters 22 V, 22 N 13
Hángzhou Hangchow (PW) 16 V
hǎo good, well; fine, O.K. (SV) 1 V,
  19 N 13
hǎo (postverb) 19 N 10

hào   number; day of the month (M)   9 V,
    11 V; (M for bus routes)   S 9 N 2
hǎo-bu-hǎo?   O.K.?   5 N 8
háo-jiǔ-bú-jiàn   Haven't seen you for a
    long time   5 V
hǎo-ma?   O.K.?   5 N 8
hǎochu   advantage (N)   22 V, 22 N 5
hǎoxiē   good many   17 N 9
hē   drink (TV)   17 V
he!   Gosh! My!   19 V
hēi   black (SV)   4 V
hěn   very (AD)   1 V, 14 N 11, 17 N 10
hóng   red (SV)   4 V
hóng chá   black tea   21 N 7
hóng shāo   red-cooked (see footnote,
    p. 313)
hòu   rear (PW)   7 V
hòu   afterwards (AD)   9 V
hú   lake (N)   7 V
hú   pot (N, M)   21 V
Húběi   Hupeh Province (PW)   7 V, 7 N 11
Húnán   Hunan Province (PW)   7 V, 7 N 11
huá, huà   stroke (M)   22 V
huà   speech, language (N)   2 V
huà   paint, draw (TV)   14 V
huá quán   play 'guess-fingers' (see
    footnote, p. 273);   S 17 N 1
huàfǎ   way of painting (N)   22 N 5
huānyíng   welcome (TV)   13 V
huàr   painting, drawing (N)   14 V
huí   return (to) (TV)   13 V
huì   able to, can (V)   2 V, 8 N 8
huìhuà   conversation (N)   22 V
huó   live (IV)   14 V
huǒji   waiter, clerk (N)   21 V; S 21 N 1
huòzhě   or; perhaps (MA)   9 V, 9 N 10

if   19 N 3
imminent action   13 N 6
indefinite reference   7 N 9
inferiority   17 N 4
intensification   13 N 15, 14 N 10–11

Japanese   (see footnote, p. 380)
jī   chicken (N)   19 V
jǐ   how many? (NU)   3 V, 3 N 9
jì   remember, memorize (TV)   22 V,
    22 N 5
jīhui   opportunity (N)   15 V
jíle   in the extreme, extremely   13 V,
    13 N 15, 14 N 11
jìxu   continue (AV)   23 V
jiā   home, house (SV); (suffix)
    23 N 3
jiàn   see, meet (TV)   5 V

jiàn   (measure for matters, tasks, etc.)
    20 V
jiǎndān   simple, uncomplicated (SV)   8 V
jiānglái   in the future, hereafter (TW)
    15 V
jiàngyóu   soy sauce   21 V
jiāo   teach (TV)   15 V
jiǎo   dime (M)   S 3 V, 3 N 1
jiào   be called (IV)   10 V
jiào   (in passive)   23 N 7
jiàoyuán   teacher (N)   10 V
jiàoshòu   professor (also, a title) (N)
    16 V
jiǎozi   dumplings (N)   21 V
jiē   greet, receive (TV)   20 V
jiè   borrow (TV)   8 V
jiéhūn   marry (IV)   17 V
jièshao   introduce (TV)   16 V
jìn   near (SV)   8 V
jìn   enter (TV)   16 V
jīnnián   this year (TW)   11 V
jīntian   today (TW)   5 V
jīng   capital (N)   23 V, 23 N 5
jīngyan   experience (N, V)   21 V
jiǔ   nine (NU)   4 V
jiǔ   wine (N)   17 V
jiù   immediately, then (AD)   10 V, 11 N 5,
    13 N 3, 19 N 3
jiù   (with question words)   21 N 1
jiù   (with yī)   20 N 1
jiù   definitely, indeed, precisely (AD)
    5 V
jiù   only, merely (AD)   2 V
Jiùjīnshān   San Francisco (PW)   S 16 N 2
jiùshi   even (MA)   21 V, 21 N 2
jiùshi . . . dōu   even if. . . still   21 N 2
jiùshi . . . yě   even if. . . still   21 N 2
jiúyǎng   Pleased to meet you   16 V;
    S 16 N 2
jù   (measure for sentences)   16 V
juéde   have the feeling that (TV)   21 V
jùzi   sentence (N)   22 V

kāi   open (door, etc.), drive (car) (TV)
    16 V
kāishǐ   begin (to do) (AV)   15 V
kàn   look at, see, read (TV)   8 V
kànfǎ   way of looking (at something) (N)
    22 N 5
kànjian   see (TV)   11 V
kǎo   roast (TV)   21 V
kǎo   take or give an examination (in a
    subject, for a school) (TV)   13 V
kǎoshì   take or give an examination (IV)
    13 V